FLORENCE, TUSCANY AND UMBRIA

7TH EDITION

Where to Stay and Eat
for All Budgets

Must-See Sights
and Local Secrets

Ratings You Can Trust

Fodor's Travel Publications   New York, Toronto, London, Sydney, Auckland
www.fodors.com

FODOR'S FLORENCE, TUSCANY AND UMBRIA

Editors: Lisa Dunford, Chris Swiac

Editorial Production: Linda K. Schmidt
Editorial Contributors: Peter Blackman, Judy Edelhoff, Stephanie Gruner, Satu Hummasti, Shannon Kelly, Ann Reavis, Patricia Rucidlo, Sarah Sper
Maps: David Lindroth *cartographer;* Bob Blake and Rebecca Baer, *map editors*
Design: Fabrizio La Rocca, *creative director;* Guido Caroti, *art director;* Moon Sun Kim, *cover designer;* Melanie Marin, *senior picture editor*
Cover Photo (rape field in Tuscany): Wolfgang Meier/FPG International/Getty Images
Production/Manufacturing: Robert B. Shields

Seventh Edition

ISBN 1–4000–1477–8

ISSN 1533–1628

SPECIAL SALES

This book is available for special discounts for bulk purchases for sales promotions or premiums. Special editions, including personalized covers, excerpts of existing books, and corporate imprints, can be created in large quantities for special needs. For more information, write to Special Markets/Premium Sales, 1745 Broadway, MD 6-2, New York, New York 10019, or e-mail specialmarkets@randomhouse.com.

AN IMPORTANT TIP & AN INVITATION

Although all prices, opening times, and other details in this book are based on information supplied to us at press time, changes occur all the time in the travel world, and Fodor's cannot accept responsibility for facts that become outdated or for inadvertent errors or omissions. So **always confirm information when it matters,** especially if you're making a detour to visit a specific place. Your experiences—positive and negative—matter to us. If we have missed or misstated something, **please write to us.** We follow up on all suggestions. Contact the Florence, Tuscany and Umbria editor at editors@fodors.com or c/o Fodor's at 1745 Broadway, New York, New York 10019.

DESTINATION FLORENCE, TUSCANY & UMBRIA

arefully tended silver-green olive trees, hills lined with majestic cypresses, and lands crisscrossed with vines abound in Tuscany and Umbria. They provide a hauntingly luscious backdrop for exploring the art, sampling the food, and tasting the local wines in this part of Italy. There's a reason why many movies have been shot here and why many people want to move here: the air and the light seem, somehow, different—the air clearer and crisper; colors seem heightened; and the sunsets and sunrises are often quietly spectacular. Major cities such as Florence, Siena, Perugia, and Orvieto teem with artistic treasures, from their soaring Italian Gothic cathedrals to their wealth of Renaissance painting and sculpture. Smaller hill towns like San Gimignano and Todi offer a step back in time; it doesn't seem as if life has changed much since the Middle Ages. But there's more to this place than this abundance of art: Tuscany has beautiful beaches and sumptuous islands off its coast, while land-locked Umbria offers a perfect place to hike, bicycle, wine-taste, or simply be. The local food, which relies heavily on the quality of its ingredients, tastes especially heavenly when paired with the region's exceptional wines. Buon viaggio!

Tim Jarrell, Publisher

CONTENTS

Maps

CloseUps

ABOUT THIS BOOK

The best source for travel advice is a like-minded friend who's just been where you're headed. But with or without that friend, you'll be in great shape to find your way around your destination once you learn to find your way around your Fodor's guide.

SELECTION

Our goal is to cover the best properties, sights, and activities in their category, as well as the most interesting communities to visit. We make a point of including local food-lovers' hot spots as well as neighborhood options, and we avoid all that's touristy unless it's really worth your time. You can go on the assumption that everything in this book is recommended wholeheartedly by our writers and editors. Flip to On the Road with Fodor's to learn more about who they are. It goes without saying that no property pays to be included.

RATINGS

Orange stars ★ denote sights and properties that our editors and writers consider the very best in the area covered by the entire book. These, the best of the best, are listed in the Fodor's Choice section in the front of the book. Black stars ★ highlight the sights and properties we deem Highly Recommended, the don't-miss sights within any region. In cities, sights pinpointed with numbered map bullets ❶ in the margins tend to be more important than those without bullets.

SPECIAL SPOTS

Pleasures & Pastimes and text on chapter-title pages focus on experiences that reveal the spirit of the destination. Also watch for Off the Beaten Path sights. Some are out of the way, some are quirky, and all are worthwhile. When the munchies hit, look for Need a Break? suggestions.

TIME IT RIGHT

Check On the Calendar up front and chapters' Timing sections for weather and crowd overviews and best days and times to visit.

SEE IT ALL

Use Fodor's exclusive Great Itineraries as a model for your trip. Either follow those that begin the book, or mix regional itineraries from several chapters. In cities, Good Walks guide you to important sights in each neighborhood; ► indicates the starting point of walks and itineraries in the text and on the map.

BUDGET WELL

Hotel and restaurant price categories from ¢ to $$$$ are defined in the opening pages of each chapter—expect to find a balanced selection for every budget. For attractions, we always give standard adult admission fees; reductions are usually available for children, students, and senior citizens. Look in Discounts & Deals in Smart Travel Tips for information on destination-wide ticket schemes. Want to pay with plastic? AE, D, DC, MC, V following restaurant and hotel listings indicate whether American Express, Discover, Diner's Club, MasterCard, or Visa are accepted.

BASIC INFO

Smart Travel Tips lists travel essentials for the entire area covered by the book; city- and region-specific basics end each chapter. To find the best way to get around, see the transportation section; see individual modes of travel ("Car Travel," "Train Travel") for details.

ON THE MAPS

Maps throughout the book show you what's where and help you find your way around. Black and orange numbered bullets ❶ ➊ in the text correlate to bullets on maps.

BACKGROUND

We give background information within the chapters in the course of explaining sights as well as in CloseUp boxes and in chapter 9, "Understanding Florence, Tuscany, and Umbria" at the end of the book. To get in the mood, review the Books & Movies section. The glossary can be invaluable.

FIND IT FAST

Within the book, chapters are divided into small regions, within which towns are covered in logical geographical order; attractive routes and interesting places between towns are flagged as En Route. Heads at the top of each page help you find what you need within a chapter.

DON'T FORGET

Restaurants are open for lunch and dinner daily unless we state otherwise; we mention dress only when there's a specific requirement and reservations only when they're essential or not accepted—it's always best to book ahead. Hotels have private baths, phones, TVs, and air-conditioning and operate on the European Plan (aka. EP, meaning without meals). We always list facilities but not whether you'll be charged extra to use them, so when pricing accommodations, find out what's included.

SYMBOLS

Many Listings

- ★ Fodor's Choice
- ★ Highly recommended
- ⊠ Physical address
- ✛ Directions
- ⬤ Mailing address
- ☎ Telephone
- 🖷 Fax
- ⊕ On the Web
- ✎ E-mail
- 🎟 Admission fee
- ☉ Open/closed times
- ► Start of walk/itinerary
- ▭ Credit cards

Outdoors

- ⛺ Camping

Hotels & Restaurants

- 🏨 Hotel
- 🛏 Number of rooms
- ♨ Facilities
- ⭐ Meal plans
- ✕ Restaurant
- ⚏ Reservations
- 🏛 Dress code
- ✕🏨 Hotel with restaurant that warrants a visit

Other

- ☺ Family-friendly
- 🛈 Contact information
- ⇨ See also
- ⊠ Branch address
- ☞ Take note

ON THE ROAD WITH FODOR'S

A trip takes you out of yourself. Concerns of life at home completely disappear, driven away by more immediate thoughts—about, say, what marvels will beguile the next day, or where you'll have dinner. That's where Fodor's comes in. We make sure that you know all your options, so that you don't miss something that's around the next bend just because you didn't know it was there. Because the best memories of your trip might well have nothing to do with what you came to Florence, Tuscany and Umbria to see, we guide you to sights large and small all over the region. You might set out to tour Florence's famous Duomo or climb Pisa's Leaning Tower, but back at home you find yourself unable to forget a perfect day spent strolling in the hill towns of Umbria. With Fodor's at your side, serendipitous discoveries are never far away.

Our success in showing you every corner of Florence, Tuscany and Umbria is a credit to our extraordinary writers. Although there's no substitute for travel advice from a good friend who knows your style, our contributors are the next best thing—the kind of people you would poll for travel advice if you knew them.

After completing his master's degree in art history, Peter Blackman settled permanently in Italy in 1986. Since then he's worked as a biking and walking tour guide, managing to see more of Italy than most of his Italian friends put together. When he's not leading a trip, you'll find Peter at his home in Chianti, reading, writing, listening to opera, and planning his next journey.

Stephanie Gruner is a journalist based in Lucca, Italy. Her stories frequently appear in the European "Weekend" section of *The Wall Street Journal*. Before moving to Italy, Stephanie spent three years at *The Wall Street Journal* in London, during which time she appeared weekly on CNBC Europe and was a 2002 finalist for a British Business Journalist of the Year Award. Prior to the WSJ, Stephanie was a staff writer at *Inc.* magazine.

Judy Edelhoff, a native Floridian, moved to Rome in 1998 to serve as special assistant to a U.S. ambassador. She has written about art, food, archaeology, wine, theater, and customs in Italy for the *International Herald Tribune*; is an associate editor and food and art critic at a monthly magazine; and has broadcast live from Rome for CNN on Italian law and politics. In Umbria, Judy has picked Sagrantino grapes, mushrooms, and saffron, and in 2004 she followed the 500 Miglia antique automobiles as they departed from Rome and made their way toward Monte Carlo.

In 1997 Ann Reavis decided to put her career as a trial lawyer in San Francisco on hold for a nine-month sojourn in Tuscany. She has been living in Florence ever since, working as a freelance writer and operating a small custom tour company.

Florence-based Patricia Rucidlo has two master's degrees, in Italian Renaissance history and art history. When she's not extolling the virtues of the colors to be found in a Pontormo masterpiece or defending the Medici, she's either leading wine tours in Chianti, catering private dinner parties, or working on a cookbook.

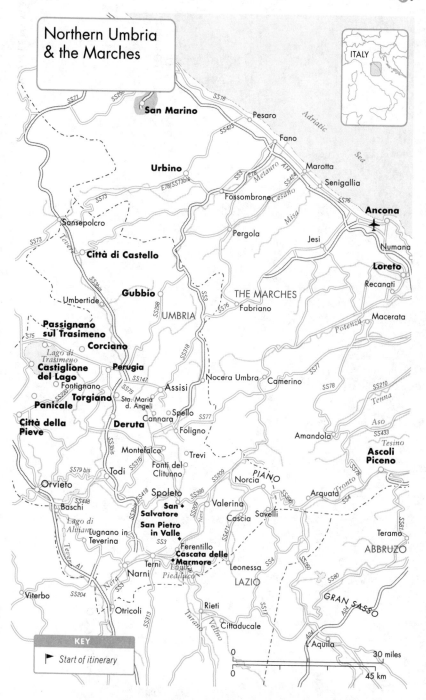

Northern Umbria & the Marches

KEY

▶ *Start of itinerary*

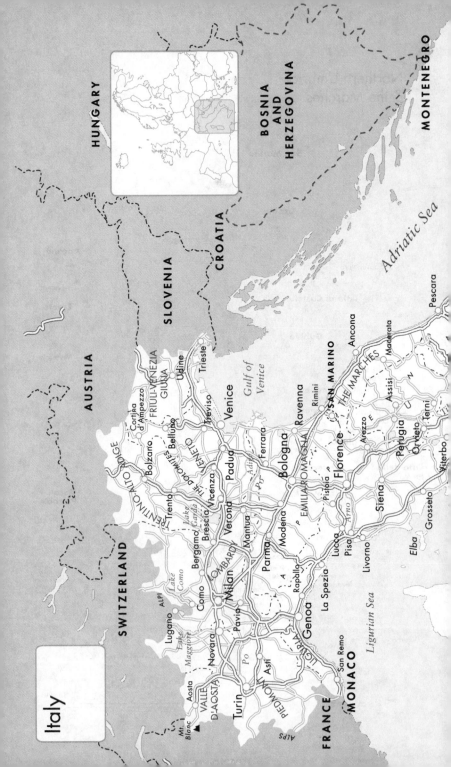

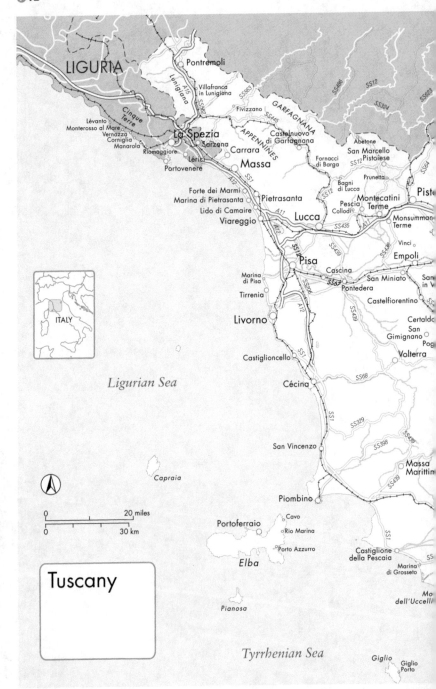

Tuscany

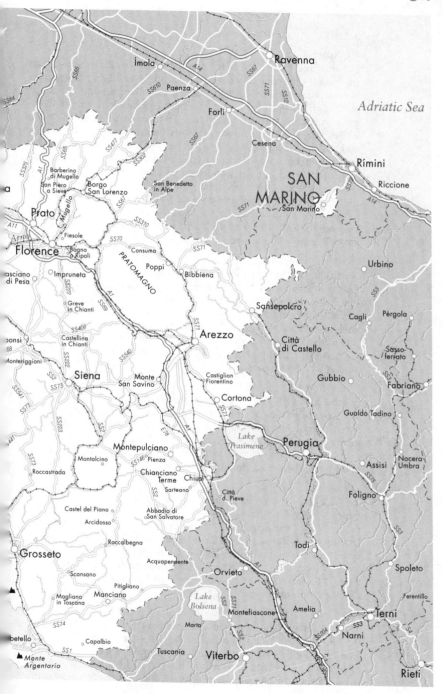

1 Florence

Florence, the "Athens of Italy" and the key to the Renaissance, hugs the banks of the Arno River, where it lies folded among the emerald cypress-studded hills of north-central Tuscany. Elegant and somewhat aloof, as if set apart by its past greatness, this historic center of European civilization still shares with Rome the honor of first place among Italian cities for the magnitude of its artworks, among them Botticelli's goddess and Michelangelo's powerful *David*. Down every street and *vicolo* (alley) and in every piazza you'll make new discoveries of Romanesque, Gothic, or Renaissance architecture; sheltered within these churches, cloisters, and towers are masterly paintings and sculptures of the Quattrocento and Cinquecento periods. Equally splendid are the magnificent chapels and palaces of the Medici—whose patronage rocketed Florence to the forefront of the Renaissance—which stand unabashed amid the city's vibrant modern pulse.

2 North of Florence

North and west of Florence are hills and mountains, snowcapped peaks, thermal waters, and miles of Mediterranean coast. The Apuan Alps split this area nearly in half, with the Lunigiana and the Garfagnana on either side: east of the Alps you're in Tuscany's Rockies; west of them the land flattens out to meet the Tyrrhenian Sea. Michelangelo, not to mention men 1,500 years before him, quarried marble in Carrara. The Ligurian coast, encompassing the Cinque Terre and Forte dei Marmi, dazzles with its panoramic vistas.

3 Cities West of Florence

Nestled in valleys and fed along the Arno, the cities west of Florence were coveted by Florence: they provided access to the sea (Pisa) and were rich industrial centers (Prato). San Miniato al Monte, high on a hill, commands views of two valleys. Although the landscape isn't Tuscany's most majestic, the area is rich with superb Renaissance art and gurgling thermal waters, such as in Montecatini Terme.

4 Chianti

The vineyard-quilted lands spreading south from Florence to Siena—Greve, Radda, Castellina—make up the heart of Chianti. Ilex and cypress, castles and wineries, and sleepy hill towns dot the magical landscape, which has seduced many an expatriate who couldn't summon the will to return home. The market town Greve, just 20 minutes south of Florence, is the gateway to sublime Chianti wine and splendid views. Montepulciano and Montalcino, south of Siena, produce some of Italy's most esteemed wines.

5 Siena and the Hill Towns

The time traveler will be entranced by medieval Siena, "the Pompeii of the Middle Ages," as it was called by the philosopher Taine. Radiating from the Gothic bastion are ocher and emerald lands teeming with olive groves, vineyards, and rolling hills nurtured by the Elsa and the Arbia. Perched dramatically above a fertile valley, San Gimignano—with its skyline of medieval towers—may jettison you into a Who-turned-back-the-clock? sensation of Mark Twain's Connecticut Yankee when he arrived in King Arthur's court. With a glass of Vernaccia di San Gimignano in hand, you'll feel like lingering long. But the old Etruscan hill town of Volterra, with sweeping views of two valleys, is not to be overlooked.

⑥ Arezzo, Cortona, and Southern Tuscany

Heading south from Florence toward Rome to the heart of southern Tuscany, you'll find Arezzo, with its treasures by Piero della Francesca. Compact, perfect Pienza, a fusion of Renaissance and Gothic styles planned by Pope Pius II, overlooks a golden valley. In mystical Cortona, with sweeping views of Lago Trasimeno, you can take pleasure in the scattering of churches and medieval art, but street scenes revealing an old-fashioned way of life are just as essential. Mountainous Elba is rimmed with seductive beaches; Giglio, its sister island to the south, is tinier and rockier.

⑦ Perugia and Northern Umbria

Nestled east of Florence and stretching to the Adriatic, Perugia and Northern Umbria—including the eastern Marches region—boast dramatically rolling, checkerboarded hills in hues of green and gold, ablaze with sunflowers and poppies. The area encompasses the valley cradling the Tiber, which is exceptionally lush and rich. Undiscovered splendor awaits in the cities: Perugia, a magnet for visitors since the Middle Ages, has a magnificent piazza; Gubbio, to the northeast, is a tiny jewel built against a steep hill; and the beauty of the Renaissance court comes alive in Urbino.

⑧ Assisi, Spoleto, and Southern Umbria

There's magic in the air in this noble area just east of the Tiber. Assisi, birthplace of St. Francis, is surrounded by wheat fields and olive groves, and the tufa plateau of Orvieto—with its own magnificent Duomo—gives the hallowed town a warm, reddish glow. Hilltop Deruta has been making ceramics for more than 600 years, and medieval Todi seems nearly celestial behind its three sets of walls.

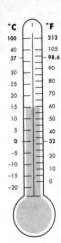

The main tourist season runs from April to mid-October. For serious sightseers the best months are from fall to early spring. The so-called low season may be cooler and inevitably rainier, but it has its rewards: less time waiting in lines and closer-up, unhurried views of what you want to see.

Tourists crowd the major art cities at Easter, when Italians flock to resorts and to the countryside. From March through May, busloads of eager schoolchildren on excursions take cities of artistic and historical interest by storm. Italian beach vacations are best taken in June and September, to avoid the August crowds.

Climate

Weatherwise, the best months for sightseeing are April, May, June, September, and October—generally pleasant and not too hot. The hottest months are July and August, when humidity can make things unpleasant and brief afternoon thunderstorms are common in inland areas. Winter is relatively mild in most places on the main tourist circuit but always includes some rainy spells.

If you can avoid it, don't travel at all in Italy in August, when much of the population is on the move, especially around Ferragosto, the August 15 national holiday; many cities are deserted during this time and many restaurants and shops are closed. (Of course, with residents away on vacation, this makes crowds less of a bother for tourists.) Except for a few year-round resorts, coastal resorts usually close up from October or November to April; they're at their best in June and September, when everything is open but uncrowded.

🔳 Forecasts **Weather Channel Connection** ☎ 900/932-8437, 95¢ per minute from a Touch-Tone phone ⊕ www.weather.com.

FLORENCE

Jan.	48F	9C	May	73F	23C	Sept.	79F	26C
	36	2		54	12		59	15
Feb.	52F	11C	June	81F	27C	Oct.	68F	20C
	37	3		59	15		52	11
Mar.	57F	14C	July	86F	30C	Nov.	57F	14C
	41	5		64	18		45	7
Apr.	66F	19C	Aug.	86F	30C	Dec.	52F	11C
	46	8		63	17		39	10

ON THE CALENDAR

Tuscany and Umbria's top seasonal events are listed below, and any one of them could provide the stuff of lasting memories. It's revealing that the Italian *festa* can be translated either as "festival" or "holiday" or "feast"—food is usually fundamental to Italian celebrations. Contact the Italian Government Tourist Board (☎ 212/245–4822 ⊕ italiantourism.com) for exact dates and further information.

WINTER

December	At Christmas, churches throughout Umbria have nativity scenes, or crèches, on display. They're a reminder that it was St. Francis who began the tradition of re-creating the nativity scene. In Armenzano and Petrignano you can see "living" nativity scenes, which are staged with actors.
January	Roman Catholic Epiphany (Epifania) Celebrations and decorations are evident throughout Italy.
February	The Festa dell'Olio, in Spello on the last Sunday of Carnevale, is a celebration of the olive and its oil. Streetside booths offer bruschetta, traditionally made with bread, sometimes rubbed with garlic, and topped with olive oil and salt. Look for other local delicacies, too.
Late February–April	During Carnevale in Viareggio, masked pageants, fireworks, a flower show, and parades are among the two weeks of festivities in this Tuscan coastal town. Carnevale in San Gimignano is smaller, with locals, dressed up in colorful costumes, marching through the streets. The biggest fete is, of course, held in Venice.
	The Easter Sunday Scoppio del Carro, or "Explosion of the Cart," in Florence is an eruption of fireworks; they shoot out of a highly ornate carriage after a mechanical dove swoops from the Duomo's high altar to set them off. Settimana Santa (Holy Week), the week after Easter, features parades and outdoor events in every major city and most small towns; the festivities in Florence are particularly notable.

SPRING

Late April–Early July	The Maggio Musicale Fiorentino (Florence May Music Festival; ⊕ www.maggiofiorentino.com) is a three-month series of internationally acclaimed concerts and recitals. It's the oldest and most prestigious Italian festival of the performing arts. Check for schedules and tickets.
Mid-May	During the Festa dei Ceri (Race of the Candles) in mid-May, a procession to the top of Mt. Ingino in Gubbio, young men in local costume carry huge wooden pillars. The Palio della Balestra (Palio of the Archers) is a medieval crossbow contest in Gubbio that dates back to 1461 and is held the last Sunday in May.

SUMMER	
June	The Battle of the Bridge in Pisa is a medieval parade and contest that takes place the first Sunday in June. Calcio Storico, soccer games in 16th-century costume representing Florence's six neighborhoods, are held in Florence on the feast day of St. John the Baptist (June 24), commemorating a match played in 1530. Festivities include fireworks displays. The Feast of the Republic, on June 2, formerly the royal national holiday, is celebrated with a flurry of Italian flags. The Luminaria feast day on June 16 honors St. Ranieri, the patron saint of Pisa. Palaces along the Arno glow with white lights and fireworks. The four former maritime republics—Amalfi, Genoa, Pisa, and Venice—compete each year on the first Sunday in June at the Regatta of the Great Maritime Republics. The 2,000-meter upstream race is held in each city on a rotating basis. A parade with participants dressed in the traditional costumes of each republic precedes the event. The regatta will take place in Pisa in 2006. During the last 10 days of June, Bevagna holds the Mercato delle Gaite, a medieval festival that re-creates daily life between 1250 and 1350.
Late June–Early July	The Festival dei Due Mondi (Festival of Two Worlds), in Spoleto, is perhaps Italy's most famous performing-arts festival, bringing in a worldwide audience for concerts, operas, ballets, film screenings, and crafts fairs for a two-week celebration. Plan well in advance.
June–August	Estate Fiesolana is a two-month long festival of theater, music, dance, and film that takes place in the churches and the archaeological area of Fiesole.
July	Pistoia Blues draws international blues artists who perform for three evenings in the city's main square. La Giostra dell'Orso (Bear Joust), on July 25, celebrates St. James, patron saint of Pistoia. The Umbria Jazz Festival, in Perugia, brings in many of the biggest names in jazz each summer. The Giostra della Quintana is a joust held in Foligno's Campo dei Giochi, the town stadium, twice yearly: on the first Saturday in July and on the second Sunday in September. Foligno's 10 rioni compete, with 600 to 700 participants dressed in meticulously researched and designed traditional 17th-century clothing. Several thousand spectators attend.
July–August	Siena's Palio horse races, held on July 2 and August 16, are colorful bareback races with participants competing for the *palio* (banner). Lucca's Puccini Festival in late July to early August celebrates the city's native son.
July–September	Estate Musicale Lucchese runs throughout the summer in Lucca.
August	For three weeks Montefalco celebrates the La Fuga del Bove (Escape of the Ox) festival. Each day brings historic processions in costume, traditional drummers and musicians, and games and

athletic competitions among the four quarters. Temporary taverns are set up nightly in some of the town's spectacular courtyards.

| August–September | Siena Music Week, from late August to early September, features opera, concerts, and chamber music. Spoleto hosts a prestigious concorso di canto (vocal competion) from mid-August to mid-September. |

FALL

September	The 500 Miglia is a procession of 40 or more antique automobiles that each year leisurely makes its way from Rome to Monte Carlo in about a week, spending almost three days tooling through southern Umbria. September 8 and 9 are the dates for Spoleto's annual Onion Festival, a tradition that goes back at least to the 1400s, sometimes referred to as the festival of Loreto. (If you don't get enough onions in two days, Cannara has a ten-day onion festival the same month.) The Giostra del Saracino (Joust of the Saracen) in early September is a tilting contest with knights in 13th-century armor in Arezzo. The Giostra della Quintana (Joust of the Quintana; ⊕ www.quintana.it) is a 17th-century-style joust and historical procession in Foligno, held on the second Sunday in September. Montefalco's local wine, Sagrantino di Montefalco, is celebrated when it's in its nascent stage, during September's Festa Della Vendemmia (Grape, or Harvest, Festival). You can attend exhibits, tastings, and lectures to celebrate the grape harvest. The twice-yearly Giostra della Quintana joust is held in Foligno in July and on the second Sunday in September (⇨ Summer, *above*).
October	The Festa di San Francesco (Feast of St. Francis) is celebrated in Assisi, his birthplace, on October 2. The first Sunday in October is the Palio Dei Terzieri, in Trevi, with a pageant followed by a relay race of three carts—representing the three sectors of the city—pulled by local men. The third Sunday in October is Trevi's Black Celery Festival. Black celery, cultivated since the 1700s in Trevi, grows only between town and the Clitunno River in limited production. The fourth Sunday in Trevi is Scenes of Medieval Life and Times, which brings locals to the main square to feast on roasted chestnuts and watch medieval pageantry. The high point of Assisi's festival year comes every October 3 and 4 with the Festa di San Francesco, commemorating the anniversary of St. Francis's death. The festival includes a symbolic offering of olive oil to illuminate all of Italy, as well as art exhibitions and folklore performances.
November	In early November, olive oil producers participate in Frantoi Aperti for tastings of new olive oil from the recent harvest. Various olive oil mills let you sample their freshly pressed oils, which are a vivid bright green color, and tour their facilities.

PLEASURES & PASTIMES

The Art of Enjoying Art

Travel veterans will tell you that the endless series of masterpieces in Italy's churches, palaces, and museums can cause first-time visitors—eyes glazed over from a heavy downpour of images, dates, and names—to lean, Pisa-like, on their companions for support. After a surfeit of Botticellis and Bronzinos and the 14th Raphael, even the miracle of the High Renaissance may begin to pall. The secret, of course, is to act like a turtle—not a hare—and take your sweet time. Instead of trotting after briskly efficient tour guides, allow the splendors of the age to unfold slowly. Get out and explore the actual settings—medieval chapels, Rococo palaces, and Romanesque town squares—for which these marvelous examples of Italy's art and sculpture were conceived centuries ago and where many of them may still be seen in situ.

Museums are only the most obvious places to view art; there are always the trompe-l'oeil renderings of Assumptions that float across baroque church ceilings and piazza scenes that might be Renaissance paintings brought to life. Instead of studying a Gothic statue in Florence's Bargello, spend an hour in the medieval cloisters of the nearby convent of San Marco; by all means, take in Michelangelo's *David* in Florence's Accademia, but then meander down the 15th-century street, a short bus ride away, where he was born. You'll find that after three days of trotting through museums, a walk through a quiet neighborhood will act as a much-needed restorative of perspective.

Il Caffè

The Italian day begins and ends with coffee, and more cups of coffee punctuate the time in between. To live like the Italians do, drink as they drink, standing at the counter or sitting at outdoor tables of the corner bar. (In Italy, the term always means coffee bar—establishments serving primarily alcoholic beverages are called pubs or American bars.) A primer: *Caffè* means coffee, and Italian standard issue is what Americans call espresso—short, strong, and usually taken very sweet. *Cappuccino* is a foamy half-and-half of espresso and steamed milk; *cacao* (cocoa powder) on top is acceptable, cinnamon not. If you're thinking of having a cappuccino for dessert, think again—Italians drink only caffè or *caffè macchiato* (with a spot of steamed milk) after lunchtime. Confused? Homesick? Order *caffè americano* for a reasonable facsimile of good old filtered joe.

La Passeggiata

A favorite Italian pastime is the *passeggiata,* literally the promenade. In the late afternoon and early evening, especially on weekends, couples, families, and packs of teenagers stroll the main streets and piazzas of Italy's towns. It's a ritual of exchanged news and gossip, window-shopping, flirting, and gelato-eating that adds up to a uniquely Italian experience. To join in, simply hit the streets for a bit of wandering. You may feel more like an observer than a participant, until you realize that observing is what la passeggiata is all about.

Shopping

"Made in Italy" has become synonymous with style, quality, and craftsmanship, whether it refers to high fashion or Maserati automobiles. The best buys are leather goods of all kinds—from gloves to bags to jackets—silk goods, knitwear, gold jewelry, ceramics, and local handicrafts. The most important thing to keep in mind when shopping in Italy is that every region has its specialties. Florence is known for gold jewelry, antiques, paper products, and leather and straw goods; Assisi for embroidery; and Deruta and Gubbio for ceramics.

Thermal Baths

Thanks to its location in the Mediterranean region—one of the world's most active volcano belts—Italy is rich in thermo-mineral springs. Consequently, the Italians have developed a special attitude about what we call spas since the ancient Romans advanced the idea of *mens sana in corpore sano* (a sound mind in a healthy body). Taking the waters remains a unique part of Italian culture; it is state-supported and medically supervised. Never mind Greco-Roman worship of the body in templelike baths; choices now range from antiaging cures to U.S.-style exercise classes to fangotherapy (medicinal mud therapy). Today more and more travelers are taking vacations from their vacations by visiting one of Italy's sybaritic spas. At these centers, drinking and bathing cures are based on naturally produced thermal mineral waters, with mornings devoted to sipping and strolling as well as occasional forays into espresso bars. Then come hot mud packs, massage, anticellulite treatments, and sinus-targeted steam inhalations. But forget the Roman origins and don't say spa (in Italian, s.p.a. denotes a business corporation): The term in Italy is *terme* (baths).

FODOR'S CHOICE

The sights, restaurants, hotels, and other travel experiences on these pages are our editors' top picks—our Fodor's Choices. They're the best of their type in Tuscany and Umbria—not to be missed and always worth your time. In the destination chapters that follow, you will find all the details.

HOTELS

$$$$ **Villa La Vedetta,** Florence. Sumptuous rooms, a superb restaurant, a stellar staff, and unbeatable views of Florence below are the reasons to splurge here.

$$$ **Locanda dell'Amorosa,** Sinalunga, near Abbazia di Monte Oliveto Maggiore. The "inn" is a stunning, luxury hotel in a 14th-century hamlet with a small stone church and a cypress-lined drive. The superb restaurant complements these lush surroundings.

$$–$$$ **Relais Fattoria Vignale,** Radda in Chianti. Vineyards and plum and olive trees surround manor-house lodging with a choice of a sophisticated ristorante or rustic wine bar for dining.

$$ **Alla Corte degli Angeli,** Lucca. This charming hotel with friendly service has attractive, sunny rooms with wood floors and wood-beam ceilings, and is right off the main shopping drag.

$$ **Le Tre Vaselle,** Torgiano. This tranquil hotel in the center of a winemaking town makes a pleasant base for exploring the attractions of Northern Umbria.

$$ **Hotel San Luca,** Spoleto. The owners here are the key to the guests' comfort; they are ready to find the best bicycle routes, plan your gourmet itinerary, prepare a group lunch, or pamper you with thoughtful touches like tea by the fireplace.

$$ **Villa Pambuffetti,** Montefalco. Enjoy seclusion in style in this elegant villa run by a local noble family that also produces wine. Guests still dress for dinner in a restaurant that chic locals like to patronize. Cooking courses are offered, too.

$$ **Villa Poggio San Felice,** Florence. This 15th-century villa just outside the city center provides a perfect place to combine gracious country living with city life.

$-$$ **Ristorante Il Pinturicchio,** Spello. Pinturicchio's dedication to excellence was able to keep the Borgias happy, and this namesake restaurant is just as dedicated to serving you with an exquisite meal.

$ **Calcione Country and Castle,** Arezzo. You're on a centuries-old family homestead at this sophisticated yet rustic *agriturismo* convenient to Siena, San Gimignano, and Cortona.

¢ | **Residenza Johanna I,** Florence. Italians in the know and well-informed budgeteers flock to this intimate, hands-off place (you'll even have your own key to let yourself in).

RESTAURANTS

$$$$ | **Cibrèo,** Florence. Chef Fabrio Picci reinterprets regional classics, served in Tuscan surroundings gone upscale. Its location next to a marketplace promises the freshest of ingredients—and imagination.

$$$$ | **Ristorante Arnolfo,** Colle di Val d'Elsa. The sublime dishes here daringly straddle the line between innovation and tradition—almost always with spectacular results.

$$–$$$$ | **Taverna del Lupo,** Gubbio. Famous throughout the region, this is a great place to enjoy traditional Umbrian cooking at its earthy, hearty best.

$$$ | **Il Giglio DíOro,** Orvieto. The fine cuisine and al fresco dining across from Orvieto's Duomo shows that you can have a spectacular view and dine well, too; the wine cellar has an excellent selection that includes some rare wines.

$$$ | **Il Molino,** Spello. Seated under the medieval vaulted ceiling you can enjoy Umbria's finest ingredients prepared in both classic and innovative ways.

$–$$ | **Antico Noe,** Florence. The food more than makes up for the lack of ambience, as the chef relies completely on seasonal ingredients which he picks up each morning at one of the local markets.

$–$$ | **Osteria del Coro,** Siena. Chef-owner Stefano Azzi produces tasty local fare as well as thin-crust pizzas; all of this can be washed down with wine from a carefully culled list.

ART AND ARCHITECTURE

Basilica di San Francesco, Arezzo. Come to see the Pietro della Francesca's frescoes, *The Legend of the True Cross,* executed on three walls of the choir of this 14th-century church.

Basilica di San Francesco, Assisi. The Giotto fresco cycle illustrating the life of St. Francis is counted among the masterpieces of the Renaissance, and the soaring double basilica, still recovering from damage sustained in a 1997 earthquake, makes them a majestic home.

Cripta, Siena. Routine excavation work under Siena's Duomo unearthed this crypt with startlingly vivid frescoes painted some 800 years ago.

Duomo, Orvieto. Few cathedrals can claim masterpieces inside and out, but here you'll find Italy's most perfect Gothic facade matched by the phenomenal intensity and variety of Luca Signorelli's frescoes—among the best in Umbria—in the Cappella di San Brizio.

Galleria degli Uffizi, Florence. One of the world's greatest art collections is housed in this Giorgio Vasari–designed palazzo. Botticelli, Caravaggio, Piero della Francesca, Rembrandt, Raphael—they're all here, along with a rare Michelangelo panel painting, the *Doni Tondo.*

Galleria Nazionale dell'Umbria, Perugia. In this, one of Italy's finest small museums, you will find a truly fine selection of Umbrian art that is well lit, well displayed, informatively presented, and truly a joy to visit.

Museo d'Arte Sacra e Archeologico, Asicano. A 2002 refurbishment of a 15th-century palazzo has given new luster to this fine collection of 13th- and 14th-century paintings from the Sienese school.

Palazzo Ducale, Urbino, the Marches. In no other place in Italy are the tenets of the Renaissance so unequivocally displayed: the nobility of man, as expressed by the measured harmony of his architecture, and the process of enlightenment, achieved by studying the past and all things beautiful.

Santa Croce, Florence. The resting place of Michelangelo, Galileo, and Machiavelli also contains the most important art of any church in Florence.

Villa Reale, Marlia, north of Lucca. This onetime home of Napoleon's sister is considered by some to be Lucca's finest villa. There's a water garden, a grotto, and a theater carved from hedges.

PURE TUSCANY AND UMBRIA

Abbazia di Sant'Antimo, Montalcino. In a peaceful valley, surrounded by gently rolling hills, olive trees, and thick oak woods, Sant'Antimo is one of Italy's most beautifully situated abbeys.

San Gimignano. A guided walk in the nearby countryside is a precious opportunity to explore the Tuscan scenery so appreciated from the windows and ramparts of this medieval town. When you've had your fill, return to San Gimignano to taste the wines and to see its famous towers.

Terme di Saturnia, Saturnia. Pamper yourself at a luxury spa where, in addition to beauty treatments, you have three excellent restaurants from which to choose.

Terme Tettuccio, Montecatini Terme. Relax in the manner of bygone days in a neoclassical limestone-and-marble pavilion surrounded by fountains and gardens. Fellini's 8½ was shot here in the early 1960s.

Torre Pendente, Pisa. Yes, the Leaning Tower is touristy, but it's touristy fun. Climb it if you have the energy.

VIEWS

Truffles in Umbria. After a long walk through the narrow, winding streets of an Umbrian town—the air rich with the smell of hearth fires and simmering pots—there's nothing like sitting down to a plate of homemade pasta dressed with the area's prized truffles.

Piazza del Duomo, Spoleto. Descending the stairs toward Spoleto's medieval cathedral, you see the broad piazza flanked by low medieval buildings. It fans out and spills down toward the pale stone sanctuary, which is studded with rose-color windows and mosaics and set against a verdant backdrop of Umbria's hills.

San Gimignano. Stand on the steps of the Collegiata church at sunset as the swallows swoop in and out of the famous medieval towers, twittering softly as they coast on the air.

SMART TRAVEL TIPS

ADDRESSES

Addresses in Italy are fairly straightforward: the street name is followed by the street number. However, you might see an address with a number plus "bis" or "A"—for instance, "Via Verdi 3/bis" or "Via Mazzini 8/A." This indicates that 3/bis and 8/A are the next entrance or door down from Via Verdi 3 and Via Mazzini 8, respectively. Addresses with a number followed by "r" (e.g., Via Santo Spirito 35/r) refer to *rosso* (red), the color of the number painted on the wall. "Red" addresses are always businesses.

In rural areas, some addresses give only the route name or the distance in kilometers along a major road (e.g., Via Fabbri, Km 4.3), or sometimes only the name of the small village in which the site is located.

AIR TRAVEL

Air travel to Italy is frequent and virtually problem-free. Sometimes, however, airport- or airline-related union strikes may cause delays of a few hours. These delays are usually reported in advance. Alitalia, Italy's national flag carrier, has the most nonstop flights to Rome and Milan. Frequent nonstop flights link London with Pisa (British Air, Ryanair). More frequent flights are available from the United States and Canada aboard Lufthansa, Air France, United, or Continental; these stop once in Europe before they or their code-sharing partners continue on to Florence or Pisa.

BOOKING

When you book, look for nonstop flights and remember that "direct" flights stop at least once. Try to avoid connecting flights, which require a change of plane. Two airlines may operate a connecting flight jointly, so ask whether your airline operates every segment of the trip; you may find that the carrier you prefer flies you only part of the way. To find more booking tips and to check prices and make online flight reservations, log on to www.fodors.com.

CARRIERS

When flying internationally, you must usually choose between a domestic carrier, the national flag carrier of the country you are visiting, and a foreign carrier from a third country. You may, for example, choose to fly Alitalia to Italy. National flag carriers have the greatest number of nonstops. Domestic carriers may have better connections to your hometown and serve a greater number of gateway cities. Third-party carriers may have a price advantage.

Alitalia—in addition to other major European airlines and smaller, privately run companies such as Meridiana and Air One—also has an extensive network of flights within Italy. Ask your domestic or Italian travel agent about discounts.

On international flights, Alitalia serves Rome, Milan, and Venice. The major international hubs in Italy are Milan and Rome, served by (in addition to Alitalia) Continental Airlines, Delta Air Lines, American Airlines, United Airlines, Northwest Airlines, US Airways, and their European code-sharing partners.

Alitalia and British Airways provide direct service from Heathrow and Gatwick. From Manchester, there are direct British Airways flights daily to Milan and Rome. Meridiana has direct flights daily to Florence from Gatwick. Lower-priced charter flights to a range of Italian destinations also are available throughout the year.

Alitalia and Air Canada have the most flights connecting Canada and Italy. Qantas flies to Rome from various cities in Australia, via Bangkok. Alitalia and Air New Zealand fly from Auckland to Rome with a stop in London.

🛫 **Major Airlines Air Canada** ☎ 888/247-2262, 0870/524-7226 in the U.K., 800/919091 in Italy ⊕ www.aircanada.com. **Air New Zealand** ☎ 0800/ 352-266 in New Zealand, 800/876126 in Italy ⊕ www.airnz.co.nz. **Alitalia** ☎ 800/223-5730, 800/ 361-8336 in Canada, 0990/448-259 in the U.K., 1300/653-747 in Australia, 06/65641 in Rome, 848/ 865641 elsewhere in Italy ⊕ www.alitalia.it. **American Airlines** ☎ 800/433-7300, 06/66053169 in Rome ⊕ www.aa.com. **British Airways** ☎ 800/ 247-9297, 0845/773-3377 in the U.K., 02/8904-8800 in Australia, 09/356-8690 in New Zealand, 199/ 712266 in Italy ⊕ www.britishairways.com. **Continental Airlines** ☎ 800/231-0856, 800/296230 in Italy ⊕ www.flycontinental.com. **Delta Air Lines**

☎ 800/241-4141, 08705/074-074 in the U.K., 1300/ 303-744 in Australia, 800/864114 in Italy ⊕ www. deltaairlines.com. **Northwest Airlines** ☎ 800/225-2525 or 800/441-1818 ⊕ www.nwa.com. **Qantas** ☎ 06/52482725 in Rome ⊕ www.qantas.com. **United Airlines** ☎ 800/241-6522, 02/69633707 in Milan ⊕ www.unitedairlines.com. **US Airways** ☎ 800/428-4322, 848/813177 in Italy ⊕ www. usairways.com.

🛫 Smaller Airlines **Air One** ☎ 8488/48880 in Italy ⊕ www.flyairone.it. **Meridiana** ☎ 020/ 7839-2222 in London, 199/111333 in Italy, 055/ 2302314 in Florence ⊕ www.meridiana.it. **Ryanair** ☎ 0870/156-9569 in London, 199/114114 in Italy ⊕ www.ryanair.com.

CHECK-IN AND BOARDING

Airports in Italy have been ramping up security measures, which include random baggage inspection and bomb-detection dogs.

Always **find out your carrier's check-in policy.** Plan to arrive at the airport about two hours before your scheduled departure time for domestic flights and 2½ to 3 hours before international flights. You may need to arrive earlier if you're flying from one of the busier airports or during peak air-traffic times. To avoid delays at airport-security checkpoints, try not to wear any metal. Jewelry, belts and other buckles, steel-toe shoes, barrettes, and underwire bras are among the items that can set off detectors.

Assuming that not everyone with a ticket will show up, airlines routinely overbook planes. When everyone does, airlines ask for volunteers to give up their seats. In return, these volunteers usually get a several-hundred-dollar flight voucher, which can be used toward the purchase of another ticket, and are rebooked on the next flight out. If there are not enough volunteers, the airline must choose who will be denied boarding. The first to get bumped are passengers who checked in late and those flying on discounted tickets, so get to the gate and check in as early as possible, especially during peak periods.

Always **bring a government-issued photo I.D.** to the airport; even when it's not required, a passport is best.

CUTTING COSTS

The least expensive airfares to Italy are priced for round-trip travel and must usually be purchased in advance. Airlines generally allow you to change your return date for a fee; most low-fare tickets, however, are nonrefundable. It's smart to call a number of airlines and check the Internet; when you are quoted a good price, book it on the spot—the same fare may not be available the next day, or even the next hour. Always check different routings and look into using alternate airports. Also, price off-peak flights, which may be significantly less expensive than others. Travel agents, especially low-fare specialists (⇨ Discounts & Deals), are helpful.

Consolidators are another good source. They buy tickets for scheduled flights at reduced rates from the airlines, then sell them at prices that beat the best fare available directly from the airlines. (Many also offer reduced car-rental and hotel rates.) Sometimes you can even get your money back if you need to return the ticket. Carefully read the fine print detailing penalties for changes and cancellations, purchase the ticket with a credit card, and confirm your consolidator reservation with the airline.

🎦 Consolidators **AirlineConsolidator.com** ☎ 888/468-5385 ⊕ www.airlineconsolidator.com; for international tickets. **Best Fares** ☎ 800/880-1234 or 800/576-8255 ⊕ www.bestfares.com; $59.90 annual membership. **Cheap Tickets** ☎ 800/377-1000 or 800/652-4327 ⊕ www.cheaptickets.com. **Expedia** ☎ 800/397-3342 or 404/728-8787 ⊕ www.expedia.com. **Hotwire** ☎ 866/468-9473 or 920/330-9418 ⊕ www.hotwire.com. **Now Voyager Travel** ✉ 45 W. 21st St., Suite 5A New York, NY 10010 ☎ 212/459-1616 🖷 212/243-2711 ⊕ www.nowvoyagertravel.com. **Onetravel.com** ⊕ www.onetravel.com. **Orbitz** ☎ 888/656-4546 ⊕ www.orbitz.com. **Priceline.com** ⊕ www.priceline.com. **Travelocity** ☎ 888/709-5983, 877/282-2925 in Canada, 0870/111-7061 in the U.K. ⊕ www.travelocity.com.

ENJOYING THE FLIGHT

State your seat preference when purchasing your ticket, and then repeat it when you confirm and when you check in. For more legroom, you can request one of the few emergency-aisle seats at check-in, if you're capable of moving obstacles comparable in weight to an airplane exit door (usually between 35 pounds and 60 pounds)—a Federal Aviation Administration requirement of passengers in these seats. Seats behind a bulkhead also offer more legroom, but they don't have under-seat storage. Don't sit in the row in front of the emergency aisle or in front of a bulkhead, where seats may not recline.

Ask the airline whether a snack or meal is served on the flight. If you have dietary concerns, request special meals when booking. These can be vegetarian, low-cholesterol, or kosher, for example. It's a good idea to pack some healthful snacks and a small (plastic) bottle of water in your carry-on bag. On long flights, try to maintain a normal routine, to help fight jet lag. At night, get some sleep. By day, eat light meals, drink water (not alcohol), and **move around the cabin** to stretch your legs. For additional jet-lag tips consult *Fodor's FYI: Travel Fit & Healthy* (available at bookstores everywhere).

Many airlines, including those that fly to Italy, prohibit smoking on all of their international flights; others allow smoking only on certain routes or certain departures. Smoking is prohibited on flights within Italy. Ask your carrier about its policy.

FLYING TIMES

Flying time is 8½ hours from New York, 10–11 hours from Chicago, 11½ hours from Dallas (via New York), 11½ hours from Los Angeles, 2 hours from London (to Milan), and 23½ hours from Sydney to Rome.

HOW TO COMPLAIN

If your baggage goes astray or your flight goes awry, complain right away. Most carriers require that you **file a claim immediately.** The Aviation Consumer Protection Division of the Department of Transportation publishes *Fly-Rights,* which discusses airlines and consumer issues and is available online. You can also find articles and information on mytravelrights.com, the Web site of the nonprofit Consumer Travel Rights Center.

🎦 Airline Complaints **Aviation Consumer Protection Division** ✉ U.S. Department of Transportation,

Office of Aviation Enforcement and Proceedings, C-75, Room 4107, 400 7th St. SW, Washington, DC 20590 ☎ 202/366-2220 ⊕ airconsumer.ost.dot.gov. **Federal Aviation Administration Consumer Hotline** ✉ for inquiries: FAA, 800 Independence Ave. SW, Washington, DC 20591 ☎ 800/322-7873 ⊕ www.faa.gov.

RECONFIRMING

Check the status of your flight before you leave for the airport. You can do this on your carrier's Web site, by linking to a flight-status checker (many Web booking services offer these), or by calling your carrier or travel agent. Always confirm international flights at least 72 hours ahead of the scheduled departure time.

AIRPORTS

The major gateways to Italy include Rome's Aeroporto Leonardo da Vinci (airport code FCO), better known as Fiumicino, and Milan's Aeroporto Malpensa 2000 (MIL). Flights to Florence make connections at Fiumicino and Malpensa; you can also take the FS airport train to Rome's Termini Station or a bus to Milan's central train station (Centrale) and catch a train to Florence or Perugia.

Alitalia and other European carriers fly into the smaller airports. Florence is serviced by Aeroporto A. Vespucci (FLR), which is also called Peretola, and by Aeroporto Galileo Galilei (PSA), which is about a mile outside the center of Pisa and about one hour from Florence. The train to Florence stops within 100 feet of the entrance to the Pisa airport terminal.

When you take a connecting flight to Florence and Pisa, be aware that your luggage might not make it onto the second plane with you. The lost-luggage service is efficient, however, and your delayed luggage is usually delivered to your hotel or holiday rental within 12 to 24 hours.

🛪 Airport Information **Aeroporto A. Vespucci** (FLR, also called Peretola) ✉ 6 km [4 mi] northwest of Florence ☎ 055/373498. **Aeroporto Galileo Galilei** (PSA) ✉ 2 km [1 mi] south of Pisa, 80 km [50 mi] west of Florence ☎ 050/500707 ⊕ www.pisa-airport.com. **Aeroporto Leonardo da Vinci** (FCO, also called Fiumicino) ✉ 35 km [20 mi] southeast of Rome ☎ 06/5953640 ⊕ www.adr.com.

Aeroporto Malpensa 2000 (MIL) ✉ 45 km [28 mi] north of Milan ☎ 02/74851 ⊕ www.sea-aeroportimilano.it.

BIKE TRAVEL

The number of travelers touring Tuscany and Umbria by bicycle has been on the rise. The back roads provide gorgeous scenery, and the Tuscan and Umbrian hills are challenging to even the best-conditioned riders. The greatest hazards to bikers are the fast cars and big trucks that travel the back roads and the lack of shoulders on the roads. Rather than ride alone, most bikers join organized tours. On your own, you can rent various types of bikes for €12 to €18 a day.

BIKES IN FLIGHT

Most airlines accommodate bikes as luggage, provided they are dismantled and boxed; check with individual airlines about packing requirements. Some airlines sell bike boxes, which are often free at bike shops, for about $20 (bike bags can be considerably more expensive). International travelers can often substitute a bike for a piece of checked luggage at no charge; otherwise, the cost is about $100. Most U.S. and Canadian airlines charge $40–$80 each way.

BOAT AND FERRY TRAVEL

Ferries connect the mainland with the Tuscan islands, including Elba, Capraia, Pianosa, Giglio, and Giannutri. To many destinations there is also hydrofoil (*aliscafo*) service, which is generally twice as fast as ferries and double the price. Service is considerably more frequent in summer months. Passenger and car ferries travel to Elba. If you're traveling in July or August, try to make reservations at least a month ahead. The Toremar and Moby Lines ferry (*traghetti*) companies accept major credit cards and cash, but not traveler's checks.

Two ferry lines operate along the coast of Cinque Terre: Golfo Paradiso, which operates from June to September from Genoa and Camogli to the Cinque Terre villages of Monterosso al Mare and Vernazza; and the smaller, but more frequent, Golfo dei Poeti, which stops at each village (from

Portovenere to Riomaggiore, except for Corniglia) four times a day.

Boat & Ferry Information Golfo Paradiso ⊠ Via Scalo 3, Camogli ☎ 0187/772091 ⊕ www.cinqueterre.it. **Golfo dei Poeti** ⊠ Via Mazzini 21 La Spezia ☎ 0187/732987 ⊕ www.cinqueterre.it. **Moby Lines** ⊠ Piazzale Premuda, Piombino ☎ 0565/221212 ⊕ www.mobylines.it. **Toremar** ⊠ Piazzale Premuda 13/14, Piombino ☎ 0565/31100 ⊕ www.toremar.it.

BUSINESS HOURS

Business hours vary from region to region in Italy. In Florence businesses can be open between 7 AM and 10 PM, but they cannot be open more than 13 hours a day. More than half of the stores close on Sunday and on national holidays. Many businesses stay closed Monday morning but open in the afternoon. In August, places shut down for two to four weeks.

BANKS & OFFICES

Banks are open weekdays 8:30–1:30 and 2:45–3:45. For post office hours, *see* Mail & Shipping.

CHURCHES

Most churches are open from early morning until noon or 12:30, when they close for three hours or more; they open again in the afternoon, closing about 7 PM or later. Major cathedrals and basilicas, such as the Duomo in Florence, are open all day. Note that sightseeing in churches during religious rites is discouraged.

GAS STATIONS

Gas stations are generally open Monday through Saturday 7–7 with a break at lunchtime. Gas stations on toll roads are open around the clock.

MUSEUMS & SIGHTS

Museum hours vary and often change with the seasons. Many museums are closed one day a week, often Monday. Small private museums may close for lunch. Always check locally.

PHARMACIES

Most pharmacies are open 9–1 and around 3:30–8. Cities such as Florence have two or three all-night pharmacies; signs usually posted in pharmacy windows provide information about the nearest one.

SHOPS

Many shops are open 9–1 and 3:30–7:30 Monday through Saturday. Barbers and hairdressers, with some exceptions, are closed Sunday and Monday. Some tourist-oriented shops in the larger cities and towns may be open all day, as well as on Sunday, as are some department stores and supermarkets.

BUS TRAVEL

Italy's bus network is extensive, although buses aren't as attractive an option as in other European countries, partly because of the low cost and convenience of train travel. Schedules are often drawn up with commuters and students in mind and may be sketchy on weekends. Regional bus companies often provide the only means (not including car travel) of getting to out-of-the-way places. Even when this isn't the case, buses can be faster and more direct than local trains, so it's a good idea to **compare bus and train schedules.**

Most of the major cities in Tuscany and Umbria have urban bus services. These buses are inexpensive, but they can become jammed, particularly at rush hours. Bus service outside cities is organized on a regional level and often operated by private companies. SITA operates throughout Italy; Lazzi Eurolines operates in Tuscany and central Italy. Inter-city buses are clean, air-conditioned, and comfortable. Neither city nor private buses permit smoking.

CLASSES

Both public and private buses offer only one class of service. Cleanliness and comfort levels are high on private buses, which have plenty of legroom and comfortable seats but no toilets.

CUTTING COSTS

Public bus lines offer student and monthly passes. Private lines offer one-, three- and six-month passes. Children under 3 feet in height ride free if they're traveling with an adult and don't require their own seat.

TICKETS & SCHEDULES

You may purchase tickets for city buses with cash from a machine at the station, at newsstands, or at tobacco shops. You must validate the bus ticket in the machine on the bus. For the private lines, tickets may be purchased with cash or a major credit card at the bus station, on the bus, or at travel agencies bearing the bus line's logo. Be sure to validate the ticket either at the bus station or on the bus as soon as you board. Bus schedules for private lines may be obtained online or at the bus station; city buses do not have schedules.

RESERVATIONS

Neither the private nor the public bus lines accept reservations.

◪ Bus Information **ATAF** ⊠ Stazione Centrale di Santa Maria Novella, Florence ☎ 055/5650642 or 055/5650222 ⊕ www.ataf.it. **Lazzi Eurolines** ⊠ Via Mercadante 2, Florence ☎ 055/363041 ⊕ www. lazzi.it. **SITA** ⊠ Via Santa Caterina da Siena 17/r, Florence ☎ 055/214721.

CAMERAS AND PHOTOGRAPHY

Tuscany is one of the world's premier spots for art and nature photography. For most purposes, an ISO 200 speed film is sufficient, although ISO 400 is a bit more versatile—and better for low-light situations. For action shots and lower light, you may want to choose a higher-speed film. Digital cameras are also a good choice for amateur and professional photographers.

Not everyone appreciates being photographed, particularly in smaller towns where locals have sometimes been exploited by photographers. Always ask for permission before taking a photograph of someone. Many museums and churches don't allow flash or tripods and may restrict cameras altogether.

The *Kodak Guide to Shooting Great Travel Pictures* (available at bookstores everywhere) is loaded with tips.

◪ Photo Help **Kodak Information Center** ☎ 800/242-2424 ⊕ www.kodak.com.

EQUIPMENT PRECAUTIONS

Don't pack film or equipment in checked luggage, where it is much more susceptible to damage. X-ray machines used to view checked luggage are extremely powerful and are therefore likely to ruin your film. Try to ask for hand inspection of film, which becomes clouded after repeated exposure to airport X-ray machines, and keep videotapes and computer disks away from metal detectors. Always keep film, tape, and computer disks out of the sun. Carry an extra supply of batteries, and be prepared to turn on your camera, camcorder, or laptop to prove to airport security personnel that the device is real.

FILM AND DEVELOPING

All major brands (Kodak, Polaroid, Fuji) of film are available in Tuscany and Umbria. Expect to pay between €4.20 and €6 for a roll of 36-exposure color-print film; often film comes in a three-roll package (approximately €12). One-hour and 24-hour developing are readily available in cities; midsize towns usually have 24-hour and three-day developing available. Local developers are reliable. The cost of 24-hour development of a roll of 36-exposure print film is about €8 to €12.50.

VIDEOS

While VHS videotapes and players are common, be forewarned that Italy, like other countries in Europe, uses a different video system than the one used in the United States. This means you won't be able to play the videotapes you bring from home on Italian equipment, and tapes purchased in Italy won't work in an American VCR. This is also true of DVDs and DVD players.

CAR RENTAL

Renting a car is essential for exploring the countryside, but not if you plan to stick to city travel. Major car-rental companies offer Ford-type cars (such as Ford Fusion) and Fiats in various sizes and in good condition, all with air-conditioning. The local rental companies provide good service, and depending on the time of year, they may have greater availability than the well-known international companies.

Because most Italian cars have standard transmissions, automatics are more expensive and must be reserved in advance. Mileage is usually unlimited, although certain offers limit included mileage to

150 km a day, after which you must pay for additional miles.

Hiring a car with a driver can come in handy, particularly if you plan to do some wine tasting. Ask at your hotel for recommended drivers, or inquire at the local tourist-information office. Typically, drivers are paid by the day, and are usually rewarded with a tip of about 15% on completion of the journey.

🚗 Major Agencies **Alamo** ☎ 800/522-9696 ⊕ www.alamo.com. **Avis** ☎ 800/331-1084, 800/879-2847 in Canada, 0870/606-0100 in the U.K., 02/9353-9000 in Australia, 09/526-2847 in New Zealand ⊕ www.avis.com. **Budget** ☎ 800/527-0700, 0870/156-5656 in the U.K. ⊕ www.budget.com. **Dollar** ☎ 800/800-6000, 0800/085-4578 in the U.K. ⊕ www.dollar.com. **Hertz** ☎ 800/654-3001, 800/263-0600 in Canada, 0870/844-8844 in the U.K., 02/9669-2444 in Australia, 09/256-8690 in New Zealand ⊕ www.hertz.com. **National Car Rental** ☎ 800/227-7368, 0870/600-6666 in the U.K. ⊕ www.nationalcar.com.

CUTTING COSTS

Most major U.S. car-rental companies have offices or affiliates in Italy, but the rates are generally better if you make a reservation from abroad rather than from within Italy. Each company's rental prices are uniform throughout Italy, so you won't save money by, for example, picking up a vehicle from a city rental office rather than from an airport location. For a good deal, book through a travel agent who will shop around.

Do look into wholesalers, companies that do not own fleets but rent in bulk from those that do and often offer better rates than traditional car-rental operations. Prices are best during off-peak periods. Rentals booked through wholesalers often must be paid for before you leave home.

🚗 Local Agencies **Program** ☎ 055/282916 in Florence, 050/500296 in Pisa.

🚗 Wholesalers **Auto Europe** ☎ 207/842-2000 or 800/223-5555 🖷 207/842-2222 ⊕ www.autoeurope.com. **Destination Europe Resources** (DER) ✉ 9501 W. Devon Ave., Rosemont, IL 60018 ☎ 800/782-2424 🖷 800/282-7474 ⊕ www.der.com. **Kemwel** ☎ 877/820-0668 or 800/678-0678 🖷 207/842-2147 ⊕ www.kemwel.com.

INSURANCE

When driving a rented car, you are generally responsible for any damage to or loss of the vehicle. Collision policies that car-rental companies sell for European rentals typically don't cover stolen vehicles. Indeed, all car-rental agencies operating in Italy require that you buy a theft-protection policy. Before you rent—and purchase collision coverage—see what coverage you already have under the terms of your personal auto-insurance policy and credit cards. Be aware that **coverage may be denied if the named driver on the rental contract is not the driver at the time of the incident.**

REQUIREMENTS AND RESTRICTIONS

In Italy your own driver's license is acceptable. An International Driver's Permit is a good idea; it's available from the American and Canadian automobile associations, and, in the United Kingdom, from the Automobile Association or Royal Automobile Club. These international permits are universally recognized, and having one in your wallet may save you a problem with the local authorities. In Italy you must be 21 years old to rent an economy or subcompact car, and most companies require customers under age 23 to pay by credit card. Upon rental, all companies require credit cards as a warranty; to rent bigger cars (2,000 cc or more), you must often show two credit cards. There are no special restrictions on senior-citizen drivers. Book car seats, required for children under age 3, in advance. The cost is generally about €36 for the duration of the rental.

SURCHARGES

Before you pick up a car in one city and leave it in another, ask about drop-off charges or one-way service fees, which can be substantial. Also inquire about early-return policies; some rental agencies charge extra if you return the car before the time specified in your contract while others give you a refund for the days not used. To avoid a hefty refueling fee, fill the tank just before you turn in the car, but be aware that gas stations near the rental outlet may overcharge. It's almost never a deal to buy the tank of gas that's in the car when you rent it; the understanding is that you'll return it empty, but some fuel usually remains. The cost for an additional driver (spouse included) is €4.50–€6.

CAR TRAVEL

Tuscany and Umbria have an extensive network of *autostrade* (toll highways), complemented by equally well maintained but free *superstrade* (expressways). The ticket you are issued upon entering an autostrada must be returned when you exit and pay the toll; on some shorter autostrade, mainly connecting highways, the toll is paid upon entering. Viacards, debit payment cards on sale at many autostrada locations (€25 at toll booths), make paying tolls easier and faster by avoiding the hunt for change to pay the toll. Pass through the Viacard lane at toll booths, slipping the card into the designated slot. A *raccordo* is a ring road surrounding a city. *Strade regionale and strade provinciale* (regional and provincial highways, denoted by *S, SS, SR,* or *SP* numbers) may be single-lane roads, as are all secondary roads; directions and turnoffs aren't always clearly marked.

Signs on country roads are usually pretty good, but be prepared for fast and impatient fellow drivers.

EMERGENCY SERVICES

Autostrade have emergency telephones at regular intervals. Automobil Club Italiano (ACI) offers 24-hour road service. Dial 803/116 from any phone at any time to reach the ACI dispatch operator. ACI also has a multilingual service to answer travelers' questions (cost: 57 European cents a minute). Many international car-rental companies also provide emergency service or information. Check your paperwork or ask when renting.

🚗 **Automobil Club Italiano (ACI)** ☎ 803/116 emergency service, 166/664477 multilingual travelers' service ⊕ www.aci.it.

GASOLINE

Gas stations are located at frequent intervals along the main highways and autostrade. In case you run out of gas along the toll roads or the main free *superstrade,*

emergency telephones are provided. To find the phone, look on the pavement at the shoulder of the highway where painted arrows and the term "SOS" point in the direction of the nearest phone. Usually on the periphery of towns and cities, they're rarely found in the center of municipalities. Gas stations on autostrade are open 24 hours. Otherwise, gas stations are generally open Monday through Saturday 7–7 with a break at lunchtime. Many stations have automatic self-service pumps that accept only bills of 5, 10, 20, and 50 euros and **don't give change** or a receipt (*ricevuta*). It's not customary to tip the attendant when full service is provided.

As of this writing, gas is (*benzina*) costs about €1.15 a liter. It's available in unleaded (*verde*) and super unleaded (*super*). Many rental cars in Italy take only diesel (*gasolio*) which costs about 95 European cents a liter; **ask about the fuel type before you leave the rental place.**

PARKING

Parking space is at a premium in most towns and cities, but especially in the *centri storici* (historic centers), which are filled with narrow streets and restricted circulation zones. It's advisable to **leave your car only in guarded parking areas.** In Florence such indoor parking costs €23–€30 for 12–24 hours; outside attended parking costs about €10–€20. Parking in an area signposted ZONA DISCO (disk zone) is allowed for limited periods (from 30 minutes to two hours or more—the limit is posted); if you don't have the cardboard disk (inquire at the local tourist office) to show what time you parked, you can use a piece of paper. The *parcometro,* the Italian version of metered parking in which you put coins into a machine for a stamped ticket that you leave on the dashboard, has been introduced in many cities.

Parking regulations are strictly enforced both in the cities and small towns. Fines run as high as €70 (more for taking a space designated for people with disabilities) and towing is possible in Florence. Car-rental companies may use your credit card to be reimbursed for any fines you incur during your rental period. In Tuscany and Umbria vandalism and theft of cars are rare. Nevertheless, **don't leave luggage or valuables in your car,** especially in cities and large towns where thieves target rental cars.

ROAD CONDITIONS

Driving on the back roads of Tuscany and Umbria isn't difficult as long as you're on the alert for bicycles and passing cars. In addition, street and road signs are often missing or placed in awkward spots, so a good map and patience are essential. Be aware that some maps may not use the *SR* or *SP* (*stradale regionale* and *stradale provinciale*) highway designations, which took the place of the old *SS* designations in 2004. They may use the old *SS* designation or no numbering at all. Autostrade are well maintained, as are most interregional highways. The condition of provincial (county) roads varies, but road maintenance at this level is generally good in Italy. In many small hill towns the streets are winding and extremely narrow; consider parking at the edge of town and exploring on foot.

Most autostrade have two lanes in both directions; the left lane is used only for passing. Italians drive fast and are impatient with those who don't, so tailgating is the norm here; the only way to avoid it is to get out of the way.

ROAD MAPS

Michelin and Touring Club Italia, which has shops in major Italian cities, produce good road maps. The Michelin Web site is good for driving instructions and maps (⊕ www.viamichelin.com). You can also get free street maps for most Tuscan and Umbrian towns at local information offices.

RULES OF THE ROAD

Driving is on the right. Regulations are largely as in Britain and the United States, except that the police have the power to levy on-the-spot fines. In most Italian towns the use of the horn is forbidden in certain, if not all, areas; a large sign, ZONA DI SILENZIO (silent zone), indicates where. Speed limits are 130 kph (80 mph) on autostrade and 110 kph (70 mph) on state and provincial

roads, unless otherwise marked. Enforcement of these limits varies from region to region. Penalties, however, are stiff, including high fines and suspension of driving privileges. Penalties for driving after drinking are heavy, too, including license suspension and the additional possibility of six months' imprisonment. The relevant blood-alcohol level is 0.05.

Right turns on red lights are forbidden. Headlights aren't compulsory when it's raining and snowing, but it's always a good idea to turn them on. Seat belts are required for adults, and infant and children's car seats are compulsory for babies and toddlers weighing up to 20 pounds and 38 pounds, respectively.

Many towns have central zones where only taxis and buses are permitted; rental cars may be allowed for pickups or drop-offs at central hotels.

CHILDREN IN TUSCANY AND UMBRIA

It's a good idea to provide older children who are allowed to wander on their own with a copy of their passport and the address and phone number of your hotel or rental apartment.

Although not widespread, discounts for children do exist in Italy. Always ask about a *sconto bambino* (child's discount) before purchasing tickets. Children under a certain height ride free on municipal buses and trams. Children under 18 who are European Union citizens are admitted free to state-run museums and galleries, and there are similar privileges in many municipal and private museums.

If you are renting a car, don't forget to arrange for a car seat when you reserve. For general advice about traveling with children, consult *Fodor's FYI: Travel with Your Baby* (available in bookstores everywhere).

FLYING

If your children are two or older, ask about children's airfares. As a general rule, infants under two not occupying a seat fly at greatly reduced fares or even for free. But if you want to guarantee a seat for an infant, you have to pay full fare. Consider flying during off-peak days and times; most airlines will grant an infant a seat without a ticket if there are available seats. When booking, confirm carry-on allowances if you're traveling with infants. In general, for babies charged 10% to 50% of the adult fare, you are allowed one carry-on bag and a collapsible stroller; if the flight is full, the stroller may have to be checked or you may be limited to less.

Experts agree that it's a good idea to use safety seats aloft for children weighing less than 40 pounds. Airlines set their own policies: if you use a safety seat, U.S. carriers usually require that the child be ticketed, even if he or she is young enough to ride free, because the seats must be strapped into regular seats. And even if you pay the full adult fare for the seat, it may be worth it, especially on longer trips. Do **check your airline's policy about using safety seats during takeoff and landing.** Safety seats are not allowed everywhere in the plane, so get your seat assignments as early as possible.

When reserving, request children's meals or a freestanding bassinet (not available at all airlines) if you need them. But note that bulkhead seats, where you must sit to use the bassinet, may lack an overhead bin or storage space on the floor.

FOOD

In restaurants and trattorias you may find a high chair or a cushion for a child to sit on, but rarely is a children's menu offered. Order a *mezza porzione* (half-portion) of any dish, or ask the waiter for a *porzione da bambino* (child's portion). Casual establishments such as trattorias are usually good choices for eating out with children. It's best to take only exceptionally well behaved children to higher-end restaurants; indeed, it's rare to see Italian children in them.

Although you won't find spaghetti and meatballs on menus, approximations of it, such as spaghetti *al pomodoro* (spaghetti with tomato sauce) are suitable substitutions. Italian children are fond of spaghetti with Parmesan, and even if it's not on the menu, most chefs are happy to prepare it. Other foods likely to find favor include pasta with butter (*pasta al burro*), fried or roast chicken (*pollo fritto* or *pollo arrosto*), french fries (*patate fritte*), pizza, and ice cream (*gelato*). McDonald's is an option, too; the chain is found throughout Tuscany and Umbria; Florence has four branches.

LODGING

Most hotels in Italy allow children under a certain age to stay in their parents' room at no extra charge, but others charge for them as extra adults; be sure to find out the cutoff age for children's discounts. Some five-star hotels and *agriturismi* are off-limits to children.

Many hotels provide cots or cribs with prior arrangement; four- and five-star hotels normally have these on hand. Babysitting isn't found as easily, especially at budget hotels. Pools in city hotels are a rarity, and video games virtually unheard-of. If you stay at a hotel with satellite TV, you'll have access to some English-language news programs, but little more. Even *The Simpsons* is dubbed into Italian.

PRECAUTIONS

Although safe to drink, Italian tap water is heavily chlorinated, which is one reason most Italians drink bottled water. Apple juice (*succo di mele*) is readily available in most bars and supermarkets, as are other fruit juices and popular soft drinks.

Mosquitoes can be pesky in warm weather. Travel with your usual brand of children's insect repellant. There are several Italian brands—Autun, for instance—that also do the trick. They're available in pharmacies and supermarkets.

SIGHTS AND ATTRACTIONS

Places that are especially appealing to children are indicated by a rubber-duckie icon (🦆) in the margin.

SUPPLIES AND EQUIPMENT

Baby formula and disposable diapers are available in all pharmacies; supermarkets also sell disposable diapers. The cost of diapers in Italy is similar to that in other countries, but American brands such as Pampers and Huggies cost slightly more here than in the United States. COOP, a reliable local brand, runs about €13 for 50 diapers, while Pampers cost about €9 for 20 and Huggies go for about €11 for 34.

American brands of baby food aren't widely available. Italian baby formula (premixed and powder) generally contains more vitamins than its American counterparts; Plasmon is a good brand. Italian bottles are identical to American ones, but no-spill glasses for toddlers are hard to find, so bring a couple with you. Jars of baby food and boxes of cereal are sold in grocery stores (local brands are Plasmon and Mellin).

COMPUTERS ON THE ROAD

Getting online in Italian cities isn't difficult: public Internet stations and Internet cafés, some open 24 hours, are becoming more and more common. Prices differ from place to place, so spend some time to find the best deal. This isn't always readily apparent: a place might appear to have higher rates, but if it belongs to a chain, it might not charge you an initial flat fee again when you visit a branch in another city. Wi-Fi hotspots are often within high-end hotels, major airports and train stations, Internet cafés, and shopping centers. Although there is no official map of Italian hotspots, you can check ⊕ www.hotspots.com for locations in Tuscany and Umbria. Some hotels have in-room modem lines, but, as with phones, using the hotel's line is relatively expensive. Always check modem rates before plugging in. You may need an adapter for your computer for the European-style plugs. If you are traveling with a laptop, carry a spare battery and an adapter. Never plug your computer into any socket before asking about surge protection. IBM sells a pea-size modem tester that plugs into a telephone jack to check whether the line is safe to use.

CONSUMER PROTECTION

Whether you're shopping for gifts or purchasing travel services, **pay with a major credit card** whenever possible, so you can cancel payment or get reimbursed if there's a problem (and you can provide documentation). If you're doing business with a particular company for the first time, contact your local Better Business Bureau and the attorney general's offices in your state and (for U.S. businesses) the company's home state as well. Have any complaints been filed? Finally, if you're buying a package or tour, always consider travel insurance that includes default coverage (⇨ Insurance).

BBBs Council of Better Business Bureaus ✉ 4200 Wilson Blvd., Suite 800, Arlington, VA 22203 ☎ 703/276-0100 📠 703/525-8277 ⊕ www.bbb.org.

CUSTOMS AND DUTIES

When shopping abroad, keep receipts for all purchases. Upon reentering the country, **be ready to show customs officials what you've bought.** Pack purchases together in an easily accessible place. If you think a duty is incorrect, appeal the assessment. If you object to the way your clearance was handled, note the inspector's badge number. In either case, first ask to see a supervisor. If the problem isn't resolved, write to the appropriate authorities, beginning with the port director at your point of entry.

IN AUSTRALIA

Australian residents who are 18 or older may bring home A$400 worth of souvenirs and gifts (including jewelry), 250 cigarettes or 250 grams of cigars or other tobacco products, and 1,125 ml of alcohol (including wine, beer, and spirits). Residents under 18 may bring back A$200 worth of goods. Members of the same family traveling together may pool their allowances. Prohibited items include meat products. Seeds, plants, and fruits need to be declared upon arrival.

Australian Customs Service 📫 Regional Director, Box 8, Sydney, NSW 2001 ☎ 02/9213-2000 or 1300/363-263, 02/9364-7222 or 1800/020-504 quarantine-inquiry line 📠 02/9213-4043 ⊕ www.customs.gov.au.

IN CANADA

Canadian residents who have been out of Canada for at least seven days may bring in C$750 worth of goods duty-free. If you've been away fewer than seven days but more than 48 hours, the duty-free allowance drops to C$200. If your trip lasts 24 to 48 hours, the allowance is C$50.

You may not pool allowances with family members. Goods claimed under the C$750 exemption may follow you by mail; those claimed under the lesser exemptions must accompany you. Alcohol and tobacco products may be included in the seven-day and 48-hour exemptions but not in the 24-hour exemption. If you meet the age requirements of the province or territory through which you reenter Canada, you may bring in, duty-free, 1.5 liters of wine *or* 1.14 liters (40 imperial ounces) of liquor *or* 24 12-ounce cans or bottles of beer or ale. Also, if you meet the local age requirement for tobacco products, you may bring in, duty-free, 200 cigarettes and 50 cigars. Check ahead of time with the Canada Customs and Revenue Agency or the Department of Agriculture for policies regarding meat products, seeds, plants, and fruits.

You may send an unlimited number of gifts (only one gift per recipient, however) worth up to C$60 each duty-free to Canada. Label the package UNSOLICITED GIFT—VALUE UNDER $60. Alcohol and tobacco are excluded.

🖪 **Canada Customs and Revenue Agency** ✉ 2265 St. Laurent Blvd., Ottawa, Ontario K1G 4K3 ☎ 800/461-9999 in Canada, 204/983-3500, 506/636-5064 ⊕ www.ccra.gc.ca.

IN ITALY

Travelers from the United States, Canada, the United Kingdom, Australia, and New Zealand should experience little difficulty clearing customs at any airports in Italy.

Of goods obtained anywhere outside the EU, the allowances are (1) 200 cigarettes or 100 cigarillos (under 3 grams) or 50 cigars or 250 grams of tobacco; (2) 2 liters of still table wine or 1 liter of spirits over 22% volume; and (3) 50 milliliters of perfume and 250 milliliters of toilet water.

Of goods obtained (duty and tax paid) within another EU country, the allowances are (1) 800 cigarettes or 400 cigarillos (under 3 grams) or 200 cigars or 1 kilogram of tobacco; (2) 90 liters of still table wine or 10 liters of spirits over 22% volume or 20 liters of spirits under 22% volume or 110 liters of beer.

There is no quarantine period in Italy, so if you want to travel with Fido or Fifi, it's possible. Contact your nearest Italian consulate to find out what paperwork is needed for entry into Italy; generally, it is a certificate noting that the animal is healthy and up-to-date on its vaccinations. Keep in mind, however, that the United States has some stringent laws about reentry: pets must be free of all diseases, especially those communicable to humans, and they must be vaccinated against rabies at least 30 days before returning. This means that if you are in Italy for a short-term stay, you must find a veterinarian or have your pet vaccinated before departure. (This law does not apply to puppies less than three months old.) Pets should arrive at the point of entry with a statement, in English, attesting to this fact.

🖪 **Ministero delle Finanze, Direzione Centrale dei Servizi Doganali, Divisione I** ✉ Via Carucci 71, Rome 00143 ☎ 06/50242117. **Dogana Sezione Viaggiatori** ✉ Aeroporto Leonardo da Vinci, Rome 00054 ☎ 06/65954343.

IN NEW ZEALAND

All homeward-bound residents may bring back NZ$700 worth of souvenirs and gifts; passengers may not pool their allowances, and children can claim only the concession on goods intended for their own use. For those 17 or older, the duty-free allowance also includes 4.5 liters of wine or beer; one 1,125-ml bottle of spirits; and either 200 cigarettes, 250 grams of tobacco, 50 cigars, *or* a combination of the three up to 250 grams. Meat products, seeds, plants, and fruits must be declared upon arrival to the Agricultural Services Department.

🖪 **New Zealand Customs** ✉ Head office: The Customhouse, 17–21 Whitmore St., Box 2218, Wellington ☎ 09/300-5399 or 0800/428-786 ⊕ www.customs.govt.nz.

IN THE U.K.

If you are a U.K. resident and your journey was wholly within the European Union, you probably won't have to pass through customs when you return to the United Kingdom. If you plan to bring back large quantities of alcohol or tobacco, check EU limits beforehand. In most cases, if you bring back more than 200 cigars, 3,200 cigarettes, 400 cigarillos, 10 liters of spirits, 110 liters of beer, 20 liters of fortified wine, and/or 90 liters of wine, you have to declare the goods upon return. Prohibited items include unpasteurized milk, regardless of country of origin.

HM Customs and Excise ⊠ Portcullis House, 21 Cowbridge Rd. E, Cardiff CF11 9SS ☎ 0845/010–9000 or 0208/929–0152 advice service, 0208/929–6731 or 0208/910–3602 complaints ⊕ www.hmce. gov.uk.

IN THE U.S.

U.S. residents who have been out of the country for at least 48 hours may bring home, for personal use, $800 worth of foreign goods duty-free, as long as they haven't used the $800 allowance or any part of it in the past 30 days. This exemption may include 1 liter of alcohol (for travelers 21 and older), 200 cigarettes, and 100 non-Cuban cigars. Family members from the same household who are traveling together may pool their $800 personal exemptions. For fewer than 48 hours, the duty-free allowance drops to $200, which may include 50 cigarettes, 10 non-Cuban cigars, and 150 ml of alcohol (or 150 ml of perfume containing alcohol). The $200 allowance cannot be combined with other individuals' exemptions, and if you exceed it, the full value of all the goods will be taxed. Antiques, which U.S. Customs and Border Protection defines as objects more than 100 years old, enter duty-free, as do original works of art done entirely by hand, including paintings, drawings, and sculptures. This doesn't apply to folk art or handicrafts, which are in general dutiable.

You may also send packages home duty-free, with a limit of one parcel per addressee per day (except alcohol or tobacco products or perfume worth more than $5). You can mail up to $200 worth of goods for personal use; label the package PERSONAL USE and attach a list of its contents and their retail value. If the package contains your used personal belongings, mark it AMERICAN GOODS RETURNED to avoid paying duties. You may send up to

$100 worth of goods as a gift; mark the package UNSOLICITED GIFT. Mailed items do not affect your duty-free allowance on your return.

To avoid paying duty on foreign-made high-ticket items you already own and will take on your trip, register them with Customs before you leave the country. Consider filing a Certificate of Registration for laptops, cameras, watches, and other digital devices identified with serial numbers or other permanent markings; you can keep the certificate for other trips. Otherwise, bring a sales receipt or insurance form to show that you owned the item before you left the United States.

For more about duties, restricted items, and other information about international travel, check out U.S. Customs and Border Protection's online brochure, *Know Before You Go*.

U.S. Customs and Border Protection ⊠ for inquiries and equipment registration, 1300 Pennsylvania Ave. NW, Washington, DC 20229 ⊕ www.cbp. gov ☎ 877/287–8667, 202/354–1000 ⊠ for complaints, Customer Satisfaction Unit, 1300 Pennsylvania Ave. NW, Room 5.2C, Washington, DC 20229.

DISABILITIES AND ACCESSIBILITY

Italy has begun to provide facilities such as ramps, telephones, and restrooms for people with disabilities, but such arrangements remain the exception, not the rule. Travelers' wheelchairs must be transported free of charge, according to Italian law, but the logistics of getting a wheelchair on and off trains and buses can make this requirement irrelevant. Seats are reserved for people with disabilities on public transportation, but few buses have lifts for wheelchairs. High, narrow steps for boarding trains create additional problems. In many monuments and museums, even in some hotels and restaurants, architectural barriers make access difficult. The Italian Government Tourist Board (ENIT; ⇨ Visitor Information) can give you a list of hotels that provide access and addresses of Italian associations for travelers with disabilities.

Contact the nearest Italian consulate about bringing a Seeing Eye dog into Italy. This requires an import license, a current certificate detailing the dog's inoculations, and a letter from your veterinarian certifying the dog's health.

🔠 Internet Resources **Access-Able Travel Service** ⊕ www.access-able.com.com; **Accessible Europe** ⊕ www.accessibleurope.com. **Consorzio Cooperative Integrate** ⊕ www.coinsociale.it.

RESERVATIONS

When discussing accessibility with an operator or reservations agent, ask hard questions. Are there any stairs, inside *or* out? Are there grab bars next to the toilet *and* in the shower/tub? How wide is the doorway to the room? To the bathroom? For the most extensive facilities meeting the latest legal specifications, opt for newer accommodations. If you reserve through a toll-free number, consider also calling the hotel's local number to confirm the information from the central reservations office. Get confirmation in writing when you can.

SIGHTS AND ATTRACTIONS

Getting around in Italy with a wheelchair is difficult but not impossible, as many of the top sights and attractions are accessible. In Florence, the Uffizi, Palazzo Pitti, Duomo, Baptistery, and the Accademia are all accessible. Local tourist offices provide maps and lists, rated on degrees of ease and difficulty, of banks, supermarkets, sights, hotels, and restaurants.

TRANSPORTATION

Most buses in Italy cannot accommodate wheelchairs; only a few have special ramps, so check with the private bus lines when planning a trip. All of Italy's airports are accessible to people who use wheelchairs. Except for the Pisa airport and Florence, most train stations rely on stairs and few have elevators or accessible passageways between tracks; contact the ticket or information office or the uniformed trackside employees for assistance crossing the tracks. Rental cars with hand controls aren't available in Tuscany and Umbria.

🔠 Complaints **Aviation Consumer Protection Division** (⇨ Air Travel) for airline-related problems. **Departmental Office of Civil Rights** ✉ for general inquiries, U.S. Department of Transportation, S-30,

400 7th St. SW, Room 10215, Washington, DC 20590 ☎ 202/366-4648 🖷 202/366-9371 ⊕ www.dot.gov/ost/docr/index.htm. **Disability Rights Section** ✉ NYAV, U.S. Department of Justice, Civil Rights Division, 950 Pennsylvania Ave. NW, Washington, DC 20530 ☎ ADA information line 202/514-0301, 800/514-0301, 202/514-0383 TTY, 800/514-0383 TTY ⊕ www.ada.gov. **U.S. Department of Transportation Hotline** ☎ for disability-related air-travel problems, 800/778-4838 or 800/455-9880 TTY.

TRAVEL AGENCIES

In the United States, the Americans with Disabilities Act requires that travel firms serve the needs of all travelers. Some agencies specialize in working with people with disabilities.

🔠 Travelers with Mobility Problems **Access Adventures/B. Roberts Travel** ✉ 206 Chestnut Ridge Rd., Scottsville, NY 14624 ☎ 585/889-9096 ⊕ www.brobertstravel.com ✍ dltravel@prodigy.net, run by a former physical-rehabilitation counselor. **Flying Wheels Travel** ✉ 143 W. Bridge St., Box 382, Owatonna, MN 55060 ☎ 507/451-5005 🖷 507/451-1685 ⊕ www.flyingwheelstravel.com.

DISCOUNTS AND DEALS

Be a smart shopper and compare all your options before making decisions. A plane ticket bought with a promotional coupon from travel clubs, coupon books, and direct-mail offers or purchased on the Internet may not be cheaper than the least expensive fare from a discount ticket agency. And always keep in mind that what you get is just as important as what you save.

DISCOUNT RESERVATIONS

To save money, look into discount reservations services with Web sites and toll-free numbers, which use their buying power to get a better price on hotels, airline tickets (⇨ Air Travel), and even car rentals. When booking a room, always **call the hotel's local toll-free number** (if one is available) rather than the central reservations number—you'll often get a better price. Always ask about special packages or corporate rates.

When shopping for the best deal on hotels and car rentals, look for guaranteed exchange rates, which protect you against a falling dollar. With your rate locked in, you won't pay more, even if the price goes up in the local currency.

F Airline Tickets **Air 4 Less** ☎ 800/AIR4LESS; low-fare specialist.

F Hotel Rooms **Accommodations Express** ☎ 800/444-7666 or 800/277-1064 ⊕ www.acex. net. **Hotels.com** ☎ 800/246-8357 ⊕ www.hotels. com. **Steigenberger Reservation Service** ☎ 800/ 223-5652 ⊕ www.srs-worldhotels.com. **Turbotrip. com** ☎ 800/473-7829 ⊕ www.turbotrip.com.

PACKAGE DEALS

Don't confuse packages and guided tours. When you buy a package, you travel on your own, just as though you had planned the trip yourself. Fly/drive packages, which combine airfare and car rental, are often a good deal. In cities, ask the local visitor's bureau about hotel and local transportation packages that include tickets to major museum exhibits or other special events. If you **buy a rail/drive pass**, you may save on train tickets and car rentals. All Eurailpass holders get a discount on Eurostar fares through the Channel Tunnel and often receive reduced rates for buses, hotels, ferries, sightseeing cruises, and car rentals.

EATING & DRINKING

The restaurants we list are the cream of the crop in each price category. Properties indicated by an ✕⊡ are lodging establishments whose restaurant warrants a special trip. Not too long ago, ristoranti tended to be more elegant and expensive than trattorie and osterie, which serve traditional, home-style fare in an atmosphere to match. But the distinction has blurred considerably, and an osteria in the center of town might be far fancier (and pricier) than a ristorante across the street. Although most restaurants in Tuscany and Umbria serve traditional local cuisine, you can find Asian and Middle Eastern alternatives in Florence, Perugia, and other cities. Menus are posted outside most restaurants (in English in tourist areas); if not, you might step inside and ask to take a look at the menu (but don't ask for a table unless you intend to stay).

Italians take their food as it is listed on the menu, seldom if ever making special requests such as "dressing on the side" or "hold the olive oil." If you have special dietary needs, however, make them known; they can usually be accommodated. Although mineral water makes its way to almost every table, you can order a carafe of tap water (*acqua di rubinetto* or *acqua semplice*) instead, but keep in mind that such water is highly chlorinated.

Wiping your bowl clean with a (small) piece of bread is considered a sign of appreciation, not bad manners. Spaghetti should be eaten with a fork only, although a little help from a spoon won't horrify locals the way cutting spaghetti into little pieces might. Order your espresso (Italians don't usually drink cappuccino after breakfast time) after dessert, not with it. Don't ask for a doggy bag.

The handiest and least expensive places for a quick snack between sights are probably bars, cafés, and pizza *al taglio* (by the slice) spots. Bars in Italy are primarily places to get a coffee and a bite to eat, rather than drinking establishments. Most have a selection of *panini* (sandwiches, often warmed up on the griddle) and *tramezzini* (sandwiches served on triangles of untoasted white bread). In larger cities, bars also serve prepared salads, fruit salads, cold pasta dishes, and yogurt around lunchtime. Most bars offer beer and a variety of alcohol, as well as wines by the glass. A café (*caffè* in Italian) is like a bar but usually with more tables. If you place your order at the counter, ask if you can sit down: some places charge extra for table service. In self-service bars and caffès, cleaning up your table before you leave is considered good manners. Note that in some places you have to pay before you place an order and then show your *scontrino* (receipt) when you move to the counter. Pizza al taglio shops are easy to negotiate. They sell pizza by weight: just point out which kind you want and how much. Very few pizza al taglio shops have seats.

MEALS & SPECIALTIES

The Italian breakfast (*la colazione*) is typically a cappuccino and a sweet roll served at the local bar. For a larger breakfast, consider dining rooms of large hotels. For lunch Italians may eat a couple of small panini while standing at a local bar or self-serve caffè. A more substantial lunch (*il pranzo*) consists of one or two courses at a trattoria. Dinner (*la cena*) out is likely to be two or three courses at a restaurant or trattoria or pizza and beer at a pizzeria.

Menus separate dishes into *antipasti* (starters), *primi piatti* (first courses), *secondi piatti* (second courses), *contorni* (side dishes), and *dolci* (desserts). At ristoranti, trattorie, and osterie, you're generally expected to order at least a two-course meal: a *primo* and a *secondo*; an antipasto followed by either primo or secondo; or, perhaps, a secondo and a *dolce*. Italian cuisine is still largely regional, so ask about the local specialties.

In an *enoteca* (wine bar) or pizzeria, it's not inappropriate to order one dish. An enoteca menu is often limited to a selection of cheeses, cured meats, salads, and desserts; if there's a kitchen, you may also find soups, pasta, meat, and fish. Most pizzerias don't offer just pizza, and although the other dishes on the menu are supposed to be starters, there's no harm in skipping the pizza. Typical pizzeria fare includes *affettati misti* (selection of cured pork), simple salads, and various kinds of bruschetta and *crostino* (similar to bruschetta, sometimes topped with cheese and broiled). All pizzerias have fresh fruit, ice cream, and simple desserts. But pizza at a caffè is to be avoided—it's usually frozen and reheated in a microwave oven.

MEALTIMES
Breakfast is usually served 7–10:30, lunch 12:30–2, and dinner 7:30–9:30 or 10. In Florence, however, lunch is generally served 1–2:30 (many places don't start serving until 1 PM), dinner 8–10:30; peak times are about 1:30 for lunch and 9 for dinner. Enoteche also are open in the morning and late afternoon for a snack at the counter. Most pizzerias open at 8 PM and close around midnight or 1 AM, or later in summer and on weekends. Most bars and caffès are open 7 AM–8 or 9 PM; a few stay open until midnight or so.

Unless otherwise noted, the restaurants listed in this guide are open daily for lunch and dinner.

PAYING
Major credit cards are widely accepted in Italian eating establishments, though cash is usually the preferred, and sometimes the only, means of payment—especially in small towns and rural areas. (More restaurants take Visa and MasterCard than American Express.) When you've finished your meal and are ready to go, **ask for the check** (*il conto*); unless it's well past closing time, no waiter will put a bill on your table until you've requested it.

Prices for goods and services in Italy include tax. The price of fish dishes is often given by weight (before cooking), so the price you see on the menu is for 100 grams of fish, not for the whole dish. (An average fish portion is about 350 grams.) Tuscan *bistecca fiorentina* is also often priced by weight.

Most restaurants charge a separate "cover" charge per person, usually listed on the menu as *pane e coperto* (or just *coperto*); this charge is not for the service. It should be a modest charge (€1–€2.50 per person), except at the most expensive restaurants. Some restaurants instead charge for bread, which should be brought to you (and paid for) only if you order it. A charge for service (*servizio*) may be included either as part of the menu prices or the total bill; if it is, tipping is unnecessary. It is customary to leave a small tip (one to five euros) in appreciation of good service when the service charge is not included in the bill. Tips are always given in cash. Whenever in doubt, ask about the servizio and pane e coperto policies upon ordering to avoid unpleasant discussions about payment later.

When you leave a dining establishment, take your meal bill or receipt with you; although not a common experience, the Italian finance (tax) police can approach you within 100 yards of the establishment at which you've eaten and ask for a receipt. If you don't have one, they can fine you and will fine the business owner for not providing the receipt. The measure is intended to prevent tax evasion; it's not necessary to show receipts when leaving Italy.

RESERVATIONS AND DRESS

Reservations are always a good idea in restaurants and trattorie, especially on weekends and holidays. We mention them only when they're essential or not accepted. Book as far ahead as you can, and reconfirm as soon as you arrive in town. (Large parties should always call ahead to check the reservations policy.) Pizzerias and enoteche usually accept reservations only for large groups.

We mention dress only when men are required to wear a jacket or a jacket and tie. But unless they're eating outdoors at a sea resort and perfectly tanned, Italian men never wear shorts or running shoes in a restaurant—no matter how humble—or in an enoteca. Shorts are acceptable in pizzerias and caffès. The same "rules" apply to women's casual shorts, running shoes, plastic sandals, and clogs.

WINE, BEER, AND SPIRITS

The grape has been cultivated in Italy since the time of the Etruscans, and Italians justifiably take pride in their local product. Though almost every region produces good-quality wine, Tuscany is one of the most renowned areas. Wine in Italy is considerably less expensive than almost anywhere else, so it's often affordable to order a bottle of wine at a restaurant rather than to stick with the house wine (which, nevertheless, may be quite good). Many bars have their own *aperitivo della casa* (house aperitif); Italians are imaginative with their mixed drinks, so you may want to try one.

You may purchase beer, wine, and spirits in any bar, grocery store, or enoteca, any day of the week. Italian and German beer is readily available, but it's more expensive than wine.

There's no minimum drinking age in Italy. Italian children begin drinking wine mixed with water at mealtimes when they are teens (or thereabouts). Italians are rarely seen drunk in public, and public drinking, except in a bar or eating establishment, isn't considered acceptable behavior. Bars usually close by 9 PM; hotel and restaurant

bars stay open until midnight. Brew pubs and discos serve until about 2 AM.

ECOTOURISM

Tuscany and Umbria have recycling programs in place. If you rent a house or apartment, ask the manager about the location of neighborhood bins for recycling glass, plastic, and paper.

ELECTRICITY

To use electric-powered equipment purchased in the U.S. or Canada, **bring a converter and adapter.** The electrical current in Italy is 220 volts, 50 cycles alternating current (AC); wall outlets take Continental-type plugs, with two round prongs.

If your appliances are dual-voltage, you'll need only an adapter. Don't use 110-volt outlets marked FOR SHAVERS ONLY for high-wattage appliances such as blow-dryers. Most laptops operate equally well on 110 and 220 volts and so require only an adapter.

EMBASSIES AND CONSULATES

🏴 Australia **Australian Embassy** ⊠ Via Allesandria 215, Rome ☎ 06/852721 🖶 06/85272300 ⊕ www.australia-embassy.it.
🏴 Canada **Canadian Embassy** ⊠ Via G.B. de Rossi 27, Rome ☎ 06/445981.
🏴 New Zealand **New Zealand Embassy** ⊠ Via Zara 28, Rome ☎ 06/4417171 ⊕ www.nzemb.org.
🏴 United Kingdom **British Consulate** ⊠ Via Lungarno Corsini 2, Florence ☎ 055/219112. **British Embassy** ⊠ Via XX Settembre 80A, Rome ☎ 06/4825441.
🏴 United States **U.S. Consulate** ⊠ Via Lungarno Vespucci 38, Florence ☎ 055/2398276. **U.S. Embassy** ⊠ Via Veneto 121, Rome ☎ 06/46741 ⊕ www.usembassy.it.

EMERGENCIES

No matter where you are in Italy, **dial 113 for all emergencies,** or find somebody (your concierge, a passerby) who will call for you, as not all 113 operators speak English; the Italian word to use to draw people's attention in an emergency is *aiuto* (help; pronounced "ah-YOU-toh"). *Pronto soccorso* means first aid, and when said to an operator will get you an *ambulanza* (ambulance). If you just need a doctor, you should ask for *un medico*; most hotels can refer you to a local doctor. Don't forget to ask the doctor for *una rice-vuta* (an invoice) to show your insurance company in order to get a reimbursement. Other useful Italian words to use in an emergency are *al fuoco* (fire; pronounced "ahl fuh-WOE-co") and *al ladro* (follow the thief; pronounced "ahl LAH-droh").

Italy has a national police force (*cara-binieri*) as well as local police (*polizia*). Both are armed and have the power to arrest and investigate crimes. Always report the loss of your passport to either the carabinieri or the police, as well as to your embassy. Local traffic officers are known as *vigili* (though their official name is *polizia municipale*)—they are responsible for, among other things, giving out parking tickets and clamping cars, so before you even consider parking the (illegal) Italian way, make sure you are at least able to spot their white (in summer) or black uniforms. Many are women. Should you find yourself involved in a minor car accident in town, you should contact the vigili. Many police stations have English-speaking staff to deal with travelers' problems. When reporting a crime, you'll be asked to fill out and sign a report form (*una denuncia*); keep a copy of your insurance company.

A country-wide toll-free number is used to call the carabinieri in case of emergency.
Carabinieri ☎ 112. **Emergencies** ☎ 113.

ENGLISH-LANGUAGE MEDIA

English-language books, newspapers, magazines, and television are easy to find in major cities such as Florence, Siena, Lucca, Viareggio, and Forte dei Marmi, but less so in other towns and villages. Most major hotels, even those in rural areas, have satellite television, which will have at least one English-language station.

BOOKS

In Florence and Perugia, English-language books are easily found.

NEWSPAPERS AND MAGAZINES

The best source for news in English is the *International Herald Tribune,* which is sold at most news agents in the major cities and major tourist towns. *USA Today* and most of the London newspapers are also available. You can find the Sunday *New York Times* in some places, but be prepared to pay an exorbitant amount for it. Various national versions of *Vogue* are obtainable, as are *Time, Newsweek, Elle, The Economist, InStyle, The New Yorker, Vanity Fair, The Tatler,* and *People,* among others. But they don't come cheap: *Vanity Fair,* for example, costs more than €8. In Florence, *Firenze Spectacolo,* a monthly events magazine, has a good entertainment overview section in English.

RADIO AND TELEVISION

Radio broadcasts are almost completely in Italian. Near Lucca and Livorno, however, you may be able to pick up the radio station of the U.S. military depot at Camp Darby.

Unless you have satellite TV (with access to CNN or SkyNews), or unless you speak Italian, Italian television is inaccessible, as everything is either filmed in Italian or dubbed into it. MTV is sometimes broadcast in English with Italian subtitles, and from 2 AM–5:30 AM the La7 TV station rebroadcasts CNN.

ETIQUETTE AND BEHAVIOR

Italy is full of churches, and many of them contain significant works of art. Because they are places of worship, care should be taken to dress appropriately. Shorts, miniskirts, tank tops, spaghetti straps, and sleeveless garments are taboo in most churches; short shorts are inappropriate anywhere. When touring churches—especially in the summer when it's hot and no sleeves are desirable—carry a sweater or shawl to wrap around your shoulders before entering the church, and always remember to take off your hat. Do not enter a church with food, and don't drink from your water bottle while inside. If a service is in progress, don't go inside. And if you have a cell phone, turn it off before entering.

Social behavior in Tuscany and Umbria tends to be more conservative and formal than in other parts of Italy. Upon meeting and leave-taking, both friends and strangers wish each other good day or good evening (*buon giorno, buona sera*); *ciao* isn't used between strangers. "Please" is *per favore*, "thank you" is *grazie,* and "you're welcome" is *prego.* When meeting, strangers will shake hands. Italians who are friends greet each other with a kiss, usually first on the right cheek, and then on the left. Very good friends might then kiss again on the right—but that's somewhat rare.

Table manners are formal; rarely do Italians share food from their plates. Flowers, chocolates, or a bottle of wine are appropriate hostess gifts when invited to dinner at the home of an Italian.

BUSINESS ETIQUETTE
Showing up on time for business appointments is the norm and expected in Italy. There are more business lunches than business dinners, and even business lunches aren't common, as Italians view mealtimes as periods of pleasure and relaxation. Business cards are used throughout Italy, and business suits are the norm for both men and women.

GAY AND LESBIAN TRAVEL
Same-sex couples should meet with no raised eyebrows from locals when traveling in Tuscany and Umbria. Nevertheless, overt displays of homosexual affection in public are rare. Florence, Perugia, Pisa, Viareggio, and Forte dei Marmi all have gay bars, and there are gay-friendly beaches at Torre del Lago, Parco dell'Uccellina, and Viareggio.

🖪 **Gay- and Lesbian-Friendly Travel Agencies** **Different Roads Travel** ⊠ 8383 Wilshire Blvd., Suite 520, Beverly Hills, CA 90211 ☎ 323/651-5557 or 800/429-8747 (Ext. 14 for both) 🖷 323/651-5454 ✑ lgernert@tzell.com. **Kennedy Travel** ⊠ 130 W. 42nd St., Suite 401, New York, NY 10036 ☎ 212/840-8659, 800/237-7433 🖷 212/730-2269 ⊕ www.kennedytravel.com. **Now, Voyager** ⊠ 4406 18th St., San Francisco, CA 94114 ☎ 415/626-1169 or 800/255-6951 🖷 415/626-8626 ⊕ www.nowvoyager.com. **Skylink Travel and Tour/Flying Dutchmen Travel** ⊠ 1455 N. Dutton Ave., Suite A, Santa Rosa, CA 95401 ☎ 707/546-9888 or 800/225-5759 🖷 707/636-0951; serving lesbian travelers.

🖪 Information in Italy **Azione Gay e Lesbica** ☝ c/o Andrea del Sarto, Via Manara 12, Florence ☎ 055/671298 ⊕ www.azionegayelesbica.it.

Circolo di Cultura Omosessuale Mario Mieli ⊠ Via Corinto 5, Rome ☎ 06/5960-4622 ⊕ www.mariomieli.org.

HEALTH
The Centers for Disease Control and Prevention (CDC) in Atlanta caution that most of southern Europe is in the "intermediate" range for risk of contacting traveler's diarrhea. Part of this risk may be attributed to an increased consumption of olive oil and wine, which can have a laxative effect on stomachs used to a different diet. The CDC also advises all international travelers to swim only in chlorinated swimming pools, unless they are absolutely certain the local beaches and freshwater lakes are not contaminated.

As of this writing, there has been one reported case of mad-cow disease in a human in Italy. The Italian desire for beef hasn't abated, and *vitello* (veal), *vitellone* (young beef), and *manzo* (beef) are considered safe to eat by both the Italian government and the European Union. Nevertheless, many restaurants and butchers have been widening their repertoire of meat dishes.

Medical care in Tuscany and Umbria is excellent. English-speaking medical assistance is available in Florence, Pisa, Perugia, Siena, and Lucca.

OVER-THE-COUNTER REMEDIES
It's always best to travel with your own medicines. The regulations regarding what medicines require a prescription aren't likely to be the same in Italy as in your home country—all the more reason to bring what you need with you. In general, medications that require prescriptions outside of Italy require them in Italy, too. You can buy aspirin (*aspirina*), ibuprofen (Cibalgina, Moment), antihistamines (*antistaminico*), and cough medicines (*sciroppo per la tosse*) at any pharmacy (*farmacia*). Tylenol and acetaminophen aren't available; a nonaspirin substitute called *paracetamolo*, also sold as Tachipirina or Efferalgan, is.

HOLIDAYS
National holidays include New Year's Day (January 1); Epiphany (January 6); Easter Sunday and Monday (March 27–28 in

2005; April 16–17 in 2006); Liberation Day (April 25); Labor Day or May Day (May 1); Assumption of Mary, also known as Ferragosto (August 15); All Saints' Day (November 1); Immaculate Conception (December 8); Christmas Day and Boxing Day (December 25 and 26).

The feast days of patron saints are observed locally. Many businesses and shops may be closed in Florence on June 24 (St. John the Baptist). (See also ⇨ Festivals and Seasonal Events.)

INSURANCE

The most useful travel-insurance plan is a comprehensive policy that includes coverage for trip cancellation and interruption, default, trip delay, and medical expenses (with a waiver for preexisting conditions).

Without insurance you'll lose all or most of your money if you cancel your trip, regardless of the reason. Default insurance covers you if your tour operator, airline, or cruise line goes out of business—the chances of which have been increasing. Trip-delay covers expenses that arise because of bad weather or mechanical delays. Study the fine print when comparing policies.

If you're traveling internationally, a key component of travel insurance is coverage for medical bills incurred if you get sick on the road. Such expenses aren't generally covered by Medicare or private policies. U.K. residents can buy a travel-insurance policy valid for most vacations taken during the year in which it's purchased (but check preexisting-condition coverage). British and Australian citizens need extra medical coverage when traveling overseas.

Always **buy travel policies directly from the insurance company**; if you buy them from a cruise line, airline, or tour operator that goes out of business, you probably won't be covered for the agency or operator's default, a major risk. Before making any purchase, review your existing health and home-owner's policies to find what they cover away from home.

🚩 Travel Insurers In the U.S.: **Access America** ✉ 2805 N. Parham Rd., Richmond, VA 23294 ☎ 800/284–8300 🖶 804/673–1491 or 800/346–

9265 ⊕ www.accessamerica.com. **Travel Guard International** ✉ 1145 Clark St., Stevens Point, WI 54481 ☎ 715/345–0505 or 800/826–1300 🖶 800/955–8785 ⊕ www.travelguard.com.

🚩 Insurance Information In the U.K.: **Association of British Insurers** ✉ 51 Gresham St., London EC2V 7HQ ☎ 020/7600–3333 🖶 020/7696–8999 ⊕ www.abi.org.uk. In Canada: **RBC Insurance** ✉ 6880 Financial Dr., Mississauga, Ontario L5N 7Y5 ☎ 800/668–4342 or 905/816–2400 🖶 905/813–4704 ⊕ www.rbcinsurance.com. In Australia: **Insurance Council of Australia** ✉ Insurance Enquiries and Complaints, Level 12, Box 561, Collins St. W, Melbourne, VIC 8007 ☎ 1300/780808 or 03/9629–4109 🖶 03/9621–2060 ⊕ www.iecltd.com.au. In New Zealand: **Insurance Council of New Zealand** ✉ Level 7, 111–115 Customhouse Quay, Box 474, Wellington ☎ 04/472–5230 🖶 04/473–3011 ⊕ www.icnz.org.nz.

LANGUAGE

In the main tourist cities, such as Florence, most hotels have English speakers at their reception desks, and you can always find someone who speaks at least a little English otherwise. Remember that the Italian language is pronounced exactly as it is written. You may run into a language barrier in the countryside, but a phrase book and the use of pantomime and expressive gestures will go a long way. Try to **master a few phrases for daily use** and familiarize yourself with the terms you'll need for deciphering signs and museum labels.

LANGUAGES FOR TRAVELERS

A phrase book and language-tape set can help get you started. *Fodor's Italian for Travelers* (available at bookstores everywhere) is excellent.

LODGING

The lodgings we list are the cream of the crop in each price category. We always list the facilities that are available, but we don't specify whether they cost extra; when pricing accommodations, always ask what's included and what costs extra. Properties are assigned price categories based on the range between their least and most expensive standard double rooms at high season (excluding holidays). Properties indicated by an ✕▦ are lodging establishments whose restaurants warrant a special trip.

Tuscany has a varied and abundant number of hotels, B&Bs, *agriturismi,* and rental properties. In both the cities and the country you can find very sophisticated, luxurious palaces and villas as well as rustic farm houses and small hotels. Tuscan establishments are generally run with pride and are very clean.

Assume that hotels operate on the European Plan (EP, with no meals) unless we specify that they use the Continental Plan (CP, with a Continental breakfast), Breakfast Plan (BP, with a full breakfast), Modified American Plan (MAP, with breakfast and dinner), or the Full American Plan (FAP, with all meals).

APARTMENT & VILLA RENTALS

If you want a home base that's roomy enough for a family and comes with cooking facilities, consider a furnished rental. These can save you money, especially if you're traveling with a group. Home-exchange directories sometimes list rentals as well as exchanges.

🏠 Local Agents **The Best in Italy** ✐ Via Ugo Foscolo 72, Florence 50124 ☎ 055/223064 🖶 055/2298912 ⊕ www.thebestinitaly.com. **Pitcher & Flaccomio Ltd** ✉ Via Pietro Thouar 2, Florence 50122 ☎ 055/2343354 🖶 055/2347240 ⊕ www.pitcherflaccomio.com. **Windows on Tuscany** ✉ Via dei Serragli 6/r, Florence 50124 ☎ 055/268510 🖶 055/2381524 ⊕ www.windowsontuscany.com
🏠 International Agents **At Home Abroad** ✐ 163 Third Ave., No. 319, New York, NY 10003 ☎ 212/421-9165 🖶 212/533-0095 ⊕ www.athomeabroadinc.com. **Drawbridge to Europe** ✉ 98 Granite St., Ashland, OR 97520 ☎ 541/482-7778 or 888/268-1148 🖶 541/482-7779 ⊕ www.drawbridgetoeurope.com. **Hideaways International** ✉ 767 Islington St., Portsmouth, NH 03801 ☎ 603/430-4433 or 800/843-4433 🖶 603/430-4444 ⊕ www.hideaways.com, annual membership $145. **Solemar** ✉ 1990 N.E. 163rd St., Suite 110, North Miami Beach, FL 33162 ☎ 305/940-2299 or 800/882-6864 🖶 305/940-2911 ⊕ www.visit-toscana.com. **Villanet** ✉ 1251 N.W. 116th St., Seattle, WA 98177 ☎ 206/417-3444 or 800/964-1891 🖶 206/417-1832 ⊕ www.rentavilla.com.
🏠 Italy Agencies **Cuendet USA** ✉ 165 Chestnut St., Allendale, NJ 07401 ☎ 201/327-2333. **Eurovillas** ✉ 3212 Jefferson St., Suite 298, Napa, CA 94558

☎ 800/767-0275 🖶 707/648-2066. **Rentvillas.com** ✉ 1742 Calle Corva, Camarillo, CA 93010 ☎ 805/987-5278 or 800/726-6702 🖶 805/482-7976 ⊕ www.rentvillas.com. **Vacanze in Italia** ✉ 22 Railroad St., Great Barrington, MA 01230 ☎ 413/528-6610 or 800/533-5405.
🏠 In the U.K. **CV Travel** ✉ 43 Cadogan St., London SW3 2PR, England ☎ 020/7581-0851. **Magic of Italy** ✉ 227 Shepherds Bush Rd., London W6 7AS, England ☎ 020/8748-7575.

BED & BREAKFASTS

You can find cozy B&Bs in Florence and Siena as well as in more rural areas. In towns and villages, B&Bs tend to be personal, homey, simple, and clean. In the Tuscan countryside you can find private villas that offer B&B accommodations; many are very upscale.
🏠 Reservation Services **Bed & Breakfast Italy** ⊕ www.bed-and-breakfast-in-italy.com. **5 Terre.com** ⊕ www.5terre.com. **Florence By Net** ✉ Piazza Pitti 22, Florence 50100 ⊕ www.florence.ala.it/bandb.htm.

CAMPING

Camping is particularly common in beach towns and in the mountains. Campgrounds are generally crowded in summer (usually with Italians and Germans) and vary in amenities depending on the place: some have showers, toilets, sinks, bars, restaurants, and shade trees. These campgrounds, which tend to draw families that rent the same space year after year, can be noisy and full of children. Camping in the national parks and on the beaches is more rustic and private, but also more restrictive. (Sleeping on the beach is illegal in Italy, which is not to say that people don't do it.) You may be required to break camp every morning and clear your space.

FARM HOLIDAYS AND AGRITOURISM

Rural accommodations in the *agriturismo* (agritourism) category are increasingly popular with both Italians and visitors to Italy; you stay on a working farm or vineyard. Accommodations vary in size and range from luxury apartments, farmhouses, and villas to very basic facilities. Agriturist has compiled *Agriturismo,* which is available only in Italian but includes more than 1,600 farms in Italy;

pictures and the use of international symbols to describe facilities make the guide a good tool. Local APT tourist offices also have information.

▣ Agencies Agriturist ✉ Corso Vittorio 101, 00186 Rome ☎ 06/685-2342. **Essentially Tuscany** ✉ 30 York St., Nantucket, MA 02554 ☎☎ 508/228-2514. **Italy Farm Holidays** ✉ 547 Martling Ave., Tarrytown, NY 10591 ☎ 914/631-7880 ☎ 914/631-8831. **Terra Nostra** ✉ Via XXIV Maggio 43, 00187 Rome ☎ 06/46821. **Turismo Verde** ✉ Via Flaminia 56, 00196 Rome ☎ 06/361-1051.

HOME EXCHANGES

If you would like to exchange your home for someone else's, join a home-exchange organization, which will send you its updated listings of available exchanges for a year and will include your own listing in at least one of them. It's up to you to make specific arrangements.

▣ Exchange Clubs HomeLink International ✉ Box 47747, Tampa, FL 33647 ☎ 813/975-9825 or 800/638-3841 ☎ 813/910-8144 ⊕ www.homelink. org; $110 yearly for a listing, online access, and catalog; $70 without catalog.

HOSTELS

No matter what your age, you can save on lodging costs by staying at hostels. In some 4,500 locations in more than 70 countries around the world, Hostelling International (HI), the umbrella group for a number of national youth-hostel associations, offers single-sex, dorm-style beds and, at many hostels, rooms for couples and family accommodations. Membership in any HI national hostel association, open to travelers of all ages, allows you to stay in HI-affiliated hostels at member rates; one-year membership is about $28 for adults (C$35 for a two-year minimum membership in Canada, £14 in the U.K., A$52 in Australia, and NZ$40 in New Zealand); hostels charge about $10–$30 per night. Members have priority if the hostel is full; they're also eligible for discounts around the world, even on rail and bus travel in some countries.

For information about hostels in Italy, also check out www.ostellionline.org.

▣ Organizations Hostelling International–USA ✉ 8401 Colesville Rd., Suite 600, Silver Spring, MD

20910 ☎ 301/495-1240 ☎ 301/495-6697 ⊕ www. hiusa.org. **Hostelling International–Canada** ✉ 205 Catherine St., Suite 400, Ottawa, Ontario K2P 1C3 ☎ 613/237-7884 or 800/663-5777 ☎ 613/237-7868 ⊕ www.hihostels.ca. **YHA England and Wales** ✉ Trevelyan House, Dimple Rd., Matlock, Derbyshire DE4 3YH, U.K. ☎ 0870/870-8808, 0870/770-8868, 0162/959-2600 ☎ 0870/770-6127 ⊕ www.yha.org.uk. **YHA Australia** ✉ 422 Kent St., Sydney, NSW 2001 ☎ 02/9261-1111 ☎ 02/9261-1969 ⊕ www.yha.com.au. **YHA New Zealand** ✉ Level 1, Moorhouse City, 166 Moorhouse Ave., Box 436, Christchurch ☎ 03/379-9970 or 0800/278-299 ☎ 03/365-4476 ⊕ www.yha.org.nz.

HOTELS

All hotels listed have private bath unless otherwise noted.

Italian hotels are awarded stars (one to five) based on their facilities and services. Keep in mind, however, that these are general indications and that a charming three-star might make for a better stay than a more expensive four-star. In the major cities, room rates are on a par with other European capitals: deluxe and four-star rates can be downright extravagant. In those categories, **ask for one of the better rooms,** because the less-desirable rooms— and there usually are some—don't give you what you're paying for. Except in deluxe and some four-star hotels, rooms may be very small by U.S. standards, and bathrooms usually have showers rather than bathtubs. Hotels with three or more stars always have bathrooms in all rooms.

In all hotels, a rate card inside the door of your room or inside the closet door tells you exactly what you pay for that particular room (rates in the same hotel may vary according to the location and type of room). On this card, breakfast and any other options must be listed separately. Any discrepancy between the basic room rate and that charged on your bill is cause for complaint to the manager and to the police.

Although by law breakfast is supposed to be optional, most hotels quote room rates including breakfast. When you book a room, specifically **ask whether the rate includes breakfast** (*colazione*). You are under no obligation to take breakfast at your hotel, but in practice most hotels expect you to do so. The trick is to "offer" guests "complimentary" breakfast and have its cost built into the rate. However, it's encouraging to note that many of the hotels we recommend provide generous buffet breakfasts instead of simple, even skimpy "Continental breakfasts." Remember, if the latter is the case, you can eat for less at the nearest coffee bar.

Hotels in the $$ and $ categories may charge extra for optional air-conditioning. In older hotels the quality of the rooms may be very uneven; if you don't like the room you're given, request another. This applies to noise, too. Front rooms may be larger or have a view, but they also may have a lot of street noise. If you're a light sleeper, request a quiet room when making reservations. Rooms in lodgings listed in this guide have a shower and/or bath, unless noted otherwise. (All hotels listed have private bath unless otherwise noted.) Remember to specify whether you care to have a bath or shower—not all rooms have both. It's always a good idea to have your reservation, dates, and rate confirmed by fax or e-mail.

High season in Italy, when rooms are at a premium, generally runs from Easter through the beginning of November, and then for two weeks at Christmas time. During low season and whenever a hotel isn't full, it's often possible to negotiate a discounted rate. Major cities have no official off-season as far as hotel rates go, but some hotels do offer substantial discounts during the slower parts of the year and on weekends. Always **inquire about special rates.** Major cities have hotel-reservation service booths in train stations.

RESERVING A ROOM
Toll-Free Numbers Best Western ☎ 800/528-1234 ⊕ www.bestwestern.com. **Choice** ☎ 800/424-6423 ⊕ www.choicehotels.com. **Comfort Inn** ☎ 800/424-6423 ⊕ www.choicehotels.com. **Hilton** ☎ 800/445-8667 ⊕ www.hilton.com. **Holiday Inn** ☎ 800/465-4329 ⊕ www.ichotelsgroup.com. **Radisson** ☎ 800/333-3333 ⊕ www.radisson.com. **Sheraton** ☎ 800/325-3535 ⊕ www.starwood.com/sheraton.

MAIL AND SHIPPING
The Italian mail system is notoriously slow. Allow up to 15 days for mail to and from the United States, Canada, Australia, and New Zealand. It takes about a week to and from the United Kingdom and within Italy. Posta Prioritaria (for Italy only) and Postacelere (for Italy and abroad) are special-delivery services from the post office that guarantee delivery within 24 hours in Italy and three to five days abroad.

Post offices are open Monday through Saturday 9–12:30; central and main district post offices stay open until 6 PM weekdays for some operations, 9–12:30 on Saturday. On the last day of the month, post offices close at midday.

OVERNIGHT SERVICES
Overnight mail is generally available in all major cities and at resort hotels. Pickups are daily, excluding weekends. Service is reliable. A Federal Express letter to the United States costs about €15, to the United Kingdom, €17, and to Australia and New Zealand €19. Overnight delivery usually means 24–36 hours.

In Florence and Perugia, many Internet cafés offer overnight mail services at reasonable rates using major overnight carriers; if your hotel can't help you out, try an Internet café.
Major Services DHL ☎ 199/199345. **Federal Express** ☎ 800/123800. **Mailboxes, Etc.** ⊕ www.mbe.com. **SDA** ☎ 800/016027.

POSTAL RATES
Airmail letters and postcards (lightweight stationery) sent *ordinaria* (standard service) to the United States and Canada cost 65 European cents for the first 20 grams, €1 for 21 to 50 grams, and €1.30 for 51 to 100 grams. Always stick the blue airmail tag on your mail, or write "Airmail" in big, clear letters to the side of the address. Expect postcards and letters sent *ordinaria* to take up to 15 days to arrive. Postcards and letters sent *ordinaria* (for the first 20 grams) to the United Kingdom, as well as to any other EU country, including Italy, cost 45 European cents.

Posta Prioritaria (stationery and small packages up to 2 kilograms) and the more expensive Postacelere (up to 20 kilograms) are special delivery services from the post office that guarantee delivery within 24 hours in Italy and three to five days abroad. Lightweight stationery sent as Posta Prioritaria to the United States and Canada costs 80 European cents for the first 20 grams, €1.50 for 21 to 50 grams, and €1.80 for 51 to 100 grams; to the United Kingdom, Italy, and all other EU countries it costs 62 European cents. Buy the special golden Posta Prioritaria stamps and use the Prioritaria blue stickers.

Postacelere will deliver packages weighing up to 30 kilograms within three to five working days. Postacelere rates to the United States and Canada are between €35.05 (€28.15 to the United Kingdom and Europe) for parcels up to 500 grams (a little over a pound) and €195.90 (€137.61 to the United Kingdom and Europe) for packages weighing 30 kilograms. Other package services to check are Quick Pack Europe, for delivery within the EU; and EMS ExpressMail Service, a global three- to five-day service for letters and packages which can be less expensive than Postacelere.

You can buy stamps at most tobacconists and post offices.

🖪 Postal Information **Informazioni Poste Italiane** ☎ 803/160, 31-European-cent information call in Italian about rates and local post offices' opening hours, 800/009966, toll-free Postacelere information ⊕ www.poste.it.

RECEIVING MAIL

Correspondence can be addressed to you in care of the Italian post office. Letters should be addressed to your name, "c/o Ufficio Postale Centrale," followed by "Fermo Posta" on the next line, and the name of the city (preceded by its postal code) on the next. You can **collect it at the central post office** by showing your passport or photo-bearing I.D. and paying a small fee. American Express also has a general-delivery service. There's no charge for cardholders, holders of American Express Traveler's checks, or anyone who booked a vacation with American Express.

SHIPPING PARCELS

You can ship parcels via air or surface. Air takes about two weeks, and surface anywhere up to three months. When purchasing antiques, ceramics, or other objects, ask whether the vendor will do the shipping for you; in most cases this is a possibility.

MONEY MATTERS

As in most countries, prices vary from region to region and are a bit lower in the countryside than in cities. Umbria and the Marches offer good value for the money. Admission to the Galleria degli Uffizi is €9.50. A movie ticket is €7. A daily English-language newspaper is €2. A taxi ride (1⅓ km [1 mi]) costs €8.50.

Prices throughout this guide are given for adults, in euros. Substantially reduced fees are sometimes available for children, students, and senior citizens from the EU; citizens of non-EU countries rarely get discounts. For information on taxes, *see* Taxes.

ATMS

Fairly common in banks in large and small towns, as well as in airports and train stations, ATMs are the easiest way to get euros in Italy. All major banks are members of Cirrus and/or Plus. You won't find an ATM (*bancomat* in Italian) in hotels or grocery stores, however. Before you leave home, **memorize your PIN in numbers,** not letters, because ATM keypads in Italy don't show letters. Check with your bank to confirm that you have an international PIN (*codice segreto*), to find out your maximum daily withdrawal allowance, and to learn what the bank fee is for withdrawing money.

CREDIT CARDS

In Italy, Visa and MasterCard are preferred over American Express, but in tourist areas American Express is usually accepted. While increasingly common, credit cards aren't accepted at all establishments, and some places require a minimum expenditure. If you want to pay with a card in a small hotel, store, or restaurant, it's a good idea to make your intentions known early on. **Notify your credit**

card companies of your travel plans before you leave home; the recent fraud prevention programs frequently suspend a cardholder's credit when foreign activity is detected on the card.

Throughout this guide, the following abbreviations are used: **AE**, American Express; **DC**, Diners Club; **MC**, MasterCard; and **V**, Visa.

Discover is rarely accepted in Italy.

🗐 Reporting Lost Cards **American Express** ☎ 336/668–5110 international collect, 06/72282 in Italy. **Diners Club** ☎ 702/797–5532 collect, 800/ 864064 in Italy. **MasterCard** ☎ 800/870866 in Italy. **Visa** ☎ 800/821001 in Italy.

CURRENCY

The euro is the main unit of currency in Italy, as well as in 11 other European countries. Under the euro system, there are eight coins: 1, 2, 5, 10, 20, and 50 *centesimi* (cents, at 100 centesimi to the euro), and 1 and 2 euros. There are seven notes: 5, 10, 20, 50, 100, 200, and 500 euros.

CURRENCY EXCHANGE

For the most favorable rates, **change money through banks.** Although ATM transaction fees may be higher abroad than at home, ATM rates are excellent because they're based on wholesale rates offered only by major banks. You won't do as well at exchange booths in airports or rail and bus stations, in hotels, in restaurants, or in stores. To avoid lines at airport exchange booths, get a bit of local currency before you leave home.

At this writing, the exchange rate is about 81 European cents to US$1, 63 European cents to C$1, 56 European cents to A$1, 53 European cents to NZ$1, and €1.46 to the pound sterling.

🗐 Exchange Services **International Currency Express** ✉ 427 N. Camden Dr., Suite F, Beverly Hills, CA 90210 ☎ 888/278–6628 orders 🖷 310/278–6410 🌐 www.foreignmoney.com. **Travel Ex Currency Services** ☎ 800/287–7362 orders and retail locations 🌐 www.travelex.com.

TRAVELER'S CHECKS

Do you need traveler's checks? It depends on where you're headed. If you're going to rural areas and small towns, go with

cash; traveler's checks are best used in cities. Lost or stolen checks can usually be replaced within 24 hours. To ensure a speedy refund, buy your own traveler's checks—don't let someone else pay for them: irregularities like this can cause delays. The person who bought the checks should make the call to request a refund. Request checks in the local currency, the euro, to obtain the best exchange rate.

PACKING

The weather is considerably milder, in the winter at least, in Italy than in the northern and central United States or Great Britain. In summer, stick with very light clothing, as things can get steamy in the height of summer; a sweater may be necessary for cool evenings, especially in the mountains and on islands even during the hot months. Sunglasses, a hat, and sunblock are essential. Brief summer afternoon thunderstorms are common in inland cities, so an umbrella will come in handy. In winter, bring a coat, gloves, hats, scarves, and boots. Even in mild areas, central heating may not be up to your standards, and interiors can be cold and damp; take wools or flannel rather than sheer fabrics. Bring sturdy shoes for winter and comfortable walking shoes in any season.

Italians dress exceptionally well. They do not usually wear shorts. Men aren't required to wear ties or jackets anywhere, except in some of the grander hotel dining rooms and top-level restaurants, but are expected to look reasonably sharp—and they do. Formal wear is the exception rather than the rule at the opera nowadays, though people in expensive seats usually do get dressed up.

A certain modesty of dress (no bare shoulders or knees) is expected in churches, and strictly enforced in many.

For sightseeing, **pack a pair of binoculars;** they will help you get a good look at painted ceilings and domes. If you stay in budget hotels, **take your own soap.** Many such hotels do not provide it or give guests only one tiny bar per room.

In your carry-on luggage, pack an extra pair of eyeglasses or contact lenses and enough of any medication you take to last a few days longer than the entire trip. You may also ask your doctor to write a spare prescription using the drug's generic name, as brand names may vary from country to country. In luggage to be checked, **never pack prescription drugs, valuables, or un-developed film.** And don't forget to carry with you the addresses of offices that handle refunds of lost traveler's checks. Check *Fodor's How to Pack* (available at online retailers and bookstores everywhere) for more tips.

To avoid customs and security delays, carry medications in their original packaging. Don't pack any sharp objects in your carry-on luggage, including knives of any size or material, scissors, nail clippers, and corkscrews, or anything else that might arouse suspicion.

To avoid having your checked luggage chosen for hand inspection, don't cram bags full. The U.S. Transportation Security Administration suggests packing shoes on top and placing personal items you don't want touched in clear plastic bags.

CHECKING LUGGAGE

You're allowed to carry aboard one bag and one personal article, such as a purse or a laptop computer. Make sure what you carry on fits under your seat or in the overhead bin. Get to the gate early, so you can board as soon as possible, before the overhead bins fill up.

Baggage allowances vary by carrier, destination, and ticket class. On international flights you're usually allowed to check two bags weighing up to 70 pounds (32 kilograms) each, although a few airlines allow checked bags of up to 88 pounds (40 kilograms) in first class. Some international carriers don't allow more than 66 pounds (30 kilograms) per bag in business class and 44 pounds (20 kilograms) in economy. On domestic flights the limit is usually 50 to 70 pounds (23 to 32 kilograms) per bag. In general, carry-on bags shouldn't exceed 40 pounds (18 kilograms). Most airlines won't accept bags that weigh more than 100 pounds (45 kilograms) on domestic or international flights. Expect to pay a fee for baggage that exceeds weight limits. Check baggage restrictions with your carrier before you pack.

Airline liability for baggage is limited to $2,500 per person on flights within the United States. On international flights it amounts to $9.07 per pound or $20 per kilogram for checked baggage (roughly $640 per 70-pound bag), with a maximum of $634.90 per piece, and $400 per passenger for unchecked baggage. You can buy additional coverage at check-in for about $10 per $1,000 of coverage, but it often excludes a rather extensive list of items, shown on your airline ticket.

Before departure, itemize your bags' contents and their worth, and label the bags with your name, address, and phone number. (If you use your home address, cover it so potential thieves can't see it readily.) Include a label inside each bag and **pack a copy of your itinerary.** At check-in, make sure each bag is correctly tagged with the destination airport's three-letter code. Because some checked bags will be opened for hand inspection, the U.S. Transportation Security Administration recommends that you leave luggage unlocked or use the plastic locks offered at check-in. TSA screeners place an inspection notice inside searched bags, which are resealed with a special lock.

If your bag has been searched and contents are missing or damaged, file a claim with the TSA Consumer Response Center as soon as possible. If your bags arrive damaged or fail to arrive at all, file a written report with the airline before leaving the airport.

🆕 Complaints **U.S. Transportation Security Administration Contact Center** ☎ 866/289-9673 ⊕ www.tsa.gov.

PASSPORTS AND VISAS

When traveling internationally, carry your passport even if you don't need one (it's always the best form of I.D.) and **make two photocopies of the data page** (one for someone at home and another for you, carried separately from your passport). If you lose your passport, promptly call the nearest embassy or consulate and the local police.

U.S. passport applications for children under age 14 require consent from both parents or legal guardians; both parents must appear together to sign the application. If only one parent appears, he or she must submit a written statement from the other parent authorizing passport issuance for the child. A parent with sole authority must present evidence of it when applying; acceptable documentation includes the child's certified birth certificate listing only the applying parent, a court order specifically permitting this parent's travel with the child, or a death certificate for the nonapplying parent. Application forms and instructions are available on the Web site of the U.S. State Department's Bureau of Consular Affairs (⊕ travel.state.gov).

ENTERING ITALY

Citizens of Australia, Canada, New Zealand, and the U.S. need only a valid passport to enter Italy for stays of up to 90 days. U.K. citizens need only a valid passport to enter Italy for an unlimited stay.

PASSPORT OFFICES

The best time to apply for a passport or to renew is in fall and winter. Before any trip, check your passport's expiration date, and, if necessary, renew it as soon as possible.

🇦🇺 Australian Citizens **Passports Australia** Australian Department of Foreign Affairs and Trade ☎ 131-232 ⊕ www.passports.gov.au.

🇨🇦 Canadian Citizens **Passport Office** ⊠ to mail in applications: 200 Promenade du Portage, Hull, Québec J8X 4B7 ☎ 819/994-3500 or 800/567-6868 ⊕ www.ppt.gc.ca.

🇳🇿 New Zealand Citizens **New Zealand Passports Office** ☎ 0800/22-5050 or 04/474-8100 ⊕ www.passports.govt.nz.

🇬🇧 U.K. Citizens **U.K. Passport Service** ☎ 0870/521-0410 ⊕ www.passport.gov.uk.

🇺🇸 U.S. Citizens **National Passport Information Center** ☎ 877/487-2778, 888/874-7793 TDD/TTY ⊕ travel.state.gov.

RESTROOMS

Standards of cleanliness and comfort vary greatly in Tuscany and Umbria. The type of toilet might be small and low with no seat or even a porcelain hole in the floor with places for your feet. In cities, restaurants, hotel common areas, department stores, and McDonald's eateries tend to have the cleanest restrooms. Pubs and bars rank among the worst. Gas stations also have facilities; again, the cleanliness varies greatly. Carry tissues with you wherever you go, in case there's no paper.

In Florence, all public eating and drinking establishments are required to provide toilet facilities to both customers and the general public alike. However, it is appropriate to pay for a little something—a mineral water or coffee—before you use the facilities. Other private businesses can refuse to make their toilets available to the passing public.

Pay and attendant-supervised restrooms are available in large towns and cities. (You can get a map of the pay toilets in Florence at city tourist-information offices.) Expect to pay or tip 50 European cents. There are restrooms in most museums and all airports and train stations; in major train stations you'll also find well-kept pay toilets for 25 to 60 European cents. Churches, post offices, and public beaches don't have restrooms.

SAFETY

The best way to protect yourself against purse snatchers and pickpockets is to wear a concealed money belt or a pouch on a string around your neck. Don't wear an exterior money belt or a waist pack, both of which peg you as a tourist. If you carry a bag or camera, be absolutely sure it has straps; you should sling it across your body bandolier-style and adjust the height to hip level or higher. Always be astutely aware of pickpockets, especially when on city buses, when making your way through train corridors, and in busy piazzas.

If you carry a purse or wallet, store only enough money there to cover casual spending. Distribute the rest of your cash and any valuables (including credit cards and your passport) between a deep front pocket, an inside jacket or vest pocket, and a hidden money pouch. Do not reach for the money pouch while in public.

LOCAL SCAMS

In Florence you may encounter "gypsies" who are adept pickpockets. One tactic the children use is to approach a tourist and proffer a piece of cardboard with writing on it. While you attempt to read the message *on* it, the children's hands are busy *under* it, trying to make off with purses or valuables. If you see such a group, avoid them—they are quick and know more tricks than you do. If traveling via rental car, it's not a bad idea when making stops along the highway to have someone remain near the car, as such cars are easily recognizable to professional thieves. Purse-snatching is not uncommon, and thieves operate on *motorini* (mopeds) as well as on foot.

WOMEN IN TUSCANY AND UMBRIA

If you carry a purse, choose one with a zipper and a thick strap that you can drape across your body; adjust the length so that the purse sits in front of you at or above hip level. (Don't wear a money belt or a waist pack.) Store only enough money in the purse to cover casual spending. Distribute the rest of your cash and any valuables between deep front pockets, inside jacket or vest pockets, and a concealed money pouch.

Women traveling alone in Tuscany and Umbria encounter few special problems. Younger women have to put up with male attention, but it's rarely dangerous. Ignoring whistling and questions is a good way to get rid of unwanted attention; a firm *no, vai via* ("no, go away") usually works, too.

SENIOR-CITIZEN TRAVEL

To qualify for any age-related discounts, **mention your senior-citizen status up front** when booking hotel reservations (not when checking out) and, if you're an EU citizen over age 65, before buying museum tickets. Movie theaters also may offer discounts; look for signs at ticket counters that mention 65 *anni* (65 years). When renting a car, ask about promotional car-rental discounts, which can be cheaper than senior-citizen rates.

🏳 Educational Programs **Elderhostel** ✉ 11 Ave. de Lafayette, Boston, MA 02111-1746 ☎ 877/426– 8056, 978/323–4141 international callers, 877/426–2167 TTY 🖨 877/426-2166 ⊕ www.elderhostel.org.

SHOPPING

"Made in Italy" has become synonymous with style, quality, and craftsmanship. The best buys are leather goods of all kinds—from gloves to bags to jackets—silk goods, knitwear, gold jewelry, ceramics, and local handicrafts. The most important thing to keep in mind when shopping in Tuscany and Umbria is that every region has its specialties: Florence is known for leather, gold jewelry, paper goods, and antiques; Assisi produces wonderful embroidery; and Deruta and Gubbio have been ceramics centers for centuries.

The notice PREZZI FISSI (fixed prices) means just that—it's a waste of time to bargain unless you're buying a sizable quantity of goods or a particularly costly object. Always try to bargain, however, at outdoor markets (except food markets) and with street vendors. For information on VAT refunds, *see* Taxes.

WATCH OUT

If you have purchased any work of art (painting, sculpture, miniature, cameo, etc.), make sure the piece is certified as being less than 50 years old. Any art deemed older than that must receive clearance from the Italian government to leave the country.

If you have purchased an antique, the dealer will provide you with a certificate attesting to the integrity of the piece and the price paid. Some dealers will ship the object for you; others leave it to you to arrange shipping.

SIGHTSEEING GUIDES

Every province in Italy has licensed tour guides who are allowed by Italian law to take groups and individuals to selected sites. Some of them are eminently qualified in relevant fields such as history and art history; others have simply managed to pass the test. Inquire at any tourist office for a licensed, English-speaking guide. When you speak to the guide, ask about his or her qualifications and specialties. Also check to make sure that the guide's English is understandable. The rates are fixed; find out what they are before hiring the guide. It's illegal for the guide to charge you more than the fixed fee. Tipping is appreciated but not obligatory.

Some places, such as the Duomo in Florence, offer free guided tours in English by a volunteer staff. Such guides may be longer on enthusiasm than knowledge.

STUDENTS IN ITALY

In major art cities, such as Florence, a popular student destination, lodging and sources of information geared to students' needs are plentiful. Students from EU member nations, if they possess valid ID cards, sometimes receive discounts at museums, galleries, exhibitions, and entertainment venues, and on some transportation. Students who aren't EU citizens generally pay the usual entrance fees.

TRAVEL AGENCIES

To save money, **look into deals available through student-oriented travel agencies.** To qualify you'll need a student ID card. Members of international student groups are also eligible.

📅 IDs and Services **STA Travel** ✉ 10 Downing St., New York, NY 10014 ☎ 212/627-3111, 800/777-0112 24-hr service center 🖷 212/627-3387 🌐 www.sta. com. **Travel Cuts** ✉ 187 College St., Toronto, Ontario M5T 1P7, Canada ☎ 800/592-2887 in the U.S., 416/979-2406 or 866/246-9762 in Canada 🖷 416/979-8167 🌐 www.travelcuts.com.

TAXES

HOTELS

The service charge and the 9% IVA, or VAT tax, are included in the rate except in five-star deluxe hotels, where the IVA (12% on luxury hotels) may be a separate item added to the bill upon departure.

RESTAURANTS

Any tax added to the cost of food in restaurants, trattorie, osterie, and cafés will already be included in the menu price and will not be designated on the bill.

VALUE-ADDED TAX

Value-added tax (IVA or V.A.T.) is 20% on clothing, wine, and luxury goods. On consumer goods, it is already included in the amount shown on the price tag, whereas on services, it may not be.

Under Italy's IVA-refund system, a non-EU resident is entitled to a V.A.T. refund. Shop with your passport and ask the store for an invoice itemizing the article(s), price(s), and the amount of tax.

When making a purchase of €151 or more, **ask for a V.A.T. refund form** and find out whether the merchant gives refunds—not all stores do, nor are they required to. Have the form stamped like any customs form by customs officials when you leave the country or, if you're visiting several European Union countries, when you leave the EU. Be ready to show customs officials what you've bought (pack purchases together, in your carry-on luggage); budget extra time for this. After you're through passport control, take the form to a refund-service counter for an on-the-spot refund, or mail it to the address on the form (or the envelope with it) after you arrive home.

A refund service processes claims from most types of stores. You receive the total refund stated on the form. Global Refund is a Europe-wide service with 210,000 affiliated stores and more than 700 refund counters—located at major airports and border crossings. Its refund form is called a Tax Free Check. The service issues refunds in the form of cash, check, or credit-card adjustment. If you don't have time to wait at the refund counter, you can mail in the form instead.

📅 V.A.T. Refunds **Global Refund** ✉ 99 Main St., Suite 307, Nyack, NY 10960 ☎ 800/566-9828 🖷 845/348-1549 🌐 www.globalrefund.com.

TELEPHONES

Telephone service in Tuscany and Umbria is organized and efficient. Cell phones, however, are in wide use by Italians, resulting in a decrease in the number of public pay phones. Travelers who plan to stay in Italy and the surrounding EU countries should consider the practicality of buying or renting a cell phone. Although cell phones used in Italy cannot be used in the U.S., Australia, and New Zealand, and vice versa, the cost of purchasing a basic phone runs between €80 and €125. The cost of renting a cell phone is about €20 a week plus the cost of a calling card or 10 to 25 European cents a minute for calling time and no charge for the phone (a €100 to €125 refundable deposit is normal). Public pay phones usually require a phone card (*carta telefonica*) that can be purchased at newsstands, and some still take coins in addition to the cards. Hotel and rental apartment/house phones operate the same as phones in the U.S. and U.K., but each minute is measured and will be charged to you.

AREA & COUNTRY CODES
The country code for Italy is 39. Area codes for major cities are as follows: Florence, 055; Perugia, 075; Pisa, 050; Siena, 0577. For example, a call from New York City to Florence would be dialed as 011 + 39 + 055 + phone number.

When dialing an Italian number from abroad, do not drop the initial 0 from the local area code. The country code is 1 for the United States and Canada, 61 for Australia, 64 for New Zealand, and 44 for the United Kingdom.

CELL-PHONE RENTAL
Rental cell phones are available in cities and large towns. Many Internet cafés offer them, but shop around for the best deal.
🖪 Rental Agencies **Cells4Rent@Internet Train**
✉ Via dell'Oriuolo 40r, Florence ☎ 055/2638968
🌐 www.cells4rent.com. **Platform 3000** ✉ Via Ghibellina 110, Florence ☎ 055/471714 🌐 www.platform3000.itb. **Webpuccino** ✉ Via dei Conti 22r, Florence ☎ 055/2776469 🌐 www.webpuccino.it.

DIRECTORY AND OPERATOR ASSISTANCE
For general information in English, dial 176. To place international telephone calls via operator-assisted service, dial 170 or long-distance access numbers (⇨ International Calls).

INTERNATIONAL CALLS
Hotels tend to overcharge for long-distance and international calls; it's best to make such calls from public phones, using telephone cards.

You can **make collect calls from any phone by dialing 172–1011,** which will get you an English-speaking operator. Rates to the

United States are lowest on Sunday around the clock and 10 PM–8 AM (Italian time) on weekdays and Saturday.

From major Italian cities, you can place a direct call to the United States by reversing the charges or using your phone calling-card number. You automatically reach a U.S. operator and thereby avoid all language difficulties.

LOCAL AND LONG-DISTANCE CALLS
For all calls within Italy—local and long distance—you must dial the regional area code (*prefisso*), which begins with a 0, such as 055 for Florence. If you are calling from a public phone, you must deposit a coin or use a calling card to get a dial tone. Rates vary during the day; it's less expensive to call within Italy during nonworking hours (before 9 AM and after 7 or 8 PM).

LONG-DISTANCE SERVICES
AT&T, MCI, and Sprint access codes make calling long-distance relatively convenient, but you may find the local access number blocked in many hotel rooms. First ask the hotel operator to connect you. If the hotel operator balks, ask for an international operator, or dial the international operator yourself. One way to improve your odds of getting connected to your long-distance carrier is to travel with more than one company's calling card (a hotel may block Sprint, for example, but not MCI). If all else fails, call from a pay phone.
🖪 Access Codes **AT&T Direct** ☎ 172–1011. **MCI WorldPhone** ☎ 172–1022. **Sprint International Access** ☎ 172–1877.

PHONE CARDS
Prepaid *carte telefoniche* (calling cards) are prevalent throughout Italy and more convenient than coins. You buy the card (values vary) at post offices, tobacconists, most news stalls, and bars. Tear off the corner of the card and insert it in the slot on a public pay phone. When you dial, its value appears in the window. After you hang up, the card is returned so you can use it until its value runs out. The phone card called Time Europa (€25) is a good value, allowing you to call Europe and the

United States at only 28 European cents a minute during peak hours, although conventional phone cards remain cheaper when used from 10 PM to 8 AM and on Sunday. Shop around for long-distance cards; the prices have been going down.

PUBLIC PHONES

All large towns and most small ones have public pay phones (*telefono pubblico*). They usually can be found in bars and at gas stations or near the center piazza. These phones usually accept phone cards but some still take coins in addition to the cards. Italy has moved to adopt the prefix "800" for toll-free or "green" numbers, but there may be some of the original prefix "172" still in operation.

TIME

Italy is six hours ahead of New York (so when it's 1 PM in New York it's 7 PM in Florence). Italy is one hour ahead of London, 10 hours behind Sydney, and 12 hours behind Auckland. Like the rest of Europe, Italy uses the 24-hour (or "military") clock, which means that after 12 noon you continue counting forward: 13:00 is 1 PM, 23:30 is 11:30 PM.

TIPPING

The following guidelines apply in major cities, but Italians tip smaller amounts in smaller cities and towns. In restaurants in Tuscany and Umbria a service charge of 10% to 15% sometimes appears on your check. It's not necessary to tip in addition to this amount. If service is not included, leave a tip of €2 to not more than 10%. No one tips in bars in Florence.

Tip checkroom attendants 50 European cents per person and restroom attendants 25 European cents (more in expensive hotels and restaurants). Italians rarely tip taxi drivers, which is not to say that you shouldn't do it. A tip of 10%, depending on the length of the journey, is appreciated—particularly if the driver helps with luggage. Railway and airport porters charge a fixed rate per bag. Tip an additional 25 European cents per person, and more if the porter is especially helpful. Give a barber €1–€1.50 and a

hairdresser's assistant €1.50–€4 for a shampoo or cut, depending on the type of establishment.

On sightseeing tours, tip guides about €1 per person for a half-day group tour, more if they are very good. In museums and other sights where admission is free, a contribution (25–50 European cents) is expected. Service-station attendants are tipped only for special services, for example, 50 European cents for checking your tires.

In hotels, give the *portiere* (concierge) about 10% of his bill for services, or €2.50–€5 if he has been generally helpful. For two people in a double room, leave the chambermaid about 75 European cents per day, or about €5 a week, in a moderately priced hotel; tip a minimum of 50 European cents for valet or room service. Double amounts in an expensive hotel. In very expensive hotels, tip doormen 50 European cents for calling a cab and €1 for carrying bags to the check-in desk, bellhops €1.50–€2.50 for carrying your bags to the room, and €1.50–2.50 for room service.

TOURS AND PACKAGES

Because everything is prearranged on a prepackaged tour or independent vacation, you spend less time planning—and often get it all at a good price.

BOOKING WITH AN AGENT

Travel agents are excellent resources. But it's a good idea to collect brochures from several agencies, as some agents' suggestions may be influenced by relationships with tour and package firms that reward them for volume sales. If you have a special interest, find an agent with expertise in that area; the American Society of Travel Agents (ASTA) has a database of specialists worldwide. You can log on to the group's Web site to find one near you.

Make sure your travel agent knows the accommodations and other services of the place being recommended. Ask about the hotel's location, room size, beds, and whether it has a pool, room service, or programs for children, if you care about these. Has your agent been there in person or sent others whom you can contact?

Do some homework on your own, too: local tourism boards can provide information about lesser-known and small-niche operators, some of which may sell only direct.

BUYER BEWARE

Each year consumers are stranded or lose their money when tour operators—even large ones with excellent reputations—go out of business. So check out the operator. Ask several travel agents about its reputation, and try to **book with a company that has a consumer-protection program.** (Look for information in the company's brochure.) In the United States, members of the United States Tour Operators Association are required to set aside funds ($1 million) to help eligible customers cover payments and travel arrangements in the event that the company defaults. It's also a good idea to choose a company that participates in the American Society of Travel Agents' Tour Operator Program; ASTA will act as mediator in any disputes between you and your tour operator.

Remember that the more your package or tour includes, the better you can predict the ultimate cost of your vacation. Make sure you know exactly what is covered, and beware of hidden costs. Are taxes, tips, and transfers included? Entertainment and excursions? These can add up.

7 Tour-Operator Recommendations **American Society of Travel Agents** (⇨ Travel Agencies). **National Tour Association (NTA)** ⊠ 546 E. Main St., Lexington, KY 40508 ☎ 859/226-4444 or 800/682-8886 🖶 859/226-4404 ⊕ www.ntaonline.com. **United States Tour Operators Association (USTOA)** ⊠ 275 Madison Ave., Suite 2014, New York, NY 10016 ☎ 212/599-6599 🖶 212/599-6744 ⊕ www.ustoa.com.

TRAIN TRAVEL

The fastest trains on the Ferrovie dello Stato (FS), the Italian State Railways, are the Eurostar trains, operating on several main lines, including Rome–Milan via Florence and Bologna. Supplement is included in the fare; seat reservations are mandatory at all times. Most trains do not have smoking and nonsmoking cars, but a few still have both. If smoke bothers you, ask for seats away from the smoking car, as the poorly designed partitions aren't smoke-proof. Some Eurostar trains (the ETR 460 trains) have little aisle and luggage space (though there is a space near the door where you can put large bags). To avoid having to squeeze through narrow aisles, board only at your car (look for the number on the reservation ticket). Car numbers are displayed on their exterior. The next-fastest trains are the Intercity (IC) trains, for which you pay a supplement and for which seat reservations may be required and are always advisable. *Interregionale* trains usually make more stops and are a little slower. *Regionale* and *locale* trains are the slowest; many serve commuters.

There is refreshment service on all long-distance trains, with mobile carts and a cafeteria or dining car. Tap water on trains is not drinkable.

Traveling by night can be inexpensive, but never leave your belongings unattended (even for a minute) and make sure the door of your compartment is locked.

Train service between Milan, Florence, Rome, and Naples is frequent throughout the day. For the most part, trains stick to the schedule, although delays may occur in the peak tourist season. Train strikes of various kinds are also frequent, so it's a good idea to make sure the train you want to take is in fact running.

7 From the U.K. **British Rail** ☎ 020/7834-2345. **French Railways** ☎ 0891/515-477.

CLASSES

Many Italian trains have first and second classes, but regional trains frequently don't have first class. On interregional trains the higher first-class fare gets you little more than a clean doily on the headrest of your seat, but on long-distance trains you get wider seats, more legroom, and better ventilation and lighting. At peak travel times, first-class train travel is worth the difference. Remember always to **make seat reservations in advance,** for either class. One advantage of traveling first class is that the cars are almost always not crowded—or, at the very least, less crowded than the second-class compartments. A first-class ticket, in Italian, is *prima classe*; second is *seconda classe*.

CUTTING COSTS

To save money, **look into rail passes.** But be aware that if you don't plan to cover many miles, you may come out ahead by buying individual tickets. If you're traveling only in Tuscany and Umbria, rail passes won't save you money.

If Italy is your only destination in Europe, **consider purchasing an Italian Flexi Rail Card** (aka Trenitalia Pass), which allows a limited number of travel days within one month. Four days of travel cost $239 (first class) or $191 (second class); additional days cost $24 (first class) or $19 (second class). If you are traveling with others, you should consider the discounted **Italian Flexi Rail Card Saver** (aka Trenitalia Pass Saver), which allows a limited number of travel days within one month for groups of two or more people. Four days of travel cost $203 (first class) or $163 (second class); additional days are $20 (first class) and $16 (second class).

The Italian Kilometric Ticket (*biglietto chilometrico*), popular with many visitors, was canceled by the Italian government in late 2003.

Once in Italy, inquire about the Carta Verde (Green Card) if you're under 26 (€26 for one year), which entitles the holder to a 15% discount on first- and second-class travel. Those under 26 should also inquire about discount travel fares under the Billet International Jeune (BIJ) and Euro Domino Junior schemes. Also in Italy you can purchase the Carta d'Argento (Silver Card) if you're over 60 (€26 for a year), which allows a 40% discount on first-class rail travel and a 20% discount on second-class travel. Travelers with disabilities who require assistance can acquire the Carta Blu (Dark-Blue Card; €10 for five years), which entitles their companions to free tickets. For further information, check out the Ferrovie dello Stato (FS) Web site (⊕ www.trenitalia.it).

Don't assume that a rail pass guarantees a seat on the trains you wish to ride; you need to book seats ahead even if you use a rail pass. There's a nominal fee (usually €2.50) for the reservation.

🚆 Information and Passes CIT Rail ⊠ 9501 W. Devon Ave., Suite 502, Rosemont, IL 60018 ☏ 800/248-7245. DER Tours ⊠ Box 1606, Des Plaines, IL 60017 ☏ 800/782-2424 🖷 800/282-7474. Rail Europe ⊠ 226-230 Westchester Ave., White Plains, NY 10604 ☏ 914/682-5172 or 800/438-7245 ⊕ www.raileurope.com ⊠ 2087 Dundas E., Suite 105, Mississauga, Ontario L4X 1M2 ☏ 416/602-4195.

TICKETS AND SCHEDULES

You can buy train tickets for nearby destinations (within a 200-km range) at tobacconists and at ticket machines in stations. Tickets are good for two months after the date of issue, but right before departure you must **validate tickets in the yellow machines in the departure area.** Once stamped, tickets are valid for six hours on distances of less than 200 km (124 mi) or for 24 hours on longer distances. If you wish to stop along the way and your final destination is more than 200 km away, you can stamp the ticket a second time before it expires so as to extend its validity to a maximum of 48 hours from the time it was first stamped. If you forget to stamp your ticket in the machine, or you didn't make it to the station in time to buy the ticket, you must seek out a conductor and pay a €5.15 fine. Don't wait for the conductor to find out that you're without a valid ticket (unless the train is overcrowded and walking becomes impossible), as he might charge you a much heavier fine. However, you often can get out of paying the fine if you immediately write the time, date, and name of the departure station on the back of the ticket and sign it—essentially "validating" it and making it unusable for another trip.

🚆 Train Information Ferrovie dello Stato (FS) ☏ 147/888-088 in Italy ⊕ www.fs-on-line.com.

PAYING

You can pay for your train tickets in cash or with any major credit card such as American Express, Diner's Club, MasterCard, and Visa.

RESERVATIONS

Trains can be very crowded; it is always a good idea to make a reservation. In summer, it's fairly common to stand for a good part of the journey.

To avoid long lines at station windows, **buy tickets and make seat reservations up to two months in advance** at travel agencies displaying the FS emblem. Tickets can be purchased at the last minute, but seat reservations can be made at agencies (or the train station) up until about three hours before the train departs from its city of origin. For trains that require a reservation (all Eurostar and some Intercity), you may be able to get a seat assignment just before boarding the train; look for the conductor on the platform, but do this only as a last resort.

TRANSPORTATION

Driving is the best mode of transportation in the region, if not essential. Buses (⇨ Bus Travel), which are usually more comfortable and more expensive than trains, offer more-frequent service to certain smaller cities and towns in Tuscany and Umbria, where train service is spotty. Ferries and hydrofoils (⇨ Boat and Ferry Travel) travel between the islands and the mainland.

Tuscany and Umbria have an intricate network of autostrade routes, good highways, and secondary roads, making renting a car (⇨ Car Rental) a better but expensive alternative (because of high gas prices and freeway tolls) to public transportation. A rental car can be a good investment for carefree countryside rambles, offering time to explore more-remote towns. Having a car in major cities, however, often leads to parking and traffic headaches, plus the additional expense of garage and parking fees.

TRAVEL AGENCIES

A good travel agent puts your needs first. Look for an agency that has been in business at least five years, emphasizes customer service, and has someone on staff who specializes in your destination. In addition, **make sure the agency belongs to a professional trade organization.** The American Society of Travel Agents (ASTA) has more than 10,000 members in some 140 countries, enforces a strict code of ethics, and will step in to help mediate any agent-client disputes involving ASTA members. ASTA also maintains a directory of agents Web site. (If a travel agency is also acting as your tour operator, *see* Buyer Beware *in* Tours & Packages.)

🖪 Local Agent Referrals **American Society of Travel Agents (ASTA)** ✉ 1101 King St., Suite 200, Alexandria, VA 22314 ☎ 703/739-2782 or 800/965-2782 24-hr hotline 🖷 703/684-8319 ⊕ www. astanet.com. **Association of British Travel Agents** ✉ 68-71 Newman St., London W1T 3AH ☎ 020/7637-2444 🖷 020/7637-0713 ⊕ www.abta.com. **Association of Canadian Travel Agencies** ✉ 130 Albert St., Suite 1705, Ottawa, Ontario K1P 5G4 ☎ 613/237-3657 🖷 613/237-7052 ⊕ www.acta.ca. **Australian Federation of Travel Agents** ✉ Level 3, 309 Pitt St., Sydney, NSW 2000 ☎ 02/9264-3299 or 1300/363-416 🖷 02/9264-1085 ⊕ www.afta.com. au. **Travel Agents' Association of New Zealand** ✉ Level 5, Tourism and Travel House, 79 Boulcott St., Box 1888, Wellington 6001 ☎ 04/499-0104 🖷 04/499-0786 ⊕ www.taanz.org.nz.

VISITOR INFORMATION

Learn more about foreign destinations by checking government-issued travel advisories and country information. For a broader picture, consider information from more than one country.

🖪 At Home **Italian Government Tourist Board (ENIT)** ✉ 630 5th Ave., New York, NY 10111 ☎ 212/245-4822 🖷 212/586-9249 ✉ 401 N. Michigan Ave., Chicago, IL 60611 ☎ 312/644-0990 🖷 312/644-3019 ✉ 12400 Wilshire Blvd., Suite 550, Los Angeles, CA 90025 ☎ 310/820-0098 🖷 310/820-6357 ✉ 1 Pl. Ville Marie, Suite 1914, Montréal, Québec H3B 3M9 ☎ 514/866-7667 🖷 514/392-1429 ✉ 1 Princes St., London W1R 8AY ☎ 020/7408-1254 🖷 020/7493-6695 ⊕ www.italiantourism.com.

🖪 Tourist Offices in Tuscany & Umbria **Florence** ✉ Via Cavour 1/r, next to Palazzo Medici-Riccardi, 50129 ☎ 055/290832 ⊕ www.firenze.turismo.toscana.it. **Lucca** ✉ Piazza Guidiccioni 2 ☎ 0583/491205 ⊕ www.cribecu.sus.it/lucca. **Perugia** ✉ Piazza IV Novembre ☎ 075/5723327 ⊕ www.perugiaonline.it. **Tuscany** ✉ Rocco Loggiato

Porto 10, Via Cavaliere de Vittorio Veneto ☎ 0583/644354 ⊕ www.welcometuscany.it.
🔒 Government Advisories **U.S. Department of State** ✉ Overseas Citizens Services Office, 2100 Pennsylvania Ave. NW, 4th floor, Washington, DC 20520 ☎ 202/647-5225 interactive hotline or 888/407-4747 ⊕ www.travel.state.gov. **Consular Affairs Bureau of Canada** ☎ 800/267-6788 or 613/944-6788 ⊕ www.voyage.gc.ca. **U.K. Foreign and Commonwealth Office** ✉ Travel Advice Unit, Consular Division, Old Admiralty Building, London SW1A 2PA ☎ 0870/606-0290 or 020/7008-1500 ⊕ www.fco.gov.uk/travel. **Australian Department of Foreign Affairs and Trade** ☎ 300/139-281 travel advice, 02/6261-1299 Consular Travel Advice Faxback Service ⊕ www.dfat.gov.au. **New Zealand Ministry of Foreign Affairs and Trade** ☎ 04/439-8000 ⊕ www.mft.govt.nz.

WEB SITES

Do check out the World Wide Web when planning your trip. You'll find everything from weather forecasts to virtual tours of famous cities. Be sure to visit Fodors.com (⊕ www.fodors.com), a complete travel-planning site. You can research prices and book plane tickets, hotel rooms, rental cars, vacation packages, and more. In addition, you can post your pressing questions in the Travel Talk section. Other planning tools include a currency converter and weather reports, and there are loads of links to travel resources.

For more information specifically on Italy, visit ⊕ www.initaly.com, ⊕ www.slowtrav.com, and ⊕ www.wel.it.

FLORENCE

1

Updated by
Patricia Rucidlo

"YOU CANNOT IMAGINE ANY SITUATION more agreeable than Florence," wrote the peripatetic Mary Wortley Montagu in 1740. This agreeable situation called Florence has captured the hearts and minds of most of the visitors who have made their way here. Florence (Firenze in Italian) casts a spell in the way that few cities can—perhaps because of its sublime art; perhaps because of the views at sunset over the Arno; perhaps because eating and drinking in Florence delight the palate. Maybe it's because the city hasn't changed all that much since the 16th century. Though Florence was briefly the capital of a newly united Italy (1865–71), its place in the sun rests squarely on its illustrious, more-distant past.

Though Florence can lay claim to a modest importance in antiquity, it didn't fully emerge into its own until the 11th century. In the early 1200s, Florence, like most of Italy, was rent by civic unrest. Two factions, the Guelphs and the Ghibellines, competed for power. The Guelphs supported the Papacy, and the Ghibellines supported the Holy Roman Empire. Bloody battles—most notably the famous one at Montaperti in 1260—tore Florence and other Italian cities apart. Sometimes the Guelphs were in power and exiled the Ghibellines; at other times, the reverse was true. By the end of the 13th century the Guelphs ruled securely and Ghibellinism had been vanquished. This didn't end civic strife, however: the Guelphs split into the Whites and the Blacks for reasons still debated by historians. Dante, author of *The Divine Comedy,* was banished from Florence in 1301 because he was a White.

Local merchants had organized themselves into guilds by 1250 and in that year proclaimed themselves the *"primo popolo"* ("first people"). It was the first attempt at democratic, republican rule. Though the episode lasted only 10 years, it constituted a breakthrough in Western history. Such a daring stance by the merchant class can be attributed to its new-found power, as Florence was emerging as one of the economic powerhouses in 13th-century Europe. Florentines were papal bankers; they instituted the system of international letters of credit; and the gold florin became the international standard of currency. With this economic strength came a building boom. Public and private palaces, churches, and basilicas were built, enlarged, or restructured. Sculptors such as Donatello and Ghiberti were commissioned to decorate them; painters such as Giotto and Botticelli were commissioned to fresco their walls.

Though ostensibly a republic, Florence was blessed (or cursed, depending on point of view) with one very powerful family, the Medici, who came into power in the 1430s and became the de facto rulers of Florence for about three hundred years. The Medici originally came from north of Florence, and it wasn't until the time of Cosimo il Vecchio (1389–1464) that the family's foothold in Florence was securely established. Florence's golden age occurred during the reign of his grandson Lorenzo de' Medici (1449–92). Lorenzo was not only an astute politician, but also a highly educated man and a great patron of the arts. Called "Il Magnifico" ("the Magnificent"), he gathered around him poets, artists, philosophers, architects, and musicians and organized all manner of cultural events, festivals, and tournaments.

You can see most of Florence's outstanding sights in three days. Plan your day around the opening hours of museums and churches; to gain an edge on the tour groups in high season, go very early in the morning or around closing time. If you can, allow a day to explore each neighborhood.

If you have 3 days

Spend Day 1 exploring Florence's centro storico, which will give you an eyeful of such masterpieces as Ghiberti's bronze doors at the Battistero (these are copies; the originals are in the nearby Museo dell'Opera del Duomo), Giotto's Campanile (bell tower), Brunelleschi's cupola majestically poised atop the Duomo, and Botticelli's epic *Primavera* and *Birth of Venus* at the Galleria degli Uffizi. On Day 2, wander north of the Duomo and take in the superb treasury of works ranging from Michelangelo's *David* at the Galleria dell'Accademia to the lavish frescoes at the Cappella dei Magi in the Palazzo Medici-Riccardi and the Museo di San Marco (don't miss San Lorenzo, Michelangelo's Biblioteca Medicea Laurenziana, and the Cappelle Medicee). On this afternoon (or on the afternoon of Day 3) head southeast to Santa Croce or west to Santa Maria Novella. On the third day, cross the Ponte Vecchio to the Arno's southern bank and explore the Oltrarno, being sure not to miss the Brunelleschi-designed church of Santo Spirito and the frescoes in the church of Santa Maria del Carmine. Skip the disappointing Boboli Gardens, which are overgrown and ill-tended.

If you have 5 days

Break down the tours in the above itinerary into shorter ones, adding a few sights such as Piazzale Michelangelo, halfway up a hill on the Arno's southern bank, and San Miniato—both with expansive views of the city. Climb Giotto's Campanile, which rewards you with sweeping views of the city and hills beyond. If you're feeling more adventurous, climb the narrow, twisting stairs to the top of the Duomo. Take Bus 7 from the station or Piazza del Duomo to enchanting Fiesole. Spend more time in the Galleria degli Uffizi and Bargello or at one of the smaller museums, such as the Museo dell'Opificio delle Pietre Dure, around the corner from the Galleria dell'Accademia. The little-visited but nevertheless wonderful Istituto e Museo di Storia della Scienza is worth a trip, as is the Museo di Santa Maria Novella.

If you have 8 days

Add an all-day excursion south to Siena or a couple of half-day trips to the Medici villas around Florence. Visit more of Florence's interesting smaller churches; there's a dazzling fresco by Perugino at Santa Maria Maddalena dei Pazzi and a brilliant Pontormo in the Oltrarno's Santa Felicita. On the trail of additional, lesser-known artistic gems, check out Andrea del Castagno's fresco of the *Last Supper* in the former refectory at Sant'Apollonia, northwest of the Museo di San Marco. It's worth the trip to see Andrea del Sarto's stunning grisaille frescoes in the Chiostro dello Scalzo, north of the Museo di San Marco. The church of Santo Spirito, west of Piazza Pitti, is a fine example of 15th-century architectural rationalism. Take the bus and visit Pontormo's faded but splendid frescoes at the Certosa in Galluzzo, or visit the Museo Stibbert for an excellent window on what high-end collecting meant in the 19th century.

Lorenzo's son, Piero (1471–1503), proved inept at handling the city's affairs. He was run out of town in 1494, and Florence briefly enjoyed its status as a republic while dominated by the demagogic Dominican friar Girolamo Savonarola (1452–98). Savonarola preached against perceived pagan abuses and convinced his followers to destroy their books, art, women's wigs, and jewelry in public "bonfires of the vanities." Eventually, he so annoyed Pope Alexander VI that he was declared a heretic and hanged.

After a decade of internal unrest, the republic fell and the Medici were recalled to power. But even with the return of the Medici, Florence never regained its former prestige. By the 1530s all the major artistic talent had left the city—Michelangelo, for one, had settled in Rome. The now ineffectual Medici, eventually attaining the title of grand dukes, remained nominally in power until the line died out in 1737, after which time Florence passed from the Austrians to the French and back again until the unification of Italy (1865–70), when it briefly became the capital under King Vittorio Emanuele II (1820–78).

Florence was "discovered" in the 18th century by upper-class Europeans making the grand tour. It became a mecca for travelers, particularly the Romantics, who were inspired by the elegance of its *palazzi* and its artistic wealth. Today millions of modern visitors follow in their footsteps. As the sun sets over the Arno and, as Mark Twain described it, "overwhelms Florence with tides of color that make all the sharp lines dim and faint and turn the solid city to a city of dreams," it's hard not to fall under the city's magic spell.

EXPLORING FLORENCE

Numbers in the text correspond to numbers in the margin and on the Florence map.

Sightseeing in Florence is easy: everything you want to see is concentrated in the relatively small historic center of the city. But the area packs in so much that you may find yourself slogging from one mind-boggling sight to another and feeling overwhelmed. If you are not an inveterate museum enthusiast, take it easy. Don't try to absorb every painting or fresco that comes into view. There is second-rate art even in the Galleria degli Uffizi and Palazzo Pitti (*especially* the Pitti), so find some favorites and enjoy them at your leisure.

In between your blitzes into the Renaissance and beyond, stop to breathe in the city, the marvelous synergy between history and modern Florentine life. Florence is a living, bustling metropolis that has managed to preserve its predominantly medieval street plan and mostly Renaissance infrastructure while successfully adapting to the insistent demands of 21st-century life. During the 12th and 13th centuries, Florence, like most other Italian towns, was a forest of towers—more than 200 of them. Today only a handful survive, but if you look closely, you'll find them as you explore the *centro storico* (historic center).

Art

The abundance of Renaissance art in Florence is staggering. To avoid an art hangover, accept the fact that no matter how determined you may be, you won't see everything. You're likely to have a more satisfying experience if you pick and choose sights that strike your interest, give yourself the freedom to follow your whims, and ignore any pangs of guilt if you'd rather nap at your hotel than stand in line at the Uffizi. Florence isn't a city that can be "done"; instead, it's a place you can return to again and again, confident that there will always be more treasures to discover.

Eating Out

Florentines are justifiably proud of their robust food, claiming that it served as the basis for French cuisine when Catherine de' Medici took a battery of Florentine chefs with her after she became queen of France in the 16th century. You can sample such specialties as creamy *fegatini* (a chicken-liver spread) and *ribollita* (minestrone thickened with bread and beans and swirled with extra virgin olive oil) in bustling, convivial *trattorie*, where you share long wooden tables set with paper place mats. Like the Florentines, you can take a break at an *enoteca* (wineshop and/or wine bar) during the day and discover some little-known but excellent Chiantis and Super Tuscans.

Shopping

Since the days of the medieval guilds, Florence has been synonymous with fine craftsmanship and good business. Such time-honored Florentine specialties as antiques (and reproductions), bookbinding, jewelry, lace, leather goods, silk, and straw attest to this. The Pitti fashion shows and the burgeoning textile industry in nearby Prato have added fine clothing to the long list of merchandise available in the shops of Florence.

Timing

Walking through the streets and alleyways in Florence is a discovery in itself, but to save time and energy (especially on your third or so day in the city), make use of the efficient bus system. Buses also provide the least fatiguing way to reach Piazzale Michelangelo, San Miniato, and Forte di Belvedere. It's easy to make excursions to, say, Fiesole or the Medici villas by city bus. Most churches are usually open from 8 or 9 until noon or 12:30 and from 3 or 4 until about 6. The Duomo, luckily, has continuous hours.

Centro Storico: From the Duomo to the Ponte Vecchio

Florence's centro storico, stretching from the Piazza del Duomo south to the Arno, is possibly one of the most beautiful spots in the world. Indeed, this relatively small area is home to some powerful artistic treasures. The smorgasbord of churches, medieval towers, Renaissance palaces, and world-renowned museums and galleries is not only testimony to the artistic and architectural genius of the past millennium but also a shrine to some of the most outstanding aesthetic achievements of Western history.

A Good Walk

Start at the **Duomo** ❶ ⌐ and **Battistero** ❷ and climb the **Campanile** ❸ if you wish; then visit the **Museo dell'Opera del Duomo** ❹ behind the Duomo. From there, take a quick walk down Via Oriuolo and duck in to the **Museo Firenze com'era** ❺. It's teeming with maps, many from the 15th century, which give you a good idea of what Florence looked like during the Renaissance. From here you could head south from the Museo dell'Opera del Duomo along Via del Proconsolo to the **Bargello** ❻ opposite the ancient **Badia Fiorentina** ❼, restructured in 1285. Or stroll back past the Piazza del Duomo, head directly south from the Duomo on Via dei Calzaiuoli, and turn right on Via degli Speziali to reach the **Piazza della Repubblica** ❽, a good place for people-watching. Take Via Orsanmichele to **Orsanmichele** ❾, then continue on to Via dei Calzaiuoli and head south (if you're coming from the Badia Fiorentina, walk west on Via della Condotta to Via dei Calzauioli and turn left). The street opens up onto the **Piazza della Signoria** ❿, with its Loggia dei Lanzi and **Palazzo Vecchio** ⓫. Right on the square is the **Raccolta d'Arte Contemporanea Alberto della Ragione** ⓬. This collection of 20th-century art provides an interesting juxtaposition to the Renaissance. The **Galleria degli Uffizi** ⓭, perhaps Italy's most important art gallery, is at the south side of the piazza. If time permits, walk through the **Corridoio Vasariano.** Exit the Uffizi on Via de' Castellani. Walk away from the river, and take the first left onto Via Vacchereccia. The street dead-ends into the corner of shop-lined Via Por Santa Maria, where you find the **Mercato Nuovo** ⓮. Follow Via Por Santa Maria to the river; walk east along the north bank of the Arno to Piazza dei Giudici to see the **Istituto e Museo di Storia della Scienza** ⓯. Backtrack west along the Arno to the **Ponte Vecchio** ⓰.

TIMING   Though much of Florence's centro storico is closed to traffic, you still must dodge mopeds, cyclists, and masses of fellow visitors as you walk the narrow streets, especially in the area bounded by the Duomo, Piazza Signoria, Galleria degli Uffizi, and Ponte Vecchio. It takes about 90 minutes to walk the route, with 45 minutes to 1 hour each for the Museo dell'Opera del Duomo and the Palazzo della Signoria; 1 to 1½ hours for the Bargello; and a minimum of 2 hours for the Uffizi (reserve tickets in advance to avoid long lines). Allot another 45 minutes for the Corridoio Vasariano. The Museo Firenze com'era can be visited in about half an hour; allow 45 minutes for the Raccolto d'Arte Contemporanea Alberto della Ragione.

What to See

❼ **Badia Fiorentina.** Originally endowed by Willa, Marquess of Tuscany, in 978, this ancient church is an interesting mélange of 13th-century, Renaissance, baroque, and 18th-century architectural refurbishing. Its graceful bell tower, best seen from the interior courtyard, is beautiful for its unusual construction—a hexagonal tower built on a quadrangular base. The interior of the church (open Monday afternoons only) was halfheartedly remodeled in the baroque style during the 17th century. Three tombs by Mino da Fiesole (circa 1430–84) line the walls, including the *monumento funebre di Conte Ugo* (tomb sculpture of Count Ugo), widely regarded as Mino's masterpiece. Executed in 1469–81, it shows Mino at his most lyrical: the faces seem to be lit from within—no small feat in marble. The best-known work of art here is the delicate *Vision of St. Bernard,* by Filippino Lippi (circa 1457–1504), on the left as you enter. The painting—one of Lippi's finest—is in superb condition; note the Virgin Mary's hands, perhaps the most beautifully rendered in the city. On the right side of the church, above the **cappella di San Mauro,** is a monumental organ dating from 1558. Constructed by Onofrio Zeffirini da Cortona (1510–86), it's largely intact but is missing its 16th-century keyboard. ⊠ *Via Dante Alighieri 1, Bargello* ☎ *055/264402* 🖭 *Free* ☉ *Mon. 3–6.*

★ ❻ **Bargello.** During the Renaissance, this building was headquarters for the *podestà,* or chief magistrate. It also was used as a prison, and the exterior served as a "most wanted" billboard: effigies of notorious criminals and Medici enemies were painted on its walls. Today it houses the **Museo Nazionale,** home to what is probably the finest collection of Renaissance sculpture in Italy. The concentration of masterworks by Michelangelo (1475–1564), Donatello (circa 1386–1466), and Benvenuto Cellini (1500–71) is remarkable; the works are distributed among an eclectic collection of arms, ceramics, and miniature bronzes, among other things. For Renaissance-art lovers, the Bargello is to sculpture what the Uffizi is to painting.

In 1401 Filippo Brunelleschi (1377–1446) and Lorenzo Ghiberti (circa 1378–1455) competed to earn the most prestigious commission of the day: the decoration of the north doors of the Baptistery in Piazza del Duomo. For the contest, each designed a bronze bas-relief panel depicting the sacrifice of Isaac; the panels are displayed together in the room devoted to the sculpture of Donatello, on the upper floor. The judges chose Ghiberti for the commission; see if you agree with their choice. ⊠ *Via del Proconsolo 4, Bargello* ☎ *055/2388606* ⊕ *www.arca.net/db/musei/bargello.htm* 🖭 *€4* ☉ *Daily 8:15–1:50* ☉ *Closed 2nd and 4th Mon. of month and 1st, 3rd, and 5th Sun. of month.*

❷ **Battistero** (Baptistery). The octagonal Baptistery is one of the supreme monuments of the Italian Romanesque style and one of Florence's oldest structures. Local legend has it that it was once a Roman temple dedicated to Mars; modern excavations, however, suggest that its foundations date from the 4th to 5th and the 8th to 9th centuries AD, well after the collapse of the Roman Empire. The round Romanesque arches on the exterior probably date from the 11th century. The interior dome mosaics from the beginning of the 14th century are justly renowned, but—glittering beauties though they are—they could never outshine the building's famed bronze Renaissance doors decorated with panels crafted by Lorenzo Ghiberti. The doors—or at least copies of them—on which Ghiberti worked most of his adult life (1403–52) are on the north and east sides of the Baptistery, and the Gothic panels on the south door were designed by Andrea Pisano (circa 1290–1348) in 1330. The original Ghiberti doors were removed to protect them from the effects of pollution and acid rain and have been beautifully restored; the panels are now on display in the Museo dell'Opera del Duomo.

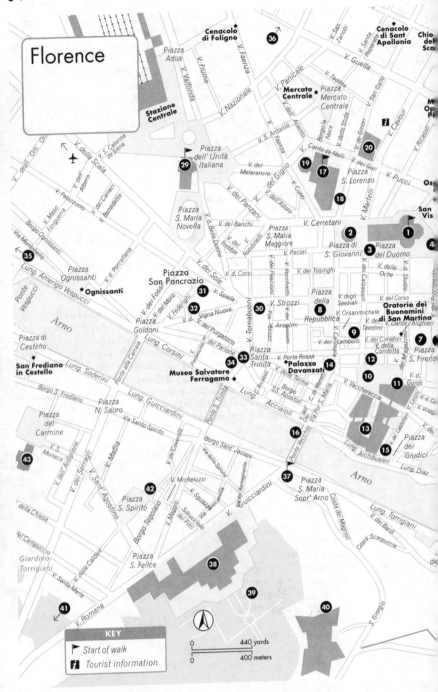

Florence

Piazza Adua
V. Faenza
Cenacolo di Foligno
36
V. San Zanobi
V. Santa Reparata
Cenacolo di Sant Apollonia
Chio del Sca

V. Valfonda
V. Fiume
V. Nazionale
V. Panicale
V. Guelfa
V. Taddea
V. Cavour

Stazione Centrale
Mercato Centrale
Piazza Mercato Centrale
V. S. Antonio
V. dall' Ariento
V. della Stufa
V. de Ginori
San Gallo

Piazza dell' Unità Italiana
V. S. Faenza
Borgo la Noce
Canto de Nelli
19
17
20
Piazza S. Lorenzo
V. de Gori
V. del Melarancio
V. del Giglio
V. dell' Alloro
V. dei Conti
18
V. Pucci

V. della Scala
V. degli Orti Ori
V. S. Caterina da Siena
Piazza S. Maria Novella
V. dei Panzani
V. Cerretani
V. Martelli
Osp
San Vis

V. degli' Alberti
V. Maso Finiguerra
V. Palazzuolo
V. dei Canacci
V. Benedetta
V. dei Banchi
V. delle Belle Donne
V. del Trebbio
V. Rondinelli
Piazza S. Maria Maggiore
V. Pecori
Piazza di S. Giovanni
2
3
Piazza del Duomo
1
4

Borgo Ognissanti
Via Montebello
35
Piazza Ognissanti
V. d. Porcellana
Piazza San Pancrazio
V. del Sole
V. d. Corso
V. Vecchietti
V. dei Tosinghi
V. delle Oche

Ognissanti
V. dei Fossi
31
V. Spada
Piazza della Repubblica
8
V. degli Speziali
Oratorio dei Buonomini di San Martino
V. del Corso
V. Dante Alighieri
7

Ponte Vespucci
Piazza di Cestello
Arno
V. dei Federighi
32
Vigna Nuova
V. d. Mora
V. del Purgatorio
V. d. Parione
Piazza Goldoni
V. dei Pescioni
V. Strozzi
Pza Strozzi
V. Anselmi
30
V. de Sassetti
Orsanmichele
V. dei Tavolini
9
V. Calimala
V. dei Cimatori
V. della Condotta
12
Piazza S. Firenz
V. d. Magazzini

San Frediano in Cestello
Piazza N. Sauro
Lung. Corsini
Lung. Soderini
Piazza Santa Trinita
33
34
Museo Salvatore Ferragamo
V. Porta Rossa
Palazzo Davanzati
V. delle Terme
14
10
11
V. Vacchereccia
V. d. Gondi
Levni

Borgo S. Frediano
Lung. Guicciardini
Via Santo Spirito
Ponte S. Trinita
Lung. Acciaioli
Borgo SS. Apostoli
Via Por S. Maria
Via de Castellani
13
15
Piazza dei Giudici
Lung. Diaz

Piazza del Carmine
V. S. Monaca
V. dell' Ardiglione
V. dei Serragli
V. Mattia
Sant' Agostino
Borgo Sant' Jacopo
16
Ponte Vecchio
Lung. Archibusieri
Arno

43
Piazza S. Spirito
42
V. Michelozzi
V. Sprone
V. della Sprone
V. dello Sdrucciolo de' Pitti
37
Piazza S. Maria Sopr' Arno
Lung. Torrigiani
V. dei Bardi
Costa dei Magnoli

della Chiesa
Borgo Tegolaio
Via Maggio
V.
Guicciardini
Costa Scarpuccia

el Campuccio
Giardino Torrigiani
Piazza S. Felice
38
V. Santa Maria
V. Romana
41
39
40
S. Giorgio
V. delle Caldaie

KEY

▶ *Start of walk*
ℹ *Tourist information*

0 ——— 440 yards
0 ——— 400 meters

Ghiberti's north doors depict scenes from the life of Christ; his later, east doors (dating from 1425–52), facing the Duomo facade, render scenes from the Old Testament. Both merit close examination, for they are very different in style and illustrate the artistic changes that marked the beginning of the Renaissance. Look at the far right panel of the middle row on the earlier (1403–24) north doors (*Jesus Calming the Waters*). Ghiberti here captured the chaos of a storm at sea with great skill and economy, but the artistic conventions he used are basically pre-Renaissance: Jesus is the most important figure, so he is the largest; the disciples are next in size, being next in importance; the ship on which they founder looks like a mere toy.

The exquisitely rendered panels on the east doors are larger, more expansive, more sweeping—and more convincing. The middle panel on the left-hand door tells the story of Jacob and Esau, and the various episodes of the story—the selling of the birthright, Isaac ordering Esau to go hunting, the blessing of Jacob, and so forth—have been merged into a single beautifully realized street scene. Ghiberti's use of perspective suggests depth: the background architecture looks far more credible than on the north-door panels, the figures in the foreground are grouped realistically, and the naturalism and grace of the poses (look at Esau's left leg and the dog next to him) have nothing to do with the sacred message being conveyed. Although the religious content remains, the figures and their place in the natural world are given new prominence and are portrayed with a realism not seen in art since the fall of the Roman Empire nearly a thousand years before.

As a footnote to Ghiberti's panels, one small detail of the east doors is worth a special look. To the lower left of the Jacob and Esau panel, Ghiberti placed a tiny self-portrait bust. From either side, the portrait is extremely appealing—Ghiberti looks like everyone's favorite uncle—but the bust is carefully placed so that you can make direct eye contact with the tiny head from a single spot. When that contact is made, the impression of intelligent life—of *modern* intelligent life—is astonishing. It's no wonder that these doors received one of the most famous compliments in the history of art from an artist known to be notoriously stingy with praise: Michelangelo declared them so beautiful that they could serve as the Gates of Paradise. ⊠ *Piazza del Duomo* ☎ *055/ 2302885* ⊕ *www.operaduomo.firenze.it* 🎫 *€3* 🕙 *Mon.–Sat. noon–7, Sun. 8:30–2.*

❸ **Campanile.** The Gothic bell tower designed by Giotto (circa 1266–1337) is a soaring structure of multicolor marble originally decorated with reliefs that are now in the Museo dell'Opera del Duomo. A climb of 414 steps rewards you with a close-up of Brunelleschi's cupola on the Duomo next door and a sweeping view of the city. ⊠ *Piazza del Duomo* ☎ *055/ 2302885* ⊕ *www.operaduomo.firenze.it* 🎫 *€6* 🕙 *Daily 8:30–7:30.*

★ ☺ ⌐ ❶ **Duomo** (Cattedrale di Santa Maria del Fiore). In 1296 Arnolfo di Cambio (circa 1245–circa 1310) was commissioned to build "the loftiest, most sumptuous edifice human invention could devise" in the Romanesque style on the site of the old church of Santa Reparata. The immense Duomo wasn't completed until 1436, the year it was conse-crated. The imposing facade dates only from the 19th century; it was added in the neo-Gothic style to complement Giotto's genuine Gothic 14th-century campanile. The real glory of the Duomo, however, is Fil-ippo Brunelleschi's dome, presiding over the cathedral with a dignity and grace that few domes, even to this day, can match.

Brunelleschi's **cupola** was an ingenious engineering feat. The space to be enclosed by the dome was so large and so high above the ground that traditional methods of dome construction—wooden centering and scaffolding—were of no use. So Brunelleschi developed entirely new building methods, which he implemented with equipment of his own design (including a novel scaffolding method). Beginning work in 1420, he built not one dome but two, one inside the other, and connected them with common ribbing that stretched across the intervening empty space, thereby considerably lessening the crushing weight of the struc-ture. He also employed a new method of bricklaying, based on an an-cient Roman herringbone pattern, interlocking each new course of bricks with the course below in a way that made the growing structure self-supporting. The result was one of the great engineering breakthroughs of all time: most of Europe's later domes, including St. Peter's in Rome, were built employing Brunelleschi's methods, and today the Duomo has come to symbolize Florence in the same way that the Eiffel Tower symbolizes Paris. The Florentines are justly proud, and to this day the Florentine phrase for "homesick" is *nostalgia del cupolone* ("home-sick for the dome").

The interior is a fine example of Florentine Gothic. Much of the cathe-dral's best-known art has been moved to the nearby Museo dell'Opera del Duomo. Notable among the works that remain are two towering equestrian frescoes honoring famous soldiers: *Niccolò da Tolentino,* painted in 1456 by Andrea del Castagno (circa 1419–57), and *Sir John Hawkwood,* painted 20 years earlier by Paolo Uccello (1397–1475); both are on the left-hand wall of the nave. A vast and crowded fresco of the *Last Judgment,* painted by Vasari and Zuccaro, covers the dome inte-rior. Originally Brunelleschi wanted mosaics to cover the interior of the great ribbed cupola, but by the time the Florentines got around to com-missioning the decoration, 150 years later, tastes had changed. Too bad: it's a fairly dreadful *Last Judgment,* and hardly worth the effort of craning your neck to see it.

You can explore the upper and lower reaches of the cathedral. The re-mains of a Roman wall and an 11th-century cemetery have been exca-vated beneath the nave; the way down is near the first pier on the right. The climb to the top of the dome (463 steps) is not for the faint of heart, but the view is superb. ✉ *Piazza del Duomo* ☎ *055/2302885* ⊕ *www. operaduomo.firenze.it* ✇ *Free, crypt €3, cupola €6* ⊙ *Crypt: week-days 10–5, Sat. 10–5:45, 1st Sat. of month 10–4. Cupola: weekdays 8:30–7, Sat. 8:30–5:40, 1st Sat. of month 8:30–4. Duomo: Mon.–Wed. and Fri. 10–5, Thur. 10–3:30, Sat., 10–4:45, Sun. 1:30–4:45, 1st Sat. of month 10–3:30.*

⑬ Galleria degli Uffizi. The venerable Uffizi Gallery occupies the top floor of
FodorśChoice   the U-shape **Palazzo degli Uffizi** (Uffizi Palace) fronting on the Arno, de-
★   signed by Giorgio Vasari (1511–74) in 1560 to hold the *uffizi* (administrative offices) of the Medici grand duke Cosimo I (1519–74). Later, the
Medici installed their art collections here, creating what was Europe's first
modern museum, open to the public (at first only by request) since 1591.

Among the collection's highlights are Paolo Uccello's *Battle of San Romano,* its brutal chaos of lances one of the finest visual metaphors for
warfare ever captured in paint; the *Madonna and Child with Two Angels,* by Fra Filippo Lippi (1406–69), in which the impudent eye contact
established by the angel in the foreground would have been unthinkable
prior to the Renaissance; the *Birth of Venus* and *Primavera* by Sandro
Botticelli (1445–1510), the goddess of the former seeming to float on water
and the fairy-tale charm of the latter exhibiting the painter's idiosyncratic
genius at its zenith; the portraits of the Renaissance duke Federico da
Montefeltro and his wife, Battista Sforza, by Piero della Francesca (circa
1420–92); the *Madonna of the Goldfinch,* by Raphael (1483–1520), which,
though darkened by time, captures an aching tenderness between mother
and child; Michelangelo's *Doni Tondo* (the only panel painting that can
be securely attributed to him); *Self-Portrait as an Old Man* by Rembrandt
(1606–69); the *Venus of Urbino* by Titian (circa 1485–1576); and the
splendid *Bacchus* by Caravaggio (circa 1571–1610). In the last two
works, both great paintings, the approaches to myth and sexuality are
diametrically opposed, to put it mildly. If panic sets in at the prospect of
absorbing all this art at one go, visit in the late afternoon, when it's less
crowded. A bar inside the gallery is a good place for a coffee break; for
a close-up view of the Palazzo Vecchio, step out onto the terrace. Advance tickets can be purchased from Consorzio ITA. ✉ *Piazzale degli
Uffizi 6, Piazza della Signoria* ☎ *055/23885* ✉ *Advance tickets* ✉ *Consorzio ITA, Piazza Pitti 1, 50121* ☎ *055/294883* ⊕ *www.uffizi.firenze.
it* ☎ *€6.50, reservation fee €3* ☼ *Tues.–Sun. 8:15–6:50.*

⑮ Istituto e Museo di Storia della Scienza (Museum of the History of Science). Although it tends to be obscured by the glamour of the neighboring Uffizi, this science museum has much to commend it: Galileo's
own instruments, antique armillary spheres—some of them real works
of art—and other reminders that the Renaissance made not only artistic but also scientific history. ✉ *Piazza dei Giudici 1, Piazza della Signoria* ☎ *055/265311* ⊕ *www.imss.fi.it* ☎ *€6.50* ☼ *Mon. and Wed.–Sat.
9:30–5, Tues. 9:30–1; Oct.–May, also open 2nd Sun. of month 10–1.*

**need a
break?**   GustaVino (✉ Via della Condotta 37/r, Piazza della Signoria
☎ 055/2399806 ⊕ www.gustavino.it) calls itself an "enoteca with
cucina," which means that you can drink and eat. Its handy location
(a minute or two from Piazza Signoria) makes it a perfect spot to
recover after a trip to the Uffizi. Sharing a kitchen with GustaVino,
La Canova di Gustavino (✉ Via della Condotta 29/r, Piazza della
Signoria ☎ 055/2399806) serves *piatti veloci* (literally, fast dishes).
The extensive list of primi includes spaghetti and ribollita, and prices
hover between €7 and €9.

MEET THE MEDICI

THE MEDICI WERE THE DOMINANT FAMILY of Renaissance Florence, wielding political power and financing some of the world's greatest art. You'll see their names at every turn around the city. These are some of the clan's more notable members:

Cosimo il Vecchio (1389–1464), incredibly wealthy banker to the popes, was the first in the family line to act as de facto ruler of Florence. He was a great patron of the arts and architecture; he was the moving force behind the family palace and the Dominican complex of San Marco.

Lorenzo il Magnifico (1449–92), grandson of Cosimo il Vecchio, presided over a Florence largely at peace with her neighbors. A collector of cameos, a writer of sonnets, and lover of ancient texts, he was the preeminent Renaissance man.

Leo X (1475–1521), also known as Giovanni de' Medici, became the first Medici pope, helping extend the family power base to include Rome and the Papal States. His reign was characterized by a host of problems, the biggest one being a former friar named Martin Luther.

Catherine de' Medici (1519–89) was married by her cousin Pope Clement VII to Henry of Valois, who later became Henry II of France. Wife of one king and mother of three, she was the first Medici to marry into European royalty. Lorenzo il Magnifico, her great-grandfather, would have been thrilled.

Cosimo I (1537–74), the first grand duke of Tuscany, should not be confused with his ancestor Cosimo il Vecchio. A country boy, he grew up north of Florence and returned as a 17-year-old who quickly caught on to the foibles and intrigues of Florentine government.

🔥 ⑭ **Mercato Nuovo** (New Market). The open-air loggia, built in 1551, teems with souvenir stands, but the real attraction is a copy of Pietro Tacca's bronze *Porcellino* (which translates as "little pig" despite the fact the animal is, in fact, a wild boar). The Porcellino is Florence's equivalent of the Trevi Fountain: put a coin in his mouth, and if it falls through the grate below (according to one interpretation), it means you'll return to Florence someday. The statue dates from around 1612, but the original version, which is held in Palazzo Pitti, is an ancient Greek work. ✉ *Corner of Via Por Santa Maria and Via Porta Rossa, Piazza della Repubblica* 🕐 *Market Tues.–Sat. 8–7, Mon. 1–7.*

❹ **Museo dell'Opera del Duomo** (Cathedral Museum). Ghiberti's original Baptistery door panels and the *cantorie* (choir loft) reliefs by Donatello and Luca della Robbia (1400–82) keep company with Donatello's *Mary Magdalen* and Michelangelo's *Pietà* (not to be confused with his more famous *Pietà* in St. Peter's in Rome). Renaissance sculpture is in part defined by its revolutionary realism, but in its palpable suffering Donatello's *Magdalen* goes beyond realism. Michelangelo's heart-wrenching *Pietà* was unfinished at his death; the female figure supporting the body of Christ on the left was added by Tiberio Calcagni (1532–65), and never has the difference between competence and genius been manifested so clearly. ⊠ *Piazza del Duomo 9* ☎ *055/2302885* ⊕ *www.operaduomo.firenze. it* ⊡ €6 ⊙ *Mon.–Sat. 9–7:30, Sun. 9–1:40.*

❺ Museo Firenze com'era. The name of this museum translates as "Florence as it was"; it has prints, paintings, and other exhibits designed to show how Florence looked once upon a time. A diorama renders Roman Florence, of which little remains in the city today. The rest of the museum is dedicated to Florence during and after the Renaissance. Of particular interest is any pre-19th-century print or painting: check out the unfinished facade of the Duomo and the one of Santa Croce. Also note the sweeping size of various *piazze* and the wide streets—clearly, fantasies and wishful thinking on the part of the artists. ⊠ *Via dell'Oriuolo 24, Duomo* ☎ *055/2616545* ⊡ €2.70 ⊙ *Fri.–Sat. and Mon.–Wed. 9–2, Sun. 9–1.*

Oratorio dei Buonomini di San Martino. Founded by Antoninus, Bishop of Florence, in 1441 to offer alms to the *poveri vergognosi* (the ashamed poor), this one-room oratory is decorated with 15th-century frescoes by the school of Ghirlandaio that vividly depict the confraternity's activities. More than 500 years later, the Compagnia dei Buonuomini, or Confraternity of the Good Men, continues to perform charitable works, linking Renaissance notions of charity to the 21st century. ⊠ *Piazza San Martino, Bargello* ☎ *No phone* ⊡ *Free* ⊙ *Mon.–Thurs. and Sat. 10–noon and 3–5, Fri. 10–noon.*

❾ Orsanmichele. This multipurpose structure, which is closed indefinitely for restoration at this writing, began as an 8th-century oratory and then in 1290 was turned into an open-air loggia for selling grain. Destroyed by fire in 1304, it was rebuilt as a loggia-market. Between 1367 and 1380 the arcades were closed and two stories added above; finally, at century's end it was turned into a church. Inside is a beautifully detailed 14th-century Gothic tabernacle by Andrea Orcagna (1308–68). The exterior niches contain sculptures dating from the early 1400s to the early 1600s by Donatello and Verrocchio (1435–88), among others, that were paid for by the guilds. Although it is a copy, Verrocchio's *Doubting Thomas* (circa 1470) is particularly deserving of attention. Here you see Christ, like the building's other figures, entirely framed within the niche, and St. Thomas standing on its bottom ledge, with his right foot outside the niche frame. This one detail, the positioning of a single foot, brings the whole composition to life. Most of the sculptures have since been replaced by copies; however, it's possible to see nearly all of them at the **Museo di Orsanmichele** (also closed at this writing for restoration). ⊠ *Via dei Calzaiuoli, Piazza della Repubblica* ☎ *055/284944* ⊡ *Free* ⊙ *Closed for restoration.*

Palazzo Davanzati. The prestigious Davanzati family owned this 14th-century palace, which has one of the few surviving fresco scenes (in a private palazzo) from this early period of the Renaissance. Because of a long and agonizing restoration, at this writing only the palazzo lobby, with photographs of the restoration process, is open. ⊠ *Piazza Davanzati 13, Piazza della Repubblica* ☎ *055/2388610* ⊡ *Free* ⊙ *Lobby Tues.–Sun. 9–2.*

⓫ Palazzo Vecchio (Old Palace). Florence's forbidding, fortresslike city hall was begun in 1299, presumably designed by Arnolfo di Cambio, and its massive bulk and towering campanile dominate the Piazza della Signoria. It was built as a meeting place for the heads of the seven major guilds that governed the city at the time; over the centuries it has served lesser purposes, but today it is once again City Hall. The interior courtyard is a good deal less severe, having been remodeled by Michelozzo (1396–1472) in 1453; a copy of Verrocchio's bronze *puttino* (little infant boy), topping the central fountain, softens the space.

The main attraction is on the second floor: two adjoining rooms that supply one of the most startling contrasts in Florence. The first is the vast **Sala dei Cinquecento** (Room of the Five Hundred), named for the 500-member Great Council, the people's assembly established by Savonarola, that met here. The sala was decorated by Giorgio Vasari, around 1563–65, with huge—almost grotesquely huge—frescoes celebrating Florentine history; depictions of battles with nearby cities predominate. Continuing the martial theme, the sala also contains Michelangelo's *Victory* group, intended for the never-completed tomb of Pope Julius II (1443–1513), plus other sculptures of decidedly lesser quality.

The second room is the little **Studiolo,** to the right of the sala's entrance. It was the study of Cosimo I's son, the melancholy Francesco I (1541–87). It was designed by Vasari and decorated by Vasari and Bronzino (1503–72) and is intimate, civilized, and filled with complex, questioning, allegorical art. It makes the Sala dei Cinquecento's vainglorious proclamations ring more than a little hollow. ⊠ *Piazza della Signoria* ☎ *055/ 2768465* ⊡ *€6* ☾ *Mon.–Wed. and Fri.–Sat. 9–7, Thurs. 9–2, Sun. 9–7.*

ↄ Museo dei Ragazzi. Florence's "Children's Museum" may be the best-kept public-access secret in Florence. A series of interactive tours includes "Encounters with History," during which participants meet and talk with Giorgio Vasari or Galileo Galilei and explore secret passageways. Events occur at three separate venues (Palazzo Vecchio, Museo Stibbert, and the Istituto e Museo di Storia della Scienza). Tours are in English and must be booked in advance: walk-ins do not happen. ⊠ *Piazza della Signoria 1* ☎ *055/2768224* ⊕ *www.museoragazzi.it* ⊡ *€6* ☾ *By reservation only.*

❽ Piazza della Repubblica. The square marks the site of the ancient forum that was the core of the original Roman settlement. The street plan in the area around the piazza still reflects the carefully plotted Roman military encampment. The Mercato Vecchio (Old Market), which had been here since the Middle Ages, was demolished and the current piazza was constructed between 1885 and 1895 as a neoclassical showpiece. The piazza is lined with outdoor cafés, affording an excellent opportunity for people-watching.

★ ❿ Piazza della Signoria. This is by far the most striking square in Florence. It was here, in 1497, that the famous "bonfire of the vanities" took place, when the fanatical friar Savonarola induced his followers to hurl their worldly goods into the flames; it was also here, a year later, that he was hanged as a heretic and, ironically, burned. A bronze plaque in the piazza pavement marks the exact spot of his execution.

The statues in the square and in the 14th-century **Loggia dei Lanzi** on the south side vary in quality. Cellini's famous bronze *Perseus* holding the severed head of Medusa is certainly the most important sculpture in the loggia. Other works here include *The Rape of the Sabine* and *Hercules and the Centaur*, both late-16th-century works by Giambologna (1529–1608), and in the back, a row of sober matrons dating from Roman times. (At this writing, *The Rape of the Sabine* is expected to be moved and replaced with a copy.)

In the square, the Neptune Fountain, created between 1550 and 1575, takes something of a booby prize. It was created by Bartolomeo Ammannati, who considered it a failure himself. The Florentines call it Il Biancone, which may be translated as "the big white man" or "the big white lump." Giambologna's equestrian statue, to the left of the fountain, pays tribute to Grand Duke Cosimo I. Occupying the steps of the Palazzo Vecchio are a copy of Donatello's proud heraldic lion of Florence, the *Marzocco* (the original is now in the Bargello); a copy of Donatello's *Judith and Holofernes* (the original is in the Palazzo Vecchio); a copy of Michelangelo's *David* (the original is in the Galleria dell'Accademia); and Baccio Bandinelli's *Hercules* (1534). The Marzocco, the Judith, and the David were symbols of Florentine civic pride—the latter two had stood up to their oppressors. They provided apt metaphors for the republic-loving Florentines, who often chafed at Medici hegemony.

★ ⓰ **Ponte Vecchio** (Old Bridge). This charmingly simple bridge is to Florence what the Tower Bridge is to London. It was built in 1345 to replace an earlier bridge that was swept away by flood, and its shops housed first butchers, then grocers, blacksmiths, and other merchants. But in 1593 the Medici grand duke Ferdinand I (1549–1609), whose private corridor linking the Medici palace (Palazzo Pitti) with the Medici offices (the Uffizi) crossed the bridge atop the shops, decided that all this plebeian commerce under his feet was unseemly. So he threw out the butchers and blacksmiths and installed 41 goldsmiths and 8 jewelers. The bridge has been devoted solely to these two trades ever since.

The **Corridoio Vasariano** (✉ Piazzale degli Uffizi 6, Piazza della Signoria ☎ 055/23885 or 055/294883), the private Medici corridor, was built by Vasari in 1565. Though the ostensible reason for its construction was one of security, it was more likely designed so that the Medici wouldn't have to walk amid the commoners. The corridor is notoriously fickle with its operating hours; at this writing it was temporarily closed, but it can often be visited by prior special arrangement. Call for the most up-to-date details.

Take a moment to study the Ponte Santa Trinita, the next bridge downriver, from either the bridge or the corridor. It was designed by Bartolomeo Ammannati in 1567 (possibly from sketches by Michelangelo), blown up by the retreating Germans during World War II, and painstakingly reconstructed after the war. The view from the Ponte Santa Trinita is beautiful, which might explain why so many young lovers seem to hang out there.

⑫ Raccolta d'Arte Contemporanea Alberto della Ragione. If Renaissance-art fatigue has set in, consider this small museum for a change of pace. In 1970 the Genoese Alberto della Ragione donated his collection of contemporary Italian art to the city. It includes a not-too-interesting De Chirico (*Les Bains Mysterieux*); a lovely Marini sculpture, *Cavallino* (*Little Horse*), from 1934; and some other lesser-known gems. Works by Felice Casorati, Gino Severini, and Renato Guttoso—preeminent 20th-century artists—are here, as are three lovely paintings by author Carlo Levi, who wrote the heartbreaking *Christ Stopped at Eboli*. The museum was closed as of this writing, but planned to reopen with visiting hours on Saturdays. Call for the latest information. ⊠ *Piazza della Signoria 5* ☎ *055/283078* ᠍ *€2.07* ☉ *Closed for restoration.*

San Michele Visdomini. Aficionados of the 16th-century Mannerists should stop in this church, which has a *Sacra Conversazione* by Jacopo Pontormo (1494–1556). The early work, said by Vasari to have been executed on paper, is in dire need of a cleaning. Its palette is somewhat bereft of the lively colors typically associated with Pontormo. ⊠ *Via dei Servi at Via Bufalini, Duomo* ☎ *No phone* ᠍ *Free* ☉ *Daily 7–noon and 3–6.*

Ospedale Santa Maria Nuova. Folco Portinari, the father of Dante's Beatrice, founded this sprawling complex in 1288. It was originally a hostel for visiting pilgrims and travelers. During the Black Death of 1348, it served as a hospice for those afflicted. At another point it served as an office where money could be exchanged and deposited and letters could be received; Michelangelo did his banking here. It had been lavishly decorated by the top Florentine artists of the day, but most of the works, such as the frescoes by Domenico Veneziano and Piero della Francesca, have disappeared or been moved to the Uffizi for safekeeping. Today it functions as a hospital in the modern sense of the word, but you can visit the single-nave church of **Sant'Egidio,** in the middle of the complex, where the frescoes would have stood. Imagine, too, Hugo van der Goes's (1435–82) magnificent *Portinari Altarpiece,* which once crowned the high altar; it's now in the Uffizi. Commissioned by Tommaso Portinari, a descendent of Folco, it arrived from Bruges in 1489 and created quite a stir. Bernardo Rossellino's immense marble tabernacle (1450), still in the church, is worth a look. ⊠ *Via Sant'Egidio and Piazza di Santa Maria Nuova, San Lorenzo.*

Michelangelo Country: From San Lorenzo to the Accademia

Sculptor, painter, architect, and yes, even poet, native son Michelangelo was a consummate genius. Some of his finest work remains in his hometown. The Biblioteca Medicea Laurenziana is perhaps his most fanciful work of architecture. The key to understanding Michelangelo's genius is in the magnificent Cappelle Medicee, where his sculptural and architectural prowess can be clearly seen. Planned frescoes weren't completed, which is unfortunate because they would have shown in one space the artistic triple threat that he certainly was. The towering and beautiful *David,* his most famous work, resides in the Galleria dell'Accademia.

A Good Walk

Start at the church of **San Lorenzo** ⑰ ⌐, visiting the **Biblioteca Medicea Laurenziana** ⑱ and its famous anteroom before circling the church to the northwest and making your way through the San Lorenzo outdoor market on Via del Canto de' Nelli to the entrance of the **Cappelle Medicee** ⑲. Retrace your steps through the market and take Via dei Gori east to Via Cavour and the **Palazzo Medici-Riccardi** ⑳, once the home of Florence's most important family throughout the Renaissance. Follow Via Cavour two blocks north to Piazza San Marco and the church of the same name, attached to which is the **Museo di San Marco** ㉑; it houses marvelous works by the pious and exceptionally talented painter–friar Fra Angelico. If you have time, go northwest from Piazza San Marco to see Castagno's *Last Supper* at Sant'Apollonia and then north to the Chiostro dello Scalzo. From Piazza San Marco, walk a half block south on Via Ricasoli (which runs back toward the Duomo) to the **Galleria dell'Accademia** ㉒. Return to the east side of Piazza San Marco and take Via Cesare Battisti east into Piazza della Santissima Annunziata, one of Florence's prettiest squares, site of the **Spedale degli Innocenti** ㉓ and, at the north end of the square, the church of **Santissima Annunziata** ㉔. The Pinacoteca at the Spedale degli Innocenti is worth a quick look: Domenico Ghirlandaio's 1488 *Adorazione dei Magi* is particularly lovely. One block southeast of the entrance to Santissima Annunziata, through the arch and on the left side of Via della Colonna, is the **Museo Archeologico** ㉕. Continue down Via della Colonna to **Santa Maria Maddalena dei Pazzi** ㉖, which harbors a superb fresco by Perugino. Return to Via della Colonna and continue heading southeast; take a right on Via Luigi Carlo Farini, where you'll find the **Sinagoga** ㉗ and its Museo Ebraico. Take a break and have a Mediterranean-kosher lunch at Ruth's or stop at a trattoria. Another option is a picnic lunch in Piazza d'Azeglio, a small but delightful park minutes from the Sinagoga. Retrace your steps on Via Luigi Carlo Farini. The park begins at the corner of Via Farini and Via della Colonna. After lunch, visit the **Cimitero dei Protestanti** ㉘, where you may pay your respects at the tomb of Elizabeth Barrett Browning.

TIMING The walk alone takes about 1½ hours, plus 45 minutes for the Cappelle Medicee, 20 minutes for the Palazzo Medici-Riccardi, 40 minutes for the Museo di San Marco, 30 minutes for the Galleria dell'Accademia (*David*), and 40 minutes for the Museo Archeologico. Note that the Museo di San Marco closes at 1:50 on weekdays. The Cimitero dei Protestanti can be visited in under half an hour. After visiting San Lorenzo, resist the temptation to explore the market that surrounds the church before going to the Palazzo Medici-Riccardi; the market is open until 7 PM, so you can come back later, when the churches and museums have closed.

What to See

⑱ **Biblioteca Medicea Laurenziana** (Laurentian Library). Michelangelo the architect was every bit as original as Michelangelo the sculptor. Unlike Brunelleschi (the architect of the Spedale degli Innocenti), however, he wasn't obsessed with proportion and perfect geometry. He was interested in experimentation and invention and in the expression of a personal vision at times highly idiosyncratic.

It was never more idiosyncratic than in the Laurentian Library, begun in 1524 and finished in 1568, and its famous **vestibolo**. This strangely shaped anteroom has had scholars scratching their heads for centuries. In a space more than two stories high, why did Michelangelo limit his use of columns and pilasters to the upper two-thirds of the wall? Why didn't he rest them on strong pedestals instead of on huge, decorative curlicue scrolls, which rob them of all visual support? Why did he recess them into the wall, which makes them look weaker still? The architectural elements here do not stand firm and strong and tall, as inside San Lorenzo, next door; instead, they seem to be pressed into the wall as if into putty, giving the room a soft, rubbery look that is one of the strangest effects ever achieved by classical architecture. It's almost as if Michelangelo purposely set out to defy his predecessors—intentionally flouting the conventions of the High Renaissance to see what kind of bizarre, mannered effect might result. His innovations were tremendously influential and produced a period of architectural experimentation, known as mannerism, that eventually evolved into the baroque. As his contemporary Giorgio Vasari put it, "Artisans have been infinitely and perpetually indebted to him because he broke the bonds and chains of a way of working that had become habitual by common usage."

The anteroom's staircase (best viewed straight-on), which emerges from the library with the visual force of an unstoppable lava flow, has been exempted from the criticism, however. In its highly sculptural conception and execution, it is quite simply one of the most original and fluid staircases in the world. ⊠ *Piazza San Lorenzo 9, entrance to the left of San Lorenzo* ☎ *055/210760* ⊕ *www.bml.firenze.sbn.it* ⊠ *Special exhibitions €5* ⊙ *Daily 8:30–1:30.*

★ ⑲ **Cappelle Medicee** (Medici Chapels). This magnificent complex includes the **Cappella dei Principi,** the Medici chapel and mausoleum that was begun in 1605 and kept marble workers busy for several hundred years, and the **Sagrestia Nuova** (New Sacristy), designed by Michelangelo and so called to distinguish it from Brunelleschi's Sagrestia Vecchia (Old Sacristy) in San Lorenzo.

Michelangelo received the commission for the New Sacristy in 1520 from Cardinal Giulio de' Medici (1478–1534), who later became Pope Clement VII and who wanted a new burial chapel for his cousins Giuliano (1478–1534) and Lorenzo (1492–1519). The result was a tour de force of architecture and sculpture. Architecturally, Michelangelo was as original and inventive here as ever, but it is, quite properly, the powerful sculptural compositions of the side-wall tombs that dominate the room. The scheme is allegorical: on the wall tomb to the right are figures representing Day and Night, and on the wall tomb to the left are figures representing Dawn and Dusk; above them are idealized sculptures of the two men, usually interpreted to represent the active life and the contemplative life. But the allegorical meanings are secondary; what is most important is the intense presence of the sculptural figures and the force with which they hit the viewer. Michelangelo's contemporaries were so awed by this force (in his sculpture here and elsewhere) that they invented a word to describe the phenomenon: *terribilità* (dreadfulness). To this day it's used only when describing his work, and it is in evidence here at the peak of its power. During his stormy relations with the Medici, Michelangelo once hid out in a tiny subterranean room that is accessed from the left of the altar. The room contains sketches once thought to be Michelangelo's. Though art historians now think otherwise, they're still an interesting example of centuries-old graffiti. If you want to see them, tell the ticket vendor and reserve: admission is on the hour at 9, 10, 11, and noon and is limited to 12 people per hour. Your chance of getting in is better if you try for one of the earlier times. ⊠ *Piazza di Madonna degli Aldobrandini, San Lorenzo* ☎ *055/294883 reservations* 🎫 *€5* ⊙ *Daily 8:15–5. Closed 1st, 3rd, and 5th Mon. and 2nd and 4th Sun. of month.*

Cenacolo di Sant'Apollonia. The frescoes of the refectory of a former Benedictine nunnery were painted in sinewy style by Andrea del Castagno, a follower of Masaccio (1401–28). The *Last Supper* is a powerful version of this typical refectory theme. From the entrance, walk around the corner to Via San Gallo 25 and take a peek at the lovely 15th-century cloister that belonged to the same monastery but is now part of the University of Florence. ⊠ *Via XXVII Aprile 1, San Marco* ☎ *055/2388607* ⊙ *Daily 8:15–1:50. Closed 1st and 3rd Sun. of month.*

> **off the beaten path**

CHIOSTRO DELLO SCALZO – Often overlooked, this small, peaceful 16th-century cloister was frescoed in grisaille by Andrea del Sarto (1486–1530), with scenes from the life of St. John the Baptist, Florence's patron saint. ⊠ *Via Cavour 69, San Marco* ☎ *055/ 2388604* ⊙ *Mon., Thurs., and Sat. 9–1:50.*

㉘ Cimitero dei Protestanti. Formally known as the Protestant Cemetery but more familiarly known as the Cimitero degli Inglesi, or English Cemetery, this final resting place for some 1,400 souls was designed in 1828 by Carlo Reishammer for the Swiss community in Florence. Just outside Florence's 14th-century walls (no longer visible), the cemetery grew to accommodate other foreigners (in other words, Protestants) living in Florence. Perhaps its most famous permanent resident is Elizabeth Barrett Browning (1809–61), who spent the last 15 years of her life in the city. Other expats, including Arthur Clough, Walter Savage Landor, Frances Trollope (mother of Anthony), and the American preacher Theodore Parker are buried in this cemetery, also referred to as the "Island of the Dead." (Swiss painter Arnold Böcklin [1827–1901] used the cemetery as inspiration for his haunting painting *Island of the Dead.*) ⊠ *Piazzale Donatello 38, Santa Croce* ☎ *055/582608* 🎫 *Free; suggested €2 per person for large groups* ⊙ *Nov.–Mar., Mon. 9–noon, Tues.–Fri. 3–5; Apr.–Sept., Mon. 9–noon, Tues.–Fri. 3–6.*

★ ⊙ ㉒ Galleria dell'Accademia (Accademia Gallery). The collection of Florentine paintings, dating from the 13th to the 18th centuries, is largely unremarkable, but the sculptures by Michelangelo are worth the price of admission. The unfinished *Slaves,* fighting their way out of their marble prisons, were meant for the tomb of Michelangelo's overly demanding patron Pope Julius II (1443–1513). But the focal point is the original *David,* moved here from Piazza della Signoria in 1873. *David* was commissioned in 1501 by the Opera del Duomo (Cathedral Works Committee), which gave the 26-year-old sculptor a leftover block of marble that had been ruined by another artist. Michelangelo's success with the block was so dramatic that the city showered him with honors, and the Opera del Duomo voted to build him a house and a studio in which to live and work.

Today *David* is beset not by Goliath but by tourists, and seeing the statue at all—much less really studying it—can be a trial. Save yourself a long and tiresome wait in line by reserving tickets in advance. A Plexiglass barrier surrounds it, following a 1991 attack upon the sculpture by a hammer-wielding artist who, luckily, inflicted only a few minor nicks on the toes. A 2004 restoration in honor of his 500th birthday has, at the very least, cleaned up the sculpture. The statue is not quite what it seems. It is so poised and graceful and alert—so miraculously alive—that it is often considered the definitive embodiment of the ideals of the High Renaissance in sculpture. But its true place in the history of art is a bit more complicated.

As Michelangelo well knew, the Renaissance painting and sculpture that preceded his work were deeply concerned with ideal form. Perfection of proportion was the ever-sought Holy Grail; during the Renaissance, ideal proportion was equated with ideal beauty, and ideal beauty was equated with spiritual perfection. But *David*, despite its supremely calm and dignified pose, departs from these ideals. Michelangelo didn't give the statue perfect proportions. The head is slightly too large for the body, the arms are too large for the torso, and the hands are dramatically large for the arms. The work was originally commissioned to adorn the exterior of the Duomo and was intended to be seen from a distance and on high. Michelangelo knew exactly what he was doing, calculating that the perspective of the viewer would be such that, in order for the statue to appear proportioned, the upper body, head, and arms would have to be bigger as they are farther away from the viewer's line of vision. But he also did it to express and embody, as powerfully as possible in a single figure, an entire biblical story. David's hands *are* big, but so was Goliath, and these are the hands that slew him. ⊠ *Via Ricasoli 60, San Marco* ☏ *055/294883 reservations, 055/2388609 gallery* 🎟 *€6.50, reservation fee €3* 🕐 *Tues.–Sun. 8:15–6:50.*

Giardino dei Semplici. Created by Cosimo I in 1550, this delightful garden was designed by favorite Medici architect Niccolò Tribolo. Many of the plants here have been grown since the 16th century. Springtime, especially May, is a particularly beautiful time to visit, as multitudes of azaleas create a riot of color. ⊠ *Via Pier Micheli 3, San Marco* ☏ *055/2757402* 🎟 *€3* 🕐 *Nov.–Mar. weekdays 9–1; Apr.–Oct. Tues. 9–1 and 3–6, Wed.–Fri. 9–1* ⊕ *www.unifi.it-msn.*

☺ **Mercato Centrale.** Some of the food at this huge, two-story market hall is remarkably exotic. The ground floor contains meat and cheese stalls, as well as some very good bars that have *panini* (sandwiches), and the second floor teems with vegetable stands. ⊠ *Piazza del Mercato Centrale, San Lorenzo* ☏ *no phone* 🕐 *Mon.–Sat. 7–2.*

CloseUp

FLORENCE'S TRIAL BY FIRE

One of the most striking figures of Renaissance Florence was Girolamo Savonarola, a Dominican friar who, for a moment, captured the conscience of the city. In 1491 he became prior of the convent of San Marco, where he adopted a life of austerity and delivered sermons condemning Florence's excesses and the immorality of his fellow clergy. Following the death of Lorenzo de' Medici, Savonarola was instrumental in the formation of the republic of Florence, ruled by a representative council with Christ enthroned as monarch. In one of his most memorable acts, he urged Florentines to toss worldly possessions—from frilly dresses to Botticelli paintings—onto a "bonfire of the vanities" in Piazza della Signoria. Savonarola's antagonism toward church hierarchy led to his undoing: he was excommunicated in 1497, and the following year was hanged and burned on charges of heresy. Today, at the Museo di San Marco, you can visit Savonarola's cell and see his arresting portrait.

㉕ Museo Archeologico (Archaeological Museum). Of the Etruscan, Egyptian, and Greco-Roman antiquities here, the Etruscan collection is particularly notable—one of the largest in Italy. The famous bronze *Chimera* was discovered (without the tail, a reconstruction) in the 16th century. ⊠ *Via della Colonna 38, Santissima Annunziata* ☎ *055/23575* ⊕ *www.comune.fi.it/sogetti/sat* ☜ *€4* ☾ *Mon. 2–7, Tues. and Thurs. 8:30–7, Wed. and Fri.–Sun. 8:30–2.*

Museo dell'Opificio delle Pietre Dure. Adjacent to this fascinating small museum is an *opificio*, or workshop, that Ferdinand I established in 1588 to train craftsmen in the art of working with precious and semiprecious stones and marble (*pietre dure* means hard stone). Four hundred–plus years later, the workshop is renowned as a center for the restoration of mosaics and inlays in semiprecious stones. The museum is highly informative and includes some magnificent antique examples of this highly specialized and beautiful craft. ⊠ *Via degli Alfani 78, San Marco* ☎ *055/26511* ☜ *€2* ☾ *Mon., Wed., and Fri.–Sat. 8:15–1:50, Thurs. 8:15–7.*

㉑ Museo di San Marco. A former Dominican convent adjacent to the church of San Marco now houses this museum, which contains many stunning works by Fra Angelico (circa 1400–55), the Dominican friar famous for his piety as well as for his painting. When the friars' cells were restructured between 1439 and 1444, he decorated many of them with frescoes meant to spur religious contemplation. His unostentatious and direct paintings exalt the simple beauties of the contemplative life. Fra Angelico's works are everywhere, from the friars' cells to the superb panel paintings on view in the museum. Don't miss the famous *Annunciation,* on the upper floor, and the works in the gallery off the cloister as you enter. Here you can see his beautiful *Last Judgment;* as usual, the tortures of the damned are far more inventive and interesting than the pleasures of the redeemed. ⊠ *Piazza San Marco 1* ☎ *055/2388608* ☜ *€4* ☾ *Week-*

days 8:15–1:50, weekends 8:15–6:50. Closed 1st, 3rd, and 5th Sun., and 2nd and 4th Mon. of month.

⑳ Palazzo Medici-Riccardi. The main attraction of this palace, begun in 1444 by Michelozzo for Cosimo de' Medici, is the interior chapel, the so-called **Cappella dei Magi** on the upper floor. Painted on its walls is Benozzo Gozzoli's famous *Procession of the Magi,* finished in 1460 and celebrating both the birth of Christ and the greatness of the Medici family. Like his contemporary Ghirlandaio, Gozzoli wasn't a revolutionary painter and today is considered by some not quite first rate, because of his technique, which was old-fashioned even for his day. Gozzoli's gift, however, was for entrancing the eye, not challenging the mind, and on those terms his success here is beyond question. The paintings are full of activity yet somehow frozen in time in a way that fails utterly as realism but succeeds triumphantly as soon as the demand for realism is set aside. Entering the chapel is like walking into the middle of a magnificently illustrated children's storybook, and this beauty makes it one of the most enjoyable rooms in the city. ⊠ *Via Cavour 1, San Lorenzo* ☎ *055/2760340* 🎟 *€4* 🕙 *Thurs.–Tues. 9–7.*

▶ ⑰ San Lorenzo. Filippo Brunelleschi designed this basilica, as well as that of Santo Spirito in the Oltrarno, in the early 15th century. He never lived to see either of them finished. The two interiors are similar in design and effect and proclaim with ringing clarity the beginning of the Renaissance in architecture. San Lorenzo, however, has a grid of dark, inlaid marble lines on the floor, which considerably heightens the dramatic effect. The grid makes the rigorous geometry of the interior immediately visible and is an illuminating lesson on the laws of perspective. If you stand in the middle of the nave at the church entrance, on the line that stretches to the high altar, every element in the church—the grid, the nave columns, the side aisles, the coffered nave ceiling—seems to march inexorably toward a hypothetical vanishing point beyond the high altar, exactly as in a single-point-perspective painting. Brunelleschi's **Sagrestia Vecchia** (Old Sacristy) has stucco decorations by Donatello; it's at the end of the left transept. ⊠ *Piazza San Lorenzo* ☎ *055/290184* 🎟 *€2.50* 🕙 *Mon.–Thur. 9:30–5, Fri. and Sat. 10–5.*

㉖ Santa Maria Maddalena dei Pazzi. One of Florence's hidden treasures, a cool and composed *Crucifixion* by Perugino (circa 1445/50–1523), is in the chapter house of the monastery below this church. Here you can see the Virgin Mary and St. John the Evangelist with Mary Magdalen and Sts. Benedict and Bernard of Clairvaux posed against a simple but haunting landscape. The figure of Christ crucified occupies the center of this brilliantly hued fresco. Perugino's colors radiate—note the juxtaposition of the yellow-green cuff against the orange tones of the Magdalen's robe. ⊠ *Borgo Pinti 58, Santa Croce* ☎ *055/2478420* 🎟 *Suggested €1* 🕙 *Mon.–Sat. 10–12 and 5–7, Sun. 9–10:45 and 3–6:50.*

㉔ Santissima Annunziata. Dating from the mid-13th century, this church was restructured in 1447 by Michelozzo, who gave it an uncommon (and lovely) entrance cloister with frescoes by Andrea del Sarto (1486–1530), Pontormo (1494–1556), and Rosso Fiorentino (1494–1540). The interior is a rarity for Florence: a sumptuous example of the baroque. But it's not really a fair example, because it's merely 17th-century baroque decoration applied willy-nilly to an earlier structure—exactly the sort of violent remodeling exercise that has given the baroque a bad name. The **Cappella dell'Annunziata,** immediately inside the entrance to the left, illustrates the point. The lower half, with its stately Corinthian columns and carved frieze bearing the Medici arms, was commissioned by Piero de' Medici in 1447; the upper half, with its erupting curves and impish sculpted cherubs, was added 200 years later. Each is effective in its own way, but together they serve only to prove that dignity is rarely comfortable wearing a party hat. Fifteenth-century-fresco enthusiasts should also note the very fine Holy Trinity with St. Jerome in the second chapel on the left. Done by Andrea del Castagno (circa 1421–57), it shows a wiry and emaciated St. Jerome with Paula and Eustochium, two of his closest followers. ⊠ *Piazza di Santissima Annunziata* ☎ *055/ 266186* ⊗ *Daily 7–12:30 and 4:30–6:30.*

㉗ Sinagoga. Jews were well settled in Florence by 1396, when the first money-lending operations became officially sanctioned. Medici patronage helped Jewish banking houses to flourish, but by 1570 Jews were required to live within the large "ghetto," near today's Piazza della Repubblica, by the decree of Cosimo I, who had cut a deal with Pope Pius V (1504–72): in exchange for ghettoizing the Jews, he would receive the title of Grand Duke of Tuscany.

Construction of the modern Moorish-style synagogue, with its lovely garden, began in 1874 as a bequest of David Levi, who wished to endow a synagogue "worthy of the city." Falcini, Micheli, and Treves designed the building on a domed Greek cross plan with galleries in the transept and a roofline bearing three distinctive copper cupolas visible from all over Florence. The exterior has alternating bands of tan travertine and pink granite, reflecting an Islamic style repeated in Giovanni Panti's ornate interior. Of particular interest are the cast-iron gates by Pasquale Franci, the eternal light by Francesco Morini, and the Murano glass mosaics by Giacomo dal Medico. The gilded doors of the Moorish ark, which fronts the pulpit and is flanked by extravagant candelabra, are decorated with symbols of the ancient Temple of Jerusalem and bear bayonet marks from vandals. The synagogue was used as a garage by the Nazis, who failed to inflict much damage in spite of an attempt to blow up the place with dynamite. Only the columns on the left side were destroyed, and even then, the Women's Balcony above did not collapse. Note the Star of David in black and yellow marble inlaid in the floor. The original capitals can be seen in the garden.

Some of the oldest and most beautiful Jewish ritual artifacts in all of Europe are displayed in the small **Museo Ebraico,** upstairs. Exhibits document the Florentine Jewish community and the building of the synagogue. The donated objects all belonged to local families and date from as early as the late 16th century. Take special note of the exquisite needlework and silver pieces. A small but well-stocked gift shop is downstairs. ⊠ *Via Farini 4, Santa Croce* ☎ *055/2346654* ☒ *Synagogue and museum* €3 ⊗ *Apr.–May and Sept.–Oct., Sun.–Thurs. 10–5, Fri. 10–2; Jun.–Aug.,*

Sun.–Thurs. 10–6, Fri. 10–2; Nov.–Mar., Sun.–Thurs. 10–3, Fri. 10–2.
English-guided tours 10:10, 11, 12, 1, 2 (no tour at 2 on Fri).

> **need a break?**
>
> The only kosher–vegetarian restaurant in Tuscany is **Ruth's** (⊠ Via Farini 2/a, Santa Croce ☎ 055/2480888), adjacent to Florence's synagogue. On the menu: inexpensive vegetarian and Mediterranean dishes and a large selection of kosher wines. It's closed for Friday dinner and Saturday lunch.

㉓ Spedale degli Innocenti. Built by Brunelleschi in 1419 to serve as a foundling hospital, it takes the historical prize as the very first Renaissance building. Brunelleschi designed its portico with his usual rigor, building it out of the two shapes he considered mathematically (and therefore philosophically and aesthetically) perfect: the square and the circle. Below the level of the arches, the portico encloses a row of perfect cubes; above the level of the arches, the portico encloses a row of intersecting hemispheres. The entire geometric scheme is articulated with Corinthian columns, capitals, and arches borrowed directly from antiquity. At the time he designed the portico, Brunelleschi was also designing the interior of San Lorenzo, using the same basic ideas. But because the portico was finished before San Lorenzo, the Spedale degli Innocenti can claim the honor of ushering in Renaissance architecture. The 10 ceramic medallions depicting swaddled infants that decorate the portico are by Andrea della Robbia (1435–1525/28), done in about 1487.

Within the Spedale degli Innocenti is a small museum, or **Pinacoteca** (⊠ €2.60 ☼ Thurs.–Tues 8:30–2). Most of the objects are minor works by major artists, but well worth a look is Domenico Ghirlandaio's (1449–94) *Adorazione dei Magi* (*Adoration of the Magi*), executed in 1488. His use of color, and his eye for flora and fauna, shows that art from north of the Alps made a great impression on him. ⊠ *Piazza di Santissima Annunziata 12* ☎ *055/20371* ⊠ *€3* ☼ *Thurs.–Tues. 8:30–2.*

Santa Maria Novella to the Arno

Piazza Santa Maria Novella is near the train station, and like similar areas in many other European cities, it is marked by a degree of squalor, especially at night. Nevertheless, the streets in and around the piazza have their share of architectural treasures, including some of Florence's most tasteful palazzi.

A Good Tour

Start in the Piazza Santa Maria Novella, its north side dominated by the church of **Santa Maria Novella** ㉙ ▶; then take Via delle Belle Donne, which leads from the east side of the piazza to a minuscule square, at the center of which stands a curious shrine known as the Croce al Trebbio. Take Via del Trebbio east and turn right onto Via Tornabuoni, Florence's finest shopping street. At the intersection of Via Tornabuoni and Via Strozzi is the gargantuan **Palazzo Strozzi** ㉚. If you want a dose of contemporary art, head straight down Via della Spada to the **Museo Marino Marini** ㉛. One block west from Via Tornabuoni and Palazzo Strozzi, down

Via della Vigna Nuova, is Leon Battista Alberti's groundbreaking **Palazzo Rucellai** ㉜. Follow the narrow street opposite the palazzo (Via del Purgatorio) east almost to its end; then zigzag right and left, turning east on Via Parione to reach Piazza di Santa Trinita, where, in the middle, stands the **Colonna della Giustizia** ㉝. Halfway down the block to the south (toward the Arno) is the church of **Santa Trinita** ㉞, home to Ghirlandaio's glowing frescoes. Then go east on Borgo Santi Apostoli, a typical medieval street flanked by tower houses, and take a right on Via Por Santa Maria to get to the Ponte Vecchio. Alternatively, walk from Piazza Santa Trinita to Ponte Santa Trinita, which leads into the Oltrarno. If you want to detour to **Le Cascine** ㉟, make a left as you exit the Museo Salvatore Ferragamo, and head directly for the Arno. At the Arno, make a right, and continue along the river until you hit the park. Another option is to head up Via Tornabuoni toward the station at Santa Maria Novella, making a left at Via Spada and a right onto Via delle Belle Donne. At the station, take Bus 4 to the **Museo Stibbert** ㊱.

TIMING The walk takes about 30 minutes, plus 30 minutes for Santa Maria Novella and 15 minutes for Santa Trinita. A visit to the Santa Maria Novella museum and cloister takes about 30 minutes. If you decide to include a trip to the Cascine, add another hour for walking and picnicking. Allow about 2½ hours to get to Museo Stibbert and to visit its collection.

What to See

off the
beaten
path

CENACOLO DI FOLIGNO – This delightful *Last Supper*, executed sometime in the 1470s, has been variously attributed to Perugino or to one of his followers. Its placement, at the end of a long room—the former refectory for a group of nuns—is simply breathtaking; because the white walls are otherwise unadorned, the fresco packs quite a visual punch. In the middle of the lunette in the upper center, Christ appears in the Garden of Gethsemane with the sleeping apostles. The delicate brush strokes of the leaves in the trees are exquisite. Judas, as is typical of so many representations of the Last Supper, is shown seated at the other side of the table quite apart from the other eleven apostles. Note how the artist has carefully labeled each apostle except for Judas. The tondi surrounding the fresco show portraits of prominent Franciscans such as St. Anthony of Padua, Francis of Assisi, St. Bernardino of Siena, and St. Louis of Toulouse. ✉ *Via Faenza 42, Santa Maria Novella* ☎ *055/286982* 💲 *Free* 🕙 *Mon., Tues., and Sat. 9–noon.*

㉝ **Colonna della Giustizia.** In the center of **Piazza Santa Trinita** is this column from Rome's Terme di Caracalla, given to the Medici Grand Duke Cosimo I by Pope Pius IV in 1560. Typical of Medici self-assurance, the name translates as the Column of Justice. The column was raised here by Cosimo in 1565 to mark the spot where he heard the news that Florentine ducal forces had prevailed over a ragtag army composed of Florentine republican exiles and their French allies at the 1554 battle of Marciano near Prato; the victory made his power in Florence all but absolute. ✉ *Piazza Santa Trinita, Santa Maria Novella.*

Croce al Trebbio. In 1338 the Dominican friars (the Dominican church of Santa Maria Novella is down the street) erected this little granite column near Piazza Santa Maria Novella to commemorate a famous local victory: it was here in 1244 that they defeated their avowed enemies, the Patarene heretics, in a bloody street brawl. ⊠ *Via del Trebbio, Santa Maria Novella.*

③⑤ Le Cascine. In the 16th century this vast park belonged to the Medici, who allegedly used it for hunting, one of their favorite pastimes. It was opened to the public in the 19th century. The park runs for nearly 3 km (2 mi) along the Arno and has roughly 291 acres. It's ideal for strolling on sunny days, and there are paths for jogging, allées perfect for biking, grassy fields for picnicking, and lots of space for rollerblading (as well as a place to rent skates). At the northern tip of the park is the **piazzaletto dell'Indiano,** an oddly moving monument dedicated to Rajaram Cuttraputti, Marajah of Kolepoor, who died in Florence in 1870. The park hosts sports enthusiasts, a weekly open-air market, and discotheques. But be warned: at night, there's a booming sex-for-sale trade. ⊠ *Main entrance: Piazza Vittorio Veneto, Viale Fratelli Roselli (at the Ponte della Vittoria).*

③① Museo Marino Marini. A 21-foot-tall bronze horse and rider, one of the major works by artist Marini (1901–80), dominates the space of the main gallery here. The museum itself is an eruption of contemporary space in a deconsecrated 9th-century church, designed with a series of open stairways, walkways, and balconies that allow you to peer at Marini's work from all angles. In addition to his Etruscanesque sculpture, the museum houses Marini's paintings, drawings, and engravings. ⊠ *Piazza San Pancrazio, Santa Maria Novella* ☎ *055/219432* 🎫 *€4* ⊙ *Mon. and Wed.–Sat. 10–5.*

Museo Salvatore Ferragamo. If a temple for footwear existed, it would be here. The shoes in this finely arranged collection were designed by Salvatore Ferragamo (1898–1960) beginning in the early 20th century; they are elegant and the presentation dramatic. Born in southern Italy, the late master jump-started his career in Hollywood by creating shoes for the likes of Mary Pickford and Rudolph Valentino. He then returned to Florence and set up shop in the 13th-century Palazzo Spini Ferroni. The collection includes about 10,000 shoes, and those exhibited are frequently rotated. ⊠ *Via dei Tornabuoni 2, Santa Maria Novella* ☎ *055/3360456* 🎫 *Free* ⊙ *Weekdays 9–1 and 2–6.*

③⑥ Museo Stibbert. Federico Stibbert (1838–1906), born in Florence to an Italian mother and an English father, liked to collect things. Over a lifetime of doing so, he amassed some 50,000 objects. This museum, which was also his home, displays many of them. He had a fascination with medieval armor and also collected costumes, particularly Uzbek costumes, which are exhibited in a room called the Moresque Hall. These are mingled with an extensive collection of swords, guns, and other devices whose sole function was to kill people. The paintings, most of which date from the 15th century, are largely second rate. The house itself is an interesting amalgam of neo-Gothic, Renaissance, and English eccentric. To get here, take Bus 4 from the station at Santa Maria Novella, get off at the stop marked FABBRONI 4, and follow signs to the museum. ⊠ *Via Federico Stibbert 26* ☎ *055/475520* 🎫 *€5* ⊙ *Mon.–Wed. 10–2; Fri.–Sun. 10–6. Tours every half hr.*

Ognissanti. The Umiliati owned this hodgepodge of a church before the Franciscans took it over in the mid-16th century. (They were ousted in 2001, and replaced by the Benedictines, who moved out in 2003.) Beyond the fanciful baroque facade by Matteo Nigetti (1560–1649) are a couple of wonderful 15th-century gems. On the right in the nave is *Madonna della Misericordia* by Ghirlandaio; a little farther down is Botticelli's *St. Augustine in His Study.* A companion piece, directly across the way, is Ghirlandaio's *St. Jerome.* Pass through the rather dreadfully frescoed cloister to check out Ghirlandaio's superb *Last Supper*—which proves definitively that Leonardo da Vinci was not the only Tuscan painter who could do them well. ⊠ *Piazza Ognissanti, Santa Maria Novella* ☎ *055/2398700* 🎫 *Free* ⊙ *Church daily 7–noon and 3–6; Last Supper Mon.–Tues. and Sat. 9–noon.*

㉜ Palazzo Rucellai. Architect Leon Battista Alberti (1404–72) designed perhaps the very first private residence inspired by antique models—which goes a step further than the Palazzo Strozzi. A comparison between the two is illuminating. Evident on the facade of the Palazzo Rucellai, dating between 1455 and 1470, is the ordered arrangement of windows and rusticated stonework seen on the Palazzo Strozzi, but Alberti's facade is far less forbidding. Alberti devoted a far larger proportion of his wall space to windows, which lighten the facade's appearance, and filled in the remainder with rigorously ordered classical elements borrowed from antiquity. The result, though still severe, is less fortresslike, and Alberti strove for this effect purposely (he is on record as saying that only tyrants need fortresses). Ironically, the Palazzo Rucellai was built some 30 years *before* the Palazzo Strozzi. Alberti's civilizing ideas here, it turned out, had little influence on the Florentine palazzi that followed. To Renaissance Florentines, power—in architecture, as in life—was equally as impressive as beauty. While you are admiring the facade (the palazzo isn't open to the public), turn around and look at the Loggia dei Rucellai across the street. Built in 1463–66, it was the private "terrace" of the Rucellai family, in-laws to the Medici. Its soaring heights and grand arches are a firm testament to the family's status and wealth. ⊠ *Via della Vigna Nuova, Santa Maria Novella.*

㉚ Palazzo Strozzi. The Strozzi family built this imposing palazzo in an attempt to outshine the nearby Palazzo Medici. Based on a model by Giuliano da Sangallo (circa 1452–1516) dating from around 1489 and executed between 1489 and 1504 under il Cronaca (1457–1508) and Benedetto da Maiaino (1442–97), it was inspired by Michelozzo's earlier Palazzo Medici-Riccardi. The palazzo's exterior is simple, severe, and massive: it's a testament to the wealth of a patrician, 15th-century Florentine family. The interior courtyard, entered from the rear of the palazzo, is another matter altogether. It is here that the classical vocabulary—columns, capitals, pilasters, arches, and cornices—is given uninhibited and powerful expression. Blockbuster art shows frequently occur here. ⊠ *Via*

Tornabuoni, Piazza della Repubblica ☎ *055/2776461* ⊕ *www.firenzemostre.com* ✉ *Free except during exhibitions* ⊘ *Daily 10–7.*

▶ ㉙ **Santa Maria Novella.** The facade of this church looks distinctly clumsy by later Renaissance standards, and with good reason: it is an architectural hybrid. The lower half was completed mostly in the 14th century; its pointed-arch niches and decorative marble patterns reflect the Gothic style of the day. About 100 years later (around 1456), architect Leon Battista Alberti was called in to complete the job. The marble decoration of his upper story clearly defers to the already existing work below, but the architectural motifs he added evince an entirely different style. The central doorway, the four ground-floor half-columns with Corinthian capitals, the triangular pediment atop the second story, the inscribed frieze immediately below the pediment—these are borrowings from antiquity, and they reflect the new Renaissance style in architecture, born some 35 years earlier at the Spedale degli Innocenti. Alberti's most important addition, however, the S-curve scrolls that surmount the decorative circles on either side of the upper story, had no precedent whatever in antiquity. The problem was to soften the abrupt transition between wide ground floor and narrow upper story. Alberti's solution turned out to be definitive. Once you start to look for them, you will find scrolls such as these (or sculptural variations of them) on churches all over Italy, and every one of them derives from Alberti's example here.

The architecture of the interior is, like that of the Duomo, a dignified but somber example of Florentine Gothic. Exploration is essential, however, because the church's store of art treasures is remarkable. Highlights include the 14th-century stained-glass rose window depicting the *Coronation of the Virgin* (above the central entrance); the Cappella Filippo Strozzi (to the right of the altar), containing late-15th-century frescoes and stained glass by Filippino Lippi; the *cappella maggiore* (the area around the high altar), displaying frescoes by Ghirlandaio; and the Cappella Gondi (to the left of the altar), containing Filippo Brunelleschi's famous wood crucifix, carved around 1410 and said to have so stunned the great Donatello when he first saw it that he dropped a basket of eggs.

Of special interest for its great historical importance and beauty is Masaccio's *Trinity,* on the left-hand wall, almost halfway down the nave. Painted around 1426–27 (at the same time he was working on his frescoes in Santa Maria del Carmine), it unequivocally announced the arrival of the Renaissance. The realism of the figure of Christ was revolutionary in itself, but what was probably even more startling to contemporary Florentines was the barrel vault in the background. The mathematical rules for employing perspective in painting had just been discovered (probably by Brunelleschi), and this was one of the first works of art to employ them with utterly convincing success.

In the cloisters of the **Museo di Santa Maria Novella** (✉ Piazza Santa Maria Novella 19 ☎ 055/282187 ✉ €2.60 ⊘ Wed.–Mon. 9–2), to the left of Santa Maria Novella, is a faded fresco cycle by Paolo Uccello depicting tales from Genesis, with a dramatic vision of the Deluge. Earlier and better-preserved frescoes painted in 1348–55 by Andrea da Firenze are in the chapter house, or the **Cappellone degli Spagnoli** (Spanish Chapel), off the cloister. ✉ *Piazza Santa Maria Novella* ☎ *055/210113* 🎫 *€2.50* 🕓 *Mon.–Thurs. and Sat. 9–3, Sun. 9–2.*

34 **Santa Trinita.** Started in the 11th century by Vallambrosian monks and originally Romanesque in style, the church underwent a Gothic remodeling during the 14th century. (Remains of the Romanesque construction are visible on the interior front wall.) Its major works are the fresco cycle and altarpiece in the Cappella Sassetti, the second to the high altar's right, painted by Ghirlandaio from around 1480 to 1485. Ghirlandaio was a wildly popular but conservative painter for his day, and generally his paintings show little interest in the laws of perspective with which other Florentine painters had been experimenting for more than 50 years. But his work here possesses such graceful decorative appeal it hardly seems to matter. The wall frescoes illustrate scenes from the life of St. Francis, and the altarpiece, depicting the *Adoration of the Shepherds,* veritably glows. ✉ *Piazza Santa Trinita, Santa Maria Novella* ☎ *055/216912* 🕓 *Mon.–Sat. 9–12 and 3:30–6.*

The Oltrarno: Palazzo Pitti, Giardino di Boboli, Santo Spirito

A walk through the Oltrarno takes in two very different aspects of Florence: the splendor of the Medici, manifest in the riches of the mammoth Palazzo Pitti and the gracious Giardino di Boboli; and the charm of the Oltrarno, literally "the other side of the Arno," a slightly gentrified but still fiercely proud working-class neighborhood with artisans' and antiques shops.

A Good Tour

Starting from Santa Trinita, walk toward the Arno on Via Tornabuoni, make a left onto the Lungarno degli Acciaiuoli, and cross the Arno over the Ponte Vecchio. If you want to take a Mannerist detour to see the Pontormo *Deposition* at **Santa Felicita** ㉟ ▶, head down Via Guicciardini and stop in the first piazza on your left. Head toward **Palazzo Pitti** ㊳, Florence's largest palace, by continuing on Via Guicciardini; it lies before you as you emerge onto Piazza Pitti. Behind the palace is the **Giardino di Boboli** ㊴. Then head for the Giardino del Cavaliere, which requires a gently demanding uphill climb. At the top, **Forte di Belvedere** ㊵ commands a wonderful view and sometimes has art exhibits. From here it's an easy walk to Bus 37, which takes you to the **Certosa** ㊶. Return via bus and alight at the Santo Spirito stop to take in Piazza Santo Spirito, dominated at its north end by the unassuming and unfinished facade of the church of **Santo Spirito** ㊷. Take Via Sant'Agostino, diagonally across the square from the church entrance, and follow it west to Via dei Serragli. Cross and follow Via Santa Monaca west through the heart of the Oltrarno to Piazza del Carmine and the church of **Santa Maria del Carmine** ㊸, where the famous fresco cycle by Masaccio, Masolino, and Filippino Lippi fills the Cappella Brancacci. Go to the far end of Piazza del Carmine and turn right onto Borgo San Frediano; then follow Via di Santo Spirito and Borgo Sant'Jacopo east to reach the Ponte Vecchio.

TIMING The walk alone takes about 45 minutes; allow one hour to visit the Galleria Palatina in Palazzo Pitti and more if you visit the other galleries. Spend at least 30 minutes to an hour savoring the graceful elegance of the Giardino di Boboli. When you reach the crossroads of the Sdrucciolo dei Pitti and Via Michelozzi, you have a choice. If it's around noon, you may want to postpone the next stop temporarily to see the churches of Santo Spirito, Santa Felicita (if you didn't stop in before going to Palazzo Pitti), and Santa Maria del Carmine before they close for the afternoon. Otherwise, proceed to Palazzo Pitti. The churches can be visited in 15 minutes each. The trip to and the tour of the Certosa take about two hours total.

What to See

㊶ Certosa. The incredible Carthusian complex was largely funded in 1342 by the wealthy Florentine banker Niccolò Acciaolo, whose guilt at having amassed so much money must have been at least temporarily assuaged with the creation of such a structure to honor God. In the grand cloister are stunning frescoes of *Christ's Passion* by Pontormo. Though they suffer from much paint loss, their power is still unmistakable. Also of great interest are the monks' cells; apparently the monks could spend most of their lives tending their own private gardens without dealing with any other monks. To get here, you must take Bus 37 and get off at the stop marked CERTOSA, or you need a car. ⊠ *From Florence, take Viale Petrarca to Via Senese and follow it for about 10 mins; the Certosa is on the right* ☎ *055/2049226* ⊠ *Suggested €3 to €4* ⊗ *Tues.–Sun. 9–11:30 and 3–4:30.*

㊵ Forte di Belvedere (Fort Belvedere). The impressive structure was built in 1590 to help defend the city against siege. But what was once a first-rate fortification is now a first-rate exhibition venue. Farther up the hill is Piazzale Michelangelo, but as the natives know, the best views of Florence are right here. To the north, all the city's monuments are spread out in a breathtaking panorama. To the south, the nearby hills furnish a complementary rural view, in its way equally memorable. The fortress is adjacent to the top of the Giardino di Boboli. ⊠ *Porta San Giorgio, San Niccolò* ⊠ *Varies with exhibit.*

㊴ Giardino di Boboli (Boboli Gardens). The main entrance to these landscaped gardens is from the right wing of ⇨ **Palazzo Pitti.** The gardens began to take shape in 1549, when the Pitti family sold the palazzo to Eleanor of Toledo, wife of the Medici grand duke Cosimo I. The initial landscaping plans were laid out by Niccolò Tribolo (1500–50). After his death, work was continued by Vasari, Ammannati, Giambologna, Bernardo Buontalenti (circa 1536–1608), and Giulio (1571–1635) and Alfonso Parigi (1606–56), among others. Italian landscaping is less formal than French but still full of sweeping drama. A copy of the famous *Morgante,* Cosimo I's favorite dwarf astride a particularly unhappy tortoise, is near the exit. Sculpted by Valerio Cioli (circa 1529–99), the work seems to illustrate the perils of culinary overindulgence. Because the gardens aren't always well kept, a visit here can be disappointing. ⊠ *Enter through Palazzo Pitti* ☎ *055/294883* ⊠ *€4, combined ticket with Museo delle Porcellane and Museo degli Argenti* ⊗ *Apr.–May and Sept.,* *daily 8:15–6:30; Jun.–Aug., daily 8:15–7:30; Nov.–Mar. and Oct., daily 8:15–4:30. Closed 1st and last Mon. of month.*

③ **Palazzo Pitti.** This enormous palace is one of Florence's largest architectural set pieces. The original palazzo, built for the Pitti family around 1460, comprised only the main entrance and the three windows on either side. In 1549 the property was sold to the Medici, and Bartolomeo Ammannati was called in to make substantial additions. Although he apparently operated on the principle that more is better, he succeeded only in producing proof that more is just that: more.

Today the palace houses several museums: The **Museo degli Argenti** displays a vast collection of Medici household treasures. The **Galleria del Costume** showcases fashions from the past 300 years. The **Galleria d'Arte Moderna** holds a collection of 19th- and 20th-century paintings, mostly Tuscan. Most famous of the Pitti galleries is the **Galleria Palatina**, which contains a broad collection of paintings from the 15th to 17th centuries. The rooms of the Galleria Palatina remain much as the Medici left them. Their floor-to-ceiling paintings are considered by some to be Italy's most egregious exercise in conspicuous consumption, aesthetic overkill, and trumpery. Still, the collection possesses high points, including a number of portraits by Titian and an unparalleled collection of paintings by Raphael, notably the double portraits of Angelo Doni and his wife, the sullen Maddalena Strozzi. The price of admission to the Galleria Palatina also allows you to explore the former **Appartamenti Reali** containing furnishings from a remodeling done in the 19th century. ⊠ *Piazza Pitti* ☎ *055/210323* ▣ *Galleria Palatina €6.50; Galleria d'Arte Moderna and Galleria del Costume combined admission €5; Museo degli Argenti, Museo delle Porcellane, and Giardino di Boboli combined admission €4* ۞ *All but Galleria Palatina closed 2nd and 4th Sun. and 1st, 3rd, and 5th Mon. of month.*

▶ ③ **Santa Felicita.** This late-baroque church (its facade was remodeled between 1736 and 1739) contains the Mannerist Jacopo Pontormo's *Deposition*, the centerpiece of the Cappella Capponi (executed 1525–28) and a masterpiece of 16th-century Florentine art. The remote figures, which transcend the realm of Renaissance classical form, are portrayed in tangled shapes and intense pastel colors (well preserved because of the low lights in the church), in a space and depth that defy reality. Note, too, the exquisitely frescoed *Annunciation,* also by Pontormo, at a right angle to the *Deposition.* The granite column in the piazza was erected in 1381 and marks a Christian cemetery. ⊠ *Piazza Santa Felicita, Via Guicciardini, Palazzo Pitti* ۞ *Mon.–Sat. 9–noon and 3:30–6, Sun. 9–1.*

④ **Santa Maria del Carmine.** The **Cappella Brancacci**, at the end of the right transept of this church, houses a masterpiece of Renaissance painting: a fresco cycle that changed the course of Western art. Fire almost destroyed the church in the 18th century; miraculously, the Brancacci Chapel survived almost intact. The cycle is the work of three artists: Masaccio and Masolino (1383–circa 1447), who began it around 1424, and Filippino Lippi, who finished it some 50 years later after a long interruption during which the sponsoring Brancacci family was exiled. It was

Masaccio's work that opened a new frontier for painting, as he was among the first artists to employ single-point perspective; tragically, he died in 1428 at the age of 27, so he didn't live to experience the revolution his innovations caused.

Masaccio collaborated with Masolino on several of the paintings, but by himself he painted the *Tribute Money,* on the upper-left wall; *St. Peter Baptizing,* on the upper altar wall; the *Distribution of Goods,* on the lower altar wall; and most famous, the *Expulsion of Adam and Eve,* on the chapel's upper-left entrance pier. If you look closely at the last painting and compare it with some of the chapel's other works, you should see a pronounced difference. The figures of Adam and Eve possess a startling presence primarily thanks to the dramatic way in which their bodies seem to reflect light. Masaccio here shaded his figures consistently, so as to suggest a single, strong source of light within the world of the painting but outside its frame. In so doing, he succeeded in imitating with paint the real-world effect of light on mass, and he thereby imparted to his figures a sculptural reality unprecedented in his day.

These matters have to do with technique, but with the *Expulsion of Adam and Eve* his skill went beyond mere technical innovation. In the faces of Adam and Eve, you see more than finely modeled figures; you see terrible shame and suffering depicted with a humanity rarely achieved in art. Reservations to see the chapel are mandatory, but can be booked on the same day. Your time inside is limited to 15 minutes—a frustration that's only partly mitigated by the 40-minute DVD about the history of the chapel you can watch either before or after your visit. ✉ *Piazza del Carmine, Santo Spirito* ☎ *055/276558, 055/2768224 reservations* 🖼 €4 ⊙ *Mon. and Wed.–Sat. 10–5, Sun. 1–5.*

42 **Santo Spirito.** The plain, unfinished facade gives nothing away, but the interior, although it appears chilly compared with later churches, is one of the most important examples of Renaissance architecture in Italy. The interior is one of a pair designed in Florence by Filippo Brunelleschi in the early 15th century (the other is San Lorenzo). It was here that Brunelleschi supplied definitive solutions to the two major problems of interior Renaissance church design: how to build a cross-shape interior using classical architectural elements borrowed from antiquity and how to reflect in that interior the order and regularity that Renaissance scientists (among them Brunelleschi himself) were at the time discovering in the natural world around them.

Brunelleschi's solution to the first problem was brilliantly simple: turn a Greek temple inside out. To see this clearly, look at one of the stately arcades separating the side aisles from the central nave. Whereas ancient Greek temples were walled buildings surrounded by classical colonnades, Brunelleschi's churches were classical arcades surrounded by walled buildings. This brilliant architectural idea overthrew the previous era's religious taboo against pagan architecture once and for all, triumphantly claiming that architecture for Christian use.

Brunelleschi's solution to the second problem—making the entire interior orderly and regular—was mathematically precise: he designed the ground plan of the church so that all its parts were proportionally related. The transepts and nave have exactly the same width; the side aisles are precisely half as wide as the nave; the little chapels off the side aisles are exactly half as deep as the side aisles; the chancel and transepts are exactly one-eighth the depth of the nave; and so on, with dizzying exactitude. For Brunelleschi, such a design technique would have been a matter of passionate conviction. Like most theoreticians of his day, he believed that mathematical regularity and aesthetic beauty were flip sides of the same coin, that one was not possible without the other. In the **refectory** of Santo Spirito (✉ Piazza Santo Spirito 29 ☎ 055/287043), adjacent to the church, you can see Andrea Orcagna's painting of the Crucifixion. The refectory is open Tuesday through Sunday 9–2; admission is €2.05. ✉ *Piazza Santo Spirito* ☎ *055/210030* *Church free, refectory €2.20* ⏲ *Church: Thurs.–Tues. 10–noon and 4–5:30; Wed. 9–noon. Refectory: Apr.–Sept., Tues.–Sat. 9–2; Oct.–Mar. Tues.–Sat. 9–1:30.*

need a break?

Cabiria (✉ Piazza Santo Spirito 4/r ☎ 055/215732), across the piazza from the church of Santo Spirito, draws funky locals and visitors in search of a cappuccino, quenching ade, or expertly mixed drink. When it's warm, sit outside on the terrace.

From Santa Croce to San Miniato al Monte

The Santa Croce quarter, on the southeast fringe of the historic center, was built up in the Middle Ages outside the second set of medieval walls. The centerpiece of the neighborhood was (and is) the basilica of Santa Croce, which could hold great numbers of worshipers; the vast piazza could accommodate any overflow and also served as a fairground and playing field for traditional, no-holds-barred soccer games. A center of leather working since the Middle Ages, the neighborhood is still packed with artisans producing their exquisitely crafted leather goods.

A Good Walk

Begin your walk at the church of **Sant'Ambrogio** ㊹ ⚑, which is at the intersection of Via dei Pilastri and Via di Mezzo. Duck in and check out the damaged, but still highly enjoyable 15th- century frescoes by Cosimo Rosselli in the left aisle. Exit the church and proceed on Via Pietrapiana to **Piazza dei Ciompi** ㊺. From here, take Borgo Allegri until it meets Via San Giuseppe. Make a right here, and follow it until you reach the church of **Santa Croce** ㊻; stop for a moment to admire the beautiful **Piazza Santa Croce** ㊼. From here you can take a quick jaunt up Via delle Pinzochere to **Casa Buonarroti** ㊽ to see works by Michelangelo. Return to Santa Croce, and at the southwest end of the piazza go south on Via de' Benci. Detour to the **Museo Horne** ㊾, former home of an assiduous 19th-century collector. Cross the Arno via Ponte alle Grazie. Turn left onto Lungarno Serristori and continue to Piazza Giuseppe Poggi; a series of ramps and stairs climbs to **Piazzale Michelangelo** ㊿, where the city lies before you in all its glory. From Piazzale Michelangelo, take the stairs behind La Loggia restaurant to the church of San Salvatore al Monte, and go south on the lane leading to the stairs that lead to **San Miniato al Monte** (51), cutting through the fortifications hurriedly built by Michelangelo in 1529 when Florence was threatened by troops of the Holy Roman Emperor Charles V (1500–58). You can avoid the long walk by taking Bus 12 or 13 at the west end of Ponte alle Grazie and getting off at Piazzale Michelangelo or at the stop after for San Miniato al Monte; you still have to climb the monumental stairs to and from San Miniato, but you can then take the bus from Piazzale Michelangelo back to the center of town.

TIMING   The walk alone takes about 2½ hours one way, plus 15 to 30 minutes in Sant'Ambrogio, 30 minutes in Santa Croce, 30 minutes in the Museo di Santa Croce, and 30 minutes in San Miniato. Depending on the amount of time you have, you can limit your sightseeing to Santa Croce and Casa Buonarroti or continue on to Piazzale Michelangelo. The walk to Piazzale Michelangelo is a long uphill hike, with the prospect of another climb to San Miniato from there. If you decide to take a bus, remember to buy your ticket before you board. Also, because you go to Piazzale Michelangelo for the view, skip it if it's a hazy day.

What to See

off the beaten path

AMERICAN MILITARY CEMETERY – About 8 km (5 mi) south of Florence on the road to Siena is one of two American cemeteries in Italy (the other is in Nettuno). It contains 4,402 bodies of Americans who died in Italy during World War II. Spread across a gently rolling hill, the simple crosses and Stars of David bearing only name, date of death, and state seem to stretch endlessly. At the top of the hill is a place for reflection and large mosaic maps depicting the Allied assault in 1943. The two fronts—called the Gothic Line and the Gustav Line—are vividly rendered. So, too, is the list containing 1,409 names of those missing in action. ⊠ *From Florence, take Via Cassia south to Località Scopeti* ☎ *055/2020020* ⊑ *Free* ☉ *Daily 9–5.*

48 **Casa Buonarroti.** If you are really enjoying walking in the footsteps of the great genius, you may want to complete the picture by visiting the Buonarroti family home, even though Michelangelo never actually lived in the house. It was given to his nephew, and it was the nephew's son, also called Michelangelo, who turned it into a gallery dedicated to his great-uncle. The artist's descendents filled it with art treasures, some by Michelangelo himself—a marble bas-relief; the *Madonna of the Steps,* carved when Michelangelo was only a teenager; and his wooden model for the facade of San Lorenzo—and some by other artists that pay homage to him. ⊠ *Via Ghibellina 70, Santa Croce* ☎ *055/241752* ⊕ *www.casabuonarroti.it* ⊑ *€6.50* ☉ *Wed.–Mon. 9:30–4.*

off the beaten path

MUSEO DEL CENACOLO – This way-off-the-beaten-path museum (the name translates as the Museum of the Last Supper) has a stunning fresco by Andrea del Sarto. Begun sometime around 1511 and finished 1526–27, the fresco depicts the moment when Christ announced that one of his apostles would betray him. Andrea has rendered the scene in subtle yet still brilliant colors. Also on display are a couple of lesser-known works by Pontormo and copies of other 16th-century works. (Down the street is the church of San Salvi, founded by John Gualbert and begun in 1048. Though it suffered damage during the siege of 1529–30, the interior has a modest but lovely *Madonna and Child* by Lorenzo di Bicci as well as a 16th-century wood cross on the altar.) To get here, take Bus 6 from Piazza San Marco and get off at the Lungo L'Affrico stop—it's the first stop after crossing the railroad tracks. ⊠ *Via San Salvi 16* ☎ *055/ 2388603* ⊠ *Free* ☉ *Tues.–Sun. 8:15–1:50.*

㊾ Museo Horne. Englishman Herbert P. Horne (1864–1916), architect, art historian, and collector, spent much of his life in his 15th-century palazzo surrounded by carefully culled paintings, sculptures, and other decorative arts mostly from the 14th to 16th centuries. His home has since been turned into a museum, which aims to display the objects much as they would have been displayed in his lifetime. Most of the collection is decidedly B-list, but it's worth a visit to see how a gentleman lived in the 19th century. Many of the furnishings, such as the 15th-century *lettuccio* (divan), are exemplary. ⊠ *Via dei Benci 6, Santa Croce* ☎ *055/244661* ⊠ *€5* ☉ *Mon.–Sat. 9–1.*

㊺ Piazza dei Ciompi. Now the site of a daily flea market, this piazza was a working-class neighborhood of primarily wool- and silk-trade workers in the 14th century. The disenfranchised wool workers, forbidden entry to the Arte della Lana (the Wool Guild, to which belonged the wool merchants and managers), briefly seized control of the government. It was a short-lived exercise in rule by the nonrepresented and was eventually overpowered by the ruling upper class. The loggia was executed much later, in 1567, by Giorgio Vasari.

㊿ Piazzale Michelangelo. From this lookout you have a marvelous view of Florence and the hills around it, rivaling the vista from the Forte di Belvedere. It has a copy of Michelangelo's *David* and outdoor cafés packed with tourists during the day and with Florentines in the evening. In May, the **Giardino dell'Iris** (Iris Garden) off the piazza is abloom with more than 2,500 varieties of the flower. The **Giardino delle Rose** (Rose Garden) on the terraces below the piazza is also in full bloom in May and June.

㊼ Piazza Santa Croce. Originally outside the city's set of 12th-century walls, this piazza grew with the Franciscans, who used the large square for public preaching. During the Renaissance it was used for *giostre* (jousts), including one sponsored by Lorenzo de' Medici. "Bonfires of the vanities" occurred here, as well as soccer matches in the 16th century. Lined with many palazzi dating from the 15th century, it remains one of Florence's loveliest piazze and is a great place to sit and people-watch.

⑤ San Miniato al Monte. This church, like the Baptistery, is a fine example of Romanesque architecture and one of the oldest churches in Florence, dating from the 11th century. The lively green-and-white marble facade has a 12th-century mosaic topped by a gilt bronze eagle, emblem of San Miniato's sponsors, the Calimala (cloth merchants' guild). Inside are a 13th-century inlaid-marble floor and apse mosaic. Artist Spinello Aretino (1350–1410) covered the walls of the **Sagrestia** with frescoes depicting scenes from the life of St. Benedict. The nearby **Cappella del Cardinale del Portogallo** (Chapel of the Portuguese Cardinal) is one of the richest 15th-century Renaissance works in Florence. Built to hold the tomb of a Portuguese cardinal, Prince James of Lusitania, who died young in Florence in 1459, it has a glorious ceiling by Luca della Robbia, a sculptured tomb by Antonio Rossellino (1427–79), and inlaid pavement in multicolor marble. ⊠ *Viale Galileo Galilei, Piazzale Michelangelo, Lungarno South* ☎ *055/2342731* ⊘ *Apr.–Oct., daily 8–noon and 3–7; Nov.–Mar., daily 8–noon and 3–4:30.*

㊻ Santa Croce. Like the Duomo, this church is Gothic, but (also like the Duomo) its facade dates from only the 19th century. The interior is most famous for its art and its tombs. As a burial place, the church is a Florentine pantheon, probably containing more skeletons of Renaissance celebrities than any other church in Italy. Among others, the tomb of Michelangelo is immediately to the right as you enter; he is said to have chosen this spot so that the first thing he would see on Judgment Day, when the graves of the dead fly open, would be Brunelleschi's dome through Santa Croce's open doors. The tomb of Galileo Galilei (1564–1642), who produced evidence that Earth is not the center of the universe—and who was not granted a Christian burial until 100 years after his death because of it—is on the left wall, opposite Michelangelo's. The tomb of Niccolò Machiavelli (1469–1527), the Renaissance political theoretician whose brutally pragmatic philosophy so influenced the Medici, is halfway down the nave on the right. The grave of Lorenzo Ghiberti, creator of the Baptistery doors, is halfway down the nave on the left. Composer Gioacchino Rossini (1792–1868) is entombed at the end of the nave on the right. The monument to Dante Alighieri (1265–1321), the greatest Italian poet, is a memorial rather than a tomb (he is buried in Ravenna); it is on the right wall near the tomb of Michelangelo.

FodorśChoice
★

The collection of art within the church complex is by far the most important of any church in Florence. Historically, the most significant works are probably the Giotto frescoes in the two adjacent chapels immediately to the right of the high altar. They illustrate scenes from the lives of St. John the Evangelist and St. John the Baptist (in the right-hand chapel) as well as scenes from the life of St. Francis (in the left-hand chapel). Time has not been kind to them; over the centuries, wall tombs were introduced into the middle of them, whitewash and plaster covered them, and in the 19th century they were subjected to a clumsy restoration. But the reality that Giotto introduced into painting can still be seen. He did not paint beautifully stylized religious icons, as the Byzantine style that preceded him prescribed; he instead painted drama—St. Francis surrounded by grieving friars at the very moment of his death. This was a radical shift in emphasis, and it changed the course of western art. Before Giotto, the role of painting was to symbolize the attributes of God; after him, it was to imitate life. His work is indeed primitive, compared with later painting, but in the proto-Renaissance of the early 14th century it caused a sensation that was not equaled for another 100 years. He was, for his time, the equal of both Masaccio and Michelangelo.

Among the church's other highlights are Donatello's *Annunciation,* one of the tenderest and most eloquent expressions of surprise ever sculpted (on the right wall two-thirds of the way down the nave); 14th-century frescoes by Taddeo Gaddi (circa 1300–66) illustrating scenes from the life of the Virgin, clearly showing the influence of Giotto (in the chapel at the end of the right transept); and Donatello's *Crucifix,* criticized by Brunelleschi for making Christ look like a peasant (in the chapel at the end of the left transept). Outside the church proper, in the **Museo dell'Opera di Santa Croce,** off the cloister, is the 13th-century *Triumphal Cross* by Cimabue (circa 1240–1302), badly damaged by the flood of 1966. A model of architectural geometry, the **Cappella Pazzi,** at the end of the cloister, is the work of Brunelleschi. ⊠ *Piazza Santa Croce 16* ☎ *055/2466105* 🕮 *Basilica and museum (combined ticket): €4* ⊙ *Easter–Oct., Mon.–Sat. 9–5:30, Sun. 1–5; Nov.–Easter, daily 1–5.*

▶ 🟤 **Sant'Ambrogio.** Named for the Bishop of Milan, this 10th-century church once belonged to an order of Benedictine nuns. Just this side of austere, the church is one of the oldest in Florence. Though its facade is 19th-century, inside are 15th-century panel paintings and a lovely but rather damaged 1486 fresco by Cosimo Roselli, in the chapel to the left of the high altar. The tabernacle of the Blessed Sacrament was carved by Mino da Fiesole, who, like Verrocchio, il Cronaca, and Francesco Granacci (1469/77–1543), is buried here. ⊠ *Piazza Sant'Ambrogio, Santa Croce* ☎ *No phone* 🕮 *Free* ⊙ *Daily 8–noon and 3–6.*

WHERE TO EAT

A typical Tuscan repast starts with an antipasto of *crostini* (grilled bread spread with various savory toppings) or cured meats such as prosciutto *crudo* (cured ham thinly sliced) and *finocchiona* (salami seasoned with fennel). *Primi piatti* (first courses) can consist of local versions of pasta dishes available throughout Italy. Peculiar to Florence, however, are the vegetable-and-bread soups such as *pappa al pomodoro* (bread-and-tomato soup), *ribollita* (minestrone thickened with bread and beans and swirled with extra virgin olive oil), and in the summer, a salad called *panzanella* (tomatoes, onions, vinegar, oil, basil, and bread). Before they are eaten, these are often christened with *un "C" d'olio,* a generous C-shape drizzle of the sumptuous local olive oil.

Unparalleled among the *secondi piatti* (main courses) is *bistecca alla fiorentina*—a thick slab of local Chianina beef, often seasoned with olive oil, salt, and pepper, grilled over charcoal, and served very rare. *Trippa alla fiorentina* (tripe stewed with tomato sauce) and *arista* (roast loin of pork seasoned with rosemary) are also local specialties, as are many other roasted meats that pair especially well with Chianti. A *secondo* is usually served with a *contorno* (side dish) of white beans, sautéed greens, or artichokes in season, all of which can be drizzled with more of that fruity olive oil. Desserts in Florence are more or less an afterthought. The meal often ends with a glass of *vin santo* (literally, "holy wine"), an ochre-colored sweet dessert wine that pairs beautifully with biscotti. Dining hours are earlier here than in Rome, starting at 1 for the midday meal and at 8 for dinner. Many of Florence's restaurants are small, so reservations are a must.

Those with a sense of culinary adventure should not miss the tripe sandwich, served from stands throughout town. This Florentine favorite comes with a fragrant *salsa verde* (green sauce) or a piquant red hot sauce—or both.

	WHAT IT COSTS In euros				
	$$$$	$$$	$$	$	¢
AT DINNER	over €22	€18–€22	€13–€17	€7–€12	under €7

Prices are for a second course (secondo piatto).

Centro Storico

ECLECTIC
$–$$

✕ **Birreria Centrale.** The feel here is more Munich beer hall than Florentine trattoria; indeed, although the menu lists plenty of Italian dishes, it also emphasizes sausages and goulash. The *würstel rossi con crauti, speck, e patate alla tedesca* (a large and quite plump hotdog with sauerkraut, cured beef, potatoes, and pickles), for instance, comes with a dollop of spicy mustard. Heavy wooden tables are set closely together, and copies of 19th-century paintings adorn the intensely yellow walls, along with two frescoed Michelangelesque nudes that cavort over a brick arch. There's outside seating in warm weather—a great place to enjoy a beer. ✉ *Piazza Cimatori 1/r, Duomo* ☎ *055/211915* ▤ *AE, MC, V* ☸ *Closed Sun.*

ITALIAN
$$$–$$$$

✕ **Osteria n. 1.** The name "Osteria" is the only pretentious aspect of this romantic restaurant in an old palazzo in the historic center. The place is suffused with a rosy glow from the tablecloths and cream-color walls, lined with painted landscapes and the occasional coat of arms. The food is expertly prepared—try *tagliatelle verdi ai broccoli e salsiccia* (flat noodles with sausage and broccoli) before moving on to any of the grilled meats. ✉ *Via del Moro 18–20/r, Santa Maria Novella* ☎ *055/284897* ▤ *AE, DC, MC, V* ☸ *Closed Sun. and 20 days in Aug. No lunch Mon.*

$$–$$$

✕ **La Posta.** Only steps from Piazza della Repubblica, this restaurant has been around since 1822. Ceilings reach high above the cloth-covered tables in the three dining rooms. Under the fine ministrations of owner Enzo Vocino, La Posta has a large menu with typical Tuscan treats as well as less-common offerings such as *filetto alla tartara* (steak tartare) prepared tableside. The chef has a deft touch with fried vegetables, particularly the light *fiori di zucca* (zucchini blossoms). Reserve in warmer months for the lovely outdoor tables. ✉ *Via dei Lamberti 20, Piazza della Repubblica* ☎ *055/212701* ▤ *AE, DC, MC, V* ☸ *Closed Tues.*

☕ $–$$

✕ **Il Latini.** Although it may well be the noisiest, most crowded trattoria in Florence, it's also one of the most fun precisely because it is so lively. The genial host, Torello ("little bull") Latini, presides over his four big dining rooms, and somehow it feels as if you're eating in his own home. Ample portions of *ribollita* prepare the palate for the hearty meat dishes that follow. Both Florentines and tourists alike tuck into the *agnello fritto* (fried lamb) with aplomb. Though reservations are advised, there's always a wait anyway. ⊠ *Via dei Palchetti 6/r, Santa Maria Novella* ☎ *055/210916* ⊟ *AE, DC, MC, V* ☯ *Closed Mon. and 15 days at Christmas.*

$–$$ ✕ **Osteria del Porcellino.** Contemporary paintings line the candlelit room of this intimate restaurant serving perfectly inventive fare. *Pappa con melanzane e funghi porcini,* a bread-based soup with eggplant and porcini mushrooms, updates an often tired classic. *Pollo con harissa* (chicken with a peppered Moroccan sauce) is zesty and spicy—two adjectives not often associated with Tuscan food. Service is courteous and prompt and the wine list short but comprehensive. ⊠ *Via Val di Lamona 7/r, Piazza della Repubblica* ☎ *055/264148* ⊟ *AE, DC, MC, V* ☯ *No lunch weekday.*

$–$$ ✕ **Ottorino.** The waiters wear jackets and bow ties as they sashay through the brick-vaulted, high-ceiling rooms. The decor is simple—white walls, white tablecloths—but the menu is not. The chef's flights of fancy show up in the daily specials; the menu also includes Tuscan standards. Primi such as *tortelli di carciofi con speck e pecorino* (large squares of pasta stuffed with artichokes and pecorino and sauced with cured ham and butter) do little for the waistline but much to lift the spirits. ⊠ *Via delle Oche 12-16/r, Duomo* ☎ *055/281747 or 055/215151* ⊟ *AE, DC, MC, V* ☯ *Closed Sun.*

$ ✕ **Osteria delle Belle Donne.** Down the street from the church of Santa Maria Novella, this gaily decorated spot, festooned with ropes of garlic and other vegetables, has an ever-changing menu and stellar service led by the irrepressible Giacinto. Even the checkered cloth napkins are cheery. The kitchen has Tuscan standards, but shakes up the menu with alternatives such as *sedani con bacon, verza, e uova* (thick noodles sauced with bacon, cabbage, and egg). If you want to eat al fresco, request a table outside when booking. ⊠ *Via delle Belle Donne 16/r, Santa Maria Novella* ☎ *055/2382609* ⊟ *AE, DC, MC, V.*

¢–$ ✕ **Le Mosacce.** Come to this tiny, cramped, and boisterous place for a quick bite to eat. The menu, written in three languages, includes hearty, stick-to-the-ribs Florentine food such as *ribollita*. Seating is communal, and fellow diners share the big, straw-covered flask of wine. Service is prompt and efficient; two nimble cooks with impeccable timing staff the small kitchen. ⊠ *Via del Proconsolo 55/r, Duomo* ☎ *055/294361* ⌲ *Reservations not accepted* ⊟ *AE, DC, MC, V* ☯ *Closed weekends.*

San Lorenzo & Beyond

ITALIAN ✕ **Taverna del Bronzino.** Want to have a sophisticated meal in a 16th-
★ **$$$$** century Renaissance artist's studio? There's nothing outstanding about the decor in the former studio of Santi di Tito, a student of Bronzino's, save for its simple formality, with white tablecloths and place settings. Lots of classic, superb Tuscan food, however, graces the artful menu, and the presentation is often dramatic. A wine list of solid, affordable choices rounds out the menu. The service is outstanding. Reservations are advised, especially for eating at the wine cellar's only table. ⊠ *Via delle Ruote 25/r, San Marco* ☎ *055/495220* ⊟ *AE, DC, MC, V* ☯ *Closed Sun. and 3 wks in Aug.*

★ **$-$$** ✕ **Le Fonticine.** Owner Silvano Bruci is from Tuscany and his wife, Gianna, is from Emilia-Romagna, and their fine-dining oasis near the train station combines the best of two Italian cuisines. Start with the mixed-vegetable antipasto plate and then move on to any of their house-made pastas. The feathery light tortelloni *nostro modo* are stuffed with fresh ricotta and served with a tomato and cream sauce, and should not be missed. The restaurant's interior, filled with the Brucis' painting collection, provides a cheery space for this soul-satisfying food. ⊠ *Via Nazionale 79/r, San Lorenzo* ☎ *055/282106* ▤ *AE, DC, MC, V* ⊘ *Closed Sun., Mon., Nov. 24–Jan. 5, and July 25–Aug. 25.*

$ ✕ **Il Ritrovo.** Marco del Re, in the kitchen, and his partner Rosetta in the front, have a simple and romantic subterranean 15th-century room with candlelit tables. Here they serve Tuscan classics, as well as other concoctions like cold beets with a dill mayonnaise. Highlights of the menu include *arrosto di vitello* (roast veal fragrantly spiked with rosemary) and *arrosto di coniglio* (roast rabbit stuffed with sausage). Affable service complements the well-chosen wine list. ⊠ *Via de' Pucci 4/a, San Lorenzo* ☎ *055/281688* ▤ *AE, DC, MC, V* ⊘ *Closed Mon. and 3 wks in Aug.*

★ **¢-$** ✕ **Mario.** Florentines flock to this narrow family-run trattoria near San Lorenzo to feast on Tuscan favorites served at simple tables under a wooden ceiling dating from 1536. A distinct cafeteria feel and genuine Florentine hospitality prevail: you'll be seated wherever there's room, which often means with strangers. Yes, there's a bit of extra oil in most dishes, which imparts calories as well as taste, but aren't you on vacation in Italy? Worth the splurge is *riso al ragù* (rice with ground beef and tomatoes). ⊠ *Via Rosina 2/r, corner of Piazza del Mercato Centrale, San Lorenzo* ☎ *055/218550* ⌣ *Reservations not accepted* ▤ *No credit cards* ⊘ *Closed Sun. and Aug. No dinner.*

¢ ✕ **Antica Sosta degli Aldobrandi.** A handful of rustic wooden tables provide a relaxing place to catch your breath, perhaps after you've visited the Capelle Medicee across the street. On the menu are breakfast and lunch, as well as a list of made-to-order sandwiches. The *Lorenzo il Magnifico* (turkey, pesto, and pecorino) is a filling rendition of the turkey sandwich, which is somewhat hard to come by in this town. The list of wines by the glass includes mostly Antinori estates selections. ⊠ *Piazza Madonna 5-6/r* ☎ *055/2399199* ▤ *No credit cards* ⊘ *Closed Sun.*

¢ ✕ **La Mescita.** Come early (or late) to grab a seat at this tiny little spot frequented by Florentine university students and businesspeople. You can get a sandwich to go, or sit and enjoy the day's *primi* (such as a terrific *lasagne*) and follow it with their *polpettona* (meat loaf), which has a lively tomato sauce. Though seats are cramped and the wine is no great shakes, the service is friendly and the food hits the spot. Groups of 15 or more can reserve in the evenings for special meals. ⊠ *Via degli Alfani 70/r,* ☎ *No phone* ▤ *No credit cards* ⊘ *Closed Sun. No dinner.*

Santa Maria Novella to the Arno

ITALIAN ✕ **Harry's Bar.** You come to Harry's for the swank setting—it's cozy, with
$$$$ a tiny bar, pink tablecloths, and plenty of well-heeled customers captured in rosy lighting. Where else could you hope to see a gold-bedecked

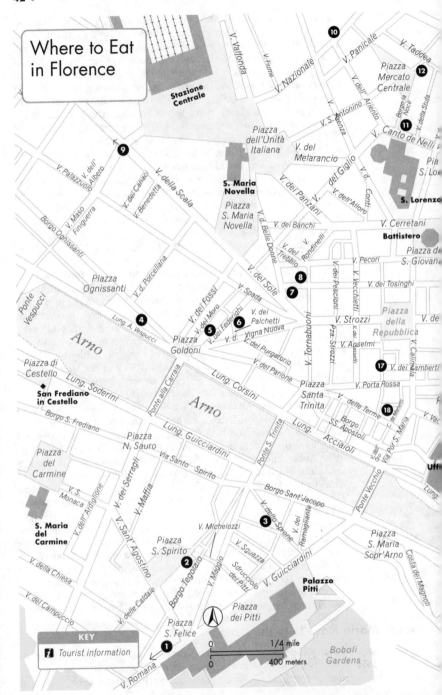

Where to Eat in Florence

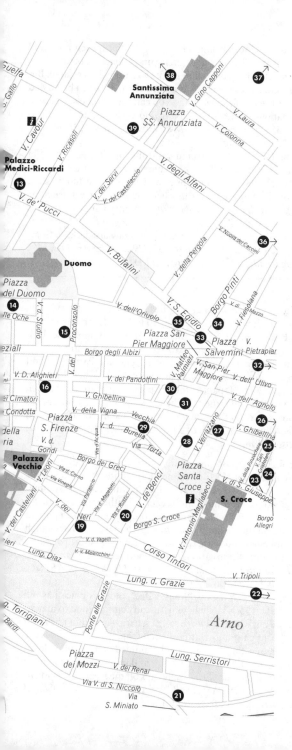

Florentine matron toting a Pekinese? Enjoy a Bellini (peach juice and Prosecco) or, better yet, Harry's absolutely superb martini, before tucking into the menu. The perfectly bilingual staff is more than affable. But don't expect any culinary punches: this is nursery food—often bland and unseasoned—for the privileged set, and you can eat better elsewhere in Florence. Reservations are advised. ⊠ *Lungarno Vespucci 22/r, Lungarno North* ☏ *055/2396700* ▤ *AE, DC, MC, V* ☺ *Closed Sun., 1 wk over Christmas, and 1 wk in Aug.*

$$–$$$ ✕ **Cantinetta Antinori.** After a rough morning of shopping on Via Tornabuoni, stop for lunch in this 15th-century palazzo in the company of Florentine ladies (and men) who lunch and come to see and be seen. The panache of the food matches its clientele: expect treats such as *tramezzino con pane di campagna al tartufo* (country pâté with truffles served on bread) and the *insalata di gamberoni e gamberetti con carciofi freschi* (crayfish and prawn salad with shaved raw artichokes). ⊠ *Piazza Antinori 3, Santa Maria Novella* ☏ *055/292234* ▤ *AE, DC, MC, V* ☺ *Closed weekends, 20 days in Aug., and Dec. 25–Jan. 6.*

The Oltrarno

ECLECTIC ✕ **Domani.** Chef Yukihiro Kojima was born in Japan and classically
$ trained in French technique before moving to Italy and teaming up with chef Alberto Borborini to create this one-of-a-kind Japanese–Italian–French restaurant. It's a bit odd to see bouillabaisse on the same menu as spaghetti *alla carbonara* (with bacon, eggs, and Parmesan) and *maiale saltato con kimchi* (pork with pickled cabbage), but that's the beauty of this place. The Japanese food is particularly good, and well priced; Mr. Kojima says it's the food he grew up on. The restaurant's two large rooms are rather unremarkable, but it's all about the food here. ⊠ *Via Romana 80/r, Palazzo Pitti* ☏ *055/221166* ▤ *AE, DC, MC, V* ☺ *Closed Mon.*

ITALIAN ✕ **Quattro Leoni.** The eclectic staff at this trattoria in a small piazza is
☺ **$–$$** an appropriate match for the diverse menu. In winter you can sample the offerings in one of two rooms with high ceilings, and in summer you can sit outside and admire the scenery. Traditional Tuscan favorites, such as *taglierini con porcini* (long, thin, flat pasta with porcini mushrooms), are on the menu, but so, too, are less typical dishes such as the earthy cabbage salad with avocado, pine nuts, and drops of *olio di tartufo* (truffle oil). Reservations are a good idea. ⊠ *Piazza della Passera, Via dei Vellutini 1/r, Palazzo Pitti* ☏ *055/218562* ▤ *AE, DC, MC, V* ☺ *No lunch Wed.*

¢–$ ✕ **La Casalinga.** *Casalinga* means "housewife," and this place has the nostalgic charm of a 1950s kitchen with Tuscan comfort food to match. If you eat *ribollita* anywhere in Florence, eat it here—it couldn't be more authentic. Mediocre paintings clutter the semipaneled walls, tables are set close together, and the place is usually jammed. The menu is long, portions are plentiful, and service is prompt and friendly. Save room for dessert: the *sorbetto al limoncello* perfectly caps off the meal. ⊠ *Via Michelozzi 9/r, Santo Spirito* ☏ *055/218624* ▤ *AE, DC, MC, V* ☺ *Closed Sun., 1 wk at Christmas, and 3 wks in Aug.*

¢–$ ✕ **Osteria Antica Mescita San Niccolò.** It's always crowded, always good, and always cheap. The osteria is next to the church of San Niccolò, and if you sit in the lower part you'll find yourself in what was once a chapel dating from the 11th century. The subtle but dramatic background plays off nicely with the food, which is simple Tuscan at its best. The *pollo con limone* is tasty pieces of chicken in a lemon-scented broth. In winter try the *spezzatino di cinghiale con aromi* (wild boar stew with herbs). Reservations are advised. ⊠ *Via San Niccolò 60/r, San Niccolò* ☎ *055/2342836* ▤ *AE, MC, V* ☺ *Closed Sun. and Aug.*

Santa Croce

AMERICAN-CASUAL
☺ ¢–$
✕ **Danny Rock.** There's a bit of everything at this restaurant, which is always hopping with Italians eager to eat well-made cheeseburgers and fries or one of the many tasty crepes (served both sweet and savory). You can also find a basic plate of spaghetti as well as a respectable pizza here. Interior decor isn't high on the list: you dine at a green metal table with matching chairs. The young-at-heart feel might explain why the main dining room has a big screen showing *Looney Tunes*. ⊠ *Via Pandolfini 13/r, Santa Croce* ☎ *055/2340307* ▤ *AE, DC, MC, V.*

ITALIAN
$$$$
Fodor's Choice
★
✕ **Cibrèo.** The food at this upscale trattoria is fantastic, from the creamy crostini *di fegatini* (a savory chicken-liver spread) to the melt-in-your-mouth desserts. If you thought you'd never try tripe—let alone like it—this is the place to lay any doubts to rest: the *trippa in insalata* (cold tripe salad) with parsley and garlic is an epiphany. Construe chef Fabio Picchi's unsolicited advice as a sign of his enthusiasm for cooking; it's warranted, as the food is among the best and most creative in town. Around the corner is Cibreino, Cibrèo's budget version, with a shorter menu and a no-reservations policy. ⊠ *Via A. del Verrocchio 8/r, Santa Croce* ☎ *055/2341100* ⩇ *Reservations essential* ▤ *AE, DC, MC, V* ☺ *Closed Sun. and Mon., July 25–Sept. 5, and Dec. 31–Jan. 7.*

$$$$
✕ **Enoteca Pinchiorri.** A sumptuous Renaissance palace with high, frescoed ceilings and bouquets in silver vases provides the backdrop for this restaurant, one of the most expensive in Italy. Some consider it one of the best, and others consider it a non-Italian rip-off, as the kitchen is presided over by a Frenchwoman with sophisticated, yet internationalist, leanings. Prices are high and portions are small; the vast holdings of the wine cellar, as well as stellar service, dull the pain, however, when the bill is presented. Interesting pasta combinations such as the *ignudi*—ricotta-and-spinach dumplings with a lobster-and-coxcomb fricassee—are always on the menu. ⊠ *Via Ghibellina 87, Santa Croce* ☎ *055/242777* ⩇ *Reservations essential* ▤ *AE, MC, V* ☺ *Closed Sun., Mon., Aug. No lunch Tues. or Wed.*

$$$–$$$$
✕ **Alle Murate.** Creative versions of classic Tuscan dishes are served in this sleek and sophisticated spot. The *involtini di vitella ripieni di melanzane coi fagiolini al dente* (veal rolls stuffed with eggplant garnished with green beans) is remarkably light and flavorful. The main dining room has a rich, uncluttered look, with warm wood floors and paneling and soft lights. In a smaller adjacent room called the *vineria* you get the same splendid service but substantially reduced prices. There's no middle ground with the wine list—there's only a smattering of inexpensive

bottles before it soars to exalted heights. ⊠ *Via Ghibellina 52/r, Santa Croce* ☎ *055/240618* ☰ *AE, DC, MC, V* ☺ *Closed Mon. No lunch.*

★ $$$ ✕ **La Giostra.** The clubby La Giostra, which means "carousel" in Italian, is owned and run by Prince Dimitri Kunz d'Asburgo Lorena, and his way with mushrooms is as remarkable as his charm. The unusually good pastas may require explanation from Soldano, one of the prince's good-looking twin sons. In perfect English he'll describe a favorite dish, *taglierini con tartufo bianco,* a decadently rich pasta with white truffles. Leave room for dessert: this might be the only show in town with a sublime tiramisu *and* a wonderfully gooey Sacher torte. ⊠ *Borgo Pinti 12/r, Santa Croce* ☎ *055/241341* ☰ *AE, DC, MC, V.*

$–$$$ ✕ **Enoteca del Boccanegra.** Simon Boccanegra, a famous Ghibelline *condottiere* (mercenary), has a restaurant and an enoteca named in his honor. Though the restaurant is quite good, it's the less expensive, less formal enoteca that's the real winner here. Wooden tables and candles provide a romantic glow in this intimate space (it seats about 30 on a good night). Simple, top-quality Tuscan fare dominates the menu. The wine list is well priced and ample. The kitchen stays open well past the usual 10:30 PM Florentine closing. ⊠ *Via Verdi 27/r, Santa Croce* ☎ *055/2001098* ☰ *AE, DC, MC, V* ☺ *No lunch. Closed Sun.*

$$ ✕ **Cantina Barbagianni.** *"Diverso dal solito"* (different from the usual) is the leitmotif here, and this attitude is reflected in the funky furnishings (lots of strategically placed drapery) and avant-garde paintings on the walls. Cristina, the proprietor, presides over it all with great ease. The regularly changing menu strays far from the typical Tuscan path: *l'anatra con mirtillo* (duck with blueberries) is a rare thing in these parts, and the chef is to be commended for his inventiveness. The *risotto al carciofi con scamorza* (artichoke risotto with smoked cheese) is fragrant and tasty. ⊠ *Via Sant'Egidio 13, Santa Croce* ☎ *055/2480508* ☰ *AE, DC, MC, V* ☺ *Closed Sun.*

☺ $–$$ ✕ **Baldovino.** David and Catherine Gardner, expat Scots, have created this lively, brightly colored restaurant down the street from the church of Santa Croce. From its humble beginnings as a pizzeria, it has evolved into something more. It's a happy thing that pizza is still on the menu, but now it shares billing with sophisticated primi and secondi. The menu changes monthly and has such treats as *filetto di manzo alla Bernaise* (filet mignon with light béarnaise sauce). Baldovino also serves pasta dishes and grilled meat until the wee hours. ⊠ *Via San Giuseppe 22/r, Santa Croce* ☎ *055/241773* ☰ *DC, MC, V* ☺ *Closed Mon. and 2 wks in Aug.*

$–$$ ✕ **Cantinetta il Francescano.** Plain wooden tables, muted indigo-gray walls, and fresh flowers provide the backdrop for simple Tuscan food served by a gracious and caring staff. Have a quick lunch here (it's just down the street from Santa Croce), or linger over a candlelit dinner. Start with one of the tasty antipasti, such as the *mozzarella di buffala con pomordori* (buffalo mozzarella with tomato sauce), and follow with one of the hearty pastas; or opt for the *tagliata,* which is done two ways. The standard version has sliced, rare beef topped with arugula and Parmesan; the succulent *tagliata di pollo* is flattened and grilled chicken topped with arugula. Reservations are advised. ⊠ *Largo Bargellini 16, Santa Croce* ☎ *055/241605* ☰ *MC, V* ☺ *Closed Tues.*

$–$$ ✕ **La Maremma.** A 2004 refurbishment including brightly colored walls and white table linens has put some zest into this simple trattoria. It excels at Tuscan classics as well as other dishes from around Italy. Nicely apportioned *primi* (the version here of the Roman *spaghetti alla carbonara* is terrific) prime the taste buds for what follows: the *pollo al aceto* (chicken with balsamic vinegar) is luscious. Service is courteous and prompt; the wine list is affordable and well thought out. ⊠ *Via Verdi 16/r, Santa Croce* ☎ *055/244615* ▤ *AE, DC, MC, V* ☉ *Closed Wed.*

★ **$–$$** ✕ **Osteria de'Benci.** A few minutes from Santa Croce, this charming osteria serves some of the most eclectic food in Florence. Try the spaghetti *degli eretici* (in tomato sauce with fresh herbs). The grilled meats are justifiably famous; the *carbonata* is a succulent piece of grilled beef served rare. When it's warm, you can dine outside with a view of the 13th-century tower belonging to the prestigious Alberti family. Right next door is Osteria de'Benci Caffè (¢–$), serving selections from the menu from 8 AM to midnight. ⊠ *Via de'Benci 11-13/r, Santa Croce* ☎ *055/2344923* ▤ *AE, DC, MC, V* ☉ *Closed Sun. and 2 wks in Aug.*

☾ **¢–$$** ✕ **Benvenuto.** At this Florentine institution, beloved for decades by locals and Anglophone Renaissance scholars alike, the service is ebullient, the menu long (with often unwittingly humorous English typographical errors), and the food simple, Tuscan, and tasty. The list of primi and secondi is extensive, and there are daily specials as well. Don't miss the *scaloppine all Benvenuto* (veal cutlets with porcini). ⊠ *Via della Mosca 16/r, at Via de' Neri, Santa Croce* ☎ *055/214833* ▤ *AE, DC, MC, V* ☉ *Closed Sun.*

$ ✕ **Acquacotta.** With its closely spaced, red-checked tablecloths, you couldn't get any more "Italian" than this. You almost expect the chef to come out of the kitchen with an accordion and serenade you while you eat. Not to worry: service is offhand (sometimes dismissive), and the chef has better things to do than break into song. The highlight of the menu, with the usual list of grilled meats and pasta starters, is the *acquacotta,* literally "cooked water"—a favorite from southern Tuscany that rarely appears on Florentine menus. It's a vegetable-based soup with mushrooms and onions that's topped with a poached egg. ⊠ *Via dei Pilastri 51/r, Santa Croce* ☎ *055/242907* ▤ *MC, V* ☉ *Closed Sun. and Aug.*

$ ✕ **Antico Noe.** If Florence had a dive restaurant, this would be it. The 30-seat place on one of the more unsavory half blocks in town (benign local addicts seem to congregate here, and the police patrol frequently) serves Tuscan classics with flair; Florentines are especially fond of it and rave about the *taglietelle ai porcini.* The mixed meat plate is fine, the *lardo di colonnata* (don't ask, just eat it) sublime. The wine list is short but includes great bargains. ⊠ *Volta di San Piero 6/r, Santa Croce* ☎ *055/2340838* ▤ *AE, DC, MC, V* ☉ *Closed Sun. and 2 wks. in Aug.*

Fodor'sChoice ★

$ ✕ **Pallottino.** With its tiled floor, photograph-filled walls, and wooden tables, Pallottino is the quintessential Tuscan trattoria, with hearty, heartwarming classics such as pappa al pomodoro and *peposa alla toscana* (beef stew laced with black pepper). The menu changes frequently to reflect what's seasonal; the staff is friendly, as are the diners who often share a table and, eventually, conversation. ⊠ *Via Isola delle Stinche*

1/r, Santa Croce ☎ *055/289573* 🖃 *AE, DC, MC, V* ⊙ *Closed Mon. and 2–3 wks in Aug.*

MOROCCAN ✕ **Sésame.** Fusion has been very slow in coming to Italy, but this spot
$–$$ was among the first to settle into the Florentine dining scene. A series
of romantically lit rooms, a lounge area complete with hookahs, a restful outdoor garden, and stellar staff won over the local cognoscenti. The menu mixes the best of French cuisine (such as truffles) with Moroccan (like spicy tagines). This is one of the few places in town where you can eat oysters from Brittany. 🖂 *Via delle Conce 20/r* ☎ *055/2001381* ♿ *Reservations essential* 🖃 *AE, DC, MC, V* ⊙ *No lunch.*

Beyond the City Center

ECLECTIC ✕ **Targa.** It looks and feels like California on the Arno at this sleek, airy
$$–$$$ restaurant a short ride from the city center. Owner–chef Gabriele Tarchiani has spent time in the United States, which shows in the plants that fill the interior as well as the creative touches on the frequently changing menu. Somewhat unusual combinations such as the *fusilli al ragù di anatra e finferli* (fusilli with a minced duck and wild mushroom sauce) provide the perfect prelude for the exquisitely prepared *secondi* that follow. Leave room for dessert—they're culinary masterpieces. No wonder Florentines come here to celebrate special occasions. 🖂 *Lungarno Colombo 7 (east of city center)* ☎ *055/677377* ♿ *Reservations essential* 🖃 *AE, DC, MC, V* ⊙ *Closed Sun.*

ITALIAN ✕ **Zibibbo.** Benedetta Vitali, formerly of Florence's famed Cibrèo, has a
$–$$$ restaurant of her very own. It's a welcome addition to the sometimes claustrophobic Florentine dining scene—particularly as you have to drive a few minutes out of town to get here. Off a quiet piazza, it has two intimate rooms with rustic, maroon-painted wood floors and a sloped ceiling. *Tagliatelle al sugo d'anatra* (wide pasta ribbons with duck sauce) are aromatic and flavorful, and *crocchette di fave con salsa di yogurt* (fava bean croquettes with a lively yogurt sauce) are innovative and tasty. 🖂 *Via di Terzollina 3/r (northwest of city center)* ☎ *055/433383* 🖃 *AE, DC, MC, V* ⊙ *Closed Sun.*

¢–$$ ✕ **l'Giuggiolo.** They call themselves an osteria–pizzeria, and certainly many Florentines flock here to indulge in the sinfully rich, thin-crusted pizzas turned out by a skilled pizzaiuolo. However, the real thrills come from the fantastic offerings from the osteria part of the menu. Start with the *bavarese di pomodoro fresco su salsa al basilico* (a chilled tomato concoction spiked with garlic and sauced with basil), sample one of the divine pastas, and then move on to any of the meats, like the *millefoglie di manza con pomodori secchi e parmigiano* (thinly sliced rare roast beef with sun-dried tomatoes and Parmesan). 🖂 *Viale Righi 3* ☎ *055/606240* ♿ *Reservations essential* 🖃 *AE, DC, MC, V.*

Bars & Caffè

Caffè, or bars, in Italy serve not only coffee concoctions and pastries but also sweets, drinks, and panini, and some have hot pasta and lunch dishes. They are usually open from early in the morning to late at night and are closed Sunday.

At night **Capocaccia** (✉ Lungarno Corsini 12/14r, Lungarno Sud ☎ 055/ 210751) can be a chaotic scene, but in the daytime it's significantly calmer. Light lunches and a good list of panini are on the menu, and you can nosh at an outdoor table with a view of the Arno. If you're craving Sunday brunch, Capocaccia has that too. **Caffè Giacosa** (✉ Via della Spada 10/r Santa Maria Novella ☎ 055/2776328 ⊕ www.caffegiacosa.it) opens early in the morning for coffee, serves tasty light lunches, and makes excellent cocktails in the evening. **Gran Caffè** (✉ Piazza San Marco 11/r ☎ 055/215833) is down the street from the Accademia, so it's a perfect stop for a marvelous panino or sweet while raving about the majesty of Michelangelo's *David*.

Around the corner from the church of Santa Maria Novella, **i 5 Tavoli** (✉ Via del Sole 26/r, Santa Maria Novella ☎ 055/294438) has only five tables (as its name implies), many fine sandwiches, hot pasta specials, and a very good (and inexpensive) cheeseburger. **i Visacci** (✉ Borgo Albizi 80/r, Santa Croce ☎ No phone), which has great panini and a fine selection of beers on tap (in addition to the ubiquitous wine), is a good place for a light lunch or an aperitivo. **Nannini** (✉ Borgo San Lorenzo 7/r, San Lorenzo ☎ 055/212680) has light lunches and excellent coffee. Down the street from the church of Santissima Annunziata is **Oliandolo** (✉ Via Ricasoli 38-40/r, Santissima Annunziata ☎ 055/211296), with an enticing list of panini. Classy **Procacci** (✉ Via Tornabuoni 64/r, Santa Maria Novella ☎ 055/211656) is a Florentine institution dating back to 1885; try one of the panini tartufati and swish it down with a glass of Prosecco. It's closed Sunday and Monday. Perhaps the best spot for people-watching is **Rivoire** (✉ Via Vaccherreccia 4/r, Piazza della Signoria ☎ 055/214412). Stellar service, light snacks, and terrific aperitivi are the norm. Think twice, however, before ordering more substantial fare; it falls flat. **Rose's** (✉ Via del Parione 26/r, Santa Maria Novella ☎ 055/ 287090) draws businesspeople at lunch and people with multiple body piercings at night. The Italian lunch menu switches to sushi in the evening. **Sant'Ambrogio Caffè** (✉ Piazza Sant'Ambrogio 7–8/r, Santa Croce ☎ 055/241035) has outdoor summer seating with a view of an 11th-century church (Sant'Ambrogio) directly across the street.

Enoteche

Wine bars have been popping up all over Florence, and most of them have light fare as well as lengthy wine lists—perfect places for lunch or dinner. Most are closed on Sunday.

In the heart of the centro storico is **Cantinetta dei Verrazzano** (✉ Via dei Tavolini 18/20/r, Piazza della Signoria ☎ 055/268590), where serious wines may be had as well as tasty baked treats in the morning and light lunches. **Casa del Vino** (✉ Via dell'Ariento 16/r San Lorenzo ☎ 055/215609) makes creative *panini*, such as *sgrombri e carciofini sott'olio* (mackerel and marinated baby artichokes), and has an ever-changing list of significant wines by the glass. They also have a well-stocked collection of bottles to go, at more than fair prices. It's hard to believe that **Coquinarius** (✉ Via delle Oche 15/r, Duomo ☎ 055/2302153) is as close to the Duomo as it is; the place is serene, sophisticated, and perfect for resting one's soul. **Enoteca Baldovino** (✉ Via San Giuseppe 18/r, Santa Croce ☎ 055/2347220) is a cozy little place with candlelit tile tables. Try the *piatti misti* (mixed plate of various specials of the day) while sipping a glass of wine. When it's warm, you can sit outside on a quiet, narrow side street. It's closed Monday.

Fuori Porta (✉ Via Monte al Croce 10/r, San Niccolò ☎ 055/2342483), in the Oltrarno, is a stone's throw from Forte Belvedere. You can sit down (inside or out), have wine by the glass or by the bottle, and pick from a lengthy list of crostini and crostoni with various toppings. A hop, skip, and a jump from Orsanmichele in the centro storico is **I Fratellini** (✉ Via dei Cimatori 38/r, Piazza della Signoria ☎ 055/2396096), in existence since 1875. It sells wines by the glass and has a list of 27 panini, including pecorino with sun-dried tomatoes and spicy wild-boar salami with goat cheese. There are no seats, so perch on the curb and make like a local. **Le Volpi e l'Uva** (✉ Piazza de' Rossi 1, Palazzo Pitti ☎ 055/2398132), off Piazza Santa Trinita, is an oenophile's dream: the waiters pour significant wines by the glass and serve equally impressive cheeses and little sandwiches to go with them. **Olio & Convivium** (✉ Via Santo Spirito 4 ☎ 055/2658198) has a great selection of cheeses and cured meats, wines by the glass, food products to take home (like powdered porcini mushrooms), and daily specials. At **Pitti Gola** (✉ Piazza Pitti 16, Palazzo Pitti ☎ 055/212704), you can order tasty tidbits to accompany your choices from the extensive and impressive wine list. The outdoor seats have a view of the Palazzo Pitti. **Semidivino** (✉ via San Gallo 22/r San Marco ☎ 055/4620016) has indoor and outdoor seating, a great list of wines by the glass, and light fare at both lunch and dinner.

Foreign Foods

Eating ethnic in Florence is a hit-or-miss affair. Although numerous Asian restaurants have sprung up since the 1990s, most of them are nothing to write home about. Still, if you need a break from Italian, some relief is available.

Amon (✉ Via Palazzuolo 26/28r, Santa Maria Novella ☎ 055/293146) is a standing-only spot that serves Egyptian and other Middle Eastern fare at rock-bottom prices. **Dionisio** (✉ Via San Gallo 16/r, San Lorenzo ☎ 055/217882) draws a mostly student crowd (as it's in the midst of university buildings) enjoying tasty kebabs. **KoocliKoo** (✉ Borgo Pinti 2/r ☎ 055/2342201) has a nonsensical name courtesy of the owner's son when he was three years old; it's dedicated to vegetarian takeout and has such stalwarts as seitan and tofu. **Il Mandarino** (✉ Via Condotta 17/r, Piazza della Signoria ☎ 055/2396130) has excellent hot-and-sour soup and more-than-passable dumplings. Enjoy them with white linen tablecloths and a bottle of Verdicchio. If you're craving doner kebab (thin, grilled slices of beef or lamb), look no further than **Mavi** (✉ Via de'Benci 15/r, Santa Croce ☎ 055/2466760). Portions are copious, and the hot sauce is darn hot. Doner kebabs at **Turkaz** (✉ Via de'Servi 65/r, Santissima Annunziata ☎ 055/2399959) have a killer hot sauce; you can order hot rice and meat dishes to eat in or take out. Most dishes at **Mister Hang** (✉ Via Ghibellina 134/r, Santa Croce ☎ 055/2344810) are Chinese, but the place also has Thai options. **Ramraj** (✉ Via Ghibellina 61/r, Santa

Croce ☎ 055/240999) has Indian food to take away. **Saigon Restaurant** (✉ Via del Ponte alle Mosse 2-8/r ☎ 055/350541), outside the centro storico on the other side of Porto al Prato, has a mixed Chinese and Vietnamese menu. Scotch bonnet peppers and sour cream are novelties in Florence (and, indeed, Italy), but they can be found at **El Tacos** (✉ Via dei Benci 47/r, Santa Croce ☎ 055/241970), popular with locals as well as foreign students. **Tijuana** (✉ Via Ghibellina 156-158/r ☎ 055/2341330) is open only at night; it's frequented by young Florentines craving enchiladas and fatijas.

Gelaterie & Pasticcerie

The convenient **Caffè delle Carrozze** (✉ Piazza del Pescee 3-5/r, Piazza Signoria ☎ 055/2396810) is around the corner from the Uffizi; their *gelati* are the best in the historic center. The *pasticceria* (bakery) **Dolci e Dolcezze** (✉ Piazza C. Beccaria 8/r, Sant'Ambrogio ☎ 055/2345458), on colorful Borgo La Croce, has the prettiest and tastiest cakes, sweets, and tarts in town. It's closed Monday. **Gelaterie Carabe** (✉ Via Ricasoli 60/r, San Marco ☎ 055/289476) specializes in things Sicilian (including cannoli). Its *granità* (granular flavored ices), made only in the summer, are tart and flavorful—perfect thirst-quenchers. Lemon is a good choice. Florentines with serious sweet tooths come to **I Dolci di Patrizio Corsi** (✉ Borgo Albizi 15/r, Santa Croce ☎ 055/2480367), which has a bewildering selection of chocolate- and cream-filled sweets. It's closed on Sunday afternoons. **Vestri** (✉ Borgo Albizi 11/r, Santa Croce ☎ 055/2340374) is devoted to chocolate in all its guises. The small but sublime selection of chocolate-based gelati includes one with hot peppers. Most people consider **Vivoli** (✉ Via Isola delle Stinche 7/r, Santa Croce ☎ 055/292334) the best gelateria in town, though the cioccolata con caffè is overrated.

Pizzerias

Pizzas in Florence can't compete with their counterparts in Rome or Naples, but you can sample a few good approximations.

Ⓒ **Baldovino** (✉ Via San Giuseppe 22/r, Santa Croce ☎ 055/241773) makes pizzas to delight the kids and more sophisticated stuff to satisfy parents. In the Oltrarno, try **Borgo Antico** (✉ Piazza S. Spirito 6/r, San Spirito ☎ 055/210437), which serves pizza and other trattoria fare. The pizza at **Il Pizziauolo** (✉ Via dei Macci 113/r, Santa Croce ☎ 055/241171) is probably as close as you're going to get in Florence to the Rome and Naples versions. It has a thick crust, Naples style. The pizza *con salsicce e friarielli* (with sausage and a bitter green that's native around Naples) deserves respect. The *pizziauoli* (pizza-makers) successfully merge Roman (thin) crust with Neapolitan (thick) crust at **Le Campane** (✉ Borgo La Croce 85-87/r, Santa Croce ☎ 055/2341101). Two doors down from its main entrance, the **Osteria del Caffè Italiano** (✉ Via Isole delle Stinche 11/r, Santa Croce ☎ 055/289368) has a little pizzeria which locals swear by. Come early to grab one of the few tables, and don't mind the fact that service here is intentionally rushed: turning tables is paramount. **Pugi** (✉ Piazza San Marco 9/b San Marco ☎ 055/280981), which is handily across the street from San Marco, sells the popular *pizza a taglio* (pizza by the slice); their *focaccie* and other breads are equally good.

Rosticcerie & Tavole Calde

Rosticcerie and *tavole calde* are good alternatives to the more-formal trattorie, osterie, and ristoranti dining options. You can assemble an entire meal at a rosticcerie, which has antipasti, pastas, roasted chicken and other meats, vegetable side dishes, and desserts; sometimes seating is also available. Tavole calde (literally, "hot tables") are sometimes synonymous with rosticcerie, but while a rosticceria almost always has whole roast chickens, that's not always the case with a tavola calda. Both are significantly less expensive than full sit-down service—another part of their appeal.

At **Alfio e Beppe** (⊠ Via Cavour 118-120/r, San Marco ☎ 055/214108), you can watch chickens roast over high flames as you decide which of the other delightful things you're going to eat with it. The daily specials at **Da Rocco** (⊠ Piazza Ghiberti, Santa Croce ☎ No phone), in the Mercato Sant'Ambrogio, can include *polpettine alla pizzaiuolo* (veal meatballs in tangy tomato-oregano sauce). Portions are generous. In summer, try the *panzanella*, a salad made with bread crumbs, tomatoes, and basil and doused with extra virgin olive oil. Near the Uffizi is **Guiliano Centro** (⊠ Via de' Neri 74/r, Piazza della Signoria ☎ 055/2382723), with a mouth-watering assortment of food including crisp *pollo fritto* (fried chicken). **La Ghiotta** (⊠ Via Pietrapiana 7/r, Santa Croce ☎ 055/241237) sells whole and half chickens, grilled or roasted, among other things. The baked fennel is also a treat. Near Santa Maria Novella is **La Spada** (⊠ Via del Moro 66/r, Santa Maria Novella ☎ 055/218757). Walk in and inhale the fragrant aromas of meats cooked in the wood-burning oven. La Spada also has a complete line of take-out.

Salumerie

Salumerie, specialty food shops strong on fine fresh ingredients such as meats and cheeses, are great for picking up a picnic lunch or assembling dinner.

Antico Salumificio Anzuini-Massi (⊠ Via de'Neri 84/r, Santa Croce ☎ 055/294 901) shrink-wraps their own pork products, making it a snap to take home some *salame di cinghiale* (wild boar salami). If you find yourself in the Oltrarno and hungry for lunch or a snack, drop into **Azzarri Delicatesse** (⊠ Borgo S. Jacopo 27b/cr, Santo Spirito ☎ 055/2381714) for a sandwich, meat for the grill, wine, or French cheeses. The cheese collection at **Baroni** (⊠ Mercato Central, enter at Via Signa, San Lorenzo ☎ 055/289576) may be the most comprehensive in Florence. **Conti** (⊠ Mercato Centrale, enter at Via Signa, San Lorenzo ☎ 055/2398501), closed Sunday, sells top-quality wines, olive oils, and dried fruits; they'll shrink-wrap the highest-quality dried porcini for traveling. Looking for some cheddar cheese to pile in your panino? **Pegna** (⊠ Via dello Studio 8, Duomo ☎ 055/282701) has been selling both Italian and non-Italian food since 1860. It's closed Saturday afternoon in July and August, Wednesday afternoon September through June, and Sunday year-round. **Perini** (⊠ Mercato Centrale, enter at Via dell'Aretino, San Lorenzo ☎ 055/2398306), closed Sunday, sells prosciutto, mixed meats, sauces for pasta, and a wide assortment of antipasti. They're generous with their free samples.

WHERE TO STAY

No stranger to visitors, Florence is equipped with hotels for all budgets; for instance, you can find both budget and luxury hotels in the *centro storico* (historic center) and along the Arno. Florence has so many famous landmarks that it's not hard to find lodging with a panoramic vista. The equivalent of the genteel *pensioni* of yesteryear still exist, though they are now officially classified as hotels. Usually small and intimate, they often have a quaint appeal that usually doesn't preclude modern plumbing.

Florence's importance not only as a tourist city but as a convention center and the site of the Pitti fashion collections guarantees a variety of accommodations. The high demand also means that, except in winter, reservations are a must. If you find yourself in Florence with no reservations, go to **Consorzio ITA** (✉ Stazione Centrale, Santa Maria Novella ☎ 055/282893). You must go there in person to make a booking.

WHAT IT COSTS In euros				
	$$$$	**$$$**	**$$**	**$**	**¢**
FOR 2 PEOPLE	over €290	€210–€290	€140–€209	€80–€139	under €80

Prices are for two people in a standard double room in high season, including tax and service.

Centro Storico

$$$$ ⊞ **Grand Hotel Minerva.** Despite its size, this hotel, on a beautiful Renaissance square overlooking the church of Santa Maria Novella and minutes from the train station, is intimate. With their wicker furniture and bright fabrics, public rooms recall the 1960s. The doors to each room display full-size photographs of historic Florentine doors. Bathrooms are colorfully tiled and spacious. ✉ *Piazza Santa Maria Novella 16, Santa Maria Novella, 50123* ☎ *055/27230, 055/2723182 reservations* 🖷 *055/ 268281* ⊕ *www.grandhotelminerva.com* 🛏 *83 rooms, 16 suites* 🍴 *Restaurant, in-room safes, some in-room hot tubs, minibars, cable TV, in-room VCRs, pool, bicycles, bar, dry cleaning, laundry service, concierge, Internet, meeting rooms, parking (fee), some pets allowed, no-smoking rooms* ▤ *AE, DC, MC, V* ⬮❘ *BP.*

$$$$ ⊞ **Hotel degli Orafi.** A key scene in *A Room with a View* was shot in this pensione, which is today a luxury hotel adorned with chintz and marble. Many rooms have luscious views of the Arno, and a few have their own terraces. Breakfast is served in opulent surroundings—check out the crystal chandelier and the frescoed ceiling. The affable English-speaking staff go out of their way to be helpful. ✉ *Lungarno Archibusieri 4, Piazza della Signoria, 50121* ☎ *055/26622* 🖷 *055/26622111* ⊕ *www.hoteldegliorafi.it* 🛏 *42 rooms* 🍴 *In-room data ports, in-room*

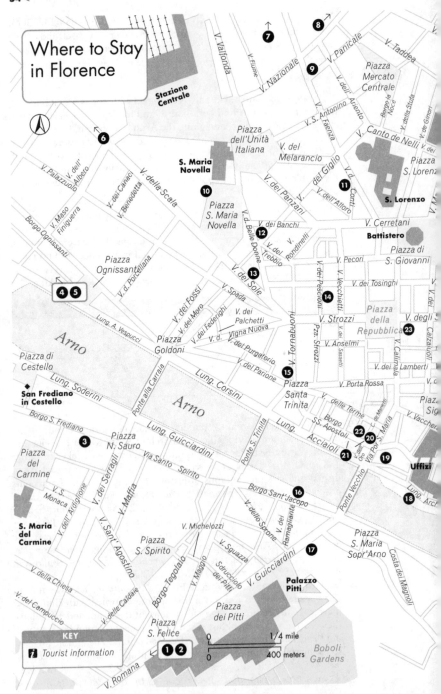

Where to Stay in Florence

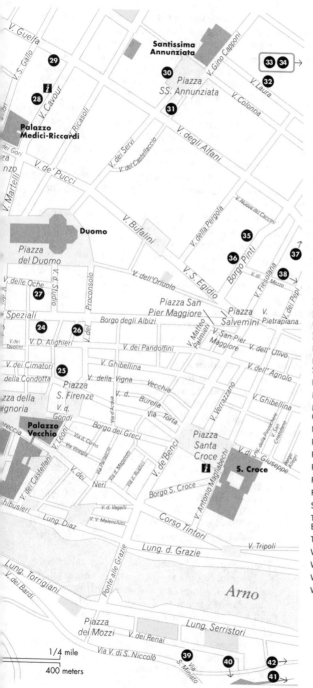

safes, minibars, cable TV, library, babysitting, laundry service, concierge, parking (fee), no-smoking rooms ⊟ *AE, DC, MC, V* ⦿ *BP.*

★ **$$$$** ▦ **Hotel Helvetia and Bristol.** Painstaking care has gone into making this hotel one of the prettiest and most intimate in town. It has the extra plus of being in the center of the centro storico, making it a luxurious base from which to explore the city. From the cozy yet sophisticated lobby with its pietra serena columns to the guest rooms decorated with prints, you might feel as if you're a guest in a sophisticated manor house. The restaurant serves sumptuous fare in a romantic setting. ⊠ *Via dei Pescioni 2, Piazza della Repubblica, 50123* ☎ *055/26651* ⊟ *055/ 288353* ⊕ *www.royaldemeure.com* ⬄ *44 rooms, 23 suites* ⚬ *Restaurant, room service, in-room safes, some in-room hot tubs, minibars, cable TV, in-room VCRs, bar, babysitting, dry cleaning, laundry service, concierge, Internet, meeting room, parking (fee), some pets allowed, no-smoking rooms* ⊟ *AE, DC, MC, V.*

$$$$ ▦ **Hotel Savoy.** From the outside, it looks very much like the turn-of-the-19th-century building that it is. Inside, sleek minimalism and up-to-the-minute amenities prevail. Sitting rooms have a funky edge, their cream-color walls dotted with contemporary prints. Muted colors dress the rooms, which have streamlined furniture and soaring ceilings; many have views of the Duomo's cupola or the Piazza della Repubblica. The deep marble tubs might be reason enough to stay here—but you'll also appreciate the efficient and courteous staff. ⊠ *Piazza della Repubblica 7, 50123* ☎ *055/ 27351* ⊟ *055/2735888* ⊕ *www.roccofortehotels.com* ⬄ *98 rooms, 9 suites* ⚬ *Restaurant, room service, in-room data ports, in-room fax, in-room safes, minibars, cable TV with movies and video games, in-room VCRs, gym, massage, bar, children's programs (ages 0–12), dry cleaning, laundry service, concierge, Internet, business services, meeting rooms, parking (fee), no-smoking rooms* ⊟ *AE, DC, MC, V.*

$$$ ▦ **Hermitage.** A stone's throw from the Ponte Vecchio, this is a fine little hotel with an enviable location. All rooms are decorated differently with lively wallpaper; some have views of Palazzo Vecchio and others of the Arno. The rooftop terrace, where you can have breakfast or an aperitivo, is decked with flowers. The lobby suggests a friend's living room—its warm yellow walls are welcoming. Double glazing and air-conditioning help keep street noise at bay. (The hotel has an elevator at the top of a short flight of stairs from the street.) ⊠ *Vicolo Marzio 1, Piazza della Signoria 50122* ☎ *055/287216* ⊟ *055/212208* ⊕ *www. hermitagehotel.com* ⬄ *27 rooms, 1 suite* ⚬ *In-room safes, cable TV, babysitting, laundry service, parking (fee), some pets allowed* ⊟ *MC, V* ⦿ *CP.*

$$$ ▦ **Hotel Benivieni.** The quiet, tranquil former 15th-century palace is one block away from the Duomo. Rooms are spacious, with high ceilings, hardwood floors, and sweeping draperies. A winter garden provides a wonderful place to while away some time. The affable Caldana family, wholly fluent in English, ably staffs the front desk. ⊠ *Via delle Oche 5, Duomo, 50122* ☎ *055/2382133* ⊟ *055/2398248* ⊕ *www. hotelbenivieni.it* ⬄ *15 rooms* ⚬ *In-room safes, cable TV, babysitting, dry cleaning, laundry service, Internet, parking (fee), some pets allowed, no-smoking rooms* ⊟ *AE, DC, MC, V* ⦿ *BP.*

$$ 🏨 **Torre Guelfa.** Enter this hidden hotel through an immense wooden door on a narrow street, and continue through an iron gate and up a few steps to an elevator that takes you to the third floor. A few more steps and you're in a 13th-century Florentine *torre* (tower). The Torre Guelfa once protected the fabulously wealthy Acciaiuoli family; now it's one of the best small hotels in the center of Florence. Each guest room is different, some with canopied beds, some with balconies. Those on a budget might want to consider one of the six less-expensive rooms on the second floor, which are comparable to the rest of the rooms except that they have no TVs. ⊠ *Borgo Santi Apostoli 8, Santa Maria Novella, 50123* ☎ *055/2396338* 🖶 *055/2398577* 🛏 *24 rooms, 2 suites* ♻ *Some in-room safes, babysitting, dry cleaning, laundry service, Internet, parking (fee), some pets allowed, no-smoking rooms; no TV in some rooms* ▭ *AE, MC, V* ❅ *CP.*

$–$$ 🏨 **Alessandra.** The location, a block from the Ponte Vecchio, and the clean, ample rooms make this a good choice. The building, known as the Palazzo Roselli del Turco, was designed in 1507 by Baccio d'Agnolo, a contemporary of Michelangelo's. Though little remains of the original design save for the high wood ceilings, there's still an aura of grandeur. Several of the rooms have views of the Arno, and the sole suite is spacious and a steal for this category. Friendly hosts Anna and Andrea Gennarini speak fluent English. ⊠ *Borgo Santi Apostoli 17, Santa Maria Novella 50123* ☎ *055/283438* 🖶 *055/210619* ⊕ *www.hotelalessandra. com* 🛏 *26 rooms, 19 with bath, 1 suite, 1 apartment* ♻ *In-room safes, some minibars, cable TV, dry cleaning, laundry service, Internet, parking (fee), no-smoking rooms* ▭ *AE, MC, V* ❅ *Closed Dec. 10–26* ❅ *BP.*

$ 🏨 **Albergo Firenze.** A block from the Duomo, this hotel is on one of the oldest piazzas in Florence. Though the reception area and hallways have all the charm of a college dormitory, the similarity ends upon entering the spotlessly clean rooms. A good number of triple and quadruple rooms make this an inviting place for families. For the location, the place is a great bargain. ⊠ *Piazza Donati 4, Duomo 50122* ☎ *055/214203* 🖶 *055/212370* ⊕ *www.hotelfirenze-fi.it* 🛏 *58 rooms* ♻ *Parking (fee)* ▭ *No credit cards* ❅ *CP.*

$ 🏨 **Soggiorno Sani.** Hosts Elizabeth and Remo have taken their former no-frills accommodation and spruced it up a bit, adding such amenities as air-conditioning and the occasional private bath to make a stay here more serene. Some rooms have a tremendous view of Orsanmichele or the Casa di Dante. There's no reception area or desk service, but if you're looking for a place to lay your head at exceptionally low prices, you're in luck. ⊠ *Piazza dei Giuochi 1, Duomo 50123* ☎ *055/211235* 🖶 *055/ 2654386* ⊕ *www.sanibnb.it* 🛏 *6 rooms with 1 shared bath* ♻ *In-room safes, refrigerators, parking (fee)* ▭ *MC, V* ❅ *CP.*

⟳ ¢–$ 🏨 **Cristina.** A friendly and enthusiastic staff runs this tiny hotel one block from the Uffizi and the Bargello. It's a couple of flights up to reach the place, and there's no elevator, but the price and location make it a bargain. Rooms are large and clean, and have desks and comfortable beds. A few rooms can accommodate up to four, which makes this a practical budget option for families. ⊠ *Via della Condotta 4, Duomo 50122* ☎🖶 *055/214484* 🛏 *9 rooms, 4 with bath* ♻ *Fans, babysitting, park-*

ing (fee), some pets allowed, no-smoking rooms; no a/c, no room phones, no room TVs ☰ *AE, DC, MC, V.*

San Lorenzo & Beyond

$$ ▣ **Porta Faenza.** A 12th-century medieval well discovered during renovations is a focal point in the lobby of this good-value hotel; rooms and bathrooms are spacious and decorated in Florentine style. Italian Antonio Lelli and his Canadian wife, Rose, go out of their way to make you feel at home. ⊠ *Via Faenza 77, Santa Maria Novella 50123* ☎ *055/284119* 🖶 *055/210101* ⊕ *www.hotelportafaenza.it* ⮐ *25 rooms* ⏃ *In-room data ports, in-room safes, cable TV, bar, babysitting, laundry service, Internet, meeting room, parking (fee), some pets allowed, no-smoking floor* ☰ *AE, DC, MC, V* �𝄃⊙�𝄃 *BP.*

★ $ ▣ **Bellettini.** You're in good hands at this small hotel on three floors run by sisters Marzia and Gina Naldini and their husbands. The top floor has two rooms with a view, and all the good-sized guest rooms have Venetian or Tuscan provincial furnishings; bathrooms are bright and modern. Public rooms are simple but comfortable. A handful of triples and quadruples are available. An ample buffet breakfast includes tasty homemade cakes. ⊠ *Via dei Conti 7, Santa Maria Novella 50123* ☎ *055/213561* 🖶 *055/283551* ⊕ *www.hotelbellettini.com* ⮐ *28 rooms* ⏃ *In-room safes, minibars, cable TV, bar, Internet, parking (fee), some pets allowed* ☰ *AE, DC, MC, V* �𝄃⊙�𝄃 *BP.*

Near Piazza San Marco & Beyond

$$-$$$ ▣ **Il Guelfo Bianco.** The 15th-century building has all modern conveniences, but its Renaissance charm still shines. Rooms have high ceilings (some are coffered) and windows are triple-glazed. Contemporary prints and paintings on the walls contrast nicely with classic furnishings. Larger-than-usual single rooms have French-style beds and are a good choice for those traveling alone. Breakfast can be enjoyed in a small outdoor garden when weather permits. Though the hotel is in the centro storico, it still feels somewhat off the beaten path. ⊠ *Via Cavour 29, San Marco 50129* ☎ *055/288330* 🖶 *055/295203* ⊕ *www.ilguelfobianco.it* ⮐ *35 rooms, 7 suites* ⏃ *In-room data ports, in-room safes, minibars, cable TV, babysitting, dry cleaning, laundry service, concierge, Internet, business services, parking (fee), some pets allowed, no-smoking rooms* ☰ *AE, DC, MC, V* ⟮⊙⟯ *CP.*

⟲ $$ ▣ **Hotel Casci.** In this refurbished 14th-century palace, the home of Giacchino Rossini in 1851–55, the friendly Lombardi family runs a hotel with spotless rooms. Guest rooms are functional, and many of them open out onto various terraces (a view doesn't necessarily follow, however). It's on a very busy thoroughfare, but triple-glazed windows allow for a sound night's sleep. Many rooms easily accommodate an extra bed or two, so this is a good option for people traveling with children. ⊠ *Via Cavour 13, San Marco 50129* ☎ *055/211686* 🖶 *055/2396461* ⊕ *www.hotelcasci.com* ⮐ *25 rooms* ⏃ *In-room safes, refrigerators, cable TV, babysitting, dry cleaning, laundry service, Internet, parking (fee), some pets allowed, no-smoking rooms* ☰ *AE, DC, MC, V* ⟮⊙⟯ *BP.*

$$ 🏨 **Hotel delle Arti.** If Florence had town houses, this would be one: the entrance to the public room downstairs feels as if you're in someone's living room. Pale, pastel walls, polished hardwood floors, and muted fabrics give rooms a simple, elegant look. Breakfast is taken on the top floor, and a small terrace provides city views. The highly capable staff is completely fluent in English. ⊠ *Via dei Servi 38/a, Santissima Annunziata 50122* ☎ *055/2645307* 🖷 *055/290140* ⊕ *www.hoteldellearti.it* 📞 *9 rooms* ♻ *Minibars, cable TV, babysitting, dry cleaning, laundry service, business services, some pets allowed (fee)* 🛏 *AE, DC, MC, V* ⭑◯⭒ *BP.*

$$ 🏨 **Loggiato dei Serviti.** Though this hotel was not designed by Brunelleschi, Florence's architectural genius, it might as well have been. The Loggiato is tucked away on one of the city's loveliest squares; a mirror image of the architect's famous Spedale degli Innocenti is across the way. Occupying a 16th-century former convent, the building was once an inn for traveling priests. Vaulted ceilings, tasteful furnishings (some antique), canopy beds, and rich fabrics make this spare Renaissance building with modern comforts a find. ⊠ *Piazza Santissima Annunziata 3, 50122* ☎ *055/289592* 🖷 *055/289595* ⊕ *www.loggiatodeiservitihotel.it* 📞 *38 rooms* ♻ *In-room data ports, in-room safes, minibars, cable TV, bar, babysitting, dry cleaning, laundry service, parking (fee), some pets allowed* 🛏 *AE, DC, MC, V* ⭑◯⭒ *CP.*

★ **$$** 🏨 **Morandi alla Crocetta.** You're made to feel like privileged friends of the family at this charming and distinguished residence near Piazza Santissima Annunziata. The former convent is close to the sights but very quiet, and it's furnished comfortably in the classic style of a gracious Florentine home. One room retains original 17th-century fresco fragments, and two others have small private terraces. The Morandi is not only an exceptional hotel but also a good value. It's very small, so try to book well in advance. ⊠ *Via Laura 50, Santissima Annunziata 50121* ☎ *055/2344747* 🖷 *055/2480954* ⊕ *www.hotelmorandi.it* 📞 *10 rooms* ♻ *In-room data ports, in-room safes, minibars, cable TV, dry cleaning, laundry service, concierge, Internet, parking (fee), some pets allowed* 🛏 *AE, DC, MC, V.*

¢ 🏨 **Residenza Johanna I.** Savvy travelers and those on a budget should look no farther, as this *residenza* (residence) is a tremendous value for **FodorsChoice** quality and location. Though it's very much in the centro storico, the place is rather homey. You're given a large set of keys to let yourself into the building after 7 PM, when the staff goes home. Simple rooms have high ceilings and pale pastel floral prints. Morning tea and coffee (but no breakfast) are served in your room. ⊠ *Via Bonifacio Lupi 14, San Marco 50129* ☎ *055/481896* 🖷 *055/482721* ⊕ *www.johanna.it* 📞 *11 rooms* ♻ *Fans, parking (fee); no a/c, no room phones, no room TVs* 🛏 *No credit cards.*

Santa Maria Novella to the Arno

$$$$ 🏨 **Gallery Art Hotel.** High design resides at this art showcase near the Ponte Vecchio. The coolly understated public rooms have a revolving collection of photographs by artists like Helmut Newton adorning the walls; the reception area is subtlely but dramatically lit. Rooms are sleek and uncluttered and dressed mostly in neutrals. Luxe touches, such as leather headboards and kimono robes, abound. Both the bar and restaurant attract sophisticated, fashionable locals; brunch happens on the weekends. ⊠ *Vicolo dell'Oro 5, Santa Maria Novella 50123* ☎ *055/27263* 🖷 *055/268557* ⊕ *www.lungarnohotels.com* 🛏 *65 rooms, 9 suites* ♿ *Restaurant, room service, in-room data ports, in-room fax, in-room safes, minibars, cable TV with movies, massage, bar, babysitting, dry cleaning, laundry service, concierge, Internet, business services, parking (fee), no-smoking rooms* ▭ *AE, DC, MC, V* ⦿ *BP.*

$$$$ ☒ **Grand.** Long the mainstay of sophisticated, moneyed travelers, this Florentine classic provides all the luxurious amenities. Rooms are decorated in either Renaissance or Empire style; the former have rich, deeply hued damask brocades, crisp prints, and patterned fabric which offsets white walls, while the latter have simple lines and solid colors. The overall effect is sumptuous, and the views—either of the Arno or overlooking a small rectangular courtyard lined with potted orange trees—are equally impressive. Public rooms dazzle with dark-wood fittings and shiny white marble. Il Fiorino, the sleek restaurant, has a cutting-edge menu. ⊠ *Piazza Ognissanti 1, Lungarno North 50123* ☎ *055/288781* 🖷 *055/217400* ⊕ *www.starwood.com* 🛏 *107 rooms* ♿ *Restaurant, room service, in-room data ports, in-room safes, minibars, cable TV with movies, gym, bar, piano bar, babysitting, dry cleaning, laundry service, concierge, Internet, business services, meeting rooms, parking (fee), some pets allowed, no-smoking rooms* ▭ *AE, DC, MC, V.*

★ $$$ ☒ **Beacci Tornabuoni.** Florentine pensioni don't come any more classic than this. It has old-fashioned style and enough modern comfort to keep you happy, and it's in a 14th-century palazzo. The sitting room has a large fireplace, the terrace has a tremendous view of some major Florentine monuments, and the wallpapered rooms are inviting. On Monday, Wednesday, and Friday nights from May through October, the dining room opens, serving Tuscan specialties. ⊠ *Via Tornabuoni 3, Santa Maria Novella 50123* ☎ *055/212645* 🖷 *055/283594* ⊕ *www.bthotel.it* 🛏 *28 rooms* ♿ *Restaurant, minibars, cable TV, bar, babysitting, dry cleaning, laundry service, Internet, parking (fee), some pets allowed* ▭ *AE, DC, MC, V* ⦿ *BP.*

$$ ☒ **Le Vigne.** The small, family-run hotel looks out over one of Florence's most beautiful and central squares. Despite soaring high ceilings, the feeling is comfortable and homey, with rooms furnished in 19th-century Florentine style. Nice touches include complimentary afternoon tea and homemade breakfast jams and cakes. There's also a children's play area. ⊠ *Piazza Santa Maria Novella 24, 50123* ☎ *055/294449* 🖷 *055/2302263* ⊕ *www.florence.ala.it/le_vigne* 🛏 *25 rooms* ♿ *In-room safes, cable TV, bar, babysitting, dry cleaning, laundry service, parking (fee), some pets allowed* ▭ *AE, DC, MC, V* ⦿ *BP.*

$$ ☒ **Villa Azalee.** The 19th-century villa deftly recalls its previous incarnation as a private residence. Quilted, floral-print slipcovers dress the furniture; throw rugs pepper the floors. Many rooms have views of the hotel's garden, and some have private terraces. The hotel is five minutes on foot from the train station and steps from the Fortezza da Basso (site of the Pitti fashion shows). ⊠ *Viale Fratelli Rosselli 44, Santa Maria*

Novella 50123 ☎ *055/214242* 🖷 *055/268264* ⊕ *www.villa-azalee.it* ⇆ *25 rooms* ♦ *Minibars, cable TV, bicycles, bar, dry cleaning, laundry service, parking (fee), some pets allowed* ▭ *AE, DC, MC, V* ⏐◯⏐ *BP.*

$ 🏨 **Nuova Italia.** A genial English-speaking family runs this hotel near the train station and within walking distance of the sights. Its homey rooms are clean and simply furnished. Air-conditioning and triple-glazed windows ensure restful nights. Some rooms can accommodate extra beds. ⊠ *Via Faenza 26, Santa Maria Novella 50123* ☎ *055/268430* 🖷 *055/210941* ⊕ *nuovaitalia.hotelinfirenze.com* ⇆ *20 rooms* ♦ *Cable TV, babysitting, dry cleaning, laundry service, parking (fee), some pets allowed, no-smoking rooms* ▭ *AE, MC, V* ⏐◯⏐ *CP* ⊙ *Closed Dec. 8–Dec. 26.*

¢–$ 🏨 **Pensione Ferretti.** Look out onto the tiny Piazza Santa Maria Novella at this pensione, which is close to the historic center. English-speaking owner Luciano Michel and his South African–born wife, Sue, do just about anything to make you feel at home (including providing 24-hour free Internet access). Though it's housed in a 16th-century palazzo, accommodations are simple and no-frills. Ceiling fans make warmer months more bearable. ⊠ *Via delle Belle Donne 17, Santa Maria Novella 50123* ☎ *055/2381328* 🖷 *055/219288* ⊕ *www.emmeti.it/Hferretti* ⇆ *16 rooms, 6 with bath, 1 apartment* ♦ *Fans, Internet, parking (fee), some pets allowed; no a/c, no room TVs* ▭ *AE, DC, MC, V* ⏐◯⏐ *CP.*

The Oltrarno & Beyond

$$$$ 🏨 **Lungarno.** Many rooms and suites here have private terraces that jut out right over the Arno, granting views of the Palazzo Vecchio and Duomo opposite. Four suites in a 13th-century tower preserve details like exposed stone walls and old archways and look over a little square with a medieval tower covered in jasmine. The very chic interiors approximate breezily elegant homes, with lots of crisp white fabrics with blue trim. A wall of windows and a sea of white couches make the lobby bar one of the most relaxing places in the city to stop for a drink. Inquire about the Lungarno Suites, across the river; they include kitchens, making them attractive if you're planning a longer stay. ⊠ *Borgo San Jacopo 14, Lungarno South 50125* ☎ *055/27261* 🖷 *055/268437* ⊕ *www.lungarnohotels.com* ⇆ *60 rooms, 13 suites* ♦ *Restaurant, in-room data ports, in-room fax, cable TV with movies, bar, babysitting, dry cleaning, laundry service, concierge, Internet, meeting rooms, parking (fee), no-smoking rooms* ▭ *AE, DC, MC, V* ⏐◯⏐ *BP.*

$$$$ 🏨 **Palazzo Magnani Feroni.** The perfect place to play the part of a Florentine aristocrat is at this 16th-century palazzo, which despite its massive halls and sweeping staircase could almost feel like home. Suites include large sitting rooms and bedrooms, all decorated with luxurious fabrics, chandeliers, and Renaissance-inspired furniture. The rooftop terrace, complete with bar, has citywide views that startle. Though it's only a five-minute walk from the Ponte Vecchio, the street is surprisingly quiet. ⊠ *Borgo San Frediano 5, Santo Spirito 50124* ☎ *055/2399544* 🖷 *055/2608908* ⊕ *www.florencepalace.com* ⇆ *11 suites* ♦ *Room service, in-room data ports, in-room safes, minibars, cable TV, exercise equip-*

ment, billiards, bar, dry cleaning, laundry service, parking (fee), no-smoking rooms ⊟ *AE, DC, MC, V* ⫟◯⫠ *BP.*

$$$$
Fodor'sChoice
★
✕⊞ **Villa La Vedetta.** A private family villa–turned–luxury hotel perches on the hills of the Arno's south bank, providing phenomenal views of Florence. Cool black, gray, and red tones complement contemporary Baccarat chandeliers and 19th-century consoles in public rooms. Carefully coordinated color schemes prevail in both the sleeping areas and the bathrooms. The stellar staff is fluent in English and are virtually equal in number to the guests. The Onice Restaurant ($$$–$$$$) has an inventive Italian menu that alludes to the five years the chef spent cooking in Thailand. ⊠ *Viale Michelangelo 78, 50125* ☎ *055/681631* 🖷 *055/6582544* ⊕*www.villalavedettahotel.com* ⭬*10 rooms, 8 suites* ⟁ *Restaurant, room service, in-room data ports, in-room safes, minibars, cable TV, pool, sauna, 2 bars, babysitting, dry cleaning, laundry service, Internet, meeting rooms, free parking, some pets allowed, no-smoking rooms* ⊟ *AE, DC, MC, V.*

$$
⊞ **Annalena.** The story goes that Annalena, a 15th-century maiden, married a Medici; another man, smitten with her and angry at her refusal to capitulate, murdered her husband and her young son. The devastated widow then turned her private home into a convent. Is it true? Well, it certainly is romantic, as is the former convent, now pensione, that bears her name. With its high ceilings and spacious rooms, it's a perfect place to unwind. Some rooms overlook a private garden, and one has a private terrace; there are also a handful of triples and quads available. ⊠ *Via Romana 34, Santo Spirito/San Frediano 50125* ☎*055/229600* 🖷 *055/222403* ⊕ *www.hotelannalena.it* ⭬ *20 rooms* ⟁ *Minibars, cable TV, babysitting, laundry service, parking (fee), some pets allowed; no a/c in some rooms* ⊟ *AE, DC, MC, V* ⫟◯⫠ *BP.*

$$
⊞ **Hotel Silla.** The entrance to this slightly off-the-beaten-path hotel is through a 15th-century courtyard lined with potted plants and sculpture-filled niches. The hotel, formerly a palazzo dating from the 15th century, is up a flight of stairs and has two floors. Rooms are simply furnished and walls are papered; some have views of Via de' Renai and the Arno, while others overlook a less-traveled road. Breakfast may be taken in a room that preserves an Empire feel (including two chandeliers from the early 19th century); when it's warm, a large, sunny terrace is the perfect place to read or to write that postcard. ⊠ *Via de' Renai 5, San Niccolò 50125* ☎ *055/2342888* 🖷 *055/2341437* ⊕ *www.hotelsilla.it* ⭬ *35 rooms* ⟁ *In-room safes, minibars, cable TV, bar, babysitting, dry cleaning, laundry service, concierge, parking (fee), some pets allowed; no smoking* ⊟ *AE, DC, MC, V* ⫟◯⫠ *BP.*

$
⊞ **Albergo La Scaletta.** For a tremendous view of the Boboli Garden, look no farther than this exquisite pensione near the Ponte Vecchio and Palazzo Pitti. Simply furnished yet rather large rooms and a sunny breakfast room make this place, run by a mother-and-son team, cozy. In warm weather, two flower-bedecked terraces are open; one has a stunning 360-degree view of Florence. ⊠ *Via Guicciardini 13, Palazzo Pitti 50125* ☎ *055/283028* 🖷 *055/289562* ⊕ *www.lascaletta.com* ⭬ *11 rooms, 10 with bath* ⟁ *Dining room, parking (fee), some pets allowed; no TV in some rooms* ⊟ *MC, V* ⫟◯⫠ *BP.*

Santa Croce

$$$$ 🏨 **Hotel Regency.** The noise and crowds of Florence seem far from this stylish hotel in a residential district near the Sinagoga, though you're not more than 10 minutes from the Accademia and Michelangelo's *David*. Across the street is Piazza d'Azeglio, a small public park that somehow evokes 19th-century Middle Europe. Rooms dressed in richly colored fabrics and antique-style furniture remain faithful to the hotel's 19th-century origins as a private mansion. The restaurant here is equally sophisticated. ⊠ *Piazza d'Azeglio 3, Santa Croce 50121* ☎ *055/245247* 🖷 *055/2346735* ⊕ *www.regency-hotel.com* 🛏 *30 rooms, 4 suites* ⌂ *Restaurant, room service, in-room safes, minibars, cable TV, bar, babysitting, dry cleaning, laundry service, concierge, Internet, parking (fee), some pets allowed, no-smoking rooms* ☰ *AE, DC, MC, V* ℔ *BP.*

$$$–$$$$ 🏨 **J&J.** On a quiet street within walking distance of the sights sits this unusual hotel, a converted 16th-century convent. Ideal for honeymooners, families, and small groups of friends are the large, suitelike rooms; some are on two levels, and many are arranged around a central courtyard. Pale travertine tiles used to refit some bathrooms provide a pleasing, ultramodern juxtaposition to more traditional furnishings. Smaller rooms are more intimate, and some open onto a little shared courtyard. The gracious owners enjoy chatting in the light and airy lounge; breakfast is served in a glassed-in Renaissance loggia or in the central courtyard. ⊠ *Via di Mezzo 20, Santa Croce 50121* ☎ *055/26312* 🖷 *055/240282* ⊕ *www.jandjhotel.com* 🛏 *19 rooms, 7 suites* ⌂ *In-room data ports, cable TV, bar, babysitting, dry cleaning, laundry service, parking (fee), no-smoking rooms* ☰ *AE, DC, MC, V* ℔ *CP.*

★ $$$–$$$$ 🏨 **Monna Lisa.** Housed in a 15th-century palazzo, with parts of the building dating from the 13th century, this hotel retains some of its original wood-coffered ceilings from the 1500s, as well as its original marble staircase. Though some rooms are small, they are tasteful, and each is done in different floral wallpaper. The public rooms retain a 19th-century aura, and the intimate bar, with its red velveteen wallpaper, is a good place to unwind. ⊠ *Borgo Pinti 27, Santa Croce 50121* ☎ *055/2479751* 🖷 *055/2479755* ⊕ *www.monnalisa.it* 🛏 *45 rooms* ⌂ *In-room safes, minibars, cable TV, bar, babysitting, dry cleaning, laundry service, concierge, parking (fee), some pets allowed, no-smoking rooms* ☰ *AE, DC, MC, V* ℔ *BP.*

$$ 🏨 **Hotel Liana.** With this hotel, it's possible to experience palazzo life without breaking the bank. Steps from the *viali* (the outer limit defining the centro storico) but still very much within the bounds of the historic center, the Liana, originally a 19th-century villa, retains the feel of another era. The lobby has high ceilings and large windows; a sweeping staircase leads to the breakfast room, which has a period fresco on its ceiling. A small bar offers the makings of an aperitivo; sip it in the gazebo in the garden. ⊠ *Via Alfieri 18, Santa Croce 50121* ☎ *055/ 245303 or 055/245304* 🖷 *055/2344596* ⊕ *www.hotelliana.com* 🛏 *20 rooms, 2 suites* ⌂ *Some in-room safes, some minibars, bar, dry cleaning, parking (fee), some pets allowed; no a/c in some rooms* ☰ *AE, DC, MC, V* ℔ *BP.*

¢　🏨 **Albergo Losanna.** Most major sights are within walking distance of this tiny pensione steps away from the *viali*, the edge of the city center. Though dated and a little worn around the edges, the property is impeccably clean and the rooms have high ceilings; the mother and son who run the place are enthusiastic and cordial. Try to get a room facing away from the street; though there aren't any views, you won't hear as much street noise. ⊠ *Via V. Alfieri 9, Santa Croce 50121* 📠 *055/245840* ⊕ *www.albergolosanna.com* 🛏 *8 rooms, 3 with bath* ⚲ *Parking (fee); no a/c in some rooms, no room TVs* ▤ *MC, V* ⵗ *CP.*

¢　🏨 **Istituto Oblate dell'Assunzione.** Twelve nuns run this convent, which is minutes from the Duomo. Rooms are spotlessly clean and simple; some of them have views of the cupola, and others look out onto a carefully tended garden where you are encouraged to relax. Several rooms have three and four beds, making them well suited for families. Curfew is at 11:30 PM. You can join mass every morning at 7:30. The nuns provide half or full pension for groups of 10 or more. ⊠ *Borgo Pinti 15, Santa Croce 50121* 📞 *055/2480582* 🖷 *055/2346291* 🛏 *50 rooms, 25 with bath* ⚲ *Parking (fee), no-smoking rooms; no a/c in some rooms, no room phones, no room TVs* ▤ *No credit cards.*

Outside the City

$$$$　🏨 **Torre di Bellosguardo.** *Bellosguardo* means "beautiful view"; given the view of Florence you get here, the name is fitting. The hotel, perched atop a hill minutes from the *viale* (the outer limit defining the centro storico), is reached via a narrow road dotted with olive trees. Dante's friend Guido Calvacanti supposedly chose this serene spot for his country villa, but little remains from the early 14th century. The reception area, a former ballroom, has soaring ceilings with frescoes by Francavilla (1553–1615). Guest rooms, all with high ceilings, are simple and have heavy wooden furniture. ⊠ *Via Roti Michelozzi 2, 50124* 📞 *055/2298145* 🖷 *055/229008* ⊕ *www.torrebellosguardo.com* 🛏 *9 rooms, 7 suites* ⚲ *Minibars, pool, bar, babysitting, dry cleaning, laundry service, concierge, free parking, some pets allowed; no a/c in some rooms, no room TVs* ▤ *AE, MC, V.*

★ $$$$　🏨 **Villa La Massa.** You approach the tall and imposing villa, 15 minutes out of town, via a gravel drive lined with flowers. The public rooms are outfitted in Renaissance style, with a color scheme of deep green, gold, and crimson. Guest rooms have high ceilings, some with frescoes, plush carpeting, and deep bathtubs. A pool and beautiful views of the Arno are bonuses. The restaurant is superb and serves Tuscan classics as well as less-standard fare; a pianist quietly plays old standards while you eat. A shuttle bus runs every hour to and from the center of Florence. You have access to nearby tennis courts. ⊠ *Via della Massa 24, Candeli 50012* 📞 *055/62611* 🖷 *055/633102* ⊕ *www.villalamassa.com* 🛏 *19 rooms, 18 suites* ⚲ *Restaurant, in-room data ports, in-room safes, minibars, room TVs with movies, golf privileges, pool, bar, babysitting, dry cleaning, laundry service, concierge, Internet, business services, meeting rooms, parking (fee), some pets allowed, no-smoking rooms* ▤ *AE, DC, MC, V* ⊗ *Closed Dec.–Mar.* ⵗ *CP.*

$$ 🏠 **Relais Villa l'Olmo.** Alberto and Claudia Giannotti have turned a former 16th-century country villa into an elegantly comfortable agriturismo 20 minutes south from the center of Florence. If you're looking for a country experience but crave easy access to the city, this place outside the small town of Impruneta does the trick. Many of the apartments look out over a gently terraced field of olive trees. (The estate produces top-notch olive oil, as well as some respectable wine.) The cheerful apartments are suitable for couples; some are adjoining, making them good options for families or groups. Unlike many agriturismi, there's no minimum stay during high season here. ⊠ *Via Impruneta 19, Impruneta 50023* ☎ *055/2311311* 📠 *055/2311313* ⊕ *www.relaisfarmholiday.it* 🛏 *8 apartments, 2 cottages, 1 farmhouse* ⚘ *Picnic area, BBQs, fans, in-room safes, kitchens, refrigerators, cable TV with movies, golf privileges, 3 pools, massage, mountain bikes, babysitting, dry cleaning, laundry facilities, laundry service, Internet, free parking, some pets allowed, no-smoking rooms* 🖃 *AE, DC, MC, V.*

$$ 🏠 **Villa Poggio San Felice.** Livia Puccinelli Sannini, the descendant of a
Fodor's Choice famed 19th-century Florentine hotelier, and her husband have turned
★ her family's former country villa (documented in the 15th century) into a serene hotel outside the city limits. It retains the intimate feel of a single-family home with only five high-ceilinged rooms; some have divine views of Brunelleschi's cupola down below, and others have working fireplaces. Simple landscaped gardens are peaceful. Though a daily shuttle service runs to the center of town, a car is vital. ⊠ *Via San Matteo in Arcetri 24, 50125* ☎ *055/220016* 📠 *055/2335388* ⊕ *www.villapoggiosanfelice.com* 🛏 *4 rooms, 1 suite* ⚘ *Golf privileges, pool, wading pool, babysitting, laundry service, Internet, free parking, some pets allowed* 🖃 *AE, MC, V* ⦿◎ *BP* ⊗ *Closed Jan. 10–Feb. 28.*

NIGHTLIFE & THE ARTS

The Arts

Festivals & Special Events

Teatro Tenda (⊠ Lungarno Aldo Moro 3 ☎ 055/6503068), a large exhibition space, is the venue for many events throughout the year, including a large Christmas bazaar run by the Red Cross and rock concerts. Around St. Patrick's Day (March 17), Teatro Tenda hosts the week-long **Irlanda in Festa** (Ireland Festival), with "seminars" on Irish beer as well as lots of Irish music.

On **Holy Thursday** at the Duomo, a centuries-old ritual is reenacted with members of the Compagnia della Misericordia, a lay association that during the Renaissance comforted those condemned to death and provided dowries for poor girls as well as other services for its members. (Today the confraternity runs an efficient emergency-ambulance service.) A solemn procession of priests and confraternity members wends its way into the Duomo, and then the priests wash the feet of the confraternity members. It is a moving ritual, and a visual link to the Renaissance.

On Easter Sunday, Florentines and foreigners alike flock to the Piazza del Duomo to watch the **Scoppio del Carro** (the Explosion of the Cart): a monstrosity of a carriage, pulled by two huge oxen decorated for the occasion, makes its way through the city center and ends up in the piazza. Through an elaborate wiring system, an object representing a "dove" is sent from inside the church to the Baptistery across the way. The dove sets off an explosion of fireworks that comes streaming from the carriage. You have to see it to believe it. If you don't like crowds, don't worry: video replays figure prominently on the nightly newscasts afterward.

On June 24 Florence grinds to a halt to celebrate the **Festa di San Giovanni** (Feast of St. John the Baptist) in honor of its patron saint. Many shops and bars close, and at night a fireworks display along the Arno attracts thousands.

The **Fortezza da Basso** (✉ Viale Strozzi 1 ☎ 055/49721), a vast space perfect for large events, hosts a remarkable festival of food and ethnic arts in early December, as well as other happenings throughout the year. The fashion world flocks to Florence several times a year for high-end designer shows that are held here. Visit the local tourist information center to see what's on while you're in town.

Film

The daily Florentine newspaper *La Nazione* (⊕ www.lanazione.it) has movie listings. Note that most American films are dubbed into Italian rather than subtitled. **Festival dei Popoli** (✉ Borgo Pinti 82/r, Santa Croce ☎ 055/244778 ⊕ www.festivaldeipopoli.org) is a week-long documentary–and–feature film festival that happens in November or December with screenings at various venues around town.

The **Fulgor** (✉ Via Maso Finiguerra 22/r, Lungarno North ☎ 055/2381881) screens English-language films on Thursday. The **Odeon** (✉ Piazza Strozzi, Piazza della Repubblica ☎ 055/214068 ⊕ www.cinehall.it) shows first-run English-language films on Monday, Tuesday, and Thursday at its magnificent art-deco theater. The **British Institute of Florence** (✉ Palazzo Lanfredini, Lungarno Guicciardini 9, Lungarno Sud ☎ 055/26778270 ⊕ www.britishinstitute.it) runs English-language film series; they have a bent toward classic movies.

Music

The **Accademia Bartolomeo Cristofori** (✉ Via di Camaldoli 7/r, Santo Spirito/San Frediano ☎ 055/221646 ⊕ www.accademiacristofori.it), also known as the Amici del Fortepiano (Friends of the Fortepiano), sponsors fortepiano concerts throughout the year. **Amici della Musica** (⊕ www.amicimusica.fi.it) organizes concerts at the **Teatro della Pergola** (Box office ✉ Via Alamanni 39, Santissima Annunziata ☎ 055/210804 ⊕ www.pergola.firenze.it).

The **Maggio Musicale Fiorentina**, a series of internationally acclaimed concerts and recitals, is held in the **Teatro Comunale** (✉ Corso Italia 16, Lungarno North ☎ 055/211158 ⊕ www.maggiofiorentina.com). Within Italy, you can purchase tickets from late April through July directly at the box office (✉ Via Alamanni 39 ☎ 055/210804) or by phone (☎ 800/ 112211). Other events—opera, ballet, and additional concerts—occur regularly throughout the year at different venues in town.

The **Orchestra da Camera Fiorentina** (✉ Via E. Poggi 6, Piazza della Signoria ☎ 055/783374) performs various concerts of classical music throughout the year at Orsanmichele, the grain market–turned–church; this is a fine case of the architecture being at least as interesting as the music.

The concert season of the **Orchestra della Toscana** (✉ Via Ghibellina 101, Santa Croce ☎ 055/210804) runs from November to June. You can hear organ music in the baroque church of **Santa Margherita in Maria de' Ricci** (✉ Via il Corso, Piazza della Signoria ☎ 055/215044). Free concerts begin every night at 9:15, except Monday.

Visiting rock stars, trendy bands from Germany, and some American groups play at **Tenax** (✉ Via Pratese 46 ⊕ www.tenax.org).

Opera

Operas are performed in the **Teatro Comunale** (✉ Corso Italia 12, Lungarno North ☎ 055/211158) from September through April.

Theater

Theater lovers might want to try an evening at **Teatro della Pergola** (✉ Via della Pergola 12/r, Santissima Annunziata ☎ 055/22641 ⊕ www. pergola.firenze.it). The season runs from mid-October to mid-April. If the idea of hearing a play in Italian is too forbidding, visit the lovely theater. Built in 1656 by Ferdinando Tacca, and once the private theater of the grand dukes, it was opened to the public in 1755. The theater has undergone several metamorphoses; its present incarnation dates to 1828, and the atrium was constructed nine years later. Call to arrange a guided visit.

Nightlife

Florentines are rather proud of their nightlife options. Most bars now have some sort of happy hour, which usually lasts for many hours and often has snacks that can substitute for a light dinner. Discos typically don't open until very late in the evening and don't get crowded until 1 or 2 in the morning. Though the cover charges might seem steep, finding free passes around town is fairly easy.

Bars

Young Florentines aching to see and be seen come to **Angels** (✉ Via del Proconsolo 29-31/r ☎ 055/2398762 ⊕ www.ristoranteangels.it), which pulls double duty as a restaurant. If you want to sip a sparkling aperitivo or simply check your e-mail, stop in at the **Astor** (✉ Piazza del Duomo 20/r, Duomo ☎ 055/2399000), open from early in the morning till late at night. The bar at **Beccofino** (✉ Piazza degli Scarlatti 1/r, [Lungarno Corsini] Lungarno Sud ☎ 055/290076) serves one of the best martinis in town. **Capocaccia** (✉ Lungarno Corsini 12/14r, Lungarno Sud ☎ 055/210751) makes great Bloody Marys, and it's the place to be at cocktail time. At night young Florentines crowd the doors and spill out into the street. **Danny Rock** (✉ Via Pandolfini 13/r, Santa Croce ☎ 055/2340307) bills itself as a "pub restaurant"; you can enjoy its divine cheeseburger (or have a plate of pasta) while watching Bugs Bunny cartoons on a big screen. One of the hottest spots in town is the bar at the **Gallery Art Hotel** (✉ Vicolo dell'Oro 5, Santa Maria Novella ☎ 055/27263). For a swanky experience, lubricated with trademark bellinis and the best martinis in Florence, head to **Harry's Bar** (✉ Lungarno Vespucci 22/r, Lungarno North ☎ 055/2396700). The oh-so-cool vibe at **La Dolce Vita** (✉ Piazza del Carmine 6/r, Santo Spirito ☎ 055/284595 ⊕ www.dolcevitaflorence.com) attracts Florentines and the occasional visiting American movie star. **Negroni** (✉ Via dei Renai 17/r, San Niccolò ☎ 055/243647 ⊕ www.negronibar.com) teems with well-dressed young Florentines at happy hour. **Rex** (✉ Via Fiesolana 23–25/r, Santa Croce ☎ 055/2480331) attracts a trendy, artsy clientele. **Zoe** (✉ Via dei Renai 13/r, San Niccolò ☎ 055/243111) calls itself a "caffetteria," and while coffee may indeed be served, twentysomething Florentines flock here for the fine (and expensive) cocktails. Here's people-watching at its very best, done while listening to the latest CDs imported from England. **Zona 15** (✉ Via del Castellaccia 53-55/r [Piazza Brunelleschi], Duomo ☎ 055/211678) is coolly chic with its pale interior, blond woodwork, and metallic surfaces. Lunch, dinner, cocktails, and live music draw Florentine cognoscenti and others.

Nightclubs

BeBop (✉ Via dei Servi 76/r, Santissima Annunziata ☎ No phone) has loud, live music, and Beatles nights. **Central Park** (✉ Via Fosso Macinante 2 ☎ 055/353505) is a great spot for those who want to put on their dancing shoes for some house and hip-hop music. **Jazz Club** (✉ Via Nuova de' Caccini 3, corner of Borgo Pinti, Santa Croce ☎ 055/2479700) puts on live music in a smoky basement. When last call's come and gone, go where the bartenders unwind after their shift. **Loch Ness** (✉ Via de' Benci 19/r, Santa Croce ☎ No phone) keeps the drinks flowing until 5 AM. Live music, a well-stocked bar, and a cavernous underground space make for a rollicking good evening at **Loonees** (✉ Via Porta Rossa 15, Piazza della Repubblica ☎ 055/212249).

Maracaná (✉ Via Faenza 4, Santa Maria Novella ☎ 055/210298) is a restaurant and pizzeria featuring Brazilian specialties; at 11 PM it transforms itself into a cabaret floor show, and then into a disco until 4 AM. Book a table if you want to eat. **Meccanò** (✉ Le Cascine, Viale degli Olmi 1 ☎ 055/331371) is a multimedia experience in a high-tech disco with a late-night restaurant. People sip cocktails against a backdrop of exotic flowers, leopard-print chairs and chintz, and red walls and floors on the two crowded floors at **Montecarla** (✉ Via de' Bardi 2, San Niccolò ☎ 055/2340259). **Space Electronic** (✉ Via Palazzuolo 37, Santa Maria Novella ☎ 055/293082) has two floors, with karaoke downstairs and an enormous disco upstairs. It's full of Italian military types prowling for young foreign women. **Yab** (✉ Via Sassetti 5/r, Piazza della Repubblica ☎ 055/215160) celebrated its 25th anniversary in 2004; it never seems to go out of style.

SPORTS & THE OUTDOORS

Biking

Bikes are a great way to tour the centro storico, as the town center has no hills. Patience, however, must be maintained while dodging hordes of tourists and those pesky *motorini* (mopeds). The Cascine, a former Medici hunting ground turned into a large public park with paved pathways and lots of trees, admits no cars. The historic center can be circumnavigated via bike paths lining the *viali,* a road that runs along the center's circumference. **Florence by Bike** (⊠ Via San Zanobi 120-122/r, San Lorenzo ☎ 055/488992 ⊕ www.florencebybike.it) leads day trips into Chianti; you start on bicycles in Florence's centro storico in the morning, and return there in the late afternoon. **I Bike Italy** (⊠ Borgo degli Albizi 11, Santa Croce ☎☎ 055/2342371 ⊕ www.ibikeitaly.com) runs one-day tours of the countryside outside Florence.

Health Clubs

Palestra Ricciardi (⊠ Borgo Pinti 75, Santa Croce ☎ 055/2478444 or 055/2478462) has stretching, aerobics, step aerobics, and bodybuilding classes; it also has free weights, stationary bikes, treadmills, and rowing machines. Daily admission is €10, and a monthly pass is €82.

Running

Don't even think of running on the narrow city streets, as tour buses and triple-parked Alfa Romeos leave precious little space for pedestrians. Instead, head for **Le Cascine,** the park along the Arno at the western end of the city. You can run to Le Cascine along the Lungarno (stay on the sidewalk), or take Bus 17 from the Duomo. A cinder track lies on the hillside below **Piazzale Michelangelo,** across the Arno from the city center. The locker rooms are reserved for members, so come ready to run. A scenic, but not serene, run can be had along the Lungarno, those streets that frame both sides of the Arno.

Soccer

Italians are passionate about *calcio* (soccer), and the Florentines are no exception; indeed, *tifosi* (fans) of Fiorentina, the local team, are fervent supporters. The team plays home matches at the **Stadio Comunale** (Municipal Stadium; ⊠ Top of Viale Manfredo Fanti, northeast of the center) in Campo di Marte, usually on Sunday from late August to May. Tickets are sold at the ticket booth **Chiosco degli Sportivi** (⊠ Via Anselmi, southwest side of Piazza della Repubblica ☎ 055/292363). A medieval version of soccer, **Calcio Storico,** is played around the Festa di San Giovanni on June 24 each year by teams dressed in costumes representing the six Florence neighborhoods. Games take place in Piazza Santa Croce, where they have allegedly been played since the middle of the 16th century.

SHOPPING

Window-shopping in Florence is like visiting an enormous contemporary-art gallery, for many of today's greatest Italian artists are fashion designers, and most keep shops in Florence. Discerning shoppers may find bargains in the street markets. Shops are generally open 9–1 and 3:30–7:30 and are closed Sunday and Monday morning most of the year. Summer (June–September) hours are usually 9–1 and 4–8, and some shops close Saturday afternoon instead of Monday morning. When looking for addresses of shops, you'll see two color-coded numbering systems on each street. The red numbers are commercial addresses and are indicated, for example, as 31/r. The blue or black numbers are residential addresses. Most shops take major credit cards and ship purchases, but because of possible delays it's wise to take your purchases with you.

Markets

Le Cascine's open-air market is held every Tuesday morning. Food, bargain clothing, and gadgets are sold. The **Mercato Centrale** (⊠ Piazza del Mercato Centrale, San Lorenzo) is a huge indoor food market that has a staggering selection of things edible. The clothing and leather-goods stalls of the **Mercato di San Lorenzo** in the streets next to the church of San Lorenzo have bargains for shoppers on a budget. It's possible to strike gold at the **Mercato di Sant'Ambrogio** (⊠ Piazza Ghiberti, off Via dei Macci, Santa Croce), where clothing stalls abut the fruit and vegetables. Every Thursday morning from September through June, the covered loggia in Piazza Repubblica hosts a **Mercato dei Fiori** (⊠ Piazza Repubblica); it's awash in a lively riot of plants and flowers. If you're looking for cheery, inexpensive trinkets to take home, you might want to stop and roam through the stalls under the loggia of the **Mercato del Porcellino** (⊠ Via Por Santa Maria at Via Porta Rossa, Piazza della Repubblica). You can find bargains at the **Piazza dei Ciompi flea market** (⊠ Sant'Ambrogio, Santa Croce) Monday through Saturday and on the last Sunday of the month. The second Sunday of every month brings the **Spirito flea market.** On the third Sunday of the month, vendors at the Fierucola organic fest sell such delectables as honeys, jams, spice mixes, and fresh vegetables.

Shopping Districts

Florence's most fashionable shops are concentrated in the center of town. The fanciest designer shops are mainly on **Via Tornabuoni** and **Via della Vigna Nuova.** The city's largest concentrations of antiques shops are on **Borgo Ognissanti** and the Oltrarno's **Via Maggio.** The **Ponte Vecchio** houses reputable but very expensive jewelry shops, as it has since the 16th century. The area near **Santa Croce** is the heart of the leather merchants' district.

Specialty Stores

Antiques

Galleria Luigi Bellini (⊠ Lungarno Soderini 5, Lungarno South ☎ 055/214031) claims to be Italy's oldest antiques dealer, which may be true, since father Mario Bellini was responsible for instituting Florence's international antiques biennial. **Giovanni Pratesi** (⊠ Via Maggio 13, Santo Spirito ☎ 055/2396568) specializes in Italian antiques; in this case, it's furniture, with some fine paintings, sculpture, and decorative objects turning up from time to time. Vying with Galleria Luigi Bellini as one of Florence's oldest antiques dealers, **Guido Bartolozzi** (⊠ Via Maggio 18/r, Santo Spirito ☎ 055/215602) deals predominately in period Florentine pieces. At **Paolo Paoletti** (⊠ Via Maggio 30/r, Palazzo Pitti ☎ 055/214728), look for Florentine antiques with an emphasis on Medici-era objects from the 15th and 16th centuries. **Roberto Innocenti e C. S.N.C.** (⊠ Via Matteo Palmieri 29/r, Santa Croce ☎ 055/2478668) specializes in more recent antiques, like art deco, art nouveau, and Jugendstil.

Books & Paper

Alberto Cozzi (⊠ Via del Parione 35/r, Santa Maria Novella ☎055/294968) keeps an extensive line of Florentine papers and paper products. The artisans in the shop rebind and restore books and works on paper. **Alice's Masks Art Studio** (⊠ Via Faenza 72/r, Santa Maria Novella ☎ 055/287370) preserves the centuries-old technique of papier-mâché masks. On hand are masks typical of 18th-century Venice, as well as some more whimsical ones: a mask of Vincent van Gogh is painted with brushstrokes reminiscent of his own inimitable style. **Centro Di** (⊠ Via dei Renai 20/r, San Niccolò ☎ 055/2342666) publishes art books and exhibition catalogs for some of the most important organizations in Europe. One of Florence's oldest paper-goods stores, **Giulio Giannini e Figlio** (⊠ Piazza Pitti 37/r ☎ 055/212621) is *the* place to buy the marbleized stock, which comes in many shapes and sizes, from flat sheets to boxes and even pencils. Photograph albums, frames, diaries, and other objects dressed in handmade paper can be purchased at **Il Torchio** (⊠ Via dei Bardi 17, San Niccolò ☎055/2342862). The stuff is high-quality, and the prices lower than usual. **La Tartaruga** (⊠ Borgo Albizi 60/r, Santa Croce ☎ 055/2340845) sells brightly colored, recycled paper in lots of guises (such as calendars and stationery), as well as toys for children. Long one of Florence's best art-book shops, **Libreria Salimbeni** (⊠ Via Matteo Palmieri 14–16/r, Santa Croce ☎055/2340905) has an outstanding selection. **Pineider** (⊠ Piazza della Signoria 13/r, Piazza della Signoria ☎ 055/284655) has shops throughout the world, but the business began in Florence and still does all its printing here. Stationery and business cards are the mainstay, but the stores also sell fine leather desk accessories as well as a less stuffy, more lighthearted line of products.

Clothing

The usual fashion suspects—Prada, Gucci, Versace, to name but a few—all have shops in Florence.

The sleek, classic **Giorgio Armani** boutique (⊠ Via Tornabuoni 48/r, Santa Maria Novella ☎ 055/219041) is a centerpiece of the dazzling high-end shops clustered in this part of town. **Bernardo** (⊠ Via Porta Rossa 87/r, Piazza della Repubblica ☎ 055/283333) specializes in men's trousers, cashmere sweaters, and shirts with details like mother-of-pearl buttons. **Cabó** (⊠ Via Porta Rossa 77-79/r, Piazza della Repubblica ☎ 055/215774) carries that sinuous Missoni knitwear as well as some of the Fendi line. Trendy **Diesel** (⊠ Via dei Lamberti 13/r, Piazza della Signoria ☎ 055/2399963) started in Vicenza; its gear is on the "must-have" list of many self-respecting Italian teens. The outlandish designs of native son **Roberto Cavalli** (⊠ Via Tornabuoni 83/r, Santa Maria Novella ☎ 055/2396226) appeal to Hollywood celebrities and to those who want a more-expensive Britney Spears look. **Emporio Armani** (⊠ Piazza Strozzi 16/r, Santa Maria Novella ☎ 055/284315), sister store of the Giorgio Armani boutique, has slightly more affordable, funky, nightclub- and office-friendly garb. **Prada** (⊠ Via Tornabuoni 67/r, Santa Maria Novella ☎ 055/267471), known to mix schoolmarmish sensibility with sexy cuts and funky fabrics, appeals to an exclusive clientele. The aristocratic Marchese di Barsento, **Emilio Pucci** (⊠ Via Tornabuoni 20-22/r, Santa Maria Novella ☎ 055/2658082), became an international name in the late 1950s when the stretch ski clothes he designed for himself caught on with the dolce vita crowd—his pseudopsychedelic prints and "palazzo pajamas" became all the rage. You can take home a custom-made suit or dress from **Giorgio Vannini** (⊠ Via Borgo Santi Apostoli 43/r, Santa Maria Novella ☎ 055/293037), who has a showroom for his prêt-à-porter designs. The signature couture collection of **Gianni Versace** (⊠ Via Tornabuoni 13–15/r, Santa Maria Novella ☎ 055/2396167) revolutionized the catwalk with rubber dresses and purple leather pants; sister Donatella continues the line of high-priced, over-the-top couture for rock stars and movie celebs. **Versus** (⊠ Via Vigna Nuova 36–38/r, Santa Maria Novella ☎ 055/217619) is the more playful—and more affordable—Versace line.

The intrepid shopper might want to check out some other, lesser-known shops. Young Florentines have a soft spot in their hearts for the clingy, one-of-a-kind frocks designed by Angela Baldi at her tiny shop, **Babele** (⊠ Borgo Pinti 34/r, Santa Croce ☎ 055/244729). **Blunuata** (⊠ Via del Proconsolo 69/r, Duomo ☎ 055/212460) sells casual, well-made clothes for men and women; it's the closest Italy comes to Gap-style clothes. Gals with a sense of derring-do and fashion flair should check out the stockings and tights at **Emilio Cavallini** (⊠ Via della Vigna Nuova 24/r, Santa Maria Novella ☎ 055/2382789). They come in outrageous and stylish prints. **Geraldine Tayar** (⊠ Sdrucciolo de Pitti 6/r, Palazzo Pitti ☎ 055/290405) makes clothing and accessories of her own design in eclectic fabric combinations. **Il Guardaroba/Stock House** (⊠ Borgo Albizi 78/r, Santa Croce ☎ 055/2340271) is where savvy Florentines shop for designer clothes at affordable prices. If you're looking for something hot to wear to the clubs, check out **Liu-Jo** (⊠ Via Calimala 14/r, Piazza della Repubblica ☎ 055/216164). The surreal window displays at **Luisa Via Roma** (⊠ Via Roma 19–21/r, Duomo ☎ 055/217826) hint at the trendy yet tasteful clothing inside this fascinating, *alta moda* (high-style) boutique, which stocks the world's top designers as well as Luisa's own line. **Maçel** (⊠ Via Guicciardini 128/r, Palazzo Pitti ☎ 055/287355) has collections by lesser-known Italian designers, many of whom use the same factories as the A-list. The women's clothing here is sophisticated and sexy. **Paolo Pardini** (⊠ Borgo Albizzi 70/r, Santa Croce ☎ 055/2001340) has a refined line of women's knitware in cashmere and other wools. Florentine designer **Patrizia Pepe** (⊠ Piazza San Giovanni 12/r, Duomo ☎ 055/264056) has body-conscious clothes perfect for all ages, especially for women with a tiny streak of rebelliousness. Members of the junior set desiring to look well clad, Florentine style, should consider stopping at **Piccolo Slam** (⊠ Via dei Lamberti 13/r, Piazza della Signoria ☎ 055/214504). **Principe** (⊠ Via del Sole 2, Santa Maria Novella ☎ 055/292764) is a Florentine institution with casual clothes for men, women, and children at far-from-casual prices. It also has a great housewares department. For cutting-edge fashion, the fun and funky window displays at **Spazio A** (✉ Via Porta Rossa 109-115/r, Piazza della Repubblica ☎ 055/212995) merit a stop. The shop carries such well-known designers as Alberta Ferretti and Narciso Rodriguez, as well as lesser-known Italian, English, and French designers.

Gifts & Housewares

Aromatherapy has been elevated to an art form at **Antica Officina del Farmacista Dr. Vranjes** (✉ Borgo La Croce 44/r, Santa Croce ☎ 055/241748 ✉ Via San Gallo 63/r ☎ 055/494537). Dr. Vranjes makes scents for the body and for the house. For housewares, nothing beats **Bartolini** (✉ Via dei Servi 30/r, Santissima Annunziata ☎ 055/211895) for well-designed practical items. **Brandimarte** (✉ Via L. Bartolini 18/r, Santo Spirito/San Frediano ☎ 055/2286242), a silversmith workshop, can be toured by prior arrangement; it makes everything from salt and pepper shakers to gigantic serving trays, for sale in the attached showroom. **La Bottega dell'Olio** (✉ Piazza del Limbo 2/r, Santa Maria Novella ☎ 055/2670468) sells olive oil in all its permutations. The shop, which is tucked into a small piazza, has a great collection of fine olive oils, as well as bath products made from olive oil. **La Scagliola** (✉ Piazza Pitti14/r, Palazzo Pitti ☎ 055/211523) practices the 17th-century art of scagliola, a less-expensive alternative to pietre dure; it's a composite that imitates marble, used here to form handsome tabletops, boxes, and picture frames. **Mandragora Art Store** (✉ Piazza del Duomo 50/r, Duomo ☎ 055/292559) is one of the first attempts in Florence to cash in on the museum-store craze. Florence has been famous for its straw products for centuries, and **Martini** (✉ Via S. Veridiana 6/r, Santa Croce ☎ 055/2480612) has been producing fine baskets, trays, and other household goods since 1921.

The essence of a Florentine holiday is captured in the sachets of the **Officina Profumo Farmaceutica di Santa Maria Novella** (✉ Via della Scala 16, Santa Maria Novella ☎055/216276), an art nouveau emporium of herbal cosmetics and soaps that are made following centuries-old recipes created by friars. **Paolo Carandini** (✉ Via de' Macci 73/r, Santa Croce ☎ 055/245397) works exclusively in leather, producing exquisite objects such as picture frames, jewelry boxes, and desk accessories. **Pitti Mosaici** (✉ Piazza de' Pitti 23/r, Palazzo Pitti ☎ 055/282127) continues the pietre dure tradition that was all the rage of 16th-century Florence. Stones are worked into exquisite tables, pictures, and jewelry. **Rampini Ceramiche** (✉ Borgo Ognissanti 32/34, Lungarno North ☎ 055/219720) sells exquisitely crafted, and expensive, ceramics. **Sbigoli Terrecotte** (✉ Via Sant'Egidio 4/r, Santa Croce ☎ 055/2479713) carries traditional Tuscan terra-cotta and ceramic vases, pots, and cups and saucers. What to get that gal (or guy) who has everything? Drop into the **Shabby Shop** (✉ Via del Parione 12/r, Santa Maria Novella ☎ 055/294826), which specializes in antique silver—mostly English, dating from George I to George III (1698–1811), and jewelry from the 1950s. For the record: there's nothing shabby about this shop.

Jewelry

Carlo Piccini (⊠ Ponte Vecchio 31/r, Piazza della Signoria, ☎ 055/292030) has been around for several generations, selling antique jewelry as well as making pieces to order; you can also get old jewelry reset here. **Cassetti** (⊠ Ponte Vecchio 54/r, Piazza della Signoria, ☎ 055/2396028) combines precious and semiprecious stones and metals in contemporary settings. **Gatto Bianco** (⊠ Borgo Santi Apostoli 12/r, Santa Maria Novella ☎ 055/282989) has breathtakingly beautiful jewelry worked in semiprecious and precious stones; the feel is completely contemporary. **Gherardi** (⊠ Ponte Vecchio 5/r, Piazza della Signoria ☎ 055/211809), Florence's king of coral, has the city's largest selection of finely crafted pieces, as well as cultured pearls, jade, and turquoise. **La Gazza Ladra** (⊠ Piazza Salvemini 6, Santa Croce ☎ 055/2466008) is an off-the-beaten-path and young-at-heart shop with affordable necklaces and rings, mostly in silver. The two women who run **Oreria** (⊠ Borgo Pinti, 87/a, Santa Croce ☎ 055/244708) create divine designs using silver and semiprecious stones. Send suitors to purchase significant gifts here. One of Florence's oldest jewelers, **Tiffany** (⊠ Via Tornabuoni 25/r, Santa Maria Novella ☎ 055/215506) has supplied Italian (and other) royalty with finely crafted gems for centuries. Its selection of antique-looking classics has been updated with a selection of contemporary silver.

Linens & Fabrics

Antico Setificio Fiorentina (⊠ Via L. Bartolini 4, Santo Spirito/San Frediano ☎ 055/213861) has been providing damasks and other fine fabrics for royalty and those who aspire to it since 1786. Visits by appointment are preferred. **Blue Home** (⊠ Vicolo dell'Oro 12/r, Santa Maria Novella ☎ 055/2658262) sells sumptuous fabrics which can be rendered into sofas, rugs, and other home furnishings to create divinely inspired interiors. Antique and contemporary rugs are also on hand. **Loretta Caponi** (⊠ Piazza Antinori 4/r, Santa Maria Novella ☎ 055/213668) is synonymous with Florentine embroidery, and the luxury lace, linens, and lingerie have earned the eponymous signora worldwide renown. **Sant'Jacopo Show** (⊠ Borgo Sant'Jacopo 66/r, Santo Spirito ☎ 055/2396912) is an offbeat shop specializing in mannequins, decorations, and shop fixtures. Luxurious silks, beaded fabrics, lace, wool, and tweeds can be purchased at **Valli** (⊠ Via Strozzi 4/r, Piazza della Repubblica ☎ 055/282485). It carries fabrics created by Armani, Valentino, and other high-end designers. **Valmar** (⊠ Via Porta Rossa 53/r, Piazza della Repubblica ☎ 055/284493) is filled with tangled spools of cords, ribbons, and fringes, plus buttons, tassels, sachets, and hand-embroidered cushions you can take home—or bring in your own fabric, choose the adornments, and you can have a cushion or table runner made.

Outlets

The **Fendi Outlet** (⊠ Via Pian dell'Isola 66 ☎ 055/834981) is about a half-hour car or train ride from Florence. One-stop bargain shopping awaits at **The Mall** (⊠ Via Europa 8 ☎ 055/8657775), where the stores sell goods by such names as Bottega Veneta, Giorgio Armani, Loro Piana,

Sergio Rossi, and the decidedly non-Italian Yves St. Laurent. Cognoscenti drive or taxi about 45 minutes out of town to the **Prada Outlet** (⊠ Levanella Spacceo, Estrada Statale 69, Montevarchi ☎ 055/91911).

Shoes & Leather Accessories

The colorful, foot-friendly shoes at **Camper** (⊠ Via Por Santa Maria 47/r, Piazza della Signoria ☎ 055/2670342) are made in Spain, but they cost less here than they do in the United States. The ultimate fine leathers are crafted into classic shapes at **Casadei** (⊠ Via Tornabuoni 33/r, Santa Maria Novella ☎ 055/287240), winding up as women's shoes and bags. The late Salvatore Ferragamo earned his fortune custom-making shoes for famous feet, especially Hollywood stars. The classy **Ferragamo** store (⊠ Via Tornabuoni 2/r, Santa Maria Novella ☎ 055/292123), in a 13th-century Renaissance palazzo, displays designer clothing and accessories, but elegant footwear still underlies the Ferragamo success. **Lily of Florence** (⊠ Via Guicciardini 2/r, Palazzo Pitti ☎ 055/294748) has high-quality, classic shoe designs at reasonable prices and in American sizes. **Pollini** (⊠ Via Calimala 12/r, Piazza della Repubblica ☎ 055/214738) has beautifully crafted shoes and leather accessories for those willing to pay that little bit extra. For sheer creativity in both color and design, check out the shoes at **Sergio Rossi** (⊠ Via Roma 15/r, Duomo ☎ 055/294873) and fantasize about where you'd wear them.

Beltrami (⊠ Via della Vigna Nuova 70/r, Santa Maria Novella ☎ 055/287779), which sells shoes and some apparel, has long been synonymous with style; classic looks are beautifully updated. **Cellerini** (⊠ Via del Sole 37/r, Santa Maria Novella ☎ 055/282533) is an institution in a city where it seems that just about everybody wears an expensive leather jacket. **Coccinelle** (⊠ Via Por Santa Maria 49/r, Piazza della Signoria ☎ 055/2398782) sells leather accessories in bold colors and funky designs. **Furla** (⊠ Via Calzaiuoli 47/r, Piazza della Repubblica ☎ 055/2382883) makes beautiful leather bags and wallets in up-to-the-minute designs. **Giotti** (⊠ Piazza Ognissanti 3–4/r, Lungarno North ☎ 055/294265) has a full line of leather goods, including clothing. At peak tourist times, status-conscious shoppers often stand in line outside **Gucci** (⊠ Via Tornabuoni 73/r, Santa Maria Novella ☎ 055/264011), ready to buy anything with the famous initials. Beware, however, of shop assistants with severe attitude problems. **Il Bisonte** (⊠ Via del Parione 31/r, off Via della Vigna Nuova, Santa Maria Novella ☎ 055/215722) is known for its natural-looking leather goods, all stamped with the store's bison symbol. **Madova** (⊠ Via Guicciardini 1/r, Palazzo Pitti ☎ 055/2396526) has high-quality leather gloves in a rainbow of colors and a choice of linings (silk, cashmere, and unlined). Shoe styles at **Romano** (⊠ Via Speziali 10/r, Piazza della Repubblica ☎ 055/216535) span the staid to the offbeat at appealing prices.

A consortium of leatherworkers plies its trade at **Scuola del Cuoio** (⊠ Piazza Santa Croce 16 ☎ 055/355644 ⊕ www.leatherschool.com), in the former dormitory of the convent of Santa Croce; high-quality, fairly priced jackets, belts, and purses are sold here.

SIDE TRIPS FROM FLORENCE

Fiesole

A half-day excursion to Fiesole, in the hills 8 km (5 mi) above Florence, gives you a pleasant respite from museums and a wonderful view of the city. From here the view of the Duomo, with Brunelleschi's powerful cupola, gives you a new appreciation for what the Renaissance accomplished. Fiesole began life as an ancient Etruscan and later Roman village that held some power until it succumbed to barbarian invasions. Eventually it gave up its independence in exchange for Florence's protection. The medieval cathedral, ancient Roman amphitheater, and lovely old villas behind garden walls are clustered on a series of hilltops. A walk around Fiesole can take from one to two or three hours, depending on how far you stroll from the main piazza.

The trip from Florence by car or bus takes 20–30 minutes. Take Bus 7 from the Stazione Centrale di Santa Maria Novella, Piazza San Marco, or the Duomo. (You can also get on and off the bus at San Domenico.) There are several possible routes for the two-hour walk from central Florence to Fiesole. One route begins in a residential area of Florence called Salviatino (Via Barbacane, near Piazza Edison, on the Bus 7 route), and after a short time, offers peeks over garden walls of beautiful villas, as well as the view over your shoulder at the panorama of Florence in the valley.

The **Duomo** reveals a stark medieval interior. In the raised presbytery, the **Cappella Salutati** was frescoed by 15th-century artist Cosimo Rosselli, but it was his contemporary, sculptor Mino da Fiesole (1430–84), who put the town on the artistic map. The Madonna on the altarpiece and the tomb of Bishop Salutati are fine examples of the artist's work. ⊠ *Piazza Mino da Fiesole* ☎ *055/59400* ⊗ *Nov.–Mar., daily 7:30–noon and 2–5; Apr.–Oct., daily 7:30–noon and 3–6.*

The beautifully preserved 2,000-seat **Anfiteatro Romano** (Roman Amphitheater), near the Duomo, dates from the 1st century BC and is still used for summer concerts. To the right of the amphitheater are the remains of the **Terme Romani** (Roman Baths), where you can see the gymnasium, hot and cold baths, and rectangular chamber where the water was heated. A beautifully designed **Museo Archeologico,** an intricate series of levels connected by elevators, is built amid the ruins and contains objects dating from as early as 2000 BC. The nearby **Museo Bandini** is a small collection of interesting paintings. It's filled with the private collection of Canon Angelo Maria Bandini (1726–1803); he fancied 13th- to 15th-century Florentine paintings, terra-cotta pieces, and wood sculpture, which he later bequeathed to the Diocese of Fiesole. ⊠ *Via Portigiani 1* ☎ *055/59477* ⊠ *€6.50, includes access to the archaeological park and museums* ⊗ *Apr.–Sept., daily 9:30–7; Oct.–Mar., Wed.–Mon. 9:30–5.*

The hilltop church of **San Francesco** has a good view of Florence and the plain below from its terrace and benches. Halfway up the hill you'll see sloping steps to the right; they lead to a lovely wooded park with trails that loop out and back to the church.

If you really want to stretch your legs, walk 4 km (2½ mi) toward the center of Florence along Via Vecchia Fiesolana, a narrow lane in use since Etruscan times, to the church of **San Domenico.** Sheltered in the church is the *Madonna and Child with Saints* by Fra Angelico, who was a Dominican friar here. ⊠ *Piazza San Domenico, off Via Giuseppe Mantellini* ☎ *055/59230* 🎫 *Free* ☉ *Daily 8–noon.*

From the church of San Domenico, it's a five-minute walk northwest to the **Badia Fiesolana,** which was the original cathedral of Fiesole. Dating back to the 11th century, it was first run by Camaldolese monks before going to the Benedictines and then the Augustinians. Thanks to Cosimo il Vecchio, the complex was substantially restructured. The facade, never completed due to the death of Cosimo, contains elements of its original Romanesque decoration. The attached convent once housed Cosimo's valued manuscripts; today it's the site of the European Institute, for pre- and postdoctoral studies. Its mid-15th-century cloister is well worth a look. ⊠ *Via della Badia dei Roccettini 11* ☎ *055/ 59155* ☉ *Weekdays 9–6, Sat. 9:30–12:30.*

Where to Stay & Eat

¢–$$ ✕ **San Domenico.** Three-quarters of the way up the hill to Fiesole, this rather industrial-looking spot has tasty *pizze* as well as pastas. If you're hiking in the nearby hills, or going to see the Fra Angelico at the church of San Domenico, this is a perfect place to break for lunch. Outdoor seating in the summer looks directly on to a somewhat busy two-lane road. No matter: the air's still better here than in town and that makes the pizza taste so much better. ⊠ *Piazza San Domenico* ☎ *055/59182* ▤ *AE, DC, MC, V* ☉ *Closed Mon.*

$$$$ 🏨 **Villa San Michele.** The cypress-lined driveway provides an elegant preamble to this incredibly gorgeous (and very expensive) hotel nestled in the hills of Fiesole. The 16th-century building was originally a Franciscan convent designed by Santi di Tito. Not a single false note is struck in the reception area (formerly the chapel), the dining rooms (a covered cloister and former refectory), or the tasteful antiques and art that decorate the rooms. The open-air loggia, where lunch and dinner are served, provides one of the most stunning views of Florence—a good thing, too, as the food is overpriced and bland. ⊠ *Via Doccia 4, 50014* ☎ *055/ 59451* 🖷 *055/5678250* ⊕ *www.villasanmichele.com* ➷ *19 rooms, 26 suites* ⌂ *Restaurant, room service, in-room data ports, in-room fax, in-room safes, minibars, cable TV with movies, in-room VCRs, pool, gym, mountain bikes, piano bar, babysitting, dry cleaning, laundry service, concierge, Internet, free parking, some pets allowed, no-smoking rooms* ▤ *AE, DC, MC, V* ☉ *Closed Dec.–Easter* ❖Ⅰ *CP.*

$$ 🏨 **Villa Aurora.** The attractive hotel on the main piazza takes advantage of its hilltop spot, with beautiful views in many of the rooms, some of which are on two levels with beamed ceilings and balconies. The building, constructed as a theater in 1860, was transformed into a hotel in the late 19th century. It's fit for queens, and quite a few of them—Queen Victoria and Margherita di Savoia among others—have stayed here.

Rooms are sophisticated but understated, as is the hotel. ⊠ *Piazza Mino da Fiesole 39, 50014* ☎ *055/59100* 🖷 *055/59587* ⊕ *www. aurorafiesole.com* ⇨ *23 rooms, 2 suites* 🔥 *Restaurant, cable TV, bar, Internet, meeting room, some pets allowed* ⊟ *AE, DC, MC, V* ⦿❘ *BP.*

Nightlife & the Arts

From June through August, **Estate Fiesolana** (⊠ Teatro Romano ☎ 055/5978403 ⊕ www.comune.fiesole.fi.it) is a festival of theater, music, dance, and film that takes place in Fiesole's churches and archaeological park.

Settignano

When Florence is overcrowded and hot—that is, for most of the summer—this village, a 20-minute car or bus trip east of Florence, is particularly appealing. Its biggest claim to fame is that it was the birthplace of many noteworthy artists, including the sculptors Desiderio di Settignano (circa 1428–64), Antonio (1427–79) and Bernardo (1409–64) Rossellino, and Bartolomeo Ammannati (1511–92). Michelangelo's wet nurse was the wife of a stonecutter in Settignano, and to her he attributed his later calling in life. Alas, though these artists' works no longer adorn their native town (Florence and other cities lay claim to them), Settignano is worth a visit simply to breathe its fresh air, walk its tiny streets, and sit in its small **piazza** with an aperitivo.

To get to the village, take Bus 10 from Florence, from the station at Santa Maria Novella or at Piazza San Marco, and ride it all the way to the end of the line, the *capolinea*. It will put you in the middle of Settignano's small piazzetta.

A 20-minute walk through scenic countryside from the piazza leads to the **Oratorio della Vannella** (⊠ Località Corbignano). The exterior, dating from 1719–21, is unremarkable, but the fresco of the *Madonna and Child Enthroned* (circa 1470), attributed to a young Sandro Botticelli (1445–1510), is housed here. It's in sad shape but is said to work miracles, and therefore was venerated by the local stonecutters and sculptors. To get here, take Via Desiderio di Settignano, walk around the very modern cemetery, turn left, and then follow the narrow path lined with olive trees. The oratory is open for 6 PM mass the last Sunday of each month; otherwise, you can call the tourist-information office in Fiesole (☎ 055/598720) to open the doors.

Where to Stay & Eat

$–$$ ✕ **Osvaldo.** If you're making the trip to Settignano, this is a great dining option (get off Bus 10 at the stop called Ponte a Mensola). The small, unassuming family-run trattoria is situated along a street and a tiny stream; if you sit outside (there are no views, alas), you might hear the trickle of the stream. The food is terrific, and though it is described as *cucina casalinga* (home cooking), only the portions are homestyle. Service is prompt and courteous. Count yourself lucky if the menu includes *fritti di fiori di zucca* (fried zucchini flowers)—probably the lightest fried food you'll find anywhere. ⊠ *Via G. D'Annunzio 51/r* ☎ *055/603972* ⊟ *AE, DC, MC, V* ⊘ *Closed Wed. No lunch Tues.*

$ ✕ **Trattoria Casalinga da Graziella.** Though it's a very simple, bare-bones trattoria, the *cucina casalinga* is tasty and inexpensive, and the service is courteous. Generously portioned primi stick to the ribs—the *tortelloni alla mugellana* (potato-stuffed ravioli with a tomato meat sauce) is perfectly executed. The roast piglet, cooked Sardinian style, must be reserved one night in advance. ⊠ *Via Cave di Maiano 20* ☎ *055/599963* ▭ *MC, V* ⊙ *Closed Tues.*

$ ▦ **Fattoria di Maiano.** In the foothills between Florence and Fiesole are these lovely apartments, which sleep 4 to 11 people and rent by the week. Many apartments are in a former convent, and some are scattered around the farm; all have wood floors, simple and sturdy furniture, and very modern kitchens, and most have splendid views onto olive groves (olive oil is produced by the Fattoria owners). ⊠ *Via Benedetto da Maiano 11, 50016* ☎ *055/599600* ▤ *055/599640* ⊕ *www.fattoriadimaiano. com* ⇨ *8 apartments* ⚭ *Restaurant, kitchenettes, some pets allowed; no a/c in some rooms* ▭ *DC, MC, V.*

Gracious Gardens Around Florence

Like any well-heeled Florentine, you, too, can get away from Florence's hustle and bustle by heading for the hills. Take a break from city sightseeing to enjoy the gardens and villas set like jewels in the hills around the city. Villa di Castello and Villa La Petraia, both northwest of Florence's historic center in Castello, can be explored in one trip. The Italian garden at Villa Gamberaia is an 8-km (5-mi) jaunt east of the center near Settignano. Plan for a full-day excursion, picnic lunch included, if visiting all three gardens. Spring and summer are the ideal times to visit, when flowers are in glorious bloom. Though Villa Demidoff, originally a Medici country house, is in somewhat dilapidated shape, it's worth a trip to see Giambologna's *Appenino*. For a prime taste of Medici living, venture farther afield to the family's Villa Medicea in Poggio a Caiano, south of Prato (⇨ Chapter 4).

Villa di Castello

A fortified residence in the Middle Ages, Villa di Castello was rebuilt in the 15th century by the Medici. The Accademia della Crusca, a 400-year-old institution that is the official arbiter of the Italian language, now occupies the palace, which isn't open to the public; the gardens, however, are the main attraction. From the villa entrance, walk uphill through the 19th-century park set above part of the formal garden. You'll reach the terrace, which affords a good view of the geometric layout of the garden below; stairs on either side descend to the parterre.

Though the original garden design has been altered somewhat over the centuries, the allegorical theme of animals, devised by Tribolo in 1537 to the delight of the Medici, is still evident. The artificial cave, Grotta degli Animali (Animal Grotto), displays an imaginative menagerie of sculpted animals by Giambologna and his assistants. An Ammannati sculpture, a figure of an old man representing the Appenines, is at the center of a pond on the terrace overlooking the garden. Two bronze sculptures by Ammannati, centerpieces of fountains studding the garden, can now be seen indoors in Villa La Petraia. Allow about 45 minutes to visit the garden; you can easily visit Villa La Petraia from here, making for a four-hour trip in total. The palace is closed to the public.

To get to Villa di Castello by car, head northwest from Florence on Via Reginaldo Giuliani (also known as Via Sestese) to Castello, about 6 km (4 mi) northwest of the city center in the direction of Sesto Fiorentino; follow signs to Villa di Castello. Or take Bus 28 from the city center and tell the driver you want to get off at Villa di Castello; from the stop, walk north about ½ km (¼ mi) up the tree-lined allée from the main road. ⊠ *Via di Castello 47, Castello* ☎ *055/454791* ✉ *€2, includes entrance to Villa La Petraia* ⊙ *Garden Nov.–Feb., daily 8:15–4:30; Mar.–Oct., daily 9–7. Closed 2nd and 3rd Mon. of month* ☞ *Palace closed to public.*

Villa La Petraia

The splendidly planted gardens of Villa La Petraia sit high above the Arno plain with a sweeping view of Florence. The villa was built around a medieval tower and reconstructed after it was purchased by the Medici sometime after 1530. Virtually the only trace of the Medici having lived here are the 17th-century courtyard frescoes depicting glorious episodes from the clan's history. In the 1800s the villa served as a hunting lodge of King Vittorio Emanuele II (1820–78), who kept his mistress here while Florence was the temporary capital of the newly united country of Italy.

The garden—also altered in the 1800s—and the vast park behind the palace suggest a splendid contrast between formal and natural landscapes. Allow 60 to 90 minutes to explore the park and gardens, plus 30 minutes for the guided tour of the so-called museum, the villa interior. This property is best visited after the Villa di Castello.

To get here by car, follow directions to Villa di Castello, but take the right off Via Reginaldo Giuliani, following the sign for Villa La Petraia. You can walk from Villa di Castello to Villa La Petraia in about 15 minutes; turn left beyond the gate of Villa di Castello and continue straight along Via di Castello and the imposing Villa Corsini; take Via della Petraia uphill to the entrance. ⊠ *Via della Petraia 40, Località Castello* ☎ *055/451208* ✉ *€2, includes entrance to Villa di Castello* ⊙ *Oct.–Mar., garden daily 8:15–4:30, villa tours daily at 9:15, 10, 10:45, 11:30, 12:10, 1:30, 2:20, 3, and 3:40; Apr, May, and Sept., garden daily 9–5, villa tours daily at 9:15, 10, 10:45, 11:30, 12:10, 1:30, 2:20, 3, 3:40, and 4:45; June–Aug., garden daily 9–7, villa tours daily at 9:15, 10, 10:45, 11:30, 12:10, 1:30, 2:20, 3, 3:40, 4:45, 5:35, and 6:35. Closed 2nd and 3rd Mon. of month.*

Villa Gamberaia

Villa Gamberaia, near the village of Settignano on the eastern outskirts of Florence, was the rather modest 15th-century country home of Matteo di Domenico Gamberelli, the father of noted Renaissance sculptors Bernardo, Antonio, and Matteo Rossellino. In the early 1600s the villa eventually passed into the hands of the wealthy Capponi family. They spared no expense in rebuilding it and, more importantly, creating its garden, one of the finest near Florence. Studded with statues and fountains, the garden suffered damage during World War II but has been restored according to the original 17th-century design. This excursion takes about 1½ hours, allowing 45 minutes to visit the garden. Parts of the villa are open by appointment

To get here by car, head east on Via Aretina, an extension of Via Gioberti, which is picked up at Piazza Beccaria; follow the sign to the turnoff to the north to Villa Gamberaia, about 8 km (5 mi) from the center. To go by bus, take Bus 10 to Settignano. From Settignano's main Piazza Tommaseo, walk east on Via di San Romano; the second lane on the right is Via del Rossellino, which leads southeast to the entrance of Villa Gamberaia. The walk from the piazza takes about 10 minutes. ⊠ *Via del Rossellino 72, near Settignano* ☎ *055/697205* 💶 *€10* ☉ *Garden Mon.–Sat. 9–6, Sun. 9–6.*

Villa Demidoff

Francesco I de' Medici commissioned the multitalented Bernardo Buontalenti in 1568 to build a villa and a grandiose park to accompany it. Its current name comes from Paolo Demidoff, who bought the villa in 1872 and attempted to bring back its former glory. The park, particularly the colossal and whimsical sculpture of the *Fontana dell'Appenino* (*Fountain of the Appenines*), executed by Giambologna in 1579–89, is worth the price of admission alone. It's a grotto that plays tricks on the eye; the Appenine Mountains are personified by a colossal figure that seems to rise with some amount of difficulty from the earth—the figure also is pressing upon the head of a monster. Besides providing a nice excursion from Florence, the villa is an excellent picnic spot.

To get here by car, head north from Florence on the SR65 toward Pratolino and follow signs to the villa. Or take Bus 25 from Piazza San Marco and get off at Pratolino. ⊠ *Località Pratolino, Vaglia* ☎ *055/409427* 💶 *€2.58* ☉ *Mar. and Oct., Sun. 8:30–8; Apr.–Sept., Thurs.–Sun. 8:30–8.*

FLORENCE A TO Z

To research prices, get advice from other travelers, and book travel arrangements, visit www.fodors.com.

AIRPORTS & TRANSFERS

Florence's Aeroporto A. Vespucci, called Peretola, services flights from Milan, Rome, London, and Paris. To get into the city from Peretola by car, take the A11. Pisa's Aeroporto Galileo Galilei is the closest landing point with significant international service. Take the SR67 from Pisa airport; it leads directly to Florence. For flight information, call the Florence Air Terminal or Aeroporto Galileo Galilei.

A local bus service runs from Peretola into Florence. Buy a ticket at the second-floor bar. Take Bus 62, which goes directly from the airport to the train station at Santa Maria Novella; the bus shelter is beyond the parking lot. There's no direct bus service from Pisa's airport to Florence. Buses do go to and from Pisa, but then you have to change to a slow train service.

No train service exists between the center of Florence and Peretola. A scheduled service connects the station at Pisa's Aeroporto Galileo Galilei with Florence's Stazione Centrale di Santa Maria Novella, roughly a one-hour trip. Trains start running about 7 AM from the airport, 6 AM from Florence, and continue service every hour until about 11:30 PM from the airport, 8 PM from Florence. You can check in for departing flights at the air terminal office, which is around the corner from train tracks 1 and 2.

🛈 Airport Information **Aeroporto A. Vespucci (known as Peretola)** ✉ 10 km [6 mi] northwest of Florence ☎ 055/373498 🌐 www.airport.florence.it. **Aeroporto Galileo Galilei** ✉ 12 km [7 mi] south of Pisa and 80 km [50 mi] west of Florence ☎ 050/500707 🌐 www. pisa-airport.com. **Florence Air Terminal** ✉ Stazione Centrale di Santa Maria Novella ☎ 055/216073.

BIKE & MOPED TRAVEL

Brave souls (cycling in Florence is difficult, at best) may rent bicycles at easy-to-spot locations at Fortezza da Basso, the Stazione Centrale di Santa Maria Novella, and Piazza Pitti. Otherwise try Alinari. If you want to go native and rent a noisy Vespa (Italian for "wasp") or other make of motorcycle or *motorino* (moped), you may do so at Maxirent. Massimo also rents mopeds. However unfashionable, helmets must be rented also, and by law are mandatory, much to the chagrin of many Italians.

If you have well-exercised legs and lungs, you can also take a guided half-day bicycle tour from Florence with tour groups Florence by Bike and I Bike Italy.

🛈 Bike Rentals **Alinari** ✉ Via Guelfa 85/r, San Lorenzo ☎ 055/280500. **Florence by Bike** ✉ Via San Zanobi 120-122/r San Lorenzo ☎ 055/488992 🌐 www.florencebybike. it. **I Bike Italy** ✉ Borgo degli Albizi 11, Santa Croce ☎☎ 055/2342371 🌐 www.ibikeitaly. com. **Massimo** ✉ Campo d'Arrigo 16/r ☎ 055/573689. **Maxirent** ✉ Borgo Ognissanti 155/r, Santa Maria Novella ☎ 055/265420.

BUS TRAVEL TO & FROM FLORENCE

Long-distance buses provide inexpensive if somewhat claustrophobic service between Florence and other cities in Italy and Europe. One operator is SITA; you can also try Lazzi Eurolines.

🛈 Bus Information **Lazzi Eurolines** ✉ Via Mercadante 2, Santa Maria Novella ☎ 055/363041 🌐 www.lazzi.it. **SITA** ✉ Via Santa Caterina da Siena 17/r, Santa Maria Novella ☎ 055/214721 🌐 www.sita-on-line.it.

BUS TRAVEL WITHIN FLORENCE

Maps and timetables are available for a small fee at the ATAF (Trasporti Area Fiorentina) booth next to the train station, or for free at visitor-information offices. Tickets must be purchased in advance at tobacco stores, newsstands, from automatic ticket machines near main stops, or at ATAF booths. The ticket must be canceled in the small validation machine immediately upon boarding. Two types of tickets are available, both valid for one or more rides on all lines. One costs €1 and is valid for one hour from the time it is first canceled. A multiple ticket—four tickets, each valid for 60 minutes—costs €3.90. A 24-hour tourist ticket costs €4.50. Monthly passes are also available.

Small electric buses make the rounds of the centro storico and provide an easy alternative to footing it around town. Use the same ticket as for the regular bus.

Bus Information **ATAF** ⊠ Piazza del Duomo 57/r, Duomo ☎ 800/019794 toll free.

CAR RENTAL

Local Agencies **Avis** ⊠ Via Borgo Ognissanti 128/r, Santa Maria Novella ☎ 055/2398826. **Hertz Italiana** ⊠ Via Finiguerra 33/r, Santa Maria Novella ☎ 055/317543. **Maggiore-Budget Autonoleggio** ⊠ Via Termine 1, Santa Maria Novella ☎ 055/311256.

CAR TRAVEL

Abandon all hope of using a car in the city: most of the downtown area is accessible only to locals with properly marked vehicles. Florence is connected to the north and south of Italy by the Autostrada del Sole (A1). For assistance or information, call the ACI (Automobile Club Firenze).

ACI (Automobile Club Firenze) ☎ 055/2486246.

CONSULATES

U.S. Consulate ⊠ Lungarno Vespucci 38, Lungarno Sud ☎ 055/2398276. **U.K. Consulate** ⊠ Lungarno Corsini 2, Lungarno Sud ☎ 055/284133.

ENGLISH-LANGUAGE BOOKSTORES

BM Bookshop ⊠ Borgo Ognissanti 4/r, Santa Maria Novella ☎ 055/294575. **Edison** ⊠ Piazza della Repubblica 27/r, Piazza della Repubblica ☎ 055/213110. **Feltrinelli International** ⊠ Via Cavour 12-20/r, Duomo ☎ 055/219524. **Libreria Martelli** ⊠ Via Martelli 22/r Duomo ☎ 055/2657603. **McRae Books** ⊠ Via de'Neri 32/r, Santa Croce ☎ 055/2382456 ⊕ www.mcraebooks.com. **Paperback Exchange** ⊠ Via Fiesolana 31/r, Santa Croce ☎ 055/2478154 ⊕ www.papex.it.

EMERGENCIES

You can get a list of English-speaking doctors and dentists at the U.S. Consulate, or contact the Tourist Medical Service. If you need hospital treatment and an interpreter, you can call AVO, a group of volunteer interpreters; it's open Monday, Wednesday, and Friday 4–6 PM and Tuesday and Thursday 10–noon. Comunale No. 13, a local pharmacy, is open 24 hours a day, seven days a week. For a complete listing of other pharmacies that have rotating late-night hours, dial ☎ 192.

AVO ☎ 055/2344567. **Tourist Medical Service** ⊠ Via Lorenzo il Magnifico 59 ☎ 055/475411.

Emergency Services **Ambulance** ☎ 118. **Emergencies** ☎ 113. **Misericordia** (Red Cross) ⊠ Piazza del Duomo 20, Duomo ☎ 055/212222. **Police** ⊠ Via Zara 2, near Piazza della Libertà, San Lorenzo ☎ 055/49771.

24-Hour Pharmacies **Comunale No. 13** ⊠ Stazione Centrale di Santa Maria Novella, Santa Maria Novella ☎ 055/289435.

LODGING

Villa-Rental Agencies **The Best in Italy** ⊠ Via Foscolo 72, Florence 50124 ☎ 055/223064 ☐ 055/2298912 ⊕ www.thebestinitaly.com. **Custom Travel and Special Events** ⊠ Via dell'Ardiglione 19, Santo Spirito/San Frediano ☎ 055/2645526 ⊕ www.customitaly.com. **Florence and Abroad** ⊠ Via San Zanobi 58, San Lorenzo 50129 ☎ 055/470603 ⊕ www.florenceandabroad.com.

INTERNET CAFÉS

Internet Train is the best known and most reliable Internet café chain operating in the city center.

Warning: Pickpocketing is a problem at many Internet cafés throughout the city and professionals seem to prey on foreigners: always know where your purse or wallet is (preferably on your lap or in a zipped pocket) and be aware that pickpockets work in teams.

📁 Internet Cafés **Internet Train** ⊠ Via Guelfa 54-56/r ☎ 055/2645146 ⊕ www.internettrain.it ⊠ Via dell'Oriuolo 40/r, Duomo ☎ 055/2638968 ⊠ Borgo Sant']acopo 30/r, Lungarno Sud ☎ 055/2657935 ⊠ Via Zannoni 1/r, San Lorenzo ☎ 055/2645284 ⊠ Via del Parione, Santa Maria Novella ☎ 055/2645563 ⊠ Via de'Benci 36/r, Santa Croce ☎ 055/2638555 ⊠ Borgo La Croce 33/r, Santa Croce ☎ 055/2347852 ⊠ Galleria Commerciale, Santa Maria Novella ☎ 055/2399720 ⊠ Via Porta Rossa 38/r, Piazza Repubblica ☎ 055/2741037. **Webpuccino** ⊠ Via dei Conti 22r ☎ 055/2776469 ⊕ www.webpuccino.it.

MAIL & SHIPPING

📁 Post Offices **Florence** ⊠ Via Pellicceria 3, Piazza della Repubblica ☎ 055/27361 ⊠ Via Pietrapiana 53/55, Santa Croce ☎ 055/211415.

📁 Major Overnight Services **DHL** ⊠ Via della Cupola 234/5 ☎ 800/123800 toll free. **Federal Express** ⊠ Via Gioberti 3 ☎ 055/8974001, 800/123800 toll free.

SAFETY

Florence is subject to the same types of petty thievery that are practiced in Italy's other large, heavily touristed cities. Pickpockets are known to frequent crowded places, particularly buses. Purse-snatchers sometimes operate on mopeds, making them quick and potentially dangerous. Groups of gypsy children have a number of ruses to part you from your property. Although the odds are against you falling prey to such crimes, it's always wise to keep your valuables well guarded, to be alert to your surroundings, and to err on the side of caution if you find yourself in suspicious circumstances.

TAXIS

Taxis usually wait at stands throughout the city (in front of the train station and in Piazza della Repubblica, for example), or you can call for one. The meter starts at €2.30, with a €3.60 minimum and extra charges at night, on Sunday, or for radio dispatch. A tip of at least 10% is much appreciated.

📁 Taxi Companies **Taxis** ☎ 055/4390 or 055/4798.

TOURS

BUS TOURS The major bus operators have half-day itineraries, all of which use comfortable buses staffed with English-speaking guides. Morning tours begin at 9, when buses pick visitors up at the main hotels. Stops include the cathedral complex, the Galleria dell'Accademia, Piazzale Michelangelo, and the Palazzo Pitti (or, on Monday, the Museo dell'Opera del Duomo). Afternoon tours stop at the large hotels at 2 PM and take in Piazza della Signoria, the Galleria degli Uffizi (or the Palazzo Vecchio on Monday, when the Uffizi is closed), nearby Fiesole, and, on the return, the church of Santa Croce. A half-day tour costs about €24.75, including museum admissions.

ATAF also runs a red double-decker bus service that starts from the station at Santa Maria Novella and does a big loop of all the major sites; you can hop on and hop off whenever you want.

◪ Fees & Schedules **ATAF** ⊠ Piazza del Duomo 57/r, Duomo ☎ 800/019794 toll free. **Lazzi Eurolines** ⊠ Via Mercadante 2, Santa Maria Novella ☎ 055/363041 ⊕ www.lazzi. it. **SITA** ⊠ Via Santa Caterina da Siena 17/r, Santa Maria Novella ☎ 055/214721 ⊕ www. sita-on-line.it.

TRAIN TRAVEL

Florence is on the principal Italian train route between most European capitals and Rome, and within Italy it is served frequently from Milan, Venice, and Rome by Intercity (IC) and nonstop Eurostar trains. Stazione Centrale di Santa Maria Novella, the main station, is in the center of town. Be sure to avoid trains that stop only at the Campo di Marte or Rifredi stations, which aren't convenient to the center.

◪ Train Information **Stazione Centrale di Santa Maria Novella** ☎ 8488/888088 ⊕ www.trenitalia.com.

TRAVEL AGENCIES

◪ Local Agent Referrals **American Express** ⊠ Via Dante Alighieri 22/r, Duomo ☎ 055/50981. **Brunelleschi Travel** ⊠ Via dell'Oriuolo 50–52/r, Santa Croce ☎ 055/2340228. **CIT Italia** ⊠ Piazza Stazione 51/r, Santa Maria Novella ☎ 055/284145 or 055/212606. **Travelex** ⊠ Lungarno Acciaiuoli 7/r, Lungarno Sud ☎ 055/289781.

VISITOR INFORMATION

◪ Tourist Information **Fiesole** ⊠Via Portigiani 3, 50014 ☎055/598720 ⊕www.comune. fiesole.fi.it. **Florence** (Agenzia Promozione Turistica, or APT) ⊠ Via Cavour 1/r, next to Palazzo Medici-Riccardi, San Lorenzo 50100 ☎ 055/290832 ⊕ www.comune.firenze. it ⊠ Stazione Centrale di Santa Maria Novella, Santa Maria Novella 50100 ☎ 055/212245 ⊠ Borgo Santa Croce 29/r, Santa Croce ☎ 055/2340444.

NORTH OF FLORENCE

2

By Patricia
Rucidlo
Updated by
Ann Reavis

CRAGGY, OFTEN SNOWCAPPED MOUNTAINS border sparsely populated valleys; narrow roads wind up and down incredible heights—this is Tuscan mountain territory, and even when it's hot elsewhere, it's cooler here. The steep terrain rolls down into pine-forested hills and eventually meets the wide sandy beaches of the Ligurian Sea. Aided by the natural mountain barriers, cities and towns in the Garfagnana and the Lima Valley north of Florence were involved with the defense of the great Tuscan cities Lucca and Florence during the Middle Ages and the Renaissance. The majestic Alpi Apuane (Apuane Alps) mountain chain cuts a swath between the Garfagnana and the Lunigiana regions. Trails run through the starkly beautiful landscapes of the protected Parco Naturale delle Alpi Apuane. At the edge of the Alps, quarries at Carrara and Pietrasanta in Versilia have been sources of marble for builders and sculptors—Michelangelo among them—for more than 2,000 years. Along the Versilian Coast are the wide, sandy beaches of the resort towns Viareggio and Forte dei Marmi. Seductively close to Tuscany's northwestern edge—technically in the region of Liguria—are the five seaside towns called the Cinque Terre, where pastel houses cling to sheer cliffs and fishermen haul in their catches from a turquoise sea.

Exploring North of Florence

This is a geographically diverse area: north of Florence you can both enjoy soaring mountain vistas and laze on the beach. The best way to explore the region is by car, as part of the fun is stopping to take in the dramatic scenery. Towns are fairly spread out, and driving the narrow, winding mountain roads adds considerable time. If you have to rely on public transportation, bus service to the region can get you around; train service, however, is extremely limited.

About the Restaurants

In the hills of the Mugello and the mountains of the Garfagnana, family-style *osterias* (down-to-earth taverns), serving hearty sauces and grilled meats, incorporate the native chestnut and pine woods in their decor. Along the coast, especially in the Cinque Terre, cafés and trattorias ring sunny piazzas or cling to terraced hillsides. Restaurants in the Lunigiana and the Mugello areas are generally less expensive than those in major Tuscan cities. Seafood restaurants are easily found in Forte dei Marmi and Viareggio and the many other resort towns dotting the coast, where prices are frequently higher. In the five villages of the Cinque Terre, attractive outdoor trattorias abound, but be prepared to pay a premium for the ambience.

About the Hotels

Excluding the beach resort towns, lodging is generally less expensive here than in many other parts of Italy. Some real bargains can be found in off-the-beaten-path towns. Consider staying at an *agriturismo* (agritourism), a farm and/or vineyard that has opened rooms or apartments—from rustic to stately—to guests. Many area hotel restaurants serve delicious fare, and half (breakfast and lunch) and full board (breakfast, lunch, and dinner) are usually available as supplements to your room rate. In January 2005 a nationwide law came into effect requiring lodging establishments to convert to no smoking if they do not have approved ventilation systems. Time will tell what changes this will engender in Italian hotels, inns, and at agriturismo properties.

WHAT IT COSTS In Euros				
	$$$$	$$$	$$	$	¢
RESTAURANTS	over €22	€18–€22	€13–€17	€7–€12	under €7
HOTELS	over €290	€210–€289	€140–€209	€80–€139	under €80

Restaurant prices are for a second course (secondo piatto) per person. Hotel prices are for two people in a standard double room in high season, including tax and service.

Timing

To drive around and marvel at the gorgeous scenery north of Florence, a trip anytime from spring through autumn can be beautiful and rewarding. If the torrid July and August temperatures in the major Tuscan cities become oppressive, head to the mountains of the Mugello or Garfagnana. Hiking, trekking, and mountain-biking vacations in the Alpi Apuane are spectacular in the summer months. The Cinque Terre area is packed in July and August: to truly enjoy the tiny villages and the hiking trail between the five towns, go in May and June or September and early October. July and August are the popular months to be at the coast in Forte dei Marmi and Viareggio: the towns are bustling with people and the beaches are crowded. In the fringe of the tourist season (June or September) the water is warm enough to take a swim and there are fewer people. Another good time to visit Viareggio is during Carnevale, the period before Lent that culminates in a huge street party on Shrove Tuesday; it's said that Viareggio's celebrations are second only to those in Venice.

THE MUGELLO

The lands of the Mugello—surrounding the upper reaches of the Sieve River and the vineyard-rich Val di Sieve—were distributed in the 1st century AD to those soldiers who fought for the Roman general Sulla (138–78 BC); they took over land previously inhabited by the Etruscans. The region's strategic defensive position and its rich agricultural resources attracted Florence, which conquered it in the 14th century. The area's native sons include the artists Giotto (1266–1337), Fra Angelico (1387–1455), and Andrea del Castagno (circa 1421–57). The small town of San Piero a Sieve gave birth to the Medici dynasty. Now the Mugello is quiet, its days of glory gone. Though parts of it are industrialized, flat, and uninteresting, other parts are extremely beautiful, with sharp hills and dramatic sunsets.

Borgo San Lorenzo

❶ *32 km (20 mi) north of Florence.*

The artist Giotto was supposedly born here—though some other places, including Vespignano, which claims to have the house that Giotto was

Numbers in the text correspond to numbers in the margin and on the Mugello and the Northwestern Tuscany and the Ligurian Coast maps.

If you have 3 days:
Garfagnana & Versilia

For a period this short, to minimize the time spent getting from place to place it's best to pick a specific area and explore it in depth. Drive either from Florence or Lucca to the Garfagnana and spend the first night in ▣ **Castelnuovo di Garfagnana** ❿ ▶. On Day 2, drive or hike in the nearby **Parco dell'Orecchiella** ⓫. The second night should be spent in ▣ **Barga** ❾, taking in one of the frequent cultural events. On Day 3, drive to ▣ **Forte dei Marmi** ㉒ or ▣ **Viareggio** ㉔ via SR445 and SP13 to **Carrara** ⓴, where you can tour one or two of the marble caves before heading to the wide, sandy beaches on the Ligurian Sea.

If you have 3 days:
The Mugello and Gargnana

Though there's wonderful art to be seen and wonderful food to be eaten, the scenery takes precedence when you are touring this area. Drive north from Florence on SR302 into the rolling hills of the Mugello. Visit the two Medici villas at Trebbio and **Cafaggiolo** ❹ ▶ and stop at the Bosco ai Frati monastery near **San Piero a Sieve** ❸, having lunch along the way. In the afternoon, tour the picturesque town **Scarperia** ❷ and its Museum of Knives and Swords, and the Liberty-style buildings of Borgo San Lorenzo. Spend the first night in **Borgo San Lorenzo** ❶. The next morning, head south, back toward Florence; before reaching Florence, turn west, taking the A11 to Montecatini Terme. Then pick up the SR633 and take it to the SR12, which you follow north for a good 1½ hours to ▣ **Abetone** ❼, the mountain resort in the Garfagnana. Spend the night here after watching the sun set behind the peaks and dining on the northern Tuscan cuisine. From Abetone, drive south along winding roads to **Bagni di Lucca** ❽, and then head north to **Barga** ❾. Stop to see Barga's Duomo and admire the panorama from its little piazza before proceeding to ▣ **Castelnuovo di Garfagnana** ❿ to spend the second night. On Day 3, drive or hike in the nearby **Parco dell'Orecchiella** ⓫.

If you have 5 days

For an ideal mix of mountains and sea, start in Florence, head to the Garfagnana and the Lunigiana hills, spend time on the beaches, and finish on the cliffs of the Cinque Terre. Take A11 out of Florence to Montecatini Terme. Then pick up the SR633 and take it to the SR12, which you follow north for a good 1½ hours to ▣ **Abetone** ❼ ▶, the mountain resort in the Garfagnana. Spend the night here after watching the sun set behind the peaks and dining on the northern Tuscan cuisine. From Abetone, drive south along winding roads to **Bagni di Lucca** ❽, and then head north to **Barga** ❾. Stop to see Barga's Duomo and admire the panorama from its little piazza before proceeding to ▣ **Castelnuovo di Garfagnana** ❿ to spend the second night. On Day 3, drive or hike in the nearby **Parco dell'Orecchiella** ⓫. Then head to the Lunigiana on SR445 and stay in ▣ **Equi Terme** ⓬. On Day 4, drive to ▣ **Forte dei Marmi** ㉒ or ▣ **Viareggio** ㉔ via **Carrara** ⓴ and the marble caves. Stay overnight in either Forte dei Marmi or Viareggio, doing nothing but sampling the fresh seafood and walking along the shore. On Day 5, drive to La Spezia and take

2

the train to ⊡ **Riomaggiore** ⑮, the southernmost village of the five Cinque Terre towns. From Riomaggiore you could hike to ⊡ **Manarola** ⑯ on the Blue Trail and spend the afternoon at a portside café or continue on foot to **Corniglia** ⑰ and by train to ⊡ **Vernazza** ⑱ or ⊡ **Monerosso al Mare** ⑲. Take your pick of Cinque Terre towns in which to spend the night before journeying back to Florence the next day.

born in, would dispute this. What is inarguable is that Borgo San Lorenzo, the largest town in the Mugello (population 16,000), has Roman origins and that in the Middle Ages it was controlled by Florence. It saw some heavy fighting during World War II, and the plaque commemorating the heroism of its citizens, which can be seen on the wall of the Palazzo Pretorio, is moving in its strong and unapologetic language. Borgo San Lorenzo has many Liberty-style buildings, excellent examples of the decorative arts of the early 20th century.

Documents refer to a church on the site of **San Lorenzo** as early as 941, and there is evidence to suggest that the foundation was built over a Roman temple dedicated to Bacchus. The 1263 bell tower, rebuilt from one dating from 1193, is a fine example of Roman-Byzantine architecture. Inside the church are works of art spanning the centuries, the most important of which is a Madonna attributed to Giotto. It is the only work of his still to be found in his native territory. ⊠ *Via San Francesco, off Piazza Garibaldi* ☎ *No phone* 🎫 *Free* ⊙ *Daily 9–7.*

off the beaten path

MUSEO DI CASA DI GIOTTO – There's no evidence that the Museum of the House of Giotto was once the artist's house, but inside are reproductions of his major works. There's also a tiny chapel, the **Cappellina della Bruna,** which has some 15th-century fresco fragments. You can get the key to the chapel at the museum. ⊠ *Off SR551, Vespignano, 3 km (2 mi) east of Borgo San Lorenzo* ☎ *055/ 8448251* 🎫 *€1.50* ⊙ *Apr.–Oct., Tues. and Thurs. 3–6, weekends 10–noon and 4–6; Nov.–Mar., Tues. and Thurs. 4–7, weekends 10–noon and 4–7.*

Where to Stay & Eat

$ ✕ **La Casa del Prosciutto.** Sitting at the foot of a tiny 14th-century bridge in Vicchio, this rustic, small osteria is a real find—one worth the detour for lunch. Grilled and cured meats are the specialty, but all of the courses are terrific, from an appetizer of *crostini alla Toscana* (toasted bread with various toppings) to luscious pastry and fruit desserts. Try the *tortelli del Mugello,* a regional specialty of pasta stuffed with potatoes, here served with a sauce of porcini mushrooms, or the duck. There is also an *alimentari* (deli) that prepares panini with delectable local prosciutto, cheeses, and Tuscan bread. ⊠ *Via Ponte a Vicchio 1, Vicchio, 7 km (4½ mi) east of Borgo San Lorenzo* ☎ *055/844031* 🍴 *Reservations essential* 🖃 *AE, DC, MC, V* ⊙ *Restaurant closed Mon. and Tues. Deli and restaurant closed Jan. and July. No dinner.*

$$ ⊡ **Park Hotel Ripaverde.** Although the hotel's glass exterior might not be inviting, the modern, clean interior is comfortable. Rooms are con-

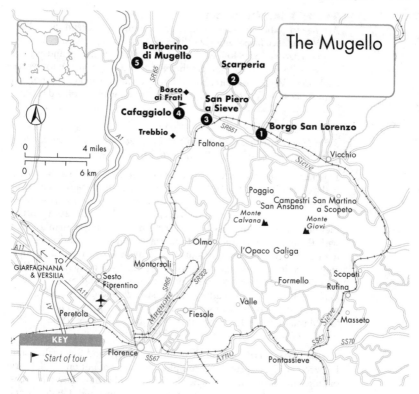

temporary with upholstered chairs in floral fabrics that coordinate with the curtains and bedspreads and cornflower-blue wood desks. The restaurant serves regional and typical Italian specialties. The exercise room has a sauna and whirlpool. Half and full board are available. ⊠ *Viale Giovanni XXIII 36, 50032* ☎ *055/8496003 or 055/8459279* 🖷 *055/ 8459379* ⊕ *www.berchielli.it* ➦ *51 rooms, 6 suites* ⚘ *Restaurant, in-room safes, refrigerators, cable TV, gym, sauna, bar, Internet, meeting rooms, some pets allowed* ▭ *AE, DC, MC, V* ⦿❘ *CP.*

$ 🏨 **Casa Palmira.** Make yourself at home in a rural bed-and-breakfast that has guest rooms with hardwood floors, patchwork quilts, and country antiques. The common areas include a large lounge with a fireplace and a flower/vegetable garden. Cooking lessons are available in the Tuscan kitchen, and courses in tai chi, fresco painting, and photography can be arranged. Dinner is available on request. Ask about their transportation service to the Florence airport and local train stations. Only about 20 km (12 mi) north of Florence on SR302, this makes a convenient base for touring. ⊠ *Via Faentina-Polcanto, Località Feriolo, 50030 Polcanto, 11 km (7 mi) southwest of Borgo San Lorenzo* ☎ *055/ 8409749* 🖷 *055/8409749* ⊕ *www.casapalmira.it* ➦ *7 rooms, 5 with bath* ⚘ *Mountain bikes, Internet, airport shuttle; no a/c, no room TVs* ▭ *No credit cards* ⊙ *Closed mid-Jan.–mid-Mar.* ⦿❘ *CP.*

Sports & the Outdoors

Arrange to go hot-air ballooning or paragliding on weekends with **Aeroclub Volovelistico Mugello** (⊠ Località Figliano, 5 km north east of Borgo San Lorenzo ☎ 055/8408665 ⊕ www.mugellogliding.aero) and explore the Mugello from the air. To get there, follow the signs for AVIOSUPERFICIE VOLO A VELA in the direction of Luco di Mugello and Grezzano, and at the SCUOLA DI VOLO sign, turn for the school, which is on a dirt road.

Scarperia

❷ *8 km (5 mi) northwest of Borgo San Lorenzo, 4 km (2½ mi) north of San Piero a Sieve, 30 km (19 mi) north of Florence.*

Florence created a strategic defensive post in the Mugello at Scarperia in the early 1300s. In the 16th and 17th centuries the fast-growing township was the center of the cutlery-manufacturing trade for Tuscany—knives and scissors as well as daggers and swords. By the 20th century the more than 40 businesses had been reduced to fewer than 10, but with the emerging popularity of the yearly market fair, an ever-growing number of individual artisans has turned the town into a popular stop for collectors and aficionados of knifeware. The annual **Mostra Mercato dei Ferri Taglienti** (Market Exhibit of Knives and Swords)—displaying old and modern cutlery, knives, swords, and daggers along with demonstrations of the skills of modern-day craftsmen—is held during late May and during late September in the town center. ☎ 055/8468165 ⊜ 055/8468862 ⊕ *www.zoomedia.it/Scarperia.*

The **Museo dei Ferri Taglienti** (Museum of Knives and Swords), in the Palazzo dei Vicari, provides a complete overview of not only 500 years of knife- and sword-making in northern Tuscany but also shows the techniques that modern artisans use to craft knives by hand. Guided tours are given every hour. ⊠ *Palazzo dei Vicari, Piazza dei Vicari* ☎ 055/8468027 ⊕ *www.zoomedia.it/Scarperia/* ⊠ *€3.50, €5 with guided tour* ☉ *June 15–Sept. 15, Wed.–Fri. 3:30–7:30, Sat. 3–7, Sun. 10–1 and 3–7; Sept. 16–June 14, Sat. 3–7, Sun. 10–1 and 3–7.*

The **Oratorio della Madonna dei Terremoti** (Oratory of the Madonna of the Earthquakes) has a 15th-century fresco of the Madonna and Child that some believe is by Fra Filippo Lippi (1406–69). ⊠ *Viale John F. Kennedy 18* ☎ *No phone* ⊠ *Free* ☉ *Daily 9–7.*

The 14th-century facade and courtyard of the City Hall, **Palazzo Pretorio**, are adorned with stone and ceramic coats of arms. Frescoes of a religious nature and of local coats of arms decorate the interior. ⊠ *Via dei Bastioni 3* ☎ *055/8430671 or 055/8468165* ⊠ *Free* ☉ *Mon.–Sat. 9–1 and 4–7.*

The Augustinian church of **Ss. Jacopo e Filippo**, though dating from the 14th century, was reconstructed in the 19th and early 20th centuries. Inside are frescoes attributed to Bicci di Lorenzo (circa 1373–1452). Note the marble tondo, *The Madonna and Child*, by Benedetto da Maiano (circa 1442–97) in the chapel to the left of the main altar. ⊠ *Via San Martino 17* ☎ *No phone* ⊠ *Free* ☉ *Daily 9–7.*

2

Cuisine

The food north of Florence clearly reflects the local area you are exploring. In the Mugello, sample the *tortelli del Mugello* (ravioli with potato stuffing, sauced in a variety of ways). In the Lunigiana region try the *ravioli alle ortiche* (spinach ravioli stuffed with nettles and lightly dressed with a creamy nut sauce), the vegetable tarts, and lasagna made with chestnut flour.

The Garfagnana Valley produces *farro* (an ancient, pearly wheat grain that resembles barley or spelt), which should definitely be tasted, either in *zuppa di farro* (farro and bean soup) or in *farro alla contadina*, (cooked in water or broth and tossed with extra virgin olive oil and chopped fresh tomatoes.) Restaurants in the Garfagnana stock Lucca's famed deep-green, fruity olive oil, which adds a distinctive flavor to every dish. The Garfagnana is also a huge chestnut-growing area; sample anything on the menu that has chestnuts, especially *polenta di castagne* (chestnut polenta). Chestnuts may be whole and roasted or ground up and used as a flour.

In the mountains you can taste dishes made from game meats (deer, wild boar, and hare). *Lardo di Colonnata* (herbed pork lard) is an obscenely delicious dish that comes from near Carrara. The lard has been cured for months in cool marble boxes and should be sampled even by the skeptical. On the coast, seafood, seafood, and more seafood is what you should be eating. Mixed seafood platters come raw or *fritto* (fried); you can get whole fish and squid grilled; or you may try a pasta sauce that has clams, scampi, mussels, or lobster in it.

Hiking

Wide-open spaces, cliff-side views, turquoise sea, alpine heights: every portion of the area north of Florence invites an afternoon ambling through dense forests, beside lakes and rivers, and along the ridges high above the sea. The Parco dell' Orecchiella in the Garfagnana has extensive forests with trails for hiking, biking, and horseback riding; in winter this region is popular with Tuscan downhill and cross-country skiers. The Parco Naturale delle Alpi Apuane encompasses several towns. Trek up its highest peak, Monte Pisanino, which rises more than 6,000 feet and towers over an artificial lake, Lago di Vagli, which covers the submerged village of Fabbricca. The tiny stone villages of Vagli di Sotto and Vagli di Sopra sit alongside the lake, and a hiking trail connects the towns. There is also some great terrain for mountain bikers in the Forte dei Marmi area. In the Cinque Terre you can take a lengthy hike, with stops at villages, or walk for as little as 30 minutes from Riomaggiore to Manarola. This area is less touristed than many in Italy, so trails are not often crowed. The notable exception is along the Sentiero Azzurro trail of the Cinque Terre in midsummer.

The Seaside

The area north of Florence is frequently thought of as a place for forest and mountain pastimes, but the pleasures of simply walking on a great beach and relaxing at a café portside in a small fishing town should not be missed. The seaside towns of Viarregio, Forte di Marmi, and Marina di Massa all have popular beaches. From October to June the sand is clear and you can walk for miles enjoying the lapping of the sea. During this time the water is cold, and fresh sea breezes encourage you to don a sweater or jacket. You won't meet many people and you can enjoy watching the sunset in peace. June through August, these beaches are packed and lively. *Bagni* (bathhouses) open and the beaches fill with colorful umbrellas and beach chairs. The most coveted spots are right at the shore, where the small waves break on the sand. Many of the bagni have snack bars and showers. For about €20 you can get your own chair and umbrella for the day.

In the Cinque Terre, port-side piazzas are ringed by cafés and trattorias where you can spend hours watching the activities of the fishing port and passersby. Be sure to try the sweet, local wine, Sciacchetrá, with a basket of *fritto misto* (mixed fried food), which may include fried fish, squid, shrimp, and vegetables.

Where to Stay

$$$–$$$$ ⊡ **Sonesta Resort and Country Club.** New facilities are added each year to the sophisticated resort encompassing the lavish villa and dramatic grounds of a 16th-century noble family. The luxurious rooms and common areas are decorated with fine fabrics in earth tones and elegant antique furnishings. You can walk out from many rooms to access the golf course. The restaurant serves traditional Tuscan cuisine with a nouveau flair, and it presents an extensive wine list with many rare vintages. Packages are available that include golf, cooking, art, history, and language classes. ⊠ *Via S. Gavino 27, 50038* ☎ *055/8468282 or 055/84350* 🖷 *055/8430439* ⊕ *www.sonesta.com/tuscany_resort/* 🛏 *46 rooms, 2 suites* ♢ *Restaurant, in-room safes, minibars, cable TV, driving range, 18-hole golf course, pool, health club, hot tub, bar, Internet, meeting rooms* ⊟ *DC, V* ☺ *Closed Jan. and Feb.* ⊠ *EP.*

$ ⊡ **Villa Ebe.** A restored 15th-century villa sits amid rolling countryside, but within minutes of Scarperia, Borgo San Lorenzo, San Piero a Sieve, and the Autodromo. Each of the voluminous rooms is decorated differently—with fabric-draped four-poster beds, beds with tester canopies, or beds made from ornate ironwork. A comfortable chintz covers many chairs. Homey touches include baskets of candy, and some of the rooms have kitchenettes. The large garden is landscaped in the traditional Tuscan manner. The villa can be rented in its entirety for large multiday house parties during the winter off-season. ⊠ *Via di Ferracciano 20, Località Figliano, 50038 Borgo San Lorenzo, 3 mi (5 km) east of Scarperia* ☎ *055/848019 or 055/8457507* 🖷 *055/848567* ⊕ *www.ebeweb.it* 🛏 *14 rooms* ♢ *Restaurant, some kitchenettes, bar; no a/c* ⊟ *DC, V* ☺ *Closed Oct.–May* ⊠ *EP.*

Sports & the Outdoors

Outside Scarperia, the **Autodromo Internazionale del Mugello** (⊠ 1 km [½ mi] east of Scarperia ☎ 055/8499111 🖷 055/8499251 ⊕ www. mugellocircuit.it) is a 5-km (3-mi) racetrack built by the Florence Auto Club for Formula 2 race-car meets and world-championship motorcycle races. The track has a full schedule of events every weekend from mid-April through October.

The **Poggio dei Medici Golf and Country Club** (✉ Via S. Gavino 27, 3 km [2 mi] east of Scarperia town center ☎ 055/84350 🖶 055/8430439 ⊕ www.poggiodeimedici.com) provides the ideal Tuscan backdrop for its 18-hole, par 72, course designed to United States Golf Association standards. A driving range and putting green are on-site. A 1500s villa houses the club's restaurant. The club welcomes day visitors; the greens fee is €80.

San Piero a Sieve

❸ *4 km (2½ mi) south of Scarperia, 6 km (4 mi) west of Borgo San Lorenzo, 26 km (16 mi) north of Florence.*

A grand Medici fort guards this little crossroads town. During the Renaissance, the fort belonged first to the Ubaldini before becoming a Florentine possession. It is a private residence today. The 11th-century parish church of **San Pietro** is worth a stop. It was greatly modified in the late 18th century, but retains the octagonal multicolor terra-cotta baptismal font from the early 16th century that is attributed to the school of Giovanni della Robbia (1469–circa 1529); there's also a panel painting, the *Madonna and Child,* that may have been executed by Lorenzo di Credi (circa 1456–1537). ✉ *Via Provinciale* ☎ *055/848751* 💲 *Free* ⊙ *Daily 8–7.*

The **Fortezza di San Martino** was built as a defensive fortification by Buontalenti on orders of Cosimo I (1519–74), the first grand duke of Tuscany, in the 1570s. ⊕ *1 km (½ mi) southwest of San Piero a Sieve, turn left on dirt road south of village limits and follow signs* ☎ *055/848751 or 055/8487536* ☞ *Closed for renovation at this writing; call for hours and admission price.*

At **Bosco ai Frati**, a Franciscan monastery set in the countryside, you get the feeling that not much has changed since St. Francis visited in 1212. It was here in 1273 that St. Bonaventure, Francis's biographer, was washing dishes when he heard the news that he had been made a cardinal. Cosimo de' Medici, a patron of the monastery, commissioned the young Michelozzo to redo the facade in 1420. The most important work of art remaining in the monastery is a wood sculpture of the Crucifixion by Donatello (circa 1386–1466) that dates from 1430. According to local legend, it was carved from a pear tree in the monastery's garden. ✉ *Off SR65, 2 km (1 mi) northwest of San Piero a Sieve* ☎ *055/848111* 💲 *Free* ⊙ *Daily 9–11:30 and 3–5.*

Where to Stay & Eat

¢–$ ✕🏨 **Hotel Ebe.** A great deal of care has been taken with the rooms at the charming, family-run Hotel Ebe, built in the 1960s. Pastel satin spreads adorn curvaceous ironwork beds. Only a third of the rooms have air-conditioning, so in midsummer ask for one of these. In addition to Tuscan dishes at the attached restaurant, you can eat *seitan* (wheat gluten), Italian style—six members of the delle Fabbriche family are devoted to vegetarianism and the menu reflects that fact. The family also owns the Villa Ebe, near Scarperia. ✉ *Via Mozzete 1/A, 50027* ☎ *055/848019*

🏠 *055/848567* ⊕ *www.ebeweb.it* 📞 *24 rooms, 4 suites* ⚬ *Restaurant, cable TV; no a/c in some rooms* ▤ *DC, V* ⦿ *EP.*

Cafaggiolo

▶ **4** *3 km (2 mi) east of San Piero a Sieve, 28 km (17 mi) north of Florence.*

Cafaggiolo is probably most famous for its **Villa Medicea di Cafaggiolo.** In 1454 Cosimo de' Medici (the Elder, 1389–1464) commissioned Michelozzo to convert this structure, originally a fortress, into a country hunting manor for the Medici. Lorenzo the Great spent part of his childhood here. The villa's castellated walls and massive tower decorated with a huge clock are impressive. The house and gardens are open for touring, and there's is cooking school and group banquet facilities on-site. ⊠ *Off SR65, Via Nazionale 16* 📞 *055/8479293* 🏠 *055/8498103* ⊕ *www. castellodicafaggiolo.it* 🎟 *€5* ⊙ *Apr. 15–Oct. 15, Wed. and Fri. 2:30–6:30, weekends 10–12:30 and 2:30–6:30; Oct. 16–May 14, weekends 10–12:30 and 2:30–6:30.*

off the
beaten
path

CASTELLO DEL TREBBIO – The 14th-century Castello del Trebbio was transformed—on the orders of the Medici patriarch Cosimo the Elder—from a medieval fortress into an elegant villa with an imposing tower by Michelozzo in the 15th century. The narrow, serpentine road that leads to the villa is lined with cypresses and creates a sense of drama. Amerigo Vespucci, the mapmaker who named America, lived here in 1476 to escape the plague in Florence. The villa is privately owned and closed to tours, but by previous appointment you can visit the gardens, which are designed in the classical Italian style with a focus on terraces, trees, and sculpted hedges (individual travelers can arrange to join scheduled groups). Don't bother coming without calling—nothing can be seen from the road. ⊠ *SR65, Trebbio, 3 km (2 mi) south of Cafaggiolo* 📞 *055/ 8458793 or 055/848296* 🎟 *€10.50* ⊙ *Garden tours weekdays by appointment.*

Where to Eat

$–$$ ✕ **Girodibacco Osteria.** Dishes that use truffles are the specialty of this rustic, tavern-style restaurant: the savory risotto *Il Magnifico* has truffles, mushrooms, and vegetables for example. Other Tuscan options include *ribollita* (a thick soup of white beans, bread, cabbage, and onions), *pappa al pomodoro* (a bread-and-tomato soup), and grilled meats. There's also a bar in front that serves great espresso. Girodibacco is about 300 feet down the road from Villa Medicea di Cafaggiolo. ⊠ *Via Nazionale 8* 📞 *055/8418173* 🏠 *055/8486865* ▤ *AE, DC, MC, V* ⊙ *Closed Mon.*

Barberino di Mugello

5 *5 km (8 mi) northwest of Cafaggiolo, 34 km (21 mi) north of Florence.*

Barberino di Mugello, the largest town on the western rim of the Mugello, has views of both the glorious Tuscan countryside and industrial complexes. Of note in the town center are the 15th-century city hall, Palazzo Pretorio, emblazoned with colorful coats-of-arms, and the Logge Medicee, open-sided galleries designed by Michelozzo (1396–1472).

Next to the town's parish church is the **Oratorio Dei Ss. Sebastiano e Rocco** (Oratory of Sts. Sebastian and Rocco), which dates from the 18th century. ⊠ *Corso Bartolomeo Corsini* ☎ *No phone* ⊠ *Free* ⊗ *Mon.–Sat. 4:30 PM–5:30 PM, Sun. 8 AM–9 AM.*

off the beaten path	**PASSO DELLA FUTA** – For a magnificent view of the Mugello region, drive 14 km (9 mi) north of Barberino di Mugello via SR65 to the top of Passo della Futa, a mountain pass at an altitude of 2,800 feet.

Where to Eat & Stay

$ ✕ **Cosimo de' Medici.** The number of trucks parked in the lot is an indicator of a good cook and a great deal—this is the Italian version of a diner. The decor is extremely plain, but the Tuscan food is plentiful and tasty. Grilled meats are a specialty, and the pastas are made in-house—try the *pappardelle alla lepre* (wide pasta in a wild-hare meat sauce) or farfalle *alla Cosimo,* sauced with herb pesto. Don't miss the *salsiccia di cinghiale* (wild boar sausage). ⊠ *Via del Lago 19* ☎ *055/ 8420370* ⊟ *AE, DC, MC, V* ⊗ *Closed Mon. and 20 days in Aug. No dinner Sun.*

$ ✕ **Marisa.** The *bistecca alla fiorentina,* the Florentine T-bone steak, is a great bargain here, as is the *lombatina di vitella al limone* (grilled veal chop with lemon). Enjoy your meal in one of two large, air-conditioned dining rooms or out on the veranda. The restaurant also sells Tuscan products—local salami, cheeses, olive oil, and *biscottini* (small, hard cookies). *Panini* (sandwiches) are available to take away for a picnic lunch. ⊠ *Exit 18 off the A1, Viale del Lago 21* ☎ *055/8420045* ⊟ *No credit cards* ⊗ *Closed Tues.*

¢–$ ▦ **Poggio di Sotto.** Perched on a *poggio* (little hill), this agriturismo is a series of small, ocher-color buildings looking onto some pretty Mugellan countryside (with the inevitable view of industry on one side). The accommodations are simple—white walls, rectangular wood headboards—and very well kept. Although there's no air-conditioning, it's not needed in the Mugello. You can borrow a mountain bike from the proprietor and explore the area if you wish; horseback riding is also nearby. A small on-site restaurant serves local specialties. The half-board option costs €20 per person per night. ⊠ *Via Galliano 15/A, Località Galliano, 50030* ☎ *055/8428447 or 055/8428448* ⊞ *055/8055/8428449* ⊕ *www.wel.it* ⊷ *9 rooms* ⚮ *Restaurant, mountain bikes, some pets allowed (fee); no a/c* ⊟ *AE, MC, V* ⦿ *EP.*

THE GARFAGNANA

The heart of the Alpi Apuane, the Garfagnana is one of the most visually stunning areas in all of Tuscany. Roads marked by constant hairpin turns wind around precipitous, jagged peaks and through old stone villages. Cool mountain air tempers even the sultriest summer. Most of the major cities and towns can be found along the Serchio, Italy's third-largest river, which runs north–south. The Val di Lima (Lima Valley), formed by the Lima River, has for centuries been known for its curative thermal waters and its lush chestnut groves.

San Marcello Pistoiese

6 *77 km (48 mi) west of Barberino di Mugello, 66 km (41 mi) northwest of Florence.*

The largest small town in the surrounding mountains bustles in summer and winter, but calms down during spring and fall. Set amid spectacular scenery; you can drive across a dramatic suspension bridge over the Lima River.

The **Museo Ferrucciano** has exhibits on the history of the area as well as on the 1530 battle, waged in the nearby village of Gavinana, in which the Republic of Florence resisted the troops of Charles V of Spain. ⊠ *Piazza Francesco Ferrucci* ☏ *0573/621289* 📠 *055/630623* 💶 *€1.55* ☉ *July–Aug., daily 10–noon and 5–7; Sept.–June, Thurs. and Sat. 3–6.*

The **Pieve di San Marcello** church dates from the 12th century. The interior was redone in the 18th century, and most of the art inside is from that period. ⊠ *Piazza Arcangeli* ☏ *0573/630179* 💶 *Free* ☉ *Daily 9–1 and 3–6.*

Sports & the Outdoors

You can rent mountain bikes and equipment for paragliding from **Nonsolovolo** (⊠ Via XXIV Maggio 10 Lizzano Pisotiese ☏ 0573/677700 ⊕ www.nonsolovolo.it). The Web site is in Italian only.

Abetone

7 *20 km (12 mi) northwest of San Marcello Pistoiese, 86 km (53 mi) northwest of Florence.*

Abetone is one of the most-visited vacation spots in the Apennine Mountains, where Tuscans, Emilia-Romagnans, and others come to ski. Set above two valleys, the resort town is on the edge of a lush and ancient forest of more than 9,000 acres. The numerous ski trails are mostly for beginner and intermediate levels (the entire area has only two expert slopes). Summer is the time to trek or mountain bike in and around the beautiful hills and mountains.

en route | Stop at the **San Pellegrino in Alpe** monastery en route from Abetone to Castelnuovo di Garfagnana to see the staggering view and the large wooden cross. Story has it that a 9th-century Scot, Pellegrino by name, came to this spot to repent. Inside the monastery, the **Museo Etnografico** is devoted to rural life and has over 4,000 items on display. ⊠ *Off SR12, Via del Voltone 14, San Pellegrino in Alpe, 16 km (10 mi) northeast of Castelnuovo di Garfagnana, 28 km (17 mi) northwest of Abetone* ☏ *0573/649072* 💶 *Monastery free, museum €2.60* ☉ *June–Sept., daily 9:30–1 and 2:30–7; Oct.–May, Tues.–Sun. 9–noon and 2–5.*

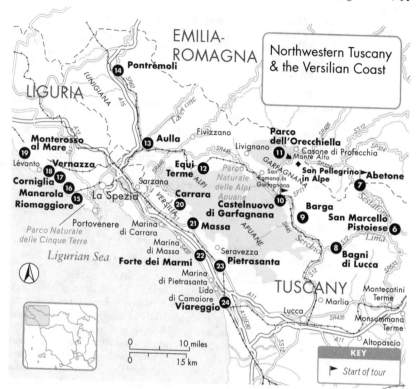

EMILIA-
ROMAGNA

Northwestern Tuscany
& the Versilian Coast

Pontrèmoli ⑭

LIGURIA

Fivizzano

**Parco
dell'Orecchiella** ⑪
Livignano   Casone di Profecchia
Monte Alto

⑬ **Aulla**

**Monterosso
al Mare** ⑲
Lèvanto ⑱ **Vernazza**
Corniglia ⑰
⑯
Manarola ⑮
Riomaggiore

**San Pellegrino
in Alpe**
Sarzana
**Equi
Terme** ⑫
Parco
Naturale
delle Alpi
Apuane

La Spezia
Carrara
⑳
**Castelnuovo
di Garfagnana**
⑩

Abetone ⑦

Barga
⑨

**San Marcello
Pistoiese** ⑥

Portovenere   Marina
di Carrara
**Parco Naturale
delle Cinque Terre**
⑳① **Massa**

**Bagni
di Lucca** ⑧

Ligurian Sea
Marina
di Massa
Seravezza
Forte dei Marmi ㉒ ㉓ **Pietrasanta**

TUSCANY
Montecatini
Terme

Marina
di Pietrasanta
Lido
di Camaiore
Viareggio ㉔

Marlia

Lucca
Monsummano
Terme

Altopascio

0 _____ 10 miles
0 _____ 15 km

KEY

▶ *Start of tour*

Where to Stay & Eat

$–$$ ✕ **La Capannina.** Fresh local ingredients—chestnuts, mushrooms, freshwater fish, cheeses, olive oil, and herbs—are the keys to the fabulous cooking of owners Luigi Ugolini and Romea Politi. The traditional rustic Tuscan soups and pastas are filling, but save room for dessert, especially anything made with the local chestnuts. This mountainside restaurant also has seven associated rooms for rent (€70 nightly). ⊠ *Via Brennero 256* ☎ *0573/60562* ▭ *AE, DC, MC* ⊘ *Closed Mon. and 2 wks in May and Oct.*

¢–$ ✕ **La Locanda dello Yeti.** Stop at this restful osteria after a day on the slopes or a trek through the forest. The specialty of the house is mushrooms—on *crostini* (toasted bread), polenta, or pasta. Mushrooms also garnish the fine grilled meats. The local house wine is refreshing. ⊠ *Via Brennero 324* ☎ *0573/606974* ⌁ *Reservations essential* ▭ *MC, V* ⊘ *Closed Tues.*

¢–$ ▦ **Hotel Bellavista.** Originally a 19th-century villa that belonged to the Strozzi family—powerful bankers in Renaissance Florence—this is now a contemporary inn. Some of the public rooms have a quaint Victorian charm to them, but the guest rooms are of more recent decor, with basic wooden furniture and no frills. Ask for one of the eight with a whirlpool tub. In winter you can use this as a base to ski to the slopes; in summer the Bellavista is perfectly situated for trekking and mountain biking. ⊠ *Via Brennero 383, 51021* ☏ *0573/60245* 📠 *0573/60028* ⊕ *www.bellavista-abetone.it* ⤳ *40 rooms, 2 suites* ♿ *Restaurant, some in-room hot tubs, bar; no a/c* 🖃 *AE, MC, V* ⊘ *Closed May, Oct., and Nov.* ⏶ *CP.*

Sports

SKIING The area has 37 ski slopes, amounting to about 50 km (31 mi) of ski surface, all accessible through the purchase of a single Multipass. Check the Abetone section of the **Pistoiese ski area** (⊕ www.lamontagnapistoiese. it) Web site for information on the Multipass pass. **Consorzio Impianti** (⊠ Via Brennero 429 ☏ 0573/60557), the group that manages ski facilities, has information on the Multipass as well as maps, directions, and area information. **F. Ballantini** (⊠ Via Brennero 615 ☏ 0573/60482) rents skis.

Bagni di Lucca

❽ *36 km (22 mi) southwest of Abetone, 27 km (17 mi) north of Lucca, 101 km (63 mi) northwest of Florence.*

Pretty Bagni di Lucca was a fashionable spa town in the early 19th century—in part because of its thermal waters. The Romantic poet Percy Bysshe Shelley (1792–1822) installed his family here during the summer of 1818. He wrote to a friend in July of that year that the waters here were exceedingly refreshing: "My custom is to undress and sit on the rocks, reading Herodotus, until perspiration has subsided, and then to leap from the edge of the rock into this fountain." In 1853, Robert and Elizabeth Browning spent the summer in a house on the main square. Its heyday behind it, the town is now a quiet, charming place where elegant thermal spas still enliven the temperate summer days.

The **Centro Termale Bagni di Lucca** has two natural steam-room caves, as well as spa services such as mud baths, massage, hydrotherapy, and facials. ⊠ *Piazza San Martino 11* ☏ *0583/87221* ⊕ *www. termebagnidilucca.it* 🎟 *€10* ⊘ *May–Sept., daily 9–6.*

Where to Eat

$-$$ ✕ **La Ruota.** About 3 km (2 mi) west of Bagni di Lucca in the tiny village of Fornoli, La Ruota is known for dishes that are traditional in the region along the Serchio River, such as smoked trout, tortelli with duck sauce, steak with porcini mushrooms, and fried frog legs. ⊠ *Via Giovanni XXIII 29, Fornoli* ☏ *0583/805627* ⌂ *Reservations essential* ⊘ *Closed July and Tues. No dinner Mon.* 🖃 *AE, DC, MC, V.*

Barga

❾ *17 km (11 mi) northwest of Bagni di Lucca, 111 km (69 mi) northwest of Florence.*

Barga is a lovely little hill town with a finely preserved medieval core. It produced textiles—particularly silk—during the Renaissance and wool in the 18th century. You won't find textiles here today; now the emphasis is on tourism. Here, the black American squadrons, known as the Buffalo Soldiers, are remembered for their bravery defending this mountainous area during World War II.

The **Duomo,** dedicated to St. Christopher, is an elegant limestone Romanesque cathedral that saw four separate building campaigns; the first began in the 9th century. Inside, the intricately carved high pulpit has two pillars that sit on the backs of stone lions, one pillar with a dragon being stabbed by a man, and the fourth pillar rests on a dwarf. From the Duomo you can get a beautiful panorama of the surrounding countryside. ⊠ *Via del Duomo* ☎ *No phone* ⚏ *Free* ☉ *Daily 9–7.*

off the
beaten
path

GROTTA DEL VENTO – About 14 km (9 mi) southwest of Barga, after following a winding road flanked by both sheer cliffs and fabulous views, you come to Tuscany's Cave of the Wind. As the result of a steady internal temperature of 10.7°C (about 51°F), the "wind" is sucked into the cave in the winter and blown out in the summer. It has a long cavern with stalactites, stalagmites, "bottomless" pits, and subterranean streams. One-, two-, and three-hour guided tours of the cave are given. (In winter only the one-hour tour is offered.) ⊠ *SP 39, west at Galliciano, Fornovolasco* ☎ *0583/722024* ᐧ *0583/722053* ⊕ *www.grottadelvento.com* ⚏ *€6.50 for 1 hr, €10 for 2 hrs, €15 for 3 hrs* ☉ *Daily 10–6.*

Where to Stay

$$–$$$ ▦ **Il Ciocco.** A huge resort and convention center, Il Ciocco has its own soccer stadium, basketball court, and equestrian center. There's even an on-site ATM. Most rooms have balcony views of the surrounding pine-forested hills and the distant Alpi Apuane. Furnishings include dark-wood desks, some chandeliers, and some wood paneling. Apartments and chalets are available for rental by the week; half and full board are available. ⊠ *Off SP7, 55020 Castelvecchio Pascoli, 7 km (4½ mi) north of Barga* ☎ *0583/7191 or 0583/719204* ᐧ *0583/723197* ⊕ *www.ciocco. it* ⇨ *220 rooms, 15 suites, 56 apartments, 12 chalets* ⚐ *Restaurant, pizzeria, some kitchens, minibars, cable TV with movies, 8 tennis courts, pool, health club, indoor hot tub, massage, sauna, mountain bikes, archery, basketball, boccie, hiking, horseback riding, roller-skating rink, soccer, volleyball, cinema, dance club, recreation room, shops, children's programs (ages 6–17), laundry service, business services, convention center, Internet, helipad, travel services, some pets allowed; no a/c in some rooms* ▤ *AE, DC, MC, V* ⎟◯⎟ *BP.*

Nightlife & the Arts

From mid-July to mid-August, the stony streets of Barga come alive with the participants and spectators of the **Opera Barga** (⊠Teatro dell' Accademia dei Differenti, Piazza Angelio 4 ⊕ www.barganews.com/operabarga), a highly regarded opera festival held at the **Teatro dell' Accademia dei Differenti** (Theater of the Academy of the Different). The Opera Barga was started in 1967 when a workshop was offered to young singers and musicians. The Opera Barga puts on smaller, lesser known operas of the baroque period together with more modern and even contemporary compositions. The Barga visitor center has additional information.

Listen to the newest music during **Barga Jazz** (⊠ Teatro dell' Accademia dei Differenti, Piazza Angelio 4 ⊕ www.barganews.com/bargajazz), a jazz orchestra competition (in July and August). The scores presented each year are selected by a special committee and a winner is selected by an international jury. The visitor center has information about these and other concerts.

Castelnuovo di Garfagnana

▶ ⑩ *13 km (8 mi) northwest of Barga, 121 km (75 mi) northwest of Florence.*

Castelnuovo di Garfagnana might be the best base for exploring the Garfagnana, as it is central with respect to the other towns. During the Renaissance the town's fortunes were frequently tied to those of the powerful Este family of Ferrara.

La Rocca (The Fortress) dates from the 13th century and has a plaque commemorating writer Ludovico Ariosto's brief tenure here as commissar general for the Este. Ariosto (1474–1533) wrote the epic poem *Orlando Furioso* (1516), among other works. You can only see the impressive walls and great entryway of the fort from the outside—at this time entry into La Rocca is not prohibited. ⊠ *Piazza Umberto I.*

The **Duomo**, a cathedral dedicated to St. Peter, was begun in the 11th century and was reconstructed in the early 1500s. Inside is a crucifix dating from the 14th to 15th century. There's also an early-16th-century terra-cotta attributed to the school of Della Robbia. ⊠ *Piazza del Duomo* ☎ *0583/62170* ⌖ *Free* ⊙ *Daily 9–7.*

Preserved ancient forests and barren rocky peaks create the dramatic scenery in the **Parco Naturale delle Alpi Apuane,** a national park area that encompasses several towns. Its highest peak, Monte Pisanino, rises more than 6,000 feet and towers over an artificial lake, Lago di Vagli, which covers the submerged village of Fabbricca. The tiny stone villages of Vagli di Sotto and Vagli di Sopra sit alongside the lake. Plan on a half or full day hiking in the Natural Park of the Apuane Alps. Remember to wear comfortable sports shoes or hiking boots and bring plenty of drinking water. A two-lane winding road through the park (SP13) connects Castelnuovo di Garfagnana to the seacoast. To get to Vagli di Sotto and Vagli di Sopra, go north of Castelnuovo di Garfagnana on SR445 to Poggio and then turn west on SP50. ☎ *0583/644354* ⊕ *www.parcapuane.toscana.it* ⌖ *Free.*

Where to Stay & Eat

$ ✕ **Osteria Vecchio Mulino.** An antique marble serving counter, wooden tables, and rush-seat chairs make this tiny eatery inviting. A mixed antipasto plate has vegetables *sott'olio* (marinated in olive oil), beans, and marinated anchovies. Traditional local dishes with *farro* (a pearly wheat grain), polenta, pecorino cheese, and salami round out the menu. Finish your meal with their famous *caffé al vetro con miele di castagno* (coffee in a glass with chestnut honey). This osteria keeps deli hours (7:30 AM to 8 PM) and you can order a picnic of sliced meats and sandwiches to take away. ✉ *Via Vittorio Emanuele 12* ☎ *0583/62192* ⊕ *www. ilvecchiomulino.com* 🖃 *AE, DC, MC, V* ⊗ *Closed Mon. and 3 wks in Oct. or Jan.*

¢–$ ✕🏠 **La Lanterna.** Take the few minutes' drive up a long, winding road from the center of town to a modern inn with beautiful mountain views. Wall-to-wall carpeting complements neutral color schemes and fairly motel-like furnishings. The restaurant ($–$$) serves bountiful regional specialties; the menu, featuring farro in several guises, is fantastic and inexpensive. The chef has a gift for sauces—try the pork in a radicchio sauce and anything (pasta or meat) with a porcini mushroom sauce. Half board is available. ✉ *Località le Monache, 55032 Piano Pieve, 1½ km (1 mi) southwest of Castelnuovo di Garfagnana* ☎ *0583/62272* 🖶 *0583/641418* ⊕ *www.hotellalanterna.com* 🛏 *42 rooms* ☄ *Restaurant, cable TV, meeting rooms, some pets allowed* 🖃 *AE, DC, MC, V* ❗ *BP* ⊗ *Restaurant closed Tues.*

Sports & the Outdoors

HIKING & The **Centri Accoglienza Parco** (✉ Piazza Erbe 1 ☎ 0583/644242) can help
CLIMBING you with hiking information, particularly for the Parco Naturale delle Alpi Apuane.

For detailed maps and information about trekking in the mountains surrounding Castelnuovo di Garfagnana, contact the **Club Alpino Italiano** (Italian Alpine Club; ✉ Via Vittrio Emanuele ☎ 0583/65577 ⊕ www.cai.it).

Parco dell'Orecchiella

⓫ *15 km (9 mi) north of Castelnuovo di Garfagnana, 121 km (72 mi) north-west of Florence.*

Orecchiella Park is 52 square km (21 square mi) of protected land dedicated to the preservation of local flora and fauna, including eagles, mouflon, and deer. The southeastern boundary of the park is accessible via SR324, a pretty 30-minute drive on the winding two-lane road from Abetone. There is a botanical garden and, for avid hikers, many trails marked with the length of time necessary to complete them—anywhere from 2½ to 5 hours. To find the visitor center drive to Castiglione Garfagnana, follow signs to Corfino, thereafter travel 7 km (4 mi) on SP48 and then follow the sign to turn into the park—the visitor center is just inside the gate. The botanical garden is 2 km (1¼ mi) from the visitor center. ✉ *7 km (4 mi) north of Corfino* ☎ *0583/619098 for information, 0583/955525 National Forest Administration* 🎟 *Park €1.50, garden €2* ⊗ *Apr.–May., Sun. 9* AM–*twilight; June, weekends 9–7; July–Aug., daily 9–7; Sept., daily 9* AM–*twilight; Oct.–Nov. 1, weekends 9* AM–*twilight.*

Where to Eat

¢–$ ✕ **Bar Ristorante Orecchiella.** Signora Ilda presides in the kitchen, serving grilled meats—*cinghiale* (wild boar) is often on the menu—and rich pasta dishes. This little place is quite rustic, set in the woods in San Romano in Garfagnana, near the main parking lot at Parco dell'Orecchiella. ✉ *Parco dell'Orecchiella, 7 km (4 mi) north of Corfino on SP48 San*

Romano in Garfagnana ☎ *0583/619010* ▬ *No credit cards* ⊘ *Closed Mon.–Sat. Nov.–Mar. and Fri. mid-Sept.–Oct. and Apr.–mid-June.*

THE LUNIGIANA

The Lunigiana (Land of the Moon) area was of strategic importance in pre-Roman times as a commercial center for trading between the Celts and the Ligurians. It maintained its economic strength during the early Middle Ages, serving as a junction between cities north of the Alps and those south. It also was a stopping point for pilgrims en route to Rome. The territory was hotly contested between the Milanese, the Genoese, and the Florentines during the Renaissance. This is the place where medieval fantasies run wild: the hills are steep, the mountains are plentiful, and there are lots of castles—more than 100 of them, still whole or in ruins—that provide testimony to the Lunigiana's tumultuous past. Built in the 13th and 14th centuries, the castles and defensive towers set amid the rocky, forested landscape create a powerful effect.

Equi Terme

⑫ *34 km (21 mi) west of Parco dell'Orecchiella, 147 km (91 mi) northwest of Florence.*

This pretty little spa town nestled in the mountains is a great place for an affordable spa experience. Though the Romans first discovered these waters (a warm 27°C [81°F]), it wasn't until the end of the 19th century that the thermal springs became a draw. At the **Stabilimento Termale di Equi Terme,** there's a large pool with warm thermal waters for a lengthy soak under the clear blue mountain sky, and many spa services—sauna, massage, water therapy, and water massage, among others—provided within. Treatments run from €9 to €27. ⊠ *Piazza delle Terme 1* ☎☎ *0585/949300* ▨ *€12* ⊘ *Treatments May–Oct., daily 8:30–12:30 and 2–6. Pool June–Sept., daily 10–6:30.*

Where to Stay & Eat

¢ ✕▦ **La Posta.** This slightly ramshackle, but fun place to stay and eat is directly across a little stream from the Hotel Terme. The rooms are basic—each has high ceilings, a double bed or two narrow twin beds, and a bedside table, but the restaurant ($$–$$$) is a real treat. The *ravioli alle ortiche* (spinach ravioli stuffed with nettles and lightly dressed with a creamy nut sauce) is a good choice; the house special, *lasagne la spagnola,* made—as the proprietor says—with "top-secret" ingredients, definitely includes five cheeses and tastes as light as a feather. Half and full board are available. ⊠ *Via Provinciale 26, 54022* ☎ *0585/97937* ⇨ *7 rooms ⟁ Restaurant; no a/c, no room TVs, no room phones* ▬ *AE, DC, MC, V* ⊘ *Closed Jan. and Feb.* ⦿ *CP.*

¢ ▦ **Hotel Terme.** More than a century old, this cool and comfortable hotel is a great place to unwind; next door is a spa that has all sorts of soothing things for body and soul. Some of the rooms have antique pieces, but the emphasis is on cleanliness and functionality. A small river runs near it, which might be the only noise you hear. The restaurant serves local specialties, and the menu changes frequently. ⊠ *Via Noce Verde*

51, 54022 ☎ 0585/97830 🖷 0585/97831 ⤴ *20 rooms* ⌂ *Restaurant, pool, bar, Internet, meeting room; no a/c* ▤ *AE, DC, MC, V* ⫟ *CP.*

Aulla

⑬ *22 km (13 mi) northwest of Equi Terme, 23 km (14 mi) northeast of La Spezia, 169 km (104 mi) northwest of Florence.*

Aulla is a sleepy little town just off the A15. It was heavily bombed by the United States during World War II, so much of what you see is postwar reconstruction.

However, on the outskirts of town is a park with an old castle, **La Brunella,** that affords some superb views. The castle dates from the 16th century, and you can see remnants of a 9th-century abbey dedicated to St. Caprasio on-site. English couple Aubrey Waterfield and Lina Duff Gordon bought the property in the early 1900s and turned it into a country home; they also created its garden. D. H. Lawrence (1885–1930) was one of their visitors. Inside the complex is the **Museo di Storia Naturale della Lunigiana** (Museum of Natural History of the Lunigiana), which provides an overview of the plants and animals of the surrounding mountain area. You can also tour the gardens, but at this time the interior of the castle is closed to visitors. ⊠ *Castle la Brunella* ☎ *0187/400252* 🖷 *0187/420727* ⤴ *Park and museum €3.50* ⊙ *Park and museum, June 15–Oct. 15, Tues.–Sun. 9–noon and 4–7; Oct. 16–June 14, Tues.–Sun., 9–noon and 3–6.*

Pontrémoli

⑭ *17 km (11 mi) north of Aulla, 40 km (25 mi) northeast of La Spezia, 186 km (125 mi) northwest of Florence.*

Where the Magra and Verde rivers meet, Pontrémoli is a town with an old center developed according to a medieval matrix. During the Middle Ages the city was a point of contact between north and south, which helped it to flourish economically. Here originated the *libri ambulanti* (traveling book fair), and a prestigious literary prize, the Premio Bancarella, is still awarded. The town is especially bursting with activity on Wednesday and Saturday, when an open-air market with fruits, vegetables, and clothing takes over the Piazza del Duomo and the adjoining Piazza Repubblica.

The 17th-century **Duomo** is an exercise in baroque excess—the lime-green walls, accentuated with pale pink on the pilasters, and the white molding throughout make it look like a gaudy wedding cake. ⊠ *Piazza del Duomo* ☎ *No phone* ⤴ *Free* ⊙ *Daily 9–noon and 3–6:30.*

The **Chiesa di Nostra Donna** (Church of Our Lady), which was finished in the 1730s, has a pretty rococo facade that's worth a look. It's on the the other side of the Magra River from the Piazza del Duomo. The Chiesa di Nostra Donna is in the **Parco della Torre,** a lovely park that makes a great place for a picnic. ⊠ *End of Via Mazzini.*

Castello di Piagnaro was built in the 9th and 10th centuries—though not much remains from that period—with alterations made between the 15th and 16th centuries. What does remain is a fully formed castle with stupefying views; it's home to the **Museo delle Statue Stele Lunigianesi,** which contains a collection of steles found in the area. Many of the large, prehistoric, carved stone slabs depict stylized warriors, and others are of women. ⊠ *Via Garibaldi* ☎ *0187/831439* ▣ *€3.50* ⊘ *Oct.–Mar., Tues.–Sun. 9–noon and 2–5; Apr.–Sept., Tues.–Sun. 9–noon and 3–6.*

A very tiny chapel built between 1883 and 1893, **La Chiesetta di Sant' Ilario** is without artistic or historic merit, but it is so cute that it's worth a visit. The exterior, with its orange and yellow paint, is almost Disneyesque in style; inside are ceiling decorations that were executed after World War II by the members of the Triani family, Pontrémoli natives. (Ask at the Duomo for chapel access.) It's a few minutes' walk from the Castello di Piagnaro. ⊠ *Via Piagnaro 13* ☎ *No phone* ▣ *Free* ⊘ *Daily 9–noon.*

Where to Eat

$ ✕ **Da Busse'.** The interior is brightly lighted, the tables are close together, and a hum emanates from the chatting diners and kitchen activity: this family eatery serves solid local fare in a casual, understated way. *Zuppa con ragu e parmigiano* (soup with meat sauce and Parmesan) has been pleasing crowds for the past 20 years. Other kitchen favorites include vegetable tarts, lasagna made with chestnut flour, and stuffed veal. The restaurant is around the corner from the Duomo. ⊠ *Piazza Duomo 31* ☎ *0187/831371* ⌣ *Reservations essential* ▭ *No credit cards* ⊘ *Closed Fri. and July.*

CINQUE TERRE

The aura of isolation that has surrounded the five Ligurian coastal villages known as the Cinque Terre (Five Lands)—Riomaggiore, Manarola, Corniglia, Vernazza, and Monterosso al Mare—together with their dramatic coastal scenery, has made them one of the Italian Riviera's premier attractions. The area was declared a UNESCO World Heritage site in 1997. In 1999 the Italian government followed by establishing the Parco Nazionale delle Cinque Terre, and creating a marine protected area off the coast.

The five villages, which cling haphazardly to steep cliffs, are linked by popular footpaths. By hiking these trails you can traverse centuries-old terraces, olive groves, and forests; take in breathtaking ocean views; and gain access to rugged, secluded beaches and grottoes (⇨ Hiking the Cinque Terre box, *below*). For much of the villages' history, the trails were the only way to get from one town to the next on land.

These days, the local train on the Genoa–La Spezia train line stops at each of the Cinque Terre. The train runs approximately every 30 minutes. A 24-hour Cinque Terre Tourist train ticket, which allows unlimited travel between the five towns, is available at the five train stations (€2.85). The stations are frequently high on the ridge, requiring a hike down to the port. A full-day train/boat/trail pass is available for €23.50.

Along the coast of Cinque Terre, two ferry lines operate: Golfo Paradiso, which operates from June to September from Genoa and Camogli to the Cinque Terre villages of Monterosso al Mare and Vernazza; and the smaller, but more frequent, Golfo dei Poeti, which stops at each village (from Portovenere to Riomaggiore, except for Corniglia) four times a day. A daily ticket costs €11.50. Boat travel involves less frequent stops than train travel.

There is a narrow, largely unpaved, serpentine road connecting each of the towns with one-lane tunnels and few parking opportunities. Car travel in the Cinque Terre is not advised.

Riomaggiore

15 *50 km (31 mi) southeast of Pontrémoli, 11 km (7 mi) west of La Spezia, 158 km (98 mi) northwest of Florence.*

At the eastern end of the Cinque Terre, Riomaggiore is the most accessible of the villages (via car or train from La Spezia). It curves around a tiny harbor that is ringed with lively cafés and dotted with fishing boats, but does not have as much old-world charm as her sister villages. Easy accessibility has brought more modern construction and increased traffic. Riomaggiore, however, is the best town from which start walking the *Sentiero Azzurro* (Blue Trail), the lower coastal walking route connecting the five villages in the national park (⇨ Hiking the Cinque Terre, *below*). According to legend, settlement along the narrow valley of the River Maior dates back to the 8th century, when Greek religious refugees came here to escape persecution by the Byzantine emperor.

Where to Stay & Eat

$–$$$ ✕ **Ripa del Sole.** Try some of the great local wine at this notable seafood restaurant with the chef's signature *scampi con tartufo bianco* (large shrimp with white truffles). Other house specialties include calamari with farro, *gamberi con fagioli e rucola* (shrimp with beans and greens), and *trofie fatte a mano con pesto* (handmade curly pasta in a pesto sauce). Enjoy your meal on the terrace in summer, or in the dining room dressed in cool white tile and tablecloths. ⊠ *Via De Gasperi 282* ☎ *0187/ 920143* ⚲ *Reservations essential* ▤ *No credit cards* ⊘ *Closed mid-Jan.–mid-Feb. and Mon. Nov.–Mar.*

$ ▦ **Villa Argentina.** Fabulous views of the turquoise water are to be had from the small Villa Argentina. Simple, wood-veneer furniture all but fills the rooms, which are clean and bright—the bathrooms are tiny. You can have a bountiful Continental breakfast for €7, which provides fuel enough for hiking the nearby Cinque Terre trails. Parking is available for €10 per day. ⊠ *Via de Gasperi 170, 19017* ☎ *0187/920213* ⇥ *15 rooms* ⚲ *Restaurant, cable TV, laundry service, some pets allowed; no a/c* ▤ *No credit cards* ⧆ *EP.*

Manarola

16 *1 ½ km (1 mi) west of Riomaggiore on foot.*

The enchanting pastel houses of Manarola spill down a steep hill overlooking a spectacular turquoise swimming cove and a bustling harbor. The whole town is built on black rock. Above the town, ancient ter-

HIKING THE CINQUE TERRE

ALTHOUGH MANY PEOPLE EXPLORE the Cinque Terre by train or boat, others find the most rewarding way to view one of the finest coastlines in Italy is on foot. The Blue Trail is the easier, coastal route, and the Red Trail is a more challenging, ridge-top hike. Trail maps and boat and train schedules are available at tourist offices in Riomaggiore and Monterosso al Mare.

The **Sentiero Azzurro** (Blue Trail) is about 13 km (8 mi) start to finish (three to five hours) from Riomaggiore to Monterosso al Mare along the coast. It's suitable for all endurance levels. Each of the four sections has fabulous views of the turquoise sea, century-old terraces, and fishing villages.

The trailhead in Riomaggiore is off Piazza Stazione: a staircase to the left of the train station entrance crosses over the tracks to the beginning of the first segment, also known as the Via dell'Amore (Lovers' Lane). This short segment is carved into the cliff, providing spectacular views of the sea (it's a good place to come at sunset). After only 30 minutes, you pass through a tunnel into Manarola, the first village stop. After Manarola turn left to the waterfront, where there's a path denoted by blue-paint markers that skirts around the headland and then climbs up a steep hillside to an abandoned railway line. Within an hour from Manarola you can arrive at the train station of Corniglia.

The marked trail does not go through Corniglia, but keeps the village on the seaward side and passes a small 14th-century Gothic church dedicated to St. Peter. About two hours later, after a difficult climb to Prevo and an easier path through the olive groves, you arrive in Vernazza, arguably the prettiest of the five villages. From there the Sentiero Azzurro climbs steeply up next to the church, dedicated to St. Margaret of Antioch.

This section has the best views of the day. At the top of the ridge the path levels out all the way to Monterosso, which is about 90 minutes from Vernazza.

Although you can start along the Sentiero Azzurro from any of the five towns at any time of day, if you're doing the full trek, it's best to start in the morning at Riomaggiore so the sun will be at your back. This also allows an easy warm-up before the path becomes increasingly difficult. (Remember, at each village you can take the train back to your start point or ahead to meet more energetic members of your group.) There's a daily fee for hiking any part of the trail (€3), and at checkpoints along the way you must either show your ticket or buy one.

Trekkers looking for a challenge and less company may wish to tackle the 9- to 12-hour **Sentiero Rosso** (Red Trail), the ridge-top path that provides spectacular views from far above each of the five villages. From the trailhead in Portovenere the path climbs steeply and in returns to the sea at Levanto. Along the way, trails drop steeply from the Red Trail to each of the Cinque Terre villages (see the footpaths map on www.cinqueterre.it). The Red Trail is free and is not as frequently maintained as the Blue Trail. Good hiking boots are necessary. Bring food, water, and sunscreen; and wear a hat, since there's little shade.

There are also a web of free **minor trails** around each of the towns. For instance, Trail No. 9 starts from the old section of Monterosso al Mare and finishes at the Santuario del Soviore (Sanctuary of Sovoire). Minor trails are not maintained as well as the Blue Trail.

races still protect abundant vineyards and olive trees. This village is the center of the wine and olive oil production of the region, and its streets are lined with shops selling local products.

Where to Stay & Eat

$ ✗☰ **Hotel Marina Piccola** You can look out at the water from the terrace, from the restaurant, or from your room at this small cliff-side hotel. Curled-iron beds stand against whitewashed walls and are covered with fresh white linens. The restaurant is oriented to the sea, with indoor seating that has wide windows and outdoor tables overlooking the water. Go for the best—choose the platter of shellfish, shrimp, crab, and lobster, steamed and served cold with lemon. The garlicky spaghetti with clams, also a specialty, is sautéed in a local olive oil. Half and full pension are available. ⊠ *Via Lo Scalo 16, 19010* ☎ *0187/920103* 🖨 *0187/ 920966* ⊕ *www.hotelmarinapiccola.com* 🛏 *10 rooms* ♨ *Restaurant, cable TV* ☰ *AE, DC, MC, V* ⧈ *CP.*

$ ☰ **Cá d'Andrean.** Who needs complicated design in a guest room when you have large windows—or access to a terrace—with sea views? Simple honey-color wood desks and beds are the only furniture in white-tile rooms. During summer, breakfast (€6) is served in a flower garden with lemon trees. ⊠ *Via Discovolo 101, 19010* ☎ *0187/920040* 🖨 *0187/ 920452* ⊕ *www.cadandrean.it* 🛏 *10 rooms* ♨ *Cable TV, bar, some pets allowed; no a/c* ☰ *No credit cards* ⊘ *Closed Nov.* ⧈ *EP.*

Corniglia

⑰ *3 km (2 mi) northwest of Manarola on foot.*

The buildings, narrow lanes, and stairways of Corniglia—the middle of the Cinque Terre—are strung together amid vineyards high on the cliffs; on a clear day views of the entire coastal strip are excellent. Lacking the beach and harbor activity of the other towns, this farming community is the most peaceful. Access to this village is limited to hikers and rail travelers, but even if you take the train, a challenging climb up 365 steps from the station to the village awaits.

The Gothic parish church of St. Peter, **Chiesa di San Pietro**, was built in 1334 on the ruins of an old 11th-century chapel and is one of the most beautiful to be found in the Cinque Terre. ⊠ *Via Serra* ☎ *No phone* 🎫 *Free* ⊘ *Daily 9–1 and 4–7.*

Where to Eat

$–$$ ✗ **A Cantina de Mananan.** You can't eat outside and there's no view at the minuscule osteria with marble tables, but owner-chef Agostino Gallenti's traditional Ligurian fare is legendary. A board on the wall lists the daily changing menu. Good bets, when available, include the anchovy starter, followed by spaghetti with either clams, crab, or pesto sauce. Another favorite is the rabbit fried in local olive oil. For a simple dessert, do as the locals do and order the milk custard drizzled with honey. ⊠ *Via Fieschi 117* ☎ *0187/821166* ♨ *Reservations essential July–Aug.* ☰ *No credit cards* ⊘ *Closed Tues. July–Aug. Might be closed Nov.–Feb.; call for hrs. No lunch July–Aug.*

Vernazza

⑱ *4 km (3 mi) northwest of Corniglia on foot.*

A charming village of narrow streets and small squares, Vernazza is arguably the most picturesque of the five towns. Because it has the best access to the sea, this village became wealthier than its neighbors—as witnessed by the elaborate arcades, loggias, and use of marble. The village's pink, slate-roof houses and colorful squares contrast with the remains of the medieval fort and castle, including two towers, in the old town. The Romans first inhabited this rocky spit of land in the 1st century.

Today Vernazza has a fairly lively social scene, because you can access the village by car, train, or boat and on foot. If you chose to undertake the full three- to five-hour hike along the seaside Blue Trail (⇨ Hiking the Cinque Terre, *above)*, this is a great place to stop for a hearty seafood lunch.

Where to Stay & Eat

$–$$ ✕ **Trattoria Gianni Franzi.** Pesto on *fagiolini* (green beans) is a Ligurian specialty, and this is the place to order it; somehow it tastes better when you're eating outside in a beautiful *piazzetta* (small square) with a view of the port. Many of the other dishes here focus on seafood. Gianni has an adjoining hotel as well. ⊠ *Piazza Marconi 5* ☎ *0187/821003* 🖷 *0187/812228* ⌘ *Reservations essential* 🖃 *AE, DC, MC, V* ☺ *Closed Jan.–Mar. and Wed.*

¢–$ 🏨 **Hotel Gianni Franzi.** Gianni Franzi restored buildings next to his trattoria in the 1990s to create this interesting hotel. Aldo Trionfo, who worked with the famous theater director Luchino Visconti, helped decorate some of the rooms, distinguished by their colorful artwork and ever-so-slightly-quirky design. Other rooms have interesting antique beds and furniture. Ask to see the room before you accept it—some have sea views, but many are tiny. A small garden for guests sits on a ledge above the sea. ⊠ *Piazza Marconi 5, 19018* ☎ *0187/821003* 🖷 *0187812228* 🌐 *www.giannifranzi.it* 🛏 *23 rooms* ⚒ *Restaurant; no a/c, no room phones, no room TVs* 🖃 *AE, DC, MC, V* ☺ *Closed Jan.–Mar.* ⅋ *CP.*

Monterosso al Mare

⑲ *3 km (2 mi) west of Vernazza on foot.*

Beautiful beaches, steep rugged cliffs, crystal-clear turquoise waters, and plentiful small hotels and restaurants make Monterosso al Mare, the largest of the Cinque Terre villages (population 1,730), one of the two busiest in midsummer. The village center bustles high on a hillside. Below, connected by stone steps, are the port and seaside promenade, where there are boats for hire. The medieval tower, Aurora, on the hills of the Cappuccini, separates the ancient part of the village from the more modern part. The village is encircled by hills covered with vineyards and olive groves and by a forest of scrubby bushes and small trees.

Monterosso has the most festivals of the five villages, starting with the Lemon Feast on the Saturday preceding Ascension Sunday, followed by the Flower Festival of Corpus Christi, celebrated yearly on the second Sunday after Pentecost. During the afternoon, the streets and alleyways of the *centro storico* (historic center) are decorated with thousands of colorful flower petals set in beautiful designs that the evening procession passes over. Finally, the Salted Anchovy and Olive Oil Festival takes place each year during the second weekend of September.

Thursday, the **market** attracts mingled crowds of tourists and villagers from along the coast to shop for everything from pots and pans to underwear to fruits, vegetables, and fish. Often a few stands sell local art and crafts as well as olive oil and wine. ☒ *Old town center* ☽ *Thurs. 8–2.*

Visit the **Chiesa di San Francesco,** which was built in the 12th century in the Ligurian Gothic style. Its distinctive black stripes and marble rose window make it one of the most photographed sites in the Cinque Terre. ☒ *Piazza Garibaldi* ☎ *No phone* 🎫 *Free* ☽ *Daily 9–1 and 4–7.*

Where to Stay & Eat

$$–$$$ ╳ **Il Pirata.** The high-quality Ligurian seafood stands out at the port-side trattoria where preferred seating is at the long table outside. Try the starters with anchovy or tiny squid. Soups and pastas with seafood are also highly recommended. Chef-owner Roberto has developed a tasting menu that lists the best the sea has to offer each day. This intimate space is less appropriate for children than others in the area. Reservations are essential on weekends. ☒ *Via Molinelli 6/8* ☎ *0187/817536* 🖃 *MC, V* ☽ *Closed Wed. and mid-Jan.–mid.-Feb.*

$$–$$$ ╳ **Miky.** Anything having to do with seafood is the specialty at this popular eatery. The *insalata di mare* (cold squid and fish salad) is more than appetizing; so are the risotto and prawns and the linguine *al mare* (with seafood). Pizza is available too: try the one topped with shrimp. Miky has a beautiful little garden in back, perfect for lunch on a sunny day. ☒ *Via Fegina 104* ☎ *0187/817608* 🖃 *AE, DC, MC, V* ☽ *Closed Nov., Dec., and Tues. Sept.–June.*

$$ ╳ **Il Ciliegio** Come at sunset to the forested edge of a ridge far above Monterosso for the ultimate romantic view of the sea. Chef-owners Rosanna and Teresa bring simple but plentiful seafood dishes to the table. Using the local olive oil, the women prepare mussels and clams over spaghetti that comes heaped high and steaming. Other options include anchovies prepared in a variety of ways—marinated, under salt, and stuffed. Local wines are on the menu, as is a tasty apple tart for dessert. Call and ask about van service to the restaurant. ☒ *Località Beo 2* ☎ *0187/817829* 🖃 *V* ☽ *Closed Mon. Hrs vary unpredictably Nov.–Mar.*

★ $$–$$$ 🏨 **Porto Roca.** In a panoramic position above the sea, Porto Roca is slightly, and blessedly, removed from the crowds that visit the Cinque Terre. The hotel is on a network of not-too-demanding hill walks and draws a faithful American clientele. Interiors contain authentic antique pieces, such as Victorian loveseats and suits of armor. Ask for one of the rooms with a fantastic sea view; the north-facing, small dark rooms tend to be damp. Half and full pension are available. ☒ *Via Corone 1, 19016*

☎ *0187/817502* 🖨 *0187/817692* ⊕ *www.portoroca.it* ➾ *43 rooms* ⚷ *Restaurant, in-room safe, refrigerators, cable TV, bar, some pets allowed (fee)* ▭ *AE, MC, V* ⊗ *Closed Nov. 4–mid-Mar.* ⦿ *BP.*

$　🔲 **Degli Amici.** Stay here if you want to be only 165 yards from the beach in the old part of Monterosso. The furniture is simple, with a modular, light-oak look, and the rooms are small, but everything is neat and clean. Relax under the lemon tree in the rose-filled garden terrace, reached from the top floor, and enjoy the view of the town and sea below. There is buffet service for breakfast, and the restaurant has a buffet of salads and vegetables for lunch and dinner in addition to the menu. Half board is available. ☒ *Via Buranco 36, 19016* ☎ *0187/817574* 🖨 *0187/817424* ⊕ *www.hotelamici.it* ➾ *43 rooms* ⚷ *Restaurant, in-room safes, cable TV, Ping-Pong* ▭ *DC, MC, V* ⊗ *Closed Nov. and Jan.* ⦿ *BP.*

VERSILIA & THE COAST

In full view of the Alpi Apuane, the Versilian coast bustles in July and August with vacationing Italians drawn by the sea breezes and fine, wide sandy beaches. From the coast, roads in Versilia climb over the rolling hills blanketed with pine forests and into the mountains, where marble quarries have been operating since long before Michelangelo (1475–1564) came to pick his own blocks of Carrara marble.

Carrara

🔟 *45 km (28 mi) southeast of Riomaggiore, 126 km (79 mi) northwest of Florence.*

Carrara, from which the famous white marble takes its name, lies in a beautiful valley midway up a spectacular mountain in the Apuane Alps. The surrounding peaks are bare of foliage and white as snow, even in summer, because they are full of marble stone. Marble has been quarried in the area for the past 2,000 years. The art historian Giorgio Vasari (1511–74) recorded that Michelangelo came to Carrara with two apprentices to quarry the marble for the never-completed tomb of Julius II (1443–1513). According to Vasari, Michelangelo spent eight months among the rocks conceiving fantastical ideas for future works.

The area around Carrara has a lot of still-active quarries—well over 100 at last count. Most of them are not open to the public for safety reasons. However, it is possible to tour specific marble caves. The **Carrara visitor information center,** 7 km (4½ mi) away in Marina di Massa, has details about which areas you can visit. ☒ *Lungomare A. Vespucci 24, Marina di Massa* ☎ *0585/240063.*

Carrara's history as a marble-producing center is well documented in the **Museo del Marmo** (Museum of Marble), beginning with early works from the 2nd century. Exhibits detail the working of marble, from quarrying and transporting it to sculpting it. ☒ *Viale XX Settembre 85* ☎🖨 *0585/845746* 💳 *€4.50* ⊗ *May–Sept., Mon.–Sat. 10–6; Oct.–Apr., Mon.–Sat. 9–5.*

Work began on the **Duomo** in the 11th century, and continued into the 14th. The cathedral is dedicated to St. Andrew, and is the first church of the Middle Ages constructed entirely of marble. Most of the marble comes from the area (the white, light blue-gray, black, and red). The tremendous facade is a fascinating blend of Pisan Romanesque and Gothic architecture. Note the human figures and animals on Corinthian capitals. ⊠ *Piazza del Duomo* ☎ *No phone* ⊠ *Free* ⊙ *Daily 9–7.*

The lovely baroque church of **San Francesco** is a study in understated elegance. It dates from the 1620s to 1660s, and even though it was built during the peak years of the baroque, the only excess can be found in the twisting marble columns that embellish the altars. ⊠ *Piazza XXVII Aprile* ☎ *No phone* ⊠ *Free* ⊙ *Daily 9–7.*

During the 19th and 20th centuries Carrara became a hotbed for anarchism, and during World War II it put up fierce resistance to the Nazis. The town is still lively thanks to its art institute. The **Accademia di Belle Arti,** founded by Maria Teresa Cybo Malaspina d'Este in 1769, draws studio art students from all over Italy. Their presence explains the energetic and artistically eclectic presence in some of the piazzas.

Where to Stay & Eat

★ **$$–$$$$** ✕ **Ninan.** Marco Garfagnini, chef of this small, exclusive eatery, prepares dishes that satisfy the palate and delight the eye: try the artful ravioli stuffed with lobster under a sauce with ground shrimp and lemon. Marco's menu pays homage to the abundant fresh seafood available, but also includes special meat dishes, such as a starter of foie gras with carmelized oranges. To satiate a sweet tooth, have the banana Bavarian cream with strawberry sauce. Call ahead during winter; the restaurant may close for a few weeks' vacation. ⊠ *Via L. Bartolini 3* ☎ *0585/ 74741* ⊙ *Closed Sun.* ▤ *MC, DC, V.*

$ ⌂ **Hotel Carrara.** Although this quiet hotel isn't actually in Carrara, it is right across the street from the Avenza-Carrara train station. Distinctive wall hangings—copies of Renaissance masterworks—complement red lampshades and bedspreads in guest rooms. The dinner-only restaurant (**$–$$**) serves seafood specialties and regional pastas and grilled meats. The included breakfast buffet is extensive. ⊠ *Via Petacchi 21, 54031 Avenza, 4 km (2½ mi) southeast of Carrara* ☎ *0585/857616* ⌨ *0585/ 50344* ⊕ *www.hotelcarrara.it* ⇥ *32 rooms* ⌂ *Restaurant, in-room safes, minibars, cable TV, Internet, some pets allowed* ▤ *AE, DC, MC, V* ⎟⊙⎟ *BP.*

$ ⌂ **Hotel Mediterraneo.** The same family has owned and managed the hotel since 1958, and they take obvious pride in the facilities and their maintenance. Unlike most coastal hotels, this one has a large, well-outfitted gym and a swimming pool surrounded by a lovely grass lawn. Breakfast is served on a terrace with both sea and mountain views. Rooms have carpeted floors, white walls, and a few modern decorative touches like black leather lounge chairs. Many have balconies, although some face the street. The restaurant's daily-changing menu derives inspiration from the sea, but there are meat options too. Half and full board are available. ⊠ *Via Genova 2/h, 54036 Marina di Carrara, 5 km (3 mi) south of Carrara* ☎ *0585/785222* ⌨ *0585/785290* ⊕ *www.*

mediterraneohotel.com 🛏 *42 rooms, 1 suite* 🔥 *Restaurant, cable TV, pool, gym, bar, meeting room; no a/c* 🖃 *AE, DC, MC, V* ✝⚬ *BP.*

Massa

㉑ *7 km (4½ mi) south of Carrara, 115 km (74 mi) northwest of Florence.*

The best reasons to visit this modern town are the large fountains, marble sculptures, and its proximity to Carrara and the marble quarries.

The **Castello Malaspina** (La Rocca) was built between the 11th and 14th centuries. The fortress's exterior alone is impressive, but be warned that getting to La Rocca requires a steep climb. ⊠ *Via della Rocca* ☎ *0585/ 490259 or 0585/44774* 🎟 *€5* ⊘ *June 15–Sept. 15, daily 9:30–noon and 4–7:30; July–Aug. also Sun. 8 PM–midnight.*

Things are livelier in **Marina di Massa**, the port area, where there's a busy beach and many eateries. ✛ *5 km (3 mi) south of Massa.*

Where to Stay & Eat

$–$$ ✕ **La Peniche.** Similar to a French bistro, La Peniche specializes in light choices such as the large salad with fish cakes. Try the spaghetti with lobster, or couscous with seafood, for a slightly heartier meal. The specialty dessert is a sinfully rich crème brûlée. The restaurant is alongside the Brugiano Canal. ⊠ *Via Lungo Brugiano 3, Marina di Massa* ☎ *0585/ 240017* ⊘ *Closed Mon.* 🖃 *DC, V.*

$–$$ 🏨 **Hotel Excelsior.** The spacious rooms in this modern hotel have panoramic views of either the sea or the Alpi Apuane; three are wheelchair accessible. The on-site restaurant, Il Sestante, serves both local and international dishes. The Carrara marble quarries are only 5 km (3 mi) away. ⊠ *Lungomare Vespucci, Via Cesare Battisti I, 54037* ☎ *0585/ 8601* 🖷 *0585/869795* ⊕ *www.hotelexcelsior.it* 🛏 *71 rooms, 7 suites* 🔥 *Restaurant, room service, in-room safes, minibars, cable TV, pool, laundry service, Internet, meeting room, some pets allowed (fee)* 🖃 *AE, DC, MC, V* ✝⚬ *CP* ⊘ *Restaurant closed Dec.–Mar.*

$–$$ 🏨 **Hotel Tirreno e Milano.** The two buildings of the once-private Liberty villa (about 100 feet from the sea) were converted into two hotels in the 1950s; they are run by the same management and share a restaurant and meeting rooms, including the reception desk. The rooms are decorated in cool pastel colors and have high ceilings that contribute to a grand sense of space. Those in the Tirreno ($$) are larger and fancier than those in the Milano ($). The Milano is frequently booked by large tour groups. Full board is required in August. ⊠ *Piazza Betti 24, 54037 Marina di Massa* ☎ *0585/246173 or 0585/240076* 🖷 *0585/240827* ⊕ *www.hoteltirrenomarinadimassa.com* 🛏 *Tirreno 27 rooms, 5 suites; Milano 55 rooms* 🔥 *Restaurant, cable TV, meeting rooms, some pets allowed* 🖃 *DC, MC, V* ⊘ *Closed Nov.–Mar.* ✝⚬ *FAP.*

Forte dei Marmi

㉒ *8 km (5 mi) south of Massa, 106 km (66 mi) northwest of Florence.*

Forte dei Marmi is a playground for wealthy Italians and equally well-heeled tourists. Its wide, sandy beaches—strands are 6 km (4 mi) long—

have the Alpi Apuane as a dramatic backdrop. The town was, from Roman times, the port from which marble quarried in Carrara was transported. In the 1920s, it became the fashionable seaside resort it is today. During the winter the town's population is about 10,000; in the summer, it swells to seven to eight times that.

Where to Stay & Eat

★ **$$$$** ✕ **Lorenzo.** The affable Lorenzo Viani has presided here for more than 20 years, and his restaurant still draws a crowd. Start with the chilled raw oysters before moving on to seafood pasta, sea bass with chopped tomatoes, or a fish tartar. Request the *menu degustazione* (tasting menu) and let chef Giocchino Pontrelli prepare the freshest items of the day. You can also choose vegetarian and *terra* (meat) tasting menus. ⊠ *Via Carducci 61* ☎ *0584/84030* ⌂ *Reservations essential* ▤ *AE, DC, MC, V* ⊘ *Closed mid-Dec.–Jan. and Mon. No lunch July–Aug.*

$$$–$$$$ ✕ **Bistrot.** For beach-side dining, this seafood restaurant can't be beat. The delicious *carpaccio di branzino* (thin slices of sea bass) is quickly seared and then served with fragrant local olive oil, basil, and tomatoes. The regal champagne risotto with lobster is a house favorite. Pastas are homemade, and the *sauté di frutti di mare,* a cross between a soup and stew, has *vongole* (clams), tomatoes, and garlic in a heavenly broth. For dessert have the hot flan made with *gianduia* chocolate and pieces of white chocolate. ⊠ *Viale Franceschi 14* ☎ *0584/89879* ▤ *AE, DC, MC, V* ⊘ *Closed Tues. Oct.–May. No lunch Aug.*

★ **$$$$** ▥ **Byron.** The pale yellow exterior only hints at the elegance inside the hotel created by joining two Liberty villas from 1899 and 1902. Refined furnishings include gem-color fabrics and dark wood. Many rooms have balconies that face the sea or the mountains. The billiard room and bar overlook a garden of pine trees and flowers. Walk across the street to get to the beach. The restaurant, La Magnolia, serves regional cuisine pool-side during the summer. Half board is mandatory June 15 to August 31; the rest of the year Continental breakfast is included in the price. Full board is always available. ⊠ *Viale Arthur-Jules Morin 46, 55042* ☎ *0584/787052* ▤ *0584/787152* ⊕ *www.hotelbyron.net* ⇱ *29 rooms, 3 suites, 3 apartments* ⌂ *Restaurant, some kitchens, cable TV, pool, billiards, bar, meeting rooms* ▤ *AE, DC, MC, V* ⊙l *MAP.*

$$–$$$$ ▥ **The Ritz.** The late artist Henry Moore found inspiration for a few of his sculptures while residing at this 1930s Beaux-Arts villa. Here there's none of the stuffiness associated with some other upscale hotels. Rooms are simple but elegant, with modern art prints on the walls, art deco–esque furniture, and large marble bathrooms. At least half board is required from June 1 to August 31; in other months a Continental breakfast is included in the room price. Full board is available year round. The hotel is one block from the area's beach clubs and a short walk from the center of town. ⊠ *Via Flavio Gioia 2, 55042* ☎ *0584/787531* ▤ *0584/ 787522* ⊕ *www.ritzfortedeimarmi.com* ⇱ *32 rooms* ⌂ *Restaurant, room service, cable TV, in-room VCRs, pool, bar, Internet, meeting rooms* ▤ *AE, DC, MC, V* ⊙l *MAP.*

$$–$$$ ▥ **Goya.** This white hotel with green shutters in the middle of town is built in the Liberty style and evokes old-world villa charm. The rooms have high ceilings, and some have their own little balconies with a view to the sea. An outdoor hot tub sits on a pleasant terrace full of chaise longues, and tables with umbrellas, surrounded by trees and a tall hedgerow. Half and full board are available. ⊠ *Via Carducci 69, 55042* ☎ *0584/787221* 🖶 *0584/787269* ⊕ *www.hotelgoya.it* ⤳ *47 rooms, 4 suites* ⟳ *Restaurant, cable TV, bicycles, outdoor hot tub* ⊟ *AE, DC, MC, V* ⊙❘ *CP.*

Nightlife & the Arts

After a day at the beach, the place to meet and greet the rich and famous is **Alma Rosa Art Music and Bar** (⊠ Viale Morin 89/a ☎ 0584/82503). The clientele during high season frequently includes Italian national soccer players and other young, good-looking celebs and politicos. A champagne tasting and a happy "hour" runs from 6 PM to 10 PM daily. Leonardo, the charming owner-bartender, speaks English. On Saturday nights there's a DJ.

Sports

BIKING **Claudio Maggi Cicli** (⊠ Viale Morin 85 ☎ 0584/89529 🖶 0584/81699 ⊕ www.ciclimaggi.it), which is near the beach, has been selling bicycle equipment and renting bikes since 1906. From May through September it's open daily 8–1 and 3–8; from October through April it's closed Wednesday and Sunday. **Maggi-Coppa** (⊠ Via A. Franceschi 4d ☎ 0584/83528), which rents bicycles, is right on the beach and keeps late hours: 8 AM–midnight daily from May through August, 8–8 daily the rest of the year.

HIKING & CLIMBING The **Forte dei Marmi Club Alpino Italiano** (⊠ Via Buonarroti 47 ☎ 0584/89808 ⊕ www.caifortedeimarmi.it) can provide information on area hiking and rock climbing, and about guided tours. The club itself is open only on Friday from 9 PM to 11 PM, and their Web site is in Italian.

SCUBA DIVING For information about the best places to scuba dive on the Versilian and Ligurian coasts, contact the **Associazione Subacquei Versilia** (⊠ Via S. Allende 38 ☎ 0584/82070 or 329/9413130).

Pietrasanta

❷❸ *5 km (3 mi) southeast of Forte dei Marmi, 104 km (65 mi) northwest of Florence.*

Historically, Pietrasanta has been the major town in Versilia for two reasons: first because of its military importance to the Romans, and later as an artistic center, thanks in part to the availability of marble in the area. Donatello and, later, Michelangelo used marble quarried nearby.

The buildings of the Renaissance **Piazza del Duomo** give you a feel for how grandly 15th-century architects conceived of urban planning. On the piazza near Via Barsanti is a plaque commemorating a contract signed on that spot by Michelangelo in 1518 for marble to build the facade of San Lorenzo in Florence (a project that was never realized).

The **Duomo** is dedicated to St. Martin and was begun in the mid-13th century. Most of the art inside dates from the 16th and 17th centuries. ⊠ *Piazza del Duomo* ☎ *058/790177* 🎟 *Free* ⊙ *Daily 8–noon and 3-7.*

The **Civico Museo Archeologico** has objects from the 3rd millennium BC as well as pottery dating from the Renaissance. The collection, housed in the 15th-century **Palazzo Moroni,** is closed for renovation at this writing, but is expected to open sometime in 2005. ⌧ *Palazzo Moroni, Piazza del Duomo* ☎ *0584/70522.*

The church of **Sant'Antonio Abate** (also known as the church of San Biagio) dates from the 14th century and is dedicated to St. Biagio. Inside are two wood polychrome sculptures of St. Biagio and St. Anthony Abate that date from the 16th century. Frescoes by Colombian artist Fernando Botero (born 1932)—*La Porta del Paradiso* (*The Gates of Heaven*) and *La Porta dell'Inferno* (*The Gates of Hell*), dating from the 1990s—are worth the visit on their own. ⌧ *Via G. Mazzini 103* ☎ *0584/70055* ⌨ *Free* ☉ *Sept.–May, daily 8–noon and 3–7:30; Jul.–Aug., daily 8–noon and 3–midnight.*

The church of **Sant'Agostino** was built in the 14th century by the Augustinians. The building no longer functions as a church, but is used for special exhibitions. It has some 15th-century frescoes and paintings from the 17th and 18th centuries ⌧ *Via Sant'Agostino* ☎ *No phone* ⌨ *Free* ☉ *Daily 9:30–12:30 and 5–7.*

The **Museo dei Bozzetti** contains a collection of sculptural sketches and models made by contemporary Italian and foreign artists, including the most important sculptors in the Versilian workshops of the 20th century. ⌧ *Via Sant'Agostino 1* ☎ *0584/795500* 🖷 *0584/795588* ⊕ *www. museodeibozzetti.com* ⌨ *Free* ☉ *June–Sept. Tues.–Sun. 9–1, 2–7, and 9–midnight; Oct–May Tues.–Sat. 2–7.*

Viareggio

㉔ *8 km (5 mi) south of Pietrasanta, 25 km (15 mi) northwest of Lucca, 97 km (60 mi) northwest of Florence.*

Tobias Smollett (1721–71), an English novelist, wrote in the 1760s that Viareggio was "a kind of sea-port on the Mediterranean . . . The roads are indifferent and the accommodation is execrable." Much has changed here since Smollett's time. For one, this beach town becomes very crowded in summer, so accommodations are plentiful. But Viareggio can be loud and brassy, so if you're looking for peace and quiet, come in the autumn and early spring.

Viareggio has numerous buildings decorated in the 1920s Liberty style, characterized by colorful wood and some with ornate exterior decoration. Locals and tourists alike stroll along the town's wide seaside promenade lined with bars, cafés, and some very fine restaurants. If you can't make it to Venice for *Carnevale* (Carnival), come here, which in some ways is more fun than Venice. The city is packed with revelers from all over Tuscany who come to join in the riot of colorful parades with giant floats and other festivities. Book lodging far in advance; be aware that hotels charge high-season prices during Carnevale.

Where to Stay & Eat

★ **$$$$** ✕ **Romano.** An ebullient host, Romano Franceschini is justifiably proud of the food produced by his wife, Franca, who oversees the kitchen. Fresh local fish and shellfish are presented in fine style on large white platters. Taste the fried zucchini flowers stuffed with ricotta and fish; the mixed seafood grill and lightly fried *calamaretti* (tiny squid) are delights. The wine list is one of the best of any coastal restaurant. Franca's special desserts are coconut *biscottini* (cookies) and an apple crumble. You may wisely wish to leave everything in Franceschini's hands and order the tasting menu (€68 without wine). ⊠ *Via Mazzini 122* ☎ *0584/31382* ⌚ *Reservations essential* ☰ *AE, DC, MC, V* ☺ *Closed Mon. and Jan. No lunch July and Aug.*

$$–$$$ 🏨 **Hotel President.** A quiet elegance pervades here. The rooms have slightly formal decor, high ceilings, and pastel walls; some look directly out at the sea, across the promenade. Two suites have hot tubs. The hotel restaurant, Ristorante Gaudi, has panoramic views of the sea. The hotel bar has an outdoor terrace and furniture from the early 1900s. Half board is available. ⊠ *Viale Carducci 5, 55049* ☎ *0584/962712* 🖷 *0584/ 963658* ⊕ *www.hotelpresident.it* ⇨ *31 rooms, 6 suites* ♻ *Restaurant, in-room safes, some in-room hot tubs, minibars, cable TV, bar, Internet, meeting rooms, some pets allowed* ☰ *AE, DC, MC, V* �🍽 *BP.*

$–$$$ 🏨 **Grand Hotel Royal.** A hotel since 1899, the Grand Hotel Royal looks majestic from the outside, and sweepingly high ceilings maintain the feeling inside. In cooler months, enjoy dinner served in the romantic salon—with arched windows, French empire–style chairs, and soft pink tablecloths—which doubled as a ballroom in the past. Dine in the garden during summer. The restaurant changes its menu daily. There's also a yellow breakfast room flooded with sunlight. Rooms have tile floors, and elegant wood-and-upholstery furniture. Some have balconies overlooking the sea (for an additional charge). In high season a three-day minimum stay is required. ⊠ *Viale Carducci 44, 55049* ☎ *0584/45151* 🖷 *0584/31438* ⊕ *www.hotelroyalviareggio.it* ⇨ *102 rooms, 2 suites* ♻ *Restaurant, minibars, cable TV, pool, bicycles, Ping-Pong, Internet, meeting rooms, no-smoking rooms* ☰ *AE, DC, MC, V* ☺ *Closed Nov.* 🍽 *CP.*

Nightlife & the Arts

For four Sundays and Shrove Tuesday in late January and early February, this little seaside town produces its world-famous **Carnevale** (☎ 0584/ 962568 ⊕ www.viareggio.ilcarnevale.com), with intricate floats, or *carri,* representing Italy's most influential celebrities and politicians and sometimes the famous and infamous from around the world. Started in the late 1800s, the Viareggio Carnevale differs from the better-known carnival held in Venice because of its parades of huge and fantastical floats. Traditionally, the floats were put together by Viareggio's shipbuilders, whose carpentry and ironworking skills translated into the construction of fabulous parade floats. In the beginning, the masked celebrants were civil and political protesters, and the floats were, and often are, used as a vehicle to lampoon popular figures of the day. Other events—music, parties, and art displays—also take place during Carnevale. The crowds are huge with many attending in costume.

Sports & the Outdoors

Club Nautico Versilia (✉ Piazza Artiglio ☎ 0584/31444 or 0584/31445) can assist sailors who wish to tour the coastal waters with maps, port and docking information, charter and craft rental resources, and information about craft repair and refueling.

NORTH OF FLORENCE A TO Z

To research prices, get advice from other travelers, and book travel arrangements, visit ⊕ www.fodors.com

AIR TRAVEL

Most visitors to the area fly into Florence's Aeroporto Amerigo Vespucci (known as Peretola). Pisa's Aeroporto Galileo Galilei is 15 mi (25 km), or about 30 minutes, from Viareggio. For the Mugello, Bologna's Aeroporto Guglielmo Marconi is also a logical option, as it is 60 mi (92 km), or 90 minutes, from Borgo San Lorenzo.

🛪 Airports **Aeroporto A. Vespucci (Peretola)** ☎ 055/373498 ⊕ www.safnet.it. **Aeroporto Galileo Galilei** ☎ 050/500707 ⊕ www.pisa-airport.com. **Aeroporto Guglielmo Marconi** ☎ 051/6479615 ⊕ www.bologna-airport.it.

BUS TRAVEL

Most bus service to areas north of Florence originates in Florence or Pisa, depending on which is closest to the area you plan to tour. The Mugello's small towns rely on bus service from Copit, SITA, and Lazzi with erratic connections to Florence; Lazzi has the most extensive service within the area north of Florence. Buses can get you around the Garfagnana and are more practical than trains. Bus service to and in the Lunigiana and along the coast is limited. It's also possible to take a bus from Pistoia or Florence to get to Abetone. A car is necessary to see Massa, Carrara, and the rest of Versilia, because bus service is sporadic. For the Cinque Terre, the Lazzi bus service will get you to La Spezia, and then you can take the train to Riomaggiore.

Copit (☎ 055/214637 in Florence ⊕ www.copit.it). **Lazzi** (☎ 055/ 351061 in Florence ⊕ www.lazzi.it). **SITA** (☎ 800/373760 ⊕ www.sita-on-line.it).

CAR RENTAL

Major international rental firms have agencies at the airports (⇨ Air Travel, above).

CAR TRAVEL

Aside from the isolated Cinque Terre, which is impractical for car travel because of the narrow roads and lack of parking (although better access and parking are available at the northern and southern towns of Monterosso al Mare and Riomaggiore), driving is the best way to get around the area north of Florence. The east–west A11 autostrada connects Viareggio, Lucca, Montecatini Terme, Pistoia, Prato, and Florence. The A1 runs north–south from Milan through Bologna, Florence, and down to Rome and Naples. En route from Florence to Bologna, the A1 passes a few miles to the west of the Mugello. And the A12 will take you from near Pisa along the Versilian coast to La Spezia, entryway to the Cinque Terre. Most of these towns are approached by lesser highways and two-lane roads.

EMERGENCIES
For emergencies there is one national number for paramedics, police, and the fire department. Pharmacies post the addresses of the nearest late-night pharmacies outside their doors.

🚹 Emergency Services ☎ 113.

TRAIN TRAVEL
With the exception of Viareggio and Borgo San Lorenzo, which are on a main state railway train service (Ferrovia dello Stato, or FS) line, the towns and cities in the area north of Florence are difficult to get to by rail. In the Garfagnana, train connections are extremely limited. Trains from Lucca to Equi Terme run four times a day; Lucca to Aulla runs less frequently and goes through Viareggio. Trains make their way to some parts of the Lunigiana, but it too is best explored by car. To properly explore Massa and Carrara, the two marble towns, a car is necessary because service is spotty and the train station in Carrara is not near the center of town. Viareggio, because it is on a major train line, is easily reachable from Florence and Rome. To get to the Cinque Terre, take a train to La Spezia and then take a local train to any of the five towns. The central station in Florence, Firenze Santa Maria Novella, is well served by Intercity (IC) and Eurostar trains.

🚹 Train Information **Ferrovia dello Stato (FS)** ☎ 892021 in Italian ⊕ www.trenitalia. com.

🚹 VISITOR INFORMATION
🚹 Tourist Information **Abetone** ✉ Via Pescinone 15 ☎ 0573/607811. **Barga** ⊕ www. barganews.com. **Borgo San Lorenzo** ✉ Via Togliatti 45 ☎ 055/845271 ⊕ www.comune. borgo-san-lorenzo.fi.it. **Carrara** ✉ Lungomare A. Vespucci 24, Marina di Massa ☎ 0585/ 240063. **Cinque Terre** ⊕ www.cinqueterre.it. **Forte dei Marmi** ✉ Via A. Franceschi 8b ☎ 0584/80091 ⊕ www.comune.forte-dei-marmi.lucca.it. **Massa** ✉ Lungomare A. Vespucci 24, Marina di Massa ☎ 0585/240063 ⊕ www.marinadimassa.it. **Monterosso al Mare** ✉ Via Fegina 38 ☎ 0187/17506 ✉ Via del Molo, below the train station ☎ 0187/ 817204. **Pietrasanta** ✉ Piazza del Duomo ☎ 0584/20331 ⊕ www.comune.pietrasanta. lu.it. **Riomaggiore** ✉ Piazza Unitá ☎ 0187/920633. **Viareggio** ✉ Vialle Carducci 10 ☎ 0584/962233 ⊕ www.comune.viareggio.lu.it.

CITIES WEST
OF FLORENCE

3

TALLEST PLACE TO PLAY
Lucca's Ramparts ⇨*p.139*

HUNTER'S HAVEN
Rustic Da Delfina restaurant ⇨*p.128*

MOST DRAMATIC HEDGES
Villa Reale's topiary theater ⇨*p.140*

BEST PLACE TO ENJOY THE SIMPLE LIFE
Working farm Fattoria di Migliarino ⇨*p.150*

AT FULL TILT
Leaning Tower of Pisa ⇨*p.148*

TOP LOCAL WINE FIND
Enoteca Vanni ⇨*p.144*

Updated by
Stephanie
Gruner

AS IN ANY AREA OF ITALY, the reasons to visit the cities west of Florence are art, architecture, history, food, and the beauty of the landscape. Undeniably, this is a great place to take a break from the crowded tourist center of Florence. And each of the cities in this region has a long and rich history.

During the Middle Ages and the Renaissance, Prato, Pistoia, Lucca, and Pisa were the bane of Florence, which waged many wars in her struggle to become the dominant force in Tuscany. Eventually these cities—with the exception of Lucca—came under Florentine influence. It's best when traveling to the region to resist the pull of Florence: the fine churches and museums in these other cities are fewer but no less impressive. Lucca's charm lies in the medieval wall that surrounds the historic center, and the beauty of Pisa's Duomo, Battistero, and Torre Pendente (Leaning Tower) complex is unsurpassed. Prato has many works by Fra Filippo Lippi, a native son, and Pistoia, with its Duomo and Battistero, preserves its medieval aura.

Exploring Cities West of Florence

The best way to see this part of Tuscany is by car, as some of the smaller cities are otherwise difficult to get to. However, cities such as Lucca, Pisa, Prato, Pistoia, Empoli, and Montecatini have regular train and bus service, which makes getting around easy. Five days is ample time to tour the area, as most of the towns are close to one another and—with the exception of Lucca and Pisa, which demand more time—can be toured relatively quickly.

Numbers in the text correspond to numbers in the margin and on the Cities West of Florence; Lucca; and Pisa maps.

About the Restaurants & Hotels

This area of Tuscany is known for its simple, hearty food. Grilled meats such as steak and pork are always a good bet. For the more adventurous, there is *cingiale* (boar) and *coniglio* (rabbit). What the region lacks in variety it more than makes up for in the quality of its meats, vegetables, and homemade pastas. Wine lovers have a broad choice. If you want, you can order Barollos, Chianti Classicos, and other famous (and expensive) wines. Otherwise, you can follow the local custom and simply order a bottle or carafe of the house wine. You will almost always be pleasantly surprised. The wines generally come from local vineyards with strong local followings.

If you can, steer clear of the larger tourist-oriented restaurants in favor of the smaller trattorias that can be found both in cities and in the country. Often, these smaller restaurants offer a limited menu that varies daily. The quality is almost always good and the prices excellent. Reservations are generally not required other than on Friday and Saturday nights and in restaurants in the center of cities.

For a taste of the country, you can stay outside Florence—particularly in the warmer months, when Florence is at its hottest and most crowded—and avail yourself of the excellent train service for day trips

Lucca and Pisa are the most-visited Tuscan cities west of Florence, and with good reason. Lucca's charm is preserved within the medieval walls surrounding the historic center, and Pisa has perhaps the most famous tower in the world. Less visited but eminently worthwhile are Pistoia and Prato, smaller cities with fine Romanesque churches, good restaurants, and fewer tourists. A different taste of Tuscany can be had by heading west to Empoli, San Miniato, and other small cities. Part of the pleasure of visiting these places comes from being slightly off the well-trod path, and a greater part comes from discovering the smaller treasures these places offer.

3

If you have
3 days

From Florence, travel to **Prato** ❶ ► and spend the morning in the Duomo, the Museo del Tessuto, and the Museo di Pittura Murale before heading off to **Pistoia** ❷ for the afternoon. In Pistoia, see the lovely Cattedrale di San Zeno, with its magnificent silver altar, and the Spedale del Ceppo, which has a multicolor terra-cotta frieze. Spend the night in ⊡ **Montecatini Terme** ❸ and take in the sights from the lively and bustling Piazza del Popolo. On Day 2, travel to **Lucca** ❺–❶⑤ in the morning. Tour the Duomo and see the early-15th-century tomb of Ilaria del Caretto. Be sure to take time to walk the walls; in the afternoon, go to ⊡ **Pisa** ⑯–㉕ and see the Torre Pendente, Duomo, and Battistero, but also go beyond the tourist spots to visit the Piazza dei Cavalieri and stroll along the Arno. Spend the night in Pisa. In the morning, travel to the area around **Empoli** ㉖. You can enjoy the view from the Torre di Federico II in **San Miniato** ㉙ and purchase hand-crafted goods in the area around **Vinci** ㉘ and **Montelupo** ㉗, or visit the small, exquisite Collegiata di Sant'Andrea back in Empoli. Head back to Florence in the afternoon.

If you have
5 days

Using Florence as a starting point, travel to ⊡ **San Miniato** ㉙ ► and book a hotel. Explore the little town and see the Medici villa in Cerreto Guidi in the morning before heading south to **Certaldo** ㉛ to pay homage to the birthplace (and final resting spot) of Giovanni Boccaccio, Certaldo's most famous son. The next morning, explore **Empoli** ㉖ and its Collegiata; then go to **Pisa** ⑯–㉕ to spend the afternoon. Stay in Pisa or at a local agriturismo. On Day 3 go to ⊡ **Lucca** ❺–❶⑤ and spend most of the day seeing the Duomo, Palazzo Pfanner, and the churches of San Frediano and San Michele. Pop into the Museo Nazionale di Palazzo Mansi and spend some time in the room with portraits of various Medici. Stay over in Lucca on the third night, leaving time for walking the town center's walls. Drive to ⊡ **Montecatini Terme** ❸ the next morning and spend the day taking the waters, or simply walking through the thermal parkland, and take the funicular up to Montecatini Alto. Stay overnight in Montecatini Terme, and return to Florence in the morning.

---

into the city. Another option might be to stay in an *agriturismo*, or farm, and experience a different kind of Tuscany, one based more in the 19th and early 20th centuries. More lavish accommodations can be found in Montecatini, where it's perfectly permissible to pamper yourself with spa treatments—people have been doing it there since the 19th century.

	WHAT IT COSTS in euros				
	$$$$	**$$$**	**$$**	**$**	**¢**
RESTAURANTS	over €22	€18–€22	€13–€17	€7–€12	under €7
HOTELS	over €290	€210–€290	€140–€209	€80–€139	under €80

Restaurant prices are per person for a second course (secondo piatto). Hotel prices are for two people in a standard double room, including tax and service.

Timing

The best time to visit these cities—particularly in the cases of Lucca and Pisa—is any time but July and August, when the tourist season is in full swing and the sun is at its hottest. If you visit during the summer months, plan to do early-morning or late-afternoon touring, when the crowds and the heat are somewhat less oppressive. Also, consider staying in one of the cooler and less congested hill towns—such as San Miniato—to avoid crowds and heat. Or discover the joys of Pistoia, Prato, and Empoli, three wonderful but rarely visited cities that each hold treasures of Renaissance art.

If you're in Pisa in June, try to see its Luminara, held June 16. Blues lovers might want to check out Pistoia Blues in July. Also in July is Pistoia's La Giostra dell'Orso (Bear Joust). Lucca's famous annual Puccini Festival is held at the end of July and in early August. The traveling gourmand might want to sample the various black-truffle celebrations that take place in and around San Miniato in October. And if you love ceramics, the two-week International Ceramics Festival in Montelupo in June includes art shows, demonstrations, and plenty of beautiful items—for buying as well as looking.

FROM FLORENCE TO COLLODI

The journey from Florence to Collodi takes you north and west of Florence via industrial Prato. Pistoia is a short distance away. After Pistoia, the countryside becomes a little hillier and much prettier. At Montecatini, wander north along the Pescia River to Pescia, a flower-market town with worthwhile art, and to Collodi, where there's an amusement park devoted to Pinocchio.

Prato

► ❶ *19 km (12 mi) northwest of Florence, 81 km (50 mi) east of Pisa.*

The wool industry in this city, one of the world's largest producers of cloth, was known throughout Europe as early as the 13th century. Business was further stimulated in the 14th century by a local cloth merchant, Francesco di Marco Datini, who built his business, according to one of his surviving ledgers, "in the name of God and of profit." One thing that distinguishes Prato from other Italian towns of its size is the presence of modern public art—most notably Henry Moore's mammoth, marble *Square Form with Cut* in the Piazza San Marco. But Prato also holds the fine, earlier artworks expected of a Tuscan city of this size.

3

Architecture

The Middle Ages left their mark on these cities. Many of their churches bear the green-and-white marble striping typical of churches built during the period, and historic centers have palaces adorned with coats of arms from various prominent families. If your taste leans toward art nouveau, look for buildings in the Liberty style, popular in the late 19th and early 20th centuries. It's most evident in Lucca, where the main thoroughfare, the Fillungo, is dotted with examples.

Cuisine

Most restaurants in the region serve dishes that will be familiar to you if you've eaten in Florence—*bistecca alla fiorentina* (grilled local Chianina beef) and *ribollita* (a vegetable soup thickened with stale Tuscan bread and cannellini beans), for instance. Pistoia and environs are famous for their *maccheroni all'anatra* (pasta in a sauce made of duck). Prato is home of the famous *biscotti di Prato,* an exquisite hard cookie made for dunking into steaming cappuccino or *vin santo,* a sweet dessert wine. Pisa can lay claim to *ceccina,* a pancake made of chickpea flour that can be eaten alone or rolled with various toppings. Montecatini has its *cialda,* a thin, sweet wafer usually topped with gelato. Lucca is famous for its *farro,* an early type of wheat also known as emmer in English. It's been cultivated for several thousand years and is unique to the region. You can eat it in soup or cooked in the manner of risotto (some wags refer to it as *farrotto*), or as a cold grain salad. And then there's the region's olive oil, which adds depth and soul to any dish it garnishes; to many palates it's the best in the world.

Sagras (Festivals)

A great way to get a feel for the region and its people is to attend a *sagra* (festival). During the summer they take place nearly every weekend in smaller towns and villages, and each celebrates some kind of food, such as *sagre dei funghi* (mushroom festivals) or *sagre della zuppa* (soup festivals). Held at night, the festivals dish out plenty of food and wine, and there's usually a square for dancing, sometimes with live music. You might want to brush up on your ballroom dancing first. Locals display a surprising degree of dancing expertise, and it's not uncommon to see couples fox-trotting or doing the tango. Mushroom festivals usually take place at the end of summer and in early fall, right after the mushroom harvest. Other festivals happen nearly every weekend in warm weather, in different towns. These are village affairs, with few people speaking English. There are no numbers to call for information. The festivals are advertised only by handwritten signs on the side of the road. Attending a sagra is a unique experience if you want to soak in small-town Italian culture.

Prato's Romanesque **Duomo,** reconstructed from 1211, is famous for its **Pergamo del Sacro Cingolo** (Chapel of the Holy Girdle), to the left of the entrance, which enshrines the sash of the Virgin Mary. It is said that the girdle was given to the apostle Thomas by the Virgin Mary when she miraculously appeared after her Assumption into heaven. The Duomo also contains 15th-century frescoes by Prato's most famous son,

Fra Filippo Lippi (1406–69). His scenes from the life of St. Stephen are on the left wall of the **Cappella Maggiore** (Main Chapel); those from the life of John the Baptist are on the right. ⊠ *Piazza del Duomo* ☎ *0574/26234, 0574/24112 reservations* ☉ *Daily 7–noon and 3:30–7.*

need a break? Prato's biscotti (literally "twice cooked") have an extra-dense texture, lending themselves to submersion in your caffè or vino santo. The best biscotti in town are at **Antonio Mattei** (⊠ Via Ricasoli 20/22 ☎ 0574/25756 ⊕ www.antoniomattei.it).

A sculpture by Donatello (circa 1386–1466) that originally adorned the Duomo's exterior pulpit is now on display in the **Museo dell'Opera del Duomo**. The museum also includes such 15th-century gems as Fra Filippo Lippi's *Madonna and Child*, Giovanni Bellini's (circa 1432–1516) *Christ on the Cross*, and Caravaggio's (1571–1610) *Christ Crowned with Thorns*. ⊠ *Piazza del Duomo 49* ☎ *0574/29339* ☞ *€3, combination ticket €5 (includes Museo di Pittura Murale and il Castello)* ☉ *Mon. and Wed.–Sat. 9:30–12:30 and 3–6:30, Sun. 9:30–12:30.*

The permanent collection in the **Museo di Pittura Murale** (Museum of Mural Painting) contains frescoes removed from sites in and around Prato such as those by Agnolo Gaddi, Nicolo Gerini, and Il Volterrano. Until 2006, on display are masterpieces by Pratese painters from the 14th and 15th centuries, as well as altarpieces by Filippo Lippi, and his collaborators, Filippino Lippi and Luca Signorelli. ☒ *Piazza San Domenico 8* ☎ *0574/ 440501* ☞ *€3, combination ticket €5 (includes Museo dell'Opera del Duomo and il Castello)* ☉ *Mon., Wed., and Thurs. 9–1; Fri. and Sat. 9–1 and 3–6.*

Prato's **Centro per l'Arte Contemporanea L. Pecci** (L. Pecci Center of Contemporary Art) contains works of artists from around the world completed after 1965. The exhibitions constantly change and often feature inaugural presentations. ☒ *Viale della Repubblica 277* ☎ *0574/5317* ⊕ *www.centropecci.it* ☞ *€7* ☉ *Mon., Thurs., and Fri. noon–7; Wed. noon–9; weekends 10–7.*

Preserved in the **Museo del Tessuto** (Textile Museum) is what made this city a Renaissance economic powerhouse. The collection includes clothing, fragments of fabric, samples, and the machines used to make them from the 14th to the 20th centuries. Check out the 15th-century fabrics with pomegranate prints, a virtuoso display of Renaissance textile wizardry. ☒ *Piazza del Commune* ☎ *0574/611503* ☞ *€4; free Sun.* ☉ *Weekdays 10–6, Sat. 10–2, Sun. 4–7. Tours by appointment.*

The church of **Santa Maria delle Carceri** was built by Giuliano Sangallo in the 1490s and is a landmark of Renaissance architecture. ☒ *Piazza Santa Maria delle Carceri, off Via Cairoli and southeast of the cathedral* ☎ *0574/27933* ☞ *Free* ☉ *Daily 7–noon and 4–7.*

The formidable **Castello** (Castle), adjacent to Santa Maria delle Carceri, is an impressive sight. The Lombard Emperor Frederick II (1194–1250) built the seat of his authority in Tuscany. Frederick's castles were designed to echo imperial Rome, and the many columns, lions, and porticos testify to his ambition. This is the only castle he built outside of Sicily and Puglia in southern Italy. ☒ *Piazza Santa Maria delle Carceri* ☎ *0574/38207* ☞ *€2, combination ticket €5 (includes Museo dell'-Opera del Duomo and Museo di Pittura Murale)* ☉ *Apr.–Sept., Wed.–Mon. 9–1 and 4–7.*

---

off the beaten path

POGGIO A CAIANO – For a look at gracious country living Renaissance style, take a detour to the Medici Villa in Poggio a Caiano. Lorenzo "il Magnifico" (1449–92) commissioned Giuliano da Sangallo (circa 1445–1516) to redo the villa, which was lavished with frescoes by important Renaissance painters such as Pontormo (1494–1556), Franciabigio (1482–1525), and Andrea del Sarto (1486–1531). You can walk around the austerely ornamented grounds while waiting for entry. ☒ *7 km (4½ mi) south of Prato (follow signs), Piazza dei Medici 14* ☎ *055/877012* ☞ *€2 (includes villa and garden)* ☉ *Jun.–Aug., daily 8:15–6:30; Sept., Apr., and May, daily 8:15–5:30; Mar. and Oct., daily 8:15–4:30; Nov.–Feb., daily 8:15–3:30. Closed 2nd and 3rd Mon. of each month. Guests are accompanied through the villa by custodians, hourly on the ½ hour before closing.*

CARMIGNANO – *The Visitation* by Pontormo is in this small village, a short car ride from Poggio a Caiano. The Franciscan church of **San Michele**, which was dedicated in 1211, houses the work. The painting dates from 1527–30, and it may well be Pontormo's masterpiece. The colors are luminous, the drapery is flowing, and the steady gaze shared between the Virgin and St. Elizabeth is breathtaking. The church's small cloister, shaded by olive trees, is always open and offers a quiet place to sit. ✉ *15 km (9 mi) south of Prato, through Poggio a Caiano, up Mt. Albano* ☎ *055/8712046* ✆ *Free* ☉ *Oct.–Apr., daily 7:30–5; May–Sept., daily 7:30–6.*

In the small town of **Artimino**, next door to Carmignano, is the **VILLA MEDICEA LA FERDINANDA DI ARTIMINO** – Built by Ferdinando I de' Medici (1549–1609) in the 1590s, it was originally used as a hunting lodge. ✉ *11 km (7 mi) south of Prato (head east from Carmignano or south from Poggio a Caiano, up Mt. Albano), Artimino* ☎ *055/871124* ✆ *Free* ☉ *Thurs.–Tues. 9:30–12:30.*

Where to Stay & Eat

$$-$$$$ ✕ **Piraña.** Named for the sharp-toothed fish swimming in an aquarium in full view of the diners, this sophisticated restaurant, done in shades of blue with steely accents, is a local favorite. Seafood, the specialty, may take the form of ravioli *di branzino in crema di scampi* (stuffed with sea bass and in a creamy shrimp sauce) and *rombo al forno* (baked turbot). It's a bit out of the way for sightseers but handy if you have a car, as it's near the Prato Est autostrada exit. ✉ *Via Valentini Giuseppe 110* ☎ *0574/ 25746* ▤ *AE, DC, MC, V* ☉ *Closed Sun. and Aug. No lunch Sat.*

$-$$$$ ✕ **La Veranda.** A short walk from the 13th-century Castello, this Prato restaurant offers an Italian version of Spanish paella, a rice dish with meat and seafood, including pork, chicken, rabbit, cuttlefish, and shrimp. Tuscan specialties include *agnello alla cacciatora* (lamb with a tangy wine-and-vinegar sauce). Despite its shabby appearance, the restaurant is popular with locals. ✉ *Via dell'Arco 10* ☎ *0574/38235* ▤ *AE, DC, MC, V* ☉ *Closed Sun. No lunch Sat.*

$$-$$$ ✕ **Baghino.** In the heart of the historic center, Baghino's menu includes typical Tuscan fare as well as more fanciful dishes such as penne *con vongole e curry* (with clams and curry). Try the ravioli alla Senese (with spinach sauce and pecorino cheese). ✉ *Via dell'Accademia 9* ☎ *0574/ 27920* ▤ *AE, DC, MC, V* ☉ *Closed Aug. No dinner Sun. or lunch Mon.*

★ $$ ✕ **Da Delfina.** Many years ago, Delfina began cooking for hungry hunters, and now she has four comfortably rustic dining rooms in her namesake restaurant surrounded vineyards and olive trees. The dishes use pure ingredients, seasonal vegetables, and savory meats accented with herbs. The *secondi* (second courses) such as *coniglio con olive e pignoli* (rabbit sautéed with olives and pine nuts) are a real treat. That dish is the specialty of the house. ✉ *Via della Chiesa 1, Artimino* ☎ *055/8718074* ⌘ *Reservations essential* ▤ *No credit cards* ☉ *Closed Mon. and 3 wks in Aug. No lunch Tues. No dinner Sun.*

$-$$ ✕ **Biagio Pignatta.** A lovely restaurant, this is a great stop after touring Artimino. If you come here in summer you can dine outdoors in a loggia with a beautiful view of Tuscan hills behind you. The food is Tuscan with some unexpected twists—including pasta with shellfish and a sublime carpaccio. The fried vegetables are as delectable as potato chips, and just as hard to stop eating. Try the crisp rosé that's made in the neighborhood. Reservations are a good idea, especially if you want an outside table. ☒ *Viale Papa Giovanni XXIII 1, Artimino* ☎ *055/8751406* ▤ *AE, DC, MC, V* ☉ *No lunch Wed. or Thurs.*

$ ✕ **La Vecchia Cucina di Soldano.** Pratesi specialties, including the odd but tasty *sedani ripieni* (stuffed celery), are served here in a completely unpretentious setting. It feels as if you're sitting in your Italian grandmother's kitchen; tablecloths have red and white checks, and the service is friendly and casual. The place teems with locals enjoying the superb *tagliolini sui fagioli* (soup with thin noodles and beans); clearly those who live here like the rock-bottom prices, too. ☒ *Via Pomeria 23* ☎ *0574/34665* ▤ *No credit cards* ☉ *Closed Sun.*

$$ ▦ **Hotel President.** Despite the unattractive 1970s exterior, the interior of this Best Western hotel, a five-minute walk from the historic center, is calm, cool, and well furnished. The rooms are spacious, and each of the four floors has a different color scheme. Pale green and pink leather couches give one of the two bars a slight art-deco feel. ☒ *Via Simintendi 20, at Via Baldinucci, 59100* ☎ *0574/30251* ▤ *0574/36064* ⊕ *www.hotel-president.net* ▨ *78 rooms* ♨ *Restaurant, in-room safes, minibars, cable TV, 2 bars, concierge, Internet, business services, meeting rooms, free parking, some pets allowed, some no-smoking rooms* ▤ *AE, DC, MC, V* ⦶ *CP.*

$ ▦ **Hotel Giardino.** In the center of Prato's historic district and a stone's throw from the main cathedral, this simple and clean hotel has friendly service. The rooms are nothing special, but the location is ideal. ☒ *Via Magnolfi, 2/4/6, 59100* ☎ *0574/261189* ▤ *0574/606591* ⊕ *www.giardinohotel.com* ▨ *28 rooms* ♨ *In-room safes, minibars, cable TV with movies, bar, Internet, business services, dry cleaning, laundry service, some free parking, some pets allowed* ▤ *AE, DC, MC, V* ⦶ *CP.*

Pistoia

❷ *18 km (11 mi) northwest of Prato, 61 km (38 mi) east of Pisa, 37 km (23 mi) northwest of Florence.*

Founded in the 2nd century BC as a support post for Roman troops, Pistoia had grown into an important trading center, but then it was caught up in the brutal Guelph-Ghibelline conflict of the Middle Ages. Reconstructed after heavy bombing during World War II, it has preserved some fine Romanesque architecture. Modern-day Pistoia's major industries include the manufacture of rail vehicles (including the cars for Washington, D.C.'s Metro) and tree and plant nurseries, which flourish on the alluvial plain around the city.

The Romanesque **Duomo**, the Cattedrale di San Zeno, dates from as early as the 5th century. It houses a magnificent silver altar dedicated to Saint James. The two half-figures on its left side are by Filippo Brunelleschi (1377–1446), the first Renaissance architect (and designer of Florence's magnificent Duomo cupola). The octagonal **Battistero**, with green-and-white-striped marble cladding, dates from the middle of the 14th century. Three of its eight sides have doorways; the main door facing the piazza is crowned with a rose window. Note the lovely little lantern that crowns the top of the building. ⊠ *Piazza del Duomo* ☎ *0573/25095* 🖼 *Free; access to altarpiece €2* ⊙ *Daily 8:30–12:30 and 3–7. Services Sun. at 9:30 AM and 6 PM.*

The Palazzo del Comune, begun around 1295, houses the **Museo Civico,** which contains works by local artists from the 13th to 19th centuries. ⊠*Piazza del Duomo 1* ☎*0573/3711* 🖼*€3.50, combination ticket €6.50 (includes Palazzo Rospigliosi and Fondazione Marino Marini)* ⊙ *Tues.–Sat. 10–6, Sun. 9–12:30.*

The **Antico Palazzo dei Vescovi** (Old Bishop's Palace) and **Museo della Cattedrale di San Zeno** contain spectacular treasures of the cathedral—including ornate pieces in gold, rings with jewels the size of small eggs, and solemn, powerful statuary. Below, however, are Roman, medieval, and even Etruscan archaeological sites uncovered in a 1970s renovation. The warren of corridors and caves below and the plain, spare rooms above both show off their treasures with simple, effective elegance. ⊠ *Piazza del Duomo* ☎ *0573/369272* 🖼 *€4* ⊙ *Tues., Thurs., and Fri. 10–1 and 3–5.*

Founded in the 13th century and still a functioning hospital, the **Ospedale del Ceppo** reveals a superb early-16th-century exterior terra-cotta frieze. Begun by Giovanni della Robbia (1469–1529), the frieze was completed by the workshop of Santi and Benedetto Buglioni between 1526 and 1528. Don't miss the 17th-century graffiti on the columns outside. ⊠ *Piazza Giovanni XIII, down Via Pacini from Piazza del Duomo* ⊙ *Closed to the public.*

In the 12th-century church of **Sant'Andrea,** the fine pulpit by Giovanni Pisano (circa 1250–1314) depicts scenes from the life of Christ in a series of high-relief richly sculpted marble panels. ⊠ *Piazzetta Sant'Andrea, Via Sant'Andrea* ☎ *0573/21912* 🖼 *Free* ⊙ *Daily 8:30–12:30 and 3–6.*

The 16th-century mannerist-style **Palazzo Rospigliosi** houses the **Museo Rospigliosi** and the **Museo Diocesano,** with a collection of mostly 16th- and 17th-century works. The Museo Rospigliosi contains a room referred to as Pope Clement IX's (1600–69) apartment, although there's no evidence that the Pistoian native, born Giulio Rospigliosi, actually stayed in these rooms. The Museo Diocesano has liturgical objects and furnishings from the diocese of Pistoia. Many of them date from the 13th, 14th, and 15th centuries. ⊠ *Via Ripa del Sale 3* ☎ *0573/28740* 🖼 *€3.50, combination ticket €6.50 (includes both museums and Museo Civico and the Fondazione Marino Marini)* ⊙ *Tues.–Sat. 10–1 and 3–6.*

Lest you think that Tuscany produced artists only in centuries long gone, the **Fondazione Marino Marini** presents many works from this modern native Pistoian (1901–80). Sculpture, etchings, paintings, engravings, and mixed media have all been installed in the elegantly renovated 14th-century Convento del Tao. ⊠ *Corso Silvano Fedi 30* ☎ *0573/30285* 🖨 *0473/31332* 🖼 *€3.50, combination ticket €6.50 (includes Palazzo Rospigliosi and Museo Civico)* ⊙ *Weekdays 10–6, Sun. 9:30–12:30.*

An architectural gem in green-and-white marble, the medieval church of **San Giovanni Fuorcivitas** holds a *Visitation* by Luca della Robbia (1400–82), a painting attributed to Taddeo Gaddi, and a holy-water font that may have been made by Fra Guglielmo around 1270. ⊠ *Via Cavour* ☎ *0573/24784* ☼ *Daily 7:30–6.*

A 20-minute drive out of town brings you to the **Giardino Zoologico,** a small zoo especially laid out to accommodate the wiles of both animals and children. ⊠ *Via Pieve a Celle 160/a; take Bus 29 from the train station.* ☎*0573/ 911219* 🎫 *€9* ☼ *Apr.–Sept., daily 9–7; Oct.–Mar., daily 9–5.*

Where to Stay & Eat

$–$$ ✕ **Corradossi.** A short walk from the Piazza del Duomo, this family-run restaurant that specializes in fish makes an excellent place to break for lunch or dinner. The food is simply prepared, the service quick and attentive, and the prices are more than reasonable. Start with the *gnocchi con gamberi* (pasta with shrimp and sliced baby zucchini); follow with the crispy *frittura di mare* (fried fish and shellfish). ⊠ *Via Frosini 112* ☎ *0573/25683* 🖃 *AE, DC, MC, V* ☼ *Closed Sun.*

★ **$–$$** ✕ **S. Jacopo.** This charming restaurant minutes from the Piazza del Duomo has white walls, tile floors, and tasteful prints and photographs on the walls that contrast nicely with the rustic blue table linens. The menu has mostly regional favorites, such as the *maccheroni S. Jacopo,* wide ribbons of house-made pasta in a duck sauce, but the restaurant can turn out perfectly grilled squid as well. Save room for dessert, especially the apple strudel. ⊠ *Via Crispi 15* ☎ *0573/27786* 🖃 *AE, DC, MC, V* ☼ *Closed Mon. No lunch Tues. Closed three weeks during Jul. and Aug.*

★ **$** ✕ **La BotteGaia.** Just off Piazza del Duomo, this popular wine bar has rustic tables set in a couple of rooms with exposed brick and stone walls. Jazz plays softly in the background. Typical wine-bar fare such as *salami e formaggi* (cured ham and cheeses) shares the menu with surprisingly sophisticated daily specials that change according to the season. In the warmer months you can dine outside with a view of the Piazza del Duomo. Visit their shop nearby (Via del Lastrone 4), which sells local mortadella and salami, chocolates, and wine. ⊠ *Via del Lastrone 17* ☎ *0573/ 365602* 🍴 *Reservations essential* 🖃 *AE, DC, MC, V* ☼ *Closed Mon. and last three weeks in Aug. No lunch Sun.*

¢–$ ✕ **Trattoria dell'Abbondanza.** Entering from a quiet side street, you walk into a small place with clean, cream-color walls that's busy but not noisy, its staff friendly but never pushy. Traditional dishes include, for first courses, *minestra di farro* (a hearty soup made with farro) and *maccheroni all'anatra* (pasta in a duck sauce). For seconds, there's *baccalà alla Livornese* (salt cod in a tomato sauce), roast rabbit, and tripe. *Torta rustica,* a cake of cornmeal and cream, makes a fine dessert. ⊠ *Via dell'Abbondanza 10/14, off Via degli Orafi* ☎ *0573/368037* 🖃 *MC, V* ☼ *Closed Wed. No lunch Thurs.*

$ 🏨 **Hotel Leon Bianco.** Most everything you want to see in Pistoia is only a few minutes' walk from this small hotel. Here you'll find a lobby decorated in chintz, a small bar at which to enjoy an *aperitivo* (aperitif), and lively innkeepers who speak perfect English. Florence is 45 minutes away by train, which makes this a good base for the budget-conscious traveler. ⊠ *Via Panciatichi 2, 51100* ☎ *0573/26675 or 0573/26676* 🖳 *0573/26704* ⊕ *www.hotelleonbianco.it* 🔊 *30 rooms* ♿ *Bar, Internet, dry cleaning, laundry service, some pets allowed, no-smoking rooms; no a/c in some rooms* ▭ *AE, DC, MC, V* ⦿ *CP.*

Nightlife & the Arts

★ In mid-July, **Pistoia Blues** brings international blues artists to town for performances in the main square. Contact (☎ 0573/994659 ⊕ www.pistoiablues.com) for more information. **La Giostra dell'Orso** (Bear Joust), on July 25, celebrates St. James, Pistoia's patron saint. During the staged event, three knights from each section of the city fight a "bear" (actually a target shaped like a bear that they strike, on horseback). The visitor center has more information on the event.

Montecatini Terme

3 *15 km (9 mi) west of Pistoia, 49 km (30 mi) west of Florence, 49 km (30 mi) northeast of Pisa.*

Immortalized in Fellini's 8½, Montecatini Terme is the home of Italy's premier *terme* (spas). Known for their curative powers—and, at least once upon a time, for their great popularity among the wealthy—the mineral springs flow from five sources and are taken for a variety of ailments, including liver and skin disorders. Those "taking the cure" report each morning to one of the town's *stabilimenti termali* (thermal establishments) to drink their prescribed cupful of water. Afterward, guests can enjoy a leisurely breakfast, read the newspaper, recline and listen to music, or walk in the parks that surround these grand old spas. The umbrella group **Terme di Montecatini** (⊠ Viale Verdi 41 ☎ 0572/778487 ⊕ www.termemontecatini.it) has information on the town's nine thermal spas. For more traditional beauty treatments, there's the **Excelsior,** which offers manicures, facials, and massage therapies with mud, algae, and oils. (⊠ Viale Verdi 61 ☎ 0572/778518, 0572/778509 for appointments).

The town's wealth of art nouveau buildings went up during its most active period of development, at the beginning of the 20th century. Like most other well-heeled resort towns, Montecatini attracts the leisured traveler, and it's trimmed with a measure of neon and glitz; aside from taking the waters and people-watching in Piazza del Popolo, there's not a whole lot to do here. There are, however, plenty of places to stay, making the town a good base from which to explore the region.

Fodor'sChoice The most attractive art nouveau structure in town, **Terme Tettuccio** has
★ lovely colonnades. Here fountains set up on marble counters dispense mineral water, bucolic scenes painted on tiles decorate walls, and an orchestra plays under a frescoed dome. ⊠ Viale Verdi 71 ☎ 0572/778501 🎫 *Morning €12.50, afternoon €5* ⊙ *Daily 7:30–noon and 5–7.*

Piazza del Popolo, the main square in town, teems with cafés and bars. It's an excellent spot for people-watching; in the evening and on weekends it seems like everyone is out walking, seeing, and being seen.

The Piazza del Popolo offers a view of the basilica of **Santa Maria Assunta.** The church and bell tower were completed in 1962. The bold geometric lines are a little incongruous among its more ornate neighbors. ⊠ *Piazza del Popolo* ☎ *No phone* ☎ *Free* ⊙ *Daily 8–noon and 3–5:30.*

<table>
<tr><td>need a
break?</td><td>*Cialde,* a local specialty, are circular wafers made with flour, sugar, eggs, and almonds from Puglia. They were invented by the Bargilli family in 1936. Try them topped with several scoops of the local gelato at **Bargilli** (⊠ Viale Grocco 2 ☎ 0572/79459), the family's shop and probably the best *gelateria* in town.</td></tr>
</table>

The older town, **Montecatini Alto,** sits atop a hill nearby and is reached by a funicular from Viale Diaz. Though there isn't much to do once you get up there, the medieval square is lined with restaurants and bars, the air is crisp, and the views of the Nievole, the valley below, are gorgeous.

Where to Stay & Eat

$$-$$$$ ✕ **La Cascina.** Just off the Piazza del Popolo, and on the way to the *terme,* this recently renovated restaurant offers seafood specialities in a relaxed setting. Start with the raw seafood antipasto and finish with the chocolate sponge cake dessert. There's plenty of outdoor seating for summer and live music on weekends. ⊠ *Viale Verdi 43* ☎ *0572/78474* ⊕ *www. incascina.it* ☐ *AE, DC, MC, V* ⊙ *Closed Mon.*

$$ ⌂ **Croce di Malta.** Taste and sophistication have been the calling cards of this hotel since 1911. It's a short walk on tree-lined streets from the center of town; it's even closer to the thermal baths. Rooms are spacious, with high ceilings; many have deep bathtubs with water jets. You can enjoy an aperitivo in the majestic lobby before dining at the guests-only restaurant ($$-$$$). The menu changes daily and offers Tuscan specialties as well as other options; the food is as elegant as the hotel. ⊠ *Viale IV Novembre 18, 51016* ☎ *0572/9201* ⌂ *0572/767516* ⊕ *www.crocedimalta.com* ⇔ *122 rooms, 22 suites* ⌂ *Dining room, room service, minibars, cable TV with movies, pool, gym, massage, bar, babysitting, dry cleaning, laundry service, concierge, business services, meeting rooms, parking (fee), some pets allowed, no-smoking floors* ☐ *AE, DC, MC, V* ⊙ *CP.*

Pescia

❹ *8 km (5 mi) west of Montecatini Terme, 19 km (12 mi) northeast of Lucca, 61 km (38 mi) northwest of Florence.*

This sleepy little town has a large flower market and some lesser-known but rather interesting Renaissance art. During the early Middle Ages it was dominated by Lucca, but by 1339 it had come under Florence's influence, where it remained throughout the Renaissance. Pescia has long been a center for coppersmithing. You can still find shops in town with men hammering and tinning copper by hand in the traditional manner. The town is also proud of its white beans. The best are grown in the dry gravel river beds of Sorana, a village just over the hills north of Pescia.

The **Santuario della Madonna di Pie di Piazza,** a little chapel built in 1447 and designed by Andrea Cavalcanti, the adopted son of Filippo Brunelleschi, is the only example of Brunelleschi's style outside of Florence. Inside is a 15th-century *Madonna and Child* on a wood panel that was transported to the church in a solemn procession in 1605. ✉ *Piazza Mazzini* ☎ *No phone* 💲 *Free* ⊙ *Daily 3–5:30.*

The church of **Santi Stefano e Nicolao** is an odd combination of Romanesque and baroque. It dates from as early as the 11th century and had alterations as late as the 18th century. A *Madonna and Child with Angels,* by the school of Andrea Orcagna (active 1343/44–1368), and a panel painting of the *Madonna and Child with Sts. Nicholas and John the Baptist* (circa 1400) are among the more interesting works in the church, but because they hang on side walls in the presbytery, they are difficult to see. ✉ *Piazza Stefano* ☎ *No phone* 💲 *Free* ⊙ *Daily 10–12:30 and 4–6.*

The **Palazzo del Podestà** presents a lovely 13th-century facade; inside, however, are banal early-20th-century sculpted works by local artist Libero Andreotti (1875–1933). ✉ *Piazza del Palagio* ☎ *0572/490057* 💲 *Free* ⊙ *Nov.–Mar., Wed. and Sun., 3–6, Fri. and Sat. 10–1 and 3–6; Apr.–Oct., Wed. and Sun. 4–7, Fri. and Sat. 10–1 and 4–7.*

The **Museo Civico** contains Tuscan paintings, a Lorenzo Monaco triptych, Etruscan objects, and works attributed to the school of Fra Angelico and Fra Bartolommeo. At this writing, the museum is closed for restoration. Contact the tourist office (☎ 0574/24112) for further information. ✉ *Piazza Santo Stefano* ☎ *0572/490057* 💲 *Free* ⊙ *Nov.–Mar., Wed. and Fri.–Sat. 10–1 and 3–6; Apr.–Oct., Wed. and Fri.–Sat. 10–1 and 4–7.*

Sant'Antonio Abate, a tiny oratory, has an amazing wood sculpture of the *Deposition,* popularly known as the "Ugly Saints." In seven pieces, it dates from the second half of the 12th century. Early 15th-century frescoes depict scenes from the life of St. Anthony the Abbot and include what is considered the oldest view of Pescia. If the door is locked, nearby businesses may know where to get the key. ✉ *Via Battisti* ☎ *No phone* 💲 *Free* ⊙ *Daily 7–7.*

The church of **San Francesco** has a wood-panel painting by Bonaventura Berlinghieri (active 1228–43) that dates from 1235; it depicts the life of St. Francis. ✉ *Piazza San Francesco* ☎ *No phone* 💲 *Free* ⊙ *Daily 8:30–noon and 4–5:45.*

Unless you're a great fan of the late baroque, the **Duomo** is a disappointment compared to Pescia's other churches. ✉ *Piazza del Duomo* ☎ *No phone* 💲 *Free* ⊙ *Daily 8–7:30.*

off the beaten path

MUSEO DELLA CARTA (Paper Museum) – Handmade Italian paper is becoming rarer and rarer, although only two generations ago more than 15 small paper factories operated on the banks of the Pescia River. Used paper and cloth were broken up in great stone basins, the soggy masses poured onto forms, and the water drained out. The sheets were then stacked, hung to dry, pressed, and pressed again. This small museum in Pietrabuona, with two informative videos (narrated in Italian), a room of old paper-making machinery, and the nearby remains of an old factory, attempts to preserve the knowledge, even if it cannot forestall the decline of the industry. ⊠ *Piazza la Croce, Pietrabuona, 3 km (2 mi) north of Pescia* ☎ *0572/476252* ⌨ *Free* ☉ *Tues., Thurs., and Sat., 9:30–noon.*

PARCO DI PINOCCHIO – In a little village 4 km (2½ mi) west of Pescia, once the summer home of Carlo Lorenzini (1826–90), author of *Pinocchio*, is a theme park devoted to the fictional marionette, where sculptures illustrate various characters and scenes from the story. It's a fine place to bring children and to have a picnic. The park makes more sense if the story is fresh in your mind—so you might want to reread it or watch the 1940 Disney film beforehand. "Collodi," the name of the village, was also Lorenzini's pen name. His mother was born in the village, and he spent summers here as a child. ⊠ *Via San Gennaro 2, Collodi* ☎ *0572/429342* ⌨ *€8.50* ☉ *Daily 8:30–sunset.*

Just around the corner from Parco di Pinocchio are the **Garzoni Gardens,** one of Italy's best restored 17th-century gardens, with a long cascading fountain, a park with hidden statuary, and a maze. ⊠ *Piazza della Vittoria* ☎ *0572/429590* ⌨ *€5.20* ☉ *Mar. 16–Nov. 14, daily 9–sunset; Nov. 15–Mar. 16, weekends 9–sunset.*

LUCCA

Ramparts built in the 16th and 17th centuries enclose a charming fortress town filled with churches (99 of them), terra-cotta-roofed buildings, and narrow cobblestone streets, along which local ladies maneuver bikes to do their daily shopping. Here Caesar, Pompey, and Crassus agreed to rule Rome as a triumvirate in 56 BC; Lucca was later the first Tuscan town to accept Christianity. The town still has a mind of its own, and when most of Tuscany was voting communist as a matter of course, Lucca's citizens rarely followed suit. The famous composer Giacomo Puccini (1858–1924) was born here; he is celebrated, along with his peers, during the summer Opera Theater and Music Festival of Lucca. The ramparts that circle the center city are the perfect place to take a stroll, ride a bicycle, kick a ball, or just stand and look down onto Lucca both within and without.

Exploring Lucca

Traffic (including motorbikes) is restricted in the walled historic center of Lucca. Walking is the best, most enjoyable way to get around. Otherwise, you can rent a bicycle; getting around on bike is easy, as the center is quite flat.

A Good Walk

Begin your walk with an overview of the *centro storico* (historical center) on the **Ramparts** ⑤ ▶. Climb the stairs to them at Piazza Vittorio Emanuele. Walking the entire ramparts takes about 45 minutes; if you decide not to, descend and start your tour at the **Museo Nazionale di Palazzo Mansi** ⑥ on Via Galli Tassi, just within the walls. Walk down Via del Toro to Piazza del Palazzo Dipinto, and follow Via di Poggio to **San Michele in Foro** ⑦. From Piazza San Michele, walk down Via Beccheria through Piazza Napoleone, and make a left through the smaller Piazza San Giovanni, which leads directly to the **Duomo** ⑧. Check out the lively facade before going into the church and looking at the Volto Santo and the *Tomb of Ilaria del Caretto*. The **Museo della Cattedrale** ⑨ is to the north of the Cathedral itself. If you have time, duck into the church of **Ss. Giovanni e Reparata** ⑩ and check out the fragments of early Christian architecture mingling with the baroque. Walk down Via dell'Arcivescovato, which is behind the Duomo and turns into Via Guinigi, toward the other side of the old city. You can climb the Torre Guinigi for an admirable view. The **Museo Nazionale di Villa Guinigi** ⑪ is a 10- to 15-minute walk east through Piazza San Francesco and on Via della Quarquonia. Backtrack to the Torre Guinigi; take Via Sant'Andrea to Via Fillungo to see the many Liberty-style buildings. Head a bit south on Via Fillungo to see the **Torre delle Ore** ⑫, whose view is especially worth a visit if you are traveling with children. Take Via Fillungo northward; at Via Fontana, make a left and follow it a short distance to Via Cesare Battisti, onto which you make a right. Head toward the church of **San Frediano** ⑬, which holds the mummified remains of St. Zita, the patron saint of domestic workers. Before returning to the Fillungo, walk behind the church, and take the narrow Via Cesare Battisti to **Palazzo Pfanner** ⑭. Retrace your steps to San Frediano, and head to Via Fillungo. Make a right and then a left, and head into the **Piazza dell Anfiteatro Romano** ⑮, where the Roman amphitheater once stood. Relax and have an aperitivo at one of the many sidewalk cafés.

TIMING   The walk takes about three hours, perhaps a little longer if you linger in the museums.

What to See

Casa Natale di Giacomo Puccini. Lucca's most famous musical son was born in this house. It includes the piano on which Puccini composed *Turandot*, scores of important early compositions, letters, costumes and costume sketches, and family portraits. ✉ *Corte San Lorenzo 9, Via di Poggio* ☎ *0583/584028* 💶 €3 ⊙ *June–Sept., daily 10–6; Oct.–Jan. and Mar.–May, Tues.–Sun. 10–1 and 3–6.*

★ ⑧ **Duomo.** The round-arched facade of the cathedral is a fine example of the rigorously ordered Pisan Romanesque style, in this case happily enlivened by an extremely varied collection of small carved columns. Take a closer look at the decoration of the facade and that of the portico below; they make this one of the most entertaining church exteriors in Tuscany. The Gothic interior contains a moving Byzantine crucifix—called the Volto Santo, or Holy Face—brought here, according to legend, in the 8th century (though it probably dates from between the 11th and early-

13th centuries). The masterpiece of the Sienese sculptor Jacopo della Quercia (circa 1371–1438) is the marble *Tomb of Ilaria del Carretto* (1407–1408). ✉ *Piazza del Duomo* ☎ *0583/490530* 🎟 *€2* ☉ *Weekdays 9:30–5:45, Sat. 9:30–6:45, Sun. 9–9:50, 11:30–11:50, and 1–5:45; Nov.–Mar., weekdays 9:30–4:45, Sat. 9:30–5:45, Sun. 9–9:50, 11:30–11:50, and 1–4:45.*

9 Museo della Cattedrale. The cathedral museum exhibits many items too precious to be in the church, most notably the finely worked golden decorations of the Volto Santo, the Byzantine crucifix that remains in the Duomo. ✉ *Piazza Antiminelli* ☎ *0583/490530* 🎟 *€3.50, combination ticket €5.50 (includes tomb in Duomo and San Giovanni's baptistery and archaeological works)* ☉ *Mid-Mar.–mid-Nov., daily, 10–6; mid-Nov.–mid-Mar., weekdays 10–2, weekends, 10–5.*

6 Museo Nazionale di Palazzo Mansi. Highlights here include the lovely *Portrait of a Youth* by Pontormo; portraits of the Medici painted by Bronzino (1503–72); and paintings by Tintoretto, Vasari, and others. ✉ *Palazzo Mansi, Via Galli Tassi 43 (near west walls of old city)* ☎ *0583/55570* 🎟 *€4, combination ticket with Museo Nazionale di Villa Guinigi €6.50* ☉ *Tues.–Sat. 8:30–7:30, Sun. 8:30–1:30.*

11 Museo Nazionale di Villa Guinigi. On the eastern end of the historic center, this museum has an extensive collection of local Romanesque and Renaissance art. The museum represents an overview of Lucca's artistic traditions from Etruscan times until the 17th century, housed in the former 15th-century villa of the Guinigi family. ✉ *Villa Guinigi, Via della Quarquonia* ☎ *0583/496033* 🎟 *€4, combination ticket with Museo Nazionale di Palazzo Mansi €6.50* ☉ *Tues.–Sat. 8:30–7:30, Sun. 8:30–1:30.*

14 Palazzo Pfanner. Here you can rest your feet and let time pass, surrounded by a harmonious arrangement of sun, shade, blooming plants, water, and mysterious statuary. The palazzo's well-kept formal garden, which abuts the city walls, centers on a large fountain and pool. Allegorical statues pose along pebbled paths that radiate outward. The palazzo, built in the 17th century, was purchased in the 19th century by the Pfanners, a family of Swiss brewers. The family, which eventually gave the town a mayor, still lives here. ✉ *Via degli Asili 33* ☎ *0583/954029* 🎟 *Garden €2.50, palazzo €2.50, garden and palazzo €4* ☉ *Mar.–mid-Nov., daily 10–6; mid-Nov.–Feb., by appointment only.*

15 Piazza dell'Anfiteatro Romano. On this site the Roman amphitheater once stood; some of the medieval buildings built over the amphitheater retain its original oval shape and brick arches. ✉ *Off Via Fillungo, near north side of the old town.*

need a break? Guido Cimino Ray Bar (✉ Anfiteatro 37–39, ☎ No phone), within the Roman amphitheater, offers good drinks and light lunches, including some novel salad combinations. You can also sit outside when it's warm. An airy upstairs gallery with a second bar and seating on small sofas and plush armchairs is the perfect spot for romance. It's closed Tuesday.

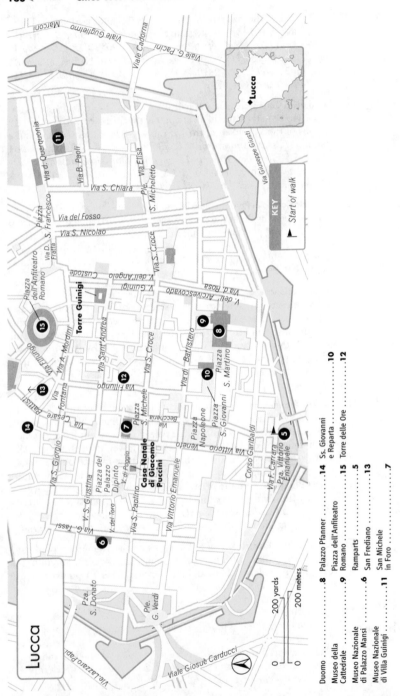

Lucca

KEY

▲ *Start of walk*

0 — 200 yards
0 — 200 meters

For a more stylish alternative, try **Girovita** (⊠ Piazza Antelminelli 2 ☎ 0583/469412). Opened in 2002, this popular hangout near the town's cathedral is elegant and lively. It serves light fare at lunch and dinner. At night its outdoor patio is packed with young people and provides one of Lucca's best people-watching spots. There's a huge selection of free *antipastis*; specialty drinks including *sorbetto,* an icy fruit drink made with fresh oranges, mandarins, or lemons from Sicily; and occasional live music. It's closed Monday night.

★ ▶ ❺ **The Ramparts.** Any time of day when the weather is clement, you can find the citizens of Lucca's historic district cycling, jogging, strolling, or playing ball in this green, beautiful, and very large park—neither inside nor outside the city but rather right on the ring of ramparts that defines Lucca. Sunlight streams through two rows of tall plane trees to dapple the *passeggiata delle mura* (walk on the walls), which is 4.2 km (2.5 mi) in length. Ten bulwarks are topped with lawns, many with picnic tables, and some with play equipment for children. Be aware at all times of where the edge is—there are no railings and the drop to the ground outside the city is a precipitous 40 feet.

⑬ **San Frediano.** The church of San Frediano, just inside the middle of the north town wall, has a spectacular 14th-century mosaic decorating its facade and contains works by Jacopo della Quercia (circa 1371–1438) and Matteo Civitali (1436–1501), as well as the lace-clad mummy of St. Zita (circa 1218–78), the patron saint of household servants. ⊠ *Piazza San Frediano* ☎ *No phone* ⊠ *Free* ☉ *Mon.–Sat. 8:30–noon and 3–5, Sun. 10:30–5.*

❼ **San Michele in Foro.** In the center of the old city is this church with a facade even more fanciful than that of the Duomo. The upper levels of the facade have nothing but air behind them (after the front of the church was built, there were no funds to raise the nave), and the winged Archangel Michael, who stands at the very top, seems precariously poised for flight. The facade was heavily restored in the 19th century and so, thanks to the times, displays busts of 19th-century Italian patriots such as Garibaldi and Cavour in addition to the earlier work. Check out the superb Filippino Lippi (1457/58–1504) panel painting of Sts. Girolamo, Sebastian, Rocco, and Helen in the right transept. ⊠ *Piazza San Michele* ☎ *No phone* ⊠ *Free* ☉ *Daily 9–noon and 3–6.*

❿ **Ss. Giovanni e Reparata.** The baptistery of this church, one piazza over from the Duomo, is lovely enough, but the unusual element here is an archaeological site, discovered in 1969, where five layers of Luccan history have been uncovered. As you walk the paths and catwalks suspended above the delicate sites in the caves under the church, you move from era to era—from the 2nd-century BC site of a Roman temple through the 5th, 8th, 9th, and 11th centuries. When seen after coming up the stairs from underground, the 12th-century church feels almost modern. ⊠ *Piazza San Giovanni* ☎ *0583/490530* ⊠ *Baptistery and archaeological site €2.50, combination ticket €5.50 (includes tomb in Duomo and Museo della Cattedrale)* ☉ *Mid-Mar.–mid-Nov., daiy 10–6; mid-Nov.–mid-Mar., weekdays 10–2, weekends 10–5.*

🕐 ⑫ **Torre delle Ore** (Tower of the Hours). The highest spot in Lucca is the top of this tower, first purchased by the city in 1490 as its "civic tower." The tower has held several clocks over the centuries; the current timepiece was installed in 1754. The reward for the climb to the top is a panoramic view. ⊠ *Via Fillungo at Via dell' Arancio* ☎ *No phone* 🎟 *€3.50, combination ticket €5.50 (includes Torre Guinigi)* ☉ *Daily 10–7.*

Torre Guinigi. The tower of the medieval Palazzo Guinigi contains one of the city's most curious sights: a grove of ilex trees has grown at the top of the tower and their roots have pushed their way into the room below. From the top you have a magnificent view of the city and the surrounding countryside. (Only the tower is open to the public, not the palazzo.) ⊠ *Palazzo Guinigi, Via Sant'Andrea* ☎ *No phone* 🎟 *€3.50, combination ticket €5.50 (includes Torre delle Ore)* ☉ *Mid-June–mid-Nov., daily 9–midnight; mid-Nov.–mid-June, daily 9:30–6.*

> **off the beaten path**
>
> Fodor'sChoice
> ★

VILLA REALE – Eight kilometers (5 mi) north of Lucca in Marlia, this villa was once the home of Napoléon's sister, Princess Elisa. Restored by the Counts Pecci-Blunt, the estate is celebrated for its spectacular gardens, laid out in the 16th century and redone in the middle of the 17th. Gardening buffs adore the legendary *teatro di verdura*, a theater carved out of hedges and topiaries; concerts are occasionally held here. During the summer, concerts are held in the gardens of other famous Lucca villas as well. Contact the Lucca tourist office (☎ 0583/583150) for details. ⊠ *Marlia; north of Lucca along the river Serchio, in the direction of Barga and Bagni di Lucca* ☎ *0583/30108* 🎟 *€6* ☉ *Jun.–Sept., guided visits Tues.–Sun. at 10, 11, noon, 3, 4, 5, and 6; Oct.–May, by appointment.*

Where to Stay & Eat

$$–$$$$ ✕ **All'Olivo.** If you're tired of the meat-oriented Tuscan cuisine, head for this restaurant hidden in a little square in the center of town that specializes in seafood. For a first course, try *spaghetti alle arselle*, made with the tiny clams found only on the Tuscan coast. Follow that with *branzino di mare al sale*, sea bass baked in a sea-salt crust, preserving all of its juices. You can eat outdoors here, even in winter. ⊠ *Piazza San Quirico 1* ☎ *0583/496264* ⊕ *www.ristoranteolivo.it* ⌂ *Reservations essential* ☰ *AE, DC, MC, V* ☉ *Closed Wed. Oct. 1–June 30.*

★ $$–$$$ ✕ **La Mora.** Detour to this former stagecoach station, now a gracious, rustic country inn 9 km (5½ mi) north of Lucca, for local specialties—from minestra di farro to homemade *tacconi* (a thin, short, wide pasta) with rabbit sauce and lamb from the nearby Garfagnana mountains. You might be tempted by the varied *crostini* (toasted bread) and delicious desserts. ⊠ *Via Sesto di Moriano 1748, Ponte a Moriano* ☎ *0583/406402* ☰ *AE, DC, MC, V* ☉ *Closed Wed., Jan. 1–15, and June 15–30.*

★ $$ ✕ **Buca di Sant'Antonio.** It's easy to see why this restaurant has been around since the 1800s. The white-walled interior adorned with copper pots, the expertly prepared food, and an able staff make dining here a real treat. The menu includes simple but blissful dishes such as *tortelli luc-*

chesi al sugo (meat-stuffed pasta with tomato–meat sauce) to more-daring entrées such as roast *capretto* (kid) with herbs. ⊠ *Via della Cervia 3* ☎ *0583/55881* ▤ *AE, DC, MC, V* ☺ *Closed Mon., 1 wk in Jan., and 1 wk in July. No dinner Sun.*

$–$$ ✕ **Il Giglio.** Just off Piazza Napoleone, this restaurant has quiet, late-19th-century charm and classic cuisine. It's a place for all seasons, with a big fireplace for chilly weather and an outdoor patio in summer. If mushrooms are in season, try the *tacchonni con funghi,* a homemade pasta with mushrooms and a local herb called *niepitela.* A local favorite during winter is the *coniglio con olive* (rabbit stew with olives). ⊠ *Piazza del Giglio 2* ☎ *0583/494508* ▤ *AE, DC, MC, V* ☺ *Closed Wed. and 15 days in Nov. No dinner Tues.*

$–$$ ✕ **Osteria del Neni.** Tucked away on a side street a block from San Michele, this delightful little place offers up tasty treats in a cozy space with paper place mats, wooden tables, and walls sponged in two hues of orange. All the pasta is made in-house, and if you're lucky enough to find ravioli *spinaci e anatra in salsa di noci* (stuffed with duck and spinach, in creamy but light walnut sauce), order it. The menu changes regularly; in summer you can eat outside. ⊠ *Via Pescheria 3* ☎ *0583/492681* ⚖ *Reservations essential* ▤ *AE, MC, V* ☺ *Closed Sun. and Jan.*

$ ✕ **Trattoria da Leo.** A few short turns away from the facade of San Michele, this noisy, informal, traditional trattoria delivers *cucina alla casalinga* (home cooking) in the best sense. Try the typical minestra di farro to start or just go straight to *secondi piatti* (entrées); in addition to the usual roast meats, there's excellent chicken with olives and a good cold dish of boiled meats served with a sauce of parsley and pine nuts. Save some room for a dessert, such as the rich, sweet, fig-and-walnut torte or the lemon sorbet brilliantly dotted with bits of sage, which tastes almost like mint. ⊠ *Via Tegrimi 1, at corner of Via degli Asili* ☎ *0583/492236* ▤ *No credit cards* ☺ *No lunch Sun.*

¢–$ ✕ **Ristorante Guinigi.** Around the corner from the Guinigi Tower in a 15th-century building is a restaurant that opened in early 2004. The elegant interior with a huge crystal chandelier, high ceilings, and candlelight all suggest a pricey menu, but excellent grilled fish and roasted meats come at reasonable prices and there's a two-course €10 lunch special. Don't miss the light and fresh *spaghetti alle Michele con gamberoni* (spaghetti with shrimp). ⊠ *Via S. Gregorio 4* ☎ *0583/491551* ▤ *AE, DC, MC, V* ☺ *Closed Tues.*

$$–$$$ ✕▥ **Locanda l'Elisa.** When Napóleon's sister, Elisa Baciocchi, arrived in Lucca to preside over it as a princess, she came with an entourage. One member built this delightful indigo villa 3 km (2 mi) south of Lucca. Surrounded by rosemary, lavender, and azaleas, the hotel preserves the intimacy of a well-furnished home; it's decorated in Empire style, with 19th-century furniture, prints, and fabrics. The attached restaurant ($$–$$$) elevates Lucchesi specialties such as *tordelli lucchese con sfoglia di farina di farro integrale al ragù d'anatra* (tortelli made with farro and served in a duck sauce) to new heights. ⊠ *Via Nuova per Pisa 1952, Massa Pisana 55050* ☎ *0583/379737* ☐ *0583/379019* ⊕ *www.locandalelisa.com* ⇄ *3 rooms, 7 suites* ⚹ *Restaurant, in-room safes, minibars, cable TV, in-room data ports, pool, massage, bar, babysitting,* *dry cleaning, laundry service, concierge, Internet, free parking, some pets allowed* ⊟ *AE, DC, MC, V* ⊘ *Closed Jan. 7–Feb. 11* ⍟ *EP.*

$$$–$$$$ ⊞ **Hotel Ilaria.** This beautifully appointed hotel faces the wide Via del Fosso. A terra-cotta terrace wraps around the side and back of the building and overlooks the garden of the neighboring Villa Botini, which has magnificent old, tall trees. Three rooms open directly onto the back terrace; two rooms are accessible to people who use wheelchairs. In early 2004, the Ilaria restored a medieval church around the corner, adding sunny and attractive suites that are on two levels. ⊠ *Via del Fosso 26, 55100* ☎ *0583/47615* ⊜ *0583/991961* ⊕ *www.hotelilaria.com* ⇌ *36 rooms, 5 suites* ⟳ *In-room safes, minibars, cable TV, bicycles, bar, babysitting, dry cleaning, laundry service, concierge, Internet, meeting rooms, free parking, some pets allowed (fee), no-smoking rooms* ⊟ *AE, DC, MC, V* ⍟ *BP.*

$$–$$$$ ⊞ **Villa La Principessa.** Some rooms in this exquisitely decorated 19th-century country mansion 3 km (2 mi) outside Lucca have handsome beamed ceilings, and doors are individually decorated. Antique furniture and portraits impart an aura of gracious living. The grounds are well manicured, the pool large and inviting. A stay here evokes the time of Napoléon's court, when many of his retinue built their summer pleasure palaces outside the city. The restaurant is open for dinner only (but closed Tuesday). ⊠ *Via Nuova per Pisa 1616, Massa Pisana 55050* ☎ *0583/370037* ⊜ *0583/ 379136* ⊕ *www.hotelprincipessa.com* ⇌ *35 rooms, 7 suites* ⟳ *Restaurant, room service, minibars, cable TV, pool, bar, babysitting, dry cleaning, laundry service, concierge, Internet, meeting rooms, some pets allowed* ⊟ *AE, DC, MC, V* ⊘ *Closed Nov.–Mar.* ⍟ *EP.*

$$ ⊞ **Alla Corte degli Angeli.** This charming hotel with a friendly staff is
FodorśChoice   right off the main shopping drag, Via Fillungo. Rooms combine Tus-
★   can authenticity, in the form of high brick and timbered ceilings and wood floors, with large modern bathrooms. Renovations in 2004 added four big rooms with frescoed ceilings, and an attractive breakfast room. ⊠ *Via degli Angeli 23, 55100* ☎ *0583/469204* ⊜ *0583/991989* ⊕ *www. allacortedegliangeli.com* ⇌ *10 rooms* ⟳ *Minibars, in-room hot tubs, lobby lounge, dry cleaning, laundry service, Internet, parking (fee), some pets allowed* ⊟ *AE, DC, MC, V* ⍟ *CP.*

★ $$ ⊞ **Palazzo Alexander.** This small, elegant boutique hotel is on a quiet side street a short walk from San Michele in Foro. The building, dating from the 12th century, has been restructured to create the ease common to Lucchesi nobility: timbered ceilings, warm yellow walls, and brocaded chairs adorn the public rooms, and the motif continues into the guest rooms, all of which have high ceilings and that same glorious damask. Top-floor suites have sweeping views of the town. One suite is on the mezzanine floor, but also has city views. ⊠ *Via S. Giustina 48, San Michele 55100* ☎ *0583/583571* ⊜ *0583/583610* ⊕ *www.palazzo-alexander. com* ⇌ *9 rooms, 3 suites, 1 apartment* ⟳ *In-room data ports, in-room safes, minibars, cable TV, bicycles, wine bar, babysitting, dry cleaning, laundry service, concierge, Internet, parking (fee), no-smoking rooms* ⊟ *AE, DC, MC, V* ⍟ *CP.*

$ ⊞ **Albergo San Martino.** Down a narrow street facing a quiet, sun-sprinkled *piazzale* (small square) stands this small hotel. The brocade bedspreads are fresh and crisp, the proprietor friendly. Although around the corner from the Duomo, the busy Corso Garibaldi, and the great walls of Lucca, the inn, tucked away as it is, feels private—a place to retreat to when you have seen all the church facades you can stand. Two of the eight rooms are wheelchair accessible. ⊠ *Via della Dogana 9, 55100* ☎ *0583/469181* 🖷 *0583/991940* ⊕ *www.albergosanmartino.it* 🛏 *6 rooms, 2 suites* ♿ *Minibars* ☰ *AE, DC, MC, V* |◯| *CP.*

$ 🏨 **La Luna.** On a quiet, airy courtyard close to the Piazza del Mercato, this family-run hotel occupies two renovated wings of an old building. The bathrooms are modern, but some rooms still have the flavor of Old Lucca. One of the suites has high frescoed ceilings and a chandelier, an echo of a nobler age. ⊠ *Corte Compagni 12, at Via Fillungo, 55100* ☎ *0583/493634* 🖷 *0583/490021* ⊕ *www.hotellaluna.com* 🛏 *27 rooms, 2 suites* ♿ *Minibars, some in-room safes, cable TV, bar, babysitting, parking (fee)* ☰ *AE, DC, MC, V* ⊙ *Closed Jan. 7–31* |◯| *EP.*

$ 🏨 **Piccolo Hotel Puccini.** Steps from the busy square and church of San Michele, this little hotel is quiet, calm, and handsomely decorated. Helpful and friendly service makes it an appealing place to stay. ⊠ *Via di Poggio 9, 55100* ☎ *0583/55421* 🖷 *0583/53487* ⊕ *www.hotelpuccini. com* 🛏 *14 rooms* ♿ *Fans, in-room data ports, in-room safes, cable TV, bar, babysitting, dry cleaning, laundry service, some pets allowed, no-smoking rooms; no a/c* ☰ *AE, MC, V* |◯| *EP.*

¢–$ 🏨 **Fattoria di Fubbiano.** Lucca is famous for producing some of the world's finest olive oil, and it could be argued that the best of all is produced here at this agriturismo 10 minutes outside Lucca's *centro storico.* In addition to olive oil, the firm also makes wine and has lodging available. There's a villa that sleeps up to 12; a small house reached by a narrow road often dotted with horses grazing at the side; and three apartments. The apartments have kitchenettes; the house and villa both have kitchens. During high season a one-week stay is strongly encouraged. ⊠ *San Gennaro, 55010* ☎ *0583/978011* 🖷 *0583/978344* ⊕ *www.fattoriadifubbiano. com* 🛏 *3 apartments, 1 farmhouse, 1 villa* ♿ *Some kitchens, some kitchenettes, 3 pools, laundry facilities; no a/c* ☰ *MC, V* |◯| *EP.*

Nightlife & the Arts

The **Estate Musicale Lucchese,** one of many Tuscan music festivals, runs throughout the summer in Lucca. Contact the Lucca tourist office for details. The **Opera Theater and Music Festival of Lucca,** sponsored by the Opera Theater of Lucca and the music college of the University of Cincinnati, runs from mid-June to mid-July; performances are staged in open-air venues. Call the Lucca tourist office, the Opera Theater of Lucca (☎ 0583/46531), or the University of Cincinnati, College-Conservatory of Music (☎ 513/566–5662) for information.

Sports & the Outdoors

A good way to spend the afternoon is to go biking around the large path atop the city's ramparts. There are two good spots right next to each other where you can rent bikes. The prices are about the same (€10–10.50 for the day and €2.10 per hour for city bikes) and they are centrally located, just beside the town wall. The people are friendlier and speak English at **Cicli Bizzarri** (⊠ Piazza Santa Maria 32 ☎ 0583/496031). There's a larger selection, including some mountain bikes at **Abbigliamento Biciclette** (⊠ Piazza Santa Maria 42 ☎ 0583/493787).

Shopping

Chocolate

Chocolate lovers will be pleased with the selection at **Caniparoli** (⊠ Via San Paolino 96 ☎ 0583/53456), a small stylish shop that specializes in homemade chocolates. Try their fruit-filled truffles and pistacchio-dusted chocolates. The store is closed in July and August.

Food

Lucca is known for its farro, an ancient barleylike grain that has found its way into regional specialties such as *zuppa* (or *minestra*) *di farro* (farro soup). It's available in food shops all over the city. Lucca is most famous for its olive oil, however, which is exported throughout the world. Look for extra-virgin oil whose label clearly indicates that it is entirely from Tuscany or, better yet, entirely from a local *fattoria*, or farm. *Olio nuovo* (new oil) is available from November, when the olive-picking season begins, until about February. This new oil is full-tasting and peppery—great for drizzling on soup, pasta, and bread—and it's also nearly impossible to find in North America. Wine from small Lucca producers is also difficult to find abroad. Visit **Enoteca Vanni** (⊠ Piazza del Salvatore 7 ☎ 0583/491902 ⊕ www.enotecavanni.com), which has a huge selection of wines, as well as an ancient cellar worth seeing. For the cost of the wine only, tastings can be organized through the shopkeepers and held in the cellar. Not far away is a smaller shop, **Massei Ugo** (⊠ Via S. Andrea 19 ☎ 0583/467656), with great wine prices and assorted local delicacies. The store's owner, Ugo Massei, doesn't speak English, but he's friendly, helpful, and a classic example of an old-fashioned Lucchese gentleman.

Markets

On the third weekend of the month there's an **antiques market** in Piazza San Martino. Vendors unveil their wares around 8:30 and start packing up around dusk. There's something for everyone, including old-fashioned glassware, ancient coins, and furniture—some antique, some just old. Check out the 19th-century tools and collections of fascist memorabilia.

Looking for old prints? Old postcards? Old comic books? Just behind the church of S. Giusto (off Via Beccheria, which runs for about two blocks between Piazza Napoleone and Piazza San Michele) are **bookstalls** that open their cupboard doors on clement days (including Sundays), from about 10 to 7. You may discover anything from hand-tinted prints of orchids to back issues of *Uomo Ragno* (Spider-Man looks and acts just the same even when he's speaking Italian).

Pasticceria

A particularly delicious version of *buccellato*—the sweet, anise-flavor bread with raisins that is a specialty of Lucca—is baked at **Pasticceria Taddeucci** (⊠ Piazza San Michele 34 ☎ 0583/494933). For a broad selection of scrumptious pastries, visit **Pasticceria Pinelli** (⊠ Via Beccheria 28 ☎ 0583/496119). It's a favorite of Lucca's elderly ladies and that's where you'll find them after church on Sunday.

PISA

If you can get beyond the kitsch that's around the Torre Pendente, the Leaning Tower, you'll find that Pisa has much to offer. Its treasures are more subtle than Florence's, to which it is inevitably compared; Pisa's cathedral-baptistery-tower complex on Piazza del Duomo is among the most dramatic in Italy.

Pisa may have been inhabited as early as the Bronze Age. It was certainly populated by the Etruscans and, in turn, became part of the Roman Empire. In the early Middle Ages it flourished as an economic powerhouse—along with Amalfi, Genoa, and Venice, it was one of the maritime republics. But the city's economic and political power ebbed in the early 15th century as it fell under Florence's domination, though it enjoyed a brief resurgence under Cosimo I in the mid-16th century. Though Pisa sustained heavy damage during World War II, the Duomo and Tower were spared, along with some other grand Romanesque structures.

Exploring Pisa

Pisa, like many other Italian cities, is best seen on foot, and most of what you'll want to see is within walking distance. The views along the Arno are particularly grand and shouldn't be missed—there's a feeling of spaciousness that isn't found along the same river in Florence.

As you set out, keep in mind the various combination-ticket options for sights on the Piazza del Duomo. The tickets are all sold at the sights themselves.

A Good Walk

Start in the Campo dei Miracoli (Field of Miracles), exploring the piazza complex containing the **Torre Pendente** ⑯ ➤, **Duomo** ⑰, **Battistero** ⑱, **Camposanto** ⑲, **Museo dell'Opera del Duomo** ⑳, and the **Museo delle Sinopie** ㉑. Walk down Via Santa Maria—the Campanile will be behind you. Somewhere along the way, to recover from the crowds at the Campo, stop to have a coffee or a gelato. Once on these streets, you are surrounded by students, professors, and the buildings housing the faculties of the University of Pisa, for centuries one of the finest Italian institutions of higher education. At Piazza Felice Cavalloti, go left on to Via dei Mille. On the right is the Romanesque church of **Santo Sisto** ㉒. Continue straight on Via dei Mille to **Piazza dei Cavalieri** ㉓, a study in Renaissance symmetry. Go straight through the piazza to Via Dini, and make a right on to Borgo Stretto, a major thoroughfare lined with cafés. On the left, before the river, is the church of San Michele in Borgo, whose early-14th-century Pisan Romanesque facade resembles a wedding cake. Walk up to Piazza Garibaldi and turn left along the Lungarno Mediceo. Practically at the Ponte della Fortezza, on the left, is the **Museo Nazionale di San Matteo** ㉔. Cross over the bridge and turn right on to Lungarno

Galileo Galilei. Take a left on the little side street Vicolo Lanfranchi, which is at the corner of Palazzo Lanfranchi. At the end of the street is the church of San Martino. Make a right onto Via San Martino and walk until you reach Piazza XX Settembre, where the large, freestanding Logge di Banchi (loggias) stand on the right. Go left onto Corso Italia, another major shopping thoroughfare. Or, if you wish to continue the walk, take a right on Corso Italia instead and walk until you reach the Arno. Make a left, and follow the curve of the sidewalk until you come upon **Santa Maria della Spina** ㉕, a Gothic gem.

TIMING   The walk takes a little more than 1½ hours without stops—but there's lots to see along the way; it could take a few hours, depending upon how long you stay in the Museo Nazionale di San Matteo.

What to See

⑱ Battistero. This lovely Gothic baptistery, which stands across from the Duomo's facade, is best known for the pulpit carved by Nicola Pisano (circa 1220–84; father of Giovanni Pisano) in 1260. Ask one of the ticket takers if he'll sing for you inside; the acoustics are remarkable (a tip of €3 is appropriate). ⊠ *Piazza del Duomo* ☎ *050/835010 or 050/835011* ⊕ *www.operaduomo.firenze.it* ☑ *€5, discounts available if bought in combination with tickets for other monuments* ☉ *Oct.–Mar. daily 9–5:40, Apr.–Sept. daily 8–7:40.*

⑲ Camposanto. According to legend, the cemetery—a walled structure on the western side of the Campo dei Miracoli—is filled with earth that returning Crusaders brought back from the Holy Land. Contained within are numerous frescoes, notably *The Drunkenness of Noah*, by Renaissance artist Benozzo Gozzoli (1422–97; presently under restoration) and the disturbing *Triumph of Death* (14th century; authorship uncertain), whose subject matter shows what was on people's minds in a century that saw the ravages of the Black Death. ⊠ *Piazza del Duomo* ☎ *050/835010 or 050/835011* ⊕ *www.duomo.pisa.it* ☑ *€5, discounts available if bought in combination with tickets for other monuments.* ☉ *Oct.–Mar. daily 9–5:40; Apr.–Sept. daily 8–7:40.*

off the beaten path

LA CERTOSA DI PISA – A *certosa* (charterhouse) is a monastery whose monks belong to the strict Carthusian order. This vast and sprawling complex, begun in 1366, was suppressed by Napoléon, and then again in 1866. Most of the art and architecture you see date from the 17th and 18th centuries. The Carthusians returned here, only to leave it permanently in 1969. Also within it is the **Museo di Storia Naturale e del Territorio.** This museum of natural history contains fossils, 24 whale skeletons that serve to trace the mammal's development over the millennia, and some exhibits of local minerals. ⊠ *10 km (6 mi) east of Pisa via road north of Arno, through Mezzana and then toward Calci and Montemagno* ☎ *050/938430* ☑ *€4* ☉ *Tues.–Sat. 8:30–6:30, Sun. 8:30–12:30, with tours on the half hour.*

⑰ Duomo. Pisa's cathedral was the first building to use the horizontal marble stripe motif (borrowed from Moorish architecture) that became common to Tuscan cathedrals. It is famous for the Romanesque panels on the

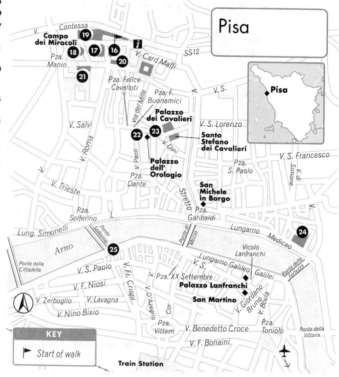

transept door facing the tower that depict the life of Christ. The beautifully carved 14th-century pulpit is by Giovanni Pisano (son of Nicola). ⊠ *Piazza del Duomo* ☎ *050/835010 or 050/835011* ⊕ *www.duomo.pisa. it* ⊠ *€2, discounts available if bought in combination with tickets for other monuments* ⊙ *Oct.–Mar. daily 10–5:40; Apr.–Sept. daily 10–7:40.*

㉑ Museo delle Sinopie. The well-arranged museum on the south side of the Piazza del Duomo holds the *sinopie* (preparatory drawings) for the Camposanto frescoes. ⊠ *Piazza del Duomo* ☎ *050/835010 or 050/ 835011* ⊕ *www.duomo.pisa.it* ⊠ *€5, discounts available if bought in combination with tickets for other monuments* ⊙ *Oct.–Mar. daily 9–5:40; Apr.–Sept. daily 8–7:40.*

㉒⁰ Museo dell'Opera del Duomo. At the southeast corner of the sprawling Campo dei Miracoli, this museum holds a wealth of medieval sculptures and the ancient Roman sarcophagi that inspired Nicola Pisano's figures. ⊠ *Piazza del Duomo* ☎ *050/835010 or 050/835011* ⊕ *www.duomo. pisa.it* ⊠ *€5 discounts available if bought in combination with tickets for other monuments.* ⊙ *Oct.–Mar. daily 9–5:40; Apr.–Sept. daily 8–7:40.*

㉔ Museo Nazionale di San Matteo. On the north bank of the Arno, this museum contains some incisive examples of local Romanesque and Gothic art. ✉ *Lungarno Mediceo* ☎ *050/541865* 🖼 *€4* ⊘ *Tues.–Sat. 9–7, holidays 9–2.*

㉓ Piazza dei Cavalieri. The piazza, which holds the fine Renaissance **Palazzo dei Cavalieri, Palazzo dell'Orologio,** and **Santo Stefano dei Cavalieri,** was laid out by Giorgio Vasari in about 1560. The square was the seat of the Ordine dei Cavalieri di San Stefano (Order of the Knights of St. Stephen), a military and religious institution that was meant to defend the coast from possible invasion by the Turks. Also in this square is the prestigious **Scuola Normale Superiore,** founded by Napoléon in 1810 on the French model. Here graduate students pursue doctorates in literature, philosophy, mathematics, and science. In front of the school is a large statue of Ferdinando I de' Medici dating from 1596. On the extreme left is the tower where the hapless Ugolino della Gherardesca (died 1289) was imprisoned with his two sons and two grandsons; legend holds that he ate them. Dante immortalized him in Canto XXXIII of *The Inferno.* Duck into the **Church of Santo Stefano** and check out Bronzino's *Nativity of Christ* (1564–65).

㉕ Santa Maria della Spina. Originally an oratory dating from the 13th century, this gem of a church has been restored several times, most recently in 1996–98, owing to flood damage. It's a delicate, tiny church, and a fine example of Tuscan Gothic. ✉ *Lungarno Gambacorti* ☎ *055/3215446* 🖼 *€1.50* ⊘ *Sept.–May., Tue.–Fri. 10–1:30 and 2:30–6, weekends 10–5; Jun.–Aug., Tue.–Fri. 11–1:30 and 2:30–6, weekends 11–8.*

㉒ Santo Sisto. Dating from the 11th century, this church reveals a simple yet elegant arcaded colonnade and stone interior. The inside is parted by colonnades with Roman capitals and includes an Arabian tombstone and the rudder of a Pisan boat dating back to the 14th century. ✉ *Piazza Francesco Buonamici* ☎ *No phone* 🖼 *Free* ⊘ *Daily 8–7:30.*

⑯ Torre Pendente (Leaning Tower). Legend holds that Galileo conducted an experiment on the nature of gravity by dropping metal balls from the top of the 187-ft-high Leaning Tower of Pisa. Historians, however, say this legend has no basis in fact—which isn't quite to say that it is false. Work on this tower, built as a campanile (bell tower) for the Duomo, started in 1173: the lopsided settling began when construction reached the third story. The tower's architects attempted to compensate through such methods as making the remaining floors slightly taller on the leaning side, but the extra weight only made the problem worse. The settling continued, and by the late 20th century it had accelerated to a point that led many to fear the tower would simply topple over, despite all efforts to prop it up. The structure since has been firmly anchored to the earth. The final phase to restore the tower to its original tilt of 300 years ago was launched in early 2000 and finished two years later. The last phase removed some 100 tons of earth from beneath the foundation. Reservations, which are essential, can be made online or by calling the Museo dell'Opera del Duomo. ✉ *Piazza del Duomo* ☎ *050/835010 or 050/835011* ⊕ *www.duomo.pisa.it* 🖼 *€15* ⊘ *Nov.–Feb., daily 9:30–5; Oct. and Mar., daily 8:30–7:30; Apr.–Sept., daily 8:30–8:30. Evening hours mid-June–mid-Sept., daily 8:30–11.*

Fodor'sChoice
★

Where to Stay & Eat

\$\$-\$\$\$ ✕ **Beny.** Apricot walls hung with etchings of Pisa make this small, single-room restaurant warmly romantic. Beny specializes in fish: its *ripieno di polpa di pesce a pan grattato con salsa di seppie e pomodoro* (fish-stuffed ravioli with tomato–octopus sauce) is a delight. Another flavorful dish is the *sformato di verdura* (a flan with Jerusalem artichokes), which comes embellished with sweet *gamberoni* (shrimp). ⊠ *Piazza Gambacorti 22* ☎ *050/25067* ▭ *AE, DC, MC, V* ☉ *Closed Sun. and two weeks mid-Aug. No lunch Sat.*

\$\$-\$\$\$ ✕ **La Mescita.** This cheerful trattoria has high, vaulted brick ceilings and stenciled walls lined with colorful contemporary prints. It's a great place to eat tasty and inventive food, such as *tagliolini con salsiccia e porri sopra salsa di cabernet sauvignon* (house-made thin noodles with sausage and leeks in wine sauce). The wine list has been carefully compiled, and service is friendly and efficient. ⊠ *Via Cavalca 2* ☎ *050/544294* ▭ *AE, DC, MC, V* ☉ *Closed Mon., 1 wk in Jan., and last 3 wks in Aug. No lunch weekdays.*

\$-\$\$\$ ✕ **La Pergoletta.** On an old-town street named for its "beautiful towers," this small, simple restaurant is in one itself. There's also a shady garden for outdoor dining. Signora Forte, the proprietor–chef, cooks such traditional Tuscan classics as *minestra di farro* (grain soup) and choice interpretations of *grigliata* (grilled beef, veal, or lamb). Her sense of whimsy accounts for some of the non-Italian ingredients that pepper her dishes. ⊠ *Via delle Belle Torri 40* ☎ *050/542458* ▭ *MC, V* ☉ *Closed Mon., and 1 wk in Aug. No lunch Sat.*

\$\$ ✕ **Al Ristoro dei Vecchi Macelli.** The "Inn by the Old Slaughterhouse" retains its name even though the slaughterhouse is no longer in use. Head here for special, sophisticated food. You can order a fixed-price seafood or meat menu or choose dishes à la carte. The menu changes regularly to reflect the season; in the cooler months look for *ravioli salsicce cavolfiore con i broccoli saltato* (ravioli stuffed with sausage and cauliflower and in a broccoli sauce). The room has low, subdued lighting; an old wooden ceiling; terra-cotta floors; and walls lined with stylish black-and-white photographs. ⊠ *Via Volturno 49* ☎ *050/20424* ▭ *AE, DC, MC, V* ☉ *Closed Wed. and 2 wks in mid-Aug. No lunch Sun.*

★ **\$-\$\$** ✕ **Osteria dei Cavalieri.** This charming white-walled restaurant, a few steps from Piazza dei Cavalieri, is reason enough to come to Pisa. They can do it all here—serve up exquisitely grilled fish dishes, please vegetarians, and prepare *tagliata* (thin slivers of rare beef) for meat lovers. Three set menus, from the sea, garden, and earth, are available, or you can order à la carte—which can be agonizing because everything sounds so good. And it is. Finish your meal with a lemon sorbet bathed in Prosecco (a dry sparkling wine), and walk away feeling as if you've eaten like a king at plebeian prices. ⊠ *Via San Frediano 16* ☎ *050/580858* ▭ *AE, DC, MC, V* ☉ *Closed Sun., two weeks in Aug., Dec. 29–Jan. 7. No lunch Sat.*

\$ ✕ **Il Re di Puglia.** In winter at "The King of Puglia," in the countryside 15 minutes outside of Pisa, you can enjoy Tuscan favorites in a large room with a fireplace. In summer you sit outside on a covered terrace. Beef, sausage, vegetables, and bruschetta are prepared on a very large grill and are all done well. Paired with the formidable wine list and friendly service, they make for a memorable meal. ⊠ *Via Aurelia Sud 7* ☏ *050/960157* ⌘ *Reservations essential* 🖃 *No credit cards* ☉ *Closed Mon.–Tues. No lunch Wed.–Sat.*

$ 🏨 **Hotel Verdi.** Down the street from Teatro Verdi, this small hotel often provides lodging for actors and musicians who are drawn by the hotel's quiet location, simple rooms with high ceilings, and intimate feel. The small bar is well stocked, and the lounge area is pleasant. ⊠ *Piazza Repubblica 5/6, 56100* ☏ *050/598947* ⎙ *050/598944* ⬀ *32 rooms* ⌂ *Bar, lounge, Internet, free parking* 🖃 *AE, DC, MC, V* ⍾ *CP.*

$ 🏨 **Royal Victoria.** In a pleasant palazzo facing the Arno, a 10-minute walk from the Campo dei Miracoli, this comfortably furnished hotel has been in the same family since 1837. The continuity may help to explain why such notables as Charles Dickens and Charles Lindbergh enjoyed staying here. Antiques and reproductions are in the lobby and in some rooms, whose style ranges from the 1800s, complete with frescoes, to the 1920s. Ask for a room in the old tower. There's also a pretty rooftop garden where you can order cocktails. ⊠ *Lungarno Pacinotti 12, 56126* ☏ *050/940111* ⎙ *050/940180* ⊕ *www.royalvictoria.it* ⬀ *48 rooms, 40 with bath* ⌂ *Room service, some fans, in-room data ports, cable TV, bicycles, babysitting, dry cleaning, laundry service, concierge, parking (fee), some pets allowed; no a/c in some rooms* 🖃 *AE, DC, MC, V* ⍾ *CP.*

★ ¢–$$ 🏨 **Fattoria di Migliarino.** Martino Salviati and his wife Giovanna have turned their working *fattoria*, or farm—on which they raise soybeans, corn, and sugar beets—into an inn. The charming, spacious apartments accommodate anywhere from two to eight people and are rustically furnished, many of them with fireplaces. There's also a farmhouse that has been converted into a bed-and-breakfast. The pool is framed by fields, and the only sound you're likely to hear is the clucking of the hens they keep for eggs. The surrounding woods can be explored on horseback or with a mountain bike. During high season there is a two-night minimum stay. ⊠ *Via del Mare 1, Migliarino, 10 km (6 mi) northwest of Pisa, 56010* ☏ *050/803046 or 335/6608411* ⎙ *050/803170* ⬀ *10 rooms in B&B, 7 apartments* ⌂ *BBQ, kitchenettes, pool, Ping-Pong; no a/c in some rooms, no room TVs* 🖃 *MC, V* ⍾ *BP, EP.*

Nightlife & the Arts

The **Luminaria** feast day, on June 16, is Pisa at its best. The day honors St. Ranieri, the city's patron saint. Palaces along the Arno are lit with white lights, and there are plenty of fireworks.

EMPOLI & CENTRAL HILL TOWNS

Off the beaten track in Empoli, San Miniato, and the neighboring hill towns are fine examples of art—especially in Empoli and Castelfiorentino—and stirring views. The terrific restaurants in this area are less expensive than in the cities to the north. This is also a good place to find local handmade products—ceramics in Montelupo, glass and leather in the Empoli–Vinci area, as well as local wine and oil, both in Certaldo and in Vinci.

Empoli

26 *50 km (31 mi) east of Pisa, 33 km (21 mi) west of Florence.*

Off the Arno roughly halfway between Florence and Pisa, Empoli is a bustling town with a long history. References to the city first appear in documents from the 800s. By 1182 it was completely aligned with Florence. In 1260, after the Battle of Montaperti, the leader of the pro-imperial faction called the Ghibellines, Farinata degli Uberti, made the decision while in Empoli not to burn Florence to the ground, a decision that Dante wrote about in Canto X of *The Inferno.*

Now Empoli is a sleepy little town only a half-hour train ride from Florence. If you're traveling in the summer, you might want to consider staying here and hopping on the train for day trips into Florence. But don't forget to see the sights in Empoli—they're worth it.

★ A woman who works at the **Collegiata di Sant'Andrea** describes it as a "little jewel," and she's completely right. In this museum, with its cloister filled with terra-cotta sculptures from the della Robbia school, including one by Andrea della Robbia, is a magnificent 15th-century fresco pietà by Masolino (circa 1383–1440); there are also a small Fra Filippo Lippi and a wonderful tabernacle attributed to Francesco Bottincini (circa 1446–97) and Antonio Rossellino (1427–79). ☒ *Just off Piazza Farinata degli Uberti* ☎ *0571/76284* ☒ *€3; combination ticket €6 (includes Museo Leonardiano in Vinci and the Museo Archeologico e della Ceramica in Montelupo)* ☉ *Tues.–Sun. 9–noon and 4–7.*

Originally founded by the Augustinians in the 11th century, **Santo Stefano** can be seen only by asking for a tour in the Collegiata di Sant'Andrea. It's worth the walk around the corner and down the street, as there are *sinopie* (preparatory drawings) by Masolino depicting scenes from the *Legend of the True Cross.* He left without actually frescoing them; it may be that the Augustinian friars were late in making payment. ☒ *Via de' Neri* ☎ *0571/76284* ☒ *Free* ☉ *Tues.–Fri. 9–noon.*

> **need a break?**
>
> **Vinegar** (☒ Piazza della Vittoria 36–37 ☎ 0571/74630) is a nice bar near the train station that sells many sorts of panini as well as coffee and aperitifs.

A short but not very scenic walk from the center of town brings you to the little **San Michele in Pontorme,** chiefly notable for the gorgeous *St. John the Baptist* and *St. Michael the Archangel,* two works dating from about 1519 by Jacopo Carrucci (1494–1556), better known as Pontormo. ☒ *Piazza San Michele* ☎ *No phone* ☒ *Free* ☉ *Ring for sacristan.*

> **off the beaten path**

VILLA MEDICEA – On the night of July 15, 1576, Isabella de' Medici, daughter of the all-powerful Cosimo I, was murdered by her husband in the Villa Medicea in the town of Cerreto Guidi for "reasons of honor"—that is, she was suspected of adultery. These days, although the villa's formal garden is in somewhat imperfect condition, the vast halls and chambers within remain majestic. Copies of portraits of various Medici, including Isabella, cover the walls. Cosimo chose to build this villa on the ruins of a castle that originally belonged to the Guidi counts, and the choice speaks volumes about what he believed himself to be. The Medici buildings sit atop the highest point in Cerreto Guidi, encircled by two narrow streets where the daily business of the town goes on. As you stand on the wide, flat front lawn, high above the streets of the town, with the villa behind you and terraced hillsides of olive groves and vineyards stretching into the distance, you can imagine what it was like to be a Medici. To see the villa, ring the bell for the custodian. ⊠ *Cerreto Guidi, 8 km (5 mi) west of Empoli* ☎ *0571/55707* ⌂ *€2* ☉ *Daily 8:15–7. Closed the 2nd and 3rd Mon. of each month.*

Where to Stay & Eat

★ **$–$$$$**   ✕ **Il Galeone.** This relaxed and friendly place is known for its fish, but the meat dishes are as delicious. Pale-pink walls and pink tablecloths play off the gray-and-white tile floors. You may have trouble deciding what to order, but give the *moscardini con fagioli e rucola* (baby squid gently heated with cannellini beans, diced tomatoes, and olive oil and served on a bed of arugula) a try; the *spiedini di seppioline e gamberoni* (kebabs of squid with shrimp) are terrific, too. Pizza is also served here. ⊠ *Via Curtatone e Montanara 67* ☎ *0571/72826* ▤ *AE, DC, MC, V* ☉ *Closed Sun. and Aug.*

¢–$ ▦ **Hotel Il Sole.** Across the street from the railway station, Il Sole has been in the hands of the Sabatini family since 1905. Each of the 12 rooms is an eclectic, unique interpretation of the Victorian style. If you are on a budget, this is a good alternative to staying in Florence, which is about a half-hour train ride away. ⊠ *Piazza Don Minzoni 18, 50053* ☎ *0571/73779* ▤ *0571/79871* ⇶ *12 rooms, 9 with bath* ⚲ *Some pets allowed; no a/c in some rooms* ▤ *AE, DC, MC, V* ⊙l *CP.*

Shopping

Large or small, formal or sporty—women are likely to find something to fit the bill at the high-quality **Modyva outlet** (☎ 0571/9501 ⊕ www. modyva.it). The store is outside Empoli, hidden away near Modyva's factory with no sign outside: retail shops had complained that the outlet was too visible from the FI-PI-LI superstrada. The prices and selection are excellent; all four of the fashion house's lines are sold here at reduced prices, with those for irregulars (meticulously marked) lowered further. The sales staff is friendly and professional. Like many other Italian businesses, Modyva is family-run, with the third generation being groomed to take on increasing leadership. To get to the outlet, take either of the Empoli Ovest exits from the FI-PI-LI autostrada and turn left at the bottom of the ramp; at the traffic light go straight across the road and into the Terrafino industrial park. Modyva's *spazio aziendale* (selling space) is in the first building on your left. It's open Monday through Saturday 9–1 and 3:30–7 and is closed in August.

Montelupo

27 *6 km (4 mi) east of Empoli, 30 km (19 mi) southwest of Florence.*

This small town, which straddles the Arno, and surrounding villages have been producing ceramics for centuries. Many of the shops in Montelupo's centro storico (historical center) are devoted to selling these ceramics, especially tableware and pots.

The **Museo archeologico e della ceramica** (Museum of Archaeology and Ceramics) has some 3,000 objects devoted to majolica, a glazed pottery that has been made in this region since the early 14th century. The museum includes a good section on archaeology and prehistoric finds, clear explanations of the technology and history of making ceramics from the earliest days to the present, and a beautifully mounted and arranged collection of local work that dates from the early-14th to the late-18th centuries. Most fascinating are the coats of arms representing important Renaissance names such as Medici and Strozzi. ⊠ *Via Bartolomeo Sinibaldi 45* ☎*0571/ 51087* ⊠*€3; combination ticket €6 (includes Museo Leonardiano in Vinci and Collegiata di Sant'Andrea in Empoli)* ⊙ *Tues.–Sun. 10–6.*

Nightlife & the Arts

FESTIVAL Every June, Montelupo is host to the weeklong **Festa della Ceramica** (☎ 0571/518993), a ceramics festival that includes exhibitions of local and international contemporary artists, demonstrations of techniques new and ancient, street theater and music—and, of course, sales of ceramics from around the world. Additional information about the ceramics festival is available from the Montelupo Fiorentino tourist office.

Shopping

CERAMICS Montelupo's ceramics museum proudly displays the work of the past, but the finest tribute to centuries of craft is the fact that top-quality ceramics are still being produced by hand in the region. Much work is in traditional styles, but there are also some artists who bring modern inspiration to their wheels. Not all of the stores will ship for you, although many will wrap the objects for you to carry home.

Bartoloni: La Ceramica Tradizionale di Montelupo (⊠ Corso Garibaldi 34 ☎0571/51242 or 0571/913569) is down the road from the Museo Archeologico e Della Ceramica. The articles produced are done in many kinds of styles. The small shop is open daily 10:30–1 and 4:30–8.

Ceramica ND Dolfi (⊠ Via Toscoromagnola 1, Località Antinoro ☎ 0571/ 51264) has been a family business for three generations. The compound, including a sun-drenched *spazio aziendale* (selling floor), the factory workshop, the family residence, and a yard where terra-cotta planters are displayed, is 3 km (2 mi) from Montelupo on the east road toward Florence. The ceramics, all priced reasonably for such high-quality handcrafted work, include big floor vases, plates suitable for wall display, and bright serving pieces for the table. The shop is open daily from 9 to 8.

Le Ceramiche del Borgo (⊠ Via G. Marconi 2/4 ☎ 0571/518856) sells the work of Eugenio Taccini, which includes bowls, platters, tiles, and plates. The large shop, which is open daily, is next to a bridge in Montelupo's historical center; the store's proprietor, Lea Taccini, speaks good English. The shop is open daily from 9 to 1 and 4 to 8.

Some serious ceramics lovers think **Maioliche Dolfi Otello** (⊠ Via Toscoromagnola Nord 8/b, Località Camaioni ☎ 0571/910105 ⊕ www.otellodolfi.it) is the best. The shop, in the same building as the factory, is a couple of miles outside Montelupo, down SS67 in the direction of Florence, and well worth the ride. In addition to fine platters, vases, pitchers, and the like, the shop produces devotional ceramics by hand, in the style of the della Robbia studio. Maioliche Dolfi Otello is open weekdays 8–noon and 1:30–6:30. You can often watch the artisans at work.

Vinci

❷❽ *10 km (6 mi) north of Empoli, 45 km (28 mi) west of Florence.*

The small hill town from which Leonardo da Vinci derived his name is a short bus ride north of Empoli. At the church of Santa Croce, near the town square, you can see the baptismal font in which Leonardo was baptized. But if you want to see the house where he was born, you'll have to travel to Anchiano, 3 km (2 mi) north of Vinci. In any case, it's worth a trip to Vinci for the views alone.

Museo Ideale Leonardo da Vinci. A small museum houses an idiosyncratic hodgepodge of items related to Leonardo, including mechanical objects from the time of Leonardo and copies of his sketches, including one of this region. ⊠ *Via Montalbano 2* ☎ *0571/56296* 🖾 *€5* ☉ *Daily 10–1 and 3–7.*

Museo Leonardiano. If you are interested in Leonardo or the history of science, this museum, atop the castle belonging to the Guidi family in the historical center of Vinci, has replicas of many of Leonardo's machines and gadgets. The typically Tuscan views are not at all bad. ⊠ *Via della Torre 2* ☎ *0571/56055* 🖾 *€5; €6 combination ticket (includes Collegiata di Sant'Andrea in Empoli and Museo Archeologico e della Ceramica in Montelupo)* ☉ *Daily 9:30–7.*

Where to Stay

$ 🏠 **Il Fondaccio.** This moderately priced agriturismo overlooks the hills near Vinci. Five apartments are available for groups of two to six people for one-week stays. One apartment is entirely wheelchair accessible. If you're traveling with children, il Fondaccio is a perfect spot from which to tour the sights (Pisa, Lucca, San Gimignano, and beaches are all nearby); the pool provides a fine option for nonsightseeing days. ⊠ *Via del Fondaccio 19, 50059* ☎ *0571/559511* 🖷 *0571/959703* ⊕ *www.fondaccio.it* ⇝ *5 apartments* ♿ *Kitchenettes, pool, bicycles, playground, kennel; no a/c, no room TVs* ▭ *No credit cards* ☉ *Closed Nov.–Mar.* ⫶○⫶ *EP.*

Shopping

CERAMICS In the historic center of Vinci near the Castello dei Conti Guidi is **Arte Più** (✉ Via del Castello 10 ☎ 0571/729151 ⊕ www.artepiuvinci.com), a small shop run by artist Roberta Campori, who lives and works in the old stone building. She hand-paints ceramics, and customers can make requests for particular patterns or scenes.

LEATHER As you drive around this part of Tuscany, you see advertisements for *venditta diretta* (direct sales) at the small local factories that work in leather and furs. Of course, not every factory is set up for doing this or carries high-quality goods, and the stock is extremely limited. In the spazio aziendale, **ESSEBI** (✉ Via del Torrino 33, behind the Cantine Leonardo da Vinci ☎ 0571/902172) has a small but excellent selection of leather jackets, pants, shirts, skirts, and coats. It also has silky-soft suede. The stock, including colors and sizes, varies depending on the season (more windbreakers in the colder months). Prices here are not low, but the cost is reasonable for what you are getting. The retail space is open Tuesday–Saturday 8:30–12:30 and 2:30–6:30. If you need to call, be sure to ask *per lo spazio* (for the space).

OLIVE OIL **L'Oleificio Cooperativo Montalbano** (✉ Via Beneventi 2/c ☎ 0571/56247), a cooperative *frantoio* (olive mill)—where many local farmers bring their olives to be pressed at late autumn's harvest—sells oil made only from fruit on these hills. Other locally made goods, including wine and vinegar and herb-flavored oils, are sold here too. Look for oil pressed as recently as possible; if kept out of the sunlight, it should keep for two years. The cooperative is open weekdays 8:30–12:30 and 2:30–6:30, Saturday 8–noon.

WINE As you walk in **Cantine Leonardo da Vinci** (✉ Bivio di Streda ☎ 0571/902444), you will see three huge vats with large nozzles, resembling those used to pump gasoline, and a choice of white and two types of red wine. It's all good, straightforward table wine (the minimum purchase is 6 liters—the equivalent of 8 bottles). This *cantina* (wine shop), open weekdays 8:30–12:30 and 2:30–6:30, also sells a range of Italian wines; look for those produced and bottled in Vinci.

San Miniato

㉙ *20 km (12 mi) southeast of Vinci, 43 km (27 mi) west of Florence.*

Dating from Etruscan and Roman times, this town was named San Miniato after the saint (also known as St. Mineas) to whom the Lombards dedicated a church in the 8th century. The Holy Roman Empire had very strong ties to San Miniato; in fact, its castle was built in 962 under the aegis of Otto I (912–973). Matilde of Tuscany was born here in the mid-11th century. Eventually the town, with its Ghibelline (pro-imperial and anticlerical) sympathies, passed into the hands of the Florentines. Today the pristine, tiny hill town's narrow, cobbled streets are lined with austere 13th- to 17th-century facades, some of them built over buildings that were already centuries old. San Miniato's artistic treasures are somewhat limited in comparison with Florence's, but the town's prettiness makes a trip well worth it.

St. Francis founded the 1211 **Convento di San Francesco** (Convent and Church of St. Francis), containing two cloisters and an ornate wooden choir. For a dose of monastic living, you can stay overnight (€35 in summer; €37 in winter for a double room). ✉ *Piazza San Francesco* ☎ *0571/ 43051* ⛶ *Free* ⊙ *Daily 9–noon and 3–7 (or ring bell).*

The **Convento e Chiesa di Santi Jacopo e Filippo** (Convent and Church of Sts. Jacob and Philip) is also known as the church of San Domenico, which refers to the fact that the Dominicans took over the church in the 14th century. Most of the interior suffers from too much baroque, but there is a lovely sculpted tomb by Bernardo Rossellino for Giovanni Chellini, a doctor who died in 1461. ✉ *Piazza del Popolo* ☎ *0571/418739* ⛶ *Free* ⊙ *Daily 8:30–noon and 3–7.*

> **need a break?**
>
> **Bar Cantini** (✉ Via Conti 1 ☎ 0571/43030) might be the meeting place for all San Miniatans; its panini are wonderful, in part because the bread is baked on site. There's also pizza by the slice, tasty *granita* (a flavored ice), and homemade ice cream.

The only thing remarkable about the **Duomo**, set in a pretty piazza, is its 13th-century facade, which has been restored. The interior is largely uninteresting; a moment of poignancy occurs when you view the plaque commemorating the 55 citizens who were killed in this church in July 1944 by German occupying forces (the Taviani brothers' 1982 movie, *The Night of San Lorenzo*, was about these events). ✉ *Piazza del Castello* ☎ *No phone* ⛶ *Free* ⊙ *Daily 8–12:30 and 3–6:30.*

Although the **Museo Diocesano** is small, the modest collection incorporates a number of subtle and pleasant local works of art. Note the rather odd Crucifixion by Fra Filippo Lippi, Verrocchio's (1435–88) *Il Redentore,* and the small but exquisite *Education of the Virgin* by Tiepolo (1696–1770). ✉ *Piazza del Castello* ☎ *0571/418071* ⛶ *€3, combination ticket €5 (includes entry to eight museums)* ⊙ *Tue.–Sun. 10–1 and 3–7.*

The **Torre di Federico II**, dating from around the time of Frederick II (1194–1250), was destroyed during World War II. A point of civic pride for the San Miniatans and visible for miles and miles around, the tower was rebuilt and reopened in 1958. The hapless, ill-fated Pier della Vigna, chancellor and minister to Frederick II, leapt to his death from the tower, earning a mention in Canto XIII of *The Inferno.* The hill on which the tower stands—a surprisingly large, flat oval of green grass—is one of the loveliest places in the area to munch a panino, enjoy the 360-degree view, or join local children in a pickup game of *calcio* (Italian soccer). Just don't let the ball go over the edge, because you'll never see it again. ✉ *Piazza del Popolo* ☎ *0571/42745* ⛶ *€5* ⊙ *Tues.–Sun. 9:30–1 and 3–7.*

Where to Stay & Eat

$–$$ ✕ **L'Antro di Bacco.** You'd never know it was here even though it's in the center of town, as you first have to enter a *salumeria* (delicatessen) and then descend. It's worth seeking out: the food is superb, and the chef has a deft touch with slightly atypical combinations. Be sure to try a plate that includes *tartufi,* the local white truffles San Miniato is famous for. A lighter menu is served at lunch. Ask for one of two tables on a tiny balcony with a glorious view of the countryside. ⊠ *Via Quattro Novembre 13* ☎ *0571/43319* ▤ *MC, V* ⊘ *Closed Sun. and 2 wks. in Aug. No dinner Wed.*

★ **$–$$** ✕ **Il Convio.** The stenciled walls, brightly colored tablecloths, and absolute calm make this charming restaurant homey. There is plenty of outdoor seating. Start with the *testaroli al pesto rosso* (local handmade noodles with sundried tomato pesto). For a main course, try the *carbonata* (a fillet steak on bread with a porcini mushroom on top). In the truffle season (October–December), many plates come with the local white truffles. Il Convio-Maiano is 2 km (1 mi) from the historic center, in San Miniato Basso. ⊠ *Via San Maiano 2* ☎ *0571/408114* ▤ *AE, DC, MC, V* ⊘ *Closed Wed.*

¢ 🏠 **Convento di San Francesco.** For a complete change of pace, you can stay in this 13th-century monastery in the company of five Franciscan friars. Rooms are simple, bordering on spartan, but quiet. You are given keys, so you're not expected back by a certain time. You can partake in some spiritual activities or skip them altogether. All rooms have baths, four rooms accommodate three people, and one room has four beds. The city center is a 10-minute walk from the monastery. ⊠ *Piazza San Francesco, 56020* ☎ *0571/43051* 🖷 *0571/43398* ⬿ *30 rooms* ⬧ *No a/c, no room phones, no room TVs, no kids under 12* ▤ *No credit cards* ⍥ *EP.*

Castelfiorentino

③⓪ *12 km (7 mi) south of San Miniato, 50 km (31 mi) southwest of Florence.*

Like San Miniato, Castelfiorentino can claim Roman origins. During the Middle Ages it was of strategic importance in the struggles between the Holy Roman Empire and the Papacy. Now it is a sleepy little town.

Admirers of Renaissance artist Benozzo Gozzoli (1420–97) have much to see at the **Biblioteca Comunale,** where the detached frescoes and sinopie from two tabernacles executed by him are on display. The Tabernacolo della Visitazione shows scenes from the life of the Virgin Mary; another tabernacle, *Madonna della Tosse* (literally, "Madonna of the Coughs"), from 1484, has exquisite renderings of major events in the life of the Virgin Mary, including the Assumption. ⊠ *Via Tilli 41* ☎ *0571/64019* 🎟 *Free* ⊘ *Tue., Thur., and Sat. 4–7, Sun. 10–noon and 4–7.*

Certaldo

③① *9 km (6 mi) south of Castelfiorentino, 56 km (35 mi) west of Florence.*

Certaldo is probably most famous for having produced Giovanni Boccaccio (1313–75), the witty and irreverent author of *The Decameron* (circa 1351). It seems as if practically every shop in town has managed to incorporate his name into its title. The town was greatly damaged during World War II, and much of what you see of its brick buildings is postwar reconstruction. The centro storico, Certaldo Alto, is high above the rest of town and has magnificent views into Chianti.

The dimly lit church of **Santissimi Jacopo e Filippo,** begun in the 12th century, is where Boccaccio is buried. A tomb slab bearing his likeness is found in the center aisle, and a Latin epitaph written by Florentine chancellor Coluccio Salutati is near it on the left wall. Also of interest are two terra-cotta tabernacles dated 1499 and 1502 from the school of the della Robbia. On the right wall is a stupendous, multicolor terra-cotta altarpiece, attributed to one of the della Robbia, depicting the *Madonna of the Snow.* ☒ *Piazza Santissimi Jacopo e Filippo* ☎ *No phone* ☜ *€3 (includes Palazzo Pretorio and Casa di Boccaccio)* ⊙ *Daily 8–noon and 4–8.*

Begun in the late-12th century, the **Palazzo Pretorio,** speckled with terra-cotta coats of arms on its facade, served as the city's town hall and also provided space for a women's prison. Now it houses a gallery for art exhibitions, a permanent display of Etruscan pottery, and fragments of 14th-century murals. All of its spaces are open to visitors; you can crawl under the low sills of the doorways leading into the prison cells (where lines are scored on the walls, presumably by inmates keeping track of the dismal days), or you can walk outside, across a wide walled-in lawn to narrow brick stairs that ascend the back garden wall to a balcony that runs the length of the palazzo, looking straight up into Chianti. Also in this complex is the church of **San Tommaso e Prospero,** which contains a Benozzo Gozzoli tabernacle (1466–67) depicting scenes from the life of Christ. You can view the sinopie that he executed for the tabernacle too. ☒ *Piazzetta del Vicariato1* ☎ *0571/661219* ☜ *€3 (includes Santissimi Jacopo e Filippo and Casa di Boccaccio)* ⊙ *May–Sept., Wed.–Mon. 10–7, Tue. 10:30–4:30; Oct. and Apr., weekdays 10:30–4:30, weekends 10–7; Nov.–Mar., Wed.–Mon. 10:30–4:30.*

At the **Casa di Boccaccio** they say that the room in which Boccaccio died is the only part of the house to have survived a World War II bombing. ☒ *Via Boccaccio 25* ☎ *0571/664208* ☜ *€3 (includes Santissimi Jacopo e Filippo and Palazzo Pretorio)* ⊙ *May–Sept., Wed.–Mon. 10–7, Tues. 10:30–4:30; Oct. and Apr., weekdays 10:30–4:30, weekends 10–7; Nov.–Mar., Wed.–Mon. 10:30–4:30.*

> **need a break?** **La Saletta di Dolci Follie** (☒ Via Roma 3, in Certaldo Basso ☎ 0571/668188), closed Tuesday, serves tasty light lunches and delectable sweets.

Where to Stay & Eat

$ ✕▣ **Osteria del Vicario.** In the historic center, this is a full-service stop for the weary traveler. Here you can have a coffee or a glass of wine, stay for dinner, or even spend the night; next to the Palazzo Pretorio complex, what was once a monastery is now an upscale bar, restaurant, and inn. Five of the rooms are former monks' cells, decorated in a well-appointed (and most unmonkish) fashion; ten additional rooms are in a building nearby. Traditional and innovative Tuscan cooking is served elegantly along with a wide selection of wines in the restaurant ($$$–$$$$; closed Wednesday). In warm weather you can dine in the open-air cloister and enjoy a view of the countryside. ☒ *Via Rivellino 3, 50052* ☎ *0571/668228* ⎙ *0571/668676* ⊕ *www.osteriadelvicario.it* ⮐ 15 *rooms* ⟂ *Restaurant, bar, babysitting, Internet, no-smoking rooms; no a/c* ⊟ *AE, DC, MC, V* ⊙ *Closed Sundays.* ⦾ *EP.*

Shopping

WINE **Cantina Sociale Certaldo** (⊠ Via Agnoletti 97, just north of Certaldo city limits ☏ 0571/667403), a typical wine cooperative, sells the local wine in bulk amounts (bring a container of at least 6 liters) as well as bottled wine from the region, which stretches over to Montalbano, up to Pontassieve, and down to Poggibonsi near Siena. This local wine, because it is intended to be consumed in a fairly short time, is a good table wine. Bulk wine is sold in red, white, and often rosé; local olive oil is also available. The cooperative is open weekdays 8:30–12:30 and 2:30–6:30, and Saturday 8:30–noon.

Livorno

③② *50 km (31 mi) northwest of Certaldo, 187 km (116 mi) west of Florence.*

The ferry hub of Livorno is a gritty city with a long and interesting history. In the early Middle Ages it alternately belonged to Pisa and then to Genova (Genoa). In 1421 Florence, seeking access to the sea, bought it. Cosimo I (1519–74) started construction of the harbor in 1571, putting Livorno on the map. After Ferdinando I de' Medici (1549–1609) proclaimed Livorno a free city, it became a haven for people suffering from religious persecution; Roman Catholics from England and Jews and Moors from Spain and Portugal, among others, settled here. The *Quattro Mori* (Four Moors), also known as the Monument to Ferdinando I, commemorates this. (The statue of Ferdinand I dates from 1595, the bronze Moors by Pietro Tacca from the 1620s.)

In the following centuries, and particularly in the 18th, Livorno boomed as a port. In the 19th century, the town drew a host of famous Britons passing through on their Grand Tours. Livorno's prominence continued up to World War II, when it was heavily bombed. Much of Livorno's architecture, therefore, now postdates the war, and it's somewhat difficult to imagine what it might have looked liked. Livorno has recovered from the war, however, as her influence in shipping—particularly container shipping—continues.

Most of Livorno's artistic treasures date from the 17th century and aren't all that interesting unless you dote on obscure baroque artists. However, Livorno's most famous native artist, Amedeo Modigliani (1884–1920), was of much more recent vintage.

There may not be much in the way of art, but it's still worth strolling around the city. The **Mercato Nuovo,** which has been around since 1894, sells all sorts of fruits, vegetables, grains, meat, and fish. Outdoor markets nearby are also chock-full of local color. The presence of Camp Darby, an American military base just outside of town, accounts for the availability of many American products.

If you have time, Livorno is at least worth a stop for lunch or dinner.

Where to Eat

$–$$$ ✕ **La Chiave.** Ask locals where to find the best food in town, and they'll send you to a small elegant restaurant near the Fortezza Nuova (New Fortress) with just ten tables and a menu that changes frequently. You can't go wrong by choosing the fresh catch of the day prepared exactly the way the chef recommends. ⊠ *Scali delle Cantine 52/54* ☎ *0586/888609* ▤ *AE, DC, MC, V* ☾ *Closed Wed. and Aug. 15–Sept. 10. No lunch.*

$ ✕ **Cantina Nardi.** It's only open for lunch, and it's well off the beaten path even if it is very much in the center of Livorno's shopping district. But getting here is worth the trouble: this tiny place, lined with bottles of wine, has a small menu that changes daily, a superb wine list, and gregarious staff. Their *baccalà alla livornese* (deep-fried salt cod served with chickpeas) is succulently crisp; soups, such as ribollita, are very soothing. ⊠ *Via Cambini 6/8* ☎ *0586/808006* ▤ *AE, MC, V* ☾ *Closed Sun. No dinner.*

CITIES WEST OF FLORENCE A TO Z

To research prices, get advice from other travelers, and book travel arrangements, visit ⊕ *www.fodors.com*

AIRPORTS
The largest airports in the region are Pisa's Aeroporto Galileo Galilei and Florence's Peretola (officially Aeroporto A. Vespucci).

🛪 Airport Information **Aeroporto A. Vespucci (Peretola)** ☎ 055/373498. **Aeroporto Galileo Galilei** ☎ 050/849300 ⊕ www.pisa-airport.com.

BUS TRAVEL
Most of the cities covered here do have bus stations, but service is often sporadic or complicated; it's easier to take the train to Pisa, Prato, Pistoia, Lucca, Montecatini Terme, Livorno, and Empoli, where service is regular and trains run frequently. Pescia is an easy bus ride from the train station at Montecatini Terme; you can purchase bus tickets at the station or at the news vendor. San Miniato and environs are best reached by car, as service is limited.

CAR RENTALS
🛪 Agencies **Avis** ⊠ Sant'Anna, Piazzale Italia 289, Lucca ☎ 0583/513614 ⊕ www.avis.com. **Hertz** ⊠ Via Montegrappa 208, Prato ☎ 0574/527774 ⊠ Aeroporto Galileo Galilei, Pisa ☎ 050/49187 ⊠ Via Pistoise 28C, Montecatini Terme ☎ 0572/905604 ⊕ www.hertz.com.

CAR TRAVEL
The A1 connects Florence to Prato; for Pistoia, Montecatini, and Lucca, follow signs for Firenze Nord, which connects to the A11. For Empoli, Pisa, and hill towns west, take the FI-PI-LI superstrada from Scandicci (just outside Florence).

Renting a car is the best way to see the cities west of Florence, as many of them are not on train lines or are served by buses that run sporadically. Prato, Pistoia, Montecatini Terme, Lucca, and Pisa are especially easy to travel between because they are all off the A11. The other cities are along secondary two-lane roads.

EMERGENCIES

Many of the smaller towns post the name and address of late-night pharmacies, which are open on a rotating basis, in the windows of the tourist-information centers as well as at individual pharmacies. Pharmacies that hang the big green cross above their doorways—most do—light up the sign when the pharmacy is open.

 Emergency Services **Ambulance** ☎ 118. **Carabinieri** (federal military police) ☎ 112. **Police** ☎ 113. **Fire** ☎ 115.

MAIL & SHIPPING

 Post Office **Lucca** ⊠ Via Vallisneri 2 ☎ 0583/43351.

 Internet Cafés **Internet Train** ⊠ IT.Empoli, Via Cavour 5/9, Empoli ☎ No phone ⊠ IT.Prato.BarCiardi, Piazza Ciardi 16, Prato ☎ 0574/22238 ⊠ IT.Prato.Garibaldi, Via Garibaldi 102, Prato ☎ 0574/31912 ⊠ IT.Prato.Repubblica, Viale della Repubblica 284, Prato ☎ 0574/596764 ⊕ www.internettrain.it.

TRAIN TRAVEL

Trains from Rome and Milan run regularly to Florence, which serves as the hub for many connections, such as those going to Prato, Pistoia, Montecatini, Lucca, Empoli, Pisa, and Livorno. Empoli is easily reached via train, but the surrounding towns—Certaldo, Castelfiorentino, San Miniato—are not.

Trains from the main station at Santa Maria Novella in Florence run regularly to Prato, Pistoia, Montecatini, and Lucca, which are all on the same line. Trains from Florence to Empoli and Pisa, on the same line, run frequently as well.

 Train Lines **FS Information** ☎ 147/888088 toll-free within Italy ⊕ www.fs-on-line. com.

TRAVEL AGENCIES

 Agencies **Angelini** ⊠ Piazza S. Michele 45, Lucca ☎ 0583/91441. **Azienda Promozione Turistica Montecatini/Vadlinievole** ⊠ Viale Verdi 66/68, Montecatini Terme ☎ 0572/ 772244.

VISITOR INFORMATION

 Tourist Information **Castelfiorentino** ⊠ Via Costituente ☎ 0571/629049. **Certaldo** ☎ 0571/656721. **Lucca** ⊠ Piazza Santa Maria 35 ☎ 0583/91991 ⊕ www.lucca.turismo. toscana.it. **Montecatini Terme** ⊠ Viale Verdi 66-68 ☎ 0572/772244. **Montelupo** ☎ 0571/518993. **Pisa** ⊠ Piazza Vittorio Emanuele II ☎ 050/42291. **Pistoia** ⊠ Palazzo dei Vescovi ☎ 0573/21622. **Prato** ⊠ Piazza delle Carceri 15 ☎ 0574/24112. **San Miniato** ⊠ Piazza del Popolo 3 ☎ 0571/418739. **Vinci** ⊠ Via delle Torre 11 ☎☎ 0571/568012.

CHIANTI

Updated by
Peter Blackman **COUNTRY ROADS WIND AROUND CYPRESS TREES** on hilltops that often appear to catch and hold on to the clouds. Planted vineyards, fields, and orchards turn those curving hills into a patchwork of colors and textures that has inspired artists and delighted travelers for centuries. Chianti has an enticing landscape, one that invites you to follow those roads to see where they go. Perhaps you'll come to a farmhouse selling splendid olive oil or the region's Chianti Classico wine; or perhaps you'll arrive at a medieval *pieve* (country church), an art-filled abbey, a *castello* (castle or fortress), or a restaurant where a flower-bedecked terrace provides respite from the summer heat as well as a spectacular panorama.

It's hard to imagine that this gentle area was once the battleground of warring Sienese and Florentine armies, but until Florence finally defeated Siena in 1555, these enchanting walled cities were strategic defensive outposts in a series of seemingly never-ending wars. Since the 1960s many British and northern Europeans have relocated here: they've been drawn to the unhurried life, balmy climate, and old villages. They've bought and restored farmhouses, many given up by the young heirs who decided not to continue life on the farm and instead found work in cities. There are so many Britons, in fact, that the area has been nicknamed Chiantishire. But don't let this be a deterrent to a visit: there's lots of Chianti to go around, and it remains strongly Tuscan in character.

Exploring Chianti

By far the best way to discover Chianti is by car, as its beauty often reveals itself along the road less traveled. The Certosa exit from the A1 highway provides direct access to the area. The Florence–Siena Superstrada (no number) is a four-lane, divided road that has exits which allow you to divert into the countryside. The Via Cassia (SR2) winds its way south from Florence to Siena through San Casciano, Tavarnelle, and Barberino Val d'Elsa, all on the western edge of the Chianti region. The Superstrada is more direct, but much less scenic, than the SR2, and it has a lot of traffic, especially on Sunday evening when Italians return from weekends in the countryside or at the beach. The Strada Chiantigiana (Chianti Road, SR222) cuts through the center of Chianti, to the east of the Superstrada, in a curvaceous path past vineyards and countryside.

The rolling hills are the region's most famous geographic feature, and you can expect to do a lot of winding up and down on the beautifully panoramic roads that link the area's hill towns. The narrow medieval streets of these old town centers are mostly closed to traffic. Park outside the city walls and walk in. Keep in mind that roads often lack shoulders in these parts and that gas stations are rarely open on Sunday.

About the Restaurants

Most restaurants in the countryside have terraces for dining in good weather and large picture windows for captivating views. Though many restaurants take credit cards, quite often village trattorias and traditional *osterie* (basic, down-to-earth taverns) don't. Lunch is usually served from

12:30 to 2:30, and many bars and trattorias serve a quick plate of pasta and salad for lunch. *Enoteche,* wine bars or shops (*enoteca* in the singular), have a large selection of local wines and sometimes serve wine by the glass, sandwiches, and simple meals.

Dinner can start as early as 7:30, but most Italians consider dining before 9 PM uncivilized. If you decide to go all out, order a *primo* (first course), *secondo* (second course), and a *dolce* (dessert or sweet), you might want to take a siesta first. During the high season, advanced booking is *always* recommended.

About the Hotels

Agriturismo (agritourism) lodging may be a good choice for those who want a more rustic holiday. In the Chianti countryside such accommodations range from a multistory stone farmhouse turned into an inn to entire medieval villages, always surrounded by a working farm, vineyard, or orchard. Having a car is essential in these isolated places.

Towns teeming with small shops, street markets, and lively *piazze* (squares) also have small hotels, pensions, and *affittacamere* (rented rooms in private homes). But Chianti is not as easy a place for spontaneous exploration as it used to be. Don't count on taking off by bicycle, car, or foot in the morning and then being able to find a romantic hideaway to spend the night—reserve well in advance. Chianti overflows with people and rooms are at a premium, especially during high season, which runs from the end of March to mid-November. Minumum stays of three days to a week may be required.

WHAT IT COSTS In Euros				
	$$$$	**$$$**	**$$**	**$**	**¢**
RESTAURANTS	over €22	€18–€22	€13–€17	€7–€12	under €7
HOTELS	over $290	€210–€290	€140–€209	€80–€139	under €80

Restaurant prices are for a second course (secondo piatto) per person. Hotel prices are for two people in a standard double room in high season, including tax and service.

Timing

Between Easter and late September, hotels and restaurants fill up and foreign license plates and rental cars cram the roads. There's a reason for the crush: summer is a glorious time to be driving in the hills and sitting on terraces.

Summer is not, however, the best time for biking. Temperatures, particularly in July and August, can soar to unbearable highs. It's better to plan bike tours for the spring or fall, when the heat is not so intense and cool breezes becomes a distinct possibility. Spring can be especially spectacular, with blooming poppy fields, bursts of yellow *ginestra* (broom), and wild irises growing by the side of the road. Fall is somewhat more soothing, when all those colors typically associated with Tuscany—burnt siena, warm ochers, mossy forest greens—predominate.

An itinerary can give you the big picture, but it's also important to look for the little picture and to know that if you see something that looks interesting, it's often a good idea to turn the wheel, head down the road, and check it out. Beautiful cypress-lined paths for walking, curving roads for biking, friendly residents for asking directions, and an abundance of fresh air and country smells await you. It may be easiest to pick one village to stay in and explore the others on day trips, as there is often a minimum stay required.

4

Numbers in the text correspond to numbers in the margin and on the Chianti map.

If you have
3 days
Leaving from Florence on Day 1, explore **San Donato in Poggio** ⑦ and surroundings, including **Passignano** ④ (even if its abbey is closed, as the town is set in stunning countryside), or 🚗 **Barberino Val d'Elsa** ⑥, before concluding with a ramble to Sant'Appiano and a miniature reproduction of the famous Florentine Duomo. Spend Day 2 exploring the hamlets and vineyards in the hills off the Strada Chiantigiana (SR222): 🚗 **Greve in Chianti** ⑧, an attractive market town with a piazza lined with wine bars, cafés, and boutiques; tiny **Panzano** ⑨; **Castellina in Chianti** ⑩, an equally charming town with a lively main street full of enoteche; 🚗 **Radda in Chianti** ⑪, a small, enchanting wine town and Volpaia, a lost-in-time hilltop castle. On Day 3 you can explore the villages you missed, or go south to **Castelnuovo Berardenga** ⑬ to enjoy an *aperitivo* in the main piazza.

If you have
7 days
If you're staying a week, you have enough time to rent out an agritoursimo apartment. Stock up your refrigerator with local groceries and wines; go for hikes in the hills; and expand the time you take meandering through the 3-day itinerary.

November through March, you might wonder who invented the term "sunny Italy"; the panoramas, however, are still beautiful, even with overcast skies, chilling winds, and sometimes, depending upon where you are, a sprinkling of snow. Many hotels, agriturismi, wine estates, and restaurants close November through March.

WESTERN CHIANTI

Just beyond Florence's reach are magnificently preserved country churches, abbeys, and little-visited towns that make for perfect jaunts and offer relief from taking in too much art. But there's art to be had as well, such as at Badia a Passignano, which shelters a 15th-century *Last Supper* by Domenico and Davide Ghirlandaio. Western Chianti also has affordable, relaxed country lodging.

Sant'Andrea in Percussina

❶ *15 km (9 mi) south of Florence.*

A 3 km (2 mi) detour from the Via Cassia, south of Tavarnuzze, leads to the tiny village where Niccolò Machiavelli (1469–1527) lived when he was exiled from Florence in 1513 by the Medici family. The unassuming building called **L'Albergaccio** (loosely, "the nasty hotel"—it was a dump) is where Machiavelli wrote *The Prince* and *Discourses*. A small, rarely open **Museo Machiavelli** shows his actual studio, kitchen, and bedroom as they might have looked when he lived here. You may be able to gain entry by asking at the Taverna Machiavelli, across the road, where he went when in need of friendship and food. ⊠ *Via dei Scopeti* ☎ *No phone* 💲 *Free.*

<table>
<tr><td>

off the
beaten
path

</td><td>

AMERICAN MILITARY CEMETERY – About 8 km (5 mi) south of Florence, on the Via Cassia on the way to San Casciano, is one of two American cemeteries in Italy (the other is in Nettuno). It contains 4,402 bodies of Americans who died in Italy during World War II. On a gentle hill, the sea of simple crosses and Stars of David bearing only name, date of death, and state seems to stretch endlessly. At the top of the hill are a place for reflection and large mosaic maps depicting the Allied assault in 1943. The two fronts—called the Gothic Line and the Gustav Line—are vividly rendered. ✛ *3 km (2 mi) south of Tavarnuzze, Località Scopeti* ☎ *055/2020020* 💲 *Free* ⊙ *Weekdays 8–5, weekends 9–5.*

</td></tr>
</table>

Where to Eat

¢–$$ ✕ **Taverna Machiavelli.** Across the road from Machiavelli's residence, this place was the neighborhood tavern in the 1500s. Five centuries later, it's a fine restaurant with a typical Tuscan menu that includes a fine *ribollita* (thick bread soup), pasta dishes with wild-boar or hare sauces, and a tasty variety of grilled meats. There's also an extensive list of local wines. You can have a *merenda* (afternoon snack) of bruschetta and a glass of wine (their own Chianti, of course). Proprietors of the restaurant will often take patrons across the street to see the Museo Machiavelli. ⊠ *Via dei Scopeti 64a* ☎ *055/828471* 💳 *MC, V* ⊙ *Closed Mon.–Tues.*

San Casciano in Val di Pesa

❷ *4 km (2½ mi) south of Sant'Andrea in Percussina, 18 km (13 mi) south of Florence.*

Parts of the original mid-14th-century walls and gates of San Casciano in Val di Pesa—one of the larger towns in Chianti—are still standing. They serve to weave the old and new parts of the town together. A large wooded city park with parking is near the city center. If you're coming from Florence on the Florence–Siena Superstrada, take the San Casciano exit.

4

Cuisine

Chianti restaurants serve Tuscan dishes similar to those in Florence, but they also have local specialties such as pasta creations made with *pici* (a long, thick, hand-rolled spaghetti). Many recipes are from the *nonna* (grandmother) of the restaurant's owner, handed down through time but never written down. In southern Chianti, *piccione* (pigeon) is served either roasted or stuffed and baked. The so-called *tonno del Chianti* (Chianti tuna) is really a dish of tender flakes of rabbit meat that look and, believe it or not, taste exactly like the fish in question—it's actually delicious.

Excellent extra-virgin olive oil is produced in Chianti, and the best way to taste it is in the form of a *fett'unta* (greasy slice), a thick slice of toasted Tuscan bread rubbed with garlic, sprinkled with salt, and dripping with olive oil. Asking for a plate or bowl to sample olive oil with bread before a meal is a dead giveaway that you're a tourist—it's the invention of American restaurateurs. Many of the Chianti wines pair marvelously with the area's ubiquitous grilled meats.

Vin santo (sweet dessert wine) is served as an apertif or as a dessert wine with *cantuccini* (hard almond cookies), which are dunked once or twice in the glass. It's made from choice white Trebbiano Toscano or Malvasia del Chianti grapes and is aged in small, partially filled oak barrels.

Biking

In spring, summer, and fall, bicyclists are as much a part of the landscape as the cypress trees. A drive on any steep Chianti road takes you past groups of bikers peddling up and down endless hills. Many are on week-long organized tours, but it's also possible to rent bikes for jaunts in the countryside or to join afternoon or day minitours. Most Tuscan roads are in excellent condition, though often narrow, winding, and steep. That said, be cautious—especially as some of the drivers on these narrow, twisting roads may have just stopped at a vineyard for a tasting.

Wineries

Those vineyards on the Chianti hillsides are not cinematic backdrops; they are working farms, and when fall comes and their grapes are harvested and processed, they produce that world-famous *vino rosso* (red wine) that has been complementing Tuscan food for ages. Chianti's heritage dates back thousands of years, but the borders that define Chianti Classico weren't officially drawn until 1932. Wine tasting lures travelers who want to give their eyes a rest after looking at all those halos in the churches and museums of Florence and Siena. Most of the vintners have figured this out and offer direct sales and samplings of their products. Some have roadside stands, and others have elaborate sampling rooms in which snacks are served. There are innumerable road-side signs for wineries offering free tastings. Though the wine-makers do this to encourage the sale of their product, purchasing their wine after a sample is by no means obligatory. Most of the smaller or more exclusive wineries are not open to the general public, but can usually be visited by appointment. Tourist-information offices in most Chianti towns have maps to guide you through an itinerary of vineyard hopping.

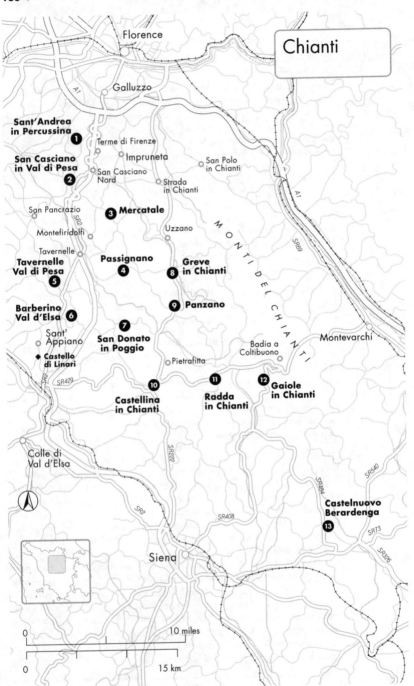

Chianti

en route   If you drive the Via dei Scopeti from Sant'Andrea in Percussina to San Casciano in Val di Pesa, look for the tiny hamlet of **Spedaletto** and the church of **Santa Maria di Casavecchia**, where there's a terra-cotta *Assumption* by Benedetto Buglioni (1461–1521). ✛ *Via dei Scopeti, 4 km (2½ mi) north of San Casciano in Val di Pesa.*

Santa Maria sul Prato, next to the remains of one of the San Casciano city gates, dates from 1335. The church oratory contains a small but surprisingly fine collection of artworks, including a crucifix by Sienese artist Simone Martini (1280s–1344) and the splendid *Madonna and Child* by Ugolino di Neri (active 1317–1327), also from Siena. A rather sober marble pulpit by Giovanni di Balduccio, a student of Giovanni Pisano (mid-1240s–1318), depicts the Annunciation. For entrance ask the custodian at the Misericordia, which is next door. ⊠ *Via Morrocchesi 19* ☎ *055/820023* ⊠ *Free* ⊙ *Daily 8:30–7:30.*

The **Museo d'Arte Sacra** in the church of **Santa Maria del Gesù** contains many works originally in small country churches in the area. The pieces, including a Sienese wood crucifix and four bronze crosses (circa 14th–15th centuries) and the carved pedestal of a marble baptismal font dating from the early 12th century, were brought here to protect them from thieves and the elements. ⊠ *Via Roma 31* ☎ *055/8229444* ⊠ *Free* ⊙ *Oct.–Apr., Sat. 4:30–7, Sun. 10–12:30 and 4–7; May–Sept., Sat. 5–7:30, Sun. 10–12:30 and 4–7.*

Where to Stay & Eat

$$$$ ✕ **La Tenda Rossa.** What began as a simple pizzeria some years ago has turned into one of Italy's finest restaurants. The menu changes frequently but has such treats as *minestra di cappelletti di baccalà* (a delicate soup with tiny pillows of pasta stuffed with dried cod). The sophisticated wine list is comprehensive and pairs beautifully with the food. ⊠ *Piazza del Monumento 9/14, Cerbaia, 5 km (3 mi) northwest of San Casciano in Val di Pesa* ☎ *055/826132* ⌂ *Reservations essential* ▤ *AE, DC, MC, V* ⊙ *Closed Sun. No lunch Mon.*

$–$$ ✕ **Cantinetta del Nonno.** Walk through the front-room *salumeria* (delicatessen), where you can buy prosciutto and other cured meats, then past an open kitchen, and then into the back dining room. If it's warm, you can sit outside on the tented terrace lined with impatiens. The menu has typical Tuscan treats as well as slightly less typical dishes such as *fusilli con pesto di rucola* (fusilli with an arugula pesto). Service is gracious and prompt. ⊠ *Via 4 Novembre* ☎ *055/820570* ▤ *MC, V* ⊙ *Closed Wed. and Nov.*

$ ✕▥ **Castello Il Corno.** A 13th-century castle forms the central core of this Renaissance-style villa complex, which feels like a luxury hotel in the middle of a farm. More than 10,000 olive trees dot the property, which also produces wine, including a high-quality *vin santo* (sweet dessert wine). The owners live in the villa, but there are two guest rooms in the castle itself, and 17 apartments in cottages. All have 19th-century furnishings. The restaurant's dishes, based on family recipes, are composed of fresh ingredients from the farm's garden. During high season (July through September), a minimum stay of one week is required.

✉ *Via di Malafrasca 64, 50026* ☎ *055/8248009* 🖷 *055/8248035* 🛌 *2 rooms, 17 apartments* ⚴ *Restaurant, cable TV, 2 pools, babysitting, meeting rooms, some pets allowed; no a/c* ▤ *AE, MC, V* ⊘ *Closed early Jan.–Feb.*

$ 🏨 **La Ginestra.** You can stay on the grounds of this agriturismo venture that makes and sells organic pasta, salami, prosciutto, honey, wine, and olive oil. All apartments have white walls and heavy, rustic wooden furniture. The villa il Mandorlo can sleep 12 people and has its own garden. A large barn can serve as a conference room or a large-scale party space. Horseback riding and tennis are available nearby. Even during high season, you are welcome to stay as little as one night. ✉ *Via Pergolata 3, Località Santa Cristina, 50020 San Pancrazio, 10 km (6 mi) south of San Casciano* ☎🖷 *055/8248196* 🛌 *6 apartments, 1 villa* ⚴ *Restaurant, kitchens, refrigerators, pool, babysitting, laundry service, meeting rooms, free parking, some pets allowed; no a/c, no room phones, no room TVs* ▤ *MC, V.*

Mercatale

❸ *6 km (4 mi) southeast of San Casciano in Val di Pesa, 25 km (16 mi) south of Florence on SR222*

As its name implies, Mercatale began in 1237 when the mayor of a neighboring town ordered the construction of a public square to serve as a marketplace for his court. The city center doesn't have much to offer in the way of important art, but its villa-lined roads make for pleasant country strolls.

en route   If you're traveling from San Casciano in Val di Pesa to Mercatale and feel the need for some art, stop after 5 km (3 mi) and visit the **Chiesa dei Cappuccini;** the church has a terra-cotta *Adoration of the Child* by Andrea della Robbia (1435–1525/28), and it's worth a detour. Continue southeast, 8 km (5 mi) south of San Casciano, toward Calcinaia and visit the **Capella dello Strozzo** (Chapel of the Strozzi). Inside is a fresco pietà, much restored, attributed to Agnolo Bronzino (1503–72).

Where to Stay

$ 🏨 **Salvadonica.** Tour area vineyards and olive groves with the friendly owners here. Each one-room apartment has a small kitchen, some wood furniture, and light-color bedspreads. A communal room, surrounded by glass, functions as the lobby. The pool has hydromassage jets. If you're interested in the real country Italian experience, try out the boccie ball court. A minimum stay of one week is required. ✉ *Via Grevigiana 82, 50024* ☎ *055/8218039* 🖷 *055/8218043* ⊕ *www.salvadonica.com* 🛌 *5 rooms, 11 apartments* ⚴ *Fans, kitchenettes, refrigerators, tennis court, pool, billiards, boccie, playground, some pets allowed; no a/c, no room TVs* ▤ *AE, DC, MC, V* ⊘ *Closed Nov.–Mar.* ⦿⦿ *CP.*

Passignano

❹ *8 km (5 mi) south of Mercatale, 29 km (18 mi) south of Florence.*

One of the finest and best-preserved works of art in Italy is in the refectory (dining hall) of the towering 11th-century **Badia a Passignano** (Abbey of Passignano): a stunningly massive, 21-ft-wide *Last Supper* (1476) by Domenico and Davide Ghirlandaio. The monastery's church of **San Michele Arcangelo**, also called San Piaggio, has a 13th-century sculpture of St. Michael slaying the dragon. All visits are conducted 20-minute tours by the resident monks. At this writing the Badia is closed for restoration, but even if you can't get in to see the *Last Supper,* it's worth the drive to see its fairy-tale surroundings and to walk on the beautiful hillside. ✣ *Via Passignano, 7 km (4 mi) east of Tavarnelle–Passignano exit off Florence–Siena Superstrada* ☎ *055/8071622.*

Where to Eat

$$$-$$$$ ✕ **Osteria di Passignano.** In an ancient wine cellar owned by the Antinori family—who also happen to own much of what you see in these parts—is a sophisticated restaurant ably run by Chef Marcello Crini and his attentive staff. The menu changes seasonally; traditional Tuscan cuisine is given a delightful twist through the sapient use of unexpected herbs, spices, and ingredients. Particularly tantalizing is the *filetto di vitello alle spezie* (spiced veal fillet), served with roast tomatoes and beans flavored with sage. The extensive wine list includes Antinori vintages as well as numerous international labels. Day-long cooking courses are available. ⊠ *Via Passignano 33* ☎ *055/8071278* ☰ *AE, D, MC, V* ☯ *Closed Sun., Jan. 2–21, and Aug. 9–24.*

$-$$ ✕ **La Cantinetta di Rignana.** On Sunday afternoons this old-style trattoria nestled among woods and vineyards teems with lively Italian families. Be sure to make a reservation. Grilled meats are the speciality of the house. Enjoy the Tuscan farmhouse dining room interior, or eat overlooking the vines in the garden. ⊠ *Via di Rignana 15, Località Rignana, 4 km (2 mi) west of Passignano* ☎ *055/852601* ⚖ *Reservations essential Sun.* ☰ *AE, D, MC, V* ☯ *Closed Tues.*

Tavarnelle Val di Pesa

❺ *11 km (7 mi) southwest of Passignano, 28 km (15 mi) south of Florence.*

The name Tavarnelle comes from *tabernulae,* which were the stopover villages between Florence and Siena for travelers on their way to Rome. Its location kept it out of the fierce battles between Florence and Siena, which explains the absence of towers and fortifications. Today the city's best defense seems to be its system of ring roads, frustrating locals as well as tourists. If you are arriving by car, the only thing to do is to follow the signs for *centro* (the center) and hope for the best. With this in mind, it's probably just as well that the main sights lie outside the town itself. Tavarnelle has an exit on the Florence–Siena Superstrada.

San Pietro in Bossolo, one of the most beautiful country churches in the area, is northeast of the city center. Dating from the 10th century, it has a 14th-century marble sanctuary and a 16th-century portico. The bell tower dates from the mid-1800s. Inside the small attached museum is a *Virgin Mary with Child and Saints*, by Coppo di Marcovaldo (active 1260–80), an early and important example of the Florentine school. ⊠ *Via della Pieve 19* 🕾 *055/8077832* 🖅 *Free* 🕙 *Nov.–Mar., weekends 3:30–6; Apr.–Oct., weekends 4:30–7.*

The church of **Santa Maria del Carmine,** built in 1466, is part of a monastery, and the main attraction is the group of industrious Carmelite nuns from Australia. When they came here in 1982, they rescued the old monastery, which had fallen into 200 years' worth of disrepair. The nuns make and sell products such as perfumed candles, creams, and lotions using traditional formulas. It's worth making sure you arrive at 5:00 any afternoon, to hear the singing of vespers in pure, beautiful voices. The pews are filled for Sunday and holiday masses with appreciative Italians and an English-speaking community who come from a wide area. Inside the church is a terra-cotta Annunciation from the school of Andrea della Robbia. To get here, look for the sign to Sambuca and the Superstrada; the monastery is on the south side of the road. ⊠ *Via di Morrocco 35, Morocco, 3km (2 mi) east of Tavarnelle Val di Pesa* 🕾 *055/8076067* 🖅 *Free* 🕙 *Daily 9–7.*

off the beaten path

SAMBUCA – Next to the Pesa River, Sambuca itself is an unattractive industrial town, but its graceful arched bridge and riverside park make the 10-minute detour worth it. The **Ponte Romano** was built in 1069 as part of the Via Francigena that brought pilgrims from northern Europe to Rome. The bridge was partially destroyed during World War II and rebuilt later. Documents indicate that Leonardo da Vinci himself once walked across this bridge. ✛ *Off Via Chianti Sulla Pesa, 6 km (4 mi) east of Tavarnelle Val di Pesa.*

Where to Stay & Eat

$–$$ ✕ **Osteria La Gramola.** Delicately stenciled floral patterns decorate the walls, and rustic tables and chairs set the stage for traditional Tuscan food done well. Both the *cinghiale in umido con le olive* (wild-boar stew with olives) and the *peposo dell'Impruneta* (peppery beef stew) are well worth trying. The menu changes with the seasons, but if you order anything with truffles, you won't go wrong. Make sure to save room for desserts like the delightfully crunchy *latte alla Portoghese* (a type of créme caramel). The wine list is extensive. ⊠ *Via delle Fonti 1* 🕾🕾 *055/8050321* 🖃 *MC, V* 🕙 *No lunch Tues.*

$ 🏠 **Fattoria Querceto.** Each of the large, two-floor apartments in this group of three restored farm buildings has a fireplace, a living room, and a modern kitchen. Some of the apartments have separate dining rooms, all have private outside areas and traditional furniture—marble-topped chests-of-drawers, wooden credenzas, or tall, free-standing wardrobes. Brick-vaulted or wood-beamed ceilings and exposed stone walls are special features in some of the rooms. Games are provided for children. You can taste and buy the wine, olive oil, honey, jellies, and eggs that are produced here. Television is available for €8 per day. A minimum one-week stay is required. ⊠ *Via Benvenuto Cellini 149, 53011 Località Pontenuovo, 5 km*

(3 mi) north of Tavarnelle ☎ *055/8070135* 🖷 *055/8070171* ⊕ *www. querceto.it* ➷ *6 apartments* ⚘ *Kitchens, pool, mountain bikes, library, laundry service, some pets allowed; no a/c, no room TVs* ▤ *MC, V.*

$ 🏨 **Park Hotel Chianti.** If you've been in the car all day and want new-world amenities instead of old-world charm, stop here. Poplar trees and thick greenery surround the beautiful pool and terrace. Don't let the fact that the hotel is near the Tavernelle exit off the Florence–Siena Superstrada turn you off; rooms have soundproof windows and are impeccable, though furnished with uninspired, motel-like, wood-veneer pieces. ⊠ *Località Pontenuovo, 50028* ☎ *055/8070106* 🖷 *055/8070121* ⊕ *www.parkhotelchianti.com* ➷ *43 rooms* ⚘ *Restaurant, in-room safes, minibars, cable TV, pool, bar, Internet* ▤ *AE, MC, V* ☾ *Closed early Dec.–early Jan.* ❙⊙❙ *CP.*

$ 🏨 **Sovigliano.** The affable Bicego family runs this 12th-century farmhouse inn. They've kept the agriturismo aspect of the operation to a minimum, maintaining the natural gardens filled with herbs, wildflowers, and pines. Firm beds have scrolled iron or straight wood headboards. The pool, surrounded by fragrant rosemary bushes, provides a perfect place to relax. There's a minimum stay of three days. ⊠ *Via Strada Magliano 9, 50028* ☎ *055/8076217* 🖷 *055/8050770* ⊕ *www.sovigliano.com* ➷ *4 rooms, 4 apartments* ⚘ *Dining room, some kitchens, refrigerators, pool, bicycles, Internet; no a/c in some rooms* ▤ *MC, V* ❙⊙❙ *CP.*

¢ 🏨 **Albergo Vittoria.** Katia Torresi, the hands-on owner, works to make sure you are happy. She provides all kinds of tips for travelers and even shares her computer if you need to send or receive e-mail. Rooms are large, the furniture is modern, and the bathrooms are new. Though Albergo Vittoria is on a busy street, quadruple-pane soundproof windows covered with heavy drapes help you forget it. ⊠ *Via Roma 57, 50028* 🖷🖷 *055/8076180* ⊕ *www.albergovittoria.it* ➷ *7 rooms* ⚘ *Dining room, fans, cable TV, babysitting, parking (fee), some pets allowed, no-smoking rooms; no a/c* ▤ *AE, DC, MC, V* ❙⊙❙ *CP.*

¢ 🏨 **La Villa.** You ring the bell at the entry door, walk through a garden, and reach the hotel in a restored 16th-century convent on the other side of a field. There's a rustic, country style to the six simply furnished apartments, which are situated around an enclosed courtyard filled with fruit trees. The young owners are enthusiastic about their work and are happy to act as guides for you. There's a minimum stay of a week during high season and a minimum of three days the rest of the year. ⊠ *Strada Romita 42, 50028* 🖷🖷 *055/8070105* ➷ *6 apartments* ⚘ *Pool, some pets allowed; no a/c, no room phones* ▤ *No credit cards.*

Barberino Val d'Elsa

❻ *3 km (2 mi) southwest of Tavarnelle Val di Pesa, 28 km (17 mi) south of Florence.*

The medieval wall surrounding this town has two gates—one faces Florence and the other Siena. Via Francesco da Barberino connects the two and is the main street of this town, which has glorious views of the surrounding hills and is a perfect jumping-off point for countryside explorations. The town dates from the 11th century, the walls from the

14th. You have to take the Via Cassia from Tavarnelle, as Barberino has no Florence–Siena Superstrada exit of its own.

The 13th-century Renaissance **Palazzo Pretorio** is decorated with the coats of arms of the *podestà* (judges) who adjudicated over civil and criminal cases during the Middle Ages and Renaissance. ⊠ *Piazza Barberini.*

A tiered walkway from Piazza Barberini leads to Via Vittorio Veneto, site of the church of **San Bartolomeo.** It's worth a visit to admire its 14th-century frescoes. ⊠ *Via Vittorio Veneto* 🕾 *No phone* 🎫 *Free* ☉ *Sun. 9–1.*

off the beaten path

CAPPELLA DI SAN MICHELE ARCANGELO – The Chapel of St. Michael the Archangel is one of the biggest surprises in Tuscany. Here in the Chianti countryside is a 1:8 scale model of Brunelleschi's Duomo of Florence, built in 1597 (this replica was designed by Santi di Tito [1536–1603]). The cupola has been restored. Originally on this site was the castle of Semifonte, which was totally destroyed by the Florentines in 1202, and orders were given not to rebuild anything here. Nearly 400 years passed before the small San Michele, celebrating Florence, was constructed to mark the spot. ⊠ *Strata Petrognano, west of town, Petrognano Semifonte, 4 km (2 ½ mi) southeast of Barberino Val d'Elsa* 🕾 *No phone* 🎫 *Free* ☉ *Sun. 3:30–7:30.*

Signs on the Via Cassia point you to this tiny village of **Sant'Appiano,** 8 km (5 mi) south of Barberino Val d'Elsa. The lovely Romanesque church, also named **Sant'Appiano,** has parts which date from the 11th century. The interior contains fragments of a fresco of the Madonna and Child by an anonymous master that dates back to the middle of the 15th century. There are also 14th- and 15th-century fresco fragments from the schools of Giotto and Ghirlandaio; a tomb dating from 1331 in the right aisle holds the remains of Gherarduccio Gheradini, one of the church's patrons. The church faces an intriguing set of ancient stone stairs that descends to the village below. Rising in the grass field between the church and the stairs are four mysterious sandstone pillars—the remains of a 5th-century baptistery that was destroyed by an earthquake in the early 19th century. ⊠ *Via Sant'Appiano 1* 🕾 *055/8075519* 🎫 *Free* ☉ *Daily by appointment.*

There's a two-room village **museum** that displays archaeological finds from the area. Open hours change erratically; it's best to phone ahead. ⊠ *Behind the church, Località Pieve di Sant'Appiano* 🕾 *055/8075622* 🎫 *€1.50* ☉ *Nov.–Mar., weekends 3–6; Apr.–Oct., weekends 4–7:30.*

off the beaten path

LINARI – A very steep road leads up to the village of Linari, which was almost completely abandoned after an earthquake in the early 19th century. On a wall beyond the Gothic entrance, across the street from Via Santa Maria 11, is an Etruscan advertisement inviting travelers and shepherds to stop at Linari for food and shelter. Today the ruins of the **Castello di Linari** and the town's houses make for an interesting and somewhat mysterious stop along the road. ⊠ *Via Sant'Appiano, 1 km (½ mi) south of Sant'Appiano, 9 km (5 ½ mi) south of Barberino Val d'Elsa.*

Where to Stay & Eat

$$–$$$ ✕ **Il Paese dei Campanelli.** An old *cantina* (wine-storage building) with bare stone walls and brick-vault ceilings houses a noteworthy restaurant. Typical Tuscan recipes fill the menu, but there are also some creative variations using less-expected ingredients such as seasonal mushrooms. The duck comes rare, and all the dishes are presented with artistry. In summer you can dine in the glorious surrounding gardens. Make reservations well in advance. ⊠ *Località Petrognano, 4 km (2½ mi) south of Barberino Val d'Elsa* ☎ *055/8075318* ⌂ *Reservations essential* ▭ V ⊘ *Closed Sun. No lunch.*

$ ✕ **L'Archibugio.** Come here for a great thin-crust pizza or a plate of inexpensively priced spaghetti. In summer you can dine on the covered terrace and enjoy a respite from the heat; in winter, you can eat inside, next to a comforting fireplace. Residents from surrounding towns fill the place year-round. ⊠ *Via Vittorio Veneto 48* ☎ *055/8075209* ▭ *No credit cards* ⊘ *Closed Wed.*

$$ ▦ **La Spinosa.** The owners have organized a group of 17th-century farmhouses into an agriturismo venture and have dedicated their lives to helping produce perfect vacations. The buildings have been renovated, but they maintain their original character through a mix of Italian farmhouse furniture and antiques. The public spaces include a game room, library, and small bar. There is a two-night minimum stay. ⊠ *Via Le Masse 8, 50021* ☎ *055/8075413* 🖷 *055/8066214* ⊕ *www.laspinosa. it* ⇨ *5 rooms, 4 suites* ⌂ *Pool, archery, volleyball, bar, library, recreation room, Internet; no a/c, no room phones* ▭ MC, V ⊘ *Closed mid-Nov.–mid-Mar.* ℺ MAP.

¢–$ ▦ **Il Paretaio.** This peaceful, extremely private retreat attracts the horsey set with its riding lessons and trail rides. Six spacious, simply decorated guest rooms with wood-beamed ceilings are in the farmhouse, while two apartments with kitchen facilities are in a separate building. A chef comes daily with fresh coffee cakes for breakfast and prepares excellent dinners; you can eat in the farmhouse dining room or in the garden. A one-week minimum stay is required. ⊠ *Strada delle Ginestre 12, Località San Filippo, 50021* ☎ *055/8059218* 🖷 *055/8059231* ⊕ *www.ilparetaio. it* ⇨ *6 rooms, 2 apartments* ⌂ *Restaurant, dining room, some kitchens, pool, horseback riding, Internet; no a/c, no room phones* ▭ *No credit cards* ℺ MAP.

San Donato in Poggio

❼ *11 km (7 mi) southeast of Barberino Val d'Elsa, 34 km (21) mi south of Florence.*

Great care has been taken by the residents of San Donato in Poggio to ensure that this gem of a medieval city maintains its ancient qualities. Cars aren't permitted in the perfectly preserved walled village, which is also free of neon signs and advertising posters. A village has existed on this site since 1033, when a fortified castle was built high on the hill between San Casciano in Val di Pesa and Colle di Val d'Elsa.

The original castle was destroyed during a conflict in 1289. A new wall was constructed immediately after the fighting ended, and it still stands, enclosing the city with two gates—one facing Siena and one facing Florence. The only remains of the original castle walls can be seen in the base of the present-day municipal bell tower. The main square, **Piazza Malaspina,** contains the Renaissance palazzo belonging to the Malaspina family as well as the 15th-century church of **Santa Maria delle Neve.**

The **Pieve di San Donato in Poggio,** north outside the town's walls, dates from 989, although the existing building is probably from the early 12th century. In the baptistery of this parish church is a baptismal font by Giovanni della Robbia that illustrates scenes from the life of St. John the Baptist. Open hours are unpredictable. ⊠ *Via della Pieve 25* ☎ *055/8072934* 🖅 *Free.*

Where to Stay

$$ 🏨 **Fattoria Casa Sola.** Each apartment in this romantic agriturismo has its own garden or terrace and views of surrounding vineyards and woods. Comfortable modern couches and lounge chairs, along with older wooden furniture, make for a pleasant mix of styles in every room. The owners are ready to supply information about local cultural events, and when there's a group of six or more they give courses in painting, cooking, or photography. A one-week minimum stay is required. ⊠ *Località Le Cortine, 50021* ☎ *055/8075028* ⊕ *www.fattoriacasasola.com* ♣ *3 km (2 mi) south of San Donato's center* 🖶 *055/8059194* 🖅 *6 apartments* ⚱ *Pool, babysitting, laundry service, Internet, some pets allowed; no a/c, no room phones, no room TVs* ☰ *MC, V.*

$ 🏨 **Le Filigare.** A pioneer in Chanti's agriturismo operations, Le Filigare is actually an entire medieval *borghetto* (village) that's been converted into a mellow, extremely private inn. Apartments are filled with a combination of antique and modern furnishings. Le Filigare is known throughout the area for its excellent wine, oil, grappa, and vin santo, all of which can be tasted and purchased from its cellars. The minimum stay is one week. ⊠ *Località Le Filigare, 50020* ☎ *055/8072796* 🖶 *055/755766* ⊕ *www.lefiligare.it* 🖅 *7 apartments* ⚱ *Kitchens, cable TV, tennis court, pool, sauna, fishing, mountain bikes, horseback riding, Ping-Pong, babysitting, playground, laundry facilities; no a/c* ☰ *AE, DC, MC, V.*

STRADA CHIANTIGIANA

Here you are in the heartland: both sides of the Strada Chiantigiana (Chianti Road, SR222) are embraced by glorious panoramic views of vineyards, olive groves, and castle towers. Travelling into Chianti from Florence, you first reach the aptly named one-street-town of Strada in Chianti. Farther south, the number of vineyards on either side of the road dramatically increases—as do the signs inviting you in for a free tasting of wine. Beyond Strada lies Greve in Chianti, completely surrounded by wineries and filled with wine shops. Farther still along the Chiantigiana are Panzano and Castellina in Chianti, both hill towns. It's from near Panzano and Castellina that branch roads head to the other main towns of eastern Chianti: Radda in Chianti, Gaiole in Chianti, and Castelnuovo Berardenga. The Strada Chiantigiana gets crowded dur-

ing the high season, but no one is in a hurry, and the slow pace gives
you time to soak up the beautiful scenery.

Greve in Chianti

❽ *16 km (10 mi) northeast of San Donato in Poggio, 28 km (17½ mi) south
of Florence.*

If there is a capital of Chianti, it is Greve, a friendly market town with
no shortage of cafés, enoteche, and crafts shops along its pedestrian street.
The sloping, asymmetrical **Piazza Matteotti** is an attractive arcade whose
center holds a statue of the discoverer of New York harbor, Giovanni
da Verrazano (circa 1480–1527). There's a lively market here Saturday
morning.

The church of **Santa Croce** has a triptych by Bicci di Lorenzo (1373–1452)
and an Annunciation by an anonymous Florentine master that dates from
the 14th century. ✛ *At the small end of Piazza Matteotii* ☎ No phone
🎫 Free ☺ Daily 9–1 and 3–7.

A mile west of Greve in Chianti is the tiny hilltop hamlet of **Montefio-
ralle;** it's the ancestral home of Amerigo Vespucci (1454–1512), the mapmaker, navigator, and explorer who named America. (His niece Simonetta
may have been the model for Sandro Botticelli's *Birth of Venus,* painted
sometime in the 1480s.)

> **off the
> beaten
> path**

LAMOLE – The tiny village of Lamole contains the **Chiesa di San
Donato a Lamole,** a Romanesque church that was greatly modified
in 1860; the only remnant of its earlier incarnation can be found in
its simple facade. Inside is a 14th-century altarpiece of saints and the
Madonna and Child, as well as a curious side chapel on the right that
is decorated with rather garish 20th-century religious works. ✉ *Off
SR222, Lamole, 10 km (6 mi) southeast of Greve* ☎ 055/8547015
🎫 Free ☺ Daily 9–12:30 and 4–6:30.

The terrace at **Ristoro di Lamole,** with its sweeping views of valleys
and a glimpse of Panzano in the distance, makes the drive to Lamole
via a maddeningly twisting road worth it. The bar–restaurant serves
superb panini and more-substantial fare ($). The primi, particularly
any featuring game, are excellent. The desserts are made in-house and
are some of the best in the area. Try the simple and delicious *torta
della nonna* (grandmother's cake) topped with pine nuts and filled
with rich yellow cream. ✉ *Off SR222, Lamole* ☎ 055/8547050.
From Greve in Chianti, drive south on SR222 for about 1 km (½ mi);
take a left and follow signs for Lamole.

Where to Stay & Eat

$–$$ ✕ **Locanda il Gallo.** Terrific thin-crust pizzas come out of the wood-burn-
ing oven here. The large, informal, country dining rooms have stone walls
and wood-beam ceilings, and there's a veranda for dining outside in summer. The restaurant is about 4 km (2½ mi) north of Greve in Chianti.
✉ *Via Lando Conti 16, Chiocchio* ☎ 055/8572266 ▭ AE, DC, MC,
V ☺ Closed Tues.

CloseUp

BACCHUS IN TUSCANY

TUSCANY IS ITALY'S CLASSIC WINE COUNTRY. *In addition to Chianti, one of Italy's top wine exports, Tuscan wine-makers produce other renowned wines. Many of these are recognizable by the* DOCG *(Denominazione di Origine Controllata e Garantita) or* DOC *(Denominazione di Origine Controllata) on their labels, notations that identify the wine not only as coming from an officially delineated wine region but also as adhering to rigorous standards of production. Don't be afraid to sample something that doesn't bear this label, however; Tuscans have been making wine for 25 centuries.*

If you think **Chianti** *is about straw-covered jugs and deadly headaches, think again. This firm, full-bodied, and powerful wine is pressed from mostly Sangiovese grapes. The* DOCG *region has seven subregions: Chianti Classico, Colli Fiorentini, Colli Senesi, Colli Aretini, Colline Pisane, Montalbano, and Rufina. The area where various types of Chianti wines are grown actually stretches from Pistoia, north of Florence, to Montalcino, south of Siena.*

Chianti Classico, *the oldest classification, is from the relatively small zone that extends from just south of Florence to just north of Siena, bordered to the east by the Chianti Mountains and to the west by the hills closest to the Florence–Siena Superstrada. Outside the Classico zone, the grapes and the wine-makers' recipes may be exactly the same, but names represent the geographic difference: Colli Fiorentini and Colli Senesi, for example, take their names from the Florentine and Sienese colli (hills) on which each is grown. Keep in mind that the most noticeable—and costly—difference is whether the wine is regular Chianti or riserva (reserve) stock, aged for at least three years.*

Some Italian wine makers, chafing at the strict limitations imposed upon them when making Chianti, sought to break free of the chains by mixing grapes and recipes. Thus was born the so-called **Super Tuscan,** *French oak–aged wines which have become the toast of Tuscany and most of Italy.*

Vino Nobile di Montepulciano, *the "Noble Wine," lays claim to its aristocratic title by virtue of royal patronage and ancient history: the Etruscans were making wine here before Rome had even been founded. In 1669, England's William III sent a delegation to Montepulciano to procure this splendid wine. The less noble but no less popular* **Rosso di Montepulciano,** *a light, fruity* DOC *red, is also produced in the area.*

Brunello di Montalcino *has a rich bouquet and structured tannins. The strain of the Sangiovese grape variety used to make it was developed in 1870 by a local wine-maker in need of vines that would be better able to cope with windy weather. The wine became popular quickly and remained so. Brunello has a younger sibling, the* DOC **Rosso di Montalcino.**

Not all of Tuscany's great wines are reds; in fact, many give the region's highest honors to a white wine, **Vernaccia di San Gimignano.** *This golden wine is made from grapes native to Liguria, and it's thought that its name is a corruption of Vernazza, a village that's part of the Ligurian coast's Cinque Terre.*

$ ✕ **Il Camineto.** The pasta is all homemade at this small, cozy country restaurant; the *gnocchi ripieno ai funghi porcini* (potato dumplings stuffed with porcini mushrooms) are a real treat. There's a terrace for summer dining under the shade of lime trees. ⊠ *Via della Montagnola 52* ☎ *055/ 8588909* ▤ *MC, V* ⊘ *Closed Tues. No lunch Mon.–Sat.*

$ ✕▦ **Castello Vicchiomaggio.** Stay in what was formerly a fortified castle that dates from 956 (it was rebuilt during the Renaissance). Today, in addition to providing lodging, it is a prestigious wine estate with a tasting facility you can visit. Throughout the nine guest apartments and two farmhouses is wonderful heavy wooden furniture. The restaurant ($$$) serves homemade pastas and specialties such as *stracotto*, beef cooked in the farm's own prize-winning Chianti Classico. ⊠ *Via Vicchiomaggio 4, 50022* ☎ *055/854079* ▦ *055/853911* ⊕ *www. vicchiomaggio.it* ⇖ *8 apartments, 2 houses* ♨ *Restaurant, in-room safes, kitchenettes, refrigerators, cable TV, pool; no a/c* ▤ *MC, V.*

$$ ▦ **Villa Vignamaggio.** Reputed to be the birthplace of Mona Lisa, the woman made famous by Leonardo da Vinci, the Villa Vignamaggio has origins in the 14th century but was overhauled in the 16th. This historic estate has guest rooms and apartments in a long, rectangular villa, as well as two small houses for rent, surrounded by manicured classical Italian gardens. Some rooms have exposed beams; some have the genuine ancient plaster walls that faux-paint treatments attempt to replicate. The place also does tastings of its very fine wine; inquire at the reception for arrangements. ⊠ *Via Petriolo 5, 50022* ☎ *055/854661* ▦ *055/8544468* ⊕ *www.vignamaggio.com* ⇖ *3 rooms, 4 suites, 13 apartments, 2 cottages* ♨ *Some kitchnens, minibars, cable TV, tennis court, 2 pools, babysitting, playground, laundry service, some pets allowed, no-smoking rooms* ▤ *AE, DC, MC, V* ⊘ *Closed mid-Nov.–mid-Mar.* ✲❙ *CP.*

$ ▦ **Albergo del Chianti.** At a corner of the main piazza, the Albergo del Chianti rooms have views of the square or out over neighborhood terraces and rooftops toward surrounding hills. Plain modern cabinets and wardrobes stand near ironwork beds, atop terra-cotta floors.The swimming pool, terrace, and grassy lawn behind the hotel are a nice surprise. ⊠ *Piazza Matteotti 86, 50022* ☎ *055/853674* ▦ *055/853763* ⊕ *www. albergodelchianti.it* ⇖ *16 rooms* ♨ *Restaurant, minibars, cable TV, pool, bar* ▤ *No credit cards* ⊘ *Closed late Dec.–early Jan.* ✲❙ *CP.*

¢–$ ▦ **Agriturismo Patrizia Falciani.** Trees surround the farm of Patrizia Falciani. Apartments are comfortable and well furnished in typical country Tuscan style, with wood-beam ceilings and terra-cotta floors throughout. Signora Falciani speaks no English but still manages to communicate with those who don't speak Italian. Washing machines, a barbecue, and a small but delightful pool are all available for guest use. Olive oil and wine are also sold here. ⊠ *Via di Melazzano 5, 50022, 1 km (½ mi) southeast of Greve in Chianti town center* ☎☎ *055/8544505* ▦ *055/2301003* ⊕ *www.patriziafalciani.it* ⇖ *7 apartments* ♨ *Fans, kitchens, refrigerators, pool, babysitting, laundry facilities, Internet, free parking, some pets allowed; no a/c* ▤ *No credit cards.*

¢ ▦ **La Camporena.** The farmhouse of La Camporena dates from the 1200s. The rooms are rustic, with typical, simply made wood furnishings. Here you can discover the joys of country living with none of the hard farm work involved: your hosts will point out the numerous walking paths in the surrounding countryside. Then you can discuss your day's adventures at dinner, over farm-fresh produce. ⊠ *Via Convertoie 27, 50022, 3 km (2 mi) south of Greve in Chianti center* 🕾 *055/853184* 🖷 *055/8544784* ⊕ *www.lacamporena.com* ↩ *17 rooms* ⌂ *Restaurant, bar, Internet, some pets allowed, no-smoking rooms; no a/c* ⊟ *AE, DC, MC, V* |◎| *CP.*

Nightlife

Chianti is by no means known for the variety and vivacity of its nightlife, which for all intents and purposes is nonexistent. The piano bar **Caffé S. Anna** (⊠ Via Italo Stecchi 1 🕾 055/853095), which opened in 2004, may just be a sign of change. Evenings of *ballo liscio* (dance music, usually conservative) and more contemporary jazz are programmed regularly throughout the year—schedules are usually lying on or near the piano.

Panzano

🟊 *7 km (4½ mi) south of Greve in Chianti, 36 km (22 mi) south of Florence.*

The magnificent views of the valleys of the Pesa and Greve rivers easily make Panzano one of the prettiest stops in Chianti. The triangular Piazza Bucciarelli is the heart of the new town. A short stroll along Via Giovanni da Verrazzano brings you up to the old town, Panzano Alto, which is still partly surrounded by medieval walls. The town's 13th-century castle is now almost completely absorbed by later buildings (the castle's central tower is now a private home).

In the church of **Santa Maria Assunta** you can see an Annunciation attributed to Michele di Ridolfo del Ghirlandaio (1503–77). ⊠ *Panzano Alto* 🎫 *Free* ☉ *Daily 7–noon and 4–6.*

An ancient church even by Chianti standards, **San Leolino** probably dates from the 10th century, but it was completely rebuilt in the Romanesque style sometime in the 13th century. The hilltop church has an exterior simplicity and 14th-century cloister worth seeing. The 16th-century terra-cotta tabernacles are attributed to Giovanni della Robbia, and there's also a remarkable triptych (attributed to the Master of Panzano) that was executed sometime in the mid-14th century. Open days and hours are unpredictable; you check with the tourist office in Greve in Chianti for the latest. ⊠ *Località San Leolino, 3 km (2 mi) south of Panzano* 🕾 *No phone* 🎫 *Free.*

Where to Stay & Eat

$$–$$$ ✕ **Oltre il Giardino.** An ancient stone farmhouse has been converted into a cozy dining area. If it's warm, enjoy your meal in the carefully planted garden, with spectacular views of the valley. Stenciled terra-cotta–colored walls and simple wood tables provide the background for very tasty Tuscan food—the *peposo* (a beef stew laced with black pepper) is particularly piquant; the *tagliatelle sul piccione* (flat noodles with a delicate squab sauce) delightfully fragrant. The wine list is particularly strong on the local variety, in this case Chianti Classico. ⊠ *Pi-*

azza G. Bucciarelli 42 ☎ *055/852828* ▤ *AE, DC, MC, V* ⊘ *Closed Mon. and mid-Nov.–mid-Dec.*

★ $ ✕ **Osteria Le Panzanelle.** Silvia Bonechi's experience in the kitchen—and a few precious recipes handed down from her *nonna* (grandmother)—coupled with the front-room hospitality of Nada Michelassi is the secret to the success of this small restaurant. These two *panzanelle* (women from Panzano) serve a short menu of tasty and authentic Tuscan dishes at what the locals refer to as *prezzi giusti* (the right prices)—both the *pappa al pomodoro* (Tuscan tomato soup) and the *peposo* (peppery beef stew) are exceptional. Whether you are eating inside or under large umbrellas on the terrace near a tiny stream, the experience is always congenial. ⊠ *Località Lucarelli 29, Lucarelli, 6 km (4 mi) southeast of Panzano on road to Radda* ☎ *0577/733511* ⌂ *Reservations essential July and Aug.* ▤ *MC, V* ⊘ *Closed Mon. and Nov.–Mar.*

¢–$ ✕ **Enoteca Baldi.** Sample the local vino while satisfying your appetite with simply prepared and presented bruschetta, soups, and pastas. In summer a few tables are set in the shade under the trees in the town's main square. ⊠ *Piazza Bucciarelli 25* ☎ *055/852843* ▤ *MC, V.*

★ $$$ ▦ **Villa La Barone.** Once the home of the Viviani della Robbia family, this 16th-century villa in a grove of ancient cypress trees retains many aspects of a private country dwelling. The honor bar allows you to enjoy an *aperitivo* on the terrace while admiring the views of the pool to the rose gardens, across the hills to the town. Guest rooms have tile white plaster walls, timber ceilings, and some tile floors. The restaurant uses fresh produce from the owner's farm in western Tuscany. Though the hotel staff may recommend it, the full, three-meal plan is not mandatory. ⊠ *Via San Leolino 19, 50020* ☎ *055/852621* 🖶 *055/852277* ⊕ *www.villalebarone.it* ⤳ *30 rooms* ⌂ *Restaurant, tennis court, pool, recreation room, babysitting, laundry service, concierge, Internet; no a/c in some rooms, no room TVs* ▤ *AE, MC, V* ⊘ *Closed Nov.–Easter* ⊧⊙⊧ *CP.*

$ ▦ **Villa Sangiovese.** On the main town square, half the rooms at this simple, well-run hotel look out to the hillside and the other half (the only ones with air-conditioning) face the piazza. An enclosed courtyard is used for summer dining, and a terraced garden has numerous shady resting places that lead down to the pool. Country-style rooms with terra-cotta tile floors are furnished with antiques. The hotel's restaurant ($$) serves regional dishes. A minimum stay of three nights is required. ⊠ *Piazza G. Bucciarelli 5, 50020* ☎ *055/852461* 🖶 *055/852463* ⤳ *17 rooms, 2 suites* ⌂ *Restaurant, pool; no a/c in some rooms, no room TVs* ▤ *MC, V* ⊘ *Closed mid-Dec.–mid-Mar. Restaurant closed Wed.* ⊧⊙⊧ *CP.*

Shopping

★ **Antica Macelleria Cecchini** (⊠ Via XX Luglio 11 ☎ 055/852020) may be the world's most dramatic butcher shop, and it teems with customers. Here, amid classical music and lively conversation, owner Dario Cecchini holds court: while quoting Dante, he serves samples of his very fine *sushi di Chianina* (raw slices of Chianina beef gently salted and peppered). He has researched recipes from the 15th century and sells pâtés and herb concoctions found nowhere else. Serious food enthusiasts should not miss the place.

Castellina in Chianti

🔟 *13 km (8 mi) south of Panzano, 59 km (35 mi) south of Florence.*

Castellina in Chianti, or simply Castellina, is on a ridge above three valleys: the Val di Pesa, Val d'Arbia, and Val d'Elsa. No matter what direction you gaze in, the panorama is bucolic. The strong 15th-century medieval walls and fortified town gate give a hint of the history of this village, which was an outpost during the continuing wars between Florence and Siena. In the main square, the Piazza del Comune, there's a 15th-century palace and a 15th-century fort, La Rocca, constructed around a 13th-century tower. It now serves as the town hall.

> **need a break?** Treat yourself to one of the terrifically fragrant ice creams at **L'Antica Delizia** (⊠ Via Fiorentina 4 ☎ 0577/741337). The fruit flavors—*fragola* (strawberry), *melone* (cantaloupe), and *limone* (lemon)—are particularly good.

Where to Stay & Eat

$$–$$$ ✗ **Albergaccio.** The fact that Albergaccio can seat only 35 diners makes dining here an intimate experience. The ever-changing menu mixes traditional and creative cuisine. In late September and October *zuppa di funghi e castagne* (mushroom and chestnut soup) is a seasonal treat; grilled meats and seafood are on the list throughout the year. Food choices are accompanied by an excellent wine list. You can dine alfresco on the terrace when it's warm. ⊠ *Via Fiorentina 25* ☎ *0577/741042* ⌧ *Reservations essential* ▤ *No credit cards* ☾ *Closed Sun. No lunch Wed.–Thurs.*

$$ ✗ **Osteria alla Piazza.** Relax amid vineyards on a countryside terrace with one of Chianti's most spectacular views of the vineyards in the valley of the River Pesa. Enjoy the sophisticated menu: the *girasole ai quattro sapori*, a giant vegetable-filled ravioli flavored with fresh tomato sauce and a few drops of cream, arrives at the table looking much like a *girasole* (sunflower). And certainly, try the delicious desserts. ⊠ *Località La Piazza, 15 km (8 mi) north of Castellina* ☎ *0577/733580* ⌧ *Reservations essential* ▤ *MC, V* ☾ *Closed Mon. and Jan.–Feb.; closed weekdays Mar. and Nov.–Dec.*

$–$$ ✗ **Ristorante Le Tre Porte.** *Bistecca alla fiorentina,* a thick slab of steak that is the specialty of the house, is usually served very rare. Paired with grilled fresh porcini mushrooms when in season (in spring and fall), it's a heady combination. The main floor of the restaurant has a small dining room serving full-course meals. Evenings, an extra room is opened downstairs, where you can order a pizza from the wood-burning oven. ⊠ *Via Trento e Trieste 4* ☎ *0577/741163* ⌧ *Reservations essential July and Aug.* ▤ *AE, DC, MC, V* ☾ *Closed Tues.*

$$–$$$ ▥ **Locanda Le Piazze.** What was once an old farmhouse has been carefully and lovingly turned into a marvelous and intimate hotel tucked in among vineyards. The three common rooms are cozy but elegant with well-stuffed upholstered couches and chairs; the breakfast room looks out on a sweeping panorama of hills. The chirping of birds is about the only noise you'll hear on the grounds awash in flowers. Timbered ceilings hang above beds with floral comforters and cool terra-cotta floors.

✉ *Locanda Le Piazze, 53011* ☎ *0577/743190* 🖷 *0577/743191* ⊕ *www. locandalepiazze.it* 🛏 *20 rooms* ♻ *Restaurant, fans, some cable TV, pool, bar, laundry service, business services, meeting room; no a/c, no TVs in some rooms* ▤ *AE, DC, MC, V* ☉ *Closed Nov.–Apr.* ⦿ *CP.*

$$–$$$ 🏠 **Villa Casalecchi.** This beautiful villa is filled with antique furniture such as ornate, carved armoires with mirrors and canopy beds. All guest rooms are in the elegant main house with marble arches and some statuary; the three apartments, in a nearby farmhouse, are more rustic and do not have air-conditioning. Dark wood paneling makes the restaurant snug. There's also a pool, which overlooks vineyards. ✉ *Località Casalecchi in Chianti, 53011* ☎ *0577/740240* 🖷 *0577/741111* ⊕ *www. villacasalecchi.it* 🛏 *16 rooms, 3 apartments* ♻ *Restaurant, in-room fax, in-room safes, cable TV, tennis court, pool, boccie, bar, babysitting, dry cleaning, laundry service, Internet, business services, meeting rooms, some pets allowed; no a/c in some rooms* ▤ *AE, DC, MC, V* ⦿ *CP.*

★ **$–$$** 🏠 **Palazzo Squarcialupi.** A 15th-century palace is a tranquil place to stay in the center of Castellina. Rooms are spacious, with high ceilings, tile floors, and 18th-century furniture; bathrooms are tiled in local stone. Many of the rooms have a view of the valley below. Common areas are elegant but comfortable—with deep, plush couches—and the breakfast buffet is ample. The multilingual staff goes out of its way to be helpful: though there's no restaurant, they will arrange for a light lunch in the warmer months. ✉ *Via Ferruccio 22, 53011* ☎ *0577/741186* 🖷 *0577/ 740386* ⊕ *www.chiantiandrelax.com* 🛏 *9 rooms, 8 suites* ♻ *Mini-bars, cable TV, bar, babysitting, dry cleaning, laundry service, Internet, some pets allowed* ▤ *AE, DC, MC, V* ☉ *Closed Nov.–Mar.* ⦿ *BP.*

$ 🏠 **Hotel Belvedere di San Leonino.** Stroll around the wonderful gardens in a restored country complex that dates from the 14th century. The guest rooms are in two houses that look out upon vineyards to the north and Siena to the south. The homey rooms have antique wardrobes and ladder-back chairs, arched windows, and tall, oak-beam ceilings. The dining room, open to guests only, has a fixed menu. In summer you can eat dinner by the pool surrounded by rolling green lawn. ✉ *Località San Leonino, 53011* ☎ *0577/740887* 🖷 *0577/740924* ⊕ *www.hotelsanleonino. com* 🛏 *28 rooms* ♻ *Dining room, cable TV, pool, babysitting, Internet; no a/c* ☉ *Closed mid-Nov.–mid-Mar.* ▤ *AE, MC, V* ⦿ *CP.*

$ 🏠 **Hotel Salivolpi.** The owners of this family-run farmhouse took special care not to alter the feeling of the house when they converted it to accommodate guest rooms: family photos, momentos of journeys, and bric-a-brac of all kinds still decorate the hotel. Each room is furnished with antiques that are typical of the late 18th and early 19th century in Chianti—heavy wooden wardrobes, marble-top chests, and woven straw–seat chairs. The large pool has a splendid view of the valley to the south of Castellina. ✉ *Via Fiorentina 89, 53011* ☎ *0577/740484* 🖷 *0577/740998* ⊕ *www.hotelsalivolpi.com* 🛏 *19 rooms* ♻ *Some fans, cable TV, pool, Internet; no a/c* ▤ *AE, MC, V* ⦿ *CP.*

Shopping

Castellina is a small town, with most of its shops located either along the main street, Via Ferruccio, or on the Piazza del Comune. But don't miss the specialty stores hidden away on Via delle Volte, which runs inside the eastern medieval walls of the town—you can reach it from either end of Via Ferruccio.

Antiquario Mario Cappelletti (✉ Via Ferruccio 34 ☎ 0577/740980) carries interesting prints, cards, and reproductions of well-known Renaissance artworks. **Cappelletti** (✉ Via Ferruccio 39–43 ☎ 0577/740420) has been producing quality leather goods at more-than-reasonable prices since 1893. The briefcases here are especially nice. **La Giravolta** (✉ Via delle Volte 32 ☎ 0577/742004) sells nothing but *i prodotti biologici* (organic products). The merchandise includes wines, candles, and spaghetti sauces. Lucia Volentieri has a delightful selection of delicately hand-painted ceramics in her **Laboratorio di Ceramica** (✉ Via Trento e Trieste 24 ☎ 0577/741133). **Le Volte Enoteca** (✉ Via Ferruccio 12 ☎ 0577/741314) has an ample and well-chosen supply of local wines such as Chianti produced by small estates and the latest in Super Tuscans.

Radda in Chianti

🕚 *10 km (6 mi) east of Castellina in Chianti, 55 km (34 mi) south of Florence.*

Radda in Chianti sits on a hill stretching between the Val di Pesa and Val d'Arbia. It is easily reached by following the SR429 from Castellina. It's another one of those tiny Chianti villages with steep streets for strolling; follow the signs that point you toward the *camminamento medioevale,* a covered 14th-century walkway that circles part of the city inside the walls.

Palazzo del Podestà, or Palazzo Comunale, is the city hall that has served the people of Radda for more than four centuries and has 51 coats of arms imbedded in the facade. ✉ *Piazza Ferrucci.*

The 16th-century **Ghiacciaia del Granducato** (Grand Duke's Ice House) supplied the ice for the main Medici ice house in the Cascine in Florence, thus providing a main ingredient for refreshing sorbets when, and if, the grand duke so desired. Snow collected during the winter was packed into the house and, because of the location partially underground and on the northern slope of the hill, could be kept through the summer. The Ice House now houses an antiques and souvenir store. ✉ *Viale Matteotti 10, outside the town walls.*

Volpaia, a small town perched on a hill 10 km (6 mi) north of Radda, was a military outpost from the 10th to the 16th centuries. It was a lodging stopover for those on the pilgrimage trail to Rome and Jerusalem. There is a small enoteca in the town's main square, Piazza della Torre, where you can sample and purchase the significant wine produced here. On August 10 people come to Volpaia for the Festa di San Lorenzo and the traditional fireworks sponsored by the family that owns a local wine estate, **Castello di Volpaia** (✉ Piazza della Cisterna 1 ☎ 0577/738066), which also has also has agriturismo lodging.

Where to Stay & Eat

$–$$ ✕ **Osteria di Volpaia.** Watch the comings and goings of the tiny hamlet of Volpaia from a terrace that overlooks the central piazza. The restaurant is at the base of the ancient town castle; dining rooms are small and unpretentious. The menu is short and includes a nice variety of mixed salads and tasty *frittate* (omelets), as well as the now practically ubiquitous bistecca alla fiorentina for those with larger appetites. ☒ *Piazza della Torre, Località Volpaia, 8 km (5 mi) north of Radda in Chianti* ☎ *0577/738905* ▤ *MC, V* ⊗ *Closed Wed.*

$$–$$$
Fodor's Choice
★

✕🏨 **Relais Fattoria Vignale.** On the outside it's an unadorned manor house with an annex across the street. Inside it's a refined and comfortable country house with multiple sitting rooms that have terra-cotta floors and nice stonework. White guest rooms with exposed brick and wood beams contain simple wooden bed frames and furniture, charming rugs and prints, and modern white-tile bathrooms. The grounds, flanked by vineyards and olive trees, are equally inviting, with lawns, terraces, and a pool. The sophisticated Ristorante Vignale ($$$$) serves excellent wines and Tuscan specialties, such as *cinghiale in umido con nepitella e vin cotto* (wild boar stew flavored with catmint and wine); the in-house enoteca ($$$) has simpler fare. ☒ *Via Pianigiani 9, 53017* ☎*0577/738300 hotel, 0577/738701 restaurant, 0577/738012 enoteca* ▤ *0577/738592* ⊕ *www.vignale.it* ➭ *35 rooms, 5 suites* ⚑ *2 restaurants, in-room safes, some in-room hot tubs, minibars, cable TV, pool, bar, wine shop, library, laundry service, concierge, Internet, meeting room, no-smoking rooms* ▤ *AE, DC, MC, V* ⊗ *Closed Jan.–Mar. 15. Restaurant closed Thurs., wine bar closed Wed.* ⧖| *BP.*

$$–$$$
🏨 **La Locanda.** At an altitude of more than 1,800 feet, this converted farmhouse is probably the highest luxury inn in Chianti, and its views are breathtaking: looking down on Volpaia and Radda, with Siena and the distant hills of Southern Tuscany as a backdrop. The infinity pool, set on the hillside, takes full advantage of the magnificent panorama. Hosts Guido and Martina Bevilacqua are on-hand to take care of and pamper you. Guest rooms are simple but tasteful, with high beamed ceilings, painted, as was once traditional in these parts, in pale pastel colors to increase the light. Take the bumpy gravel road 2 km (1 mi) west of Volpaia. ☒ *Off Via della Volpaia, 53017 Località Montanino, 13 km (8 mi) northwest of Radda in Chianti* ☎ *0577/738833* ▤ *0577/739263* ⊕ *www.lalocanda.it* ➭ *6 rooms, 1 suite* ⚑ *Pool, library; no a/c* ▤ *MC, V* ⊗ *Closed 2 wks mid-Aug. and mid-Nov.–mid.Mar.* ⧖| *CP.*

$$
🏨 **Vescine.** A former Etruscan settlement has been transformed into a secluded lodging complex of low-slung medieval stone buildings with barrel-tile roofs, connected by cobbled paths and punctuated by cypress trees. Unfussy white rooms have terra-cotta tile floors, attractive woodwork, and comfortable plain furnishings. The fire-lit reading room and bar is particularly inviting. ☒ *Località Vescine, 53017, 5 km (3 mi) west of Radda in Chianti* ☎ *0577/741144* ▤ *0577/740263* ⊕ *www.vescine. it* ➭ *20 rooms, 5 suites* ⚑ *Minibars, cable TV, tennis court, pool, library, some pets allowed* ▤ *AE, MC, V* ⊗ *Closed Nov.–Apr., except Christmastime* ⧖| *CP.*

$
🏨 **Podere Terreno.** People come from all over the world to enjoy the quiet country life in a converted wing of a 16th-century farmhouse. Seven double rooms are furnished with unadorned wood furniture. Dinners, which are included in rates along with breakfast, are inventive. The friendly

owners, who speak English, enjoy cooking, serving the wine they made themselves, and sparking conversation at the dinner table. ⊠ *Via della Volpaia, 53017 Volpaia, 5 km (3 mi) north of Radda in Chianti* ☎ *0577/ 738312* 🖷 *0577/738400* ⊕ *www.podereterreno.it* 🗩 *7 rooms* ⚑ *Restaurant, some pets allowed, no-smoking rooms; no a/c* ▤ *AE, MC, V* ⊘ *Closed Dec. 23–Dec. 28* 🍴 *MAP.*

¢ 🏠 **La Bottega di Giovannino.** The name is actually that of the wine bar run by Giovannino Bernardoni and his daughter Monica, who also rent rooms in the house next door. This is a fantastic place for the budget-conscious traveler, as rooms are immaculate and beds comfortable. Most rooms have a stunning view of the surrounding hills. All have their own bath, though most of them necessitate taking a short trip outside one's room. ⊠ *Via Roma 6–8, 53017* 🖷 *0577/738056* ⊕ *www.labottegadigiovannino.it* 🗩 *10 rooms* ⚑ *Bar; no a/c, no room phones* ▤ *MC, V.*

Shopping

Like its sister shop in Florence, **Ceramiche Rampini** (⊠ Casa Beretone, Località Beretone di Vistarenni ☎ 0577/738043 ⊕ www.rampiniceramics. com), 5 km (3 mi) south of Radda in Chianti, produces exquisite (and expensive) hand-painted ceramic objects, including plates, bowls, and candlesticks. The firm ships anywhere in the world and keeps its customers' information on file. If you break a plate or want more, they'll know exactly what your pattern is.

Locals come here to buy their nuts, bolts, and small tools, but **Tecno-Casa** (⊠ Via Roma 13 ☎ 0577/738613) also has a surprisingly varied assortment of household items, including Italian coffeemakers and cups, wine decanters, and decorative bottle stoppers.

La Bottega delle Fantasie (⊠ Via Roma 30 ☎ 0577/738978) sells colorful pillows and carefully crafted linens in sun-drenched Tuscan hues.

Gaiole in Chianti

⑫ *9 km (5½ mi) southeast of Radda in Chianti, 69 km (43 mi) south of Florence.*

A market town since 1200, Gaiole is now a central destination for touring southern Chianti. A stream runs through its center and flowers adorn many of its houses' windowboxes. The surrounding area is dotted with castles perched on hilltops (the better to see the approaching enemy): they were of great strategic importance during the Renaissance and still make dazzling lookout points.

It's a pretty drive up winding and curving roads to **Castello di Meleto,** a castle from the 13th century. Attached to it is an 18th-century villa; more importantly, there's a wine shop that serves tastes of the locally produced wine as well as honeys and jams. It's worth touring the castle if you want to get a sense of how 18th-century aristocrats lived; if that doesn't interest you, proceed directly to the enoteca for a tasting. Six apartments clustered near the castle are available for rent. ⊠ *5 km (3 mi) south of Gaiole, Località Meleto* ☎ *0577/749496 castle and cantina, 0577/ 749129 enoteca* ⊕ *www.castellomeleto.it* 🗫 *Tour and tasting €8*

◷ *Tours Mon. 3 and 4:30, Tues.–Sat. 11:30, 3, and 4:30, Sun. 11:30, 4, and 5. Wine shop mid-Mar–mid.-Nov., daily 9–7; mid.-Nov.–mid.-Mar., weekends 9–7.*

The stunning **Castello di Brolio** is the castle to visit if you have time for only one. At the end of the 12th century, when Florence conquered southern Chianti, Brolio became Florence's southernmost outpost, and it was often said, "When Brolio growls, all Siena trembles." Brolio was built about AD 1000 and owned by the monks of the Badia Fiorentina; the "new" owners, the Ricasoli family, have been in possession since 1141. Bettino Ricasoli (1809–80), the so-called Iron Baron, was one of the founders of modern Italy and is also said to have invented the original formula for Chianti wine. Today the winery is still justifiably famous. Brolio is one of Chianti's best-known labels, and the cellars may be toured by appointment. There's a sign at the Brolio gate that translates as RING BELL AND BE PATIENT. You pull a rope and the bell above the ramparts peals, and in a short time, the caretaker arrives to let you in. The grounds are worth visiting, although the grand, mostly 19th-century manor house is not open to the public (the current baron is very much in residence). There are also two apartments here available for rent by the week. ⊠ *Località Brolio, 2 km (1 mi) southeast of Gaiole* ☎ *0577/7301* 🎫 *€3* ◷ *June–Sept., daily 9–noon and 2–6:30; Oct.–May, Sat.–Thurs. 9–noon and 2–6:30.*

Vertine, 2 km (1 mi) to the west of Gaiole, is a charming hamlet documented as far back as the 10th century. The walled town is oval in shape and has a tall watchtower guarding the city gate. A walk along the still unspoiled streets gives you a glimpse of life in a Tuscan hill town as it once was, and the views of the undulating countryside from the occasional opening in the walls are spectacular. Stop for a snack after your stroll around town: **Bar Blu** (⊠ Località Vertine 38 ☎ 0577/749029) makes sandwiches to order and serves plates of cheese and cold cuts.

North of Gaiole a turnoff leads to the **Badia a Coltibuono** (Abbey of the Good Harvest), which has been owned by Lorenza de' Medici's family for more than a century and a half (the family isn't closely related to the Renaissance-era Medici). Ever since the Badia was founded by Vallombrosan monks in the 11th century, it has produced wine. Today the family continues the tradition, making Chianti Classico among other wines, along with high-quality cold-pressed olive oil and various flavored vinegars and floral honeys. A small Romanesque church with campanile is surrounded by 2,000 acres of oak, fir, and chestnut woods threaded with walking paths—open to all—that pass two small lakes. Though the abbey itself, built between the 11th and 18th centuries, is the family's home, parts are open for tours (in English, German, or Italian). Visit the jasmine-draped main courtyard, the inner cloister with its antique well, the musty old aging cellars, and the Renaissance-style garden redolent of lavender, lemons, and roses. In the shop, **L'Osteria,** you can taste and purchase Coltibuono's wine and honey, as well as pick up other items like homemade beeswax hand lotion in little ceramic dishes. The Badia is closed on public holidays. ⊠ *Off S408, Badia a Coltibuono, 4 km (2½ mi) north of Gaiole* ☎ *0577/749498 for tours, 0577/749479* *for shop* 🖷 *0577/749235* ⊕ *www.coltibuono.com* 🖴 *Abbey* €3 ⊙ *Tours May–July and Sept.–Oct., weekdays 2:30, 3, 3:30, 4; shop Mar.–Dec., daily 9–1 and 2–7.*

Where to Stay & Eat

$$–$$$ ✗ **Badia a Coltibuono.** Outside the walls of Badia a Coltibuono itself is the abbey's pleasant restaurant, with seating outside or in soft-yellow rooms divided by ancient brick arches. The *crema di peperoni e patate* (a creamless red pepper and potato soup) arrives at the table garnished with the home-grown olive oil; the *lasagnette agli asparagi al forno* (lasagna with asparagus and pecorino) is fragrant. It all pairs marvelously with the Badia's own wines. Between 2:30 and 7:30 you can order from a bistro menu that has sandwiches, salads, appetizers, and desserts. ⊠ *Off S408, Badia a Coltibuono, 4 km (2½ mi) north of Gaiole* 🖀 *0577/749031* ▭ *MC, V* ⊙ *Closed Mon.*

$$–$$$ ✗ **Osteria del Castello.** South African–born chef Seamus de Pentheny O'Kelly trained extensively in Paris and uses sophisticated techniques for his up-to-the-minute takes on Italian food. His *insalata di prosciutto con aceto balsamico* (mixed greens with blanched prosciutto drizzled with aged balsamic vinegar) is a delight, as is just about everything else on the menu. The restaurant nestles within woods a stone's throw from the Castello di Brolio. The wine list has some of Brolio's best offerings. ⊠ *Località Brolio, 2 km (1 mi) southeast of Gaiole* 🖀🖀 *0577/747277* ⚓ *Reservations essential* ▭ *AE, DC, MC, V* ⊙ *Closed Tues.*

$–$$ ✗ **La Grotta della Rana.** A perfect stop for lunch while you're exploring Chianti's wineries, this trattoria's *cucina casalinga* (home cooking) can be eaten on a lovely outdoor patio (there's also seating indoors). If you time dinner right, you might get to watch a memorable sunset while you're eating. Outstanding primi include *maccheroni alla nonna* (macaroni with asparagus in a light cream sauce dotted with truffle oil). The *misto alla griglia* (mixed grilled meats) includes succulent pork. Also notable is the *filetto al pepe verde* (Chianina beef in a creamy green-peppercorn sauce). ⊠ *Off SS408, Località San Sano, 8km (5 mi) south of Gaiole* 🖀 *0577/746020* ▭ *AE, MC, V* ⊙ *Closed Wed. and Feb.–mid-Mar.*

$ ✗ **Lo Sfizio di Bianchi.** A pleasant restaurant with outdoor seating on the main piazza of Gaiole, Lo Sfizio di Bianchi is as popular with the locals as it is with tourists. The menu, presented on small blackboards, has the occasional unexpected item, like the plate of grilled vegetables that is listed as an antipasto but almost makes a meal in itself. They also make their own delicious pastries and ice cream; skipping dessert is difficult. ⊠ *Via Ricasoli 44/46* 🖀 *0577/749501* ⚓ *Reservations essential weekends* ▭ *AE, MC, V* ⊙ *Closed Tues. No dinner Mon.*

★ $$–$$$ ✗🖫 **Castello di Spaltenna.** The term *rustic elegance* comes to life at this complex, which includes a former convent (dating to the 1300s) and a Romanesque church. Sumptuous striped fabrics or light, silky sheers drape from canopy beds; chiseled-stone fireplaces and massage-jet tubs set the minisuites apart. Windows look out on the hills, woods, and vineyards. Dine by candlelight on sophisticated classics—*filetto di manzo con fungo porcino al vino rosso* (beef fillet topped by a grilled boletus mushroom in a red wine sauce), for example—at the first-class restaurant ($$$) with a courtyard. ⊠ *Pieve di Spaltenna, 53013* 🖀 *0577/749483* 🖷 *0577/*

749269 ⊕ *www.spaltenna.it* ↪ *36 rooms, 3 suites* ⚶ *Restaurant, room service, fans, minibars, cable TV, tennis court, 2 pools (1 indoor), wading pool, sauna, billiards, bar, babysitting, dry cleaning, laundry service, Internet, business services, meeting rooms* ⊟ *AE, DC, MC, V* ⊙ *Closed early Jan.–mid-Mar.* ⎮⊚⎮ *CP.*

$$–$$$ 🏨 **Castello di Tornano.** If you'd like a bit of whimsy on your holiday, this agriturismo castle may be the place for you: next to an 11th-century tower there's a swimming pool that is roughly where the moat was, and both the prison and the chapel have been converted into rooms. The grounds are remarkably private, so if you're looking for peace and quiet, this may be the perfect choice. ⊠ *Off S408, Località Tornano, 53013, 5 km (3 mi) south of Gaiole* ☎☎ *0577/746067* ⊕ *www.castelloditornano.it* ↪ *11 suites, 7 apartments, 1 house* ⚶ *Restaurant, some in-room hot tubs, some kitchens, tennis court, pool, fishing, Ping-Pong, playground, Internet, some pets allowed* ⊟ *AE, DC, MC, V.*

$ 🏨 **Borgo Argenina.** Elena Nappa, a former interior designer, is now the consummate hostess at a centuries-old villa that she has completely renovated. Rooms are lovingly decorated with antique quilts and solid wood furnishings, and minibars (gratis) are a nod to modern times. Bianca, the resident dog, greets you at the steep drive upon your arrival, and might even hang out with you all day. Elena is an authority on the surrounding Chianti area and happily draws maps and suggests wine-tasting and -touring routes. Follow signs for San Marcellino Monti to get here. ⊠ *Off S408, 53013 Località Borgo Argenina, 15 km (9 mi) south of Gaiole* ☎ *0577/747117* 🖷 *0577/747228* ⊕ *www.borgoargenina. it* ↪ *5 rooms, 2 suites, 2 cottages, 1 villa* ⚶ *Minibars, laundry service, no-smoking rooms; no a/c* ⊟ *AE, DC, MC, V* ⎮⊚⎮ *CP.*

$ 🏨 **Hotel Residence San Sano.** An open-hearth fireplace and hand-hewn stone porticoes hark back to a time when this was a 13th-century fortress. The small hotel has modern amenities that have been added, including a beautiful outdoor pool. Shuttered windows and doors help make rooms bright and spacious. Bedsteads have unadorned, curving lines in dark or medium wood. The scent of lavender and rosemary wafts from the gardens. ⊠ *Off S408, Località San Sano, 53010 Lecchi in Chianti, 10 km (6 mi) south of Gaiole* ☎ *0577/746130* 🖷 *0577/746156* ⊕ *www.sansanohotel.it* ↪ *14 rooms* ⚶ *Restaurant, in-room safes, minibars, some cable TV, pool, laundry facilities, some pets allowed* ⊟*AE, DC, MC, V* ⊙ *Closed Jan.–Mar.* ⎮⊚⎮ *CP.*

Castelnuovo Berardenga

⓭ *20 km (12 mi) southeast of Gaiole in Chianti, 90 km (56 mi) southeast of Florence, 23 km (14 mi) east of Siena.*

The southernmost village in Chianti territory has a compact center, with hilly, curving streets. A plethora of piazzas invite wandering. Peek at the gardens of **Villa Chigi**, a 19th-century villa built on the site of a 14th-century castle (actually the "new castle" from which Castelnuovo got its name). The villa is closed to the public, but its manicured gardens are open for visiting on Sunday and holidays. ⊠ *Strada la Ragnaia* ☎ *No phone* 🎟 *Free* ⊙ *Apr.–Sept., Sun. 10–8; Oct.–Mar., Sun. 10–5.*

The neoclassical church of **San Giusto e San Clemente,** built in the 1840s on a Greek-cross plan, contains a Madonna and Child with angels by an anonymous 15th-century master. Also inside it is the *Holy Family with St. Catherine of Siena,* attributed to Arcangelo Salimbeni (1530/40–79). ☒ *Piazza Matteotti 4* ☎ *0577/355133* 🎫 *Free* ⊙ *Daily 7:30–7.*

off the beaten path

SAN GUSMÈ – Of the medieval villages that surround Castelnuovo Berardenga, hilltop San Gusmè is the oldest and most interesting. The village retains its original early 1400s layout, with arched passageways, gates topped with coats of arms, narrow squares, and steep streets. You can walk through the entire village in 20 minutes, but in those 20 minutes you may feel as if you have stepped back in time some 600 years. ☒ *SR484, 5 km (3 mi) north from Castelnuovo Berardenga, follow signs for San Gusmè.*

Where to Stay

$$$ 🏨 **Borgo San Felice.** The elegant Borgo San Felice hotel, spread across five buildings, used to be a small medieval town. Now it's given over to luxury, which is immediately apparent upon entering the reception area and public rooms: white walls, high vaulted ceilings, and furniture covered in exquisite chintz prints mingle with tasteful etchings and watercolors. Rooms have tile floors, spacious bathrooms, and windows that open out onto peace and tranquillity. The restaurant, Poggio Antico, serves sophisticated versions of Tuscan classics. ☒ *Off SS484, 53019 Località San Felice, 8 km (5 mi) northwest of Castelnuovo Berardenga* ☎ *0577/359260* 🖷 *0577/359089* ⊕ *www.borgosanfelice.com* 🛏 *43 rooms, 15 suites* ⋄ *Restaurant, room service, in-room safes, minibars, cable TV, 2 tennis courts, pool, gym, hair salon, massage, bicycles, billiards, boccie, bar, wine shop, babysitting, dry cleaning, laundry service, concierge, Internet, business services, meeting rooms, some pets allowed* 🖃 *AE, DC, MC, V* ⊙ *Closed Nov.–Mar.* ⁌◎⁍ *CP.*

CHIANTI A TO Z

To research prices, get advice from other travelers, and book travel arrangements, visit www.fodors.com.

AIRPORTS

The closest major airport is Florence's Peretola (officially Aeroporto A. Vespucci), a few minutes to an a hour and a half north of towns in Chianti. Rome's Fiumicino (officially Aeroporto Leonardo da Vinci) is about 320 km (200 mi) south of Tavernelle Val di Pesa, and Pisa's Galileo Galilei is about 85 km (53 mi) west.

🛈 Airport Information **Aeroporto A. Vespucci** (known as Peretola) ☎ 055/373498. **Aeroporto Galileo Galilei** ☎ 050/500707 ⊕ www.pisa-airport.com. **Aeroporto Leonardo da Vinci** (known as Fiumicino) ☎ 06/6594420 ⊕ www.adr.it.

BIKE TRAVEL

Any biking that you plan here will not be easy, but the slow pace of the journey, and the spectacular views along the way, more than make up for the fatigue. I Bike Italy leads one-day bike rides through the Chianti countryside from a meeting point in Florence; they provide all the equipment and lunch. Marco Ramuzzi has a bike shop in Greve in Chianti and rents bikes at daily or weekly rates—don't be surprised if you see local bikers sporting his distinctive blue-and-yellow biking outfits, he's become something of a biking guru in Chianti.

🚲 **I Bike Italy** ⊠ Borgo degli Albizi 11, Florence 📠 055/2342371 ⊕ www.ibikeitaly. com. **Marco Ramuzzi** ⊠ Via Stecchi 23, Greve in Chianti 📞 055/853037

BUS TRAVEL

Even though the best way to explore the region is by car, SENA operates a frequent daily service between Rome and Siena (2½ hours), and there is frequent service between Florence and Siena (one hour) provided by the SITA line. Service between Florence and Greve in Chianti is frequent. Radda in Chianti, however, is difficult to reach by bus from Florence; there's one outgoing bus in the early morning and a return bus in the late afternoon, but no service on Sundays and holidays. There are several buses daily to Radda from Siena.

Tra-In goes from Florence to Sant'Andrea in Percussina, San Casciano in Val di Pesa, Tavarnelle Val di Pesa, Barberino Val d'Elsa, Gaiole in Chianti, and Castelnuovo Berardenga. SITA links Florence with Sant'Andrea in Percussina, San Casciano in Val di Pesa, Tavarnelle Val di Pesa, Barberino Val d'Elsa, Gaiole in Chianti, Mercatale, Sambuca, Badia a Passignano, San Donato in Poggio, Greve in Chianti, Panzano, Castellina, and Radda in Chianti.

🚌 Bus Lines **SENA** 📞 0577/204111 in Siena ⊕ www.sena.it. **SITA** 📞 0577/204270 in Siena, 055/47821 in Florence, and 800/373760 toll free in Italy ⊕ www.sita-on-line.it. **Tra-In** 📞 0577/204111 in Siena ⊕ www.trainspa.it.

CAR RENTALS

Major international car-rental agencies have offices at the airports in the region. There are also branches in Siena and in Florence.

CAR TRAVEL

Local roads plus sensational vistas make driving a joy, and the best travel option in the region. The towns and landmarks are well signed, but you should arm yourself with a good map and nerves of steel to contend with speedy local drivers.

The area is easily reached from the Florence–Siena Superstrada. The Via Cassia (SR2) also connects Florence, Siena, and Rome, going through smaller villages. The Strada Chiantigiana (SR222) is a slower, scenic route to the east of the Superstrada, which winds through central Chianti vineyards.

EMERGENCIES

Paramedics, police, and the fire department all use a central, nationwide emergency number. Pharmacies post the addresses of the nearest late-night pharmacies outside their doors.

🚨 Emergency Services 📞 113.

LODGING

APARTMENT &
VILLA RENTALS
A good source for information about agriturist lodging is Chianti Slow Travel. They specialize in the area near Greve but also represent farmstay properties throughout Chianti. Best in Italy acts as a broker for luxury villa properties throughout Tuscany. Fine Italian Rentals represents a number of villas and small converted farmhouse properties that can sleep up to 12 people for weekly stays—their business address is in England but they are based in Chianti. If you wish, both Best in Italy and Fine Italian Rentals can organize private cooking lessons during your stay.
▪ Agents **Chianti Slow Travel** ⊠ Via Giovanni da Verrazzano 33, Greve in Chianti ☎ 055/8546299 📠 055/8544240 ⊕ www.chiantislowtravel.it. **Best in Italy** ⊠ Via Foscolo 72, Florence ☎ 055/223064 📠 055/2298912 ⊕ www.thebestinitaly.com. **Fine Italian Rentals** ⊠ 23 Old Green Rd., Kent, England ☎ 333/1588491 📠 02/700443044 ⊕ www.fineitalianrentals.com.

TAXIS

The area has few taxi companies, but in Greve you can hire cars and drivers from firms such as Giovanni Gemini, Pistolesi, and Sandra.
▪ Companies **Giovanni Gemini** ☎ 0349/4588440. **Pistolesi** ☎ 055/8544953. **Sandra** ☎ 0328/5458585.

TRAIN TRAVEL

Direct train service from Florence to the Chianti region is nonexistent, and the buses that connect Montevarchi and Chiusi, both on the Florence–Rome line, to Gaiole in Chianti and Montepulciano run very infrequently. Train service from Siena is limited to Castellina in Chianti, but the stations themselves aren't anywhere near the town centers and the connecting bus service is infrequent. Information is available from the state railway, Ferrovie dello Stato.
▪ Train Lines **Ferrovie dello Stato** (FS) ☎ 892021 toll-free within Italy ⊕ www.trenitalia.com.

TRAVEL AGENCIES

▪ Agencies **Machiavelli Viaggi** ⊠ Via Machiavelli 49, 50026 San Casciano in Val di Pesa ☎ 055/822324. **Vinea Viaggi** ⊠ Via Roma 41, 50022 Greve in Chianti ☎ 055/854352. **Xtramondo Viaggi** ⊠ Via Roma 238, 50028 Tavarnelle Val di Pesa ☎ 055/805023.

VISITOR INFORMATION

The tourist office in Tavarnelle Val di Pesa also handles Barberino Val d'Elsa inquiries. In Greve in Chianti, the office on Via Giovanni da Verrazzano is open from April to mid-October and the one on Via Giovanni da Verrazzano is open from mid-October through March.
▪ Tourist Information **Castellina in Chianti** ⊠ Piazza del Comune 1 ☎ 0577/741392 ⊕ www.comune.castellina.si.it. **Castelnuovo Berardenga** ⊠ Via Roma 8 ☎ 0577/355500. **Greve in Chianti** ⊠ Via Giovanni da Verrazzano 59 ☎ 055/8546287 ⊠ Via Giovanni da Verrazzano 33 ☎ 055/8546299 ⊕ www.comune.greve-in-chianti.com. **Radda in Chianti** ⊠ Piazza Ferrucci 1 ☎ 0577/738494. **Tavarnelle Val di Pesa** ⊠ Piazza Matteotti 39 ☎ 055/805081.

SIENA &
THE HILL TOWNS

5

ITALY'S FINEST GOTHIC TOWN HALL
Siena's Palazzo Pubblico ⇨*p.203*

ROWDIEST HORSE RACE
The twice-yearly Palio ⇨*p.211*

SITE OF THE ORIGINAL ROMAN FORUM
Fan-shaped Piazza del Campo ⇨*p.204*

BEST-KEPT DINING SECRET
Local haunt La Taverna di San Giuseppe ⇨*p.208*

MOST COMFORTABLE MONASTERY
14th-century Certosa di Maggiano ⇨*p.209*

MOST USEFUL RIVALRY
Contest to build the tallest defensive tower
in San Gimignano ⇨*p.216*

By Patricia
Rucidlo

ITALY'S MOST ENCHANTING MEDIEVAL CITY, Siena is the one stop you should make in Tuscany if you make no other. The perfectly-preserved *centro storico* (historic center), with its medieval palaces, is a delight to walk around in; traffic—including those pesky *motorini* (mopeds)—is banned. Once in the region, however, there are plenty of other places to explore: Italy's most famous hill town, San Gimignano, is known as the "medieval Manhattan" because of its enormous towers, built by rival families, that still stand today. Like Siena, it benefited from commerce and trade along the pilgrimage routes, as the wonderful art in its churches and museums attests. Equally intriguing is a visit to Volterra, an Etruscan town famous for its alabaster. Southern Tuscany is perhaps less familiar than Chianti to the north, but prestigious wines are made south of Siena, too, and the scenery is classically Tuscan. On your way down, don't miss a stop at the Abbazzia di Monte Oliveto Maggiore to see its sublime Renaissance frescoes.

Exploring Siena & the Hill Towns

Siena nestles among rolling hills rimmed with olive trees. Volterra, perched high on a hilltop, is surrounded by desolately beautiful, rocky countryside with little vegetation. Heading southwest of Siena toward Asciano there's less cultivation of the vine and fewer terraced hillsides, but the area is still prime quality farmland. Crayola Crayons invented the color "burnt sienna," a rich, orangeish brown that perfectly suggests one of the hues of the Sienese earth.

Siena is 72 km (45 mi) south of Florence: the Florence–Siena Superstrada (no number) is a four-lane, divided road with limited access. The smaller Via Cassia (SR2) winds its way south along roughly the same route as the Superstrada from Florence through Siena, but it passes through smaller villages. Siena makes a sensible, central base from which to take day or overnight trips to the hill towns and beyond.

About the Restaurants

Siena is full of restaurants—many good, many more not so good—that cater to the hordes of tourists who visit for day trips. It's easy to have a bad meal in Siena if you don't put a little thought into where you're going to eat ahead of time. Restaurant reservations are particularly necessary around the time of the Palio horse races (July 2 and August 16). Though high-end dining is a possibility in a handful of restaurants scattered around town, most eateries are far more casual and less expensive. Lunch is usually served from 12:30 to 2 in restaurants and trattorias; hours are slightly longer at *enoteche* (wine bars). Dinner hours are from 7:30 to around 10. You won't see most Sienese having lunch before 1:30, or dinner before 9 pm. Breakfast in Siena, as breakfast elsewhere in Italy, is a brioche and a cappuccino taken at a bar.

About the Hotels

Siena, San Gimignano, and Volterra are among the most visited towns in Tuscany, so there's no lack of choice for hotels across the price range. The best accommodations, however, are often a couple of miles outside town. Every year there seem to be more old villas and monasteries con-

5

Numbers in the text correspond to numbers in the margin and on the Siena & the Hill Towns, Siena, and Volterra maps.

If you have 3 days

Spend two days getting to know ⬚ **Siena** ❶–❿ ▶, exploring its medieval streets and neighborhoods as well as major sites like the Campo, Palazzo Pubblico, Duomo, and surrounding museums. Then make a day or overnight trip to see ⬚ **San Gimignano** ❸ and its medieval towers or ⬚ **Volterra** ⓮–⓴, with its sweeping views of the countryside far down below. If you'd prefer to go south, take an excursion through the countryside to the **Abbazia di Monte Oliveto Maggiore** ㉒, with its remarkable frescoes and stunning scenery.

If you have 5 days

The three-day itinerary can be easily expanded to include an extra day in ⬚ **Siena** ❶–❿ ▶ or a stop in **Colle di Val d'Elsa** ⓬ on the way to ⬚ **San Gimignano** ❸ and a night in ⬚ **Volterra** ⓮–⓴. From there head back through Siena (or stop the night and make a day trip) south, stopping at the town of **Asciano** ㉑ on the way down to the ⬚ **Abbazia di Monte Oliveto Maggiore** ㉒.

---

verted into charming, first-rate hotels, as well as simpler *agriturismo* (agritourism) farmhouses, usually available for weekly rentals. Their location makes a car necessary, but the splendor of the surroundings usually outweighs any problems getting in and out of town. Rooms are hard to come by in Siena during the weekends of the running of the Palio (July 2 and August 16); for those you need to reserve from a few months to up to a year in advance.

WHAT IT COSTS In Euros					
	$$$$	**$$$**	**$$**	**$**	**¢**
RESTAURANTS	over €22	€18–€22	€13–€17	€7–€12	under €7
HOTELS	over €290	€210–€290	€140–€209	€80–€139	under €80

Restaurant prices are for a second course (secondo piatto) per person. Hotel prices are for two people in a standard double room in high season, including tax and service.

Timing

The region enjoys particularly sparkling weather in spring and fall. In July and August, the same sun that makes the grapes ripen can also make crowded streets unpleasantly hot. During this time, it's always easier to work with the local schedule rather than against it. If you get an early start, you can enjoy the sights in the cooler morning hours and return to have an afternoon siesta while the sun is at its hottest. Siena fills to the brim in the weeks surrounding the running of the Palio on July 2 and August 16, when prices, crowds, and commotion are at their highest. In the winter months you may have towns mostly to yourself, although the choices for hotels and restaurants can be a bit more limited than when the season is in full swing. From November through February it's fairly difficult to find an open hotel in San Gimignano and Volterra: plan accordingly.

SIENA

With its narrow streets and steep alleys, a stunning Gothic Duomo, a bounty of early Renaissance art, and the glorious Palazzo Pubblico overlooking its magnificent Campo, Siena is often described as Italy's best-preserved medieval city. It is also remarkably modern: many shops sell cutting-edge clothes by up-and-coming designers. Make a point of catching the *passeggiata* (evening stroll), when the locals throng the Via di Città, the city's main street.

Sienese mythology holds that the city shares common ancestry with Rome: the legendary founder, Senius, was said to be the son of Remus and the twin brother of Rome's founder, Romulus. The city emblem—a she-wolf and suckling twins—supports the claim. Archaeological evidence suggests there were prehistoric as well as Etruscan settlements here, which undoubtedly made way for Saena Julia, the Roman town established by Augustus in the 1st century BC.

Siena rose to prominence as an essential stop on that most important of medieval roads, the Via Francigena (or Via Romea), prospering from the yearly flow of thousands of Christian pilgrims coming south to Rome from northern Europe. Siena developed a banking system—Europe's oldest bank, Monte dei Paschi, is still very much in business—and dominated the wool trade, thereby establishing itself as a rival to Florence. The two towns became regional powers and bitter enemies, each town taking a different side in the struggle that divided the peninsula between the Guelphs (loyal to the Pope) and Ghibellines (loyal to the Holy Roman Emperor). Siena took the side of the latter.

Victory over Florence in 1260 at Montaperti marked the beginning of Siena's golden age. Even though the Florentines avenged the loss nine years later, Siena continued to prosper. During the following decades Siena erected its greatest buildings (including the Duomo); established a model city government presided over by the Council of Nine; and became a great art, textile, and trade center. All of these achievements came together in the decoration of the Sala della Pace in Palazzo Pubblico. It makes you wonder wonder what greatness the city might have gone on to achieve had its fortunes been different, but in 1348 a plague decimated the population, brought an end to the Council of Nine, and left Siena economically weak and vulnerable. Siena succumbed to Florentine rule in the mid-16th century, when a year-long siege virtually eliminated the native population. Ironically, it was precisely this decline that, along with the steadfast pride of the Sienese, prevented further development, to which we owe the city's marvelous medieval condition today.

5

Cuisine

The Sienese often add a subtle flair of extra herbs and garlic to their rendition of traditional Tuscan fare. Antipastas (usually made of the simplest ingredients) are extremely satisfying. A typical starter might be *fettunta*, a slice of good, toasted bread drizzled with olive oil and rubbed with fresh garlic, and served with a variety of excellent locally cured meats, such as those made from *cinta*, a species of domestic pig rescued from near extinction. *Verdure sott'olio* (marinated vegetables) are usually artichokes, red pepper, carrots, celery, cauliflower, olives, and capers marinated in olive oil.

As you pass on to the first course, specialties include *pici* (a thick, hand-rolled spaghetti often tossed in a meat ragù or sprinkled with oiled bread crumbs and pastas such as tagliatelle or *pappardelle* (wide noodles) served with a savory ragù of *cinghiale* (wild boar) or *lepre* (hare). Pecorino, a soft sheep's cheese, makes it onto many menus in pasta dishes and appetizers. The Sienese also have many hearty soups as first courses; these are often made with lentils or beans and sometimes thickened with bread. *Panzanella*, a salad of tomato, basil, and onion, is a common first course on summer menus.

Second courses are traditionally game meats. Many prestigious wines come from the Siena area and are labeled Chianti Colli Senesi. White-wine drinkers can try Vernaccia di San Gimignano, which is a common, light white wine. Because towns in this chapter are in the midst of superb wine-producing areas, even the house wines are usually quite good. After your meal, try some delicious amber-colored *vin santo*, a sweet dessert wine, or Sienese sweets such as *ricciarelli*, a succulent almond-flavored cookie.

Shopping

Siena continues its centuries-old tradition of elaborately handcrafted needlework, which can still be purchased in local shops. Equally interesting, and newer on the scene, are women with looms making hand-woven shawls, scarves, blankets, and jackets in mohair, wool, and silk in Siena, as well as in San Gimignano and Volterra. Many shops in Siena sell woven rugs in various sizes, catering to all tastes and budgets.

If you're looking for exquisite crystal, a trip to Colle Val d'Elsa is definitely in order. They've been making crystal here for centuries, and a number of shops specialize in everything from simple vases to intricately worked decanters. Alabaster, found outside Volterra, is sold in shops throughout Volterra and in nearby San Gimignano.

Medieval Towers

Architectural remnants of Tuscany's medieval past can be found be in the number of towers dotting many towns. Built of local stone (usually a kind of sandstone), they sprang up in the 11th century and proliferated in the 12th and 13th centuries. One *torre* (tower) was constructed higher than the last, as Tuscans enjoyed their own medieval version of keeping up with the Joneses. The purpose of the towers was domestic and defensive, as they housed aristocratic, extended families and protected them when clans quarrelled, which happened frequently. San Gimignano is the Tuscan town most famous for its medieval towers; 15 of the 72 that stood during the 1300s remain today. But towers can be seen in towns all around the region, and are often part of the palace that served as the old city hall, as in Volterra. In Siena you can stay the night in a restored tower, Antica Torre.

But while much looks as it did in the early 14th century, Siena is no museum. Walk through the streets and you can see that the medieval *contrade*, 17 neighborhoods into which the city has been historically divided, are a vibrant part of modern life. You may see symbols of the *contrada*—Tartuca (turtle), Oca (goose), Istrice (porcupine), Torre (tower)—emblazoned on banners and engraved on building walls. The Sienese still strongly identify themselves by the contrada into which they were born and raised; loyalty and rivalry run deep. At no time is this more visible than during the centuries-old Palio, a twice-yearly horse race held in the Piazza del Campo, but you need not visit during the wild festival to come to know the rich culture and enchanting pleasures of Siena; those are evident at every step.

Exploring Siena

If you come by car, you're better off leaving it in one of the parking lots around the perimeter of town, as car access is difficult or just plain prohibited in most parts of the city center. Practically unchanged since medieval times, Siena is laid out in a "Y" over the slopes of several hills, dividing the city into *terzi* (thirds). Although the most interesting sites are in a fairly compact area around the Campo at the center of town in the neighborhoods of Città, Camollìa, and San Martino, be sure to leave some time to wander into the narrow streets that rise and fall steeply from the main thoroughfares. If your feet have had enough, head for one of the cabs usually at the bottom of the Campo or take one of the orange electric minibuses that ply their way through the crowds and between the major sites. Also, keep a few €1 coins at hand; illuminations in many churches are often not free.

A Good Walk

Try to avoid passing through Siena in a day; you need at least two to really explore the town. A basic walk begins with a coffee on the **Piazza del Campo** ❶ ►, the focal point of the city and considered by many to be the finest public square in Italy. Visit the **Palazzo Pubblico** ❷, with its Museo Civico and adjacent tower, the Torre del Mangia. Cross the piazza and exit via the stairs to the left of the Fonte Gaia to Via di Città. Just to the left is the 15th-century Loggia della Mercanzia, where merchants and money traders once did business. Commerce is still pretty active along Via di Città, Siena's main shopping street, which climbs to the left. Up ahead on Via di Città is the enchanting Palazzo Chigi-Saracini, where concerts are often held. Step in to admire the especially well-preserved courtyard. Continue up the hill on Via di Città and take the second street on the right, Via del Capitano, which leads to the Pi-

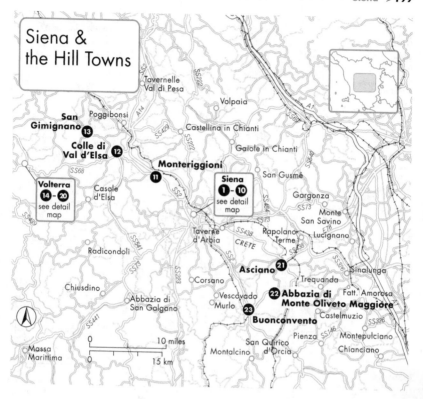

Siena &
the Hill Towns

Tavernelle
Val di Pesa

Volpaia

**San
Gimignano** 13   Poggibonsi

Castellina in Chianti

**Colle di
Val d'Elsa** 12

Gaiole in Chianti

SS68   **Monteriggioni**

11   **Siena**
Volterra   1 - 10
14 - 20   Casale   San Gusmé
see detail d'Elsa   see detail
map   map   Gargonza

Monte
San Savino

Taverne   Rapolano
Radicondoli   d'Arbia   CRETE Terme   Lucignano

Corsano

Chiusdino   Trequanda
Vescóvado   **Abbazia di**   Fatt. Amorosa
Abbazia di   Murlo 23   **Monte Oliveto Maggiore**
San Galgano   Castelmuzio
Buonconvento

0   10 miles   San Quirico   Pienza   Montepulciano
Massa   Montalcino d'Orcia   Chianciano
Marittima   0   15 km

Asciano 21   Sinalunga

---

azza del Duomo. The **Duomo** 3 is a must-see, along with the frescoes inside in the Biblioteca Piccolomini and the **Cripta** 4. The church's baptistery, the **Battistero** 5, is to one side and the nearby the **Museo dell'-Opera Metropolitana** 6 occupies what was to be a new cathedral that went unfinished. Across from the Duomo is the **Spedale di Santa Maria della Scala** 7 and its Museo Archeologico. Chief among Siena's other gems is the **Pinacoteca Nazionale** 8, an art museum, several blocks straight back down Via del Capitano (which becomes Via San Pietro). The church of **San Domenico** 9 lies in the other direction (you could take Via della Galluzza to Via della Sapienza), and nearby is the **Casa di Santa Caterina** 10, where one of Italy's patron saints was born.

TIMING   It's a joy to walk in Siena—hills notwithstanding—as it's a rare opportunity to stroll through a medieval city rather than just a town. (There is quite a lot to explore, in contrast to tiny hill towns that can be crossed in minutes.) The walk can be done in as little as a day, with minimal stops at the sights. But stay longer and take time to tour the church building and museums, and to enjoy the streetscapes themselves. Several of the sites have reduced hours on Sunday afternoon and Monday.

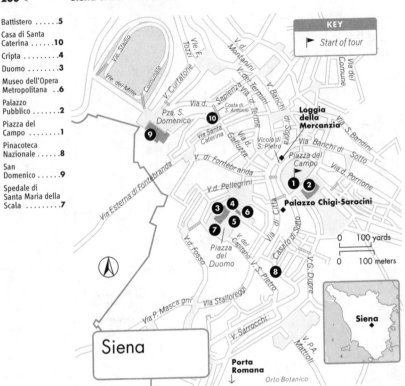

What to See

Association of Official Tour Guides. You can take a two-hour walking tour that takes in most of the major sights such as the Duomo, the Campo, and the exterior of Palazzo Pubblico, with English-speaking guides. ✉ *Piazza il Campo 56* ☎ *0577/288084* ⊕ *www.terredisiena.it* 💰 *€5* ⊙ *Mon.–Sat. at 3 PM.*

⑤ Battistero. The Duomo's 14th-century Gothic Baptistery was built to prop up one side of the Duomo. There are frescoes throughout, but the highlight is a large bronze 15th-century baptismal font designed by Jacopo della Quercia (1374–1438). It's adorned with bas-reliefs by various artists, including two by Renaissance masters: the *Baptism of Christ* by Lorenzo Ghiberti (1378–1455) and the *Feast of Herod* by Donatello. *Entrance on Piazza San Giovanni* ☎ *No phone* 💰 *€3* ⊙ *Mar. 15–Sept. 30, daily 9–7:30; Oct. 1–Oct. 31, daily 9–6; Nov. 1–Mar. 14, daily 10:30–1 and 2–5.*

⑩ Casa di Santa Caterina. Caterina Benincasa was born here in 1347, and although she took the veil of the Dominican Tertiary order at age eight, she lived here, devoting her life to the sick and poor in the aftermath of the devastating plague of 1348. She had divine visions and received the stigmata, but is most famous for her words and her argumentative skills. Her letters—many of which are preserved in the Biblioteca Comunale—were dictated because she did not know how to write. She is credited with convincing the Pope (the Frenchman Gregory XI, 1329–78) to return the papacy to Rome after 70 years in Avignon and French domination, ending the Western Schism. Caterina died in Rome in 1380 and was canonized in 1461. A few years later she was made patron saint of Siena, and the city purchased the family house and turned it into a shrine, one of the first examples of its kind in Italy. The rooms of the house, including her cell and the kitchen, were converted into a series of chapels and oratories and decorated by noteworthy artists over the following centuries with scenes from Caterina's life. In 1939 she was made a patron saint of Italy, along with St. Francis of Assisi. In 1970 she was elevated to Doctor of the Church, the highest possible honor in Christendom. ⊠ *Entrance on Costa di San Antonio, off Via della Sapienza, Camollia* ☎ *0577/280801* ☞ *Free* ☉ *Daily 9–1 and 3–5:30.*

④ Cripta. After it had lain unseen for possibly 700 years, a crypt was rediscovered under the grand *pavimento* (floor) of the Duomo during routine excavation work and was opened to the public in the fall of 2003. An unknown master executed the breath-taking frescoes here sometime between 1270–1280; they retain their original colors and pack an emotional punch even with sporadic paint loss. The *Deposition/Lamentation* gives strong evidence that the Sienese school could paint emotion just as well as the Florentine school—and do it some 20 years before Giotto. Guided tours in English take place more or less every half hour and are limited to no more than 35 persons. ⊠ *Piazza del Duomo, Città* ☎ *0577/ 283048* ⊕ *www.operaduomo.it* ☞ *€6* ☉ *Mar. 15–Sept. 30, daily 9–7:30; Oct., daily 9–6; Nov.–Mar. 14, daily 9–1:30.*

Fodor'sChoice
★

★ **③ Duomo.** Siena's Duomo is beyond question one of the finest Gothic cathedrals in Italy. The multicolored marbles and painted decoration are typical of the Italian approach to Gothic architecture—lighter and much less austere than the French. The amazingly detailed facade has few rivals in the region, although it's quite similar to the Duomo in Orvieto. It was completed in two brief phases at the end of the 13th and 14th centuries. The statues and decorative work were designed by Niccolo and Giovanni Pisano, although most of what we see today are copies, the originals having been removed to the nearby Museo dell'Opera Metropolitana for protection. The gold mosaics are 18th-century restorations. The Campanile (no entry) is among central Italy's finest, with the number of windows increasing with each level.

The Duomo's interior, with its black-and-white striping throughout and finely coffered and gilded dome, is simply striking. Step in and look back up at Duccio's (circa 1255–1319) panels of stained glass that fill the circular facade window. Finished in 1288, it's the oldest example of stained glass in Italy. The Duomo is most famous for its unique and magnificent inlaid marble floors, which took almost 200 years to complete (beginning around 1370); more than 40 artists contributed to the work, made up of 56 separate compositions depicting biblical scenes, allegories, religious symbols, and civic emblems. The floors are covered for most of the year for conservation purposes, but are unveiled every September for the entire month. The Duomo's carousel pulpit, also much appreciated, was carved by Nicola Pisano (circa 1220–84) around 1265; the *Life of Christ* is depicted on the rostrum frieze. In striking contrast to all the Gothic decoration in the nave are the magnificent Renaissance frescoes in the **Biblioteca Piccolomini,** off the left aisle. Painted by Pinturicchio (circa 1454–1513) and completed in 1509, they depict events from the life of native son Aeneas Sylvius Piccolomini (1405–64), who became Pope Pius II in 1458. The frescoes are in excellent condition and have a freshness rarely seen in work so old.

The Duomo is grand, but the medieval Sienese people had even bigger plans. They wanted to enlarge the building by using the existing church as a transept for a new church, with a new nave running toward the southeast, to make what would be the largest church in the world. But only the side wall and part of the new facade were completed when the Black Death struck in 1348, decimating Siena's population. The city fell into decline, funds dried up, and the plans were never carried out. (The dream of building the biggest church was actually doomed to failure from the start—subsequent attempts to get the project going revealed that the foundation was insufficient to bear the weight of the proposed structure.) The beginnings of the new nave, extending from the right side of the Duomo, were left unfinished, perhaps as a testament to unfulfilled dreams, and ultimately enclosed to house the adjacent ⇨ **Museo dell'Opera Metropolitana.** The ⇨ **Cripta** was discovered during routine preservation work on the church and has been opened to the public. ✉ *Piazza del Duomo, Città* ☎ *0577/283048* ▣ *€3* ◷ *Mar.–Oct., Mon.–Sat. 10:30–7:30, Sun. 1:30–6:30; Nov.–Feb., Mon.–Sat. 10:30–6:30, Sun. 1:30–5:30.*

❻ **Museo dell'Opera Metropolitana.** Built into part of the unfinished nave of what was to have been a new cathedral, the museum contains the Duomo's treasury and some of the original decoration from its facade and interior. The first room on the ground floor displays weather-beaten 13th-century sculptures by Giovanni Pisano (circa 1245–1318) that were brought inside for protection and replaced by copies, as was a tondo of the *Madonna and Child* (now attributed to Donatello) that once hung on the door to the south transept. The masterpiece is unquestionably Duccio's *Maestà,* one side with 26 panels depicting episodes from the Passion, the other side with a *Madonna and Child Enthroned.* Painted between 1308 and 1311 as the altarpiece for the Duomo (where it remained until 1505), its realistic elements, such as the lively depiction of the Christ child and the treatment of interior space, proved an enormous influence on later painters. The second floor is divided between the treasury, with a crucifix by Giovanni Pisano and several statues and busts of biblical characters and classical philosophers, and La Sala della Madonna degli Occhi Grossi (the Room of the Madonna with the Big Eyes), named after the namesake painting it displays by the Maestro di Tressa, who painted in the early 13th century. The work originally decorated the Duomo's high altar, before being displaced by Duccio's *Maestà.* There is a fine view from the tower inside the museum. ✉ *Piazza del Duomo, Città* ☎ *0577/283048* ▣ *€6* ◷ *Mid-Mar.–Sept., daily 9–7:30; Oct., daily 9–6; Nov.–mid-Mar., daily 9–1:30.*

Orto Botanico. Siena's botanical garden is a great place to relax and enjoy views onto the countryside below. Guided tours in English are available by reservation. ✉ *Via Pier Andrea Mattioli 4, Città* ☎ *0577/232874* 💰 *$8* ⊘ *Weekdays 8–12:30 and 2:30–5, Saturday 8–noon.*

★ ❷ **Palazzo Pubblico.** Considered Italy's finest Gothic town hall, Palazzo Pubblico has been the symbol of the city and the seat of its government for almost 700 years. Several of the rooms are decorated with some of Italy's finest early Renaissance frescoes. The main doorway opens onto the Cortile del Podestà (Courtyard of the Podestà), at the left of which is the entrance to the Torre del Mangia. The Magazzini del Sale (salt warehouses), where salt—once a precious commodity—was kept safe, are now used for temporary exhibits.

To the right of the Cortile del Podestà is the entrance to the **Museo Civico.** The first room is the Sala del Risorgimento, with 19th-century panels telling the story of Italian unification. Cut through to the main hall, the Sala del Mappamondo, named for a circular frescoed map of the Sienese state by Ambrogio Lorenzetti (documented to be working 1319–48), now lost. The room holds Simone Martini's (circa 1284–1344) early 14th-century *Maestà,* as well as an equestrian portrait fresco of *Guidoriccio da Fogliano,* which has also been attributed to him.

The next room in the museum, the Sala della Pace (Hall of Peace), is decorated by the largest secular pictorial cycle of the Middle Ages and one of Italy's greatest fresco cycles, the *Allegories of Good and Bad Government,* painted by Ambrogio Lorenzetti in 1337–39 on three walls. The Council of Nine commissioned him to decorate the room in which they met, perhaps to be ever reminded of the right thing to do. When you walk in you immediately face the *Mal Governo e i suoi effetti* (Bad Government and its effects). The figure of Tyranny is surrounded by a nasty bunch of negative attributes: Avarice, Pride, and Vanity hang in the air, while Cruelty, Deceit, Fraud, Fury, Discord, and War sit on either side, fondling strange animals. Interestingly, the Bad Government fresco is severely damaged. You can barely make out the figure of Justice (all tied up), her scales lying on the ground, but the conditions in the town leave little doubt as to the results of bad government: buildings in ruin, brutal soldiers everywhere, the landscape barren. Note that this was the view that visitors had on entering the room, only then turning to see the Council of Nine and the effects of their good government.

If you turn around, directly opposite is *Effetti del Buon Governo in città e in campagna* (Effects of Good Government in the city and the country). The wise old man dressed in the colors of the *comune,* represents the town council. At his feet are the twin sons of Remus, one of whom, according to legend, founded Siena. Hovering above his head are the three theological virtues: Faith, Charity, and Hope. To his sides are the virtues of good government (left to right, Peace, Force, Prudence, Magnanimity, Temperance, and Justice), each holding corresponding symbols. To the left is the figure of Justice, looking up at Wisdom while balancing her scales. The left side represents commutative justice (the distribution of wealth and power) and the right, distributive justice (the absolution of the innocent and punishment of the guilty). In the foreground are the town's 24 magistrates, who hold cords connecting them to the scales. Also included in the scene are those who execute the orders of the government (the soldiers) and those who oppose it (the prisoners); the fresco is in terrific condition. On the entrance wall is a city scene that depicts the effects of good government—easily identified as a utopian view of 14th-century Siena. The painting is full of bright, vibrant colors; well-maintained buildings; happy, productive people; and a rich fertile landscape outside the town.

The next rooms in the museum have more frescoes by Sienese artists from the 13th to 15th century, including frescoes attributed to Ambrogio Lorenzetti (*San Michele Arcangelo*) and Neroccio di Bartolomeo (1447–1500; *Predica di San Bernardino*). Off the Sala del Mappamondo is the Antechapel, with frescoes by Taddeo di Bartolo (circa 1362–1422), and the adjacent chapel with marvelous inlaid-wood choir stalls.

Built to the height of the Duomo's Campanile, thereby asserting the power of temporal rule, the **Torre del Mangia** is 330-ft tall, making it the second tallest in Italy. Its curious name comes from one of the tower's first bell ringers, Giovanni di Duccio (called Mangiaguadagni, or earnings eater). The climb up to the top is long and steep, but the superb view makes it worth every step. ⊠ *Piazza del Campo 1, Città* ☎ *0577/ 292226* 🖭 *Museo €7, torre €6, combined ticket €10* ☉ *Museo Mar. 16–Oct., daily 10–7; Nov.–Mar. 15, daily 10–6:30. Torre Mar. 16–Oct., daily 10–7; Nov.–Mar. 15, daily 10–4.*

★ ⌐ ❶ **Piazza del Campo.** Built in the 14th century on a market area that was originally the site of the Roman Forum, this fan-shape square is known simply as Il Campo (the Field). Unclaimed by any contrada, it was neutral ground and thus the logical place to set up the town government. Strips in gray stone divide the brick pavement into nine sections—one for each of the medieval Council of Nine, which fan out from the Palazzo Pubblico. Now most associated with the running of the Palio (it's hard to walk very far in Siena without seeing a poster or calendar of the twice-yearly horse race), the Campo remains the heart of Sienese life all year long. It's a pleasant place to take a rest and enjoy one of the greatest examples of medieval city planning. The surrounding buildings received neo-Gothic facades in the 19th century that evoke the original appearance of the Campo, although the daily market was relocated. Several openings lead out to the main streets of the three zones of the city. At the top of the Campo is the **Fonte Gaia,** a fountain decorated in the early 15th century by Siena's greatest sculptor, Jacopo della Quercia, with 13 reliefs of biblical events and virtues. The reliefs you see today are 19th-century copies; the originals are in the Spedale di Santa Maria della Scala.

❽ **Pinacoteca Nazionale.** The superb collection of five centuries of local painting in Siena's national picture gallery can easily convince you that the Renaissance was by no means just a Florentine thing—Siena was arguably just as important a center of art and innovation as its rival to the north, especially in the mid-13th century. Accordingly, the most interesting section of the collection, chronologically arranged, has several important "firsts." Room 1 contains a painting of the *Stories of the True Cross* (1215) by the so-called Master of Tressa, the earliest identified work by a painter of the Sienese school, and is followed in Room 2 by late-13th-century artist Guido da Siena's *Stories from the Life of Christ,* one of the first paintings ever made on canvas (earlier painters used wood panels). Rooms 3 and 4 are dedicated to Duccio, a student of Cimabue (circa 1240–1302) and considered to be the last of the proto-Renaissance painters. Ambrogio Lorenzetti's landscapes in Room 8 are the first truly secular paintings in Western art. Among later works in the rooms on the floor above, keep an eye out for the preparatory sketches used by Domenico Beccafumi (1486–1551) for the 35 etched marble panels he made for the floor of the Duomo. ⊠ *Via San Pietro 29, Città* ☎ *0577/ 281161* ⊑ *€4* ⊙ *Sun. and Mon. 8:30 AM–1:15 PM, Tues.–Sat. 8:30–7:15.*

❾ San Domenico. While the Duomo is celebrated as a triumph of 13th-century Gothic architecture, this church, built at about the same time, turned out as an oversize, hulking brick box that never merited a finishing coat in marble, let alone a graceful facade. Named for the founder of the Dominican order, the church is now more closely associated with St. Catherine of Siena. Just to the right of the entrance is the chapel in which she received the stigmata. On the wall is the only known contemporary portrait of the saint, made in the late 14th century by Andrea Vanni (circa 1332–1414). Farther down is the famous **Cappella di Santa Caterina,** the church's official shrine. Catherine, or bits and pieces of her, was literally spread all over the country—a foot is in Venice, most of her body is in Rome, and only her head and finger are here (kept in a reliquary on the altar). She was revered throughout the country long before she was officially named a patron saint of Italy in 1939. On either side of the chapel are well-known frescoes by Sodoma (aka Giovanni Antonio Bazzi, 1477–1549) of *St. Catherine in Ecstasy.* Don't miss the view of the Duomo and town center from the apse-side terrace. ⊠ *Costa di Sant'Antonio, Camollia* ☎ *0577/280893* ⊙ *Mid-Mar.–Oct., daily 7–1 and 2:30–6:30; Nov.–mid-Mar., daily 9–1 and 3–6.*

> **need a break?**
>
> Not far from the church of San Domenico, the **Enoteca Italiana** (⊠ Fortezza Medicea, Viale Maccari, Camollia ☎ 0577/288497) is a fantastically stocked wine cellar in the bastions of the Fortezza Medici. The *enoteca* (wine bar) sells wines by the glass and snacks. Take some time to peruse the labels that are on the shelves (the wines of more than 400 wineries are in stock here). It's open daily from noon to 1 AM. On Friday evenings in winter there's also a piano bar.

Sinagoga. Down a small street around the corner from Il Campo, this synagogue is worth a visit simply to view the two sobering plaques that adorn its facade. One commemorates June 28, 1799, when 13 Jews were taken from their homes in the ghetto by a fanatic mob and burned in Il Campo. The other memorializes the Sienese Jews who were deported, and never returned, during World War II. Guided tours in English are available by arrangement. ⊠ *Vicolo delle Scotte 14, San Martino* ☎ *0577/284647* ⊙ *Sun. 10–1 and 2–5.*

❼ Spedale di Santa Maria della Scala. For more than a thousand years, this complex across from the Duomo was home to Siena's hospital, but now it serves as a museum to display some terrific frescoes and other Sienese Renaissance treasures. Restored 15th-century frescoes in the Sala del Pellegrinaio (once the emergency room) tell the history of the hospital, which was created to give refuge to passing pilgrims and to those in need and to distribute charity to the poor. Incorporated into the complex is the church of the Santissima Annunziata, with a celebrated *Risen Christ* by Vecchietta (also known as Lorenzo di Pietro, circa 1412–80). Down in the dark Cappella di Santa Caterina della Notte is where St. Catherine went to pray at night. The subterranean archaeological museum contained within the *ospedale* (hospital) is worth seeing even if you're not particularly taken with Etruscan objects: the interior design is sheer brilliance—it's beautifully lighted, eerily quiet, and an oasis of cool on hot summer days. The displays—including the *bucchero* (dark, reddish clay) ceramics, Roman coins, and tomb furnishings—are clearly marked and can serve as a good introduction to the history of regional excavations. Don't miss della Quercia's original sculpted reliefs from the Fonte Gaia. Although the fountain has been faithfully copied for the Campo, there's something incomparably beautiful about the real thing. ⊠ *Piazza del Duomo, Città* 🕾 *0577/224811* 🎟 *€5.20* ☉ *Mar. 17–Oct. and Dec. 24–Jan. 6, daily 10–6; Jan. 7–Mar. 16 and Nov.–Dec. 23, daily 10:30–4:30.*

Where to Stay & Eat

★ **$$$–$$$$**   ✕ **Antica Trattoria Botteganova.** Just outside the city walls, 2 km (1 mi) north along the road that leads to Chianti, is arguably the best restaurant in Siena. Chef Michele Sorrentino's cooking is all about clean flavors, balanced combinations, and inviting presentation. Look for inspiring dishes such as spaghetti *alla chitarra in salsa di astice piccante* (spaghetti with a spicy lobster sauce). The interior, with high vaulting, is relaxed yet classy, and the service is first rate. There's a small room for nonsmokers. ⊠ *Strada per Montevarchi (SS408) 29, 2 km (1mi) northeast of Siena* 🕾 *0577/284230* 🖃 *AE, DC, MC, V* ☉ *Closed Sun.*

$$–$$$ ✕ **Le Logge.** Bright flowers provide dashes of color in this classic Tuscan dining room with stenciled designs on the ceilings. The wooden cupboards (now filled with wine bottles) lining the walls recall the turn-of-the-19th-century food store it first was. The menu, with four or five *primi* (first courses) and *secondi* (second courses) changes regularly, but almost always includes their classic *malfatti all'osteria* (ricotta and spinach dumplings in a cream sauce). Desserts such as *coni con mousse al cioccolato e gelato allo zafferano* (two diminutive ice cream cones with chocolate mousse and saffron ice cream) provide an inventive ending to the meal. ⊠ *Via del Porrione 33, San Martino* 🕾 *0577/48013* 🖃 *AE, DC, MC, V* ☉ *Closed Sun. and 3 wks in Jan.*

$–$$ ✕ **Hosteria il Carroccio.** Angle for one of the few seats here to have an intimate meal and to try dishes both creative and deliciously simple. The *palline di pecorino con lardo e salsa di pere* (pecorino cheese balls wrapped with pork fat and briefly grilled), for instance, are sublime. So, too, are the amply proportioned primi—the *pici* (a local pasta specialty resembling a thick spaghetti) is especially good. Sit at tables outside in

DUST NEVER SETTLES ON THE PALIO

JUST THREE LAPS AROUND A MAKESHIFT TRACK in Piazza del Campo, and it's all over in less than two minutes, but the spirit of Siena's Palio—the horse race that takes place every July 2 and August 16—lives all year long.

The first recorded race was run on August 16, 1310, and another Palio on July 2 was added in 1649. Soon after the event moved to the Campo (it had previously been run through the streets of the town), the current system for selecting the race entrants was established. In the system, 10 of Siena's 17 contrade (neighborhood divisions) are chosen at random to run in the July Palio. The August Palio is run with 3 of those 10 plus the 7 contrade left out the first time. Although the races are officially of equal importance, any Sienese will tell you that it's better to win the second Palio and have bragging rights for the rest of the year.

At first it might not seem like much of a race: there is barely room for the 10 horses along the course, so falls and collisions are inevitable. The competing contrade root emphatically for nameless horses (chosen at random three days before the race) and jockeys from other towns hired by each contrada. At stake is the respect or scorn of the neighboring and rival contrade, and the event is so important to the Sienese that almost nothing is too underhanded. Bribery, secret plotting, and betrayal are commonplace (so much so that the word for "jockey" in Italian, fantino, has come to mean "untrustworthy" in Siena). There have been incidents of drugging (the horses) and kidnapping (the jockeys); only sabotaging a horse's reins remains taboo.

Official festivities kick off three days prior to the Palio, with the selection and blessing of the horses, trial runs, ceremonial banquets, betting, speculation, and late-night celebrations. Residents don scarves with their contrada's colors and march through the streets in medieval costumes. The Campo is transformed into a racecourse lined with a thick layer of yellow sand. In the early afternoon each horse is brought to the church of the contrada for which it will run, where it's blessed and told "Go little horse and return a winner." The piazza begins to fill in the mid-afternoon, and spectators crowd into every available space until bells ring and the piazza is sealed off. Processions of flag wavers in traditional dress march to the beat of tambourines and drums and the roar of the crowds. The palio itself, a banner dedicated to the Virgin Mary, makes an appearance, followed by the competitors and their jockeys.

The race is set off by one horse chosen to ride up from behind, but there are always a number of false starts, adding to the already frenzied mood. Finally the horses are off, and the race is over almost before the dust settles. The winning rider is carried away on the shoulders of his jubilant supporters, back to the streets of the winning contrada, where in the past tradition dictated that the victory entitled him to the local girl of his choice. But the celebration is far from over. TV replays, winners, and losers go over the race from every possible angle—but only one contrada will celebrate long into the night, with long tables piled high with food and drink, the champion horse the guest of honor.

Note that the reserved seating in the stands is sold out months in advance of the races. The entire area in the center is free, but you need to show up early in order to secure a prime spot against the barriers. For ticket information, see Sports & the Outdoors in Siena.

summer. ⊠ *Via Casato di Sotto 32, Città* ☎ *0577/41165* ☰ *MC, V* ⊘ *Closed Wed.*

$–$$ ✕ **La Taverna di San Giuseppe.** You have to know about this place to find it on a residential street with very few tourist attractions, though it's near the Campo. The one long, cavernous dining room is crowded mostly with people speaking Italian. The menu is full of Tuscan favorites with a Sienese twist, including prosciutto *di cinta senese* (made from a local, long black and white pig, once nearly extinct, that has a band around its belly hence *cinta*, meaning belt). The restaurant also makes a version of *fegatini* (chicken livers) with spleen that's aromatic and flavorful. ⊠ *Via G. Duprè 132, San Martino* ☎ *0577/42286* ☰ *AE, DC, MC, V* ⊘ *Closed Sun.*

⟳ **$–$$**   ✕ **Osteria del Coro.** Chef–owner Stefano Azzi promotes local fare, uses
FodorśChoice   age-old Sienese recipes, and backs it all up with a stellar wine list. His
★   *pici con le briciole alla mio modo* (thick spaghetti with breadcrumbs), liberally dressed with fried *cinta senese* (a bacon made from the local, long, stout pig), dazzles. Pizza at lunch and dinner ensures the happiness of the junior set. In fact, the place was once a pizzeria, and it retains its unadorned, unpretentious air—you certainly wouldn't come because of the furnishings. ⊠ *Via Pantaneto 85–87* ☎ *0577/222482* ⌁ *Reservations essential* ☰ *No credit cards.*

$ ✕ **Osteria Castelvecchio.** On the daily-changing menu you're likely to find both Sienese standards, such as spaghetti *saporiti con gli aromi* (with tomatoes and herbs), as well as more offbeat selections such as *bocconcini di pollo alla mediterranea* (tender chicken cooked in a robust tomato-and-olive sauce). Husband-and-wife proprietors Simone Romi and Sabrina Fabi are committed to including *piatti di verdura* (vegetarian dishes) among the choices, and they've got a great wine list. A tasting menu allows you to sample just about all the daily specials. The little restaurant with high, ribbed vaults (crisscrossing arches) is in the oldest part of town. ⊠ *Via Castelvecchio 65, Città* ☎ *0577/49586* ☰ *AE, DC, MC, V* ⊘ *Closed Tues.*

¢   ✕ **da Trombicche.** Wiped out from too much sight-seeing? Consider a simple, invigorating meal at in this one-room hole-in-the-wall where locals congregrate to drink cheap, red wine and discuss sports. The collection of *verdure sott'olio* (marinated vegetables) refreshes, as does the list of daily specials reflecting the season. They do simple, tasty things with eggs here (the frittata is exceptional), and their plates of *affetati misti* (sliced, cured meats) is a bargain. So, too, are the made-to-order *panini* (sandwiches). All of this can be washed down with the eminently drinkable house red. ⊠ *Via delle Terme 66, Camollìa* ☎ *0577/288089* ☰ *No credit cards* ⊘ *Closed Sun.*

★ **$$**   ✕▥ **Palazzo Ravizza.** The pretty and romantic Palazzo Ravizza exudes a sense of gentile shabbiness. Rooms have high ceilings, antique furniture, upholstered headboards, and bathrooms decorated with hand-painted tiles. The chef at Il Capriccioso, Giuseppe Mora, is a young Sicilian trained in Switzerland. His innovative food, like the *fagottini di foglia di riso farcito con gamberi* (rice paper bundles stuffed with shrimp and sauced with basil), shows a deep knowledge of Italian cuisine as well as the world outside. In warm weather, enjoy your meal in the garden with a trickling fountain. From here it's just a 10-minute walk to the Duomo. ⊠ *Pian dei Mantellini 34, Città, 53100* ☎ *0577/280462* ☎ *0577/221597* ⊕ *www.palazzoravizza.it* ⌁ *40 rooms, 4 suites* ⌂ *Restaurant, some in-room safes, some minibars, cable TV, bar, laundry service, concierge, free parking, some pets allowed* ⊟ *AE, DC, MC, V* ⍾ *BP.*

$$$$ ☷ **Certosa di Maggiano.** A 14th-century monastery has been converted into an upscale country hotel. Rooms have the style and comfort of an aristocratic villa, with classic prints and bold colors such as daffodil yellow. Common rooms are luxurious, with fine woods and leather. In warm weather, breakfast is served on the patio next to the garden ablaze with flowers. The officious staff is a drawback. ⊠ *Siena Sud exit off Superstrada, Via Certosa 82, ½ km (1 mi) east of Siena, 53100* ☎ *0577/288180* ☎ *0577/288189* ⊕ *www.certosadimaggiano.it* ⌁ *6 rooms, 11 suites* ⌂ *Restaurant, minibars, cable TV, tennis court, pool, exercise equipment, dry cleaning, laundry service, concierge, helipad, no-smoking rooms; no kids under 12* ⊟ *AE, MC, V* ⍾ *MAP.*

$$$$ ☷ **Grand Hotel Continental.** Pope Alexander VII of the famed Sienese Chigi family gave this palace to his niece as a wedding present in 1600; through the centuries it has been a private family home as well as a grand hotel. It exudes elegance, from the pillared entrance to the linen sheets. Some guest rooms take in panoramic views, while others have 18th-century frescos and massive chandeliers. A shuttle makes constant runs to the nearby Park Hotel, which shares its golf and pool facilities with the Grand. The excellent staff is reason enough to consider a stay here. ⊠ *Banchi di Sopra 85, Camollìa, 53100* ☎ *0577/56011* ☎ *0577/5601555* ⊕ *www.royaldemeure.com* ⌁ *40 rooms, 11 suites* ⌂ *Restaurant, room service, in-room data ports, in-room safes, some in-room hot tubs, minibars, cable TV with movies, some in-room VCRs, golf privileges, piano bar, wine bar, baby-sitting, dry cleaning, laundry service, concierge, Internet, business services, meeting rooms, parking (fee), some pets allowed, no-smoking rooms* ⊟ *AE, DC, MC, V* ⍾ *BP.*

$$$$ ☷ **Park.** What began life in the 16th century as a home for the prosperous Gori family is now an elegant hotel a short ride from the centro storico. Many of the rooms—with plush carpeting, large bathrooms, and flowered drapery—face a courtyard complete with a well and a stunning view of olive trees and Siena beyond. Public rooms have soaring ceilings, highly polished terra-cotta floors, and comfortable couches. The Olivo restaurant serves regional cuisine, and the hot breakfast buffet includes splendid scrambled eggs. Staff members are extraordinarily helpful and polite. ⊠ *Via Marciano 18, 1 km (½ mi) north of Siena, 53100* ☎ *0577/290290* ☎ *0577/49020* ⊕ *www.royaldemeure.com* ⌁ *65 rooms, 1 suite* ⌂ *Restaurant, room service, minibars, cable TV, 6-hole golf course, tennis court, pool, bar, baby-sitting, dry cleaning, laundry service, concierge, Internet, business services, meeting rooms, free parking, some pets allowed, no-smoking rooms* ⊟ *AE, DC, MC, V* ⊗ *Closed Nov.–Mar.* ⍾ *BP.*

$$ ☷ **Borgo Pretale.** A small hamlet hidden in the hills to the south of Siena has been converted into this delightful hotel. Surrounded by open fields and rolling woodlands, Borgo Pretale is an amazingly tranquil place to stay, but close enough to Siena to be a base of exploration. Rooms vary in size, but all are elegantly furnished with traditional fabrics—florals and stripes—and furniture, including some canopy beds. One room of the restaurant (closed Monday) has a wall of windows looking out into the countryside. ⊠ *Località Pretale, 53018 Sovicille, 11 km (7 mi) east of Siena* ☎ *0577/345401* 🖷 *0577/345625* ⊕ *www.borgopretale.it* ⇨ *30 rooms, 5 suites* ♘ *Restaurant, tennis court, pool, gym, bicycles, bar, meeting rooms* ▭ *AE, D, MC, V* ⊙ *Closed Nov.–Easter* ⑩ *CP.*

★ **$$** 🏨 **Hotel Santa Caterina.** Manager Lorenza Capannelli and her fine staff are welcoming, hospitable, enthusiastic, and go out of their way to ensure a fine stay. Dark, straight-lined wood furniture stands next to beds with floral spreads; some have coordinating, upholstered headboards. Rooms in the back look out onto the garden or the countryside in the distance. When it's warm, breakfast is served on the flower-filled garden with a view of the Siena countryside, providing a gorgeous start to the day. The well-run hotel is outside Porta Romana—a 10-minute walk south of the Campo. ⊠ *Via Piccolomini 7, San Martino, 53100* ☎ *0577/221105* 🖷 *0577/271087* ⊕ *www.hscsiena.it* ⇨ *22 rooms* ♘ *Minibars, cable TV, baby-sitting, dry cleaning, laundry service, concierge, parking (fee), some pets allowed, no-smoking rooms* ▭ *AE, DC, MC, V* ⑩ *BP.*

$ 🏨 **Antica Torre.** The cordial Landolfo family has carefully evoked a private home with their eight guest rooms inside a restored 16th-century tower. Simply but tasteful furnished rooms have ornate, delicate-looking iron headboards, usually atop twin beds. The old stone staircase, large wooden beams, wood shutters, and original brick vaults here and there are reminders of the building's great age. Antica Torre is in a southeast corner of Siena, a 10-minute walk from Piazza del Campo. ⊠ *Via Fieravecchia 7, San Martino, 53100* ☎🖷 *0577/222255* ⊕ *www. anticatorresiena.it* ⇨ *8 rooms* ♘ *Cable TV, parking (fee)* ▭ *AE, DC, MC, V* ⑩ *BP.*

$ 🏨 **Chiusarelli.** Caryatids stud the grounds of this well-kept neoclassical villa; a small garden invites reading. Guest rooms are functional, airy, and reasonably quiet, but the handy location—near the long-distance bus terminal and parking area, and minutes away from the main sights—is the big plus here, that and the pleasant staff. Single rooms are not the usual monastic-cell size; the place is amenable to groups. Head downstairs to the restaurant for inexpensive meals. ⊠ *Viale Curtatone 15, Camollia 53100* ☎ *0577/280562* 🖷 *0577/271177* ⊕ *www.chiusarelli. com* ⇨ *48 rooms, 1 suite* ♘ *Restaurant, in-room safes, cable TV, bar, lobby lounge, Internet, meeting rooms, free parking, some pets allowed, no-smoking rooms* ▭ *AE, MC, V* ⑩ *BP.*

¢ 🏨 **Alma Domus.** If you're after a contemplative, utilitarian experience, seek out the lodging run by the committed parishioners of the Santurario Santa Caterina (Sanctuary of St. Catherine); it's just around the corner from the church of San Domenico. Rooms in the former convent are spartan and very clean, but not overly small or cell-like. Many have a view of the Duomo and the rest of Siena, which might make the 11:30 curfew liveable. ⊠ *Via Camporeggio 37, Camollia, 53100* ☎ *0577/ 44177* 🖷 *0577/47601* ⇨ *31 rooms* ♘ *No-smoking floors; no a/c, no room phones, no room TVs* ▭ *No credit cards.*

Nightlife & the Arts

The Arts

Performances of local and other classical musicians take place during a series of concerts held in churches and courtyards during the **Settimane Musicali Senesi festival** festival in the middle of July.

Estate Musicale Chigiana (⊠ Accademia Musicale Chigiana, Via di Città 89, Città ☎ 0577/22091 ⊕ www.chigiana.it) sponsors master classes and workshops during July and August, and concerts are held from June through August. Age-old venues such as Santa Maria della Scala and the church of Sant'Agostino provide the stages.

Nightlife

Join the locals for *aperitivi* (apertifs) at **Caffè del Corso** (⊠ Banchi di Sopra 22, Camollìa ☎ No phone), where aspiring artists, area workers, and savvy students hobnob until 3 AM. A happening local hangout, **L'Officina** (⊠ Piazza del Sale 3, Camollìa ☎ 0577/286301) has live music on Thursday. The other nights, DJs spin different sounds, from Latin-inspired rhythms to dance and rock. The wine bar at **Sapordivino** (⊠ Banchi di Sopra 85, Città ☎ 0577/56011) in the Grand Hotel Continental has live piano music most evenings. A well-stocked liquor collection includes a well-thought-out list of whiskeys.

Sports & the Outdoors

Siena's thrilling **Palio** (⊠ Siena Tourist Office, Piazza del Campo 56, Città ☎ 0577/280551) horse race takes place every year on July 2 and August 16. Three laps around the track in the Piazza del Campo earn participants of the Palio the respect or scorn of the other 16 contrade. Tickets usually sell out months in advance; call the Siena tourist office for more information. Note that some hotels reserve a number of tickets for guests. It's also possible you might luck out and get an unclaimed seat or two. The standing-room center of the piazza is free to all on a first-come, first-served basis, until just moments before the start.

Shopping

Siena is known for a delectable variety of cakes and cookies with recipes dating back to medieval times. Some Sienese sweets are *cavallucci* (sweet spice biscuits), *panforte* (a traditional Christmas delicacy, literally "stong bread," with honey, hazelnuts, almonds, and spices), *ricciarelli* (almond-paste cookies), and *castagnaccio* (a baked Tuscan flat cake made in the fall and winter from a batter of chestnut flour topped with pine nuts and rosemary).

Arts & Crafts

Embroidered linens, shawls, kitchen towels, tablecloths, curtains, and sheets are among the housewares sold here at **Antiche Dimore** (⊠ Via di Città 115, Città ☎ 0577/45337). The products are made by Sienese artisans. If you've always wanted a 14th- or 15th-century painting to hang on your walls, but costs of acquiring one are prohibitive, consider purchasing one of the superb copies at **Bottega dell'Arte** (⊠ Via Stalloreggi

47, Città ☎ 0577/40755) made by Chiara Perinetti Casoni. Her work in tempera and in gold leaf is of the highest quality.

At **Fioretta Bacci** (✉ Via San Pietro 7, Città ☎ 0577/282200), wool, mohair, silk, linen, and cotton are woven on site, and turned into sweaters and jackets in the colors of the rainbow. **Siena Ricama** (✉ Via di Città 61, Città ☎ 0577/288339) has been famous for centuries for its fine embroidery work, and Bruna Brizza continues the tradition in her tiny shop. Handstitching, usually on simple white and cream-color linen, adorns lampshades, tablecloths, and other housewares.

Tapestries, kilims, Oriental rugs, curtains, fabrics, and trimmings—both contemporary and ancient—fill **Tappezzerie Lippi** (✉ Via dei Termini 21-25, Camollìa ☎ 0577/280633). The store also has upholstered sofas and chairs. Stained-glass artists create and sell contemporary secular and religious works at **Vetrate Artistiche Toscane** (✉ Via della Galluzza 5, Camollìa ☎ 0577/48033).

Food & Drink

Antico Pizzicheria (✉ Via di Città 93-95, Città ☎ 0577/289164) has been a *salumeria* (delicatessen) since 1889, and for the past 19 years it's been in the capable hands of Antonio De Miccoli. The cheeses, cured meats, and made-to-order panini are top-notch. Bruno De Miccoli stocks an impressive array of verdure sott'olio, local wines, and dried herbs at **La Bottega dei Sapori Antichi** (✉ Via delle Terme 39–41, Camollìa ☎ 0577/285501)

Enoteca Italiana (✉ Fortezza Medicea, Camollìa ☎ 0577/288497), Italy's only state-sponsored enoteca, has a vast selection of wines, though prices are not lower than at any other enoteca in town. Locals flock to Sienese bakery **Nannini** (✉ Banchi di Sopra 24, Camollìa ☎ 0577/236009) to quaff a cappuccino and to pick up panforte (the chocolate panforte is a real treat) and ricciarelli to go.

HILL TOWNS WEST OF SIENA
TOWARD VOLTERRA

From Siena the Via Cassia (SR2) heading northwest toward Volterra passes two pretty towns, Monteriggioni and Colle di Val d'Elsa; both are worth visiting. From there it's a short detour north to San Gimignano, which is known for its wine and medieval towers.

Monteriggioni

⓫ *19 km (12 mi) northwest of Siena, 55 km (34 mi) south of Florence.*

Tiny Monteriggioni makes a nice stop for a quiet walk on the way north to Colle di Val d'Elsa, San Gimignano, or Volterra. It's hard to imagine that this little town surrounded by open countryside and poppy fields was ever anything but sleepy. But in the 13th century Monteriggioni served as Siena's northernmost defense against impending Florentine invasion, so it's likely that the residents of the town spent many a sleepless night. The town's formidable walls are in good condition, although the 14 square towers are not as tall as in Dante's (1265–1321) time, when the poet likened them to the four giants who guarded the horrifying central pit of hell. The town empties of day-trippers at sundown, and this hamlet becomes very tranquil.

Where to Stay & Eat

$$ ✕ **Il Pozzo.** Dig into hearty Tuscan country cooking at this rustic tavern on the village square. The specialties are homemade fresh pasta, *filetto alla boscaiola* (fillet of Chianina beef with porcini mushrooms), *piccione ripieno* (stuffed squab), and homey desserts. ⊠ *Piazza Roma 2* ☎ *0577/ 304127* ⊟ *AE, DC, MC, V* ☽ *Closed Mon., Jan. 7–Feb. 7, and Aug. 1–7. No dinner Sun.*

¢ ✕ **Bar dell'Orso.** If you're driving on the Florence–Siena Superstrada, do stop at this bar handily positioned off the exit for Monteriggioni. Here they have a stunning array of Italian pork products, cheeses, and vegetables marinated in olive oil, all available for take-out or to be made into sandwiches served on thick, crusty bread. A couple of picnic tables outside provide a place to eat. ⊠ *Località La Colonna 23* ☎ *0577/305074* ⊟ *No credit cards* ☽ *Closed Wed. No dinner.*

$$$ ▦ **Borgo San Luigi.** The San Luigi occupies a 17th-century villa lined with lavender bushes and cypress trees outside Monteriggioni. The furnishings in the villa and the workers' quarters—converted into 10 apartments—have rustic, beam celings and terra-cotta floors. Festive striped fabric in yellows, oranges, and reds, covers iron canopies in some rooms. The facilities are those of a four-star establishment, such as room service, a gym, and tennis courts. A poolside restaurant is open in summer. ⊠ *Via della Cerretta 38, 53035 Località San Luigi Strove, 4 km (2½ mi) southwest of Monteriggioni* ☎ *0577/301055* ⊟ *0577/301167* ⊕ *www.borgosanluigi.it* ⊅ *54 rooms, 10 apartments* ⟁ *Restaurant, room service, in-room fax, in-room safes, some kitchenettes, minibars, cable TV, in-room VCRs, 2 tennis courts, pool, health club, billiards, Ping-Pong, bar, baby-sitting, concierge, business services, meeting rooms, some pets allowed* ⊟ *AE, DC, MC, V* ⎺⎺⎺ *CP.*

$$$ ▦ **Hotel Monteriggioni.** A sense of freshness comes from the terra-cotta–tile floors, high wood-beamed ceilings, and soothing white walls in the hotel's guest and public rooms. The serene garden, facing a town wall, is filled with oleanders, potted geraniums, and olive trees. ⊠ *Via I Maggio 4, 53035* ☎ *0577/305009* ⊟ *0577/305011* ⊕ *www. hotelmonteriggioni.net* ⊅ *12 rooms* ⟁ *Dining room, in-room data ports, in-room safes, minibars, cable TV, pool, dry cleaning, laundry service, some pets allowed, no-smoking rooms* ⊟ *AE, DC, MC, V* ☽ *Closed Jan. 9–Feb. 28* ⎺⎺⎺ *BP.*

Colle di Val d'Elsa

⑫ *12 km (7 mi) west of Monteriggioni, 25 km (16 mi) northwest of Siena, 51 km (32 mi) south of Florence.*

Most people pass right through on their way to and from popular tourist destinations Volterra and San Gimignano—a shame, since Colle di Val d'Elsa has a lot to offer. It's another town on the Via Francigena that benefited from trade along the pilgrimage route to Rome. Colle got an extra boost in the late 16th century when it was given a bishopric, probably related to an increase in trade when nearby San Gimignano was cut off from the well-traveled road. The town is arranged on two levels, and from the 12th century onward the flat lower portion was given over to a flourishing paper-making industry; today the area is mostly modern, and efforts have shifted toward the production of fine glass and crystal.

Make your way from the newer lower town (Colle Bassa) to the prettier, upper part of town (Colle Alta); the best views of the valley are to be had from Viale della Rimembranza, the road that loops around the west end of town, past the church of San Francesco. The early-16th-century Porta Nuova was inserted into the preexisting medieval walls, just as several handsome Renaissance palazzos were placed into the medieval neighborhood to create what is now called the Borgo. The Via Campana, the main road, passes through the facade of the surreal Palazzo Campana, an otherwise unfinished building that serves as a door connecting the two parts of the upper town. Via delle Volte, named for the vaulted arches that cover it, leads straight to Piazza del Duomo. There is a convenient parking lot off the SS68, with stairs leading up the hill. Buses arrive at Piazza Arnolfo, named after the town's favorite son, Arnolfo di Cambio (circa 1245–1302), the early-Renaissance architect who designed Florence's Duomo and Palazzo Vecchio (but sadly nothing here).

The 15th-century **Chiesa di Santa Caterina** has a stained-glass window in the main altar executed by Sebastiano Mainardi (circa 1460–1513), as well as a haunting terra-cotta, the *Pietà* created by local artist Zacchia Zacchi (1473-1544). ⊠ *Via Campana* 🕾 *No phone* 🎫 *Free* ☉ *Daily 8–noon and 3–6.*

Several reconstructions have left little of the once-Romanesque **Duomo** to admire. Inside is the **Cappella del Santo Chiodo** (Chapel of the Holy Nail), built in the 15th century to hold a nail allegedly from the cross upon which Christ was crucified. (Perhaps it inspired the locals to go into the nail-making business, which became another of the town's flourishing industries.) ⊠ *Piazza del Duomo* 🕾 *No phone* 🎫 *Free* ☉ *Daily 8–noon and 4–6.*

The **Museo Civico e d'Arte Sacra** displays religious relics as well as triptychs from the Sienese and Florentine schools dating from the 14th and 15th centuries. It also contains the town's tribute to Arnolfo di Cambio, with photos of the buildings he designed for other towns and some models of the town. Down Via del Castello, at No. 63, is the house-tower where Arnolfo was born in 1245. (It's not open to the public.) Do note that, despite the posted opening times, winter hours are highly variable. ⊠ *Via del Castello 33* 🕾 *0577/923888* 🎫 *€6* ☉ *Apr.–Oct., Tues.–Sun. 10:20–12:30 and 4:30–7:30; Nov.–Mar., weekends 10:30–12:30 and 3–7.*

Where to Stay & Eat

$$$$ ✕ **Ristorante Arnolfo.** Food lovers should not miss Arnolfo, one of Tuscany's most highly regarded restaurants. Chef Gaetano Trovato sets high standards of creativity; his dishes daringly ride the line between innovation and tradition, almost always with spectacular results. The menu changes frequently and has two fixed-price options, but you are always

Fodor's Choice ★

sure to find fish in the summer and lots of fresh vegetables and herbs. You're in for a special treat if *medaglioni di sogliola e gamberi rossi con finocchi allo zafferano* (sole and shrimp with fennel delicately flavored with saffron) is a choice when you visit. ✉ *Piazza XX Settembre 52* 📞📞 *0577/920549* 🖃 *AE, DC, MC, V* ⊗ *Closed Tues., mid-Jan.–mid-Feb., and 2 wks in Aug.*

$$$–$$$$ ✕ **L'Antica Trattoria.** Tuscan classics fill the large menu, which is strong on game, particularly fowl (pheasant, pigeon, and quail). Some of the pastas, such as *tortelli di sedano in purea di fagioli* (stuffed pasta with creamy celery and sauced with a light bean purèe) differ from the usual fare. The decor is simple; in warmer months outdoor seating on a square is a possibility. Service is first-rate, and residents of Colle Val d'Elsa hold this trattoria in high esteem, but it's a little over-priced. ✉ *Piazza Arnolfo di Cambio 23, Colle Basso* 📞 *0577/923747* ⌑ *Reservations essential* 🖃 *AE, DC, MC, V* ⊗ *Closed Tues.*

$–$$ ✕ **Il Frantoio.** Once the olive-oil pressing room of a Renaissance palace, this is now the place to come for culinary experimentation. The candlelit room is cavernous yet intimate, the daily menu's fresh pastas and meat savory. Everything that's put on the table is made in-house. If they could manage to augment that somewhat limited wine list, the place would be flawless. ✉ *Via del Castello 38* 📞 *0577/923652* 🖃 *MC, V* ⊗ *Closed Mon.*

$–$$ ✕ **Molino il Moro.** The early-12th-century grain mill, now a romantic restaurant, still perches over a rushing river. The chef concocts sophisticated spins on traditional Tuscan dishes, such as the divine *filetto di coniglio in crosta con purèe di pruge* (rabbit loin with a prune puree). The wine list is short but sweet, the service note-perfect. ✉ *Via della Ruota 2* 📞 *0577/920862* 🖃 *MC, V* ⊗ *Closed Mon.*

$ ✕ **L'Angolo di Sapia.** A short-and-simple, seasonal set menu that changes frequently is one of the reasons to eat here. The other is the sweeping view from the outdoor terrace of the countryside below. You might want to start with the *piatto misto* (mixed plate, which in this case includes a slice of vegetable tart and mozzarella and tomatoes) and then continue with one of the house specialties like the *topini della torre* (gnocchi in a vibrant saffron sauce). Every evening there's a cocktail hour with ample free buffet. ✉ *Via del Castello 4, Colle Alta* 📞 *0577/921453* 🖃 *DC, MC, V* ⊗ *Closed Mon., and Tues. and Wed. Oct.–Apr. No lunch.*

¢–$ ✕ **Oste del Borgo.** A short menu lists *crostoni* (large slices of toasted bread with various savory toppings), creative salads, and tasty primi. Do leave room for dessert—the *panna cotta* (cooked cream) iced with chocolate mousse will not disappoint. The place, just one room lined with wine bottles, is cozy in winter; when it's warm you can sit outside under white umbrellas with a view of a *piazzetta* (a little piazza). Service is prompt and friendly, and the wine list is short but well thought out. ✉ *Piazza Baios, Via Gracco del Secco 58* 📞 *0577/922499* 🖃 *No credit cards* ⊗ *Closed Wed.*

★ $$$$ 🏨 **La Suvera.** Pope Julius II once owned this luxurious estate in the valley of the River Elsa. The papal villa and adjacent building have magnificent individually furnished guest rooms and suites appointed with antiques and modern comforts. A wall-size tapestry depicting the Roman army hangs beside a rich, red tester-canopy bed in the Angels Room.

La Suvera's first-rate facilities include drawing rooms, a library, an Italian garden, a park, and the Oliviera restaurant (serving organic estate wines). ⊠ *Off SS541, 53030 Pievescola (Casola d'Elsa), 15 km (9 mi) south of Colle di Val d'Elsa* ☎ *0577/960300* 🖶 *0577/960220* ⊕ *www. lasuvera.it* ⟿ *16 rooms, 16 suites* ⚒ *Restaurant, room service, in-room safes, minibars, cable TV, tennis court, pool, exercise equipment, massage, Turkish bath, mountain bikes, bar, library, dry cleaning, laundry service, concierge, Internet, meeting rooms; no kids under 12* ⊟ *AE, DC, MC, V* ⊙ *Closed Nov.–Easter* ⏻❘ *BP.*

$ ▥ **Villa Belvedere.** The Conti-Iannone family has been running this place since 1984, and they provide the intimacy that you might find in a family home. The 17th-century villa has been converted into rooms, some of which have three beds (with an option for adding a fourth), making this a good spot for families. A simply furnished classic garden provides a place to read or have a drink, and an on-site restaurant serves Tuscan specialties. On a good day you can glimpse San Gimignano. A fair amount of traffic goes by on the road in front of the hotel. Half board is available. ⊠ *Località Belvedere, 53034, 1½ km (1 mi) south on SS2* ☎ *0577/920966* 🖶 *0577/92412* ⊕ *www.villabelvedere.com* ⟿ *15 rooms* ⚒ *Restaurant, cable TV, tennis court, pool, bar, Internet, free parking, some pets allowed; no a/c* ⊟ *AE, DC, MC, V.*

¢–$ ▥ **Arnolfo Hotel.** The Arnolfo is on the main street of Colle Alta, and there are views from the windows that face the valley (Val d'Elsa). Though the rooms are simply outfitted with wood furnishings, they're not bare-bones. ⊠ *Via F. Campana 8, Colle Alta, 53034* ☎ *0577/ 922020* 🖶 *0577/922324* ⟿ *32 rooms* ⚒ *Dining room, minibars, cable TV, Internet, some pets allowed; no a/c* ⊟ *AE, DC, MC, V* ⊙ *Closed Jan. 6–Feb. 28* ⏻❘ *CP.*

Shopping

The crystal at **Cristalleria Ceramica Artistica** (⊠ Via Castello 40 ☎ 0577/ 959666) runs the gamut from conventional to inspired: particularly gorgeous are the opaque glass vases, looking as if they'd just been dug up, intact, from Etruscan tombs. Art meets contemporary design in the glass objects at **La Molleria Gelli** (⊠ Via delle Romite 26 ☎ 0577/920163). The slanted champagne flutes are a marvel of engineering, as are the wine carafes, shaped like a child's top, that perfectly balance and gently spin.

San Gimignano

⓭ *14 km (9 mi) northwest of Colle di Val d'Elsa, 38 km (24 mi) north-*
Fodor'sChoice *west of Siena, 54 km (34 mi) southwest of Florence.*
★
When you're high on a hill surrounded by soaring medieval towers in silhouette against the blue sky, it's difficult not to fall under the spell of San Gimignano. Its tall walls and narrow streets are typical of Tuscan hill towns, but it's the medieval "skyscrapers" that set the town apart from its neighbors and give it a uniquely photogenic skyline. Today 14 towers remain, but at the height of the Guelph-Ghibelline conflict there was a forest of more than 70, and it was possible to cross the town by rooftop rather than road. The towers were built partly for defensive purposes—they were a safe refuge and useful for pouring boiling oil on at-

tacking enemies—and partly for bolstering the egos of their owners, who competed with deadly seriousness to build the highest tower in town.

The relative proximity of San Gimignano, arguably Tuscany's best-preserved medieval hill town, to Siena and Florence also makes it one of Italy's most visited. But the traffic is hardly a new thing; the Etruscans were here, and later the Romans made it an outpost. With the yearly flow of pilgrims to and from Rome in the Middle Ages, the town—then known as Castel di Selva—became a prosperous market center. When locals prayed to a martyred bishop from Modena for relief from invading barbarians, relief they got, and in gratitude they rechristened the town in his honor as San Gimignano. Devastated by the Black Death of 1348, the town subsequently fell under Florentine control. Things got going again in the Renaissance, with some of the best and brightest painters in the area—Ghirlandaio (1449–94), Benozzo Gozzoli (1420–97), and Pinturicchio (circa 1454–1513)—coming to work, but soon after, the main road was moved, cutting San Gimignano off and sending it into decline.

Today San Gimignano isn't much more than a gentrified walled city, touristy but still very much worth exploring because, despite the profusion of chintzy souvenir shops lining the main drag, there's some serious Renaissance art to be seen here. Tour groups arrive early and clog the wine-tasting rooms—San Gimignano is famous for its light white Vernaccia—and art galleries for much of the day, but most sights stay open through late afternoon. In the morning you can enjoy San Gimignano's exceptionally fine countryside and return to explore the town in the afternoon and evening, when things quiet down and the long shadows cast by the imposing towers take on fascinating shapes.

Porta San Giovanni, an opening in San Gimignano's medieval walls, is the main entrance into town. Via San Giovanni leads the short way to the center of town. Souvenir shops lining the way leave no doubt about the lifeblood of the town, but better things lie ahead. Pass under Arco dei Becci, a leftover from the city's Etruscan walls, to Piazza della Cisterna, named for the cistern at its center and once the main piazza in town. The Piazza del Duomo, lined with San Gimignano's main civic and religious buildings, is just beyond the two towers built by the Ardinghelli family. A combination ticket (€7.50) for all the local sites except the private Museo di Criminologia Medioevale is available, but it's a good deal only if you plan on visiting all of them.

Proving that the Middle Ages were about more than walled towns, praying monks, mosaics, and illuminated manuscripts, the private **Museo di Criminologia Medioevale** exhibits what was once the cutting edge in torture technology. Though some scholars dispute the historical accuracy of many of the instruments, the final, very contemporary object—an electric chair imported from the United States—is real. ⊠ *Via del Castello 1–3* ☎ *0577/942243* ✆ *€8* ☼ *Nov. 2–Mar. 15, Mon.–Sat. 10–6, Sun. 10–7; Mar. 16–July 18, daily 10–7; July 19–Sept. 17, daily 10–midnight; Sept. 18–Nov. 1, weekdays 10–7, weekends 10–8.*

The town's main church is not officially a *duomo* (cathedral), because San Gimignano has no bishop. Behind the simple facade of the Romanesque **Collegiata** lies a treasure trove of fine frescoes, covering nearly every part of the interior. Bartolo di Fredi's 14th-century fresco cycle of Old Testament scenes extends along one wall. Their distinctly medieval feel, with misshapen bodies, buckets of spurting blood, and lack of perspective, contrasts with the much more reserved scenes from the *Life of Christ* (attributed to 14th-century artist Lippo Memmi), painted on the opposite wall just 14 years later. Taddeo di Bartolo's otherworldly *Last Judgment* (late 14th century), with its distorted and suffering nudes, reveals the great influence of Dante's horrifying imagery in *The Inferno* and was surely an inspiration for later painters. Proof that the town had more than one protector, Benozzo Gozzoli's arrow-riddled *St. Sebastian* was commissioned in gratitude after the locals prayed to the saint for relief from plague. The Renaissance **Cappella di Santa Fina** is decorated with a fresco cycle by Domenico Ghirlandaio illustrating the life of St. Fina. A small girl who suffered from a terminal disease, Fina repented for her sins—among them having accepted an orange from a boy—and in penance lived out the rest of her short life on a wooden board, tormented by rats. The scenes depict the arrival of St. Gregory, who appeared to assure her that death was near; the flowers that miraculously grew from the wooden plank; and the miracles that accompanied her funeral, including the healing of her nurse's paralyzed hand and the restoration of a blind choir boy's vision. ☒ *Piazza del Duomo* ☎ *0577/940316* ☜ *€3.50* ⊗ *Mar.–Oct., weekdays 9:30–7:30, Sat. 9:30–5, Sun. 1–3; Nov.–Jan. 20, Mon.–Sat. 9:30–5, Sun. 1–5.*

Even with all the decoration in the Collegiata, the fine collection of various religious articles at the **Museo d'Arte Sacra,** through the pretty courtyard, is still worth a look. The highlight is a *Madonna and Child* by Bartolo di Fredi. Other pieces include several busts, wooden statues of Christ and the Virgin Mary and the angel Gabriel, and several illuminated songbooks. ☒ *Piazza Pecori 4* ☎ *0577/942226* ☜ *€3.50* ⊗ *Apr.–Oct., weekdays 9:30–7:30, Sat. 9–5, Sun. 1–7; Nov.–Jan. 20 and Feb. 28–Mar., Mon.–Sat. 9:30–5, Sun. 1–5.*

Across the piazza from the Museo d'Arte Sacra is the **Palazzo il Popolo,** the "old" town hall (1239). Its tower was built by the municipality in 1255 to settle the raging "my-tower-is-bigger-than-your-tower" contest—as you can see, a solution that just didn't last. ☒ *Piazza Pecori.*

★ The impressive **Museo Civico** occupies what was the "new" Palazzo del Popolo; the Torre Grossa is adjacent. Dante visited San Gimignano for only one day as a Guelph ambassador from Florence to ask the locals to join the Florentines in supporting the pope—just long enough to get the main council chamber named after him, which now holds a large *Maestà* (14th century) by Lippo Memmi. Off the stairway is a small room containing the racy frescoes by Memmo di Filippuccio (active 1288–1324) depicting the courtship, shared bath, and wedding of a young, androgynous-looking couple. That the space could have been a private room for the commune's chief magistrate may have something to do with the work's highly charged eroticism.

Upstairs, famous paintings by Renaissance stars Pinturicchio (*Madonna Enthroned*) and Benozzo Gozzoli (*Madonna and Child*) and Annunciation tondi (round paintings) by Filippino Lippi (circa 1457–1504) attest to the importance and wealth of San Gimignano. Also worth seeing are Taddeo di Bartolo's *Life of San Gimignano,* with the saint holding a model of the town as it once appeared; Lorenzo di Niccolò's gruesome martyrdom scene in the *Life of St. Bartholomew* (1401); and scenes from the *Life of St. Fina* on a tabernacle that was designed to hold her head. The admission price to Torre Grossa is steeper than the climb, but on a clear day the views are spectacular. ⊠ *Piazza del Duomo* ☎ *0577/ 940008* 🎫 *Museum €5, tower €5* ⊙ *Mar.–Oct., daily 9:30–7:30; Nov.–Feb., daily 10–5:30.*

If you want to see more of that quintessential Tuscan landscape, walk up to the **Rocca di Montestaffoli.** Built after the Florentine conquest to keep an eye on the town, and dismantled a few centuries later, it's now a public garden. ⊠ *Off Porta Quercecchio* ☎ *No phone* 🎫 *Free* ⊙ *Daily dawn–dusk.*

From the Rocca take the steps down to get to the **Museo Ornitologico,** in an ex-church at the base of the former fortress. It contains a 19th-century collection of more than 300 birds. ⊠ *Via Quercecchio* ☎ *0577/ 941388* 🎫 *€1.50* ⊙ *Mar.–Oct., daily 11–6; Nov.–Feb., Sat.–Thurs. 9:30–1 and 2:30–5.*

Via San Matteo is San Gimignano's most handsome street, framed by stout medieval buildings in excellent condition, with flowers here and there lightening up the heavy stone facades. The road ends at Porta San Matteo.

need a break?	There's no shortage of places to try Vernaccia di San Gimignano, the justifiably famous white wine with which San Gimignano would be singularly associated—if it weren't for all those towers. At **Enoteca Gustavo** (⊠ Via San Matteo 29 ☎ 0577/940057) you can get a bottle of Vernaccia di San Gimignano to accompany a picnic or sit down and nibble cheese and salami.

★ Make a beeline for Benozzo Gozzoli's superlative frescoes inside the church of **Sant'Agostino.** This Romanesque–Gothic church contains Benozzo's stunning 15th-century fresco cycle depicting scenes from the life of St. Augustine. The saint's work was essential to the early development of church doctrine. As thoroughly discussed in his autobiographical *Confessions* (an acute dialogue with God), Augustine, like many saints, sinned considerably in his youth before finding God. But unlike the lives of other saints, where the story continues through a litany of miracles, deprivations, penitence, and often martyrdom, Augustine's life and work focused on philosophy and the reconciliation between faith and thought. Benozzo's 17 scenes on the choir wall depict Augustine as a man who traveled and taught extensively in the 4th–5th centuries. The 15th-century altarpiece by Piero del Pollaiolo (1443–96) depicts *The Coronation of the Virgin* and the various protectors of the city. On your way out of Sant'Agostino, stop in at the **Cappella di San Bartolo,** with a sumptuously elaborate tomb by Benedetto da Maiano (1442–97). ✉ *Piazza Sant'Agostino, off Via San Matteo* ☎ *0577/907012* 🖾 *Free* ☉ *Apr.–Oct., daily 7–noon and 3–7; Nov.–Mar., daily 7–noon and 3–6.*

Where to Stay & Eat

The **Cooperativa Hotels Promotion** (✉ Via di San Giovanni 125 ☎ 0577/ 940809 ⊕ www.hotelsiena.com) provides commission-free booking for local hotels and farmhouses.

$$ ✕ **La Mangiatoia.** Multicolored gingham tablecloths provide an interesting juxtaposition with rib-vaulted ceilings dating from the 13th century. The lighthearted feminine touch might be explained by the influence of chef Susi Cuomo, who has been presiding over her kitchen for more than 20 years. The menu is seasonal—in autumn, don't miss her *sacottino di pecorino al tartufo* (little packages of pasta stuffed with pecorino and seasoned with truffles), and in summer eat lighter fare on the intimate, flower-bedecked terrace in the back. ✉ *Via Mainardi 5, off Via San Matteo* ☎ *0577/941528* ▭ *MC, V* ☉ *Closed Tues., 3 wks in Nov., and 1 wk in Jan.*

$ ✕ **Osteria del Carcere.** Though it calls itself an *osteria* (a tavern), which implies that hot dishes are available, this much more resembles a wine bar, with a bill of fare that includes several different types of pâtés and a short list of local, seasonal soups, and salads. The sampler of goat cheeses, which can be paired with local wines, should not be missed. Opera plays softly in the background, and service is courteous. ✉ *Via del Castello 13* ☎ *0577/941905* ▭ *No credit cards* ☉ *Closed Wed and Jan. 7–Mar. No lunch Thurs.*

★ ¢ ✕ **Enoteca Gustavo.** The ebullient Maristella Becucci reigns at this tiny wine bar (three small tables in the back, two in the bar, two bar stools)— serving divine, and ample, crostini. The *crostino con carciofini e pecorino* (toasted bread with artichokes topped with semi-aged pecorino) packs a punch. So, too, does the selection of wines by the glass: the changing list has about 16 reds and whites, mostly local, all good. The cheese plate is a bit more expensive than the other choice, but it's worth it. ✉ *Via San Matteo 29* ☎ *0577/940057* ⏃ *Reservations not accepted* ▭ *AE, DC, MC, V* ☉ *Closed Tues.*

$ ✕🏨 **Bel Soggiorno.** One wall of the spacious restaurant ($$$) is glass, and beyond is a sweeping view of a Tuscan hillside. The dining room itself is simple and rustic; the food, however, is not: the *petto di faraona con mele condite, salsa al miele e pecorino di fossa* (breast of guinea fowl with apples, honey, and aged pecorino) is a real treat. Contemporary beds and sofas in white are softened by warm, umber-color plaster walls and floral artwork. If you're looking for a place within the town walls, look no further. The same family has run both the hotel and the restaurant since 1886. ✉ *Via San Giovanni 91, 53037* ☎ *0577/940375* 🖷 *0577/940375* ⊕ *www.hotelbelsoggiorno.it* 🛏 *17 rooms, 4 suites* ⏃ *Restaurant, minibar, cable TV, baby-sitting, dry cleaning, parking (fee)* ▭ *AE, DC, MC, V* ☉ *Closed Jan. 6–Feb. Restaurant closed Wed.* ⊠ *BP.*

$$$$ 🏨 **La Collegiata.** After serving as a Franciscan convent and then the residence of the noble Strozzi family, the Collegiata has become a fine hotel, with no expense spared in the transformation. Arched, multipane windows look out on the surrounding park. All rooms (some with private balconies) are furnished with a mix of wood and upolstered antiques in warm browns and reds, and precious tapestries. Bathrooms have large whirlpool baths. A summer restaurant occupies the deconsecrated church, with tables set out on the entrance. ⊠ *Località Strada 27, 53037, 1 km (½ mi) north of San Gimignano town center* ☎ *0577/943201* 🖷 *0577/940566* ⊕ *www.lacollegiata.it* ⊅ *19 rooms, 1 suite* ⟁ *Restaurant, room service, in-room hot tubs, in-room safes, cable TV, pool, bar, wine bar, Internet, meeting rooms, free parking, some pets allowed* ☰ *AE, DC, MC, V* ⊙ *Closed Jan. and Feb.*

$ ▦ **Pescille.** A rambling farmhouse has been transformed into a handsome hotel with understated contemporary furniture in the bedroooms and country-classic motifs such as farm implements hanging on the walls in the bar. From this charming spot you get a splendid view of San Gimignano and its towers. ⊠ *Località Pescille, Strada Castel San Gimignano, 53037, 4 km (2½ mi) south of San Gimignano town center* ☎ *0577/940186* 🖷 *0577/943165* ⊕ *www.pescille.it* ⊅ *38 rooms, 12 suites* ⟁ *Cable TV, tennis court, pool, gym, outdoor hot tub, bar, Internet, free parking; no a/c in some rooms* ☰ *AE, DC, MC, V* ⊙ *Closed Nov.–Mar.* ⊣⊙⊢ *BP.*

Nightlife & the Arts

San Gimignano is one of the few small towns in the area that make a big deal out of **Carnevale** festivities, with locals dressing up in colorful costumes and marching through the streets on the four Sundays preceding Shrove Tuesday from 3:30 to 6:30. If you visit in summer, check with the tourist office about concerts and performances related to the **Estate San Gimignanese** (⊠ Tourist office, Piazza del Duomo 1 ☎ 0577/940008 ⊕ www.sangimignano.com) one of Tuscany's oldest summer-arts festivals (mid-June to August).

Sports & the Outdoors

The pristine olive groves and vineyards outside the walls are easily accessible on foot, without unreasonably steep grades or ugly peripheries to pass through. The **San Gimignano Tourist Office** (⊠ Piazza del Duomo 1 ☎ 0577/940008 ⊕ www.sangimignano.com) sponsors three-hour walks in the countryside with English-speaking guides from March through October on Wednesday, Friday, and Saturday afternoons, Sunday morning, or by appointment.

Shopping

Antica Latteria di Maurizio e Tiziana (⊠ Via San Matteo 19 ☎ 0577/941952) has an arresting collection of cheeses, and perhaps the best array of verdure sott'olio in town. They also make top-notch panini. As everywhere else, the town brightens up on **open-air market** mornings, every Thursday and Saturday, in Piazza del Duomo. It's the place to pick up fresh fruits and other snacks.

VOLTERRA

As you approach the town through bleak, rugged terrain, you can see that not all Tuscan hill towns rise above rolling green fields. Volterra's fortress, walls, and gates stand mightily over Le Balze, a stunning series of gullied hills and valleys formed by erosion that has slowly eaten away at the foundation of the town—now considerably smaller than it was during its Etruscan glory days 25 centuries ago. The town began as the northernmost city of the 12 that made up the Etruscan League, and excavations in the 18th century revealed a bounty of relics, which are on exhibit at the impressively overstocked Museo Etrusco Guarnacci. The Romans and later the Florentines laid siege to the town to secure its supply of minerals and stones, particularly alabaster, which is still worked into handicrafts on sale in many of the shops around town.

Exploring Volterra

Volterra is 29 km (15 mi) southwest of San Gimignano. There are several parking lots around the perimeter of the city walls; the most convenient one is the underground parking lot at Piazza Martiri della Libertà. Driving in the old town is forbidden. A combination admission ticket (€7) is required for admittance to all three of Volterra's museums (Museo d'Arte Sacra, Pinacoteca, and Museo Etrusco Guarnacci).

A Good Walk

Begin in Piazza Martiri della Libertà and take Via Marchesi to Piazza dei Priori. It's lined with an impressive collection of medieval buildings, including the imposing **Palazzo dei Priori** ⑭ ▶, the seat of city government for more than seven centuries. Across the piazza is the Palazzo Pretorio topped by the Torre del Porcellino, named after the sculpted little boar mounted at the upper window. Walk down Via Turazza along the side of the **Duomo** ⑮ to the triangular Piazza San Giovanni, and head out the left corner of the piazza to steal a look at the ancient **Porta all'Arco Etrusco** ⑯. Return to the piazza and step inside the Duomo and its baptistery. Next to the Duomo is Palazzo Vescovile, with the **Museo Diocesano d'Arte Sacra** ⑰ (entrance around the corner), the first of Volterra's three worthwhile museums. From there proceed straight up Via Roma to the **Pinacoteca** ⑱ museum. Via dei Sarti leads to Piazza San Michele, with the eponymous church decked out in black-and-white marble stripes. Via Guarnacci goes left (north) to Porta Fiorentina and the ruins just outside the walls of the 1st-century BC **Teatro Romano** ⑲. Retrace your steps to Piazza San Michele and continue across town on Via di Sotto, through Piazza XX Settembre to Via Don Minzoni and the **Museo Etrusco Guarnacci** ⑳. Farther along the street is the edge of the Rocca (fortress), one of the few still in use in the country, which serves as the town jail. Via del Castello leads back down the hill, along the Parco Archeologico, a pleasant public park dotted with a few Etruscan stones.

TIMING   Allow at least three hours for the walk with museum stops. Off-season, it's best to make an early start in order to have time in the museums before they close. The whole town can easily be seen in a day, although its distance from everything else makes it a good stopover as well.

What to See

⑮ **Duomo.** Behind the textbook 13th-century Pisan Romanesque facade is proof that Volterra counted for something during the Renaissance, when many important Tuscan artists came to decorate the church. Three-dimensional stucco portraits of local saints are on the gold, red,

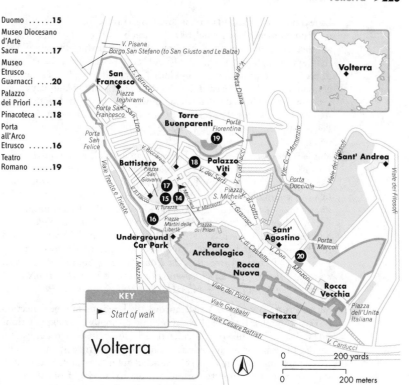

Volterra

KEY

▶ *Start of walk*

and blue ceiling (1580) designed by Francesco Capriani, including St. Linus, the successor to St. Peter as pope and claimed by the Volterrans to have been born here. The church is dedicated to Santa Maria Assunta, but local or patron saints are also venerated. The highlight of the Duomo is the brightly painted 13th-century wooden life-size *Deposition* in the chapel of the same name. The unusual Cappella dell'Addolorata (Chapel of the Grieved) has two terra-cotta Nativity scenes; the depiction of the arrival of the Magi has a background fresco by Benozzo Gozzoli. The 16th-century pulpit in the middle of the nave is lined with fine 14th-century sculpted panels, attributed to a member of the Pisano family. Across from the Duomo in the center of the piazza is the **Battistero,** with stripes that match the Duomo. Evidently this baptistery got a lot of use, as the small marble baptismal font carved by Andrea Sansovino in 1502 was moved to the wall to the right of the entrance in the mid-18th-century to make room for a larger one. ⊠ *Piazza San Giovanni* ☎ *0588/ 86192* 🎟 *Free* ⊙ *Daily 7–7.*

off the beaten path

LE BALZE – Walk along Via San Lino, through Porta San Franceso, and out Borgo Santo Stefano into Le Balze—a desolate, undulating landscape of yellow earth drawn into crags and gullies as if worn down by a desert torrent long past. This area was originally part of the

Etruscan town (called Vlathri; as usual, the current name is closer to the Roman name, Volaterrae), as evidenced by walls that extend another half mile toward the old Porta Menseri. Toward the end of the road, on the right, is the church of San Giusto (with terra-cotta statues of the town's patron saints). The church was built to replace an earlier church under which the earth had eroded. The haunting landscape is thought to have been created when rainwater collected and wore down the soil substructure. The bus for Borgo San Giusto, leaving from Piazza Martiri, goes through Le Balze (about 10 runs per day).

⑰ Museo Diocesano di Arte Sacra. The religious art collection housed in the Bishop's Palace was collected from local churches and includes an unusual reliquary by Antonio Pollaiolo with the head of Saint Octavian in silver resting on four golden lions. There's also fine terra-cotta bust of St. Linus by Andrea della Robbia (1435–1525/28). Two paintings are noteworthy: Rosso Fiorentino's (1495–1540) *Madonna di Villamagna* and Daniele da Volterra's (1509–1566) *Madonna di Ulignano*, named for the village churches (now abandoned) in which they were originally placed. ⊠ *Palazzo Vescovile, Via Roma 1* ☎ *0588/86290* ⊕ *www.comune.volterra.pi.it* ⊡ *Three-museum ticket €7* ⊙ *Mar. 16–Nov. 3, daily 9–1 and 3–6; Nov. 4–Mar. 15, daily 9–1.*

⑳ Museo Etrusco Guarnacci. An extraordinarily large and unique collection of Etruscan relics is made all the more interesting by clear explanations in English. The bulk of the collection is comprised of roughly 700 carved funerary urns: the oldest, dating from the 7th century BC, were made from tufa (volcanic rock); a handful are made of terra-cotta; and the vast majority—from the 3rd to 1st century BC—are from alabaster. The urns are grouped by subject and taken together form a fascinating testimony about Etruscan life and death. Some illustrate domestic scenes, others the funeral procession of the deceased. Greek gods and mythology, adopted by the Etruscans, also figure prominently. The sculpted figures on many of the covers may have been made in the image of the deceased, reclining and often holding the cup of life overturned. Particularly well known is *Gli Sposi* (*Husband and Wife*), a haunting, elderly duo in terra-cotta. Also on display are Attic vases, bucchero ceramics, jewelry, and household items. ⊠ *Via Don Minzoni 15* ☎ *0588/86347* ⊕ *www.comune.volterra.pi.it* ⊡ *Three-museum ticket €7* ⊙ *Mar. 16–Nov. 3, daily 9–7; Nov. 4–Mar. 15, daily 9–2.*

▶ ⑭ Palazzo dei Priori. Tuscany's first town hall was built between 1208 and 1254, with a no-nonsense facade, fortresslike crenellations, and a five-sided tower. Such fortifications were necessary and commonplace at the time; these served as a model for other similar structures throughout the region, including Florence's Palazzo Vecchio. The Florentine medallions that adorn the facade here were added after the Florentines conquered Volterra. The town leaders still meet on the first floor in the Sala del Consiglio; the room is open to the public and has a mid-14th century fresco of the *Annunciation.* ⊠ *Piazza dei Priori* ☎ *0588/87257* ⊡ *€1* ⊙ *Weekends 10–1 and 2–4.*

⑱ Pinacoteca. One of Volterra's best looking Renaissance buildings contains an impressive collection of Tuscan paintings arranged chronologically on two floors. Head straight for Room 12, with Luca Signorelli's (circa 1445–1523) *Madonna and Child with Saints* and Rosso Fiorentino's *Deposition*. Both are masterpieces, and though painted just 30 years apart, they serve to illustrate the shift in style from the early 16th century Renaissance ideals to full-blown mannerism: the balance of Signorelli's composition becomes purposefully skewed in Fiorentino's painting, where the colors go from vivid but realistic to emotively bright. Other important paintings in the small museum include Ghirlandaio's *Apotheosis of Christ with Saints* and a polyptych of the *Madonna and Saints* by Taddeo di Bartolo, which once hung in the Palazzo dei Priori. ⊠ *Via dei Sarti 1* 🕾 *0588/87580* ⊕ *www.comune.volterra.pi.it* 🎟 *Three-museum ticket €7* ⊙ *Mar. 16–Nov. 3, daily 9–7; Nov. 4–Mar. 15, daily 8:30–1:45.*

⑯ Porta all'Arco Etrusco. Even if a good portion of the arch was rebuilt by the Romans, the three dark, weather-beaten, 3rd-century BC heads carved in basaltic rock (thought to represent Etruscan gods) still face outward, greeting those who enter. A plaque recalls the efforts of the locals who saved the arch from destruction by filling it with stones during the German withdrawal at the end of World War II.

San Francesco. Look inside the church for the celebrated early-15th-century frescoes of the *Legend of the True Cross* by a local artist. It traces the history of the wood used to make the cross upon which Christ was crucified. From Piazza San Giovanni, take Via Franceschini (which becomes Via San Lino) to the church. ⊠ *Piazza Inghirami, off Via San Lino* 🕾 *No phone* 🎟 *Free* ⊙ *Daily 8–noon and 3–6.*

⑲ Teatro Romano. Just outside the walls past Porta Fiorentina are the ruins of the 1st-century BC Roman theater, one of the best preserved in Italy, with adjacent remains of the Roman *terme* (baths). ⊠ *Viale Francesco Ferrucci* 🕾 *0586/260837* 🎟 *€2* ⊙ *Mar.–May and Sept.–Nov., daily 10–1 and 2–4; Jun.–Aug., daily 10–6:45; Dec.–Feb., weekends 10–1 and 2–4.*

Where to Stay & Eat

$–$$ ✕ **Da Badò.** This is the place in town to eat traditional food elbow-to-elbow with the locals. Da Badò is family-run, and the chef's efforts concentrate on just a few dishes, so it won't take long to decide between the standards, all prepared with a sure hand: *zuppa alla volterrana* (a Tuscan soup made with vegetables and bread), *pappardelle alla lepre* (wide fettuccine in a hare sauce), and a stew of either rabbit or wild boar. A slice of homemade almond tart is a must. ⊠ *Borgo San Lazzaro 9* 🕾 *0588/86477* 🖃 *AE, DC, MC, V* ⊙ *Closed Wed.*

★ $ ✕ **Il Sacco Fiorentino.** Start with the *antipasti del Sacco Fiorentino*—a medley of sautéed chicken liver, porcini mushrooms, and polenta drizzled with balsamic vinegar. The meal just gets better when you move on to the *tagliatelle del Sacco Fiorentino*, a riot of curried spaghetti with chicken and roasted red peppers. The wine list is a marvel, as it's long and very well priced. White walls, tile floors, and red tablecloths create an understated tone that is unremarkable, but once the food starts arriving, it's easy to forgive the lack of decoration. ✉ *Piazza XX Settembre 18* ☎ *0588/88537* 🖃 *AE, DC, MC, V* ✆ *Closed Wed.*

$ 🏨 **Il Giardino di Venzano.** Terraced gardens bloom with native and exotic plants: this agriturismo is run by two transplanted Australians with serious green thumbs. The grounds and buildings are what remains of an Augustinian monastery complete with Romanesque chapel. Three apartments, each housing two to four people, have high ceilings with light-color timbers, white walls and linens, and terra-cotta tile floors. Windows provide sweeping views of the surrounding countryside. ✉ *Località Venzano, 56048 Mazzolla, 10 km (6 mi) south of Volterra* ☎☎ *0588/39095* ⊕ *www.venzanogardens.com* ⤴ *3 apartments* ⚘ *BBQs, kitchens, fans; no a/c, no room phones, no room TVs* 🖃 *No credit cards* ✆ *Closed Nov.–Apr. 14.*

$ 🏨 **San Lino.** Within the town's medieval walls, this convent turned hotel pairs some wood-beam ceilings, archways, and terra-cotta floors in public spaces with modern-day comforts such as hair dryers and some carpeting in the rooms. Guest's furnishings are contemporary wood laminate and straight-line ironwork. Sip a drink or write a postcard on the small terrace with tables, umbrellas, and potted geraniums; the pool area is framed on one side by a church with a stained-glass window of the Last Supper. The restaurant serves Tuscan classics and local specialties such as zuppa alla volterrana, a thick vegetable soup. Half board is available. ✉ *Via San Lino 26, 56048* ☎ *0588/85250* 🖨 *0588/80620* ⊕ *www. hotelsanlino.com* ⤴ *43 rooms* ⚘ *Restaurant, in-room data ports, minibars, cable TV, pool, bar, dry cleaning, laundry service, concierge, Internet, parking (fee), some pets allowed, no-smoking rooms* 🖃 *AE, DC, MC, V* ✆ *Closed Nov.–Jan.* 🍴 *BP.*

Nightlife & the Arts

On the first Sunday in September the **Astiludio festival** celebrates a flag-throwing tradition that dates back to 1406. Performances and processions are part of the activities.

Shopping

A large loom dominates in the tiny workshop/showroom where **Anna Maria Molesini** (✉ Via Gramsci 45 ☎ 0588/88411) weaves scarves, shawls, throws, and jackets. Her work, mostly in mohair, is done in lively hues and plaids. At **Camillo Rossi** (✉ Via Lungo le Mura del Mandorlo 7 ☎ 0588/86133) you can watch the artisans create household items in alabaster, and then buy their wares.

At **Cooperativa Artieri Alabastro** (✉ Piazza dei Priori 5 ☎ 0588/87590) two large showrooms in medieval buildings contain a large number of alabaster objects for sale, including bookends, ashtrays, and boxes. A former medieval monastery, **Galleria Agostiniane** (✉ Piazza XX Settembre 3 ☎ 0588/86868) is now a showcase for alabaster objects. There's also a video demonstrating how the mineral is quarried and shaped.

Volterra's **mercato** (market) is held on Saturday morning from November to April in Piazza dei Priori, and on Viale Ferrucci (just outside the city walls) from May through October. On hand are a selection of fresh fruits and vegetables, as well as vendors selling everything from corkscrews to *intimi* (underwear).

THROUGH LE CRETE
SOUTHEAST OF SIENA

Van Gogh never saw the area south of Siena known as le Crete (*creta* means "clay" in Italian), but in the bare, moonstone-color clay hills around Asciano—the rolling wheat fields, the warm light, the dramatic gullies and ravines cut by centuries of erosion—he would have perhaps found worthy subjects, as these landscapes seem carved into the earth much in the way that the furrows of paint layer his canvases.

Take the SS73 southeast out of Siena toward Taverne d'Arbia, where the SS438 branches off and goes 21 km (13 mi) to Asciano. About halfway along there's a distinct change in landscape from the farming valleys surrounding Siena to the much hillier Asciano. The road south passes through even more dramatic Crete countryside. At the Abbazia di Monte Oliveto Maggiore the road turns west and leads down to Buonconvento and the Via Cassia, the Roman consular road that runs south to Rome. A fun excursion can also be made to the east, passing through little-visited towns such as Trequanda, Sinalunga, and Montefollonico.

Asciano

㉑ *25 km (16 mi) southeast of Siena, 124 km (77 mi) southeast of Florence.*

Founded by the Etruscans around the 5th century BC, Asciano is now a sleepy little town surrounded by 13th-century walls. The tiny centro storico is eminently bike-friendly; any serious cyclists should consider a pit stop here.

Fodor'sChoice ★ Palazzo Corboli, a magnificent palace dating from the 12th century, has been refurbished and houses the **Museo d'Arte Sacra e Archeologico.** The collection of Etruscan artifacts is displayed well, but the real highlight is the collection of lesser-known 13th- and 14th-century paintings from the Sienese school. ✉ ☎ *0577/719524* 🖷 *0577/719510* 💰 *€4.13* ☉ *Tues.–Sun. 10–1 and 3–7.*

The local **Farmacia De Munari** holds the town's most important Roman artifact, a polychrome Roman mosaic from the 1st–2nd centuries AD, in the basement. To see the mosaic, you must ask for the keys at the tourist information office. ✉ *Corso Matteotti 80* ☎ *0577/718124* 💰 *Free* ☉ *Weekdays 9–1 and 4–8, Sat. 9–1.*

Abbazia di Monte Oliveto Maggiore

㉒ *8 km (5 mi) south of Asciano, 37 km (23 mi) southeast of Siena.*

Monte Oliveto Maggiore, Tuscany's most-visited abbey, sits in an oasis of olive and cypress trees amid the harsh landscape of le Crete. It was founded in 1313 by Giovanni Tolomei, a rich Sienese lawyer who, after miraculously regaining his lost sight, changed his name to Bernardo in homage to the Saint Bernard of Clairvaux, who is sometimes credited with the creation of medieval monasticism. Bernardo then founded a monastic order dedicated to the restoration of Benedictine principles. The name of the order—the White Benedictines—refers to a vision that Bernardo had in which Jesus, Mary, and his own mother were all clad in white. The monks are sometimes also referred to as Olivetans, which is the name of the hill where the monastery was built. Famous for maintaining extreme poverty—their feast-day meal consisted of two eggs—they slept on straw mats and kept a vow of silence. Although the monks look like they are eating a little better these days and are not afraid to strike up a conversation, the monastery still operates, and most of the area is off limits to visitors. One of Italy's most important book restoration centers is here, and the monks still produce a wide variety of traditional liqueurs (distilled from herbs that grow on the premises), which are available in the gift shop along with enough food products to fill a pantry, all produced by monks in various parts of Italy.

From the entrance gate, a tree-lined lane leads down to the main group of buildings, with paths veering off to several shrines and chapels dedicated to important saints of the order. The church itself is not particularly memorable, but the exquisite choir stalls (1503–1505) by Fra Giovanni da Verona are among the finest examples of *intarsia* (wood inlay) in Italy. Forty-eight of the 125 stalls have inlaid decoration, each set up as a window or arched doorway that opens onto a space (a town, a landscape) or an object (a musical instrument, a bird), rendered in marvelous perspective. Check at the entrance for the schedule of masses, as the monks often chant the liturgy.

In the abbey's main cloister, frescoes by Luca Signorelli and Sodoma depict scenes from the life of St. Benedict. Signorelli began the cycle by painting scenes from the saint's adult life as narrated by St. Gregory the Great, and although his nine scenes are badly worn, the individual expressions are fittingly austere and pensive, full of serenity and religious spirit, and as individualized as those he painted in the San Brizio chapel in Orvieto's Duomo. Later Sodoma filled in the story with scenes from the saint's youth and the last years of his life. The results are also impressive, but here for the use of color and earthier depiction. Note the detailed landscapes; the rich costumes; the animals (similar to those Sodoma was known to keep as pets); and the scantily clad boys he apparently preferred (for this he was called "the Sodomist" and described by Vasari as "a merry and licentious man . . . of scant chastity"). ⊠ *SS451* ☎ *0577/707611* 📠 *By donation* ☾ *Daily 9:15–noon and 3:15–5:45.*

Where to Stay & Eat

¢–$ ✕ **La Torre.** You can enjoy straightforward Tuscan fare in the massive tower at the abbey's entrance, or, when it's warm, on a flower-filled terrace. The *pici ai funghi* (extra-thick spaghetti with mushroom sauce) or *zuppa di funghi* (mushroom soup) take the sting out of a crisp winter day, and the grilled meats are a good bet at any time of year. If you want lighter fare, a bar serving panini is attached to the restaurant; it, too, has outdoor seating. ⊠ *Abbazia di Monte Oliveto Maggiore, 8km (5 mi) south of Asciano on SS451* ☎ *0577/707022* ▤ *AE, DC, MC, V* ☾ *Closed Tues.*

$$$–$$$$ ✕⊞ **La Chiusa.** Daniela and Umberto Lucherini bought an old farmhouse in 1974 and turned it into a significant restaurant with emphasis on Tuscan classics. An impeccable staff serves exquisitely prepared food, such as the *pappardelle alla Dania* (wide noodles tossed with tomatoes, garlic, and two cheeses). The menu changes according to the seasons, the well-culled (and expensive) wine list compliments the selections. Guest rooms live up to the high standards created in the kitchen, as the terracotta floors, crisp fabrics, and immense bathrooms (most with Jacuzzis) further a sense of luxurious well-being. ⊠ *Via della Madonnina 88, 53040 Montefollonico, 25 km (15 mi) east of Abbazia di Monte Oliveto Maggiore* ☎ *0577/669668* 🖷 *0577/669593* ⊕ *www.ristorantelachiusa.it* ↩ *15 rooms* ⟁ *Restaurant, room service, fans, some in-room hot tubs, some in-room safes, minibars, cable TV, baby-sitting, dry cleaning, laundry service, concierge, Internet, free parking, some pets allowed; no a/c* ⊟ *AE, DC, MC, V* ⊗ *Closed mid-Jan.–Mar.* ⦿⊦ *CP.*

$$$ ✕⊞ **Locanda dell'Amorosa.** What was a self-sufficient hamlet with its own
Fodor'sChoice chapel in the 14th century is now a refined inn. Some rooms have stun-
★ ning views, others a private garden or terrace. All have sumptuous fabrics flowing around windows and woven rugs on the terra-cotta floors. The grounds teem with rambling roses, thick lavender, and multicolor geraniums in spring and summer. The restaurant has candle-lit tables next to stone walls and the Tuscan menu has flights of fantasy such as *risotto primavera in spuma di piselli e prosciutto croccante,* a rice-and-spring vegetable dish in a creamy pea sauce with fried prosciutto bits. ⊠ *Località Amorosa, 53048 Sinalunga, 23 km (14 mi) east of Abbazia di Monte Oliveto Maggiore, 10 km (6 mi) west of Valdichiana exit off the A1* ☎ *0577/677211* 🖷 *0577/632001* ⊕ *www.amorosa.it* ↩ *17 rooms, 8 suites* ⟁ *Restaurant, room service, in-room data ports, in-room safes, minibars, cable TV, pool, mountain bikes, wine bar, wine shop, baby-sitting, dry cleaning, laundry service, concierge, Internet, meeting rooms, no-smoking rooms* ⊟ *AE, DC, MC, V* ⊗ *Closed Jan. and Feb.*

$ ⊞ **Fattoria del Colle.** Amid rolling vineyards and olive trees is the agriturismo Il Colle, a *fattoria* (farmhouse) that produces fine Chianti and olive oil. The main stone farmhouse retains its enormous stone fireplace and a 16th-century family chapel next door. Apartments (sleeping from 2 to 14) and a separate house sleeping 22, have traditional Tuscan wood furniture, some antique, and full kitchens; some have fireplaces. Half board is available. ⊠ *Off A1, 10 km (6 mi) west of Valdichiana exit, 53020 Trequanda, 12 km (7 mi) east of Abbazia di Monte Oliveto Maggiore* ☎ *0577/662108* 🖷 *0577/662202* ↩ *2 rooms, 19 apartments* ⟁ *Restaurant, kitchens, tennis court, 3 pools, mountain bikes, hiking, laundry service; no a/c, no room phones, no room TVs.*

Buonconvento

㉓ *9 km (5½ mi) southwest of Abbazia di Monte Oliveto Maggiore, 27 km (17 mi) southeast of Siena.*

Buonconvento reached the height of its importance when it served as a major outpost along the Roman road, Via Cassia, although it's also remembered by the history books as the place where Holy Roman Emperor Henry VII was poisoned by a Eucharist wafer. Today quiet Buonconvento is worth a stop for a look at its tiny **Museo d'Arte Sacra,** a two-room picture gallery with more than its fair share of works by Tuscan artists such as Duccio and Andrea di Bartolo. The highlight is a triptych with the *Madonna and Saints Bernardino and Catherine* by Sano di Pietro. ⊠ *Via Soccini 17* ☎ *0577/807181* 🖃 *€3.50* 🕑 *Mar.–Oct., Tues.–Sun. 10–1 and 3–7; Nov.–Feb., weekends 10–1 and 3–5.*

en route | If you're heading northwest to Siena, stray 9 km (5½ mi) west of the Via Cassia to Vescovado and follow the signs from there 2 km (1 mi) south to **Murlo,** a tiny fortified medieval *borgo* (village) that has been completely restored. An imposing bishop's palace holds the **Antiquarium Poggio Civitate,** a museum containing Etruscan relics. Although there are many more beautiful pieces on display, the almost entirely complete roof and pediment from a 5th-century BC Etruscan house are especially rare. The museum is named after the nearby site from which most of the artifacts were excavated. ⊠ *Piazza della Cattedrale 4* ☎ *0577/814099* 🖃 *€3.20* 🕑 *Mar. and Oct., Tues.–Sun. 9:30–12:30 and 3–5:30; Apr., June, and Sept., daily 9:30–12:30 and 3–7; July and Aug., daily 9:30–12:30, 3–7, and 9–11; Nov.–Feb., Tues.–Sun. 10–12:30, weekends 10–12:30 and 2:30–5.*

SIENA & THE HILL TOWNS A TO Z

To research prices, get advice from other travelers, and book travel arrangements, visit ⊕ www.fodors.com

AIR TRAVEL
Florence is the most convenient airport to the region, as you can take the Superstrada to Siena (45 minutes without traffic); Pisa's airport is about 1½ hours away. If you're coming from the United States and are set on flying nonstop, the closest destination to Siena is Rome (about three hours).

AIRPORTS
The airports nearest to the region are Florence's Peretola (officially Aeroporto A. Vespucci), Pisa's Galileo Galilei, and Rome's Fiumicino (officially Aeroporto Leonardo da Vinci).

🛪 Airport Information **Aeroporto A. Vespucci** (Peretola) ☎ 055/373498 ⊕ www.airport. florence.it. **Aeroporto Galileo Galilei** ☎ 050/500707 ⊕ www.pisa-airport.com. **Aeroporto Leonardo da Vinci** (Fiumicino) ☎ 06/6594420 ⊕ www.adr.it.

BIKE TRAVEL
Hills pose a greater difficulty here than distance, but all the towns are connected by roads that make for good cycling and rewarding panoramas. The Siena tourist office can recommend places for bike rental.

BUS TRAVEL
Tra-In buses run several times a day between Rome and Siena (2½ hours). There is frequent SITA service between Florence and Siena (one

hour), stopping in Poggibonsi. From Poggibonsi, Tra-In buses shuttle to San Gimignano, Volterra, and Colle di Val d'Elsa.

Buses are a reliable but time-consuming means of getting around the region because they often stop in every town and hamlet. On some routes, having a strong stomach helps, as the roads are twisting and winding.

Tra-In buses also run frequently within and around Siena, including through the centro storico. Tickets cost €.80 and can be bought at tobacconists or newsstands. Routes are marked with signposts.

🚌 Bus Lines **SITA** ☎ 0577/204270 in Siena, 055/47812 in Florence ⊕ www.sita-online.it. **Tra-In** ☎ 0577/204111 ⊕ www.trainspa.it.

CAR RENTALS

Siena has a handful of car-rental agencies, open weekdays and a half-day on Saturday.

🚌 Agencies **Avis** ✉ Via Simone Martini 36 ☎ 0577/270305 ⊕ www.avis.com. **Hertz** ✉ Viale Sardegna 37 ☎ 0577/45085 ⊕ www.hertz.com.

CAR TRAVEL

The area is easily reached by car on the A1 motorway (Autostrada del Sole), which runs between Rome and Florence; exit onto SR326 for Siena. From Florence, the fastest way to Siena and the hill towns is via the Florence–Siena Superstrada, which takes roughly an hour. Alternatively, the Strada Chiantigiana (SR222) is the scenic route through Tuscany's famous wine country. The Via Cassia (SR2) also connects Siena to Rome and Florence, but it's much faster to go north on the Siena–Florence Superstrada or to take SR326 east toward Sinalunga to pick up the A1.

A dense network of roads can get you into all kinds of local corners. A few towns in this area, including Monteriggioni, Buonconvento, and Asciano, can only be reached by car. Nonresidents are generally forbidden to drive in the old centers of most towns, including Siena. Traffic in and out of Siena slows during rush hour, usually between 8 and 9:30 or 10 AM and 5:30 and 7:30 PM. Both the SR2 and the A14 go through Monteriggioni and pass just east of Colle; the SR68 runs from Colle to Volterra.

EMERGENCIES

Paramedics, police, and the fire department all use a central, nationwide emergency number. Pharmacies take turns staying open late or on Sunday; for the latest information, consult the list posted outside each pharmacy, or ask at the local tourist office.

🚑 Emergency Services ☎ 113.

🚑 Hospital **Policlinico Le Scotte** ✉ Via M. Bracci 16, Le Scotte, Siena ☎ 0577/585111.

LODGING

APARTMENT & VILLA RENTALS The Best in Italy, and Custom Travel and Special Events, represent properties—from farmhouses to castles—in Tuscany, including in the country around Siena. Rental agencies and agriturismo properties have minimum-stay requirements from three days to three weeks.

🚌 Agents **The Best in Italy** ✉ Via Ugo Foscolo 72, 50124 Florence ☎ 055/223064 🖷 055/2298912 ⊕ www.thebestinitaly.com. **Custom Travel and Special Events** ✉ Via dell'Ardiglione 19, 50124 Florence ☎ 055/2645526 ⊕ www.customitaly.com.

TOURS

From Florence, American Express operates one-day bus excursions to Siena and San Gimignano with English-speaking guides. Another option is the Florence-based, American-owned and -operated Custom Travel and Special Events, which runs customized day trips from Florence to Siena and San Gimignano.

American Express ⊠ Via Dante Alighieri 22/r, Florence ☎ 055/50981. **Custom Travel and Special Events** ⊠ Via dell'Ardiglione 19, Florence ☎ 055/2645526 ⊕ www.customitaly.com.

TRAIN TRAVEL

Getting between Siena and Florence by train is quick and convenient; trains make the 80-minute trip between the two cities several times a day. Train service also runs between Siena and Chiusi–Chianciano Terme, where you can make Rome–Florence connections. Siena's train station is 2 km (1 mi) north of the centro storico, but cabs and city buses are readily available.

Train service within this region is limited, and in many cases bus trips are quicker. For instance, the nearest train station to Volterra is at Saline di Volterra (11 km [6 mi] west) with very slow connections to Cecina and the Rome–Pisa rail line along the coast. To and from Siena, trains run north to Poggibonsi and southeast to Sinalunga. Trains run from Chiusi–Chianciano Terme to Siena (1 hour) with stops in Montepulciano, Sinalunga, and Asciano. There are no direct train connections to San Gimignano or Monteriggioni.

You can check the Web site of the state railway, the Ferrovie dello Stato (FS), for information, or stop in any travel agency, as many book and print train tickets and are likely to speak English.

Ferrovie dello Stato ⊕ www.trenitalia.com.

TRAVEL AGENCIES

Siena Vacanze Senese ⊠ Piazza del Campo 56, Città ☎ 0577/45900 ⊕ www.vacanzesenesi.it. **Palio Viaggi** ⊠ La Lizza 12, Camollìa ☎ 0577/280828.

San Gimignano Mundi Travel ⊠ Via San Matteo 74 ☎ 0577/940827 ⊕ www.munditravel.com.

Volterra Pro-Volterra ⊠ Via Giusto Turazzo 2 ☎ 0588/86150 ⊕ www.provolterra.it.

VISITOR INFORMATION

Tourist bureaus in larger towns typically open from 8:30 to 1 and 3:30 to 6 or 7; bureaus in villages are usually open from Easter until early November.

Tourist Information Asciano ⊠ Corso Matteotti 18 ☎ 0577/719510 ⊕ www.terredisiena.it. **Buonconvento** ⊠ Via Soccini 41 ☎ 0577/807181. **Colle di Val d'Elsa** ⊠ Via Campana 43 ☎ 0577/922791. **Monteriggioni** ⊠ Piazza Roma 23 ☎ 0577/304810. **San Gimignano** ⊠ Piazza del Duomo 1 ☎ 0577/940008 ⊕ www.sangimignano.com. **Siena** ⊠ Piazza del Campo 56 ☎ 0577/280551 ⊕ www.comune.siena.it. **Sinalunga** ⊠ Piazza Giuseppe Garibaldi 43 ☎ 0577/636045 ⊕ www.terredisiena.it. **Tourism in Tuscany Web** ⊕ www.turismo.toscana.it. **Volterra** ⊠ Piazza dei Priori 19 ☎ 0588/87257 ⊕ www.comune.volterra.pi.it.

AREZZO, CORTONA & SOUTHERN TUSCANY

6

Updated by
Peter Blackman

SOUTHERN TUSCANY IS AS DIVERSE as Italy itself, ranging from the cool mountain enclaves of Monte Amiata to the sandy beaches at Punta Ala. It contains the wildest parts of Tuscany—the Maremma, once a malaria-ridden swampland where *butteri,* Italy's cowboys, rounded up their cattle, now a peaceful woodland fringed with beaches; Monte Amiata, a scruffy mountain landscape where goats gnaw at clumps of brown grass among scattered rocks; and the still-wild islands of the Tuscan archipelago. Some of Tuscany's best-kept secrets lie here in the south, among them the Abbazia di San Galgano, open to the sky, and the town of Pienza, built in just three years as Pope Pius II's ideal town. This is Etruscan country, where the necropolis near Sovana hints at a rich and somewhat mysterious pre-Roman civilization.

The lovely hill towns of Arezzo and Cortona carry on age-old local traditions—each September Arezzo's beautiful Franciscan, Gothic, and Romanesque churches are enlivened by the Giostra del Saracino, a costumed medieval joust. Since ancient times, Arezzo has been home to important artists: from the Etruscan potters who produced those fiery-red vessels to the poet Petrarch and Giorgio Vasari, writer, architect, and painter. Fine examples of the work of native son Luca Signorelli are preserved in Cortona.

The road between San Quirico d'Orcia and Pienza, above the Val d'Orcia, lies along views of quintessential Tuscany: round, green knolls topped by a single stone house and a cluster of cypresses. Higher hills and mountains protect the valley to the east and to the west. It is here that the hill towns of Montepulciano and Montalcino sit, surrounded by the vineyards that produce their world-famous wines. In the region's deep south, near Saturnia and Sorano, the earth is pocked with gurgling hot springs, odoriferous thermal sulfur baths, and natural geysers. The poppy and sunflower seasons in late spring and summer blanket the lands in vibrant colors, deepened by a backdrop of blue skies, earthy ocher hills, and emerald valleys.

To the west of the Val d'Orcia the landscape changes: deep valleys wind their way to the sea through high wooded hills; nearer the coast the slopes become gentler and agricultural plains begin to replace the woods. It's not uncommon to see the area's cowboys on horseback with their cattle on vast grazing areas. Lining the coast are long sandy beaches, saltwater lagoons, and islands offshore, where migratory birds and indigenous wildlife find shelter.

Exploring Arezzo, Cortona & Southern Tuscany

You can visit the whole region in about five days. This vast area can also be explored in bits and pieces, combined with visits to Chianti, the hill towns, and Umbria. Keep in mind that southern Tuscany isn't well served by trains, so if you aren't renting a car you have to plan around sometimes difficult bus schedules, and the going will be slow. The A1 (Autostrada del Sole), which runs from Florence to Rome, passes near Arezzo, Cortona, and the Val d'Orcia. SS1 (the Via Aurelia) follows the western coastline for much of the way, before jutting inland at Grosetto.

Numbers in the text correspond to numbers in the margin and on the Arezzo, Cortona, and Southern Tuscany; Arezzo; and Cortona maps.

If you have
3 days

Overnight in **Arezzo** ❶–❼ ▶ or ▦ **Cortona** ❾–❿ and visit both towns the first day. In the morning, you might head down to **Chiusi** ⓲ or go straight to the Val d'Orcia, where you spend the night. ▦ **Chianciano Terme** ⓳ is a spa town, ▦ **Pienza** ㉑ is an excellent representation of Renaissance ideals, and the walls of medieval **San Quirico d'Orcia** ㉒ are from the 15th century. ▦ **Montepulciano** ⓴ and ▦ **Montalcino** ㉔ are hill towns known for their red wines. On Day 3, head south to stay in the spa town of ▦ **Saturnia** ㉚. From here you can visit **Pitigliano** ㉘, **Sovana** ㉙, and **Sorano** ㉗, too.

If you prefer the seaside, an alternative three-day itinerary from Siena is to start making your way west, visiting the **Abbazia di San Galgano** ㊳ before spending the night in **Massa Marittima** ㊲. The next day, visit the island of ▦ **Elba** ㉟, taking the ferry from Piombino. On your third day, head south for **Monte Argentario** ㉛, seeing Porto Ercole and Porto Santo Stefano, or you can take a ferry to the island of **Giglio** ㉜.

If you have
5 days

Follow the three-day itinerary, and on Day 4 head west to **Monte Argentario** ㉛ before taking the ferry to the island of ▦ **Giglio** ㉜. Or you could drive northwest and spend the night on the island of ▦ **Elba** ㉟. Head back toward Siena on Day 5, taking time out to visit the **Abbazia di San Galgano** ㊳ and the hill towns around it.

Alternatively, if you'd like to mix nature-oriented destinations into your itinerary, after visiting ▦ **Cortona** ❾–❿ and **Arezzo** ❶–❼ on Day 1, drive north to the **Parco Nazionale Casentino** ❽ and spend the night in a monastery. Day 2 head south again to ▦ **Pienza** ㉑ and the towns of the Val d'Orcia. On Day 4 continue on, taking time to drive up **Monte Amiata** ㉖, where you could stop for a hike before spending the night in ▦ **Saturnia** ㉚ and visiting the surrounding towns. On Day 5 drive to the coast, stopping at the **Parco Naturale della Maremma** ㉝ before spending the night in ▦ **Castiglione della Pescaia** ㉞, or drive through **Monte Argentario** ㉛ and take a ferry to the island of ▦ **Giglio** ㉜, which has a rugged interior waiting to be explored on foot.

About the Restaurants

In popular tourist towns such as Monte Argentario, Saturnia, and the villages on Elba, there are excellent upscale restaurants that serve elaborate dishes. But to savor the diverse flavors of cooking in this region, look for the smaller, family-run trattorias found in every town—the service and setting are often basic, but the food can be great. Few restaurants outside Arezzo have light items on lunch menus, so be prepared to face heavy meals both at lunch and at dinner, especially in smaller, out-of-the-way towns. Hours for meals remain fairly standard: lunch between 12:30 and 2, dinner between 7:30 and 10. A fun alternative to eating in restaurants is provided by the region's many small *sagre* (festivals), which typically concentrate on local products, such as *castagne* (chestnuts). You can stroll from stand to stand sampling varied fare. Tourist offices have lists of scheduled festivals.

About the Hotels

Southern Tuscany is a great place to enjoy the *agriturismo* (agritourism) lifestyle: if you have a week to stay in a farmhouse, pick someplace central, such as Pienza, and explore the region from that base. It may be so relaxing and the food so good that you may have trouble wandering away. You can also find hotels in the region: modern affairs in cities, surfside beach resorts, and stately, timeworn villas. The Punta Ala area, near Castiglione della Pescaia, has nice, facility-rich campgrounds, ideal for budget travelers.

WHAT IT COSTS In Euros					
	$$$$	**$$$**	**$$**	**$**	**¢**
RESTAURANTS	over €22	€18–€22	€13–€17	€7–€12	under €7
HOTELS	over €290	€210–€289	€140–€209	€80–€139	under €80

Restaurant prices are for a second course (secondo piatto) per person. Hotel prices are for two people in a standard double room in high season, including VAT.

Timing

Be prepared for steamy heat in the region in July and August. Coastal areas get crowded during this time, when Italians move en masse to their beach homes, especially in August. On the other hand, July in southern Tuscany is when there's a spectacular explosion of sunflowers, creating an effect of blue sky over bright yellow fields. Spring and fall are the nicest seasons for southern sojourns, with relatively few tourists and pleasant temperatures, but beware of possible rainy seasons, especially in November and April. December to February can be fairly cold—warm boots, mittens, scarves, and heavy coats can sometimes be a necessity—and in the hilly areas near Umbria and especially Monte Amiata, it's freezing.

AREZZO

The birthplace of the poet Petrarch (1304–74), the Renaissance artist and art historian Giorgio Vasari, and Guido d'Arezzo, the inventor of musical notation, Arezzo is today best known for the magnificent Piero della Francesca frescoes in the church of San Francesco. Arezzo dates from pre-Etruscan times, when around 1000 BC the first settlers—who continue to puzzle scholars today—erected a cluster of huts. Arezzo thrived as an Etruscan capital from the 7th to the 4th centuries BC, and was one of the most important cities in the Etruscans' anti-Roman 12-city federation, resisting Rome's rule to the last. The city eventually fell and in turn flourished under the Romans. In 1248, Guglielmino degli Ubertini, a member of the powerful Ghibelline family, was elected bishop of Arezzo. This sent the city headlong into the enduring conflict between

6

Beaches Apart from the occasional rocky promontory, the coast of southern Tuscany is virtually one long stretch of fine-sand beach. Private areas are common near the resort towns to the south of Livorno and just to the north of Monte Argentario, where there are chairs and umbrellas for rent, shower facilities, and bars. Along the rest of the coast, the beaches are public, being particularly pleasant in the nature reserve at Monti dell'Uccellina and along the sandbars that connect Monte Argentario to the mainland. Avoiding Livorno and Piombino, the water is generally clean, and cleaner still off the islands of the Tuscan archipelago. Here rocky beach areas predominate—though Elba does have some white-sand beaches on its southern side. Most Tuscan beaches are crowded in July and August, but they are much less so in June and September, when the days are shorter but the water is still quite warm.

Cuisine Traditional Tuscan dishes are based around porcini mushrooms and game such as *coniglio* (rabbit) and *cinghiale* (wild boar). The local pasta specialty, *pici* (long, thick, hand-rolled spaghetti), is most commonly served *all'aglione* (with a tomato and garlic sauce) or with a rich and tasty sauce of wild boar. A similar, hand-rolled pasta is called pici or *pinci* around Siena and is made in Piedmont and Lombardy under the name *bigoli*. Chianina beef, from a prize breed of cattle raised near Montepulciano and Montalcino, is also standard fare on menus here. Try it as a *tagliata* (roasted, thinly sliced, and dribbled with extra virgin olive oil) served with arugula and cherry tomatoes. On the coast and islands, you can feast on a bounty of delectably fresh seafood such as swordfish, shrimp, clams, and mussels.

The pecorino (a sheep's-milk cheese) produced near Pienza is particularly good and should be sampled at every opportunity. It is available in three basic varieties: *fresco* (freshly made), *semi-stagionato* (partially seasoned), and *stagionato* (fully seasoned), which is grated and served with pasta dishes rather than Parmesan. Semi-seasoned pecorino is perhaps the most interesting, as the cheese rounds are first covered with either tomatoes, grapes, or ash to give the cheese a distinctive color and flavor—truffles can also be added to the cheese itself. Sliced pears, or honey and chutney, make for delicious combinations when paired with pecorino. Chestnuts also grow locally, especially on Monte Amiata, and though you can find them in desserts and coffees, you can also find them stuffed in pasta dumplings as a main dish.

Etruscan Artifacts To fully appreciate the strangely quixotic relationship that the ancient Etruscan culture had with the tufa rock that provided the fabric of the civilization, you must visit southern Tuscany. The houses and tombs, and sometimes even the roads, were carved from this soft volcanic stone, making it impossible to think about the Etruscans without also imagining the dark sandy tufa that surrounded them. Some of the best preserved and most mysterious of all their monumental tombs are in the area of Pitigliano, Sorano, and Sovana. In the necropolis of the latter, you can actually walk on a section of Etruscan road that is almost 2,500 years old. Neither should Chiusi be missed, if you are interested in things Etruscan: several tombs that still retain their brightly colored decorations and a particularly fine and thoughtfully organized achaeological museum await you there.

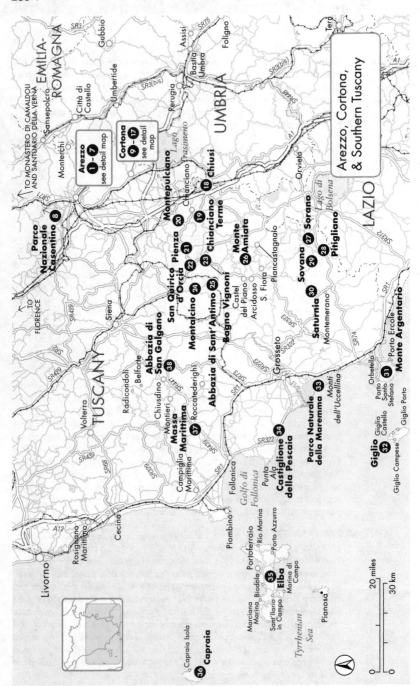

Arezzo, Cortona, & Southern Tuscany

Arezzo 1–7 see detail map

Cortona 9–17 see detail map

EMILIA-ROMAGNA

UMBRIA

TUSCANY

LAZIO

TO MONASTERO DI CAMALDOLI AND SANTUARIO DELLA VERNA

Gubbio

Sansepolcro

Città di Castello

Monterchi

Umbertide

Assisi

Bastia Umbra

Perugia

Foligno

Terni

Parco Nazionale Casentino 8

TO FLORENCE

Lago Trasimeno

Chiusi 18

Orvieto

Lago di Bolsena

Siena

Montepulciano 20

Chianciano Terme

Pienza 21

19

San Quirico d'Orcia 22 23

Sorano 27

Sovana 29 28 Pitigliano

Montalcino 24 25

Bagno Vignoni

Castel del Piano

Monte Amiata 26

Arcidosso

S. Fiora

Piancastagnaio

Abbazia di San Galgano 38

Abbazia di Sant'Antimo

Saturnia 30

Radicondoli

Belforte

Chiusdino

Roccatederighi

Grosseto

Montemerano

Porto Ercole

Volterra

Massa Marittima 37

Montieri

Campiglia Marittima

Monti dell'Uccellina

Orbetello

Monte Argentario 31

Cecina

Follonica

Punta Ala

Parco Naturale della Maremma 33

Porto Santo Stefano

Giglio Porto

Piombino

Golfo di Follonica

Castiglione della Pescaia 34

Giglio 32

Giglio Castello

Livorno

Rosignano Marittimo

Portoferraio

Rio Marina

Marciana Marina

Biodola

Elba 35

Porto Azzurro

Marina di Campo

Giglio Campese

Sant'Ilario in Campo

Pianosa

Capraia 36

Capraia Isola

Tyrrhenian Sea

20 miles

30 km

the Ghibellines (pro-emperor) and the Guelphs (pro-pope). In 1289, Florentine Guelphs defeated Arezzo in a famous battle at Campaldino. Among the Florentine soldiers was Dante Alighieri (1265–1321), who often referred to Arezzo in his *Divine Comedy*. Guelph–Ghibelline wars continued to plague Arezzo until the end of the 14th century, when Arezzo lost its independence to Florence.

Exploring Arezzo

Arezzo (population 90,000) is 64 km (41 mi) northeast of Siena and 78 km (48 mi) southeast of Florence. Although urban sprawl testifies to the fact that Arezzo is the third largest city in Tuscany (after Florence and Pisa), the old town is pretty small, and is on a low hill almost completely closed to traffic. Look for parking along the roads that circle the lower part of town, near the train station, and walk into town from there. You can explore the most interesting sights in a few hours, adding time to linger for some window-shopping at Arezzo's many antiques shops.

A Good Walk

Start at the top of Arezzo with a visit to the **Duomo** ❶ ➤. From here you can walk down Via Ricasoli and then take the first right down Via Sassoverde to **San Domenico** ❷ and the **Casa di Giorgio Vasari** ❸. Retrace your steps to the Duomo, through Piazza della Libertà and down Via dell'Orto, past the Casa del Petrarca (House of Petrarch). Turn right on Via dei Pileati, a continuation of Corso Italia (note the old library covered with Renaissance family crests), then left under the Vasari loggia and into **Piazza Grande** ❹. Lovely antiques shops line this spacious square, which is also the center of a monthly antiques fair and an annual jousting event. Leave the square, taking Via Seteria, and visit **Santa Maria della Pieve** ❺ on your right. Then turn left on Corso Italia, right on Via Cavour, and walk past Piazza San Francesco, visiting the **Basilica di San Francesco** ❻. For a look at Arezzo's ancient past, head to the lower part of town to the **Museo Archeologico** ❼. Take Via Guido Monaco all the way down and turn left onto Via Spinello, which becomes Via Niccolo'Aretino; the museum is at the corner of Via Margaritone.

TIMING The walk itself takes about a half hour, but allow a half day to see the sights and the city at a leisurely pace and to squeeze in some shopping.

What to See

Anfiteatro Romano. Periodic excavations since 1950 have brought to light segments of Arezzo's Roman amphitheater, which was probably built during the early 2nd century AD. The entire perimeter has been exposed, and you can see some of the entrance passages and the structures that supported the amphitheater's central arena. Ask at the nearby ➪ **Museo Archeologico** for entrance to the site. ⊠ *Piazza S. Agostino 12* ☎ *0575/20882 museum* ☒ *Free* ☽ *Daily 8:30–7.*

❻ **Basilica di San Francesco.** The famous Piero della Francesca frescoes depicting *The Legend of the True Cross* (1452–66) were executed on the three walls of the Capella Bacci, the choir vestibule in this 14th-century church. What Sir Kenneth Clark called "the most perfect morning light in all Renaissance painting" may be seen in the lowest section of the

FodorśChoice ★

right wall, where the troops of the Emperor Maxentius flee before the sign of the cross. The view of the frescoes from the nave of the church is limited, but a much closer look is available from the Capella Bacci by reservation. Call ahead or consult the Web site; admission is limited to 25 people every ½ hour. ⊠ *Piazza San Francesco* ☎ *0575/20630 church, 0575/302001 Capella Bacci reservations* ⊕ *www.pierodellafrancesca. it* ⊠ *Church free, Capella Bacci €6* ⊙ *Church daily 8:30–6:30. Capella Bacci Apr.–Oct., weekdays 9–6:30, Sat. 9–5:30, Sun. 1–5:30; Nov.–Mar., weekdays 9–5:30, Sat. 9–5, Sun. 1–5.*

❸ **Casa di Giorgio Vasari.** Giorgio Vasari (1511–74), the region's leading mannerist artist, architect, and art historian, designed and decorated this house after he bought it in 1540. He ended up not spending much time there, since he and his wife moved to Florence in 1554. Today the building houses archives on Vasari, and underwhelming works by the artist and his peers are on view. In the first room, which Vasari called the "Triumph of Virtue Room," a richly ornamented wooden ceiling shows Virtue combating Envy and Fortune in a central octagon. Frescoes on the walls depict, among other things, Extravagance, Charity, the Fire of Troy, and a panorama of a Rome cow field. ⊠ *Via XX Settembre 55* ☎ *0575/ 409040* ⊠ *€2* ⊙ *Mon. and Wed.–Sat. 8–7:30, Sun. 8:30–1.*

❶ Duomo. Arezzo's medieval cathedral at the top of the hill contains an eye-level fresco of a tender *Magdalen* by Piero della Francesca (1420–92); look for it in the north aisle next to the large marble tomb near the organ. Construction of the Duomo began in 1278 but twice came to a halt, and the church wasn't completed until 1510. The facade, designed by Arezzo's Dante Viviani, was added later (1901–14). ⊠ *Piazza del Duomo 1* ☎ *0575/23991* ⊙ *Daily 7–12:30 and 3–6:30.*

❼ Museo Archeologico. The Archaeological Museum in the **Convento di San Bernardo,** just outside the **Amfiteatro Romano,** exhibits a fine collection of Etruscan bronzes. ⊠ *Via Margaritone 10* ☎ *0575/20882* 💶 *€4* ⊙ *Daily 8:30–7.*

❹ Piazza Grande. With its irregular shape and sloping brick pavement, framed by buildings of assorted centuries, Arezzo's central piazza echoes Siena's Piazza del Campo. Though not quite so magnificent, it's lively enough during the outdoor antiques fair the first Sunday of the month and when the **Giostra del Saracino** (Saracen Joust), featuring medieval costumes and competition, is held here on the first Sunday of September.

❷ San Domenico. Inside the northern city walls, this church was begun by Dominican friars in 1275 and completed in the 14th century. The walls were once completely frescoed and decorated with niches and chapels. Very little remains of the original works: a famous 13th-century crucifix by Cimabue (circa 1240–1302), frescoes by Spinello Aretino (1350–1410), and some 14th- and 15th-century paintings. ⊠ *Piazza San Domenico* ☎ *0575/22906* 💶 *Free* ⊙ *Daily 7–1 and 3:30–6.*

❺ Santa Maria della Pieve (Church of Saint Mary of the Parish). The curving, tiered apse on Piazza Grande belongs to a fine Romanesque church that was originally Paleo-Christian, built on the remains of an old Roman temple. It was redone in Romanesque style in the 12th century. The facade dates from the early 13th century, but it includes granite columns from the Roman period. Interior frescoes by Piero della Francesca, Lorenzo Ghiberti (1378–1455), and Pietro Lorenzetti (circa 1290–1348) were sadly lost in the 16th, 17th, and 18th centuries. To the left of the altar there is a 16th-century episcopal throne by Vasari. ⊠ *Via Seteria and Corso Italia* ☎ *0575/377678 for tourist information* ⊙ *Daily 8–noon and 3–6.*

> **need a break?**
>
> The old-fashioned-looking **Pasticceria Carraturo** (⊠ Corso Italia 61 ☎ 0575/355757) has scrumptious pastries and cappuccino, plus a tiny restaurant in the back.

Where to Stay & Eat

$–$$ ✕ **Buca di San Francesco.** A frescoed cellar restaurant in a centuries-old building next to the church of San Francesco, this *buca* (literally "hole," figuratively "cellar") doesn't seem to have changed much since the Middle Ages. You can choose from several straightforward local specialties, including *ribollita* (minestrone thickened with beans and bread). The lean Chianina beef and the *saporita di Bonconte* (a selection of several meats) are succulent treats. ⊠ *Via San Francisco 1* 🖃🖃 *0575/23271* 🖃 *AE, DC, MC, V* ⊗ *Closed Tues. and 2 wks in July. No dinner Mon.*

$ ✕ **Antica Trattoria da Guido.** Owned by a southern Italian, this small trattoria serves tasty adaptations of Calabrian dishes, such as their homemade pasta served with *salsa ai pomodori secchi* (a spicy sauce of sun-dried tomatoes, capers, and red peppers). The display of homemade pastry desserts makes decisions difficult at the end of the meal. The dining room is a pleasant mix of rustic and modern, and the service is friendly. ⊠ *Via di San Francesco 1* 🖃 *0575/23271* 🖃 *MC, V* ⊗ *Closed Sun. and 2 wks mid-Aug.*

$ ✕ **Tastevin.** Try risotto *alla Tastevin* (with a creamy truffle sauce) or one of the seafood dishes—it's creative cooking that respects tradition. Two of the dining rooms are furnished in a warm Tuscan provincial style, one in more sophisticated bistro style. At the small bar the talented owner plays and sings Sinatra and show tunes. ⊠ *Via dei Cenci 9, near Piazza Guido Monaco* 🖃 *0575/28304* 🖃 *AE, DC, MC, V* ⊗ *Closed Sun. (except 1st Sun. of month) and 1 wk in Aug.*

$ ▦ **Calcione Country and Castle.** The elegant Marchesa Olivella Lotteringhi della Stufa has turned her six-century-old family estate (circa 1483) into a top-notch agriturismo. Think sophisticated rustic: many of the apartments have open fireplaces, and the stone houses have a private pool (the rest share the estate pool). Explore the grounds, which include olive groves, vineyards, and private lakes for fishing and windsurfing. From June to mid-September, a minimum one-week stay is mandatory. ⊠ *Calcione, 52046 Lucignano, 26 km (15 mi) southwest of Arezzo* 🖃 *0575/837100* 🖾 *0575/837153* ⊕ *www.calcione.com* ⇝ *2 houses, 1 cottage, 6 apartments* ⟁ *BBQs, kitchens, tennis court, 3 pools, 3 lakes, fishing, babysitting, some laundry facilities, some pets allowed; no a/c, no phones in some rooms, no room TVs* 🖃 *No credit cards* ⊗ *Closed Nov.–Mar.* ⥌ *EP.*

FodorśChoice
★

$ ▦ **Castello di Gargonza.** Enchantment reigns at this tiny 13th-century countryside hamlet, part of the fiefdom of the aristocratic Florentine Guicciardini. The modern Count Roberto Guicciardini reinvented the place as an agriturismo to rescue a dying village. A castle, church, and cobbled streets set the stage. Guest rooms vary in style; some are decidedly more basic than others. However, high wood-beam ceilings, terra-cotta floors, and modern bathrooms are the rule throughout. Apartments have three to eight rooms each, sleeping as many as 10 people, and have as many as four baths. A minimum three-night stay is required for most rooms; a minimum one-week stay for the apartments. ⊠ *SR73, 52048 Monte San Savino, 28 km (17 mi) southwest of Arezzo* 🖃 *0575/847021* 🖾 *0575/847054* ⊕ *www.gargonza.it* ⇝ *46 rooms, 6 apartments* ⟁ *Restaurant, some kitchenettes, minibars, pool, hiking, meeting room; no a/c, no TV in some rooms* 🖃 *AE, DC, MC, V* ⊗ *Closed 3 wks in Jan. and 3 wks in Nov.* ⥌ *BP.*

$ ▦ **Cavaliere Palace Hotel.** On a quiet backstreet in the old town, the Cavaliere is moments away from the main sights. Carpeted rooms with simple and comfortable furnishings are on the small side. The carpeted rooms in the restored 19th-century town house are small but comfy, with contemporary furnishings. ⊠ *Via Madonna del Prato 83, 52100* 🖃 *0575/*

26836 🏛 *0575/21925* ⊕ *www.cavalierehotels.com* 🛏 *24 rooms* ⚭ *Bar, restaurant, parking (fee); no a/c* 🖃 *AE, D, MC, V* ⵏⵉ *CP.*

Sports & the Outdoors

Bicycling

Ares Sport (🖂 Via Leone Leoni 2, Arezzo ☎ 0575/1820101 ⊕ www. aresweb.it) has several styles of bikes for rent.

Horseback Riding

Etruria Ippo Trekking (🖂 Viale Mecenate 18/a ☎ 0575/401597 ⊕ www. etruriaippotrekking.com) is a long-established outfit that leads group excursions on horseback.

Shopping

Ever since Etruscan goldsmiths set up their shops here more than two thousand years ago, Arezzo has been famous for its jewelry. Today the town lays claim to being one of the world's capitals of jewelry design and manufacture, and you can find an impressive display of big-time baubles in the town center's shops. Arezzo is also famous, at least in Italy, for its antiques dealers.

Antiques

Antique silver and jewelry are the specialization here at **Alma Bardi Antichità.** (🖂 Corso Italia 97 ☎ 0575/20640)

Grace Gallery (🖂 Via Cavour 30 ☎ 0575/354963) deals in antique furniture and paintings.

Come to **La Belle Epoque** (🖂 Piazza San Francesco 18 ☎ 0575/355495) to look for antique lace and embroidered linens.

Shopping for fine antique furniture and jewelry? Peruse **La Nuova Chimera** (🖂 Via San Francesco 18 ☎ 0575/350155) to your heart's content.

The first weekend of every month, between 8:30 and 5:30 each day, **Piazza Grande,** a colorful flea market selling antiques and not-so-antiques takes place here in the town's main square.

Gold

Gold jewelry is set with precious or semiprecious stones at **Aurea Monilia.** (🖂 Piazza San Francesco 15 ☎ 0575/355525)

Among the lovely pieces at **Borghini** (🖂 Corso Italia 130 ☎ 0575/24678) are beautiful gold bracelets with matching necklaces.

As **Il Diamante**'s (🖂 Via Guido Monaco 69 ☎ 0575/353450) name suggests, diamonds are the specialty here.

The earrings at **Prosperi** (🖂 Corso Italia 76 ☎0575/20746) are particularly stunning.

THE CASENTINO

East of Florence and north of Arezzo is the Casentino, a virtually unknown area of Tuscany that holds hidden treasures. In 1289 Dante fought here in the battle that ended the centuries-long struggle between the Guelphs and the Ghibellines (the site of the battle—Campaldino—is marked today by a column outside Poppi at the crossing of the SP70 and the road to Stia). Later, exiled from Florence, he returned, traveling from castle to castle, and recorded his love of the countryside in *La Divina Commedia*.

The sparsely populated region—defined as the upper valley of the Arno, which originates here as a spring on Mt. Falterona—contains enough castles, Romanesque parish churches, and unspoiled villages to keep you happily exploring for days. But the jewels in its crown are contained within the Parco Nazionale Casentino, an 89,000-acre preserve of great beauty. The heart of the park, on an Apennine ridge between the Arno and the Tiber, straddling Tuscany and Emilia-Romagna, is the antique forest tended as a religious duty for eight centuries by the monks of the Abbazia Camaldoli, designers of the world's first forestry code. Every year they have planted 4,000–5,000 saplings, resulting in large tracts of early-growth forest. Although they began by maintaining the mix of silver firs and beeches, eventually they planted only firs, creating vast, majestic stands of the deep green trees whose 150-foot, straight black trunks were once floated down the Arno to be used for the tallest masts of warships.

Parco Nazionale Casentino

★ ❽ *Pratovecchio: 55 km (34 mi) north of Arezzo, 50 km (31 mi) east of Florence.*

A drive through the park, especially on the very winding 34-km (21-mi) road between the Monastero di Camaldoli and Santuario della Verna, passing through the lovely abbey town of Badia Prataglia, reveals one satisfying vista after another, from walls of firs to velvety pillows of pastureland where sheep or white cattle graze. In autumn the beeches add a mass of red-brown to the palette, and in spring torrents of bright golden broom pour off the hillsides with an unforgettable profusion and fragrance. Walking the forests—which also include sycamore, lime, maple, ash, elm, oak, hornbeam, and chestnut trees and are laced with abundant brooks and impressive waterfalls—is the best way to see some of the wilder creatures, from deer and mouflon (wild sheep imported from Sardinia starting in 1872) to eagles and many other birds, as well as 1,000 species of flora, including many rare and endangered plants and an orchid found nowhere else. The **Grande Escursione Apenninica** (GEA) hiking route, which is accessible from both the Monastero di Camaldoli and the Sanutario della Verna, runs along a winding ridge. The park organizes theme walks in summer and provides English-speaking guides anytime with advance notice. *Headquarters ⊠ Via Brocchi 7, 52015 Pratovecchio ☎ 0575/50301 🖷 0575/504497 ⊕ www.parks.it.*

Where to Stay

$ 🏠 **Fattoria di Celli.** Set on a gentle rise in the countryside outside the castle town of Poppi, this former *fattoria*—a dormitory housing farm workers—is a tranquil place with lawns punctuated by flowers and modern sculptures, play areas for children, and picnic tables placed to appreciate mountains views. Apartments and villas have working fireplaces and exposed beams; some rooms have original stone walls. Look for hand-painted details—flowers on an armoire, a stenciled border at ceiling height, a mural on a wall. The Fattoria di Celli has a required one-week minimum stay. ⊠ *Località Celli, 52013 Poppi* ☎ *0575/583860* 🖷 *0575/ 500191* ⊕ *www.tuscany.net/celli* 🛏 *8 apartments, 5 villas ♿ Restaurant, some kitchens, tennis court, 2 pools, basketball, laundry facilities, some pets allowed; no a/c, no room TVs* 🚌 *No credit cards* †⊙| *EP.*

Monastero di Camaldoli

20 km (12 mi) northeast of Pratovecchio, 55 km (34 mi) north of Arezzo.

In 1012, Saint Romualdo, scion of a noble Ravenna family, came upon the forests of the Casentino and found their remoteness, their beauty, and their silence conducive to religious contemplation. He stayed and founded a hermitage, Monastero Camaldoli (named for Count Maldoli, who donated the land), which became the seat of a new, reformed Benedictine order. Four centuries after the order's founding by St. Benedict, Romualdo felt it had become too permissive. An important requirement of the order was preserving its ascetic atmosphere: "If the hermits are to be true devotees of solitude, they must take the greatest care of the woods." When the flow of pilgrims began to threaten that solitude, Romualdo had a monastery and hospital built 1 km (2 mi) down the mountain to create some distance. Today the hermitage, **Sacro Eremo di Camaldoli**—where the monks live in complete silence in 20 separate little cottages, each with its own walled garden—can be seen through gates, and the church and original cell of Romualdo, the model for all the others, can be visited. The church, rebuilt in the 13th century and transformed in the 18th to its present appearance, strikes an odd note in connection with such an austere order and the simplicity of the hermits' cells, because it's done up in gaudy baroque style, complete with gilt cherubs and a frescoed vault. Its most appealing artwork is the glazed terra-cotta relief *Madonna and Child with Saints* (including a large figure of Romualdo and a medallion depicting his fight with the devil) by Andrea della Robbia.

Within the monastery is the church (repeatedly restructured) containing 14th-century frescoes by Spinello Aretino, seven 16th-century panel paintings by Giorgio Vasari, and a quietly lovely monastic choir. The choir has 18th-century walnut stalls, more Vasari paintings, and a serene fresco (by Santi Pacini) of St. Romualdo instructing his white-robed disciples. In a hospital built for sick villagers in 1046 is the 1543 **Antica Farmacia** (Old Pharmacy), with original carved walnut cabinets. Here you can buy herbal teas and infusions, liqueurs, honey products, and toiletries made by the monks from centuries-old recipes as part of their daily routine balancing prayer, work, and study (the monastery is entirely self-supporting). In the back room is an exhibit of the early pharmacy's alembics, mortars, and other equipment with which the monks made herbs into medicines. You can attend short spiritual retreats organized by the monks throughout the year: contact the *foresteria* (visitors lodge) for details. ⊠ *SP 67, 52010 Camaldoli, Take SP71 to Serravalle, then follow signs* ☎ *0575/556021 Monastero, 0575/556013 Foresteria Monastero* 🏛 *0575/556001* ⊕ *www.camaldoli.it* 🎫 *Free* ☉ *Daily 9–1 and 3:30–6.*

Santuario della Verna

34 km (21 mi) southeast of Monastero di Camaldoli and of Pratovecchio.

A few hills away from the Monastero di Camaldoli, dramatically perched on a sheer-walled rock surrounded by firs and beeches, is La Verna. St. Francis of Assisi founded it in 1214; the land was given to him by a count who heard him speak and was moved by his holiness. Ten years later, after a 40-day fast, St. Francis—who had dedicated his life to following as closely as possible in Christ's footsteps—had a vision of Christ crucified, and when it it was over, Francis had received the stigmata. As Dante rendered it: "On the crag between Tiber and Arno then, in tears of love and joy, he took Christ's final seal, the holy wounds." A stone in the floor of the 1263 Chapel of the Stigmata marks the spot, and the Chapel of the Relics in the basilica contains a cloth stained with the blood that issued from his wounds. A covered corridor through which the monks pass chanting in a solemn procession each afternoon at 3 on the way to mass is lined with simple frescoes of the *Life of St. Francis* by a late 17th-century Franciscan artist. The true artistic treasures of the place, though, are 15 della Robbia glazed terra-cottas. Some were commissioned, like the huge Crucifixion in the Chapel of the Stigmata; others have been donated throughout the centuries by the faithful. Most, like a heartbreakingly beautiful Annunciation, are in the 14th- to 15th-century basilica, which has a 5,000-pipe organ that sings out joyously at masses.

Several chapels, each with its own story, can be visited, and some natural and spiritual wonders can also be seen. A walkway along the 230-foot-high cliff leads to an indentation where the rock is said to have miraculously melted away to protect St. Francis when the devil tried to push him off the edge. Most touching is the enormous Sasso Spicco (Projecting Rock), detached on three sides and surrounded with mossy rocks and trees, where St. Francis meditated. You can also view the Letto di San Francesco (St. Francis's Bed), a slab of rock in a cold, damp cave with an iron grate on which he prayed, did penance, and sometimes slept. A 40-minute walk through the woods to the top of Mt. Penna passes some religious sites and ends in panoramic views of the Arno Valley, but those from the wide, cliff-edge terrace are equally impressive, including the tower of the castle in Poppi, the Prato Magno (great meadow), the olive groves and vineyards on the lower slopes, and a changing skyscape that seems to echo the mystical feel of the monastery and the woods that surround it. Santuario della Verna's foresteria also has simple but comfortable rooms with or without bath. A restaurant ($) with basic fare is open to the public, and a shop sells souvenirs and the handiwork of the monks. ⊠ *SP208 east from Bibbiena, 52010 La Verna, 21 km (13 mi) east of Bibbiena* ☎ *0575/534211* 🏛 *0575/599320* ⊕ *www.laverna.org* 🎫 *Free* ☉ *Daily 7:30–7.*

As you leave La Verna, be glad you needn't do it as Edith Wharton (1862–1937) did on a 1912 visit during a drive across the Casentino. As she wrote, her car "had to be let down on ropes to a point about ¾ mi below the monastery, Cook steering down the vertical descent, and twenty men hanging on to a funa that, thank the Lord, didn't break."

<table>
<tr><td>

off the
beaten
path

</td><td>

CAPRESE MICHELANGELO – Some 10 km (6 mi) south of La Verna on SR54 is the small hilltop community of Caprese Michelangelo, where *the* Michelangelo was born on March 6th, 1475. The Museo Michelangelo, which opened in 1964 to celebrate the 400th anniversary of Michelangelo's death, displays photographs, plaster casts, and documents relating to the artist's work. ⊠ *Via Capoluogo 3* ☏ *0575/793776* ⊠ *€3* ⊘ *Apr.–May, Mon.–Sat. 10:30–5:30, Sun. 10:30–6; June, July, and Sept., Mon.–Sat. 9.30–6:30, Sun. 9:30–7:30; Aug., daily 9:30–7:30; Nov.–Mar., Mon.–Sat. 11–5, Sun. 11–6.*

</td></tr>
</table>

One weekend in mid-October, Caprese Michelangelo's very lively Sagra della Castagna (Chestnut Festival) takes place. Among the many other chestnut-based delights that feature in the fair, you can sample freshly made *castagnaccia* (a typically Tuscan dessert made with chestnut flour, pine nuts, and rosemary). *Tourist office* ⊠ *Via Capoluogo 10* ☏ *0575/791016* ⊕ *www.capresemichelangelo.net.*

CORTONA

Magnificently situated, with olives grove and vineyards creeping up to its walls, Cortona commands sweeping views over Lago Trasimeno and the plain of the Valdichiana. The delightful medieval streets are a pleasure to wander, and the town has two fine galleries and scattering of churches that are worth a visit.

Cortona is called "Mother of Troy and Grandmother of Rome" in popular speech, and so may be one of Italy's oldest towns. Tradition claims that it was founded by Dardanus, the founder of Troy (after whom the Dardanelles are named). He was fighting a local tribe, so the story goes, when he lost his helmet (*corythos* in Greek) on Cortona's hill. In time a town grew up that took its name (Corito) from the missing headgear. By the 4th century BC the Etruscans had built the first set of town walls, the cyclopean traces of which can still be seen in the 3-km (2-mi) sweep of the present fortifications. As a member of the Etruscans' 12-city league, Cortona became one of the federation's leading northern cities. The area's important consular road, the Via Cassia, passed the foot of Corona's hill, maintaining the town's importance under the Romans. Medieval fortunes waned, however, as the plain below reverted to marsh. After holding out against such neighbors as Perugia, Arezzo, and Siena, the *comune* was captured by King Ladislas of Naples in 1409 and sold to the Florentines two years later.

Exploring Cortona

Cortona is 28 km (17 mi) south of Arezzo, 74 km (46 mi) east of Siena, and 103 km (64 mi) southeast of Florence. The majority of Cortona's streets are very steep, and it's easy to get winded. Take it slowly and stop frequently to visit sights or just to enjoy a gelato. Fortunately, most of the main sights are grouped near the Duomo in the lower part of town, but if you want to visit the upper town, be prepared for a stiff climb. As in many other medieval hilltop towns, the city center is completely closed to traffic, and the few parking areas sprinkled outside the city walls don't make it easy to park.

A Good Tour

Start in Piazza della Repubblica ⌐, the heart of Cortona, where the Palazzo Comunale (City Hall) stands. Move on to the adjacent Piazza Signorelli, and stroll into the courtyard of the **Palazzo Casali** ❾, which houses the Museo dell'Accademia Etrusca and its important collection of Etruscan bronzes. Across Via Casali is the 19th-century Teatro Signorelli; walk north on Via Casali toward the Piazza del Duomo, the 15th-century **Duomo** ❿, and the **Museo Diocesano** ⓫, opposite. Then walk down Via Jannelli and turn left on Via Roma to head back to Piazza della Repubblica. Turning east onto Via Nazionale brings you to Piazza Garibaldi, where on the left you can visit the 14th-century church of **San Domenico** ⓬ before retracing your steps once again to your tour's start.

If you want to continue, and you're up for another climb, you can walk to four other interesting churches that are closed for renovation at this writing. Head up Via Santucci, behind the Palazzo del Capitano del Popolo, past the 13th-century church of **San Francesco** ⓭ and the 1441 Ospedale di Santa Maria della Misericordia. From Piazza San Francesco climb up the steep Via Berrettini, through Piazza Pescaia, and up to Piazza San Cristoforo. From here, a short detour on Via S. Niccolò leads to the charming church of **San Niccolò** ⓮. Back in Piazza San Cristoforo, wind up Via Santa Croce to the church of **Santa Margherita** ⓯ and the Fortezza Medicea behind it. On your way back, complete the circle by taking Via Santa Croce past the church of **San Cristoforo** ⓰, and pass by the convent of Santa Chiara on your way back down Via Berrettini to Piazza della Repubblica. You'd still have time to take the 3-km (2-mi) drive downhill along Via Guelfa to the fine Renaissance **Santa Maria del Calcinaio** ⓱, a church dedicated to medieval tanners, which could well be your most rewarding stop in Cortona.

TIMING With visits to the museums and churches, and a break along Via Nazionale before you start the climb to Santa Margherita, the tour will take two to three hours to complete. This does not include a detour to Santa Maria delle Grazie al Calcinaio, which you may want to see on your way in or out of the city.

What to See

❿ **Duomo.** Cortona's cathedral stands on an edge of the city, next to what's left of the Etruscan and medieval walls running from Porta Santa Maria to Porta Colonia. It was built on the site of an old Romanesque church, but the present Renaissance church was begun in 1480 and finished in

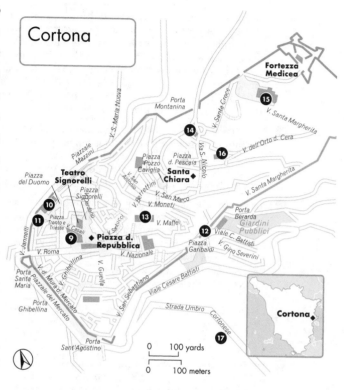

1507. An arcade along the outside wall was erected in the 16th century. Inside, the Duomo is a mixture of Renaissance and baroque styles featuring an exquisite 1664 baroque tabernacle on the high altar by Francesco Mazzuoli. ⊠ *Piazza del Duomo* 🕾 *0575/730436* 🔁 *Free* ☉ *Apr.–Oct., daily 8–7; Nov.–Mar., daily 8–6.*

⓫ **Museo Diocesano.** The Diocesan Museum houses an impressive number of large, splendid paintings by native son Luca Signorelli (1445–1523), as well as a beautiful *Annunciation* by Fra Angelico (1387/1400–1455), which is a delightful surprise in this small town. The former oratory of the Compagnia del Gesù, reached by descending the 1633 staircase opposite the Duomo, is part of the museum. The church was built between 1498 and 1505 and restructured by Giorgio Vasari in 1543. Frescoes depicting sacrifices from the Old Testament by Doceno (1508–56), based on designs by Vasari, line the walls. ⊠ *Piazza del Duomo* 🕾 *0575/ 62830* 🔁 *€5* ☉ *Apr.–Oct., daily 10–7; Nov.–Mar., Tues.–Sun. 10–5.*

⓿ **Palazzo Casali.** Built originally by the Casali family, who lived here until 1409, this palace combines 13th- to 17th-century architectural styles. Today, the palace contains the Accademia Etrusca, which has an extensive library, **La Biblioteca Comunale,** and the **Museo dell'Accademia Etrusca.** An eclectic mix of Egyptian objects, Etruscan and Roman bronzes and statuettes, and paintings lie beyond the museum's centuries-old stone staircase. Look for work by Renaissance artists such as Luca Signorelli and Pinturcchio (circa 1454–1513). From May through September, guided tours are available in English with prior arrangement. Accompanied visits, but only with Italian guides, to the Etruscan tombs on the slopes below Cortona may also be booked. ⊠ *Piazza Signorelli 9* ☎ *0575/630415* 🖾 *Museo €4.20, Biblioteca free* ☉ *Apr.–Oct., daily 10–7; Nov.–Mar., Tues.–Sun. 10–5.*

🔟 **San Cristoforo.** The 12th-century church of St. Christopher is undergoing renovation and is closed for an indefinite period. When it reopens, you can see a 14th-century fresco by unknown artists of the Umbrian Sienese school depicting the Crucifixion, the Annunciation, and the Ascension inside. ⊠ *Piazza San Cristoforo* ☎ *0575/630352.*

🔟 **San Domenico.** Inside this rather anonymous-looking 14th-century church, just outside Cortona's walls, is an altarpiece depicting the Coronation of the Virgin against a sparkling gold background by Lorenzo di Niccolò Gerini (active late 14th–early 15th centuries). Among the other works is a Madonna and Child by Luca Signorelli. ⊠ *Largo Beato Angelico* ☎ *0575/603041* 🖾 *Free* ☉ *Apr.–Oct., daily 8–noon and 3–7:30; Nov.–Mar., daily 8:30–noon and 3–6.*

> **need a break?**
>
> **Caffe degli Artisti** (⊠ Via Nazionale 18 ☎ 0575/601237) is a pleasant place to stop for a cappuccino, sandwiches at lunchtime, or the array of appetizers set out during the cocktail hour.

🔟 **San Francesco.** In the mid-13th century, this Gothic-style church was built on the site of Etruscan and Roman baths. It's closed for reconstruction at this writing, but it contains frescoes dating from 1382, a big crucifix by Giuseppe Piamontini of Florence, and the Relic of Santa Croce, a vestige from the True Cross given to Brother Elia when he served as an envoy for Federico II in Constantinople. The church had a beautiful organ, built in 1466, that was almost completely destroyed during World War II. ⊠ *Piazza San Francesco* ☎ *0575/630352.*

🔟 **San Niccolò.** A small, cypress-lined courtyard and porch stand in front of the delightful San Niccolò, a Renaissance church. At this writing the church is closed for renovation. On the main altar is a fresco by Luca Signorelli, the *Deposition of Christ,* painted around 1510. On the left wall is another fresco by Signorelli of the Madonna and Child, which was plastered over in 1768 and rediscovered in 1847. ⊠ *Via Santissima Trinità* ☎ *0575/604591.*

🔟 **Santa Margherita.** The large 1897 basilica was constructed over the foundation of a 13th-century church dedicated to the same saint. What makes the 10-minute uphill walk worthwhile is the richly decorated interior. The body of the 13th-century Saint Margherita—clothed but with skull and bare feet clearly visible—is displayed in a case on the main altar. ⊠ *Piazzale Santa Margherita* ☎ *0575/603116* 🖾 *Free* ☉ *Apr.–Oct., daily 8–noon and 3–7:30; Nov.–Mar., daily 8:30–noon and 3–6.*

★ ⑰ **Santa Maria del Calcinaio.** Legend has it that the image of the Madonna appeared on a wall of a medieval *calcinaio* (lime pit used for curing leather), the site on which the church was then built between 1485 and 1513. The linear gray-and-white interior recalls Florence's Duomo. Sienese architect Francesco di Giorgio (1439–1502) most likely designed the sanctuary: the church is a terrific example of Renaissance architectural principles. Open hours vary occasionally. ⊠ *Località Calcinaia 227, 3 km (2 mi) southeast of Cortona's center on Via Guelph* ☎ *0575/ 704930* ☒ *Free* ☉ *Daily 3:30–7.*

Where to Stay & Eat

$–$$ ✕ **Osteria del Teatro.** Photographs from theatrical productions spanning many years line the walls of this tavern off Cortona's large Piazza del Teatro. The food is simply delicious—try the *filetto al lardo di colonnata e prugne* (beef cooked with bacon and prunes); service is warm and friendly. ⊠ *Via Maffei 2* ☎ *0575/630556* ▤ *AE, DC, MC, V* ☉ *Closed Wed. and 2 wks in Nov. and in Feb.*

★ **$$$** ✕▦ **Il Falconiere.** Choose from rooms in an 18th-century villa, suites in the *chiesetta* (chapel, or little church), or for more seclusion, pick Le Vigne del Falco suites at the far end of the property, which have private entrances. Husband and wife Riccardo and Silvia Baracchi run Il Falconiere; by all means sample their estate-produced olive oil and wine. The restaurant's inventive menu includes *ignudi di ortica e ricotta con scampetti stufati e salsa al basilico* (ricotta and nettles with stuffed prawns and basil sauce), and the wine list is a product of Silvia's sommelier training. Cooking classes are available. ⊠ *Località San Martino 370, 52044, 5 km (3 mi) north of Cortona* ☎ *0575/612679* 🖷 *0575/ 612927* ⊕ *www.ilfalconiere.com* ⇖ *13 rooms, 7 suites* ⚿ *Restaurant, room service, in-room safes, minibars, cable TV, 2 pools, bar, shop, babysitting, dry cleaning, laundry service, concierge, Internet, free parking, some pets allowed (fee), no-smoking rooms* ▤ *AE, MC, V* ☉ *Restaurant closed Mon. Nov.–Mar.* ⦿ *CP.*

Shopping

Il Cocciaio. For nice ceramics, with many pieces depicting the brilliant sunflowers that blanket local fields, check here. ⊠ *Via Nazionale 54* ☎ *0575/604405.*

PIENZA & THE VAL D'ORCIA

The Val d'Orcia (Orcia Valley) is a sumptuous green valley with breathtaking views of the Orcia River, which runs through it. The area's longstanding agricultural tradition has left it utterly undeveloped, and so the vistas here are classic Tuscany—rolling hills topped by villages, wide plains, swaths of blooming fields punctuated by vineyards and olive groves. Picture-perfect Pienza, medieval San Quirico d'Orcia, and Bagno Vignoni are great photo-op stops; amateur archaeologists will enjoy pondering Chiusi's painted Etruscan tombs; and Chianciano Terme's thermal baths can provide a sybaritic treat during your stay. Hills near Montalcino border the valley in the west, and it's in that hilltop town that Siena chose to make a last desperate stand against the invading Florentines. Not to be missed is the superbly positioned Abbazia di Sant'Antimo to the south. Montepulciano, filled with town palaces and Renaissance churches—and fortified by some great red wine—is at the valley's boundary in the east.

Chiusi

⑱ *40 km (25 mi) south of Cortona, 84 km (50 mi) southeast of Siena, 126 km (78 mi) southeast of Florence.*

Chiusi was once one of the most powerful of the ancient cities of the Etruscan League, and it's now a valuable source of information about that archaic civilization. Fifth-century BC tombs found in the nearby hills have provided archaeologists with a wealth of artifacts. On the route of the ancient Via Cassia, Chiusi became a major Roman center and an important communication hub which linked Rome with the agriculturally rich Chiana Valley to the east, with Siena to the northwest, and to other major cities in central and northern Italy. When the Chiana Valley became a malaria-ridden swamp during the Middle Ages, Chiusi's importance declined, and it was not until the Medici devised a scheme to drain the valley (with plans supplied by Leonardo da Vinci) in the early 15th century that the town began to reestablish itself. Today Chiusi is on the A1 and on the main train line between Florence and Rome.

Most of the artifacts found during the excavations of Chiusi's Etruscan sites are now on display in the small but expertly laid out **Museo Nazionale Etrusco.** Relics include elegant Etruscan and Greek vases, carved Etruscan tomb chests, and a number of the strange canopic jars with anthropomorphic shapes that are particular to this area. The tombs themselves can be seen by arrangement with the museum; visits are accompanied by a member of the museum staff. These underground burial chambers are still evocative of ancient life, particularly in the Tomba della Scimmia (Tomb of the Monkey), where well-preserved frescoes depict scenes from ordinary life 2,500 years ago. The Tomba del Leone (Tomb of the Lion) and Tomba della Pellegrina (Tomb of the Pilgrim) are open by appointment during museum hours. ⊠ *Via Porsenna 93/r* ☎ *0578/20177* 🖼 *Museum €4, with tombs €6* ☉ *Museum daily 9–8 (last entrance 7:30). Tomba della Scimmia by appointment Apr.–Oct., Tues., Thurs., and Sat. at 11 and 4; Nov.–Mar., Tues., Thurs., and Sat. at 11 and 2:30.*

Where to Stay

★ **$$$** ✕🖼 **La Frateria di Padre Eligio.** It's not an overstatement to say that this former convent, founded in 1212 by St. Francis himself, remains a spiritual place. Guest rooms, occupying the original pilgrims' quarters, are simple in the finest sense—with terra-cotta floors, stone walls, exposed ceiling beams, rustic wooden furniture, and museum-quality medieval artwork to reflect upon. The restaurant is one of the most sophisticated in southern Tuscany, serving an eight-course set menu that makes full use of the Frateria's gardens and wine cellar. The flowered courtyards and grounds, spread along a wooded hillside, are immaculately maintained by young recovering addicts who've found a higher path. ⊠ *Off*

A1, Convento San Francesco, 53040 Cetona, 10 km (6 mi) southwest of Chiusi ☎ *0578/238261* 🖷 *0578/239220* ⊕ *www.lafrateria.it* ⇘ *5 rooms, 2 suites* ⚿ *Restaurant; no room phones, no room TVs* 🖃 *AE, MC, V* ⊗ *Closed Jan. 6–Feb. 12. Restaurant closed Wed.*

Chianciano Terme

⑲ *11 km (7 mi) northwest of Chiusi, 73 km (44 mi) southeast of Siena.*

People from around the world come to the *città del fegato sano* (city of the healthy liver) to experience the curative waters. The area's innumerable mineral-water springs are reputed to restore and maintain the health of the skin, among other things. This is nothing new; as early as the 5th century BC, Chianciano Terme was the site of a temple to Apollo the Healer. It's no secret, either—the Terme di Chianciano spa alone claims to draw 120,000 visitors a year, and Italian state health insurance covers visits to the baths and springs for qualified patients. But you can test the waters yourself at a number of springs. If you're not here for the waters, probably the most interesting part of Chianciano is the old town, which lies to the north. The modern town, stretching along a hillside to the south, is a series of hotels, shops, and restaurants catering to the spa clients.

Terme di Chianciano is an organization that represents three spas. The Terme Web site lists the varied spa treatments available (mornings only at Acqua Santa and Acqua Sillene). Perhaps to offset the clinical coldness of the actual treatment centers, each spa is surrounded by a large park filled with trees, flower gardens, and reflecting pools. There are facilities for such light sporting activities as tennis and boccie, and dance floors are available for summer evenings' musical events. The all-important water is served up at long counters, where the spa staff are ever ready to refill your glass. Be warned: the mineral water can have a cleansing effect on your system that may come on suddenly. ⊠ *Via delle Rose 12* ☎ *0578/68292* ⊕ *www.termechianciano.it.*

The water at **Acqua Santa,** taken as a drinking cure, is known for curing liver and digestive ailments and for detoxifying in general. ⊠ *Piazza Martiri Perugini* ☎ *0578/68411* 🖃 *€8.20* ⊗ *Daily 8–noon and 5–7.*

The waters of **Acqua Fucoli** are usually taken as a drinking cure for all manner of intestinal disorders. ⊠ *Viale G. Bacelli* ☎ *0578/68430* 🖃 *€5.70* ⊗ *June–Sept. 15, daily 4:30–7:30.*

Steamy-hot waters at **Acqua Sillene** are used for private mineral and mud tub baths. The spa has nonaquatic activities including tennis, boccie, and miniature golf (all for additional fees). ⊠ *Piazza Marconi* ☎ *0578/68551* 🖃 *€13* ⊗ *Daily 8–noon and 4–7:30.*

At **Terme Sant'Elena,** the waters are said to help with kidney and urinary-tract ailments and all manner of digestive disorders; there are boccie courts and a pretty park to stroll in while you drink. On summer afternoons you can dance to live orchestra music in the park. ⊠ *Viale dell Libertà 112* ☎ *0578/31141* ⊕ *www.acquasantelena.it* 🖃 *€6* ⊗ *Mid-Apr.–mid-Nov., 8:30–noon and 3–6, Sat. 9–noon.*

The walled medieval town of **Chianciano**, 3 km (2 mi) northeast of Chianciano Terme, is best known by its proximity to the spa town; nevertheless, the well-preserved old town is appealing. The **Museo Civico Archeologico** contains a good collection of Etruscan and Roman sculpture and pottery excavated around the area. ⊠ *Via Dante, Chiciano* ☎ *0578/30471* ⊡ *€4* ◷ *Apr.–Oct., daily 10–1 and 4–7; Nov.–Mar., weekends 10–1 and 4–7.*

To the southeast of Chianciano, 10 km (6 mi) along SP19, lies **Sarteano,** a relatively unspoiled village that dates from the 12th and 13th centuries. The town's narrow streets, which wind slowly up toward an imposing fortress, now privately owned, make for very pleasant strolling. Don't miss the small church of **San Martino**, which houses a striking Annunciation by the important Sienese painter Domenico Beccafumi (1486–1551). ⊠ *Piazza San Martino,* ☎ *No phone* ⊡ *Free* ◷ *Daily 9–12:30 and 4–7:30.*

off the
beaten
path

CETONA – Follow SP19 past Sarteano and continue on SP21 to reach the delightful village of Cetona. Time may seem to have stopped as you walk along the quiet, narrow, medieval lanes and back alleys of this village. Peer through the locked gate for a glimpse of the privately owned castle, and take in splendid views of olive orchards, cypress groves, and the quiet wooded slopes of Mount Cetona from the town's terraced streets. ⌖ *20 km (12 mi) southeast of Chianciano Terme.*

Montepulciano

➋⓿ *10 km (6 mi) northeast of Chianciano Terme, 65 km (40 mi) southeast of Siena, 114 km (70 mi) southeast of Florence.*

Perched on a hilltop, Montepulciano is made up of a pyramid of redbrick buildings set within a circle of cypress trees. At an altitude of almost 2,000 feet, it is cool in summer and chilled in winter by biting winds sweeping down its spiraling streets. The town has an unusually harmonious look, the result of the work of three architects: Antonio Sangallo "il Vecchio" (circa 1455–1534), Vignola (1507–73), and Michelozzo (1396–1472). The group endowed it with fine palaces and churches in an attempt to impose Renaissance architectural ideals on an ancient Tuscan hill town.

★ Montepulciano's pièce de résistance is the beautiful **Piazza Grande,** filled with handsome buildings. On the Piazza Grande is the **Duomo,** which has an unfinished facade that doesn't measure up to the external beauty of the neighboring palaces. On the inside, however, its Renaissance roots shine through. You can see fragments of the tomb of Bartolomeo Aragazzi, secretary to Pope Martin V (who reigned from 1417 to 1431); it was created by Michelozzo between 1427 and 1436, and pieces of it have been dispersed to museums in other parts of the world. ⊠ *Piazza Grande* ☎ *0578/757761* ⊡ *Free* ◷ *Daily 9–12:30.*

Though sections of the **Palazzo Comunale** may date from the late 13th century, it was restructured in the 1300s and again in the mid-15th century. Michelozzo oversaw this last phase. From the tower, a commanding view of Siena, Mt. Amiata (the highest point in Tuscany), and Lake Trasimeno (the largest lake on the Italian peninsula) can be enjoyed on a clear day. ⊠ *Piazza Grande* ☎ *No phone* 🎫 *Free* 🕓 *Daily 8–1.*

Michelozzo had a hand in creating the beautiful travertine facade on the church of **Sant'Agostino,** which was founded in 1285 and renovated in the early 1400s. He also sculpted the terra-cotta relief of the Madonna and Child above the door. ⊠ *Piazza Michelozzo* ☎ *0578/757761* 🎫 *Free* 🕓 *Daily 9–12:30 and 3:30–7:30.*

On the hillside below the town walls is the church of **San Biagio,** designed by Antonio Sangallo il Vecchio. A paragon of Renaissance architectural perfection, it's considered by many to be his masterpiece. Inside the church is a painting of a Madonna. According to legend, the picture was the only thing remaining in an abandoned church that two young girls entered on April 23, 1518. The two girls saw the eyes of the Madonna moving, and that same afternoon so did a farmer and a cow, who knelt down in front of the painting. In 1963 the image was proclaimed the Madonna del Buon Viaggio (Madonna of the Good Journey), the protector of tourists in Italy. ⊠ *Via di San Biagio* ☎ *0578/7577761* 🕓 *Daily 9–12:30 and 3:30–7:30.*

Where to Stay & Eat

★ $$–$$$ ╳ **La Grotta.** You might be tempted to pass right by the innocuous entrance across the street from San Biagio, but don't: the food is fantastic. Try the *tagliolini con carciofi e rigatino* (thin noodles with artichokes and bacon) or *tagliatelle di grano saraceno con asparagi e zucchine* (flat, buckwheat-flour noodles with asparagus and zucchini). Wash it down with the local wine, which just happens to be one of Italy's finest—Vino Nobile di Montepulciano. The desserts, such as an extravagantly rich triple-chocolate flan, are prepared with particular flair. ⊠ *Via di San Biagio* ☎ *0578/757479* ▤ *AE, MC, V* 🕓 *Closed Wed. and Jan. 8–Feb. 28.*

★ $$$ ▦ **Podere Dionora.** The cypress-lined drive to this secluded country retreat hints that you have found something special. The Dionora sits serenely on an estate surrounded by carefully manicured lawns, woodlands, and vineyards. Earth-toned fabrics and walls complement antiques such as sleigh or iron beds in the individually decorated rooms. Every bathroom has a sauna and hydromassage tub. A separate building, where the buffet breakfast is served and international newspapers await you each morning, has large arched windows with delightful views of lawns and vineyards on all four sides. Your charming hosts—Mario, the owner, and Giulio, the manager—are here to serve. ⊠ *Via Vicinale di Poggiano, 53045, 3 km (2 mi) east of Montepulciano town center* ☎ *0578/717496* 🖶 *0578/717498* ⊕ *www.dionora.it* ➘ *4 rooms, 2 suites* ♨ *Dining room, in-room hot tubs, pool, minibars, mountain bikes; no a/c, no room phones* ▤ *AE, D, MC, V* 🕓 *Closed Feb.* ⫲⊙⫠ *CP.*

$ ▦ **Il Marzocco.** The building, within the town walls, is from the 16th century, but the hotel's appointments—old-fashioned parlors and a billiard room—evoke the 19th century. The furniture is dark, late-19th-century style or in spindly white wood. Many guest rooms have large terraces overlooking the countryside and are big enough to accommodate extra beds, which can be pulled in. ⊠ *Piazza Savonarola 18, 53045* ☎ *0578/757262* 🖷 *0578/757530* ⊕ *www.albergoilmarzocco.it* ↵ *16 rooms* ♿ *Restaurant, fans, billiards; no a/c* ⊟ *AE, DC, MC, V* ☺ *Closed Jan. 20–Feb. 10* ⫶◯⫶ *BP.*

$ 🖸 **La Bandita.** Terra-cotta floors and lace curtains are part of the charm that abounds in this attractive old farmhouse. A fireplace and 19th-century Tuscan provincial furniture fill the large, brick-vaulted living room. Some iron beds are among the simple antiques in the guest rooms. You can walk out among the gardens surrounding the house and down to the swimming pool. ⊠ *Off A1, Via Bandita 72, 53040 Bettolle, 16 km (10 mi) north of Montepulciano* 🖀🖀 *0577/624649* ⊕ *www. locandalabandita.it* ↵ *9 rooms* ♿ *Restaurant, some pets allowed; no a/c, no room phones, no room TVs* ⊟ *AE, DC, MC, V* ☺ *Restaurant closed Tues.* ⫶◯⫶ *CP.*

Nightlife & the Arts

The **Cantiere Internazionale d'Arte** (⊠ Piazza Grande 7 ☎ 0578/757341 for tourist-information office), held in July and August, is a festival of art, music, and theater ending with a major theatrical production staged in the Piazza Grande.

Pienza

★ ㉑   *12 km (7 mi) west of Montepulciano, 52 km (31 mi) southeast of Siena, 120 km (72 mi) southeast of Florence.*

Pienza owes its appearance to Pope Pius II (1405–64), who had grand plans to transform his home village of Corsignano—the town's former name—into a compact model Renaissance town. The man entrusted with the transformation was Bernardo Rossellino (1409–64), a protégé of the great Renaissance architectural theorist Leon Battista Alberti (1404–72). His mandate was to create a cathedral, a papal palace, and a town hall (plus miscellaneous buildings) that adhered to the vainglorious pope's principles. Gothic and Renaissance styles were fused, and the buildings were decorated with Sienese paintings. The net result was a project that expressed Renaissance ideals of art, architecture, and civilized good living in a single scheme: it stands as an exquisite example of the architectural canons that Alberti formulated in the early Renaissance and that were utilized by later architects, including Michelangelo, in designing many of Italy's finest buildings and piazzas. Today the cool nobility of Pienza's center seems almost surreal in this otherwise unpretentious village, known locally for *pienzino,* a smooth sheep's-milk pecorino cheese.

In 1459, Pius II commissioned Rossellino to design the perfect palazzo for his papal court. The architect took Florence's Palazzo Rucellai by Alberti as a model and designed the **Palazzo Piccolomini** with exactly 100 rooms. Three sides of the building fit perfectly into the urban plan around it, while the fourth, looking over the valley, has a lovely loggia uniting it with the gardens in back. Guided tours (every 30 minutes) take you to visit the papal apartments, including a beautiful library, the Sala delle Armi—with an impressive weapons collection—and the music room, with its extravagant wooden ceiling forming four letter P's, for

Pope, Pius, Piccolomini, and Pienza. The last tour departs 30 minutes before closing. ⊠ *Piazza Pio II 1* ☎ *0578/748503* ☒ €3 ⊗ *Mar.–Nov. 14 and Dec.16–Feb. 14, Tues.–Sun. 10–12:30 and 3–6.*

The 15th-century **Duomo** was also built by the architect Rossellino under the influence of Alberti. The facade is divided in three parts with Renaissance arches under the pope's coat of arms encircled by a wreath of fruit. Inside, the cathedral is simple but richly decorated with Sienese paintings. The Duomo's perfection didn't last long—the first cracks appeared immediately after the building was completed, and its foundations have shifted slightly ever since as rain erodes the hillside behind. You can see this effect if you look closely at the base of the first column as you enter the church and compare it with the last. ⊠ *Piazza Pio II* ☎ *No phone* ☒ *Free* ⊗ *Tues.–Sun. 10–1 and 3–7.*

The **Museo Diocesano** is at the left of the Duomo. It's small but has a few interesting papal treasures and rich Flemish tapestries. The most precious piece is a rare mantle woven in gold with pearls and embroidered religious scenes that belonged to Pope Pius II. ⊠ *Corso Il Rossellino 30* ☎ *0578/749905* ☒ €4.10 ⊗ *Mar. 16–Oct., Wed.–Mon. 10–1 and 3–6:30; Nov.–Mar. 15, weekends 10–1 and 3–6.*

Part of the acclaimed 1996 film *The English Patient* was filmed at **Sant' Anna in Camprena,** a former Benedictine monastery where you can view frescoes by Sodoma (1477–1549) in the refectory (dining hall) and in the room where the eponymous patient lay in bed. It's best reached by car or bicycle (public transportation isn't available). For the world-weary, extremely plain rooms are available in the austere silence of the monastery. Double rooms with private bathroom and breakfast are €70 per night; those without private bathroom are €60. ⊹ *From Pienza take road to San Quirico for 1 km (½ mi) and turn right; following signs for monastery, continue 6 km (4 mi) and turn left; take tree-lined dirt road to church* ☎ *0578/748037 or 338/4079284* ☒ *Free* ⊗ *Weekends 9–6.*

Where to Stay & Eat

¢–$ ✕ **La Chiocciola.** Take the few minutes to walk from the old town for typical Pienza fare, including homemade *pici* (thick, short spaghetti) with hare or wild boar sauce. Their version of *formaggio in forno* (baked cheese) with assorted accompaniments such as fresh porcini mushrooms is reason enough to come here. ⊠ *Via dell'Acero 2* ☎ *0578/748683* ▭ *MC, V* ⊗ *Closed Wed. and 10 days in Feb.*

¢ ✕ **Osteria Sette di Vino.** Tasty dishes based on the local cheeses are the specialty at this simple and inexpensive *osteria* (down-to-earth tavern). Try versions of pici or the starter of radicchio baked quickly to brown at the edges. The local specialty pecorino appears often on the menu—the pecorino *grigliata con pancetta* (grilled with cured bacon) is divine, as is the pecorino tasting menu. Osteria Sette di Vino is on a quiet, pleasant square in the center of Pienza. ⊠ *Piazza di Spagna 1* ☎ *0578/749092* ▭ *No credit cards* ⊗ *Closed Wed., July 1–15, and Nov.*

$ ▥ **Hotel Corsignano.** A modern, comfortable property, Hotel Corsignano lies just outside the old city walls. Two light-beige buildings, the older one right on the road, are connected by a hallway. The rooms in the newer half of the hotel in the back are quieter and larger and have newer furniture (plain and made of wood). Carpeting covers the floors, except for a few in the older front rooms, which have tile. ☒ *Via della Madonnina 11, 53026* ☎ *0578/748501* 🖷 *0578/748166* ⊕ *www.corsignano. it* ➶ *40 rooms* ♻ *Dining room, in-room safes, minibars, cable TV, dry cleaning, laundry service, Internet, free parking, some pets allowed* ▭ *AE, DC, MC, V* ¶◎¶ *CP.*

¢ ▥ **Camere di Pienza.** A Renaissance building on Pienza's main street houses this tiny hotel with only four rooms. They make up for their small number in quality, with pretty, if simple, decoration and particularly nice ceilings—three with wood beams and one with a fresco. ☒ *Corso Il Rossellino 23, 53026* ☎ *0578/748500* ➶ *4 rooms* ♻ *No a/c* ▭ *No credit cards* ¶◎¶ *EP.*

San Quirico d'Orcia

㉒ *9½ km (5½ mi) southwest of Pienza, 43 km (26 mi) southeast of Siena, 111 km (67 mi) southeast of Florence.*

San Quirico d'Orcia, on the modern Via Cassia (SR2) south from Siena toward Rome, has almost-intact 15th-century walls topped with 14 turrets. The pleasantly crumbling appearance of the town recalls days of yore, and it's well suited for a stop to enjoy a gelato in a local bar or a meal and to see its Romanesque church.

The 13th-century **Collegiata** church has three majestic portals, one possibly the work of Giovanni Pisano (circa 1245/48–1318). ☒ *Piazza Chigi* ☎ *No phone* 🖃 *Free* ⊘ *Daily 8:30–12:30.*

Against the walls of San Quirico d'Orcia is the **Horti Leonini,** a public park with Italian-style gardens that retain merely a shimmer of their past opulence. ☒ *Off Piazza Libertà.*

Near Horti Leonini stands **Palazzo Chigi,** named after the family to whom the Medici gave San Quirico in 1667. Small art exhibitions are occasionally displayed in the palace courtyard, which is otherwise closed to the public. ☒ *Piazza Chigi.*

Where to Stay & Eat

$ ✕ **Trattoria al Vecchio Forno.** A meal here is truly delicious: specialties include dishes accented with porcini mushrooms, such as the excellent mushroom soup. You might also try pici with tomato or boar sauce, and roast boar and game. The menu is rounded out by a varied wine selection. There's a nice garden out back. ☒ *Via Piazzola 8* ☎ *0577/897380* ▭ *MC, V* ⊘ *Closed Wed., 10 days mid-Nov., and 2 wks mid-Jan.*

$$ ▥ **Hotel Residence Casanova.** Just 1,000 feet from the city walls a lovely old villa has been converted into an inn. Views of the Val d'Orcia are stunning, and the rooms are nicely decorated with practical, mid-tone to dark-wood Tuscan furniture that has simple curves or straight lines. Some suites have kitchens, but half board is available. The restaurant, La Taverna del Barbarossa ($$), is inside a classic Tuscan country house, with brick archways and statuary, that dates from the 13th century. Its name commemorates a meeting held here in medieval times between papal mes-

sengers and Frederick I (circa 1123–90), who was called Il Barbarossa. ⊠ *SP146, Località Casanova, 53027* ☎ *0577/898177* ⊟ *0577/898190* ⊕ *www.residencecasanova.it* ⇆ *44 rooms, 26 suites* ⚭ *Restaurant, some kitchens, cable TV, tennis court, pool, gym, sauna, spa, steam room, mountain bikes, billiards, Ping-Pong, bar, recreation room, babysitting, playground, Internet, some pets allowed (fee)* ⊟ *AE, DC, MC, V* ¹⊚¹ *CP.*

$ 🏨 **Palazzo del Capitano.** The eleven guest quarters in the 14th-century palace are named for zodiac signs (the name of the largest suite, Pisces/ Ares, makes up for the missing room), but the astrological reference stops at the painted symbol on the door. Each elegant room is individual: an antique sewing-machine table serves as a nightstand; a medieval-looking chandelier with a forged-iron ring and a globe hangs from a ceiling; striped silk covers a wood settee. Some rooms have ivory drapes hanging from baldachin beds—iron canopy beds with a painted medallion on the head piece. A lovely garden opens behind the hotel. ⊠ *Via Poliziano 18, 53027* ☎☎ *0577/899028* ⊕ *www.palazzodelcapitano.com* ⇆ *9 rooms, 2 suites* ⚭ *Restaurant, some in-room hot tubs, in-room safes, cable TV, bar* ⊟ *MC, V* ¹⊚¹ *CP.*

Bagno Vignoni

㉓ *5 km (3 mi) south of San Quirico d'Orcia, 48 km (29 mi) southeast of Siena, 116 km (70 mi) southeast of Florence.*

Bagno Vignoni has been famous since Roman times for the sulfurous waters that come bubbling up into the large rectangular pool that forms the town's main square, Piazza delle Sorgenti (Square of the Springs). Medieval pilgrims and modern hikers alike have soothed their tired feet in the pleasantly warm water that flows through open channels on its way to collecting pools and the River Orcia below. Of particular interest are the ruins of a medieval bath house on the edge of town and the Chapel of Saint Catherine, who, it seems, came here often.

Bagno Vignoni's public hot-spring swimming pool, **Piscina Val di Sole,** provides warm water relaxation for more than just your feet. Stand under the waterfall to massage and soothe weary shoulder muscles. There's no swimming allowed from 1 to 2:30 on Friday to Wednesday, and admission ends at 5 PM. Thursday there are limited hours. ⊠ *Via Ara Urcea 43* ☎ *0577/887112* ⊕ *www.piscinavaldisole* 🎟 *Fri.–Wed. €10, Thurs. €7* ☉ *Fri.–Wed. 9–6, Thurs. 9–1.*

off the beaten path

VIGNONI ALTO – A steep gravel road leads north out of Bagno Vignoni for 2 km (1 mi) to Vignoni Alto, a tiny grouping of buildings huddled at the base of a 13th-century tower. The tower, now a private home, was built to watch over the Via Francigena, and not surprisingly, a spectacular view of the entire Val d'Orcia opens up from the eastern gate of the village.

Where to Eat

¢ ✕ **Bottega di.Cacio.** A pleasantly shaded place for a light lunch is the small eatery serving pecorino cheeses, salami, and grilled vegetables *sott'olio* (preserved in olive oil). If it's something spicy you want, try the deli-

cious stuffed hot peppers. ⊠ *Piazza del Moretto 31* ☎ *0577/887477*
☱ *No credit cards* ⊘ *Closed Thurs.*

Montalcino

㉔ *19 km (12 mi) northeast of Bagno Vignoni, 41 km (25½ mi) south of Siena, 109 km (68 mi) south of Florence.*

Tiny Montalcino, with its commanding view from high on a hill, can claim an Etruscan past. It saw a fair number of travelers, as it was directly on the road from Siena to Rome. During the early Middle Ages it enjoyed a brief period of autonomy before falling under the orbit of Siena in 1201. Now Montalcino's greatest claim to fame is that it produces Brunello di Montalcino, one of Italy's most esteemed reds. Driving up to Montalcino, you pass through the Brunello vineyards. You can sample the excellent but expensive red in wine cellars in town or visit a nearby winery, such as Fattoria dei Barbi, for a guided tour and tasting; you must call ahead for reservations.

La Fortezza, a 14th-century Sienese fortress, has well-preserved battlements. Climb up the narrow, spiral steps for the 360-degree view of most of southern Tuscany. There's also an enoteca for tasting wines on-site. ⊠ *Via Panfilo dell'Oca* ☎ *0577/849211* ☱ *€3* ⊘ *Nov.–Mar., Tues.–Sun. 9–6; Apr.–Oct., daily 9–8.*

The **Museo Civico e Diocesano d'Arte Sacra** building belonged in the 13th century to the Augustinian monastic order. The ticket booth is in the glorious refurbished cloister, and the sacred art collection, gathered from area churches, is displayed on two floors in former monastic quarters. Though the art here might be called "B-list," a fine altarpiece by Bartolo di Fredi (circa 1330–1410), *Coronation of the Virgin,* makes dazzling use of gold. In addition, there's a striking 12th-century crucifix that originally adorned the high altar of the church of Sant'Antimo. Also on hand are many wood sculptures, a typical medium in these parts during the Renaissance. ⊠ *Via Ricasoli 21* ☎ *0577/846014* ☱ *€4.50* ⊘ *Jan.–Mar., Tues.–Sun. 10–1 and 2–5; Apr.–Oct., Tues.–Sun. 10–6; Nov.–Dec., Tues.–Sun. 10–1 and 2–6.*

The cellars of the venerable **Fattoria dei Barbi** date from the 17th century and hold almost 200 large, oak wine barrels. Some of Italy's most famous wines are produced here, including an excellent range of Brunellos, a fine Rosso di Montalcino, and the estate's special Super Tuscan brands, Brusco dei Barbi and Bruscone dei Barbi. Olive oil, salami, and pecorino cheese are also made on the winery's organic farm. Guided visits to the cellars are followed by wine tastings, during which you can also sample the other products. ⊠ *Località Podernovi 1* ☎ *0577/841111* ⊕ *www.fattoriadeibarbi.it* ☱ *Free* ⊘ *Weekdays at 11, noon, 3, 4, and 5.*

Where to Stay & Eat

$$$$ ✕ **Poggio Antico.** One of Italy's renowned chefs, Roberto Minnetti, abandoned his highly successful restaurant in Rome and moved to the country outside Montalcino. Now he and his wife Patrizia serve in a relaxed but regal dining room with arches and beamed ceilings. The Tuscan cuisine is masterfully interpreted by Roberto: an option on the changing menu might be *pappardelle al ragù di agnello* (flat, wide noodles in a lamb sauce) or venison in a sweet-and-sour sauce. ⊠ *On road to Grosseto, 4 km (2½ mi) south of Montalcino, Località I Poggi* ☏ *0577/849200* ⊟ *MC, V* ⊘ *Closed Mon. and 3 wks in Jan. No dinner Sun.*

$–$$ ✕ **Enoteca Osteria Osticcio.** Tullio and Francesca Scrivano have beautifully remodeled this wine shop–enoteca. Upon entering, you descend a curving staircase into a tasting room filled with rustic wooden tables; adjacent is a small dining area with a splendid view of the hills far below, and outside is a lovely little terrace perfect for sampling Brunello di Montalcino when the weather is warm. The menu is light and pairs nicely with the wines, which are the main draw. The *acciughe sotto pesto* (anchovies with pesto) are a particularly fine treat. ⊠ *Via Matteotti 23* ☏ *0577/848271* ⊟ *AE, DC, MC, V* ⊘ *Closed Sun. No dinner.*

$ ✕ **Il Grappolo Blu.** Any of the *piatti tipici* (typical plates) are worth trying here: *pici all' aglione* (thick, long noodles served with sautéed cherry tomatoes and many cloves of garlic), a local specialty, is done particularly well. The chef also has a deft touch with vegetables; if there's fennel on the menu (which is written in many languages), order it. The interior, with white walls and an odd collection of cheap prints, doesn't leave much of an impression. ⊠ *Scale di via Moglio 1* ☏ *0577/847150* ⌖ *Reservations essential* ⊟ *AE, DC, MC, V* ⊘ *Closed Fri.*

¢ ✕🏠 **Fattoria dei Barbi.** Set among the vineyards of a family-owned wine estate that produces excellent Brunello—as well as its younger cousin, Rosso di Montalcino—is this rustic taverna with a large stone fireplace. The estate farm produces many of the ingredients used in such traditional specialties as *stracotto nel brunello* (braised beef cooked with beans in Brunello wine). Two comfortable, traditionally furnished apartments are next to the restaurant; a two-night minimum stay is required throughout the year. ⊠ *Località Podernuovi, 53024* ☏ *0577/841111, 0577/841200 taverna* 🖷 *0577/841112* ⊕ *www.fattoriadeibarbi.it* ⌖ *Reservations essential* ⇌ *2 apartments* ⚒ *Fans, kitchenettes, cable TV, some pets allowed; no a/c* ⊟ *AE, DC, MC, V* ⊘ *Restaurant closed Wed. and mid-Jan.–mid-Feb. No dinner Tues. Nov.–Mar.* ❢ *EP.*

¢–$ 🏠 **La Crociona.** A quiet and serene family-owned farm, La Crociona is in the middle of a small vineyard with glorious views. The apartments, which can sleep from two to six people, have such comforts as antique iron beds and 17th-century wardrobes. There's a big terrace and you are invited to hang out around the pool and use the family barbecue, as well as to sample the owner's own wine supply. ⊠ *Località La Croce, 53024* ☏🖷 *0577/848007* ⊕ *www.lacrociona.com* ⇌ *7 apartments* ⚒ *BBQs, kitchenettes, cable TV, pool, mountain bikes, babysitting, dry cleaning, laundry facilities, Internet; no a/c, no room phones* ⊟ *MC, V* ❢ *EP.*

Abbazia di Sant'Antimo

㉕
FodorsChoice
★

10 km (6 mi) south of Montalcino, 51 km (32 mi) south of Siena, 119 km (74 mi) south of Florence.

It's well worth your while to visit this 12th-century Romanesque abbey, as it's a gem of pale stone in the silvery green of an olive grove. The exterior and interior sculpture is outstanding, particularly the nave capitals, a combination of French, Lombard, and even Spanish influences. The sacristy (rarely open) forms part of the primitive Carolingian church (founded in AD 781), its entrance flanked by 9th-century pilasters. The small vaulted crypt dates from the same period. Above the nave runs a *matroneum* (women's gallery), an unusual feature once used to separate the congregation. Equally unusual is the ambulatory, of which the three radiating chapels (rare in Italian churches) were probably copied from the French model. Stay for mass to hear the ceremony performed in Gregorian chant. Sections of the church are closed to visits during religious functions. On the drive that leads up toward Castelnuovo dell'Abate is a small shop that sells souvenirs and has washrooms. A 2½-hour hiking trail (signed as #2) leads to the abbey from Montalcino. Starting near Montalcino's small cemetery, the trail heads south through woods, along a ridge road to the tiny hamlet of Villa a Tolli, and then downhill to Sant'Antimo. ✉ *Castelnuovo dell'Abate, Sant'Antimo* ☎ *0577/835659* ⊕ *www.antimo.it* ✉ *Free* ☉ *Daily 6 AM–9 PM.*

THE MAREMMAN INLAND

The wildest part of Tuscany is here in its southern heart. And it's here that you get a sense of what the region looked like before Tuscany became a must-see on the Grand Tour. The landscape alternates between rolling hills and tufa cliffs; hill towns abound, linked by narrow, winding roads. Saturnia—with its superior hotels, restaurants, and one-of-a-kind hot springs—makes a good base to explore and sample the best of what the south has to offer: ancient Etruscan tombs and caverns at Sovana and Sorano, the famous white wine of Pitigliano, and wild mushrooms and chestnut honey from the rugged slopes of Monte Amiata, which presides over Tuscany with views from Arezzo to the sea.

Monte Amiata

㉖ *16 km (10 mi) south of Abbazia di Sant'Antimo, 86 km (52 mi) southeast of Siena, 156 km (94 mi) southeast of Florence.*

At 5,702 feet, this benign volcano is one of Tuscany's few ski slopes, but it's no Mont Blanc. Come in warmer months to take advantage of an abundance of hiking trails that cross wide meadows full of wildflowers and slice through groves of evergreens. Panoramic views of all of Tuscany present themselves on the winding road up to the summit. Along the way, you pass through a succession of tiny medieval towns, including Castel del Piano, Arcidosso, Santa Flora, and Piancastagnaio, where you can pick up picnic supplies and sample the chestnuts and game for which the mountain is famous. The thousand-year-old village of **Abbadia San Salvatore** is worth a stop—skip the nondescript new town and head straight to the *centro storico* (historic center) to explore winding stone streets with tiny churches around every corner. The abbey for which the town was named was founded in 743; its current appearance reflects an 11th-century renovation, but the original crypt remains intact. The tourist office in town has hiking trail maps for Monte Amiata. ✉ *Tourist office, Via Mentana 97, La Piazzetta* ☎ *0577/778608* 🖷 *0577/779013.*

Sorano

⊘ *38 km (23 mi) south of Abbadia San Salvatore on Monte Amiata, 138 km (86 mi) southeast of Siena, 208 km (130 mi) southeast of Florence.*

Sorano's history follows the pattern of most settlements in the area: it was an ancient Etruscan citadel, built up in the 15th century and fortified by one of the many warring families of Tuscany (in this case, the Orsini). It's the execution that sets it apart. With its tiny, twisted streets and stone houses connected by wooden stairways and ramps, Sorano looks as if it was carved from the tufa beneath it—and that's because it was. Underneath the town, visible as you approach, is a vast network of *colombari,* Etruscan-era rooms lined with hundreds of niches carved into stone walls, dating from the 1st century BC. The colombari aren't yet open to the public, but Sorano is worth a visit regardless, if only to walk its medieval alleyways and to watch old-style artisans at work. Views of the densely forested hills around town will have you reaching for your camera.

Where to Stay

$ 🏨 **Della Fortezza.** From high above Sorano, all the rooms in the austere-looking 11th-century Orsini castle have spectacular views of the town and the surrounding countryside—the location of this hotel is second to none. Wood-beam ceilings hang above white and pastel walls in most rooms, and windows have dark-wood shutters. A careful mix of antique and modern furniture—rococo chairs and upholstered couches—makes for a pleasant and comfortable stay. The hotel closes some during the winter; the length and month of the closure vary annually. ⊠ *Piazza Cairoli 5, 58010* 📞 *0564/632010* 🖨 *0564/633209* ⊕ *www. fortezzahotel.it* ⊅ *14 rooms, 1 suite* ⌂ *Dining room, minibars, cable TV, bar, Internet, free parking; no a/c, no phones in some rooms* 🖃 *AE, DC, MC, V* ⦿I *CP.*

Pitigliano

⊘ *10 km (6 mi) south of Sorano, 147 km (92 mi) southeast of Siena, 217 km (136 mi) southeast of Florence.*

From a distance the medieval stone houses of Pitigliano look as if they melt into the cliffs of soft tufa rock they are perched on. Etruscan tombs, which locals use to store wine, are connected by a network of caves and tunnels. At the beginning of the 14th century, the Orsini family moved their base from Sovana to the naturally better-fortified Pitigliano. They built up the town's defenses and fortified their home, Palazzo Orsini. Later, starting in 1543, Antonio da Sangallo the Younger added to the town's fortress aspect, building bastions and towers throughout the town and adding the 16th-century aqueduct as well.

Pitigliano has become a trendy locale for Italian vacation rentals, making the town center very lively in the summer. Restaurants serve up good food but, as a result of the tourist boom, at inflated prices. Bianco di Pitigliano (Pitigliano white wine) is a fresh and light, dry wine produced from the vines that thrive in the tufa soil of the area.

The 18th-century baroque **Duomo** has a single nave with chapels and paintings on the sides. There are two altarpieces by local artist Francesco Zuccarelli (1702–88), a rococo landscape artist and a founder of the British Royal Academy who was a favorite of George III. ⊠ *Piazza S. Gregorio* ☎ *0564/616090* ☎ *Free* ⊘ *Daily 9–7.*

Inside the **Palazzo Orsini** is the **Museo Zuccarelli**, featuring paintings by Zuccarelli as well as a Madonna by Jacopo della Quercia (1371/ 1374–1438), a 14th-century crucifix, and other works of interest. ⊠ *Piazza della Repubblica* ☎ *0564/616074* ☎ *€2.50* ⊘ *Apr.–Oct., Tues.–Sun. 10–1 and 4–7; Nov.–Mar., Tues.–Fri. 10–1 and 3–6.*

Piccola Gerusaleme di Pitigliano is the ghetto where Jews took refuge from 16th-century Catholic persecution; a thriving community lived here until the beginning of World War II. Inside the precinct are the remains of ritual bathing basins, a wine cellar, a museum of Jewish culture, a kosher butchery and bakery, and the restored synagogue, where religious services are held on the Sabbath. ⊠ *Via Firenze 116a* ☎ *0564/616006* ☎ *€2.50* ⊘ *Apr.–Oct., Sun.–Fri. 10–12:30 and 4–7; Nov.–Mar., Sun.–Fri. 10–12:30 and 3–5:30.*

Where to Stay & Eat

$$–$$$ ✕ **Il Tufo Allegro.** The name means Happy Tufa; you can be happy, too, if you eat at this fine restaurant cut directly into the tufa rock plateau on which old Pitigliano sits. The cuisine is local and Tuscan: *coniglio al finocchio selvatico* (rabbit with wild fennel) is particularly tasty, and fish also figures on the menu from time to time. ⊠ *Vicolo della Costituzione 5* ☎ *0564/616192* ⊟ *AE, DC, MC, V* ⊘ *Closed Tues. and mid-Jan.–mid-Feb. No lunch Wed. Oct.–July.*

¢ 🏠 **Locanda Il Tufo Rosa.** The space for part of this tiny guesthouse has been carved out of the tufa rock beneath the aqueduct at the entrance to the old town. Rooms are small and simply decorated with painted armoires and wood dressing tables, but immaculately clean. Beds stand right up against walls with a floral print chair rail. Only one room, the smallest, has no air-conditioning. ⊠ *Piazza Petruccioli 97, 58017* ☎ *0564/617019* ⊕ *www.iltuforosa.com* 🖷 *0564/617784* ➘ *6 rooms* △ *Minibars; no a/c in some rooms, no room phones* ⊟ *No credit cards* ⦙⊙⦙ *EP.*

Sovana

29 *5 km (3 mi) north of Pitigliano, 155 km (97 mi) southeast of Siena, 225 km (141 mi) southeast of Florence.*

This town of Etruscan origin was once the capital of the area in southern Tuscany ruled by the Aldobrandeschi family, whose reign was at its height in the 11th and first half of the 12th centuries. One member of the family, Hildebrand, was the 11th-century Catholic reformer Pope Gregory VII (circa 1020–85, served as pope 1073–1085). The 13th- to 14th-century Romanesque fortress known as the Rocca Aldobrandesca is now in ruins. Via di Mezzo, with stones arranged in a fish-scale pattern, is the main street running the length of the town.

The town extends from the fortress on the eastern end to the imposing **Duomo,** built between the 10th and the 14th centuries, on the edge of town to the west. ⊠ *Piazza del Duomo* ☎ *No phone* 🖾 *Free* ☉ *Daily 10–1 and 2:45–5:45.*

The central **Piazza del Pretorio** contains the 13th-century Palazzo Pretorio, which has a facade adorned with crests of Sovana's captains of justice, and the Renaissance Palazzo Bourbon dal Monte.

The little 14th-century church of **Santa Maria Maggiore** has frescoes from the late-15th-century Sienese Umbrian school. ⊠ *Piazza del Pretorio* ☎ *No phone* 🖾 *Free* ☉ *Daily 8:30–12:30 and 4–6:30.*

You can visit some of Italy's best-preserved monumental rock tombs, dating from the 2nd to the 3rd centuries BC, at the **Etruscan necropolis.** Some of the tombs, such as the so-called Tomba Sirena (Siren's Tomb), preserve clear signs of their original and elaborately carved decorations. Others, like the Tomba Ildebranda (Hildebrand Tomb), are spectacular evidence of the architectural complexity sometimes achieved. Don't forget to walk along the section of an Etruscan road carved directly into the tufa stone. ⊠ *1½ km (½ mi) west of Sovana town center* ☎ *0564/ 614074* ⊠ *€5.50* ☉ *Daily 9–sunset.*

Where to Eat

$–$$ ✕ **La Taverna Etrusca.** Uncomplicated Tuscan fare is served at this restaurant on Sovana's central square. Try the pici *all'aglione* (with tomatoes and lots of sautéed garlic); it's a local speciality. Grilled meat and some fish dishes highlight the list of second courses. An outdoor terrace provides plenty of fresh air. ⊠ *Piazza del Pretorio 16* ☎ *0564/616183* ▭ *AE, DC, MC, V* ☉ *Closed Wed.*

Saturnia

㉚ *25 km (15 mi) east of Sovana, 129 km (77 mi) south of Siena, 199 km (119 mi) south of Florence.*

Saturnia was settled even before the Etruscan period, but nowadays it's best known not for what lies buried beneath the ground but for what comes up from it: hot, sulfurous water that supplies the town's world-famous spa. According to an oft-repeated legend, the thermal waters were created when Saturn, restless with earth's bickering mortals, threw down a thunderbolt and created a hot spring whose miraculously calming waters created peace among them. Today these magnesium-rich waters bubble forth from the clay, drawing Italians and non-Italians alike seeking relief for skin and muscular ailments as well as a bit (well, a lot) of relaxation. Unlike better-known spa centers such as Montecatini Terme, nature still has her place here. Outside Saturnia, the hot, sulfurous waters cascade over natural limestone shelves at the **Cascate del Gorello** (Gorello Falls), affording bathers a sweeping view of the open countryside. The falls are on public land, near an abandoned farmhouse, and can be enjoyed free, 24 hours a day. They get extremely crowded—day and night—during August. ⊹ *2 km (1 mi) south of Saturnia, on road to Montemerano* ☎ *No phone.*

CloseUp

TERME, WRATH OF THE GODS

I N A COUNTRY KNOWN FOR MILLENNIA as a hotbed of seismic activity, Tuscany seems to have gotten a lucky break. While Campania and Sicily are famous for active volcanoes, and Umbria and the Marches stand on notoriously shaky ground, Tuscany's underground activity makes itself known in the form of steamy and sulfurous hot springs that have earned the region a name as a spa goer's paradise.

Tuscany is dotted throughout with small terme (thermal baths) where hot waters flow from natural springs deep under the earth's surface. Since the time of the Etruscans, Tuscany's first rulers, these hot springs have been valued for their curative properties. The Romans, in their turn, attributed the springs' origins to divine thunderbolts that split the earth open and let flow the miraculous waters. Although the findings of modern geology rob the springs of some of their mystery, their appeal endures, as the presence of thousands of people taking the waters in the Maremma attests.

Each of the springs has different curative properties, attributable to the various concentrations of minerals and gases that individual water flows pick up on their way to the surface. Carbon dioxide, for example, is said to promote drainage and strengthen the immune system, while sulfur, its characteristic rotten-egg smell notwithstanding, is said to relieve pain and aid in relaxation. Although customs and conventions vary between spa establishments, you generally pay an admission fee to swim in baths that range from hot natural lakes and waterfalls (with all the accompanying mud) to giant limestone swimming pools distinguishable from the garden variety only by their cloudy, bright blue, and steaming water. Larger establishments have treatments based on the springs, which can range

from mineral mud baths to doctor-supervised steam inhalations, all with much-touted curative effects. Believers swear that Tuscany's hot springs have a positive effect on everything from skin disorders to back pain to liver function to stress, and spa personnel will gladly offer up case histories and scientific studies to prove their point. Whatever your opinion, a good soak in a Tuscan spring is a relaxing way to take a break, and as far as geological phenomena go, it beats an earthquake or a volcanic eruption any day.

A few of the region's spas, notably the world-famous Montecatini Terme (⇨ Chapter 2), are well known outside of Tuscany. For the most part, however, the local establishments that run the springs are not well publicized; this can mean a more local flavor, lower prices, and fewer crowds: Terme di Bagni di Lucca is near Lucca (⇨ Chapter 4); Terme di Chianciano is near Chiusi; Bagno Vignoni is just south of San Quirico d'Orcia; and Terme di Saturnia is not too far from Grosseto. Local tourist offices have the most up-to-date information on smaller springs, many of which are open for only part of the year; contact an APT or Pro Loco in the area you plan to visit for recommendations on where to go for a nice, hot bath.

Fodor's Choice

★

The swimming pools and treatments at **Terme di Saturnia** spa and resort are open to nonguests. You might make an appointment for a thermal mud therapy and a hydromassage bath. Or rent a lounge chair and umbrella by the pools. ⊕ *3 km (2 mi) east of Saturnia on road to Monte-merano, after Gorello Falls* ☎ *0564/601061* ⊕ *www.saturnia-terme.it* ✉ *Full day €16, half day €12* ☾ *May–Sept., daily 9:30–7:30; Oct.–Apr., daily 9:30–5:30.*

Pre-Etruscan tombs at the **Necropoli del Puntone** aren't kept up well, but they're interesting simply for their age, as they're even older than Saturnia's legendary baths. ⊕ *1 km (½ mi) north of Saturnia, on the road to Poggio Murello, turn left and follow signs* ☎ *No phone* ✉ *Free* ☾ *Daily 24 hrs.*

Where to Stay & Eat

★ $$$$ ✕ **Da Caino.** At this excellent restaurant in the nearby town of Montemerano, specialties include tomatoes and peppers on crisp phyllo dough, ravioli *ripieni di olio extra vergine di olive* (filled with extra virgin olive oil, capers, anchovies, and fresh tomatoes), lasagna with pumpkin, and such hearty dishes as *cinghiale lardolato con olive* (wild boar larded with olives). Prices are among the highest in the region; locals consider it a serious splurge. ✉ *Via della Chiesa 4, Montemerano, 7 km (4½ mi) south of Saturnia on the road to Scansano* ☎ *0564/602817* 🍴 *Reservations essential* ☰ *DC, MC, V* ☾ *Closed Wed., Jan., and 2 wks in July. No lunch Thurs.*

$–$$$ ✕ **I Due Cippi–Da Michele.** Owner Michele Aniello captivates with a lengthy and creative menu, with emphasis placed on Maremman ingredients such as wild boar and duck. Try the *tortelli di castagne al seme di finocchio* (chestnut-stuffed pasta pillows with butter sauce and fennel seeds). In good weather you can enjoy your meal on a terrace overlooking the town's main square. ✉ *Piazza Veneto 26/a* ☎ *0564/601074* 🍴 *Reservations essential* ☰ *AE, DC, MC, V* ☾ *Closed Dec. 20–26, Jan. 10–25, and Tues. Oct.–June.*

$$$$ ▦ **Terme di Saturnia.** Spa living might not get any more top-notch than this: roam the spa resort in a plush white bathrobe (waiting in your room) before dipping into the 37.5°C (100°F) sulfurous thermal pools. Seemingly every possible health and beauty treatment is available. Sleek elegance pervades public and private rooms: tall windows have full, floor-to-ceiling draperies in rich colors like steel blue and gray or burnt umber and sage; floors are polished wood. Eclectic furniture includes some sleigh-shape benches and oval night tables. You can opt for half or full board to complete the experience. ✉ *3 km (2 mi) east of Saturnia on road to Montemerano, past Gorello Falls, 58050* ☎ *0564/ 601061* 🖶 *0564/601266* ⊕ *www.termedisaturnia.it* 🛏 *140 rooms, 10 suites* ♨ *3 restaurants, snack bar, room service, in-room safes, minibars, cable TV with movies, in-room VCRs, driving range, 2 tennis courts, 2 pools, 2 wading pools, health club, hair salon, sauna, spa, steam room, bar, piano bar, shops, dry cleaning, laundry facilities, concierge, Internet, helipad, some pets allowed* ☰ *AE, DC, MC, V* ⦿ *BP.*

$ ▦ **Villa Acquaviva.** An elegant villa painted antique rose appears at the end of a tree-lined driveway perched on top of a hill off the main road 1 km (½ mi) before Montemerano. It has expansive views and quintessential Tuscan charm. Tastefully decorated rooms—with curly ironwork or tapestries as bed headboards—are in both the main villa and a guest house. The farm that fans out around the villa produces both wine and olive oil. ⊠ *Strada Scansanese, 58050 Montemerano, 6 km (4 mi) south of Saturnia* ☎ *0564/602890* 🖷 *0564/602895* ⊕ *www.relaisvillaacquaviva. com* 🗗 *22 rooms, 3 suites* ౿ *Restaurant, in-room safes, minibars, cable TV, tennis court, pool, bar, some pets allowed, no-smoking rooms* ⊟ *MC, V* †⊙† *EP.*

★ $ 🖳 **Villa Clodia.** The former private villa in Saturnia's hilltop town center has splendid views over the neighboring hills, and the steamy clouds coming from the hot springs. Inside it's just as nice, with hand-painted decoration in spacious rooms and a cozy library with a marble fireplace. Breakfast is served in a country-style room with gingham tablecloths, but early risers may be able to stake a claim on one of the terrace tables overlooking the valley. ⊠ *Via Italia 43, 58050* ☎ *0564/601212* 🖷 *0564/601305* ⊕ *www.laltramaremma.it/it/ric/villaclodia.htm#* 🗗 *8 rooms, 2 suites* ౿ *In-room safes, minibars, pool, free parking* ⊟ *AE, DC, MC, V* ☉ *Closed Dec.* †⊙† *CP.*

$ 🖳 **Villa Garden.** The rooms at this small place, with comfortable beds, floral curtains and bedspreads, and tiled bathrooms, are named for flowers. Just a few minutes from the center of town, it's a good place to stay if you want to take the waters without breaking the bank. The buffet breakfast is filling and tasty, the staff courteous and efficient. ⊠ *Via Sterpeti 56, 58014* ☎☎ *0564/601182* ⊕ *www.laltramaremma.it/villa garden* 🗗 *10 rooms* ౿ *Minibars, cable TV, bar, Internet, free parking, some pets allowed; no a/c in some rooms* ⊟ *AE, DC, MC, V* †⊙† *CP.*

MAREMMAN COAST & TUSCAN ISLANDS

Tuscany's coast is blessed with the best of both worlds: steep hills flanked by evergreen forests and classic Tuscan views back-to-back with an enviable stretch of sandy beaches and sparkling sea. The ruined, fairy-tale Abbazia di San Galgano is a must-see, and the chain of hill towns around it are as classically pretty as anything Chianti has to offer. But this part of the Maremma is best known for its beaches and coastal towns, less developed than those to the north but even more popular among summer-vacationing cognoscenti.

The six main islands in the waters between the Tuscan coast and the French island of Corsica make up the Parco Nazionale dell'Arcipelago Toscano (Tuscan Archipelago National Park), an emerald swath of clean, deep water and small rocky islets that contains the largest protected marine area in Europe. Long, sandy beaches and tranquil coves are the bewitching gateways to an undersea world of corals, gorgons, multicolor fish, and dolphins; given the richness of its wildlife and its proximity to the mainland, it's a pleasant surprise to find that most of the park's islands are largely overlooked by outsiders. This is not to say that foreigners are anything new here: Napoléon (1769–1821) spent a glamorous exile on lush Elba in 1814–15, and Alexandre Dumas's *Le Comte de Monte-Cristo* was inspired by the tiny island of Montecristo, now a strictly protected wildlife refuge. But the islands are, thankfully, still a trip off the beaten path. Giglio and its little sister Giannutri, between Montecristo and Monte Argentario at the south of the island chain, are rocky retreats for nature lovers and beach bums. Even less touristed are remote Capraia, frequented mostly by sailors, and the former prison colony of Pianosa, whose last notorious inmates were released in 1998, leaving a massive, empty *carcere* (prison) and a landscape untouched by tourism. Montecristo can be visited only by special permission, normally given to scientific researchers—all the better to preserve this, the most pristine part of the Tuscan sea.

Of the islands, only Giglio and Elba are well equipped for visitors, with excellent hotels and restaurants and easy transportation from the mainland. Capraia has a few hotels, Giannutri has basic facilities for those who really want to get away from it all, and Pianosa makes a good day trip from Elba.

Monte Argentario

③① *Porto San Stefano 60 km (37 mi) southeast of Saturnia, 118 km (74 mi) southwest of Siena, 186 km (116 mi) southwest of Florence.*

Connected to the mainland only by three thin strips of land, Monte Argentario feels like an island. The north and south isthmuses, La Giannella and La Feniglia, have long sandy beaches popular with families, but otherwise the terrain is rugged, dotted with luxurious vacation houses (including Sophia Loren's) and wildflowers. There are beautiful views from the panoramic mountain road encircling the promontory, and a drive here is a romantic sunset excursion. The mountain itself rises 2,096 feet above the sea, and it's ringed with rocky beaches and sheer cliffs that afford breathtaking views of the coast.

On the north side, busy and colorful **Porto Santo Stefano** is Monte Argentario's main center, with markets, hotels, restaurants, and ferry service to Giglio and Giannutri, two of the Tuscan Islands. To the south in Monte Argentario, **Porto Ercole** is the haunt of the rich and famous, with top-notch hotels and restaurants perched on the cliffs.

Where to Stay & Eat

$$–$$$ ✕ **Armando.** The nautical-style family-run restaurant is known for spaghetti *alle briciole* (literally, "with crumbs"), and the kitchen here conjures up a richly inventive version, dressed with garlic, olive oil, hot peppers, and anchovies. The *moscardini con fagioli* (similar to cuttlefish, served with beans) is tastily aromatic. This may not be the place for a romantic candlelit meal, but the food makes up for the lack of allure. ⊠ *Via Marconi 1/3, Porto Santo Stefano* ☎ *0564/812568* ▭ *AE, DC, MC, V* ⊘ *Closed Wed. and Nov.–Mar.*

$$ ✕ **Gambero Rosso.** Enjoy a seaside Italian classic right at the port. Simple preparations of fresh fish have been drawn from local waters. Try the antipasto *sorpresa del Gambero* (surprise of the house), an ever-changing array of six, sometimes seven, different fish dishes (fried, chilled, or baked, for example). The chef lets his imagination run wild, and it's only to the benefit of the happy diners. It's even better if you enjoy it on the terrace with a view. ⊠ *Lungomare Andrea Doria 62, Porto Ercole*

☎ 0564/832650 ⚑ *Reservations essential* ⊟ *AE, DC, MC, V* ⊘ *Closed Wed. and mid-Nov.–mid-Jan.*

$ ✕ **La Fontanina di San Pietro.** Grape vines climbing up a trellis, cherry trees in the countryside overlooking the port: the scene here is romantic. Dine on scampi with zucchini and spaghetti *allo scoglio* (with fresh clams and mussels in a light tomato sauce), while enjoying a fruity white from the well-matched wine list. The catch of the day can be prepared a number of ways and is priced by weight; the *pescespada* (swordfish) is terrific. ⊠ *Via del Campone, outside Porto San Pietro* ☎ 0564/825261 ⊟ *AE, DC, MC, V* ⊘ *Closed Wed. and Jan.*

$$$$ ⌗ **Il Pellicano.** Worldly cares are softly washed away by the comforts of the rooms (some damask linens, tapestrylike canopies, marble highboys), the superlative attentiveness of the staff, and the hotel's magnificent garden setting. If you choose, a buffet lunch is served on a canopied terrace above the pool, with numerous smaller terraces tucked away on the sloping cliffs for a peaceful afternoon nap. Chaise longues and white umbrellas sit oceanside on the beach. Some rooms are in separate cottages. If absolute privacy, but not the cost, is your main concern, one suite has a private pool. ⊠ *Località Lo Sbarcatello, 58018, 5 km (3 mi) west of Porto Ercole* ☎ 0564/858111 🖷 0564/833418 ⊕ *www. pellicanohotel.com* ⧉ *32 rooms, 9 suites* ⬧ *2 restaurants, minibars, cable TV, 2 tennis courts, saltwater pool, health club, spa, laundry service, Internet, meeting rooms, free parking, travel services, some pets allowed* ⊟ *AE, D, MC, V* ⊘ *Closed Nov.–Mar.* ⦿| *CP.*

$–$$ ⌗ **Hotel Don Pedro.** The private beach more than makes up for the lack of a swimming pool at this midsize hotel in Porto Ercole. As a guest you can enjoy the complimentary beach chairs and umbrellas, and there's a good restaurant and a bar on the beach. Rooms are spacious and spare, with tile floors and a few pieces of painted or dark-wood furniture with lathe-turned legs and simple curves. Some have French doors that open onto a terrace. ⊠ *Via Panoramica 7, Porto Ercole 58018* ☎ 0564/833914 🖷 0564/833129 ⊕ *www.hoteldonpedro.it* ⧉ *44 rooms* ⬧ *Restaurant, beach, bar, babysitting, dry cleaning, laundry service* ⊟ *AE, MC, V* ⊘ *Closed Nov.–Easter* ⦿| *EP.*

$ ⌗ **Hotel Vittoria.** A steep walk up the hill from the center of Porto Santo Stefano leads to gorgeous view of the port. Several rooms in the 1970s-era hotel have terraces with sea views, and the 10 suites have spacious sitting areas. Bright colors, such as yellow, complement the modern, linear wooden furnishings. Tile floors keep things cool. Half board is available. ⊠ *Strada del Sole 65, 58019 Porto Santo Stefano* ☎ 0564/818580 🖷 0564/818055 ⊕ *www.hvittoria.com* ⧉ *28 rooms* ⬧ *Restaurant, tennis court, pool, baby-sitting, concierge, free parking; no a/c* ⊟ *AE, DC, MC, V* ⊘ *Closed Nov.–Mar.* ⦿| *EP.*

Giglio

❸❷ *Giglio Porto 20 km (13 mi) west of Porto Santo Stefano in Monte Argentario, 139 km (86 mi) southwest of Siena, 207 km (129 mi) south of Florence.*

Rocky, romantic Isola del Giglio (Island of the Lily) is just an hour by ferry from Porto Santo Stefano but a world away from the mainland's hustle. The island's three towns—**Giglio Porto,** the charming harbor where the ferry arrives; **Giglio Castello,** a walled village at Giglio's highest point; and **Giglio Campese,** a modern town on the west side of the island—are connected by one long, meandering road. But to really explore Giglio you need a good pair of hiking boots. A network of rugged trails climbs up the steep hills through clusters of wild rosemary and tiny daffodils, and once you leave town, chances are your only company will be the goats who thrive on Giglio's sun-baked hills.

The island's main attraction, however, is at sea level—a sparkling array of lush coves and tiny beaches, most accessible only on foot or by boat. With the exception of Giglio Campese, where the sandy beach is as popular in summer as any mainland resort, most of the little island's coastline is untouched, leaving plenty of room for peaceful sunning for those willing to go off the beaten path. ☒ *Toremar ferries, Piazzale A. Candi, Porto Santo Stefano* ☎ *0564/810803* ☒ *Dockside, Giglio Porto* ☎ *0564/809349* ⊕ *www.toremar.it* ☞ *€6.30 for passengers, €28.80 for cars.*

Where to Stay

★ **$–$$** ⊞ **Pardini's Hermitage.** The ultraprivate Hermitage is free from noise but for the lapping of waves on the rocks; terraces and flowering gardens spill down a rocky cliff to private beaches below. On the hill above, the owners raise purebred donkeys, which you can ride over the mountain, and goats that produce fresh yogurt and cheese for breakfast. Rooms feel more like those of a private home than a hotel; to complete your sense of relaxation, hydromassages and mud baths are available at the hotel's spa. You can only get here via the hotel's private boat, or by making an arduous hour-long hike. ☒ *Località Cala degli Alberi, 58013 Giglio Porto* ☎ *0564/809034* ☒ *0564/809177* ⊕ *www.hermit.it* ☞ *12 rooms* ♨ *Dining room, beach, boating, laundry service, Internet, some pets allowed; no a/c, no TV in some rooms* ☐ *No credit cards* ⊙ *Closed Oct.–Mar.* ⏃ *FAP.*

$ ⊞ **Hotel Arenella.** Isolated and quiet, sitting above the sea with great views, the Arenella has a private beach reachable by a steep 60-foot descent. Rooms in the stucco hotel's main building are larger and nicer and include suites and rooms for families; more ordinary double rooms are in a smaller building, but they have verandas. All are modestly furnished—some veneer, some rattan, some wood—and have stone floors; ask for a sea view. The property is on the mountain road leading away from Giglio Porto, 3 km (2 mi) out of town but unfortunately not on the bus route to Giglio Castello—to get here you need a car, or ask the hotel to send one to pick you up at the ferry. ☒ *Via Arenella 5, 58013 Giglio Porto* ☎ *0564/809340* ☒ *0564/809443* ⊕ *www.albergoarenella.it* ☞ *27 rooms* ♨ *Restaurant, beach, laundry service, Internet; no a/c in some rooms* ☐ *AE, MC, V* ⊙ *Closed Nov.–Easter* ⏃ *MAP.*

Sports & the Outdoors

HIKING For day-trippers, the best hike is the 1,350-foot ascent from Giglio Porto to Giglio Castello. It's a 4-km (2½- mi) trek that takes about an hour and affords marvelous views of the island's east coast. Frequent bus service to and from Castello allows the option of walking just one way. The rest of the island's trails are reasonably well marked but rough enough that it's not advisable to try them at night. Pick up maps at the tourist office in Giglio Porto.

WATER SPORTS **Dimensione Mare** (✉ Via Thaon de Revel 28, Giglio Porto ☎ 0564/ 809096) runs scuba courses and can help arrange dives. Rent motorboats for exploring the island's innumerable coves through **Giglio Noleggio** (✉ On the port, Giglio Porto ☎ 0347/0954480). You can charter your own snorkeling or beach excursion and let someone else do the driving through **Marco Bartoletti** (✉ Contrada Santa Maria 18, Giglio Porto ☎ 0564/806125 or 0336/535054).

Parco Naturale della Maremma

③③ *One-hour ferry ride and 17 km (11 mi) northeast of Giglio Porto, 88 km (55 mi) southwest of Siena, 156 km (97 mi) south of Florence.*

The well-kept nature preserve at **Monti dell'Uccellina** is an oasis of green hills sloping down to small, secluded beaches on protected coastline. Wild goats and rabbits, foxes and wild boars, as well as horses and a domesticated long-horned white ox unique to this region, make their home among miles of sea pines, rosemary, and juniper bush. The park also has scattered Etruscan and Roman ruins and a medieval abbey, the **Abbazia di San Rabano.** Enter from the south at Talamone (turn right 1 km [½ mi] before town) or from Alberese, both reachable from the SS1 (Via Aurelia). Daily limits restrict the number of cars that can enter, so in summer it's best to either reserve ahead or to leave your car in Alberese and use the regular bus service; contact the parks' information office for bookings, and English-language guides. ✉ *Information office, Via del Bersgliere 7/9, Alberese* ☎ *0564/407098* 💷 *€3–€8* 🕙 *Daily 9–1 hr before sunset.*

Castiglione della Pescaia

③④ *54 km (34 mi) northwest of Parco Naturale della Maremma, 94 km (59 mi) southwest of Siena, 162 km (101 mi) southwest of Florence.*

The medieval town built around a hilltop fortress here is as inviting as many others in Tuscany, but Castiglione's real appeal is found below, on its white sandy beaches bordered by pine forest. It's become a seaside playground of Italy's smart set by virtue of its vicinity to Florence and the north. The lovely marina has a good fresh-fish market. There are some very nice campgrounds in the area, but if you prefer sleeping in a bed, book hotels early for stays from June to October.

Punta Ala, known for alabaster, is up the road and has a pretty beach and a port with chic shops and waterfront pubs. ✛ *10 km (6 mi) northwest of Castiglione della Pescaia.*

Where to Stay

$$ 🏨 **Hotel–Residence Roccamare.** On a private sandy beach, this expensive, exclusive modern hotel is a summer resort first and foremost. Windsurfing equipment and beach chairs and umbrellas are provided, and a beautiful pool and tennis court are an alternative to seaside diversions. When

you tire of the sun, retire to airy rooms with whitewashed walls and tile floors in the main hotel or in one of the several cottages with apartments that surround it. Windows look out either on a pine grove or onto the beach. ⊠ *Strada Provinciale, 58043 Rocchette, 5 km (3 mi) west of Castiglione della Pescaia* ☎ *0564/941124* 🖷 *0564/941133* ⊕ *www. roccamare.it* ⊷ *51 rooms, 101 apartments* ☖ *Restaurant, some kitchenettes, minibars, cable TV, miniature golf, tennis court, pool, beach, windsurfing, bicycles, basketball, Ping-Pong, volleyball, free parking* ▭ *AE, DC, MC, V* ☉ *Closed Nov.–Easter* ⊠ *CP.*

$ 🏨 **Hotel Miramare.** Stay close to the center of the action in the new town. One side of the hotel is on a private beach—a must in August; the other, however, fronts the main street. Rooms are fairly lackluster, with undecorated walls and plain wooden furniture, but they are modern and clean. ⊠ *Via Vittorio Veneto 35, 58043* ☎ *0564/933524* 🖷 *0564/ 933695* ⊕ *www.hotelmiramare.info* ⊷ *35 rooms* ☖ *Restaurant, cable TV, beach, bar, babysitting, dry cleaning, laundry service, concierge, Internet, parking (fee)* ▭ *AE, DC, MC, V* ☉ *Closed Nov.–Mar.* ⊠ *CP.*

⚠ **Campeggio Santa Pomata.** Beneath the shelter of a maritime pine forest, and next to a sandy beach, you can rent sites for tents, caravans, and mobile homes. For those tired of camp stove cooking, a restaurant and bar are on-site. ⊠ *Località Santapomata, 58043* ☎ *0564/941037* ⊕ *www.campingsantapomata.it* ⊷ *340 sites* ☖ *Flush toilets, partial hookups (electric and water), drinking water, showers, restaurant, bar, food store, picnic tables, public telephone, beach* ▭ *No credit cards* ☉ *Closed Oct. 20.–Mar.*

Sports & the Outdoors

Castiglione is prime sailing and windsurfing territory. Rent boats, boards, and kayaks at the many vendors along the beach. You may want to charter one of the boats, harbored in Follonica, 23 km (14 mi) to the north, owned by **Agua** (⊠ Via San Gervasio 21/c, 50131 Florence ☎ 055/588958 ⊕ www.velanet.it/agua).

Elba

㉟ *Portoferraio 57 km (35 mi) and one-hour ferry ride west of Castiglione della Pescaia, 106 km (66 mi) southwest of Siena, 183 km (114 mi) southwest of Florence.*

Elba is the Tuscan archipelago's largest island, but it resembles nearby verdant Corsica more than it does its rocky Italian sisters, thanks to a network of underground springs that keep the island lush and green. It's this combination of semitropical vegetation and dramatic mountain scenery—unusual in the Mediterranean—that has made Elba so prized for so long, and the island's uniqueness continues to draw boatloads of visitors throughout the warm months. A car is very useful for getting around the island, but public buses stop at most towns several times a day; the tourist office has timetables.

Lively **Portoferraio,** the main port where Victor Hugo (1802–85) spent his boyhood, makes a good base. Head right when you get off the ferry to get to the centro storico, fortified in the 16th century by the Medici grand duke Cosimo I (1519–74). Most of the pretty, multicolor buildings that line the old harbor date from the 18th and 19th centuries, when the boats in the port were full of mineral exports rather than tourists. Ferries connect this city with Piombino on the mainland (one hour) and Porto Azzurro (30 minutes), also on Elba. ☒ *Toremar ferries, Calata Italia 23* ☎ *0565/918080* ⊕ *www.toremar.it* ☒ *Piombino–Portoferraio €7.10 for passengers, €36 for cars. Portoferraio–Porto Azzurro €3.50 for passengers, €28.80 for cars.*

The **Museo Archeologico** reconstructs the island's ancient history through a display of Etruscan and Roman artifacts recovered from shipwrecks. ☒ *Calata Buccari, Portoferraio* ☎ *0565/917338* ☒ *€2* ☉ *June–Sept. 9:30–2 and 6 PM–midnight; Oct.–May by appointment.*

Napoléon was famously exiled on Elba, in 1814–15, during which time he built the **Palazzina dei Mulini** out of two windmills. It still contains furniture from the period and Napoléon's impressive library, with the more than 2,000 volumes that he brought here from France. ☒ *Piazzale Napoleone 1, Portoferraio* ☎ *0565/915846* ☒ *€3, €5 with the Villa San Martino* ☉ *Mon. and Wed.–Sat. 9–7, Sun. 9–1.*

A couple of miles outside Portoferraio, the **Villa San Martino** was Napoléon's summer residence during his 10-month exile on Elba. Temporary exhibitions are held in a gallery attached to the villa. The Egyptian Room, decorated with idealized scenes of the Egyptian campaign, may have provided Napoléon the consolation of glories past. The villa's classical facade was added by a Russian prince, Anatolia Demidoff, after he bought the house in 1852. ☒ *Località San Martino* ☎ *0565/914688* ☒ *€3; €5 with the Palazzina dei Mulini* ☉ *Tues.–Sat. 9–7:30 and Sun. 9–1.*

On the south side of the Elba, **Marina di Campo** is a classic summer vacationer's town, with a long sandy beach and a charming, laid-back marina full of bars, restaurants, and shops. The waters of **Porto Azzurro** are noticeably *azzurro* (sky blue). It's worth a stop for a walk and a gelato along the rows of yachts harbored here. The island of Elba's quietest town is old-fashioned **Rio Marina,** with a pebble beach, an old mine, a leafy public park, and ferry service to Piombino.

Elba's most celebrated **beaches** are the sandy stretches at **Biodola, Procchio,** and **Marina di Campo,** but the entire island—and particularly the westernmost section, encircling Monte Capanne—is ringed with beautiful coastline. Indeed, it seems that every sleepy town has its own perfect tiny beach. Try **Cavoli** and **Fetovaia** anytime but July and August, when all the car-accessible beaches on the island are packed (there are also some accessible only by boat, such as the black-sand beach of **Punta Nera**).

Off the coast, the slopes of **Monte Capanne** are crossed by a twisting road that provides magnificent vistas at every turn; the tiny towns of **Poggio** and **Marciana** have enchanting little piazzas full of flowers and trees. You can hike to the top of Monte Capanne, or take an unusual open-basket cable car from just above Poggio.

> **off the beaten path**

PIANOSA – For years, visitors didn't come here by choice; the flat, undeveloped island was the site of a maximum-security prison that hosted some of Italy's most notorious Mafiosi. "Italy's Alcatraz" is no more, and only the caretakers of the nature preserve here—which has Roman ruins, early Christian catacombs, and a swimming area at Cala Giovanna—remain. Facilities are not developed, so come prepared with a bag lunch and plenty of water. There are plans to open the prison to the public in a few years. For now, the number of visitors allowed on the island is limited by the weekly ferry service, so be sure to reserve in advance. Ferries to Pianosa leave from Porto Azzurro. ⊠ *Toremar ferries, Porto Azzurro* ☎ *0565/31100* ⊕ *www.toremar.it.*

The most famous prisoner on **Montecristo** was fictional: Alexandre Dumas's legendary count. Today the island is a well-protected nature preserve with wild Montecristo goats and vipers, peregrine falcons, and rare Corsican seagulls who make their home amid rosemary bushes and stunted pine trees. Scientific-research teams are given priority for permission to land on the island, and an annual quota strictly limits even their number. Montecristo is in the custody of the **Corpo Forestale.** *Forest Guard* ⊠ *Follonica* ☎ *0566/40611.*

Where to Stay & Eat

$–$$$ ✕ **La Canocchia.** In the center of Rio Marina, on the eastern shore, sits an airy, 40-seat restaurant across from a public garden. Seafood takes center stage: specialties include ravioli *scampi e asparagi o calamari* (stuffed with large shrimp or squid, in light asparagus sauce) and saffron-perfumed catches of the day. The *frittura di paranza* (mixed fried fish) is crisp and light, and the *involtini di pescespada* (swordfish rolls) also shouldn't be missed. Book ahead in summer, as it can get very crowded. ⊠ *Via Palestro 3, Rio Marina* ☎ *0565/962432* ♠ *Reservations essential July–Aug.* ⊟ *MC, V* ☽ *Closed Mon. and Nov.–mid-Feb.*

$–$$ ✕ **Trattoria da Lido.** Come here for commendable *gnocchetti di pesce* (bite-size potato-and-fish dumplings) with a white cream sauce and fresh *pesce all'elbana* (whitefish baked with vegetables and potatoes). The bustling, casual trattoria is in the old center of Portoferraio, at the beginning of the road to the old Medici walls. ⊠ *Salita del Falcone 2, Portoferraio* ☎ *0565/914650* ⊟ *AE, DC, MC, V* ☽ *Closed mid-Dec.–mid-Feb.*

★ **$** ✕ **Il Cantuccio.** A small, simple, rustic eatery is a standout in the sometimes touristy Marina di Campo. Shady outdoor tables on a backstreet keep diners cool on warm nights. If the long menu seems daunting, focus on the list of specials, which often includes such local delicacies as spaghetti *alle uova di pesce* (with sea-bream caviar). The staff is friendly and well informed, particularly about wine. ⊠ *Via Largo Garibaldi 2, Marina di Campo* ☎ *0565/976775* ⊟ *AE, DC, MC, V.*

★ **$** ✕ **Il Mare.** Homemade pastas and fresh seafood are served here with a dash of style. The young chef puts her creative spin on the classics, coming up with such delights as homemade vegetable gnocchi with scampi in a butter and saffron sauce. The *semifreddi* (literally, "half cold"; chilled or partially frozen desserts) are particularly good here. Just a few steps from Rio Marina's calm and pretty port, this is an easy stop on your way to or from the ferry. ⊠ *Via del Pozzo 13, Rio Marina* ☎ *0565/962117* ⊟ *V.*

$$$$ 🏨 **Hermitage.** You have private access to a white sandy beach here at this isolated, private bay. The hotel's bar and restaurant stand beachside. A central building and surrounding cottages contain guest rooms with simple white-wood desks and beds with ironwork insets. Some rooms have balconies. During high season half board is mandatory. ⊠ *8 km (5 mi) west of Portoferraio, 57037 Biodola* ☎ *0565/974811* 🖨 *0565/ 969984* ⊕ *www.elba4star.it* 🛏 *129 rooms, 5 suites* ♨ *2 restaurants, cable TV, 6-hole golf course, 9 tennis courts, 3 pools, soccer, volleyball, 3 bars, Internet, meeting room, some pets allowed* ▭ *AE, MC, V* ⊗ *Closed Nov.–Apr.* ⦿ *MAP.*

$$$$ 🏨 **Park Hotel Napoleone.** A late-19th-century villa stands in a park next to Napoléon's Villa San Martino. Hand-painted medallions form the centerpieces of scrolled ironwork beds and chairs that are painted in colors coordinating with the draperies—some deep reds and blues. The rather high price reflects the fact that breakfast and dinner are included. Full board is available. Buses run often from the hotel to the port in Portoferraio; it's only 5 km (3 mi) west to the sandy beach of Biodola. ⊠ *Località San Martino, 57037 Portoferraio, 5 km (3 mi) west of Portoferraio's center* ☎ *0565/918502* 🖨 *0565/917836* ⊕ *www.parkhotelnapoleone. com* 🛏 *64 rooms* ♨ *Restaurant, minibars, cable TV, miniature golf, 2 tennis courts, 2 pools, mountain bikes, babysitting, dry cleaning, laundry service, Internet, free parking, some pets allowed* ▭ *DC, MC, V* ⊗ *Closed Nov.–Easter* ⦿ *MAP.*

$$ 🏨 **Hotel Rio sul Mare.** Convenient to ferries and Rio Marina's charming town center and gravel beach, this comfortable hotel has pretty sea views. Ask for one of the five rooms that have a terrace, and sling chairs, facing the sea. Use of a beach chair and umbrella are complimentary. ⊠ *Via Palestro 31, 57038 Rio Marina* ☎ *0565/924225* 🖨 *0565/924162* ⊕ *www. hotelriomarina.it* 🛏 *32 rooms* ♨ *Restaurant, minibars, refrigerators, beach, babysitting, laundry service, Internet, free parking, some pets allowed; no a/c in some rooms* ▭ *AE, DC, MC, V* ⊗ *Closed Nov.–Mar.* ⦿ *CP.*

★ $$ 🏨 **Hotel Riva del Sole.** Facing the beach, and a short walk from the center of lively Marina di Campo, lies this bright, pleasant hotel, which caters to a loyal Italian and German clientele. Breezy rooms with tile floors provide cool relief from the hot sun, and some have terraces. Marble bathrooms are an elegant touch. On warm nights the scent of oleander growing next to the hotel will truly give you sweet dreams. ⊠ *Viale degli Eroi 11, 57034 Marina di Campo* ☎ *0565/976316* 🖨 *0565/976778* 🛏 *53 rooms, 4 suites* ♨ *Restaurant, minibars, cable TV, bar, babysitting, laundry service, Internet, free parking* ▭ *AE, DC, MC, V* ⊗ *Closed Nov.–Apr.* ⦿ *EP.*

Sports & the Outdoors

Subnow (⊠ Ville degli Ulivi Camping, Località La Foce, Marina di Campo ☎ 0565/976048 ⊕ www.subnow.it) organizes daily diving excursions, for experts and beginners, into the waters of Elba's National Marine Park.

Spaziomare (⊠ Via Vittorio Veneto, Porto Azzurro ☎ 0565/95112 or 0348/6017862) has motorboats available for half- and full-day rentals and sailboats to rent by the week. Adventurous types can rent sea kayaks and mountain bikes from **Il Viottolo** (⊠ Via Pietri 6, Marina di Campo ☎ 0565/978005), which also organizes three-day guided excursions on land and sea.

Capraia

㊱ *Capraia Isola 2½-hour ferry ride southwest of Livorno. Livorno 83 km (52 mi) north of Piombino, 120 km (75 mi) northwest of Siena, 89 km (55 mi) west of Florence.*

Only a handful of people actually live on the island of Capraia, which is frequented mainly by sailors. It's a rocky and hilly unspoiled national park, with only one sandy beach, **Cala della Mortola,** on the northern end of the island; the rest of the coast is a succession of cliffs and deep green coves with pretty rock formations. The 2½-hour ferry trip departs from Livorno and pulls in at the town of **Capraia Isola,** dominated by the Fortezza di San Giorgio up above. Nearby, an archway leads to an area that was once a prison.

The **Cooperativa Parco Naturale Isola di Capraia** (⊠ Via Assunzione 42, Capraia Isola ☎☎ 0586/905071 ⊕ www.arcipelagotoscano.com) can help with villa rentals and ferry schedules.

Capraia's clear waters and undersea life draw raves from scuba divers. **Capraia Diving Service** (⊠ Via Assunzione 64, Capraia Isola ☎ 0586/ 905137 ⊕ www.capraiadiving.it) has scuba-diving equipment and boats.

Massa Marittima

㊲ *111 km (69 mi) southeast of Livorno, 48 km (30 mi) east of Piombino, 62 km (39 mi) southwest of Siena, 132 km (82 mi) southwest of Florence.*

Massa Marittima is a charming medieval hill town with a rich mining and industrial heritage—pyrite, iron, and copper were found in these parts. After a centuries'-long slump (most of the minerals having been depleted), the town is now popular simply for its old streets. The central Piazza Garibaldi, dating from the 13th to the early 14th centuries, contains the Romanesque **Duomo,** with sculptures of the life of patron saint Cerbone above the door. ⊠ *Piazza Garibaldi* ☎ *0566/902237* 🎫 *Free* ☉ *Daily 8–noon and 3–6.*

The 13th-century **Palazzo Pretorio,** on the Piazza Garibaldi, is home to the **Museo Archeologico,** with plenty of Etruscan artifacts. The most famous painting in the **Pinacoteca** (painting gallery), also housed in the palace, is Ambrogio Lorenzetti's *Maestà.* ⊠ *Piazza Garibaldi* ☎ *0566/ 902289* 🎫 *€3 (includes both museums)* ☉ *Apr.–Oct., Tues.–Sun. 10–12:30 and 4–10; Nov–Mar., Tues.–Sun. 10–1 and 3–5.*

The **Museo Arte e Storia della Miniera** (Museum of the Art and History of Mining), in the upper part of town, shows how dependent Massa Marittima has been since Etruscan times on copper, lead, and silver. Exhibits trace the history of the local mining industry, and you can visit a mine. ⊠ *Palazzetto delle Armi, Piazza Matteotti* ☎ *0566/902289* 🎫 *€5* ☉ *Museum Apr.–Sept., Tues.–Sun. 10–12:30 and 3:30–7; Oct.–Mar.,*

Tues.–Sun. 10–12:30 and 3–5. Mine visits Apr.–Sept., Tues.–Sun. 3:30–5:30.

Built to both defend and control their new possession after the Sienese conquered Massa Marittima in 1335, the **Fortezza dei Senesi** crowns the upper part of town. Just inside the imposing Sienese gate is the so-called **Torre del Candeliere** (tower of the candlemaker), a massive bastion that is connected to the outer walls by the **Arco Senese**, a high arched bridge. A visit to the tower gives access to the arch and to the upper city walls, where commanding views open before you. ⊠ *Piazza Matteotti* ☎ *0566/ 902289* 💰 *€2.50* ⏱ *Tues.–Sun. 10–1 and 3–6.*

You can see the **Antico Frantoio,** an old olive press, on a small back-street inside the Sienese Fortress walls. Mules harnessed to the heavy stone wheel pulled it around, and as it rolled, the olives on the flat sur-face were crushed by its weight, extracting the precious oil—the same technique is used today (minus the mules). ⊠ *Via Populonia 18* ☎ *0566/ 902289* 💰 *€1.50* ⏱ *Apr.–Oct., Tues.–Sun. 10:30–1; Nov.–Mar. by appointment.*

Nightlife & the Arts

On the first Sunday after May 22, and again on the first Sunday in Au-gust, Massa Marittima's three traditional neighborhood groups dress in medieval costumes, parade through the town, and compete in the **Bale-stro del Girifalco** (Falcon Crossbow Contest), where contestants try to shoot down a toy falcon.

Abbazia di San Galgano

38 *32 km (20 mi) northeast of Massa Marittima, 33 km (20 mi) southwest of Siena, 87 km (54 mi) south of Florence.*

Time has had its way with this Gothic cathedral without a rooftop, a hauntingly beautiful sight well worth a detour. The church was built in the 13th century by Cistercian monks, who designed it after churches built by their order in France. But starting in the 15th century it fell into ruin, declining gradually over centuries. Grass has grown through the floor, and the roof and windows are gone. What's left of its facade and walls makes a grandiose and desolate picture. In July and August the scene is enlivened by evening concerts arranged by the Accademia Mu-sicale Chigiana in Siena. Contact the tourist-information office at the abbey for details. ⊠ *Off SR441* ☎ *0577/756738 for tourist office* ⊕ *www.prolocochiusdino.it* 💰 *Free* ⏱ *Tourist office 9–12:30 and 2–6, church 24 hrs.*

Behind the church, a short climb brings you to the charming little **Chiesetta di Monte Siepi,** with frescoes by painter Ambrogio Lorenzetti (documented 1319–48), and a sword in a stone. Legend has it that Gal-gano, a medieval warrior and bon vivant, was struck by a revelation on this spot in which an angel told him to give up his fighting and frivolous ways forever. As token of his conversion, he plunged his sword into the rock, where it still remains today. ⊠ *Above Abbazia di San Galgano* ☎ *No phone* 💰 *Free* ⏱ *9–sunset.*

Where to Stay

$ ☒ **Rifugio Prategiano.** Horseback trail rides through Tuscany's cowboy country are an integral part of the experience at Rifugio Prategiano. Your hosts can organize picnics and suggest itineraries or organize weeklong tours. But nonriders don't have to mope at the bar—this agriturismo also has a pool and idyllic views. Rooms are plainly decorated with modern wooden wardrobes and desks; most are carpeted; some are enlivened by wood-beam ceilings. ☒ *Via dei Platani 3/b, Località Prategiano, 58026 Montieri, 17 km (11 mi) west of Abbazia San Galgano* ☎ *0566/ 997700* 🖷*0566/997891* ⊕*www.prategiano.com* ⤴*24 rooms* ⚭ *Restaurant, tennis court, pool, outdoor hot tub, horseback riding, bicycles, some pets allowed; no a/c* ▱ *MC, V* ☉ *Closed Nov.–mid-Mar.* ¶⊙∣ *CP.*

AREZZO, CORTONA & SOUTHERN TUSCANY A TO Z

To research prices, get advice from other travelers, and book travel arrangements, visit ⊕ *www.fodors.com*

AIR TRAVEL

The international airports nearest to the region are Florence's Peretola (officially Aeroporto A. Vespucci), Pisa's Galileo Galilei, and Rome's Fiumicino (officially Aeroporto Leonardo da Vinci). Pisa has a train directly to its airport.

You can fly direct from Rome, Milan, and some other European cities to Elba's La Pila airport, with Intersky and Air Alps.

🔳 Airport Information **Aeroporto A. Vespucci** (a.k.a Peretola) ☎ 055/373498 ⊕ www. airport.florence.it. **Aeroporto Galileo Galilei** ☎ 050/500707 ⊕ www.pisa-airport. com. **Aeroporto Leonardo da Vinci** (a.k.a. Fiumicino) ☎ 06/6594420 ⊕ www.adr.it. **La Pila** ☒ Marina di Campo ☎ 0565/976011.

🔳 Carriers **Air Alps** ☎ 06/4740340 ⊕ www.airalps.it. **Intersky** ☎ 05574/48800 in Austria, 0565/976011 La Pila airport on Elba ⊕ www.intersky.biz.

BOAT & FERRY TRAVEL

Passenger and car ferries link the Tuscan islands with the mainland. From Piombino, Moby Lines travels to Porto Azzurro and Portoferraio on Elba. Toremar runs ferries between Capraia and Livorno, Pianosa and Elba's Porto Azzurro, and Giglio and Porto Santo Stefano. Prices can differ drastically, so comparison shop before buying your tickets; check both counters or call both offices before booking.

Moby Lines (☒ Nuova Stazione Marittima, Piombino ☎ 0565/221212 ⊕ www.mobylines.it). **Toremar** (☒ Nuova Stazione Marittima, Piombino ☎ 0565/31100 ☒ Porto Mediceo, Livorno ☎ 0586/896113 ☒ Piazzale A. Candi, Porto Santo Stefano ☎ 0564/810803 ⊕ www. toremar.it).

BUS TRAVEL

Although tortuous roads and roundabout routes make bus travel in southern Tuscany terribly slow, it's a reliable way to get where you're going if you don't have a car; beware that schedules tend to be very spotty. Plan your trip carefully with the aid of local tourist offices; they can help with hard-to-find bus stops and ever-changing timetables, and they're more likely to have English-speaking staff than bus stations. Main bus stations in the region are in Arezzo and Cortona, but most towns in the region have bus service even if they don't have actual bus stations. Buses from Rome and Florence travel to many towns in the area. Call SITA or Rama for complete route information. Tra-In bus line goes to Montalcino and Montepulciano from Siena. Alessi bus line goes to Montepulciano from Florence. On Elba it's ATL buses that take you around the island.

🚌 Bus Lines **Alessi** ☎ 055/215155 in Florence. **ATL** ☎ 0565/914392. **Rama** ☎ 055/214721. **SITA** ☎ 055/214721 in Florence ⊕ www.sita-on-line.it. **Tra-In** ☎ 0577/204111 ⊕ www.trainspa.it

CAR RENTAL

Avis has offices in Arezzo and Chiusi. You can hire a car and driver in Montalcino (Mulinari, Pierangeli) and Montepulciano (Paolo Cencini, Stefano Bernardini). On Elba there are numerous places to rent bikes, scooters, motorcycles, or cars: at Baby Rent you can choose, among other things, BMW convertibles for touring the island in style; BW's Rent has everything from mopeds to Yamaha touring bikes, as well as a few small cars; Chiappi rents Honda and Yamaha scooters and a seven-bed camper.

🚗 Rental Agency **Avis** ⊠ Piazza della Repubblica 1/a, Arezzo ☎ 0575/354232 ⊠ Piazza Dante 22, Chiusi ☎ 0578/227993 ⊕ www.avis.com. **Baby Rent** ⊠ Piazza del Popolo 9, Portoferraio, Elba ☎ No phone ⊠ Via Mascagni, Marina di Campo, Elba ☎ 0565/977281 or 0330/777904. **BW's Rent** ⊠ Via Manganaro 23, Portoferraio, Elba ☎ 0565/930491 or 0347/7371790. **Chiappi** ⊠ Calata Italia 30, Portoferraio, Elba ☎ 0565/916779. **Mulinari** ☎ 0348/5175154. **Paolo Cencini** ☎ 0330/7322723. **Pierangeli** ☎ 0577/848656 or 0577/849113. **Stefano Bernardini** ☎ 0578/716081 or 0348/2868790.

CAR TRAVEL

The best way to travel within the region, making it possible to explore tiny hill towns and country restaurants, is by car. But the roads are better north–south than east–west, so allow time for excessively winding roads when heading east or west. Sometimes it's faster to go a little out of your way and get on one of the bigger north–south routes.

The A1 (Autostrada del Sole), which runs from Florence to Rome, passes close to Arezzo; Cortona is just off the highway linking Perugia to the A1. You can reach Pienza and the Val d'Orcia easily from the A1 or from the Via Cassia (SR2), which links Siena with Rome passes through San Quirico d'Orcia and close to other Cal d'Orcia towns. There is also a good road (SR223) linking Siena and Grosseto. From Genoa or the northern Tuscan coast, you can drive down the coastal highway (A12) as far as Rosignano Marittimo and continue south on the SS1 (the Via Aurelia).

EMERGENCIES

Pharmacies in major towns take turns staying open 24 hours; all pharmacies have a notice posted outside with the name and address of the nearest one open.

🆘 Emergency Services ☎ 113.

🏥 Hospitals **Arezzo** ⊠ Via Nenni Pietro 20 ☎ 0575/351623. **Chianciano** ⊠ Via dello Stadio 5 ☎ 0578/321015.

LODGING

APARTMENT &
VILLA RENTALS

Terra Nostra and Tuscany Farms are two professional agencies that can help you locate that perfect rental. Terra Nostra represents agritourism properties throughout the Maremma region. Tuscany Farms lists villas and agritourism houses and apartments throughout Tuscany, with a special emphasis on southern Tuscany. Many rental units have minimum stay requirements of from three days to three weeks.

🚹 Agents **Terra Nostra** ✉ Via Tolmino 18, Grosseto ☎ 0564/23680 ⊕ www.agriturismoinmaremma.com. **Tuscany Farms** ✉ Via Veneto 3, Porto Azzurro ☎ 0565/920146 ⊕ www.tuscanyfarmhouses.it.

TRAIN TRAVEL

State railway train service (Ferrovia dello Stato, or FS) is frequent between Florence and Arezzo and between Siena and Chiusi or Buonconvento, where you can change to buses for smaller towns. A regular service links Arezzo with Cortona, and with Poppi and the Casentino, but between Arezzo and the coast train service is scarce or nonexistent. There's rail service from Siena to Montepulciano, but the station isn't near the town center. Very few train routes reach the towns of southern Tuscany; it's best to use buses or cars to get around. The coast is also served by trains from Genoa and Livorno to Piombino (where you can get a ferry to Elba) and Grosseto. From Grosseto there are also frequent trains to Siena and Monte Atgentario.

🚹 Train Information **Ferrovia dello Stato** (FS) ☎ 892021 and 199/166177 ⊕ www.trenitalia.com.

VISITOR INFORMATION

Tourist offices (called, variously, Ufficio Turistico, APT, AAST, and Pro Loco) are generally open from 9 to 12:30 and 3:30 to 6 or 7.

🚹 Tourist Information **Arezzo** ✉ Piazza della Repubblica 2 ☎ 0575/377678 ⊕ www.apt.arezzo.it. **Capraia** Contact Elba office ✉ Calata Italia 26, Portoferraio, Elba ☎ 0565/914671 ⊕ www.aptelba.it. **Castiglione della Pescaia** ✉ Piazza Garibaldi ☎ 0564/933678 🖷 0564/933954. **Chianciano Terme** ✉ Via G. Sabatini 7 ☎ 0578/63538 ⊕ www.chiancianoterme.com 🖷 0578/64623. **Cortona** ✉ Via Nazionale 42 ☎ 0575/630352 ⊕ www.apt.arezzo.it. **Elba** ✉ Calata Italia 26, Portoferraio ☎ 0565/914671 ⊕ www.aptelba.it. **Giglio** ✉ On the port, Giglio Porto ☎ 0564/809400 ⊕ www.isoladelgiglio.it. **Massa Marittima** ✉ Via Todini 3/5 ☎ 0566/902756 🖷 0566/940095 ⊕ www.altamaremmaturismo.it. **Montalcino** ✉ Costa del Municipio 8 ☎ 0577/849331 ⊕ www.prolocomontalcino.it. **Monte Amiata** ✉ Via Mentana 97, La Piazzetta, Abbadia San Salvatore ☎ 0577/778608 🖷 0577/779013. **Montepulciano** ✉ Via di Gracciano nel Corso 59/r ☎ 0578/757341 ⊕ www.prolocomontepulciano.it. **Monte Argentario** ✉ Corso Umberto 55/a, Porto Santo Stefano ☎ 0564/814208. **Parco Nazionale dell'Arcipelago Toscano** ✉ Via Guerrazzi 1, Portoferraio ☎ 0565/919411 🖷 0565/919420 ⊕ www.islepark.it. **Pienza** ✉ Piazza Pio II ☎ 0578/749071. **Pitigliano** ✉ Piazza Garibaldi 51 ☎🖷 0564/617111 ⊕ www.lamaremmafabene.it. **San Quirico d'Orcia** ✉ Via Dante Alighieri 33 ☎ 0577/897211.

PERUGIA &
NORTHERN UMBRIA

7

Updated by
Peter Blackman

PERUGIA IS A LIVELY CITY, majestic, handsome, and wealthy. Students from local universities keep the streets buzzing with music and activity year-round, and an important jazz festival every July adds to the mix. With its glamorous designer shops, refined cafés, and grandiose architecture, Perugia doesn't try to hide its affluence.

It is the capital of a region rich in history, art, tradition, and breathtaking landscapes. The northern end of Umbria is squeezed between eastern Tuscany—notably Arezzo and Cortona—and the Marches, where the Renaissance architecture of the Palazzo Ducale in Urbino sets the stage. The landscapes are those depicted by the Renaissance master Perugino in his paintings: hills with a few sparse trees, flat land, and lakes.

Native Umbrian Perugino, whose real name was Pietro Vannucci (circa 1450–1523), studied under Verrocchio (1435–88) and developed his artistic career in Florence and then Rome, where he helped paint the Cappella Sistina (Sistine Chapel). He outlived his star pupil, Raffaello Sanzio (1483–1520), better known as simply Raphael, a native of Urbino. Visiting Perugino's major works in and around Perugia is a way to reconstruct the evolution of his career and also a way to see how much the artist was affected by—and re-created—the environment in which he grew up. If you follow a Perugino itinerary, remember that the Collegio del Cambio in Perugia is a must.

Gubbio, Perugia's neighbor to the north, climbs straight up a mountain, filling the bottom half with its houses and churches. Every May, costumed runners ascend to the top, to the church of Sant'Ubaldo, during the bizarre Festa dei Ceri, or Festival of the Candles (⇨ "St. Ubaldo Wins Again" CloseUp box). From Gubbio, you can take side trips to Urbino or up to the Republic of San Marino, which claims to be the oldest and smallest independent state in the world.

In Etruscan times, Perugia and Gubbio were among the last to bow to Roman rule but were eventually conquered by the Romans in the 3rd century BC. Attesting to its importance in Roman times, Gubbio has a Roman theater that could seat about 12,000 spectators. Perugia was caught in the middle of a power struggle between two Roman rulers and was burned, sacked, and destroyed in 140 BC. The city was slowly built back up and during the medieval period gave its allegiance to the popes.

After winning a war with Assisi in 1202, Perugia flourished. Churches and government buildings were erected, and the university was founded in 1308. In the 15th century, noble families became more powerful and the Baglioni family briefly ruled the city, but it quickly returned to the Papal States. In 1540 the Perugians rebelled against a tax on salt imposed by Pope Paul III (1468–1549), winning the so-called Salt War, but one of the pope's three sons, Pier Luigi Farnese (1503–47), fathered before his spiritual conversion in 1519, quickly reconquered the area. Perugia didn't become independent of the Church's rule until 1860, when the troops of Victor Emmanuel II of Savoy (1820–78) conquered it and unified the entire Italian peninsula.

Gubbio followed a different path. Its destiny, intertwined with that of Urbino in the Marches, was ruled by the Montefeltro and Della Rovere families of Urbino during the Renaissance. Like Perugia, in 1631 it fell under the rule of the Papal States, and didn't become part of Umbria until 1861, after the unification of Italy.

About the Restaurants & Hotels

Restaurants in northern Umbria have been slow to abandon the tried-and-true traditions represented by the region's hearty down-to-earth cooking. As a result, the best places to eat are often unpretentious family-run *trattorie*, where *Mamma* is in charge of the kitchen. When innovation has been sought, it's in the form of modernized versions of Umbria's tasty medieval recipes—nouvelle cuisine is foreign to these parts.

Though many restaurants take credit cards, the smaller trattorie and *locande* (simple taverns) don't. Lunch is usually served from 12:30 to 2. Perugia, because of its sizable student population, has many small *pizza a taglio* (pizza-by-the-slice) shops, which are quick and inexpensive. For something more traditionally Umbrian, look for the same type of establishment serving made-to-order *torte al testo* (flat-bread sandwiches), filled with local cheeses, salami, grilled meats, and vegetables. Dinner can start as early as 7:30, but restaurants rarely start filling before 8:30.

Virtually every historic town in Umbria has some kind of hotel, no matter how small the place may be. But be sure to book ahead—traveling to Perugia or Urbino without reservations during the high season is a chancy proposition. Northern Umbria also abounds with *agriturismi*, literally "agritourist" accommodations. These are countryside lodgings, often in restored farmhouses, with guest rooms ranging in service from bed-and-breakfast-type accommodations to fully equipped apartments. Many such lodgings have excellent restaurants on the premises, and Italian law requires that at least 70% of what is served at agriturismi is cultivated and prepared on the property. In this way, you are assured of high-quality, honest, local meals. Note that some proprietors prefer that you book a stay of at least one week, although the length of stay required varies with each location and season; still, depending on availability, the owners will do their best to accommodate your request. For further information about agritourist locations in Umbria, *see* Agritourist Agencies *in* Perugia and Northern Umbria A to Z.

WHAT IT COSTS in euros				
	$$$$	**$$$**	**$$**	**$**	**¢**
RESTAURANTS	over €22	€18–€22	€13–€17	€7–€12	under €7
HOTELS	over €290	€210–€290	€140–€209	€80–€139	under €80

Restaurant prices are per person for a second course (secondo piatto). Hotel prices are for two people in a standard double room, including tax and service.

Exploring Perugia & Northern Umbria

The steep hills and deep valleys that make Umbria so picturesque also make it difficult to explore. Driving routes must be chosen carefully to avoid tortuous mountain roads, and major towns aren't necessarily

Covering distances in this area can take longer than it might look on the map because of the winding mountain roads. Between sightseeing, you might want to set aside extra time for lounging near Lago Trasimeno or shopping for pottery in Deruta. But if you're in the area, try not to skip Perugia or Urbino.

Numbers in the text correspond to numbers in the margin and on the Northern Umbria and the Marches and the Perugia maps.

7

If you have 2 days

Spend a day in 🔲 **Perugia** ①–⑫ 🏳 and stay overnight. The next day, visit **Gubbio** ㉑ in the morning and **Urbino** ㉒ in the afternoon. On your way to or from Perugia, stop at the town of Passignano for a stroll along the **Lago Trasimeno** lakefront ⑯–⑰, where a meal of fresh fish is highly recommended.

If you have 5 days

Spend your first day exploring 🔲 **Perugia** ①–⑫ 🏳 and stay overnight. The next day visit **Torgiano** ⑬ and **Deruta** ⑭, and then head around Lago Trasimeno to **Castiglione del Lago** ⑰. If you're interested in art, an alternative route is via **Panicale** ⑲ and **Città della Pieve** ⑱ to see Perugino's works. Return to your hotel in Perugia for the second night. On the third day, visit **Città di Castello** ⑳ and then 🔲 **Gubbio** ㉑, where you can spend the next two nights. The morning of Day 4 take a day-long side trip to **Urbino** ㉒. You can spend Day 5 exploring more of the Marches: **Ancona** ㉔, **Loreto** ㉕, and **Ascoli Piceno** ㉖.

linked to each other by train, bus, or highway. But Perugia is a convenient base from which to explore the region, and you can get around fairly quickly by car. You might want to combine your trip with a southern Tuscany itinerary that includes Arezzo and Cortona or with visits to Assisi, Spoleto, and southern Umbria. You can reasonably visit the area around Perugia, see Gubbio and Città di Castello, and take a side trip to Urbino in four days. You would be shortchanging a trip to this region if you skipped Urbino (in the adjoining Marches region) and its storybook palace.

Numbers in the text correspond to numbers in the margin and on the Northern Umbria and the Marches and the Perugia maps.

Timing

Northern Umbria is fairly free of the great masses of visitors that descend upon the other regions, even in summer, when you might welcome the lush greenness of these interior tracts. In August much of the local population shifts to Adriatic resorts such as Rimini and Parco del Conero for vacation. The forested Umbrian hills also ensure a stunning autumnal landscape and an explosion of greenery in the spring. In both spring and fall the visitor count is especially low and the temperature usually moderate, but keep in mind that April and November may be rainy.

The predominantly hilly terrain of northern Umbria means that winters can be bitterly cold, and snow is common. Because many destinations here are hilltop towns, including Perugia itself, you should be prepared for harsh conditions and possible hazardous driving if you're traveling at this time of year. The winter also has its attractions, especially regarding Umbrian cuisine: January through April is the season to sample the fresh truffles for which the area is famous (though, of course, truffles are dried and can be had at any time of year), and wild mushrooms are picked from October to December.

PERUGIA

Perugia, the largest and richest of Umbria's cities, owes its elegance to the 3,000 years of history concentrated in a town that, neither too big nor too small, was clearly designed to fit the human scale. Thanks to Perugia's position on a series of hills, the medieval city remains almost completely intact. It is the best-preserved hill town of its size, and few other places in Italy better illustrate the model of the self-contained city-state that so shaped the course of Italian history.

Exploring Perugia

The best approach to the city is by train. The area around the station doesn't attest to the rest of Perugia's elegance, but buses that run directly to Piazza d'Italia, the heart of the old town, are frequent. If you are driving to Perugia and your hotel doesn't have parking facilities, leave your car in one of the parking lots near the station and take the bus or the escalator; the latter passes through fascinating subterranean excavations of the Roman foundations of the city and leads to the town center.

A Good Walk

Start in Piazza d'Italia and stroll down **Corso Vannucci** ❶ ☞ to the **Duomo** ❷, in Piazza IV Novembre. On this piazza is the original entrance to the mass of buildings that makes up the **Palazzo dei Priori** ❸, Perugia's city hall, which also houses the Sala dei Notari. The entrances to the **Collegio del Cambio** ❹, the **Galleria Nazionale dell'Umbria** ❺, and the **Collegio della Mercanzia** ❻, all also housed in the palazzo, are strung along Corso Vannucci. For another museum visit, detour back to Piazza d'Italia, and then walk down Corso Cavour (to your left) to the **Museo Archeologico Nazionale** ❼. Return to Piazza IV Novembre, breaking for lunch or an espresso at a café. Walk down Via dei Priori; on your left you'll pass the Sant'Agata church, which has Gothic archways and 14th-century frescoes. Continuing down the hill, you'll reach another church, the baroque **San Filippo Neri** ❽, in Piazza Ferri. Farther down the street, past the escalator, note the **Torre degli Sciri** ❾, the only tower of its time to survive in its original state. Walk around the tower to the Oratorio della Confraternità di San Francesco, another example of baroque architecture. After you pass the medieval city gateway, the Porta Trasimena, on your left, head to the right down Via San Francesco to the church of San Francesco al Prato. The *prato* (lawn) is a grassy square where students often lounge in nice weather. From the lawn, you can see the small **Oratorio di San Bernardino** ❿, connected to San Francesco by an archway that spans the entrance to a former convent, now the Accademia delle Belle

7

Local Cuisine

Northern Umbria is crossed by the Apennine mountains, the slopes of which curve into graceful, hilly landscapes. Called the "green heart of Italy," the terrain is hardly rugged, but Umbrians are in close touch with nature and its bounty—thus the cuisine of the northern part of Umbria is hearty. First courses such as pasta, rice, and soups (and in this region especially, lentils) are often laden with rich *tartufi neri o bianchi* (black or white truffles), while the second courses are generally meat-based. The local pasta specialty, a thick, homemade spaghetti, goes by two names, *stringozzi* (also spelled *strangozzi*) and *ombrichelli,* and most often is served *al tartufo,* with a sauce of truffles. In addition, Umbria is known to produce excellent olive oils.

A meal of fresh fish pulled from Lago Trasimeno (Lake Trasimeno) is enough to warrant a detour on your way from Tuscany to Perugia. Otherwise, some area restaurants offer fresh seafood (largely in response to consumer demand), but it's prepared according to traditional Italian methods as there are no real Umbrian seafood dishes. Once you leave Umbria and head to the coastal Marches region, however, seafood becomes more available. One characteristic dish from Ancona, *brodetto,* is a savory fish soup chock-full of the latest catch from the Adriatic. Ascoli Piceno, inland, can take credit for a particular gastronomic specialty worth noting: olive *ascolane,* stuffed green olives rolled in breading, deep fried, and served as an appetizer. Want to try a local drink? Ascoli Piceno is known for the anisette it produces.

The Outdoors

Umbria abounds with opportunities for the active traveler, and many agriturismi offer the opportunity to go horseback riding, mountain biking, golfing, or hiking, or even to practice archery.

Your tour through Umbria will keep you off the coastal regions, but you can stop at one of the communities that surround Lago Trasimeno and take a dip, go boating, or just relax. The lake, in Umbria but very close to the border with Tuscany, possesses the traits of both regions. Often overlooked by the foreign traveler, Italy's lake areas can be quite astonishing. And Trasimeno is well organized for the sport aficionado: you can swim, windsurf, and play volleyball. Swimming in the lake is quite safe; the communities of Castiglione del Lago, Lido di Trasimeno, Tuoro sul Trasimeno, Toricella, and Monte del Lago, as well as two of the islands on the lake—Isola Maggiore and Isola Pavese—have bathing establishments with lounge chairs, cabanas, and in most places, windsurfing equipment and canoes for rent. Passignano sul Trasimeno, however, has mostly ports and rocky beaches, so public bathing facilities aren't available.

The Perugino "Trail"

Umbria (north and south) is the place to tour the work of Perugino, the master who taught Raphael, and who was prestigious enough in his own day to be called in by the pope to paint frescoes in the Sistine Chapel in Rome. The vivid colors of Perugino's paintings may remind you of the vibrant hues in the works of his pupil, Raphael. Follow Perugino's works from his birthplace in Città della Pieve to Perugia, Assisi, Spello, Foligno, Montefalco, Trevi, Deruta, and other towns, to the home of his final work of 1522 in Fontignano, where he died of bubonic plague the following year.

Shopping   Pottery and wine are the two most celebrated Umbrian exports, but if you like to cook, don't overlook the opportunity to take home a bottle of rich, dark-green, Umbrian olive oil—be sure to buy extra-virgin, which comes from the first pressing of the olives.

Ceramics are sold throughout the region and are easy to find in cities such as Deruta and Perugia. There are styles to suit every taste, with decorations that range from carefully researched reproductions of 14th- and 15th-century designs to ultramodern, brightly colored abstractions. The best producers grind their own colors and use the tried-and- true techniques handed down in their families for centuries. As in all things, the smaller shops, owned by individual craftsmen, are to be trusted more for their originality and quality than the large commercial operations. All of the reputable shops will ship your purchases home with insurance, in case of breakage, included in the price.

Torgiano, south of Perugia, is the best-known Umbrian center for wine-making; here you can see the process, partake in tastings, and purchase local wines. While the Lungarotti family has a virtual monopoly on the production of the local DOC (Denominazione di Origine Controllata) wines, red Rubesco, and white Torre di Giano, they also produce a sparkling Lungarotti Brut, a so-called *metodo champenois* (a sparkling champagne-like wine).

Arti (Academy of Fine Arts), with a museum that contains Antonio Canova's (1757–1822) plaster casts. Walk up the hill along Via del Poggio, turn right on Via Armonica, and walk along the Etruscan walls to Piazza Cavallotti. Turn left on Via Cesare Battisti, past a 13th-century aqueduct, and at the end of the street you'll find the **Arco di Augusto** ⑪, next to Perugia's Università per Stranieri (University for Foreigners). Down some steps to your right, wind around to Piazza Michelotti, take a left on Via dell'Aquila, and you arrive at the church of **San Severo** ⑫.

TIMING   A thorough walk through Perugia takes about an hour; if you're stopping at all sites along this walk, you should plan on a full day with a stop for lunch.

Sights to See

⑪ **Arco di Augusto** (Arch of Augustus). Dating from the 3rd century BC, this arch was the entrance to the Etruscan and Roman acropolis. In the same square is the Università per Stranieri (University for Foreigners). ⊠ *Piazza Fortebraccio.*

★ ④ **Collegio del Cambio** (Bankers' Guild Hall). These elaborate rooms, on the ground floor of the **Palazzo dei Priori,** served as the meeting hall and chapel of the guild of bankers and money changers. The walls were frescoed from 1496 to 1500 by the most important Perugian painter of the Renaissance, Pietro Vannucci, who is better known as Perugino. The iconography prevalent in the works includes common religious themes, such as the Nativity and the Transfiguration (on the end walls), as well

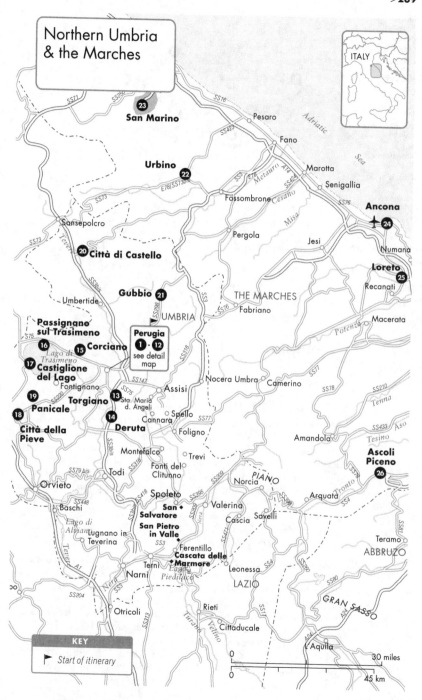

Northern Umbria & the Marches

ITALY

23 San Marino

Pesaro

Fano

Adriatic

Sea

Marotta

Urbino **22**

Fassombrone

Senigallia

Ancona **24**

Sansepolcro

Pergola

Numana

20 **Città di Castello**

Jesi

Loreto **25**

Umbertide

Recanati

Gubbio **21**

THE MARCHES

Macerata

UMBRIA

Fabriano

Passignano sul Trasimeno

16 **15** **Corciano**

Lago di Trasimeno

Perugia
1 - **12**
see detail
map

17 **Castiglione del Lago**

Fontignano

Nocera Umbra

Camerino

19

Torgiano **13**

Assisi

18 **Panicale**

Sta. Maria
d. Angeli

Spello

Città della Pieve

14 **Deruta**

Cannara

Foligno

Amandola

Montefalco

Trevi

Todi

Fonti del
Clitunno

Orvieto

PIANO

Ascoli Piceno **26**

Lago di Alviano

Spoleto

Norcia

Arquata

Baschi

San Salvatore

Valerina

Lugnano in
Teverina

San Pietro in Valle

Cascia

Savelli

Teramo

Ferentillo

Cascata delle Marmore

ABBRUZO

Terni

Leonessa

Narni

*Lago di
Piediluco*

LAZIO

GRAN SASSO

Otricoli

Rieti

Cittaducale

L'Aquila

KEY

▶ *Start of itinerary*

0   30 miles

0   45 km

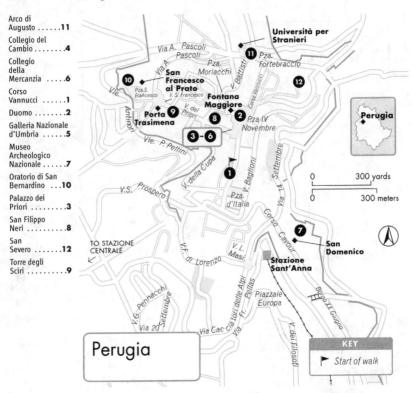

as figures intended to inspire the businessmen who congregated here. On the left wall are female figures representing the virtues, beneath them the heroes and sages of antiquity. On the right wall are the prophets and sibyls—said to have been painted in part by Perugino's most famous pupil, Raphael (1483–1520). (His hand, experts say, is most apparent in the figure of Fortitude.) On one of the pilasters is a remarkably honest self-portrait of Perugino, surmounted by a Latin inscription. The *cappella* (chapel) of San Giovanni Battista has frescoes painted by Giannicola di Paolo, another student of the Umbrian master Perugino. ⊠ *Corso Vannucci 25* ☎ *075/5728599* ☒ *€2.60; €3.10 with the Collegio della Mercanzia* ☉ *Daily 9–1 and 2:30–5:30.*

❻ Collegio della Mercanzia (Merchant's Meeting Hall). This room of carved wood, two doors away from the **Palazzo dei Priori** entrance for the Collegio del Cambio, dates back to the 1300s and was the original meeting room for merchants, especially fabric traders. Trading didn't actually take place here, but merchants met to haggle and set market prices and to standardize trade practices. ⊠ *Corso Vannucci 15* ☎ *075/5730366* ☒ *€1.03; €3.10 with Collegio della Mercanzia* ☉ *Mar.–Oct. and Dec. 20–Jan. 6, Tues.–Sat. 9–1 and 2:30–5:30, Sun. 9–1; Nov.–Dec 19 and Jan. 7–Feb., Tues., Thurs., and Fri. 8–2, Wed. and Sat. 8–4:30, Sun. 9–1.*

▶ ❶ **Corso Vannucci.** A string of elegantly connected *palazzi* (palaces) expresses the artistic nature of this city center, the heart of which is concentrated on Corso Vannucci. Stately and broad, the pedestrian-only street runs from Piazza d'Italia to Piazza IV Novembre and is the best place to soak in the uncomplicated beauty of the surroundings. Take time to appreciate the look of the bars and shops that line the street. Along the way, the entrances to many of Perugia's side streets will tempt you to wander off and explore. But don't stray too far as evening falls, when Corso Vannucci fills with Perugians out for their evening *passeggiata*, a pleasant pre-dinner stroll that may include a pause for an aperitif at one of the many bars that line the street.

need a break? You can enjoy the lively comings and goings on Corso Vannucci from the vantage point of the **Bar Sandri** (⊠ Corso Vannucci 32 ☎ 075/5724112). The 19th-century bar has wood paneling and ceiling frescoes that date from 1860. Red-vested waiters serve homemade chocolates, pastries, and ice creams, along with *tavola pronta*, a daily selection of fast first and second courses, to Sandri's lunch crowd.

❷ **Duomo.** Severe yet mystical, the Duomo, also called the Cathedral of San Lorenzo, is most famous for being the home of the wedding ring of the Virgin Mary, stolen by the Perugians in 1488 from the nearby town of Chiusi. The ring, kept high up in a red-curtained vault in the chapel immediately to the left of the entrance, is the size of a large bangle and kept under lock—15 locks, actually—and key all year except July 30 and the second-to-last Sunday in January, when it is displayed to the public. The first date commemorates the day the ring was brought to Perugia, the second Mary's wedding anniversary. The cathedral itself dates from the Middle Ages and has many additions from the 15th and 16th centuries. The most visually interesting element is the altar to the Madonna of Grace; an elegant fresco on a column at the right of the entrance depicts *La Madonna delle Grazie* and is surrounded by prayer benches decorated with handwritten notes to the Holy Mother. Around the column are small amulets—symbols of gratitude from believers who prayed for miracles and received help. Additionally, there are elaborately carved choir stalls, executed by Giovanni Battista Bastone in 1520. The altarpiece (1484), an early masterpiece by Luca Signorelli (circa 1450–1523), shows the Madonna with St. John the Baptist, St. Onophrius, and St. Lawrence. Note that sections of the church may be closed to visitors during religious services.

The **Museo Capitolare** displays a large array of precious objects associated with the cathedral, including vestments, vessels, manuscripts, and gold work. Outside the Duomo is the elaborate **Fontana Maggiore**, which dates from 1278 and was realized by Nicola and Giovanni Pisano. It is adorned with zodiac figures and symbols of the seven arts. ⊠ *Piazza IV Novembre* ☎ *075/5723832* 🎫 *Duomo free, museum €3* ☉ *Duomo Mon.–Sat. 7–12:30 and 4–6:45, Sun. 8–12:30 and 4–6:45; museum daily 10–1 and 4–6; last admission ½ hr before closing.*

❺ Galleria Nazionale dell'Umbria. The region's most comprehensive art
FodorśChoice   gallery is housed on the fourth floor of the **Palazzo dei Priori.** Enhanced
★   by skillfully lit displays and computers that allow you to focus on the
works' details and background information, the collection includes
work by native artists—most notably Pinturcchio (1454–1513) and Perugino (circa 1450–1523)—and others of the Umbrian and Tuscan
schools, among them Gentile da Fabriano (1370–1427), Duccio (circa
1255–1318), Fra Angelico (1387–1455), Fiorenzo di Lorenzo
(1445–1525), and Piero della Francesca (1420–92). In addition to housing paintings, the gallery has frescoes, sculptures, and some superb examples of crucifixes from the 13th and 14th centuries; other rooms are
dedicated to Perugia itself, showing how the medieval city evolved.
✉ *Corso Vannucci 19, Piazza IV Novembre* ☎ *075/5721009* ⊕ *www.
gallerianazionaledellumbria.it* 🎫 *€6.50* ⊗ *Daily 8:30–7:30; last admission
½ hr before closing. Closed first Mon. of each month.*

❼ Museo Archeologico Nazionale. The museum, next to the imposing church
of San Domenico, contains an excellent collection of Etruscan artifacts
from throughout the region. Perugia was a flourishing Etruscan site long
before it fell under Roman domination in 310 BC. Other than the collection here, little remains of Perugia's mysterious ancestors, although
the Arco di Augusto, in Piazza Fortebraccio, the northern entrance to
the city, is of Etruscan origin. ✉ *Piazza G. Bruno 10* ☎ *075/5727141*
⊕ *www.archeopg.arti.beniculturali.it* 🎫 *€4* ⊗ *Mon. 2:30–7:30,
Tues.–Sun. 8:30–7:30.*

★ **❿ Oratorio di San Bernardino.** Agostino di Duccio (circa 1418–81) designed
this lovely little Renaissance church with a pink-and-blue lacy stone facade in 1457–61 to honor the memory of St. Bernard, who often preached
in Perugia and became one of the city's most important saints. ✉ *Piazza
San Francesco* ☎ *075/5733957* 🎫 *Free* ⊗ *Daily 8–12:30 and 3:30–6.*

★ **❸ Palazzo dei Priori** (Palace of Priors). Actually a series of elegant, connected
buildings, the palazzo serves as Perugia's city hall and houses three of
the city's museums. The buildings string along Corso Vannucci and wrap
around the Piazza IV Novembre, where the original entrance is located.
The steps lead to the **Sala dei Notari** (Notaries' Hall). Other entrances lead to the **Galleria Nazionale dell'Umbria,** the **Collegio del Cambio,** and the **Collegio della Mercanzia.** The Sala dei Notari, which dates
back to the 13th century and was the original meeting place of the town
merchants, had become the seat of the notaries by the second half of
the 15th century. Wood beams and an interesting array of frescoes attributed to Maestro di Farneto embellish the room. Coats of arms and
crests line the back and right lateral walls; you can spot some famous
figures from *Aesop's Fables* on the left wall. The palazzo facade is
adorned with symbols of Perugia's pride and past power: the griffin is
the city symbol, and the lion denotes Perugia's allegiance to the Guelph
(or papal) cause. The two bronze figures support heavy chains that, according to local legend, came from the gates of Siena, which fell to Perugian forces in 1358. ✉ *Piazza IV Novembre* 🎫 *Free* ⊗ *June–Sept.,
Tues.–Sun. 9–1 and 3–7.*

⑧ **San Filippo Neri.** With its grandiose facade dating from 1663, this church is an interesting piece of baroque architecture. Inside are frescoes by various 18th-century artists, as well as a 1662 altarpiece by Pietro da Cortona (1596–1669) depicting the conception of Mary. ✉ *Piazza Ferri* ☎ *075/5725472* 🎫 *Free* ☉ *Daily 7:30–noon and 4–7.*

⑫ **San Severo.** The only Raphael fresco in Perugia, painted in 1505–08, resides in this little church. The lower part (six saints) was added in 1521 by Raphael's teacher, Perugino. The admission ticket allows you also to visit the **Etruscan well** in Piazza Piccinino, behind the church. ✉ *Piazza Raffaello* ☎ *075/5733864* 🎫 *€2* ☉ *Nov.–Mar., weekdays 10:30–1:30 and 2:30–5; Apr.–Oct., daily 10–1:30 and 2:30–6:30.*

⑨ **Torre degli Sciri** (Sciri Tower). The tower, which dates from the 12th to 13th centuries, is the only one of its time still standing in Perugia. At a height of 151 ft, it proclaimed to the neighborhood the wealth of the family that built it. ✉ *Via dei Priori.*

off the
beaten
path

LA CITTÀ DELLA DOMENICA – The younger set might enjoy a day at this theme park, the only attraction in Umbria most directly aimed at children and families. The playground is in the town of Montepulito, 8 km (5 mi) west of Perugia on the secondary road that leads to Corciano. The 500 acres of parkland can be toured by a train that runs through the park grounds and takes visitors on a tour through fairy-tale landscapes including Snow White's House, the Witches' Wood, Tarzan's parrot jungle, a zoo, an Indian camp, and Swan Lake. There is also a reptile house, an aquarium, a medieval museum, an exhibit of shells from around the world, and game rooms, as well as several restaurants. From November until Easter, only the aquarium and reptile house are open. ✉ *Via Col di Tenda 140, Località Montepulito, 8 km (5 mi) west of Perugia* ☎ *075/5054941* 🎫 *€10* ☉ *Easter–mid-Sept., daily 10–7; mid-Sept.–Oct., weekends 10–7; Nov.–Easter, aquarium and reptile house only, Sat. 2–7 and Sun. 10–7.*

Where to Stay & Eat

$$$ ✕ **Antica Trattoria San Lorenzo.** Brick vaults are not the only distinguishing feature of this small restaurant next to the Duomo, as both the food and the service are outstanding. Particular attention is paid to adapting traditional Umbrian cuisine to the modern palate. There is also a nice variety of seafood dishes on the menu. The *trenette alla farina di noce con pesce di mare* (flat spaghettilike noodles made with walnut flour, with fresh fish) is a real treat. ✉ *Piazza Danti 19/a* ☎ *075/5721956* ▭ *AE, D, MC, V* ☉ *Closed Sun. Nov.–May.*

$–$$$ ✕ **La Taverna.** Medieval steps lead to a rustic two-story restaurant where wine bottles and artful clutter decorate the walls. Good choices from the regional menu include *caramelle al gorgonzola* (pasta rolls filled with red cabbage and mozzarella with a Gorgonzola sauce) and grilled meat dishes, such as the *medaglioni di vitello al tartuffo* (grilled veal with truffles). ✉ *Via delle Streghe 8, off Corso Vannucci* ☎ *075/5724128* ▭ *AE, DC, MC, V* ☉ *Closed Mon.*

★ $$ ✕ **Dal Mi' Cocco.** A great favorite with Perugia's university students, this is a fun, crowded, and truly inexpensive place to enjoy a multicourse, fixed-price meal (€13 at this writing). You may find yourself seated at a long table with other diners, but some language help from your neighbors could come in handy—the menu is in pure Perugian dialect. Meals change with the seasons, and each day of the week brings some new creation *dal cocco* (from the "coconut," or head) of the chef. ⊠ *Corso Garibaldi 12* ☎ *075/5732511* ⚐ *Reservations essential* ▭ *No credit cards* ☾ *Closed Mon. and Jul. 25–Aug. 15.*

$–$$ ✕ **La Rosetta.** The restaurant, in the hotel of the same name, is a peaceful, elegant spot. In winter you dine inside under medieval vaults; in summer, in the cool courtyard. The food is simple but reliable and flawlessly served. Reservations are essential during peak seasons. ⊠ *Piazza d'Italia 19* ☎ *075/5720841* ▭ *AE, DC, MC, V* ☾ *Closed Mon.*

¢–$$ ✕ **Da Giancarlo.** Giancarlo himself is likely to greet you at this typical Umbrian restaurant. The main room has the original vaulted ceilings common in Perugia. Although the cuisine is local, hours here accommodate the traveler who may like to eat earlier than Italian diners. Giancarlo says he's known for his lentils, which he makes into wonderful soups or serves as side dishes, and also recommends the grilled Chianina, a handsome cut of beef from this prize breed of cattle raised to the west of Lago Trasimeno. Another house specialty is the *penne alla Norcina* (tubular pasta with spicy cream sauce and sausage). ⊠ *Via dei Priori 36* ☎ *075/5724314* ▭ *AE, MC, V* ☾ *Closed Fri. and last 2 wks in Aug.*

$$$$ ▦ **Brufani Palace.** A 19th-century palazzo has been turned into an elegant lodging choice. The Brufani's public rooms and first-floor guest rooms have high ceilings and are done in grand belle epoque style. Second-floor rooms are more modern; many on both floors have a marvelous view of either the Umbrian countryside or the city. ⊠ *Piazza d'Italia 12, 06121* ☎ *075/5732541* ▦ *075/5720210* ⊕ *www.brufanipalace. com* ◨ *63 rooms, 31 suites* ⚐ *Restaurant, pool, gym, bar, meeting room* ▭ *AE, DC, MC, V* ⊓ *CP.*

$$ ▦ **Castello dell'Oscano.** A splendid neo-Gothic castle, a late 19th-century villa, and a converted farmhouse hidden in the tranquil hills north of Perugia offer a complete range of accommodation styles. Step back in time in the castle, where spacious suites and junior suites, all with high oak-beamed ceilings, and some with panoramic views of the surrounding country, are decorated with 18th- and 19th-century antiques. The sweeping wooden staircase of the main lounge, and the wood-pannelled reading rooms and restaurant are particularly elegant. Standard rooms in the villa annex are smaller and more modern than those in the main building, while the apartments of the farmhouse, in the valley below the castle, provide kitchens and simple accommodation for two to five people. A one week minimum stay is required at the latter. Rooms in the castle and villa annex all have air-conditioning, and the swimming pool at the farmhouse is available to all guests. ⊠ *Strada Palaretta 19, Località Cenerente Oscano, 5 km (3 mi) north of Perugia 06134* ☎ *075/584371* ▦ *075/690666* ⊕ *www.oscano.it* ◨ *24 rooms, 8 suites, 13 apartments* ⚐ *Restaurant, cable TV, pool, gym, bicycles, Internet, bar, library, meeting rooms, no-smoking rooms; no a/c in some rooms* ▭ *AE, D, V* ⊓ *CP.*

$$ 🏨 **Locanda della Posta.** Reside at the center of Perugia's old district in an 18th-century palazzo. Renovation has left the reception and other public areas rather bland, but the rooms, all of which are carpeted, are tastefully and soothingly decorated in muted colors. Though sound-proofed, rooms at the front of the hotel face the busy Corso Vannucci and should be avoided in favor of those on the upper floors at the back of the building, which also have great views. ⊠ *Corso Vannucci 97, 06121* ☎ *075/5728925* 🖷 *075/5732562* ↪ *38 rooms, 1 suite* ⚲ *Minibars, bar, parking (fee)* ⊟ *AE, DC, MC, V* ⵜ◯ⵝ *CP.*

$ 🏨 **Hotel Fortuna.** The elegant decor in the large rooms of this friendly hotel complements the frescoes, which date from the 1700s. Some rooms have balconies. The building itself, just out of sight of Corso Vannucci, dates back to the 1300s. ⊠ *Via Bonazzi 19, 06123* ☎ *075/5722845* 🖷 *075/5735040* ⊕ *www.umbriahotels.com* ↪ *51 rooms* ⚲ *Some in-room hot tubs, cable TV, bar, meeting rooms, parking (fee)* ⊟ *AE, DC, MC, V* ⵜ◯ⵝ *CP.*

¢ 🏨 **Rosalba.** Here's a bright and friendly choice with scrupulously clean, basic rooms; the ones at the back enjoy a view. On the top floor, Room 9 has a private terrace and sleeps up to five people, making it perfect for a family or group of friends. Although somewhat out of the way, the hotel is only a matter of minutes from Corso Vannucci by virtue of a nearby public escalator stop. ⊠ *Via del Circo 7, 06100* ☎ *075/5728285* 🖷 *075/5720626* ↪ *11 rooms* ⚲ *Free parking; no room TVs* ⊟ *No credit cards* ⵜ◯ⵝ *EP.*

Nightlife & the Arts

Viva Perugia is a good source of information about what's going on in town. The monthly, sold at newsstands, has a section in English.

Music Festivals

Summer sees two music festivals in Perugia. The **Umbria Jazz Festival** (☎ 075/5732432 🖷 075/572256 ⊕ www.umbriajazz.com) is held for 10 days in July. Information on the festival is available year-round; tickets are available for purchase, with a credit card, starting at the end of April. The **Sagra Musicale Umbra** (Umbrian Music Festival; ☎ 075/5721374 ⊕ www.umbria.org), held from mid-August to mid-September, celebrates sacred music and choral symphonies.

In Perugia you can obtain information about music festivals at the **Perugia Tourist Office** (☎ 075/5736458 ⊕ www.perugia.umbria2000.it), on Piazza IV Novembre.

Shopping

Shopping is easy in Perugia. A simple walk down any of the main streets, including Corso Vannucci, Via dei Priori, Via Oberdan, and Via S. Ercolano, takes you past many well-known Italian designer-clothing and specialty shops.

The most typical thing to buy in Perugia is some Perugina chocolate, which you can find almost anywhere. The best-known chocolates made by Perugina are the chocolate-and-hazelnut-filled nibbles called Baci (literally, "kisses"). They're wrapped in silver paper that includes a sliver of paper, like the fortune in a fortune cookie, with multilingual romantic sentiments or sayings.

Perugians take their chocolate seriously: after the Umbria Jazz Festival, the **Eurochocolate Festival,** the third week in October, is Perugia's—and Umbria's—biggest event. Perugia turns into a veritable chocolate walk as the city transforms itself, even changing the names of famous avenues and piazzas to reflect the theme. Corso Vannucci becomes Morso Vannucci (a *morso* is a bite; Piazza della Reppubblica becomes Piazza della Tazza (a *tazza* is a cup); Via Mazzini becomes Chocostreet, where international chocolate makers display their best products; and Piazza Gianduiotti displays a mega *gianduiotto,* a sculptured hazelnut–chocolate affair that passersby can sample.

Crafts
Fragile (⊠ Via dei Priori 70 ☎ 075/5736120) makes and sells colorful hand-crafted wood pieces, including fanciful decorations for children's bedrooms, or for the frivolous at heart. **Il Telaio** (⇨ Fabrics, *below*) stocks a nice selection of Umbrian and Deruta pottery.

Fabrics
Fabbri Antonio (⊠ Via Oberdan 13 ☎ 075/5726609) offers beautiful, high-quality, traditionally patterned Umbrian napkins, tablecloths, and hand towels in delicate yellow, blue, and rust colors. The patterns are derived from regional Romanesque designs. **Il Telaio** (⊠ Via Rocchi 19 ☎ 075/5726603) sells woven traditional Umbrian fabrics. The name of the shop translates literally as "The Loom."

Food
Fans of Italian gastronomic specialties might like to stop by the **Casa del Parmigiano Reggiano** (⊠ Via dei Priori 9 ☎ 075/5725369) to buy some of the best local bounty: rich green Umbrian olive oils, dried salami, cheeses, wines, cookies, and Umbrian lentils.

Leather Items
Looking for Italian shoes? **Castagner** (⊠ Via Calderini 3 ☎ 075/5723236) sells such well-heeled Italian brands as Hogan, Tod's, and Fratelli Rosetti. Belts and other accessories are also available.

AROUND PERUGIA

A simple drive or train ride through the curving terrain that surrounds Perugia may make you feel as if you have traveled back to a time when life was gentler and less complex and land was respected for its beauty and the life it sustains. Hilltop towns, churches that peek out from behind screens of trees, fields of poppies and vineyards, expanses of green where animals contentedly graze—one pastoral scene after another passes before your eyes. South of Perugia, Torgiano is the center of Umbrian wine production and Deruta is the Umbrian ceramics center. A short distance east of Perugia you encounter the serene lake district of Trasimeno. The sleepy port of Passignano sul Trasimeno is on the northeast part of the lake. Around Magione, also on the east side of the lake, the land once again becomes hilly and lush.

Torgiano

⑬ *16 km (10 mi) southeast of Perugia, 27 km (17 mi) southwest of Assisi.*

Wine aficionados are certain to want to visit this home to the winery **Cantine Lungarotti**, best known for delicious Rubesco Lungarotti, San Giorgio, and chardonnay. ⊠ *Via Mario Angeloni 12* ☎ *075/988661* ✉ *Free* ☉ *Tours weekdays 8–1 and 3–6, by appointment only.*

The fascinating **Museo del Vino** (Wine Museum) has a large collection of ancient wine vessels, presses, documents, and tools that tell the story of viticulture in Umbria and beyond. The museum traces the history of wine in all its uses—for drinking at the table, as medicine, and in mythology. Next door to the Museo del Vino, the **Osteria del Museo** (⊠ Corso Vittorio Emanuele 33 ☎ 075/9880069) is a local representative for the Lungarotti winery. You can taste and buy the winery's reds and whites here. ⊠ *Corso Vittorio Emanuele 31* ☎ *075/9880200* ✉ *€4* ☉ *Apr.–Oct., daily 9–1 and 3–7; Nov.–Mar., daily 9–1 and 3–6.*

Where to Stay & Eat

$$ ×🖭 **Le Tre Vaselle.** Four charming stone buildings, linked underground,
Fodor'sChoice   house this hotel in the center of Torgiano. Its rooms are spacious, es-
★   pecially the most expensive suites, some of which have fireplaces. The floors are of typical Tuscan red-clay tiles; ceilings have wood beams. Olive groves surround the outdoor pool; a current pool and a whirlpool are indoors. The restaurant, Le Melagrane ($$$–$$$$), is a comfortable affair with red tablecloths, wood-beam ceilings, fireplaces, and exquisite local specialties. In summer you can dine alfresco on a terrace between two of the hotel buildings. ⊠ *Via Garibaldi 48, 06089* ☎ *075/9880447* 🖶 *075/9880214* ⊕ *www.3vaselle.it* ⊅ *47 rooms, 13 suites* ⌂ *Restaurant, 2 pools (1 indoor), gym, sauna, bar, meeting rooms, parking (fee)* ⊟ *AE, DC, MC, V* ⍢ *CP.*

Deruta

⑭ *7 km (4½ mi) south of Torgiano, 19 km (11 mi) southeast of Perugia.*

The 14th-century medieval hill town is most famous for the ceramic craftsmanship for which it has been esteemed since the 16th century. A drive through the countryside to visit the ceramics factories surrounding Deruta is a good way to spend a morning, but be sure to stop in the town itself.

Notable sights in Deruta include the **Museo Regionale della Ceramica** (Regional Ceramics Museum), part of which extends into the adjacent 14th-century former convent of San Francesco. Half the museum is a historic exposition of Deruta ceramics, with panels in Italian and English explaining the history, artistic techniques, and production processes. The museum also holds the country's largest collection of modern Italian ceramics. Nearly 8,000 pieces are displayed in the museum altogether, and the most notable are the Renaissance vessels using the lustro technique, a craft that originated in Arabic and Middle Eastern cultures some 500 years before coming into use in Italy in the late 1400s. Lustro, as the name sounds, gives the ceramics a rich effect, which is accomplished with the use of crushed precious materials, such as gold, silver, and other rare metals and stones. ⊠ *Largo San Francesco* ☎ *075/9711000* 🎫 *€3* 🕐 *Apr.–June, daily 10:30–1 and 3–6; July–Sept., daily 10–1 and 3:30–7; Oct.–Mar., Wed.–Mon. 10:30–1 and 2:30–5.*

Pinacoteca Comunale, the civic museum, is housed in the **Palazzo Comunale** (town hall) and displays religious paintings from the surrounding area. The museum's most important works are those painted by the Umbrian master Niccolò di Liberatore (circa 1430–1502), known as L'Alunno, and a fresco attributed to Perugino. At this writing, the museum is closed for restoration. All inquiries should be directed to the **Museo Regionale della Ceramica.** ⊠ *Piazza Consoli 13.*

Where to Stay

$ 🏨 **Antica Fattoria del Colle.** Two structures from the early 1800s make up this pleasant agritourist lodging, which includes furnishings of the same era. The friendly owners (who speak English) make your stay relaxing and peaceful. A minimum stay of two nights is required in high season. ⊠ *Colle delle Forche 6, 06053* ☎☎ *075/972201* ⊕ *www.anticafattoriadelcolle.it* 🛏 *5 rooms, 2 apartments* 🍴 *Restaurant, pool, mountain bikes, archery; no a/c, no room TVs* ⊟ *No credit cards* 🕐 *Closed Jan. 15–Mar. 15* 🍽 *MAP.*

★ ¢ 🏨 **Melody.** The plain, comfortable, modern hotel just outside the center of Deruta has a reasonably priced restaurant and a big parking area surrounded by pine trees. Rooms are commodious, some with carpeting; the newer ones have nice wood floors and wood furniture. All rooms have balconies, but those in the back are quiet and have pleasant views of the surrounding hills. ⊠ *SS E/45, km 55.8 (south side of Deruta), 06053* ☎ *075/9711022* 📠 *075/9711018* 🛏 *56 rooms* 🍴 *Restaurant, bar, meeting rooms* ⊟ *AE, DC, MC, V* 🍽 *CP.*

Shopping

Deruta is home to more than 70 ceramics workshops and boutiques. They offer a range of ceramics, including extra pieces from commissions for well-known British and North American tableware manufacturers. If you ask, most shop owners will take you to see where they actually throw, bake, and paint their wares. A drive along Via Tiberina Nord passes one ceramics factory after another.

Ceramiche El Frate (⊠ Piazza dei Consoli 29 ☎ 075/9711435) sells unusual tiles and jugs. Innovative patterns and colors brighten the traditional forms created by **Ceramiche Sberna** (⊠ Via Tiberina 146 ☎ 075/9710206); the meticulously hand-crafted and painted ceramics are on display in its factory showroom. **Fabbrica Maioliche Tradizionali** (⊠ Via Tiberina Nord 37 ☎ 075/9711220) is open for visits weekdays 8:30–1 and 2:30–4:30 and also operates one of the largest shops in the area. **Fratelli Mari** (⊠ Via Circonvallazione Nord 1 ☎ 075/9710400 ⊕ www.mari-deruta.it), one of the oldest ceramics manufacturers in Deruta, produces a variety of ceramic pieces ranging in style from the steadfastly classical to the ultramodern.

G. Grazia (✉ Via Tibertina 181 ☎ 075/972018), on the outskirts of town, has a large selection of seconds in a wide range of styles.

Maioliche Cynthia (✉ Via Umberto I 1 ☎ 075/9711255), in Deruta's central Piazza dei Consoli, specializes in reproductions of antique designs and offers a good selection. Four generations of the Veschini family have operated **Maioliche Fidia** (✉ Piazza Consoli 25 ☎ 075/972121 ⊕ www. fidiaderuta.com), which produces elegant and highly crafted ceramics in traditional designs. The factory is in the valley below town. Ceramics manufacturer **Maioliche Figli Calzuola** (✉ Via Tiberina Nord 50 ☎ 075/9711244) specializes in classically designed pieces in a great variety of shapes and sizes. Traditional patterns are the focus at **Maioliche Fima di Picchiotti Piero** (✉ Via Tiberina Nord 111 ☎ 075/9711285). **Maioliche Monotti** (✉ Via Tiberina Sud 276 ☎ 075/972002) pays special attention to the colors used in traditional designs.

Corciano

⑮ *21 km (13 mi) northeast of Deruta, 13 km (8 mi) northwest of Perugia, 97 km (60 mi) east of Siena.*

Corciano is a nicely preserved medieval hilltop village, with a view of the valley that stretches as far as Lago Trasimeno. At the **Museo della Casa Contadina** (Farmhouse Museum; ✉ Via Tarragone 16 ☎ No phone), you can see what a typical Corciano home was like before the industrial era. Check with the town's **Pro Loco** (☎ 075/5188255) for hours. Usually you can see the museum, which is free, on request.

Over the main altar of the **Chiesa di Santa Maria Assunta** (Church of the Assumption of Mary) hangs the *Assunta* (Assumed Virgin) which, having been rather energetically restored, is still attributed to Perugino. ✉ *Piazza della Vittoria 1* ☎ *No phone* 🎫 *Free* ☉ *Daily 9–12:30 and 3:30–6.*

Lago Trasimeno

Passignano sul Trasimeno: 16 km (10 mi) northwest of Corciano, 30 km (18 mi) northwest of Perugia. Castiglione del Lago: 22 km (13 mi) southwest of Passignano, 52 km (31 mi) west of Perugia.

⑯ **Passignano sul Trasimeno** is a picturesque town on the northern shore of Lago Trasimeno, complete with castle ruins and medieval walls. Beaches here are mostly rocky, and public bathing facilities aren't available, so this isn't the best spot for swimming.

⑰ In the western-shore community of **Castiglione del Lago,** evidence of Etruscan origins, castle ruins, and medieval city walls lend a mysterious, elegant air. The **Palazzo della Corgna** (✉ Piazza A. Gramsci 1 ☎ No phone) is worth a visit for its Renaissance frescoes. The palace is open daily April through October 10–1 and 3–7, but only 10–4 on weekends during the rest of the year; admission is €1.50. The city hall, or *comune* (☎ 075/96581), has additional information, but you are likely to need some rudimentary Italian when you call.

In both towns you can sail, windsurf, or take a ferry to **Isola Maggiore,** a small island in the lake with houses dating from the 15th century and a church from the 14th. The local men fish and the women still craft lace. You can pick up a schedule directly from the dock, or contact **Navigazione Lago Trasimeno** (☎🖦 075/827157 in Italian only ⊕ www. apmperugia.it).

Where to Stay & Eat

$ ✕ **Cacciatori–Da Luciano.** Fresh fish here comes straight from the lake and is exceptional. But the entire menu is sumptuous, with delectable *antipasti* (starters) and a wide range of meat and seafood courses and fine wines. Ask for a table near the windows overlooking the lake. ⊠ *Via Pompili 11, Passignano sul Trasimeno* ☎ 075/827210 ▤ *AE, DC, MC, V* ⊘ *Closed Wed. and 3 wks in Jan.*

¢–$ ✕🏠 **Kursaal.** Every room in this resort hotel has a balcony, and most of the simply decorated rooms have views of the lake. With extensive gardens and a large pool next to the private beach, the hotel is ideal for family vacations. The restaurant ($$–$$$$), overlooking Lago Trasimeno, has a veranda that's especially nice in summer. It features fish from the lake and seafood, and is closed on Monday. ⊠ *Via Europa 24 (1 km/½ mi east of the center of Passignano sul Trasimeno), Passignano sul Trasimeno 06065* ☎ *075/828085* 🖦 *075/827182* ⊕ *www.kursaalhotel. net* ❧ *16 rooms, 2 suites* ⚘ *Restaurant, pool, beach* ▤ *MC, V* ⊘ *Closed Jan.–Feb.* ❧◎ *CP.*

¢ ✕🏠 **Locanda del Galluzzo.** Sitting 2,145 feet above lake level, this small hotel offers beautiful views of the lake and the surrounding countryside, amid absolute quiet. You can stroll in the olive groves around the pool. Rooms and apartments are simple with dark-wood furniture. The restaurant ($) turns out delicious meals, and in summer you can dine on a roofed terrace with great sunset views of Lago Trasimeno. ⊠ *Via Castel Rigone 12/a, Località Trecine (5 km/3 mi east of Passignano sul Trasimeno), Passignano sul Trasimeno 06060* ☎🖦 *075/845352* ⊕ *www. locandadelgalluzzo.it* ❧ *4 rooms, 6 apartments* ⚘ *Restaurant, some kitchens, pool, bar; no a/c, no room phones* ▤ *AE, DC, MC, V* ◎ *CP.*

Città della Pieve

⑱ *26 km (16 mi) south of Castiglione del Lago, 43 km (26 mi) southwest of Perugia.*

Perugino was born in this small Etruscan town of plain redbrick buildings, flat-top towers, and churches, so it makes sense that the churches here are chock-full of his frescoes, some in better condition than others. (Also worth a peek for their Perugino frescoes are the churches of Santa Maria dei Servi and San Pietro, outside the city walls near the hospital; follow signs.)

Perugino's *Baptism of Christ* and *Madonna in Glory* in the 17th-century **Duomo,** originally a Roman structure that was transformed by Gothic and baroque renovations, are examples of the artist's later works. ⊠ *Piazza Plebiscito* ☎ *No phone* ⊘ *Daily 10–noon and 4–6.*

In **Santa Maria dei Bianchi** the *Adoration of the Magi,* painted in 1504, is particularly well restored. It depicts the Nativity scene in perfect Renaissance court style on a spring day, with the Perugian countryside in the background. At a time when Leonardo da Vinci (1452–1519) and Michelangelo (1475–1564) were exploring new scientific and religious territory, Perugino reaffirmed a classical, humanistic Renaissance style. ⊠ *Via Vannucci* ☎ *075/8299696* ⌨ *Free* ⊙ *Mon.–Sat. 10:30–12:30 and 3:30–6, Sun. 10–1 and 3–6.*

Panicale

⑲ *21 km (13 mi) northeast of Città della Pieve, 34 km (20 mi) southwest of Perugia.*

The small town of Panicale, with a population of just over 5,000, sits on a low hill about 8 km (5 mi) inland from Lago Trasimeno. The town has preserved some of its original medieval walls and gateways and is known in the area for its handcrafted lace and needlework. On the drive from Città della Pieve to Panicale, a wide-open view of Lago Trasimeno appears, showing the islands on the lake and the mountains on its far shore.

Once you've reached Panicale, head for the church of **San Sebastiano,** where Perugino painted his famous fresco the *Martyrdom of St. Sebastian.* Although it was executed in 1505, only one year later than the *Adoration of the Magi* in Città della Pieve, it is much more abstract and geometric. The painting is almost dreamlike, with St. Sebastian on a strange classical terrace and God appearing fatherlike above. The landscape in the background, however, is the same Perugian countryside found in the *Adoration of the Magi.* ⊠ *Outside the city walls, off Piazza Vittoria* ☎ *0758/37602* ⌨ *Free* ⊙ *Daily 10–noon and 4–6.*

NORTH TOWARD URBINO

The trip north from Perugia to Città di Castello and Gubbio, and across to Urbino, passes through rugged, mountainous terrain. Città di Castello can be combined with San Sepolcro in an itinerary, possibly also including Arezzo.

Città di Castello

⑳ *54 km (32 mi) north of Perugia, 42 km (26 mi) east of Arezzo.*

The noble-looking town is still surrounded in part by 16th-century walls. At its center is the Piazza Matteotti, dominated by the 14th-century **Palazzo del Podestà,** which today houses Città di Castello's administrative offices and courts.

The **Duomo** dates from the 6th century, but was renovated between 1466 and 1529; in the 17th century it received an unfinished baroque face-lift. ⊠ *Piazza del Duomo* ☎ *0758/521647* ⌨ *Free* ⊙ *Daily 10–noon and 4–6.*

The **Palazzo Albizzini** is home to the **Fondazione Palazzo Albizzini "Collezione Burri,"** which displays some 130 works by the artist Alberto Burri (1915–95), perhaps the town's most famous native son. Trained as a doctor, Burri began painting while held in a World War II detention camp in the United States. The collection reflects his work as one of Italy's most important proponents of Art Informel ("unformed" art, sometimes referred to as Lyrical Abstraction) in the 1950s and 1960s. ⊠ *Via Albizzini 1* ☎ *0758/554649* 🎫 €5 ⊗ *Tues.–Sat. 9–12:30 and 2:30–6, Sun. 9–1.*

Inside the 16th-century **Palazzo Vitelli alla Cannoniera,** built by Antonio da Sangallo the Younger (1483–1546) and with a facade by Giorgio Vasari (1511–74), is the **Pinacoteca Comunale,** second only to Perugia's art gallery for Umbrian painting. It houses paintings by Raphael (including *The Creation of Eve*), Luca Signorelli (1441–1523), and Ghirlandaio (1449–94). ⊠ *Via della Cannoniera 22/a* ☎ *0758/5206565* 🎫 €5 ⊗ *Apr.–Oct., Tues.–Sun. 10–1 and 2:30–6:30; Nov.–Mar., Tues.–Sun. 10–12:30 and 3–5:30.*

Where to Stay & Eat

★ $$$ ✕ **Il Postale di Marco e Barbara.** Friendly owners Marco and Barbara turned an old bus depot into this stellar restaurant, creating a pleasant environment while retaining such elements as old wood beams in the ceiling and an antique gas pump outside. Every two weeks the kitchen invents recipes with the freshest local vegetables, fish, and meat. Artistic and tasty antipasti might be bite-size marinated veal with sprouts and lemon cream, or little tarts of mussels and vegetables. Entrées include roast quail with cherry tomatoes and beans as well as many delicious fish and seafood choices. Throughout the year you can order a *degustazione* (tasting) menu; the chef chooses your two antipasti, first, and second courses. ⊠ *Via De Cesare 8* ☎ *075/8521356* ⌂ *Reservations essential* 🗏 *AE, DC, MC, V* ⊗ *Closed Mon. and 2 wks in Jan. No lunch Sat.*

$ ▦ **Le Mura.** Built in the early 1990s, this hotel just inside the old city walls is modern and has a friendly and efficient staff. Guest rooms are bright and comfortable, with functional furnishings. A good buffet breakfast awaits you in the morning. ⊠ *Via Borgo Farinario 24/26, 06012* ☎ *075/8521070* 🖷 *075/8521350* ⊕ *www.hotellemura.it* ⟿ *35 rooms* ⌂ *Restaurant, bar, meeting rooms, parking (fee)* 🗏 *AE, DC, MC, V* ⵏⵓ *CP.*

Nightlife & the Arts

Festival delle Nazioni di Musica da Camera (International Chamber Music Festival; ⊠ S3 bis, 80 km [50 mi] north of Perugia ☎ 075/8521142 🖷 075/8552461). Music lovers should make the trek to the International Chamber Music Festival, a two-week event held in late August and early September.

Gubbio

❷¹ *35 km (22 mi) southeast of Città di Castello, 39 km (24 mi) northeast of Perugia, 92 km (57 mi) east of Arezzo.*

There is something otherworldly about this jewel of a medieval town tucked away in a mountainous corner of Umbria. Even at the height of summer, the cool serenity and quiet of Gubbio's streets remains intact. The town is perched on the slopes of Monte Ingino, and the streets are dramatically steep. Gubbio's relatively isolated position has kept it free of hordes of high-season visitors, and most of the year the city lives up to its Italian nickname, La Città del Silenzio, City of Silence. Just don't come looking for peace and quiet during the fast and furious festivals in May. And at Christmastime, kitsch is king. From December 7 to January 10, colored lights are strung down the mountainside in a tree pattern as the town stakes its claim as the home of the world's largest Christmas tree. Parking in the central Piazza dei Quaranta Martiri—named for 40 hostages murdered by the Nazis in 1944—is easy and secure, and it is wise to leave your car in the piazza and explore the narrow streets on foot.

★ The striking Piazza Grande is dominated by the medieval **Palazzo dei Consoli,** attributed to a local architect known as Gattapone—a man still much admired by today's residents (hotels, restaurants, and bars have been named after him), though studies have suggested that the palazzo was in fact the work of another architect, Angelo da Orvieto. In the Middle Ages the Parliament of Gubbio met in this palace, which has become a symbol of the town.

The Palazzo dei Consoli houses a small museum, famous chiefly for the Tavole Eugubine, seven bronze tablets written in the ancient Umbrian language, employing Etruscan and Latin characters and providing the best key to understanding this obscure tongue. Also in the museum is a fascinating miscellany of coins, medieval arms, paintings, and majolica and earthenware pots, not to mention exhilarating views over Gubbio's roofscape and beyond from the lofty loggia. For a few days at the beginning of May, the palace also displays the famous *ceri,* the ceremonial pillars at the center of Gubbio's annual festivities. ⊠ *Piazza Grande* ☎ *075/9274298* ⊕ *www.comune.gubbio.pg.it* ⊠ *€5* ☉ *Apr.–Oct., daily 10–1 and 3–6; Nov.–Mar., daily 10–1 and 2–5.*

The **Palazzo Ducale** is a scaled-down copy of the Palazzo Ducale in Urbino. (Gubbio was once the possession of that city's ruling family, the Montefeltro.) Gubbio's palazzo contains a small museum and a courtyard. Some of the public rooms offer magnificent views. ⊠ *Via Ducale* ☎ *075/9275872* ⊠ *€2* ☉ *Tues.–Sun. 8:30–7:30.*

The **Duomo,** on a narrow street on the highest tier of the town, dates from the 13th century, with some baroque additions—in particular, a lavishly decorated bishop's chapel. ⊠ *Via Ducale* ☉ *Daily 8–12:45 and 3–7:30.*

Just outside the city walls at the eastern end of town is a **funicular** that provides a bracing ride to the top of Monte Ingino. ⊠ *Follow Corso Garibaldi or Via XX Settembre to the end* ☉ *July–Aug., daily 8:30–7:30; Sept.–June, Thurs.–Tues. 10–1:15 and 2:30–5* ⊠ *€2.60, round-trip €3.35.*

At the top of Monte Ingino is the **Basilica di Sant'Ubaldo,** repository of Gubbio's famous ceri—three 16-foot-tall pillars crowned with statues of Sts. Ubaldo, George, and Anthony. The pillars are transported to the Palazzo dei Consoli on the first Sunday of May, in preparation for the Festa dei Ceri. ⊠ *Monte Ingino* ☎ *075/9273872* ⊠ *Free* ☉ *Daily 9–noon and 4–7.*

CloseUp

ST. UBALDO WINS AGAIN

E VERY MAY 15—the eve of the day celebrating Gubbio's patron saint, St. Ubaldo—the townspeople gather for the **Festa dei Ceri** (⊕ www.festadeiceri.it), as they have since 1160. The day is rich in song and revelry, but the main event is a race during which teams of men in colorful costumes haul three enormous wooden pillars called ceri (candles) at breakneck speed to the top of Monte Ingino and the Basilica of St. Ubaldo. What makes the task so difficult? Each of the pillars weighs about 880 pounds and is carried vertically (with the aid of special frames).

The ceri, which are topped with statues of St. Ubaldo, St. George, and St. Anthony during the Corsa dei Ceri (Race of the Ceri), reside in the basilica. On the first Sunday in May, however, they're transported (in the horizontal position) in a procession to the Palazzo dei Consoli, where they're displayed ahead of the festival.

"Running" with the pillars is a serious matter and locals vie for the honor of being one of the bearers, called ceraioli. (Family tradition often dictates participation.) Teams accomplish the arduous task while surrounded by throngs of townspeople and visitors who come to absorb some of the fascinating, mystical emotion that defines the "race." Don't place any bets, though—the pillar capped with St. Ubaldo always wins.

Where to Stay & Eat

$$–$$$$ ✕ **Fornace di Mastro Giorgio.** The building dates back to the 1300s, and its original stone-and-wood structure has been kept intact. (In the 1400s the space housed a ceramics factory important in Gubbio.) The menu, with seasonal changes, includes traditional but creative fare: *gnochetti al finocchio selvatico* (potato dumplings with wild fennel), *agnolotti al tartufo nero* (ravioli-type pasta with black truffles), and *filetto alle prugne* (filet mignon with prune sauce). ⊠ *Via Mastro Giorgio 2* ☎ *075/ 9221836* ▤ *AE, DC, MC, V* ☉ *Closed Tues. No lunch Wed.*

$$–$$$$ ✕ **Taverna del Lupo.** One of the city's most famous taverns, this popu-
Fodor'sChoice lar restaurant seats 150 people and gets hectic on weekends and during
★ the high season. Lasagna made in the Gubbian fashion, with ham and truffles, is an unusual indulgence, and the *coniglio di Buon Ricordo* (rabbit stew with herbs and spices) is a specialty. Peruse the extensive wine list and save room for the excellent desserts. ⊠ *Via Ansidei 21* ☎ *075/ 9274368* ▤ *AE, DC, MC, V* ☉ *Closed Mon. Oct.–Apr.*

$–$$$ ✕ **Bosone Garden.** As the stone arches inside indicate, this was once the stables of the palace that now houses the Hotel Bosone. The menu includes a two-mushroom salad with truffles, risotto *alla porcina* (with porcini mushrooms, sausage, and truffles), and leg of pork. The garden, open in summer, seats 200. ✉ *Via XX Settembre 22* ☎ *075/9220688* 🍴 *AE, DC, MC, V* ☾ *Closed Wed. Oct.–May and 2 wks in Jan.*

$ ✕ **Grotta dell'Angelo.** The rustic trattoria is in the lower part of the old town, near the main square and tourist information office. The menu features simple local specialties, including *capocollo* (a type of salami), *stringozzi* (very thick spaghetti), and lasagna *tartufata* (with truffles). The few outdoor tables are in high demand in summer. The restaurant also offers a few small, basically furnished guest rooms, which should be booked in advance. ✉ *Via Gioia 47* ☎ *075/9273438* ⌖ *Reservations essential* 🍴 *AE, DC, MC, V* ☾ *Closed Tues. and Jan. 10–31.*

$ ▦ **Castello Cortevecchio.** The energetic owners of this truly special agriturismo have plenty organized for you. Eleven apartments are available in the 19th-century castle; a number of houses on the grounds provide additional apartments, rooms, and suites. The castle sits amid a 40-acre wooded park with a pool, stables, tennis courts, and a small soccer field. Guest rooms are simple but elegant, with furnishings in wood and marble, beamed ceilings, and clay-tile floors. ✉ *Località Nogna, 06020* ☎ *075/9241017* 🖷 *075/9241079* ⊕ *www.castellocortevecchio.it* ⟿ *10 rooms, 18 apartments, 4 suites* ⌖ *Restaurant, 2 tennis courts, pool, mountain bikes, boccie, horseback riding, soccer, bar; no a/c* 🍴 *AE, DC, MC, V* ☾ *Closed mid-Jan.–Feb. 10* ⍍ *EP.*

$ ▦ **Hotel Bosone Palace.** A former palace (Palazzo Raffaelli) serves as home to Hotel Bosone. Elaborate frescoes grace the ceilings of the two enormous suites, which are furnished with painted antiques, and the hotel's small and delightful breakfast room. Standard rooms are comfortably though soberly decorated with heavy wooden furniture. Ask for a room facing the valley and away from the sometimes noisy street. ✉ *Via XX Settembre 22, 06024* ☎ *075/9220688* 🖷 *075/9220552* ⊕ *www.mencarelligroup.com* ⟿ *28 rooms, 2 suites* ⌖ *Dining room, minibars, bar; no a/c* 🍴 *AE, DC, MC, V* ☾ *Closed 3 wks in Jan.* ⍍ *CP.*

$ ▦ **Hotel Gattapone.** The views from this spiffy, family-run hotel in the center of Gubbio are of a sea of rooftops. Rooms are a good size, modern, and comfortable; some have well-preserved wood beams on the ceilings. ✉ *Via Ansidei 6, 06024* ☎ *075/9272489* 🖷 *075/9272417* ⊕ *www.mencarelligroup.com* ⟿ *16 rooms, 2 suites* ⌖ *Bar, parking (fee); no a/c* 🍴 *AE, DC, MC, V* ☾ *Closed Jan. 8–Feb. 8* ⍍ *CP.*

Sports & the Outdoors

A costumed medieval pageant with its roots in Gubbio's warring past, ☾ the **Palio della Balestra** (Crossbow Tournament; ☎ 075/9220693) takes place on the last Sunday in May.

THE MARCHES
INCLUDING SAN MARINO

An excursion from Umbria into the Marches region allows you to see a part of Italy rarely visited by foreigners. Not as wealthy as Tuscany or Umbria, the Marches has a diverse landscape of mountains and beaches, and marvelous views. Like that of neighbors to the west, the patchwork of rolling hills of Le Marche (as it is known in Italian) is stitched with grapevines and olive trees, bearing luscious wine and olive oil.

Traveling here isn't as easy as in Umbria or Tuscany. Beyond the narrow coastal plain and away from major towns, the roads are steep and twisting. Efficient bus service connects the coastal town of Pésaro to Urbino. Train travel in the region is slow, however, and stops are limited—although you can reach Ascoli Piceno by rail.

San Marino, perched high on the upper slopes of Monte Titano, is best reached from Rimini, on the southern coast of Emilia-Romagna. A main highway connects the two; regular bus service to San Marino is available from Rimini's train station, airport, and city center.

Urbino

㉒ *75 km (45 mi) north of Gubbio, 116 km (73 mi) northeast of Perugia, 230 km (144 mi) east of Florence.*

Majestic Urbino, atop a steep hill with a skyline of towers and domes, is something of a surprise to come upon—it's oddly remote. And yet it was once a center of learning and culture almost without rival in western Europe. The town looks much as it did in the glory days of the 15th century, a cluster of warm brick and pale stone buildings, all topped with russet-color tile roofs. The focal point is the immense and beautiful Palazzo Ducale.

The city is home to the small but prestigious Università di Urbino—one of the oldest in the world—and during school term the streets are lively and filled with students. Urbino is very much a college town, with the usual array of bookshops, record stores, bars, and coffeehouses. In summer the Italian student population is replaced by foreigners who come to study Italian language and arts at several prestigious private fine-arts academies.

Urbino's fame rests on the reputation of three of its native sons: Duke Federico da Montefeltro (1422–82), the enlightened warrior-patron who built the Palazzo Ducale; Raffaello Sanzio (1483–1520), or Raphael, one of the most influential painters in history and an embodiment of the spirit of the Renaissance; and the architect Donato Bramante (1444–1514), who translated the philosophy of the Renaissance into buildings of grace and beauty. Unfortunately there is little work by either Bramante or Raphael in the city, but the duke's influence can still be felt strongly.

The **Casa Natale di Raffaello** (House of Raphael) is the house in which the painter was born and where he took his first steps in painting, under the direction of his artist father. There is some debate about the fresco of the Madonna here; some say it's by Raphael, whereas others attribute it to the father—with Raphael's mother and the young painter himself standing in as models for the Madonna and Child. ✉ *Via Raffaello 57* ☎ *0722/320105* 🎟 *€3* ⊙ *Mon.–Sat. 9–2, Sun. 10–1.*

Fodor'sChoice ⭐ The **Palazzo Ducale** (Ducal Palace) holds the place of honor in the city, and in no other palace of its era are the principles of the Renaissance stated quite so clearly. If the Renaissance was, ideally, a celebration of the nobility of man and his works, of the light and purity of the soul, then there is no place in Italy, the birthplace of the Renaissance, where these tenets are better illustrated. From the moment you enter the peaceful courtyard, you know you're in a place of grace and beauty, the harmony of the building reflecting the high ideals of the men who built it. Today the palace houses the **Galleria Nazionale delle Marche** (National Museum of the Marches), with a superb collection of paintings, sculpture, and other objets d'art, well arranged and lit. Some works were originally the possessions of the Montefeltro family; others were brought to the museum from churches and palaces throughout the region. Masterworks in the collection include Paolo Uccello's *Profanation of the Host*, Titian's *Resurrection* and *Last Supper*, and Piero della Francesca's *Madonna of Senigallia*. But the gallery's highlight is Piero's enigmatic work long known as *The Flagellation of Christ*. Much has been written about this painting, and few experts agree on its meaning. Legend had it that the three figures in the foreground represent a murdered member of the Montefeltro family (the barefoot young man) and his two killers. However, Sir John Pope-Hennessy—the preeminent scholar of Italian Renaissance art—argues that they represent the arcane subject of the vision of St. Lawrence. Academic debates notwithstanding, the experts agree that the work is one of the painter's masterpieces. Piero himself thought so: it is one of the few works he signed (on the lowest step supporting the throne). ⊠ *Piazza Duca Federico* ☎ *0722/2760* ⊕ *www.comune.urbino.ps.it* 🎫 *€4* 🕐 *Apr.–Oct., Mon. 8:30–2, Tues.–Sun. 8:30 AM–10 PM; Nov.–Mar., Mon. 8:30–2, Tues.–Sun. 8:30–7:15.*

Where to Stay & Eat

$–$$ ✕ **La Vecchia Fornarina.** Locals often fill the small, two-room trattoria near the Piazza della Repubblica to capacity. The specialty is meaty country fare, such as *coniglio* (rabbit) and *vitello alle noci* (veal cooked with walnuts) or *ai porcini* (with mushrooms). There's also a good selection of pasta dishes. ⊠ *Via Mazzini 14,* ☎ *0722/320007* ⚑ *Reservations essential* ▭ *AE, DC, MC, V.*

$–$$ ✕ **Vecchia Urbino.** In the center of town is this simple yet elegant wood-panel restaurant with views of the hills. Recommended pasta dishes include *vincisgrassi* (a meat lasagna), named after an Austrian captain who brought the recipe to Urbino more than 100 years ago, and spaghetti *alla Vecchia Urbino* (with bacon and pecorino cheese). A particularly good second course is the *coniglio al coccio* (literally, rabbit in earthenware); the rabbit is cooked in milk on the stovetop in an earthenware casserole and then baked. Prices can be higher when fresh truffles are involved in the preparation. ⊠ *Via dei Vasari 3/5* ☎ *0722/4447* ▭ *AE, DC, MC, V* 🕐 *Closed Tues.*

$ ✕ **Angolo Divino.** At this *osteria* (informal restaurant) in the center of Urbino, tradition reigns supreme: part of the menu, in pure local dialect, is translated into Italian before an English equivalent can be attempted. Dishes range from the deliciously simple *spaghetti sa la mulicca del pan (spaghetti col pane grattugiato;* spaghetti with bread crumbs) to the temptingly rich *filetto al tartuffo* (beef filet with truffles). ✉ *Via S. Andrea 14* ☎ *0722/327559* ⊟ *AE, D, MC, V* ⊗ *Closed Mon. and mid.-Oct.–mid-Nov. No dinner Sun.*

$–$$ ⊞ **Hotel Bonconte.** This classic hotel, dating from the beginning of the 20th century, is just inside the city walls and close to the Palazzo Ducale. Rooms are pleasant and include some antiques and upholstered pieces; those at the front of the hotel have views of the valley below Urbino, although they also face the street. A terrace in the tranquil garden to the rear of the hotel adjoins the cozy breakfast room and bar. ✉ *Via delle Mura 28, 61029* ☎ *0722/2463* 🖷 *0722/4782* ⊕ *www.viphotels. it/ita/hotel_bonconte.htm* 🛏 *23 rooms, 2 suites* ♨ *Bar, meeting rooms* ⊟ *AE, DC, MC, V* ♙ *EP.*

¢ ⊞ **Hotel San Giovanni.** This hotel in the old town is housed in a renovated medieval building. The rooms are basic, clean, and comfortable—with a wonderful view from Rooms 24 to 30. There's a handy restaurant-pizzeria below. ✉ *Via Barocci 13, 61029* ☎ *0722/2827* 🖷 *0722/329055* 🛏 *31 rooms, 17 with bath* ♨ *Restaurant; no a/c* ⊟ *No credit cards* ⊗ *Closed July* ♙ *CP.*

San Marino

㉓ *45 km (28 mi) northwest of Urbino, 168 km (104 mi) northeast of Florence.*

The town of San Marino is the capital of the Republic of San Marino, which measures 61 square km (23 square mi) and is landlocked on all sides by Italy. Legend has it that San Marino was founded in the 4th century AD by a humble stonecutter named Marino who settled here with a small community of Christians to escape persecution by pagan emperor Diocletian. Over the millennia, largely because of the logistical and strategic nightmares associated with attacking a fortified rock, the *repubblica* was more or less left alone by Italy's various conquerors, and it continues to this day as a politically independent state. But don't worry about changing money, showing passports, learning telephone codes, and the like; San Marino is, for all practical purposes, part of Italy.

The state consists of nine municipalities, known as the San Marino castles (or *castelli*), each run by a council called the Consiglio del Castello. Most of the republic's 26,000 residents live not in the medieval cliff town but rather along the more modern and accessible streets below the rock.

Tourist stores, tacky hotels and restaurants, and gun shops line the tangle of cobblestone streets in the town of San Marino, which climbs the side of Monte Titano. However, the views of the stunning green countryside far below more than justify a visit—the 3,300-ft-plus precipices of sheer rock make jaws drop and acrophobes quiver—and the town's *tre castelli* (three castles) are medieval architectural wonders and engineering curiosities. Starting in the center of town, you can walk castle-to-castle along a paved cliff-top ridge and take in the spectacular views of Romagna and the Adriatic Sea. A must-see in San Marino is the town's main square, Piazza della Libertà, whose battlemented and clock-topped Palazzo Pubblico is guarded by San Marino's real-life soldiers in their green uniforms. The walks make for a good day's exercise. The longest—and windiest—hike is the one between the second and third castles. Even if you arrive after castle visiting hours (8–8, shorter hours in winter), the ridge walk is worthwhile.

The **Castello della Guaita** dates from the 10th century. ⊠ *Via Salita alla Rocca* ☏ *0549/991369* 🎫 *€4.50, includes Castello della Cesta* ☉ *Mar. 20–Sept. 20, daily 8AM–8PM; Sept. 21–Mar. 19, daily 8.50–5.*

The 13th-century **Castello della Cesta** contains a museum of ancient weapons. It was built on a cliff 2,421 feet above sea level and offers great views. ⊠ *Via Salita alla Rocca* ☏ *0549/991369* 🎫 *€4.50, includes Castello della Guaita* ☉ *Mar. 20–Sept. 20, daily 8AM–8PM; Sept. 21–Mar. 19, daily 8.50–5.*

The 14th-century **Castello Montale,** the remotest of San Marino's castles, is closed to the public.

At the **Ferrari Museum** you can gaze at the automotive toys of the wealthy. Park at the border crossing. ⊠ *Strada dei Censiti 21* ☏ *0549/970614* 🎫 *€10* ☉ *Daily 10–1 and 2–6; reservations essential weekends.*

Shopping

Peer into the shops along the old town's winding streets and you're likely to notice that the republic is famous for its crossbows—and more: shopping for fireworks, firearms, and other items illegal for sale elsewhere is a popular activity here. Indeed, San Marino's legislation is looser than Italy's, and the republic is a tax haven that resembles a large duty-free shopping center. In addition to shops selling products with known brand names, plenty of stores are stocked with imitations, from perfumes to cheap stereos with labels like Panaphonic. All this may change, however; the Italian government has begun to tire of its lax little neighbor and has been stepping up border controls.

Ancona

24 *87 km (54 mi) southeast of Urbino, 139 km (87 mi) northeast of Perugia, 262 km (164 mi) east of Florence.*

Ancona was probably once a lovely city. It's on an elbow-shape bluff (hence its name; *ankon* is Greek for "elbow") that juts out into the Adriatic. But Ancona was the object of serious aerial bombing during World War II—it was, and is, an important port city—and was reduced to rubble. The city was rebuilt in the unfortunate postwar poured-concrete style, practical and inexpensive but not aesthetically pleasing. Unless you're waiting for one of the many ferries to Albania, Croatia, Greece, or Turkey, there is little reason to visit the city—with a few exceptions. The 2nd-century **Arco di Traiano** (Trajan's Arch) is worth a look, and the **Duomo San Ciriaco** and the **Loggia dei Mercanti** offer glimpses of the architecture of Ancona's past.

Settled first by Greek colonists from Syracuse, the town is now the administrative capital of the Marches and the largest Italian seaport on this central part of the Adriatic. Situated on the steep slopes of the two mountains that form its harbor, Ancona's oldest and most interesting streets provide good aerobic exercise while visiting the town on foot. The city's importance as a port means it's well served by trains, which can make it a good base for an excursion to Loreto or to Ascoli Piceno, farther south along the Adriatic coast.

Where to Stay & Eat

$–$$ ✕ **La Moretta.** This family-run trattoria is on the central Piazza del Plebiscito, and in summer there's dining outside in the square. Among the specialties here are *stoccafisso all'Anconetana* (cod baked with capers, anchovies, potatoes, and tomatoes) and the famous *brodetto* (fish stew). ⊠ *Piazza del Plebiscito 52* 🕾 *071/202317* 🖃 *AE, DC, MC, V* ⊘ *Closed Sun., Jan. 1–10, and Aug. 13–18.*

$$ 🏨 **Grand Hotel Palace.** Widely held to be the best hotel in town, it's the extras here—slippers, bath salts, and shaving kits—that earn the ranking. Rooms are on the small side but beautifully furnished with French beds dressed in yellow damask, and half have a view directly over the port. Public rooms are grand and elegant, and the breakfast room is on the top floor with a panoramic view. ⊠ *Lungomare Vanvitelli 24, 60100* 🕾 *071/201813* 🖷 *071/2074832* ⊘ *palace.ancona@libero.it* ✒ *39 rooms, 1 suite* ⟁ *Dining room, gym, bar, Internet, meeting rooms* 🖃 *AE, DC, MC, V* ⊘ *Closed Dec. 23–Jan. 1* ¶◯¶ *CP.*

Loreto

㉕ *31 km (19 mi) south of Ancona, 118 km (73 mi) southeast of Urbino.*

Loreto is famous for one of the best-loved shrines in the world, that of the **Santuario della Santa Casa** (House of the Virgin Mary), within the
★ **Basilica della Santa Casa.** Legend has it that angels moved the house from Nazareth, where the Virgin Mary was living at the time of the Annunciation, to this hilltop in 1295. The reason for this sudden and divinely inspired move was that Nazareth had fallen into the hands of Muslim invaders, whom the angelic hosts viewed as unsuitable keepers of this important shrine. Excavations made at the behest of the Church have shown that the house did once stand elsewhere and was brought to the hilltop—by either crusaders or a family named Angeli—around the time the angels (*angeli*) are said to have done the job.

The house itself consists of three rough stone walls contained within an elaborate marble tabernacle. Built around this centerpiece is the giant basilica of the Holy House, which dominates the town. Millions of visitors come to the site every year (particularly at Easter and on the Feast of the Holy House, December 10), and the little town of Loreto can become uncomfortably crowded with pilgrims. Many great Italian architects, including Bramante, Antonio da Sangallo the Younger (1483–1546), Giuliano da Sangallo (circa 1445–1516), and Sansovino (1467–1529), contributed to the design of the basilica. It was begun in the Gothic style in 1468 and continued in Renaissance style through the late Renaissance. The bell tower is by Luigi Vanvitelli (1700–73). Inside the church are a great many mediocre 19th- and 20th-century paintings but also some fine works by Renaissance masters such as Luca Signorelli and Melozzo da Forlì.

If you're a nervous air traveler, you can take comfort in the fact that the Holy Virgin of Loreto is the patron of air travelers and that Pope John Paul II has composed a prayer for a safe flight—available in the church in a half-dozen languages. ⊠ *Piazza della Madonna* ☎ *071/970104* ⊕ *www.santuarioloreto.it* ۞ *June–Sept., daily 6:45 AM–8 PM; Oct.–May, daily 6:45 AM–7 PM. Santuario della Santa Casa closed daily 12:30–2:30.*

Ascoli Piceno

㉖ *88 km (55 mi) south of Loreto, 105 km (65 mi) south of Ancona.*

Ascoli Piceno isn't a hill town but sits in a valley ringed by steep hills and cut by the fast-racing Tronto River. With almost 60,000 residents, it's one of the most important towns in the region; in Roman times it was one of central Italy's most important market towns. Despite the growth Ascoli Piceno saw during the Middle Ages and at other times, the streets in the town center continue to reflect the grid pattern of the ancient Roman city. You'll even find the word *rua*, from the Latin *ruga*, used for "street" instead of the Italian *via*. Now largely closed to vehicular traffic, the city center is a great place to explore on foot.

★ The heart of the town is the majestic **Piazza del Popolo,** dominated by the Gothic church of **San Francesco** and the **Palazzo del Popolo,** a 13th-century town hall that contains a graceful Renaissance courtyard. The square itself functions as the living room of the entire city. At dusk each evening the piazza is packed with people strolling and exchanging news and gossip—the sweetly antiquated ritual called the *passeggiata,* performed all over the country.

۞ Ascoli Piceno's **Giostra della Quintana** (Joust of the Quintana) is held on the first Sunday in August. Children love this medieval-style joust and the processions of richly caparisoned horses that wind through the streets of the old town. *Ascoli tourist office* ⊠ *Piazza del Popolo 1* ☎ *0736/253045.*

Where to Stay & Eat

★ $–$$ ✕ **Ristorante Tornasacco.** At one of Ascoli Piceno's oldest restaurants you won't find nouvelle cuisine: the owners pride themselves on meaty local specialties such as *olive ascolane* (olives stuffed with minced meat, breaded and deep-fried), *maccheroncini alla contadina* (homemade short pasta in a lamb, pork, and veal sauce), and *bistecca di toro* (bull steak). ⊠ *Piazza del Popolo 36* ☎ *0736/254151* ☰ *AE, DC, MC, V* ۞ *Closed Fri., July 15–31, and Dec. 23–28.*

¢ ▦ **Il Pennile.** Look for this modern, family-run hotel in a quiet residential area outside the old city center, amid a grove of olive trees. Some rooms have views of the city. ⊠ *Via G. Spalvieri, 63100* ☎ *0736/41645* ☎ *0736/342755* ⊕ *www.hotelpennile.com* ⇝ *33 rooms* ♤ *Minibars, gym, bar, Internet* ☰ *DC, MC, V* ⊚ *CP.*

PERUGIA & NORTHERN UMBRIA A TO Z

To research prices, get advice from other travelers, and book travel arrangements, visit www.fodors.com.

AIRPORTS

Central Italy's closest major airports are Rome's Fiumicino (officially Aeroporto Leonardo da Vinci), Pisa's Galileo Galilei, and Florence's Peretola (officially Aeroporto A. Vespucci). Tiny Aeroporto Sant'Egidio, 12 km (7 mi) east of Perugia, has flights to and from Milan, Rome (Ciampino), and Palermo. Though perhaps better known for its large military counterpart, Ancona's civic airport at Falconara has flights to and from Rome and is connected, by a number of low-cost airline companies, to London, Moscow, and several cities in Spain, Hungary, and Turkey.

🚩 Airport Information **Aeroporto A. Vespucci** (Peretola) ⊠ 5 km (3 mi) northwest of Florence ☎ 055/373498. **Aeroporto Falconara** ⊠ 5 km (3 mi) east of Ancona, ☎ 071/28271 ⊕ www.ancona-airport.com. **Aeroporto Galileo Galilei** ⊠ 2 km (1 mi) south of Pisa ☎ 050/500707 ⊕ www.pisa-airport.com. **Aeroporto Leonardo da Vinci** (Fiumicino) ⊠ 30 km (18 mi) southwest of Rome ☎ 06/6594420 ⊕ www.adr.it. **Aeroporto Sant'Egidio** ⊠ 12 km (7 mi) east of Perugia ☎ 075/592141 ⊕ www.airport.umbria.it.

BUS TRAVEL

Perugia is served by the Sulga Line with daily departures from Rome's Stazione Tiburtina and from Piazza Adua in Florence. Connections between Rome, Spoleto, and the Marches are provided by the associated bus companies Bucci and Soget.

Local bus service between all the major and minor towns of Umbria is good. Some of the routes in rural areas, especially in the Marches, are designed to serve as many places as possible and are, therefore, quite roundabout and slow. Schedules change often, so consult with local tourist offices before setting out.

🚩 Bus Lines **Bucci** and **Soget** ☎ 0721/32401 ⊕ www.autolineebucci.com. **Sulga Line** ☎ 075/5009641 ⊕ www.sulga.it.

CAR RENTALS

🚩 Agencies **Avis** ⊕ www.avis.com ⊠ Aeroporto Sant'Egidio, Perugia ☎ 075/6929796 ⊠ Stazione Ferroviaria Fontivegge, Piazza Vittorio Veneto 7, Perugia ☎ 075/5000395 ⊠ Via Piero della Francesca 20, Città di Castello ☎ 075/8558534. **Hertz** ⊕ www.hertz.com ⊠ Piazza Vittorio Veneto 4, Perugia ☎ 075/5002439 ⊠ Aeroporto Sant'Egidio, Via Aeroporto, Perugia ☎ 075/5002439.

CAR TRAVEL

Umbria has a good road network. Highway 75 bis links Perugia to Tuscany (to Siena via SR326 and E76) and to the Florence–Rome Autostrada del Sole (A1), Italy's main north–south highway; SR75 bis also goes right by Lago Trasimeno. However, travel through the mountains to Urbino can be a bit treacherous because of the winding roads; plan for plenty of travel time.

The A14 superhighway travels southeast from Bologna and follows the Adriatic coast through the entire length of the Marches; branches lead to Urbino, Ancona, Loreto, and Ascoli Piceno. SS San Marino, a state highway, takes you to the Republic of San Marino from Rimini.

EMERGENCIES

If you have ongoing medical concerns, it's a good idea to make sure someone is on duty all night where you're staying—not a given in Umbria, less so in the Marches. As elsewhere in Italy, every pharmacy in Umbria and the Marches bears a sign at the door listing area pharmacies open in off-hours. Perugia, Gubbio, and Urbino all have at least one so-called "night" pharmacy which, on a rotation basis with other pharmacies, provides 24-hour service.

🚹 Emergency Services **Ambulance** 🕾 118. **Fire department** 🕾 115. **Police** 🕾 113.

TOURS

Agriturismo (farm-stay) facilities are scattered around the Umbrian countryside. These working farms range in style from rustic establishments—offering little more than bed and breakfast—to 5-star luxury resorts with swimming pools and restaurants. They are ideal if you are traveling by car and appeciate the quiet beauty of the country more than the conveniences offered by the towns.

🚹 Agriturismo Agencies **Agriturist Umbria** ✉ Via San Bartolomeo 79, Perugia 06087 🕾 075/5997289 ⊕ www.agriturist.it. **Turismo Verde** ✉ Via Maria Angeloni 1, Perugia 06125 🕾 075/5002953 🖷 075/5002956 ⊕ www.turismoverde.it.

TRAIN TRAVEL

Several direct daily trains link Florence and Perugia. Otherwise, a change between the Florence–Chiusi–Rome line and the Perugia line is required at Terontola. The Florence–Chiusi train stops at Castiglione del Lago, on Lago Trasimeno, and sometimes at Città della Pieve as well. Daily direct service between Perugia and Rome is available, but this service isn't frequent and a change at Foligno, from the main Rome–Ancona line, is often required. Main rail lines, with fast Intercity and Eurocity trains, link Ancona with Bologna and Rome. A small, privately owned railway, Ferrovia Centrale Umbra, runs south from Città di Castello to Terni via Perugia. Gubbio and San Marino have no train service.

🚹 Train Lines **Ferrovia Centrale Umbra** 🕾 075/5729121. **Ferrovia dello Stato** (Italian State Railway) 🕾 892021 toll-free in Italy ⊕ www.trenitalia.com.

VISITOR INFORMATION

Umbria's regional tourism bureau is in Perugia.

🚹 Tourist Information **Ancona** ✉ Via Thaon de Revel 4 🕾 071/358991 ⊕ www.comune.ancona.it. **Ascoli Piceno** ✉ Piazza del Popolo 1 🕾 0736/257288 ⊕ www.ascolipiceno.com. **Assisi** ✉ Piazza del Comune 12 🕾 075/812534 ⊕ www.comune.assisi.pg.it. **Città della Pieve** ✉ Piazza Matteotti 4 🕾 075/8299375. **Città di Castello** ✉ Piazza Fanti 🕾 075/8554922. **Deruta** ✉ Piazza dei Consoli 4 🕾 075/9711559. **Gubbio** ✉ Piazza Oderisi 6 🕾 075/9220693. **Lago Trasimeno** ✉ Piazza Mazzini 10, Castiglione del Lago 🕾 075/9652484. **Perugia** ✉ Piazza IV Novembre 3 🕾 075/5736458 or 075/5723327 ⊕ www.comune.perugia.it. **San Marino** ✉ Contrada Omagnano 20 🕾 0549/882412 ⊕ www.sanmarinosite.com. **Umbria** ✉ Corso Vannucci 30, Perugia 🕾 075/5041. **Urbino** ✉ Piazza Duca Federico 35 🕾 0722/2613 ⊕ www.comune.orvieto.tr.it.

ASSISI, SPOLETO & SOUTHERN UMBRIA

8

Updated by
Judy Edelhoff

UMBRIA'S ROLLING HILLS DELIVER LANDSCAPES that might have been painted by Perugino, Raphael's master: green hills with trees that seem sculpted in place, or cascading slopes with vineyards and groves of olive trees, or forests with abundant wild mushrooms, truffles, and game— often cloaked in the same bluish haze that you see in Renaissance paintings. Here you can explore towns once settled by ancient peoples: the mysterious and sophisticated Etruscans; the simpler Umbri (the Umbrian people); and the Romans, the grand engineers who built temples, bridges, theaters, and roads—the last of which are still in use today. The absence of the overwhelming wealth of art and architecture that you find in Florence and Rome allows you to skip the mararthon here and absorb the enchanting towns and local cultures at a relaxing pace.

One of Italy's most important religious figures, St. Francis of Assisi, attracts to the charming town of Assisi in the northern Umbrian Valley religious pilgrims and those intrigued not only by his teachings and miracles but also by his joy of life and for his respect and love for nature. The region is certainly fertile ground for nature lovers: more than seven centuries after the death of St. Francis, his hometown is still surrounded by the lush forests of Mount Subasio and the agriculturally rich hills and valleys of which Umbria is justly proud.

To the south and west of the Umbrian Valley are a succession of lovely hill towns: Spello and Trevi spill down slopes; Montefalco enjoys a lofty vantage; and Bevagna and Foligno occupy the valley floor. La Rocca, a medieval fortress, announces the sophisticated hillside town of Spoleto, known for its annual summer Festival dei Due Mondi, a world-famous musical extravaganza.

Densely forested roads to the east of Spoleto take you through mountainous terrain toward Norcia, once known for its pork butchers and, not coincidentally, for its surgeons-in-training. Sadly, the butcher-shop trade has become overly commercial; you would do better to go truffle hunting in the nearby forests. The drive between Norcia and Terni takes you through some beautiful forested hills past Ferentillo, with its medieval abbey, Abbazia di San Pietro in Valle, up on the hilltop. Down below, near the Nera River, is one of Umbria's more offbeat sights, 30 or so mummies preserved in a crypt.

To the west of Terni are the walled towns of Narni and Amelia, with their architectural walks and surprising archaeological treasures. To the northwest, majestic Orvieto rises dramatically above the cliffs on which it rests like a crown, with forests, vineyards, olive groves, medieval abbeys, and Etruscan archaeological sites. Following the Tiber River, which flows into the sea not far from Rome's airport, south and east from Orvieto, you travel along a scenic, winding two-lane road to the charming medieval town of Todi.

Each town is worth exploring for its own expression of the medieval and Renaissance worlds. No two towns are the same, though some have works built or painted by some of the same masters. Inside their churches and basilicas, you have the rare opportunity to see works of art in situ—in the space for which the paintings, frescoes, or sculpture were originally created. The Roman influence is all around, from ancient consular roads like Via Flaminia that connect some of the towns, to ruins that take different forms in each town—a wall, a gate, a theater, a bridge, and so forth. Wherever you go, be sure to check out carvings on doorways and ornamentation, and look up above those tempting shop windows to find habitats whose exteriors have changed little in the past 500 or so years.

Textiles were and remain important in this region. The father of St. Francis made his fortune selling them in the 12th and 13th centuries, and today you can buy lovely textiles in most of the towns in southern Umbria—linen and cotton cloth in Montefalco and Todi; lace in Orvieto; and cashmere in Trevi and Bevagna.

The quality of southern Umbrian restaurants—whose cuisine often incorporates fresh, local truffles and porcini mushrooms—and of the broad spectrum of fine local wines is on par with or better than what you'll find in Tuscany, but at much lower prices. Cap off a day of lazily studying centuries-old artistic treasures, polishing off superb meals, and walking along narrow Romanesque streets backed by Umbria's rolling hills—straight out of a Perugino landscape painting—and this tranquil side of Tuscany and Umbria might just become an unexpected favorite.

Exploring Southern Umbria

The main towns in the region are easily accessible from Rome and Florence by road or rail, and despite the hilly terrain, getting around southern Umbria is actually a snap. The main highways run southeast from Perugia through or near the main towns, which are almost all linked by fairly frequent train and bus service. Distances are relatively short from one town to the next, but for the most flexible itinerary and to save time, a car is a must. Try to find time to follow an ancient consular road, such as Via Flaminia (SS3), which was built over 2,000 years ago to transport Romans and even today offers lovely vistas as it connects some of the towns. Assisi may be a key destination, but nearby Spello, Trevi, Bevagna, and Montefalco all make excellent bases of operation. Spoleto, too, is an excellent base thanks to its diverse resources for travelers: whether you seek sophisticated amenities in harmony with your musical tastes or a savvy staff that can help plot your bicycle route through the region, or you prefer to explore trails on horseback.

About the Restaurants

Be sure to seek out the excellent local cuisine, often better away from the tourist epicenter of Assisi, although even there you can have a good meal. Spoleto, the second major tourist center, has a much higher level of cuisine and service, probably because its international art crowd has higher expectations. For gourmet appetites, however, Spello is hard to beat, with excellent restaurants, service, sommeliers, and wine shops. You will quickly notice that prices for food and wine are often well below those in Tuscany.

Some of the region's best restaurants are not far off the beaten track—so it's well worth it to explore. To get the best results, order foods that

Numbers in the text correspond to numbers in the margin and on the Assisi, Spoleto, and Southern Umbria; Assisi; Spoleto; and Orvieto maps.

Southern Umbria is particularly well suited to touring in a limited time, as you can easily hop from one town to the next with minimal difficulty. Alternatively, any of the towns, with the exception of Norcia to the east, can be covered in day trips from Perugia. You can arrange your itinerary around some themes specific to Umbria: the paintings of Perugino, Raphael's master; the spiritual towns and places of St. Francis; the Sagrantino Wine Road; sniffing around for truffles; castles and fortresses; bicycle routes; Umbria on horseback; or local festivals.

If you have 5 days

Begin in Assisi ❶–❻ ➤ with the Basilica di San Francesco, and then seeing the town's other major sites, including the tiny Museo Civico and fortress. Using Spello or Bevagna as a base, spend the following day visiting some of the delightful hill towns in the Valle Umbra to the south, such as **Spello** ❼ or **Montefalco** ❿. Devote the third day to good walks through the narrow streets of Spoleto ⓬–㉑, including a walk across the Ponte delle Torri and around the pretty Monteluco. After spending the night in Spoleto, go east to **Norcia** ㉒ for a day hike, perhaps with a theme like truffle hunting, before returning to Spoleto for the night, or head south to the towns of **Narni** ㉖ and **Amelia** ㉗. On Day 5 visit quaint **Todi** ㉙ and the legendary Duomo and museums in nearby **Orvieto** ㉚–㉟.

If you have 7 or 8 days

Use Assisi ❶–❻ ➤ or nearby Spello ❼ ➤ as your base for the first three nights. Spend the first day discovering Assisi. The following day, make your way through the Franciscan sites outside the walls, like Eremo delle Carceri and the church of San Damiano, leaving time to explore Spello and **Foligno** ❽. The third day can be spent visiting the other small and charming hill towns of the Valle Umbra. On the fourth day head south to Spoleto ⓬–㉑. The following day, go east to **Norcia** ㉒ for a day's outing, and possibly some truffle hunting, before returning to Spoleto for the night. The sixth day could be spent between the towns of **Terni** ㉓, **Narni** ㉖, and **Amelia** ㉗, or at the waterfalls at Marmore and lovely Lake Piediluco, before heading to **Todi** ㉙. On the final day, visit Todi and the Duomo and museums in nearby **Orvieto** ㉚–㉟.

are in season. The trick is to stroll through local markets to see what's being sold.

The robust food of southern Umbria that has kept farmers and artisans going for centuries serves well to refuel visitors who climb the steep hills during the day. Wild game and fowl are more popular here than at the tables of their Roman neighbors to the south. Pork is a specialty, and beef steaks are excellent too. Meats are often roasted or grilled, sometimes basted with a rich sauce made from innards or with red wine.

Most restaurants offer truffles and porcini mushrooms, but look for subtle variations in each town. Some foods or specialties are unique to one town: Trevi's black celery is cultivated only there and is traditionally served stuffed with sausage, but you are unlikely to find it even a few miles away; the onions of Cannara are prepared in a multitude of ways in their hometown; and the "rediscovered" ancient spice saffron was reintroduced in the last few decades in pockets of Umbria like Città della Pieve and Cascia, where locals now produce a golden range of saffron-seasoned specialities from appetizers to desserts.

In the past few years the phenomenon of the *enoteca* (combination wine shop and wine bar) has taken off, making it easier to arrange wine tastings and to compare wines and producers. Wining and dining might be alfresco in a lovely town square or on a high perch with view of hills and valleys; or in a cozy converted monastery or mill—cool in summer and warmed by a fireplace in winter. Some wine information centers, like La Strada del Sagrantino in Montefalco, will give you maps and help set up appointments with your favorite wine-makers.

About the Hotels

The main towns in southern Umbria generally have one or two hotels in a high price category and a few smaller, basic—often family-run—hotels in the inexpensive-to-moderate ($–$$) range. Since the early 1990s some old villas and monasteries have been converted into small first-class hotels. These tend to be out in the countryside, but the splendor of the setting can outweigh the hassle of getting into town. If you plan to stay in the area for a few days or more, it could be economical to rent a cottage or apartment (*agriturismo*) in the countryside, an interesting alternative to the usual hotels. Reservations are always advisable, and essential if you plan to visit Spoleto during the Festival dei Due Mondi (late June to early July) or Assisi from Easter through October. Do not use Assisi as your base unless you are a passionate pilgrim; hotels and restaurants are much better elsewhere.

The local agent **Home in Italy** (✉ Via Adelaide 50/c, Perugia, 06128 ☎ 075/ 5057865 🖷 075/5006127 ⊕ www.homeinitaly.com) is a good contact for apartment and villa rentals. **Tandem** (✉ Piazza Mazzini, Trevi, 06038 ☎ 0742/780066 ⊕ www.bedandbreakfastumbria.it) is a bed-and-breakfast reservations service.

WHAT IT COSTS In Euros				
$$$$	**$$$**	**$$**	**$**	**¢**
RESTAURANTS over €22	€18–€22	€13–€17	€7–€12	under €7
HOTELS over €290	€210–€290	€140–€209	€80–€139	under €80

Restaurant prices are for a second course (secondo piatto) per person. Hotel prices are for two people in a standard double room in high season, including tax and service.

Timing

The forested hills of southern Umbria and the vivid colors of the grape vines ensure beguiling colors in the fall and an explosion of greenery

Crafts

For crafts, Bevagna is known for ironwork, Spello for woodcarving, Foligno for lace and embroidery, and Bastardo (near Montefalco) for linen and cotton textiles. Some small workshops can still be found around towns. All of the local festivals generally feature crafts of the area.

Cuisine

Truffles are the local delicacy. Try them—you'll see what all the fuss is about (⇨ "Truffle Talk" CloseUp box). Many Umbrian towns have their own excellent cured hams and salamis that go wonderfully well with the bread of the region. Lentils—for which the town of Castelluccio is known—along with farro (an ancient grain used by the Romans, similar to wheat) and a variety of beans are popular in winter soups and in summer salads, with fresh vegetables, herbs, and a drizzle of olive oil. Black celery comes from the Trevi area; look for it in local markets. Saffron, important to the area since medieval times, is raised in Cascia and other areas around Southern Umbria and makes a fragrant appearance in sauces and in a local cheese.

8

Fresh pasta is a treat that in winter is accompanied by richer sauces, often with meat or game, while summer sauces have more vegetables. Umbria's traditional pastas *ciriole* and *stringozzi* (also spelled *strangozzi*) are thicker versions of spaghetti, traditionally made without eggs, using only flour and water, served with a variety of sauces.

Freshwater fish and even shrimp are featured in local dishes—a famous dish is the *carpa in porchetta*, made with giant 40-pound carps that are dressed and roasted like suckling pigs. *Lumache* (snails) in Umbria are smaller than the French escargots and might be sautéed with wild fennel and fresh rosemary, either on pasta or still in the shell.

The best Umbrian olive oil is the extra-virgin variety from Trevi, chosen for the tables of the popes. Trevi calls itself the Olive Oil Capital, and almost everywhere you look around it olive trees are gracing the hillsides. Many *enoteche* (wine bars) now do double duty, offering olive oil tastings to compare flavor and quality.

The basic cheese of the region is a soft pecorino (sheep's-milk cheese). It's often flavored with truffles or herbs and either eaten as a spread or grated into hot pasta. Cheeses from neighboring Tuscany and Lazio also make their way to the Umbrian table. The monasteries and convents throughout the region produce various multicolor *rosolii* (sweet liqueurs) and digestive bitters, sold in all types of gift bottles.

Outdoors & Sports

Magnificent scenery makes Umbria a great place to enjoy the outdoors. The region offers excellent hiking, mountaineering, rock climbing, and horseback riding, and most tourist offices have maps of nearby trails and itineraries of walks and climbs to suit all ages and abilities. Lago di Piediluco (Lake Piediluco) is a safe, clean place to swim, and there is river rafting in the Valnerina, in the Nera River, below the waterfalls at Marmore. Southern Umbria has several famous *terme* (thermal springs), which have long been visited by travelers for their soothing, curative powers. A few thermal springs in the region are: **Terme Amerino** (✉ Via San Francesco 1, Acquasparta 05021, between Terni and Todi ☎ 0744/943921), closed Nov.–Apr.; **Terme di San Gemini** (✉ SS3 [Tiberina] Km 21, San Gemini, near Terni ☎ 0744/ 630426), closed Oct.–Apr.; and **Terme di Santo Raggio** (✉ Via P. A. Giorgi 6, near Assisi ☎ 075/816064), closed Nov.–mid-May. **Club Alpino Italiano** (CAI; ☎ 075/220433) arranges tours—some in English with advance notice— and provides detailed hiking maps.

Umbrian Wines

Sagrantino is not to be missed while in southern Umbria (⇨ "The Sagrantino Story" CloseUp box). Some experts consider it to be one of Italy's great red wines, but at prices far more accessible than some of neighboring Tuscany's wines. Another red to look for is Rosso di Montefalco, which combines the Sagrantino grape with other varieties to produce another full-bodied wine.

The Sagrantino Road, or Strada del Sagrantino, winds through the lovely rolling hills and beautifully landscaped vineyards around Montefalco. These vineyards often have historic buildings where you can see how the wines are made, tested, aged, and stored. Each winery is unique: Antonelli is gentlemanly; Caprai is bold; Terre dei Capitani is laboriously handcrafted by an artisan; some are estates and others are very "mom and pop." Try to visit several for the views, the excellent wines, and the hospitality.

Try other Umbrian full-bodied reds, too, like Rubesco and Torgiano Rosso Riserva. Some of the Sagrantino wine-makers also make whites, like Grechetto. Orvieto Classico is one of Italy's oldest varieties of white wine, but mass production has created some mediocre results, so take time to seek out some of the local wine-makers that we have recommended. Some smaller wineries are difficult to visit, as hours are limited or they are not set up to do tastings. So make good use of the local tourist office to ask for help with appointments and directions. The enoteche are valuable for advice and for sampling wines of more than one producer in one tasting or "degustazione"; ask the owner or sommelier to introduce you to some good wines produced by the smaller wineries, as that may be the only way to sample them.

If you travel to Italy in November, the *vino novello,* or "new wine," is released with similar fanfare as for *vin nouveau* in France. This young wine stays on the market for only a short time. It may be less sophisticated than other varieties, but is fresh in flavor and reasonable in price.

The "IPG" wines should not be overlooked by the budget-minded traveler. These wines, like Umbria Rosso, are specific to geographical areas and will give you specific regional differences in taste. The wines are usually less elegant but are cheaper and show that, when you select a good Italian winemaker, you can get a good table wine that is delightful to drink and won't break the bank.

and flowers in the spring. Keep in mind that winter can be cold, and that many hotels and restaurants close for some portion of it. Book accommodations far in advance if you plan to visit Spoleto in June or July during the Festival dei Due Mondi. It's always a good idea to reserve in advance in Assisi, but the city is especially crowded during Christmas, Easter, the Festa di San Francesco (October 4), and the Calendimaggio festival (early May). On the other hand, the lesser-known festivals that attract primarily residents are no time to stay away; they're an ideal opportunity to learn about provincial customs while you mingle with the locals as they are merrymaking.

ASSISI

The small town of Assisi is one of the Christian world's most important pilgrimage sites and home of the Basilica di San Francesco—built to honor St. Francis (1182–1226) and erected in swift order after his death. The inherent peace and serenity of the town allow visitors to slow their 21st-century pace, welcoming the respite after visiting some of Italy's major cities.

Like most other towns in the region, Assisi began as an Umbri settlement in the 7th century BC and was conquered by the Romans 400 years later. The town was Christianized by St. Rufino, its patron saint, in the third century, but it is the spirit of St. Francis, a patron saint of Italy and founder of the Franciscan monastic order, that is felt throughout its narrow medieval streets. The famous 13th-century basilica was decorated by the greatest artists of the period.

Assisi is pristinely medieval in architecture and appearance, owing in large part to relative neglect from the 16th century until 1926, when the celebration of the 700th anniversary of St. Francis's death brought more than 2 million visitors. Since then, pilgrims have flocked here in droves, and today several million arrive each year to pay homage to the man who made God accessible to so many. But not even the constant flood of visitors to this town of just 3,000 residents can spoil the singular beauty of this significant religious center, the home of some of the Western tradition's most important works of art. The hill on which Assisi sits rises dramatically from the flat plain, and the town is dominated by a medieval castle on the mount's top.

A series of earthquakes in the fall of 1997 devastated Umbria and Le Marche, rendering countless homes uninhabitable and causing the partial collapse of a frescoed ceiling in the Basilica di San Francesco. It was feared that the frescoes—with some of the great masterpieces of Giotto and Cimabue—reduced to rubble, were beyond repair, but an ongoing and massive effort by art restorers and volunteers is saving some of them. The Upper Basilica, closed for more than two years, has reopened (albeit with blank spaces in the ceiling where the frescoes used to be). A few of Assisi's medieval stone buildings are still propped up by scaffolds, but extensive work has restored most of the town to its former state. The earthquake's effects remain evident, however, in the cracked buildings throughout Umbria that still await repair.

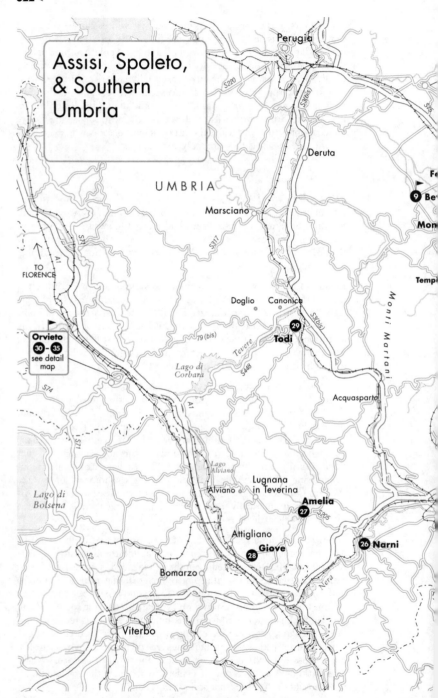

Assisi, Spoleto, & Southern Umbria

Perugia

Deruta

UMBRIA

Marsciano

Doglio Canonica

Todi 29

Orvieto
30 – 35
see detail
map

TO
FLORENCE

Lago di
Corbara

Tevere

Acquasparto

Lago di
Bolsena

Lago
Alviano

Lugnana
in Teverina

Alviano

Amelia 27

Attigliano

Giove 28

26 Narni

Bomarzo

Nera

Viterbo

Be 9

Mon

Temp

Monti Martani

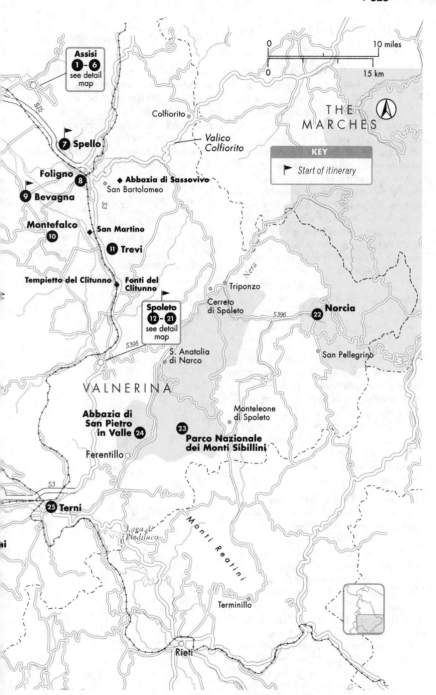

CloseUp

TRUFFLE TALK

MORE TRUFFLES ARE FOUND IN **UMBRIA** *than anywhere else in Italy. The primary truffle areas are around Spoleto (signs warning against unlicensed truffle hunting are posted at the base of the Ponte delle Torri) and the hills around the tiny town of Norcia, which holds a truffle festival every February. Even though truffles grow locally, the rare delicacy can cost a small fortune—up to $200 for a quarter pound. In November 2004 a truffle that weighed just over two pounds brought in over $50,000 at the annual truffle auction, the highest price ever paid. Fortunately, the truffles that you eat will be more reasonable (and besides, a little goes a long way in most dishes). At the 2004 truffle festival in Valtopina (north of Assisi) truffles the size of cherries went for €8–€12.*

At such a price, there is great competition among the nearly 10,000 registered truffle hunters in the province, who use specially trained dogs to sniff them out among the roots of several trees, including oak and ilex. Although there have been incidents of inferior varieties being imported from China, you can be reasonably assured that the truffle shaved onto your pasta has been unearthed locally.

The kind of truffle you taste will depend on the season. In addition to the famous black and white truffles, there are at least seven or eight other local species. The mild summer truffle, called scorzone estivo (with black outside and beige inside), is in season from May through December. The scorzone autunnale (smooth in appearance with a burnt brown color and visible veins inside) is picked from the beginning of October to the end of December. These two varieties are used especially for sauces. Norcia and Spoleto are ideal hunting territory for the tartuffo nero (reddish-black interior and fine white

veins), winter's precious black truffle, prized for its extravagant flavor; it can grow up to the size of an apple. Valtopina and Gubbio are stomping grounds for the white truffle, tartuffo bianco, which is shaved into omelettes or over pasta, pounded into sauces, chopped and mixed with oil, or used to perfume meat.

Local residents have perfected freezing, drying, or preserving truffles in oil, so you you can enjoy this delectable treat any time of year. Don't pass up the opportunity! The intense aroma of a dish perfumed with truffles is unmistakable and the flavor memorable.

Even though Assisi can become besieged with sightseers disgorged by tour buses, who clamor to visit the famous basilica, it's difficult not to be transformed by the tranquility of the quiet town and charmed by its medieval architecture as you stroll its narrow winding streets with glimpses of beautiful vistas of hills and valleys peeking through openings in the walls between buildings or from scenic overlooks in some town squares.

Exploring Assisi

Assisi lies on the Terontola–Foligno rail line, with almost hourly connections to Perugia and direct trains to Rome and Florence several times a day. The Stazione Centrale is 4 km (2½ mi) from town, with bus service about every half hour. Assisi is easily reached from the A1 Motorway (Rome–Florence) and the S75b highway. The walled town is closed to outside traffic, so cars must be left in the parking lots at Porta San Pietro, near Porta Nuova, or beneath Piazza Matteotti. (Pay your parking fee at the *cassa,* the ticket booth where the attendant is stationed, before you return to your car so that you get a ticket to insert in the machine that will allow you to exit.) It's a short but sometimes steep walk into the center of town; frequent minibuses (buy tickets from a newsstand or tobacconist near where you park your car) make the rounds for weary pilgrims.

A Good Walk

Assisi's churches are its main attractions, but be sure to take time to enjoy the city's natural surroundings, too, before you enter or after you leave its narrow cobblestone streets. Make your first stop the **Basilica di San Francesco** ❶ ➤, seeing both the Lower and Upper basilicas. Via San Francesco leads uphill from the Basilica di San Francesco, past souvenir and antiques shops, residential buildings, and at no. 10, the **Pinacoteca Comunale** ❷. Up ahead is Piazza del Comune, the town square built in the Middle Ages over Roman remains, which can be viewed through the adjacent **Foro Romano e Collezione Archeologica** ❸. Across the square is the graceful, if architecturally incongruous, **Tempio di Minerva** ❹, which is among the best-preserved Roman-era facades in Umbria. From the piazza, Via di San Rufino leads up to the **Cattedrale di San Rufino** ❺, which houses the remains of the town's "other" saint, the martyred 3rd-century bishop who brought Christianity to Assisi. To the side is the small Museo Capitolare, with detached frescoes and artifacts from the church; admission includes a visit to the 11th-century crypt. Double back to Piazza del Comune and follow Corso Mazzini to **Basilica di Santa Chiara** ❻; then continue through Porta Nuova to the church of San Damiano, a 1½-km (1-mi) walk outside the walls. Also of interest outside the walls are the Eremo delle Carceri, east of the center along Via Santuario delle Carceri, and the church of Santa Maria degli Angeli, near the train station.

TIMING Although the itinerary can be done in as little as a half day, it is a shame to be in a rush in a place as peaceful as Assisi, and a full day is recommended. An especially pleasant way to work up an appetite for dinner is to take part in the *passeggiata* (evening stroll) along the long streets

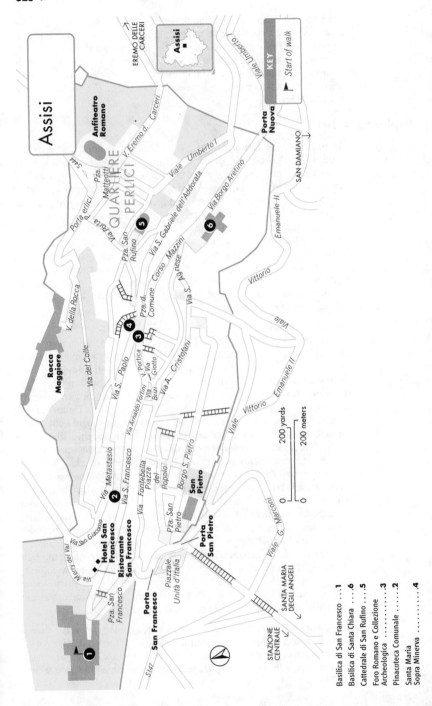

Assisi

KEY

Start of walk

(Via Fontebella, Via San Francesco) that cross the hill, where you can catch glimpses of the valley below and plenty of local color.

What to See

6 Basilica di Santa Chiara. The lovely, wide piazza in front of this church is reason enough to stop by, its panoramic view over the Umbrian plains framed by the red-and-white-striped facade of the church itself. Santa Chiara is dedicated to St. Clare, one of the earliest and most fervent of St. Francis's followers and the founder of the order of the Poor Ladies—or Poor Clares—which was based on the Franciscan monastic order. The church contains Clare's body, and in the **Cappella del Crocifisso** (on the right) is the cross that spoke to St. Francis. A heavily veiled nun of the Poor Clares order usually is stationed before the cross in adoration of the image. ⊠ *Piazza Santa Chiara* ☎ *075/812282* ⊙ *Nov.–mid-Mar daily 6:30–noon and 2–6; Mid-Mar.–Oct. daily 6:30–noon and 2–7.*

▶ **1 Basilica di San Francesco.** Followers of St. Francis began constructing the
Fodor'sChoice basilica in 1228, two years after his death. They finished what is now
★ the Lower Basilica in just a few years. Less than half a century later, Franciscan leaders from northern Europe crossed the Alps and arrived in Assisi. They built a second church right on top of the first; with soaring arches and stained glass, its Gothic style is a stark contrast to the dark and somber, Romanesque-Lombard Lower Basilica. The two levels are brought together by a 13th-century campanile (bell tower) and a Romanesque facade. Inside, the walls and ceilings are decorated with masterpieces by the greatest artists of the period.

At first, the grandeur of the basilica might seem at odds with the tenets of the Franciscan order, expressed in the credo "Carry nothing for the journey, neither purse nor bag nor bread nor money." But it is important to consider the essential role this church served for pilgrims as far back as the 14th century. Great works of art and lavish decoration were seen as an homage to saintliness, intended to elevate—as well as disquiet—the soul.

The **Upper Basilica** was devastated in the earthquakes of 1997. Portions of its vaulted ceiling collapsed over the entrance and the altar, killing four people and reducing ceiling frescoes by Giotto and his teacher, Cimabue, to dust and rubble. Although it was feared that the frescoes could never be reconstructed, art restorers have used specially designed computers to piece some sections back together. It is hoped that in the future some of the frescoes will be back on display. The ceiling has been repainted blue to take on its heavenly hue again, though patches of white plaster are visible.

Fortunately, Giotto's 28-panel fresco cycle, the *Life of St. Francis,* survived the earthquakes virtually unscathed. Giotto is often considered the first true Renaissance painter, and the innovations of his work, basic as they may seem to modern eyes, were revolutionary in his time. The roundness, depth, and weight of his figures, his knowing use of perspective, and the three-dimensionality of his painted space set the artistic stage for later masters, including Michelangelo, Leonardo, and Raphael.

View the panels of this landmark work from left to right, starting in the transept; the narration closely follows the biography of the saint by St. Bonaventure. Although St. Francis's days were mostly filled with miracles and mystic visions, Giotto doesn't dwell much on the myth of the fragile, pure, and holy poor man. Instead, he portrays a powerful, good friar who worked actively and with deep commitment for his community. Giotto's St. Francis is a robust man busy meeting people in front of real buildings and trees; rather than floating through the clouds, the saint has his feet set firmly on the ground.

The first four episodes are a prelude to the fifth, in which St. Francis renounces his worldly goods. Episodes 6 to 20 depict St. Francis's miraculous works; look for *The Sermon to the Birds,* a touching image that sums up the gentle spirit of the saint. Its airy, light depiction of nature is in contrast to *St. Francis Appearing Before Pope Innocent III in a Dream,* in which the pope dreams of a humble monk who will uphold the teachings of the church; to his left, a strong St. Francis supports a teetering church. Other famous scenes include *St. Francis Appearing to His Companions in a Flaming Chariot*; *St. Francis Proposing Trial by Fire Before the Sultan*; and *St. Francis Chasing the Devils from Arezzo.* The 19th and 20th panels solemnly illustrate St. Francis receiving the stigmata, followed by his death and funeral. Aside from a depiction of St. Clare mourning her friend, the last eight episodes refer to the canonization of St. Francis (panel 24) and the miracles he performed after his death.

In the transept of the Upper Basilica are frescoes by Cimabue (circa 1240–1302), which are in poor condition. The intarsia (inlaid wood) choir is a 16th-century masterpiece of 105 stalls; some are decorated with episodes from the lives of famous Franciscan friars, but note particularly some of the playful trompe-l'oeil windows, the magnificent medieval cityscapes, and the angel Gabriel. The vivid stained-glass windows (also in the lower church) date to the 13th century.

Around the left side of the facade and beneath a Renaissance porch is the entrance to the **Lower Basilica.** The low ceilings and dimly lit interior contrast sharply with the soaring, airy space above, but it seems an appropriate shrine for the tomb of St. Francis, beneath the main altar. Stairs at the sides of the nave lead down to the crypt. The saint's body was once visible through a window but was hidden away in the 15th century when rival towns threatened to steal it. The simple stone coffin was hidden so well, in fact, that in 1818 it took excavators 52 days to recover it; it was then reinterred in the center of the crypt, with the tombs of his four closest disciples placed at the corners.

The frescoes on the four sections of the cross-vaulting above the main altar are attributed to a student of Giotto. They represent allegories of the Franciscan virtues (*Poverty, Chastity,* and *Obedience*) and *The Triumph of St. Francis.* In the middle transept is Cimabue's *Madonna and Child Enthroned, with Four Angels and St. Francis,* which may look familiar—it features one of the best-known images of the saint. Just below are the tombs of five of St. Francis's early followers, with their portraits by Pietro Lorenzetti (circa 1280–1348) on the wall above. By the same artist, in the left transept, is a moving group of frescoes that depict the *Passion of Christ* with particular expressiveness and tension.

Also worth a look is the **Cappella di San Martino** (first on the left of the nave), with frescoes of the *Life of St. Martin* (1322) by Sienese master Simone Martini (circa 1284–1344). The cycle begins at the lower left, with the famous scene of St. Martin sharing his cloak with Christ, who is disguised as a poor man. The scenes continue with the saint's knighthood and his renunciation of the sword. The frescoes along the walls on either side of the nave, by an unknown artist, present the lives of Christ and St. Francis and served as inspiration to Giotto's more famous *Life of St. Francis* cycle in the Upper Basilica. The **Cappella della Maddalena** (last chapel in the right nave) contains frescoes of the life of St. Mary Magdalen by Giotto and assistants.

Steps lead up from the transepts of the lower church to the **Cloister,** where a well-stocked shop sells souvenirs and books and other items related to Saint Francis and Assisi. A small door leads from the Cloister to the **Treasury,** where precious religious objects belonging to the church, such as carved crucifixes, ivories, and tapestries, are on display. Admission to the Treasury is by donation. The basilica is run by Franciscan monks, who give informal tours in English; call ahead to make sure someone is available. In addition to normal services, there are special celebrations throughout the year. On October 4, the anniversary of St. Francis's death, a ceremony is held in which olive oil is offered to the saint for the lamp that burns above his tomb. Masses are sung during Easter week, and special ceremonies during Lent re-create the lives of St. Francis and Jesus. ⊠ *Piazza di San Francesco* ☎ *075/819001* ☉ *Lower Basilica Easter–Oct., daily 6:30 AM–6:50 PM; Nov.–Easter, daily 6:30–6. Upper Basilica Easter–Oct., daily 8:30–6:50; Nov.–Easter, daily 8:30–6* ☞ *Dress code strictly enforced: no bare shoulders or bare knees.*

❺ Cattedrale di San Rufino. Sts. Francis and Clare were among those baptized in Assisi's Cattedrale, which was the principal church in town until the 12th century. The baptismal font has since been redecorated, but it is possible to see the crypt of St. Rufino, the bishop who brought Christianity to Assisi and was martyred on August 11, 238 (or 236 by some accounts). Admission to the crypt includes the small **Museo Capitolare,** with its detached frescoes and artifacts. ⊠ *Piazza San Rufino* ☎ *075/ 812283* ⊕ *www.sistemamuseo.it* ☞ *Crypt and Museo Capitolare €2.07* ☉ *Cattedrale daily 7–noon and 2–sunset; Crypt and Museo, Mid-Mar.–mid-Oct., daily 10–1 and 3–6; mid-Oct.–mid-Mar., daily 10–1 and 2:30–5:30.*

❸ Foro Romano e Collezione Archeologica. Assisi didn't begin and end with St. Francis; have a look five meters below the medieval town, where you can see an archeological collection of Umbrian artifacts, housed in the crypt of a former 11th-century church of St. Nicholas (destroyed in 1929). The collection is all the more interesting for its incongruity in this medieval–Renaissance town. The *foro* (forum) may have been linked with a sacred site joined to the Tempio di Minerva. Before you walk through, be sure to request the English-language text guide—artifacts are numbered but not labeled. ⊠ *Via Portica 2* ☎ *075/813053* ⊕ *www.sistemamuseo.it* 🖭 *€3.50* ⊘ *Daily 10:30–1 and 2:30–6; call ahead, as at this writing museum is experimenting with different hours.*

❷ **Pinacoteca Comunale.** The city art gallery houses a collection of early paintings by mostly local Umbrian masters and provides a glimpse at some of Giotto's contemporaries as well as a fresco attributed to him. ⊠ *Palazzo Vallemani, Via San Francesco, next to no. 12* ☎ *075/812033* ⊕ *www.sistemamuseo.it* 🖭 *€3.50* ⊘ *Mid-Mar.–Sept., daily 10–1 and 2:30–7; Nov.–mid-Mar., daily 10–1 and 2:30–6.*

Rocca Maggiore. Although this 14th-century fortress may still be undergoing partial restoration (it largely escaped damage during the 1997 earthquakes, only to be struck by lightning in 2000, causing the collapse of a small section of wall), part of it can be visited and the views are well worth the walk up to the peak, day or night. On the way, pass through the Quartiere Perlici, a little neighborhood with narrow streets that follow a symmetrical Roman layout; in one part the houses and street trace the elliptical plan of the 1st-century Anfiteatro Romano (Roman Amphitheater) that stood on the site. ⊠ *At the end of Via della Rocca* ☎ *075/815292* ⊕ *www.sistemamuseo.it* 🖭 *€1.70* ⊘ *Daily 10–sunset.*

off the
beaten
path

SAN DAMIANO – Dating back to at least 1030, this was the church that Francis decided to restore in 1205. Nestled in an olive grove, this church seems much more in keeping with the spirit of St. Francis and his followers than the great basilica across town, and for all its austerity, its history is closely tied to that of the city's saints. This is where the crucifix (now in Santa Chiara) spoke to him: "*Vade, Francisce, et repara domum meam*" ("Go, Francis, and repair my house"). Francis took the command literally: he not only restored the building, but later set out to reform the church. St. Francis composed his *Canticle of the Creatures* here. St. Clare, after taking the Franciscan vows, lived out her life in the convent of this church, attracting a wide following and fame for her piety. In a Papal Bull in 1253, Pope Innocent IV (died 1254) confirmed her order, the Poor Clares; she died the next day. Shortly before her death, she reported having "seen" masses held in the Basilica di San Francesco. For this reason she was designated the patron saint of television in the 1950s. ⊠ *Località San Damiano, 1½ km (1 mi) south, outside the walls of Assisi* ☎ *075/812273* 🖭 *Free* ⊘ *Daily 10–noon and 2–6.*

❹ **Santa Maria Sopra Minerva.** Dating from the time of the emperor Augustus (27 BC–AD 14), this structure was originally dedicated to the Roman goddess of wisdom, in later times used as a monastery and prison before being converted into a church in the 16th century. The expectations raised by the perfect classical facade are not met by the interior, which was subjected to a thorough baroque transformation in the 17th century. ⊠ *Piazza del Comune* ☎ *075/812268* ⊘ *Weekdays 7:15–7, weekends 8:15–7. Closed 2–5:15 PM Tues. and Fri.*

ST. FRANCIS OF ASSISI

BORN TO A WELL-TO-DO TEXTILE-MERCHANT FAMILY *in 1181, Francis led a pleasure-seeking youth thanks to his father's wealth. But while serving as a young knight he was captured and spent a year in prison, which left him physically weak. Following a long illness he heard the voice of God and abandoned his military ambitions, taking his father's horse and some of his textiles to market in Foligno, where he sold everything, including the horse, to raise money to restore San Damiano church.*

After the bishop's decision in his father's court case against him, Francis publicly renounced his father's wealth and his rights to inheritance—including his clothes, which he publicly stripped off—and began a life of poverty and simplicity.

Through his dedicated works, his kind but firm nature, and his love of song, Francis quickly attracted a vast number of followers. In 1209, his order was recognized by Pope Innocent III (circa 1161–1216), and St. Francis later traveled throughout the Mediterranean to spread the word of God. He was the first saint, in 1224, to receive the stigmata. He died on October 4, 1226, in the Porziuncola, the chapel in the woods where he first preached the virtue of poverty to his disciples.

The Franciscans make up the largest of all Catholic orders. The saint's friars are identified by their simple, coarse brown habits bound by sashes of knotted rope. When you are in Assisi, consider booking one for a St. Francis–themed tour.

The fun-loving wealthy playboy turned ecologist was made patron saint of Italy in 1939. Francis is the patron saint, too, of ecologists, merchants, botanists, florists, businessmen, textile makers, and upholsterers.

Where to Stay & Eat

Assisi is not a late-night town, so don't plan on any midnight snacks. What you can count on is the ubiquitous stringozzi, as well as the local specialty *piccione all'assisana* (roasted pigeon with olives and liver). The locals eat *torta al testo* (a dense flatbread, often stuffed with vegetables or cheese) with their meals.

Although hotels in Assisi on the whole could be improved, advance reservations are essential between Easter and October or over Christmas. Latecomers are often left to choose from hotels in the modern town of Santa Maria degli Angeli, 8 km (5 mi) away. Consider instead booking a room in Spello or Bevagna, which have nicer accommodations and better cuisine, though you'll need a car to get around. As a last-minute option, you can also inquire at restaurants to see if they are renting out rooms.

Until the early 1980s, pilgrim hostels outnumbered ordinary hotels in Assisi, and they present an intriguing and economical alternative to conventional lodgings. They are usually called *conventi* or *ostelli* (convents or hostels) because they're run by convents, churches, or Catholic organizations; rooms are spartan but peaceful. Check with the tourist office for a list.

$$–$$$ ✕ **San Francesco.** An excellent view of the Basilica di San Francesco is the primary reason to come here. Locals also consider this to be the best restaurant in town, where creative Umbrian dishes are made with aromatic locally grown herbs. The seasonal menu might include gnocchi topped with a sauce of wild herbs and *oca stufata di finocchio selvaggio* (goose stuffed with wild fennel). Appetizers and desserts are especially good. ⊠ *Via di San Francesco 52* ☎ *075/812329* ▤ *AE, DC, MC, V* ⊘ *Closed Wed.*

$–$$ ✕ **Buca di San Francesco.** In summer, dine in a cool green garden; in winter, under the low brick arches of the restaurant's cozy cellars. The unique settings and the first-rate fare make this central restaurant Assisi's busiest. Try spaghetti *alla buca,* homemade pasta served with a roasted mushroom sauce. ⊠ *Via Brizi 1* ☎ *075/812204* ▤ *AE, DC, MC, V* ⊘ *Closed Mon. and July.*

¢–$$ ✕ **La Pallotta.** At this homey, family-run trattoria, the women do the cooking and the men serve the food. Try the *menu degustazione* (tasting menu) or the stringozzi *alla pallotta* (with a pesto of olives and mushrooms). The interior has a fireplace and stone walls. Connected to the restaurant is an inn whose rooms have firm beds and some views across the rooftops of town. Hotel guests get a 15% restaurant discount. ⊠ *Vicolo della Volta Pinta* ☎ *075/812649* 🖴 *075/812307* ⊕ *www.pallottaassisi.it* ▤ *AE, DC, MC, V* ⊘ *Closed Tues. and 2 wks in Jan. or Feb.*

$ ✕ **La Fortezza.** Partially enclosed by Roman walls, this family-run restaurant has personable service and reliably good food. A particular standout is *anatra al finocchio selvatico* (duck with wild fennel). ⊠ *Vicolo della Fortezza 2/b* ☎ *075/812418* ⌕ *Reservations essential* ▤ *AE, DC, MC, V* ⊘ *Closed Thurs. and Feb.*

¢–$ ✕ **La Stalla.** A onetime stable is now a rustic restaurant with hearty country fare; for something light, try the torta al testo with your choice of local cheeses, salami, grilled meats, and vegetables. Outside town, La Stalla is a good place to stop on your way to or from the Eremo delle Carceri. ⊠ *Via Santuario delle Carceri 8, 1 km (½ mi) east of center* ☎ *075/812317* ▤ *No credit cards* ⊘ *Closed Mon. Oct.–June.*

★ ¢–$ ✕ **Osteria Piazzetta dell'Erba.** Hip service (for Assisi) and sophisticated presentations attract locals to this trattoria. The owners carefully select wine at local wineries, buy it in bulk, and then bottle it themselves, resulting in high quality and reasonable prices. Choose from 10 or so appetizers, including smoked goose breast, and from four or five types of pasta, plus various salads and a good selection of torta al testo fillings. For dessert, try the homemade biscuits, which you dunk in sweet wine. Outdoor seating is available. ⊠ *Via San Gabriele dell'Addolorata 15b* ☎ *075/815352* ▤ *MC, V* ⊘ *Closed Mon. and a few wks in Jan. or Feb.*

$$ 🏨 **Hotel Subasio.** The converted monastery close to the Basilica di San Francesco is well past its prime, when guests included stars like Marlene Dietrich and Charlie Chaplin. If you can get past the sad kitsch hanging on the walls, you notice such vestiges as Venetian chandeliers. The hotel does have splendid views, comfortable sitting rooms, and flower-decked terraces, and it's a stone's throw from all those Giotto frescoes. Some rooms are grand in size and overlook the valley, while others are small and rough around the edges. Overall service can be spotty. The restaurant has a nice view, but the service and food could be better. ⊠ *Via Frate Elia 2, 06082* ☎ *075/812206* 🖷 *075/816691* ⇆ *54 rooms, 8 suites* ⚬ *Restaurant, bar, parking (fee)* ▤ *AE, DC, MC, V* ¶◎¶ *CP.*

$$ 🏨 **San Francesco.** You can't beat the location—the roof terrace and some of the rooms look out onto the Basilica di San Francesco, which is opposite the hotel. Rooms and facilities range from simple to dreary, but you may be reminded that looks aren't everything by the nice touches like slippers, a good-night piece of chocolate, and soundproofing. Fruit, homemade tarts, and fresh ricotta make for a first-rate breakfast. ⊠ *Via San Francesco 4, 06082* ☎ *075/812281* 🖷 *075/816237* ⊕ *www.hotelsanfrancescoassisi.it* ⇆ *44 rooms* ⚬ *Restaurant, minibars, bar, Internet, some pets allowed* ▤ *AE, DC, MC, V* ¶◎¶ *CP.*

$ 🏨 **Fontebella.** Between Piazza del Popolo and the Basilica di San Francesco, the Fontebella has spacious lounges and comfortable rooms (with rather small bathrooms), decorated with cheerful tapestries. The breakfast is especially ample, and the welcome warm. ⊠ *Via Fontebella 25, 06081* ☎ *075/812883* 🖷 *075/812941* ⊕ *www.fontebella.com* ⇆ *43 rooms, 3 family rooms* ⚬ *Restaurant, minibars, cable TV, bar, parking (fee)* ▤ *AE, DC, MC, V* ¶◎¶ *CP.*

$ 🏨 **Hotel Il Palazzo** Originally warehouses, stables, and inns during the 12th and 13th centuries, this building was modified in the 16th century and reopened as an inn in 1996. Very near the Basilica di San Francesco, the inn has 11 rooms—each different, some with wood beams and three with views of the valley. ⊠ *Via San Francesco 8, 06081* ☎ *075/816841* 🖷 *075/812370* ⊕ *www.hotelilpalazzo.it* ⇆ *11 rooms* ☉ *Closed Jan. and Feb.*

$ 🏨 **Hotel Umbra.** A 16th-century town house is the setting for this charming hotel in a tranquil part of the city, an area closed to traffic and near Piazza del Comune. The rooms are arranged as small suites, each with a tiny living room and balcony. Ask for an upper room with a view over the Assisi rooftops to the valley below. The restaurant, closed for lunch on Tuesday and Wednesday, has a charming vine-covered terrace leading to a secluded garden. ⊠ *Via degli Archi 6, 06081* ☎ *075/812240* 🖷 *075/813653* ⊕ *www.hotelumbra.it* ⇆ *25 suites* ⚬ *Restaurant, minibars, bar* ▤ *AE, DC, MC, V* ☉ *Closed mid-Jan.–mid-Mar.* ¶◎¶ *CP.*

The Arts

Concerts are occasionally held in Assisi's various churches; check with the **tourist office** (⊠ Piazza del Comune 12 ☎ 075/812534 ⊕ www.assisi. umbria2000.it) or look for signs around town.

Shopping

If you're in the market for a St. Francis cigarette lighter, you've come to the right place. You can sort through mountains of kitsch emblazoned with the saint's image, from key chains to Franciscan sandals to tiny blessed olive trees.

Look for some nice card shops with quality stationery and paper products. If you will not be passing through Deruta, near Perugia, Assisi has a number of shops that sell ceramics from the town; the selection is not as good but the prices are comparable. You can also pick up Umbrian truffles and all their aromatic and costly derivatives in Assisi's *alimentari* (local grocery shops) and gift shops. Assisi is well known for white-and-blue *ricamo a punto,* a traditional style of embroidery kept alive by religious institutions over the centuries. A good shop for *ricamo* items is **Rossi** (⊠ Via Frate Elia 1 ☎ 075/812555).

FROM ASSISI TO SPOLETO
THROUGH THE VALLE UMBRA

The main road (SS75) runs straight down the Valle Umbra from Assisi to Spoleto, but you'll do well to stop and smell the flowers (or talk to the birds) in the towns that line the valley. Here is your chance to do some wine tasting on the Sagrantino Road, to admire lovely town squares, and to see some unusual facades of churches. As you walk through towns, keep your eyes open for posters announcing musical performances, festivals, or other events: they will open up doors to some surprising theatrical gems, splendid courtyards, or magnificent church naves. They will give you a chance to meet the locals, who are much keener to meet the foreign visitor than those in the more famous tourist-besieged areas. Don't be surprised if they walk you to the site that you are trying to find or greet you with a cheerful "*buon giorno*" if they see you out on a quiet Sunday morning. These medieval towns are so unique that each leaves a lasting impression even if you do just a quick tour of the region. The art treasures hidden in their quiet streets would merit museums anywhere else—here, they're just part of the scenery.

Spello

▶ **❼** *12 km (7 mi) southeast of Assisi, 33 km (21 mi) north of Spoleto.*

Spello is a gastronomic paradise, especially compared to Assisi. Only a few minutes from Assisi by car or train, this hilltop town at the edge of Mt. Subasio makes an excellent strategic and culinary base for exploring nearby towns. Its hotels are well appointed and its restaurants serve some of the best cuisine and wines in the region—sophisticated in variety, and of excellent quality. Spello's art scene includes first-rate frescoes by Pinturicchio and Perugino and contemporary artists who can be observed at work in studios around town. If antiquity is your passion, the town also has some intriguing Roman ruins. And the warm, rosy-beige tones of the local *pietra rossa* stone on the buildings brighten even cloudy days.

The Romans moved in after the Umbri people, and traces remain of their walls, gates, amphitheater, and theater. Spello became a Roman colony just as Julius Caesar was riding the crest of power. Its city gates were constructed then or after, during the age of Augustus. The municipal building, or *palazzo comunale,* has an edict (carved in marble between 324 and 337) that describes Emperor Constantine's wishes for the colony. The town was later ruled by Lombards, the Baglioni family, and the Papal States. The church of Santa Maria Maggiore was built over a temple to Roman goddesses Juno and Vesta. In that church Benardino di Betto, known as Pinturicchio (1454–1513), painted the splendid frescoes in the Baglioni chapel in 1501 (in Rome he painted the frescoes for the Borgia apartments at the Vatican). The church of San Lorenzo dates from 1120; walk back behind the main altar and look at the 1533 carpenter's craftsmanship in the beautiful inlaid wood scenes in the choir. Walk uphill through town to the gate, Porta Venere, with its three arches and twelve-sided towers where the goddess Venus once had a temple. The view of the valley below shows the remains of the nearby Roman amphitheater that dates back to the first century AD. Sometimes you will find bits of Roman architecture in the hotel where you sleep or the restaurant where you dine.

Spello is 1 km (½ mi) from the train station, and buses run every 30 minutes for Porta Consolare, the Roman gate at the south end of town—the best place to enter.

From Porta Consolare continue up the steep main street that begins as Via Consolare and changes names several times as it crosses the little town, following the original Roman road. As it curves around, notice the winding medieval alleyways to the right and the more uniform Roman-era blocks to the left. Just up ahead is the basilica of **Santa Maria Maggiore**, with vivid frescoes by Pinturicchio in the Cappella Baglioni (1501). Striking in their rich colors, finely dressed figures, and complex symbolism, the *Nativity, Dispute at the Temple* (on the far left side is a portrait of Troilo Baglioni, the prior who commissioned the work), and *Annunciation* (look for Pinturicchio's self-portrait in the Virgin's room) are among Pinturicchio's finest works. They were painted after the artist had already won great acclaim for his work on the Palazzi Vaticani in Rome for Borgia pope Alexander VI. Two pillars on either side of the apse are decorated with frescoes by Perugino (circa 1450–1523), the other great Umbrian artist of the 16th century. ⊠ *Piazza Matteotti 18* ☎ *0742/301792* ✇ *Free* ☉ *May–Sept., daily 8–12:30 and 2:30–7; Oct.–Apr., daily 8–12:30 and 2:30–6.*

The **Pinacoteca Civica,** to the left of Santa Maria Maggiore, holds a rich assortment of art that once adorned the basilica, including several unusual polychrome wooden statues that were carried during Easter processions in centuries past. Look for the painting by Marcantonio Grecchi (1573–1651) with the city of Spello in it. ⊠ *Via Consolare* ☎ *0742/ 301497* ✇ *€2.60* ☉ *Apr.–Sept., Tues.–Sun. 10:30–1 and 3–6:30; Oct.–Mar., Tues.–Sun. 10–12:30 and 3–5.*

The Gothic church of **Sant' Andrea** has a painting of the *Madonna and Child with Saints* by Pinturicchio, as well as the mummified remains of the church's namesake, who was an early follower of St. Francis. ⊠ *Via Cavour* ☎ *No phone* ✇ *Free* ☉ *Closed for renovation at this writing; call for hours.*

On the north side of Piazza della Repubblica, in the center of town, sits the 13th-century **Vecchio Palazzo Comunale,** one of the oldest town halls in the region. Leave some time for strolling around town and stopping at the *belvedere* (panoramic overlook) at the top of Via Torre del

Belvedere, where you can see the ancient Porto Venere, which was named for the goddess of love but intended to keep out enemies. Just below in the valley are the remains of the Roman amphitheater, and in the distance are surrounding towns. Toward the Arch of Augustus near the Hotel Bastiglia you can see the **Monastery of the Clarisse** (closed to visitors) that for centuries kept wayward girls locked in and the outside world locked out.

Where to Stay & Eat

In addition to hotels, apartments are available to rent in Spello. Many have living rooms; all have kitchens and on-site managers. Contact **In Urbe** (⊠ Via Giulia 97, 06038 ☎ 0742/301145 ☐ 0742/301577 ⊕ www. inurbe.it) for more information. You can inquire at enoteche (wine shops) and restaurants for lodging as well; some rent mini-apartments. For contact information, see the listings below and in Shopping (for enotecas).

$–$$$ ✕ **Il Molino.** Almost a destination in itself, this former mill is considered
Fodor'sChoice one of Southern Umbria's best restaurants by locals. The sophisticated
★ food showcases the bounty of Umbria. The olive oils used and the names of the local producers are noted on the menu. Appetizers are varied, and often highlight produce found only here, like the *risina,* a tiny white bean. Pasta sauces can vary from exquisitely rich to delicate. The meat is first-rate, either elaborately prepared or grilled and topped with a signature sauce. Service is attentive, and the wine list has plenty of local and Italian options. Outside seating lets you soak up the passing street scene; inside are a series of impressive 14th-century arches. ⊠ *Piazza Matteotti, 6/7, 06038* ☎ *0742/651305* ☐ *0742/30* ☉ *Closed Tues.*

★ $–$$ ✕ **Ristorante Il Pinturicchio.** For starters, don't miss the chef's flavorful foccacia. You might follow with a frittata or hot pastry that brings out the best of the less flavorful summer truffles, and in late fall is sublime. Truffles also work themselves into the local pasta, *strangozzi* (eggless squared shoestring pasta). Or try the spinach pasta with prosciutto and cheese. All pastas are homemade. Your main dish might be lamb with wild fennel or chicken with pistachios. Dessert could be a chocolate soufflé or hazlenut cream chantilly. The wine selection is good, and the service and atmosphere are refined. ⊠ *Via Largo Mazzini 8* ☎ *0742/301003.*

¢–$$ ✕ **La Cantina.** As its name implies, this place on the main street is the place to taste wines from all over the country. The menu is seasonal and might include wild asparagus in spring and artichokes in fall and winter. The specialty of the house is grilled meat, especially the prized Tuscan Chianina beef and baby lamb chops. For dessert there's homemade apple *rocciata* (strudel). ⊠ *Via Cavour 2* ☎ *0742/651775* ☐ *AE, DC, MC, V* ☉ *Closed Wed.*

¢–$ ✕ **Bar Giardino Bonci.** The perfect place for a morning cappuccino with a view, this coffee bar also does lunch well, with simple panini and a platter with local cheeses and salami, perhaps buttressed by a glass of good local wine. Or you might stop by late afternoon to wind down with an apperitivo while you decide which of Spello's great restaurants you'll try. The large seating area in the back has a similar view of the valley as that from La Bastiglia. ⊠ *Via Garibaldi, 10* ☎ *0742/651397* ☐ *No credit cards* ☉ *No dinner.*

¢–$ ✕ **Il Cacciatore.** Wild fowl and game—especially grilled or roasted—are served at this trattoria, the name of which means "the hunter." Truffles (in season) are a specialty, served in a variety of ways, perhaps on pasta that is hand-rolled daily. Or try the *pappardelle con sugo d'oca* (ribbons of pasta dressed in goose sauce) or tagliatelle with peas and prosciutto. Though this place won't win awards for its looks, you may enjoy the view from the terrace, if weather permits. ⊠ *Via Giulia 42* ☎ *0742/ 651141* 🖶 *0742/301603* 🗖 *MC, V* ☉ *Closed Mon., 3 wks in Nov., and 2 wks in July. No lunch Mon. and Wed.–Fri.*

★ $ ✕🖼 **La Bastiglia.** This cozy hotel is a renovated grain mill, but hardwood floors and oriental-pattern rugs have replaced the rustic floors. The comfortable sitting rooms and bedrooms are filled with a mix of antique and modern pieces. Rooms on the top floor—some with terraces—have views of the valley below Spello, silvery green with its olive trees. A separate building with seven additional rooms is surrounded by a garden. Pack light, as there are plenty of steps and you carry your own bags. The hotel's wood-beamed restaurant ($$$) serves refined international cuisine and unusual adaptations of traditional recipes. The menu changes with the seasons, so look for roasted pigeon or a sorbetto of wild berries in the summer; toward winter, truffles will appear. The regionally known sommelier dispenses advice about local or international wines. ⊠ *Piazza Valle Gloria 17, 06038* ☎ *0742/651277* 🖶 *0742/301159* ⊕ *www.labastiglia. com* 🛏 *31 rooms, 2 suites* ⚲ *Restaurant, pool, bar* 🗖 *AE, DC, MC, V* ☉ *Closed early Jan.–early Feb. and late July* ¶❍¶ *CP.*

★ $–$$ 🖼 **Hotel Palazzo Bocci.** Quiet and elegant, this hotel is centrally located on Spello's main street. The original building dates back to the 14th century, but extensive restorations in the 18th and 19th centuries added bucolic ceiling and wall frescoes. You could settle in for a week and take a cooking course, or have the staff book you bicycle or horseback excursions through the countryside. The hotel has lovely sitting areas, a reading room, and a garden terrace off the bar. Several rooms have valley views. Consider splurging on the suite with the fireplace or reserving the room with the small terrace. ⊠ *Via Cavour 17, 06038* ☎ *0742/301021* 🖶 *0742/ 301464* ⊕ *www.emmeti.it* 🛏 *23 rooms* ⚲ *In-room hot tubs, minibars, cable TV, in-room safes, bar, meeting rooms* 🗖 *AE, DC, MC, V.*

Shopping

Spello is a good place to find excellent Umbrian olive oil, carved olive wood, and a variety of hemp (*canapa*) crafts. Try **Frantoio Cianetti** (⊠ Via Bulgarella 10 ☎ 0742/652781), for its own brand of cold-pressed, extra-virgin olive oil. **Angelo Passeri** (⊠ Via Giulia 18 ☎ 0330/282104) is a specialist in olive-wood carvings and produces works in an amazing variety of forms, such as animals and lamps.

Museo di Norberto (⊠ Via Cavour, 61 ☎ 0742/652044) belongs to local painter Norberto, who was born in 1927 and at age 30 began to paint images of Spello in the naive style; his paintings are pricey now, but prints are available, too. Spello native and artist **Elvio Marchionni** (⊠ Via Consolare, 78 ☎0742/301153) uses medieval techniques of mosaic and fresco that give his work the appearance of historic fragments—a technique so successful that his work adorns an altar in Santa Maria Maggiore.

At his high-end shop you can commission a work or buy a painting.

At **L'Enoteca Il Pinturicchio** (✉ Via Garibaldi 20 ☎ No phone), you can pick up foccaccia topped with local sausages, cheese, or greens. Try the local *ciauscolo* (fresh, spreadable pork salami), which is quite different here from the way it is prepared in the Marches, or *capocollo* or *lonzina* (both are cured pork meats). **Enoteca Properzio** at (✉ Via Torri di Properzio 8/A ☎ 0742/301688) is one of Italy's top wine bars—though it closes at 9 PM—and shops. Beware cool treatment if you're not a serious wine buyer. Oenophile or not, you can soberly request the €25 degustation menu.

Foligno

8 *5 km (3 mi) southeast of Spello, 18 km (11 mi) southeast of Assisi, 28 km (17 mi) north of Spoleto.*

The third-largest town in Umbria at 56,000 inhabitants, Foligno has been an important commercial center since the 13th century (this is where St. Francis came to sell his father's textiles before giving up all his worldly possessions). The town is divided into ten *rioni*, or neighborhoods, that compete every year in an elaborately staged Baroque Festival.

Although Deruta is better known for ceramics, Bevagna for ironwork, and Spello for woodcarving, all can be purchased in Foligno, once famous for dyeing textiles and papermaking but now better known for lace and embroidery (some small workshops can still be found around town). Because it was an industrial city, it was a target for severe Allied bombing in World War II; postwar reconstruction and flourishing light industry now obscure much of what must have once been a charming town.

The town also suffered some of the worst damage wrought by the 1997 earthquakes: it's not hard to imagine why the mayor broke out in tears at the sight of the collapsed 14th-century bell tower of the Palazzo Comunale (city hall). Facing that and handsomely restored, the enchanting—and puzzling—medieval facade of the Duomo survived the quake. The historic center of Foligno, which retains the old Roman street grid and some of its medieval heritage, has some Renaissance palaces and several churches worthy of a stop. Stroll along Via delle Conce (once the center for textile dyeing) and Via dei Molini for views of the canals. The main shopping street is Corso Cavour.

Find your way to Piazza della Repubblica, the central square in the old part of town. The 12th-century **Duomo** shows its better side to Piazza della Repubblica. Take some time to enjoy the elaborate marble carvings on the facade: the twelve signs of the zodiac are a curiously pagan feature over the main portal; underneath that are the symbols of the apostles; elsewhere the sun and the crescent moon appear; and on either side of the portal, fanciful animals appear, and elaborately carved grapes remind us that we are in the territory of Sagrantino. The bottom half of the facade is constructed of local stone and marble that form lovely horizontal stripes of pink and ivory; the upper half is lightened by the three bifurcated windows, and its rose window is formed of tiny columns that divide it like pie wedges. As you walk between the two ferocious lions and step inside past the bronze doors, note the geometric patterns of Cosmati mosaics that line the doorway. The interior reflects a variety of centuries of style. The two busts in the sacristy are attributed to Bernini; the *baldacchino*, with its tasseled canopy and four corkscrew columns entwined with rose tendrils, was commissioned in 1697 and looks as though it's copied after Bernini's *baldacchino* in St. Peter's in Rome. Look up in the cupola to see trompe-l'oeil rosettes painted to resemble carved marble. Exit the door which faces the Piazzetta Duomo to see the primary facade of the Duomo (it dates back to around 1133 and was renovated in the early years of the 20th century). Across the street is an excellent restaurant, Sparafucile. ⊠ *Piazza della Repubblica* 🕮 *Free* ☽ *Daily 9–noon.*

Palazzo Trinci on the north side of the square was completed around 1407 for a Lombard overlord who combined his love of Roman antiquity with the humanistic craze. The mostly Gothic interior was built over and around Roman ruins, including a prize marble stele with a bas relief of Amor and Psyche. An early-15th-century fresco cycle by Gentile da Fabriano unites ancient mythological themes with the world of chivalry and medieval courtly life. Pass through the hallway to see a Gothic stairway recycled from a previous building and a loggia that holds the *Story of the Foundation of Rome* and the Room of the Emperors. A small chapel was painted by Ottaviano Nelli in 1424. Downstairs in the palazzo is the **Multimedia Museum of Tournaments, Matches, and Games,** a research center for the competitive and deadly sport of jousting and other games from the Middle Ages to the 19th century; temporary exhibits have included a display of Renaissance costumes. The Roman-era relics in the **Museo Archeologico** came mostly from the cemetery area of Capella di Santa Maria in Campis on the old Via Flaminia (once a major Roman consular road). It's hard to escape the theme of wine: note the three marble Dionysian panels complete with cavorting centaur, one of which still has traces of red paint—a reminder that ancient Greeks and Romans often painted their sculptures. Downstairs, the olive-oil lamp shows that the oil you toss on your salads has been vital to the economy for more than a few thousand years and a nearby bronze cornucopia pays tribute the bounty of Umbria. Take a moment to look at the small bronze figurines dating back to the 6th century BC: the Goddess Cupra, the two tiny figures of Mars, god of war, in his Napoleon-like hat; and pottery that includes charming animal figures on a pot cover. The **Pinacoteca Civica,** the museum's art gallery, has works by local painters who made Foligno an important art center during the Renaissance. ⊠ *Piazza della Repubblica* 🕮 *0742/357989* 🕮 *€5* ☽ *Tues.–Sun. 10–7.*

At the other end of town from the Palazzo Trinci, follow Via Mazzini to the Romanesque church of **Santa Maria Infraportas.** There are several cycles of votive frescoes in its three naves. The **Cappella dell'Assunta** has 12th-century, Byzantine-style frescoes. ⊠ *Piazza San Domenico* 🕮 *0742/350517* 🕮 *Free* ☽ *Daily 8–12:30 and 3:30–7.*

Where to Stay & Eat

★ ¢–$ ✕ **Il Bacco Felice.** An improbably smoke-free enoteca, "Happy Bacchus" takes pride in its expert marriage of good food and good wine. The owner not only has an optimum wine selection, but personally selects the best prosciutto and cheeses; bread comes from the best bakeries in the valley. Hot vegetable soups (lentil, fava, barley) and rabbit casseroles are tasty standards here. The surprise? The owner raises his own pigs, chickens, and rabbits as well as the seasonal tomatoes and peppers that wind up on your plate. Some outdoor seating is by the facade of the Duomo. ✉ *Via Garibaldi 73–75* ☎ *0742/341019* ▤ *AE, DC, MC, V* ⊘ *Closed Mon.*

¢–$ ✕ **Sparafucile Hostaria.** Look out over the facade of the Duomo and Foligno's city hall from the outdoor seating at this enoteca. The daily changing menu often has good pork dishes or local homemade specialties like *frascarelli,* a tiny pasta that resembles rice. The friendly owner likes to showcase excellent local wines, like Sagrantino and Montefalco Rosso, while creating the kind of setting where diners often meet one another and join in ongoing conversations. ✉ *Piazzetta Duomo, 20* ☎ *0742/342602* ▤ *DC, MC, V* ⊘ *Closed Wed. No lunch Sun.*

¢–$ ▦ **Villa Roncalli.** You won't have to put up with the creaking and squealing of old floors and fixtures in this late-16th-century villa on the outskirts of town. The rooms have terra-cotta floors and modern furniture. An ample buffet breakfast with homemade bread, jams, and cakes makes it hard to leave. Be sure to let the front desk know if you have any special needs upon check-in, as you will be on your own after you get your room key. ✉ *Località Sant'Eraclio, Via Roma 25* ☎ *0742/391091* ▦ *0742/391001* ⏎ *10 rooms* ⚒ *Restaurant, pool, bar; no a/c in some rooms* ▤ *AE, DC, MC, V* ⊘ *Closed most of Jan. and last 3 wks in Aug.* ⎡◎⎤ *CP.*

The Arts

The 13th-century church of **San Domenico** (✉ Largo F. Frezzi, 8 ☎ 0742/344563) is now an auditorium that hosts concerts, special events, and temporary exhibits. The **tourist information office** (✉ Porta Romana 126 ☎ 0742/354459 ⊕ www.foligno.umbria2000.it) an tell you about upcoming concerts.

Bevagna

▶ ⑨ *9 km (5½ mi) west of Foligno, 27 km (17 mi) south of Assisi.*

Bevagna's first building boom was probably around 220 BC, when the town—then called Mevania—was constructed on the ancient Roman consular road, Via Flaminia, 148 km (92 mi) from Rome. Part of the Forum was once at the intersection of what are now Via Crescimbeni and Via Santa Margherita. In the 3rd century AD, Via Flaminia was diverted through Spoleto and Terni, thus causing Bevagna's boom to bust. Later, medieval and Renaissance homes and shops covered Roman ruins, but the shapes of ancient Roman theaters and temples can be discerned from the medieval structures that you see today, as they were built using the Roman buildings' foundations.

Although bypassed by the newer Via Flaminia, now Bevagna belongs to the Strada del Sagrantino, the wine route that links Sagrantino wine producers in the area. By the way, this town is flat, which can be a welcome change. If you approach the town by car and park in the area near Porta Todi, before you walk through the ancient gate look to your left to see a rectangular pool fed by the River Clutunno, where, until a few decades ago, local women brought their wash—an early self-service "laundromat."

The medieval town even today is divided into four distinct quarters (called *gaite* in the local dialect): San Giovanni, San Giorgio, San Pietro, and Santa Maria. The town is small and easily covered on foot, so pick up a local map to pop into churches or to trace the outline of the ancient Roman theater.

★ Begin your visit in the center of town in the asymmetrical, medieval **Piazza Filippo Silvestri,** one of Umbria's most beautiful and harmonious squares, laid out in the 12th and 13th centuries. The square's Roman Corinthian column is known as San Rocco, and the 1896 fountain replaced an ancient octagonal cistern.

The 1195 church of **San Silvestro,** by Maestro Binello, anchors the piazza on one side. A fine example of Umbrian Romanesque architecture, the lower section of the church was constructed in travertine, and the upper section in local Subasio stone; the facade remains unfinished. Note the medieval animal heads sculpted on the cornice above. ⊠ *Piazza Silvestri* ☎ *0742/361147* ✆ *Closed for renovations at this writing; contact the tourism office for reopening dates, hours, and admission price.*

Inaugurated on August 28, 1886, the **Teatro Francesco Torti** was restored and reopened on October 2, 1994. The theater seats about 200 and has three tiers of boxes, each level in a different style. Domenico Braschi and Mariano Piervittori painted the wall and ceiling frescoes in the entrance, foyer, and theater during the same period; contemporary artist Luigi Frappi painted the stage curtain with the scene of the Clitunno River. If you come through in off-hours, ask at the Pro Loco tourist office (below Palazzo dei Consoli) for a tour. The theater is inside the **Palazzo dei Consoli,** which was the seat of local magistrates from at least 1187 until the 1832 earthquake. ⊠ *Piazza Silvestri* ☎ *0742/361667* ✆ *€2.60 admission to Museo di Bevagna includes theater tour tickets* ✆ *Sept.–May, Tues.–Sun. 10:30–1 and 2:30–5; June–Aug., Tues.–Sun. 10:30–1 and 3:30–7.*

The **Museo di Bevagna** has a small collection divided between archaeology and art. Among the archaeological artifacts is an ancient tablet in Umbrian writing that is read right to left, which is how it was done before locals had to conform to Roman ways. The art collection includes a wooden Renaissance church model of Santa Maria delle Grazie and paintings by lesser known local artists from the Umbrian school. ⊠ *Palazzo del Municipio, Corso Matteotti 70* ☎ *0742/360031* ✆ *€2.60, includes Roman marine mosaics and tour of Teatro Francesco Torti* ✆ *Sept.–May, Tues.–Sun. 10:30–1 and 2:30–5; June–Aug., Tues.–Sun. 10:30–1 and 3:30–7.*

The **Roman marine mosaics** are from the 2nd century AD. Lively sea crea-tures made of black tiles adorn a white background. Lobsters, octopi, dolphins, and fanciful mythological figures face one another as if reflected in a mirror. You can track down other Roman ruins by using the free map available at the Pro Loco tourist office. You can only see the mo-saics accompanied by a museum guide. ⊠ *Le Terme, San Giovanni quar-ter* ☎ *No phone* 🎫 *€2.60* ☉ *Sept.–May., Tues.–Sun. 10:30–1 and 2:30–5; June–Aug., Tues.–Sun. 10:30–1 and 3:30–7.*

Where to Stay & Eat

In addition to hotels, you can inquire at enoteche (wine shops) and restau-rants for lodging; some rent apartments. For contact information, see the listings below.

$–$$ ✕ **Vineria Piazza Onofri.** Here is your chance to sample some local wines by the glass as you watch the parade on Bevagna's main drag, catch up on gossip, or read some of the periodicals from the nearby newsstand. The wine bar/shop combo has a limited menu for eating in (the wine by the glass is the real draw) and also sells olive oil, truffles, pastas, and other local specialties. ⊠ *Corso Matteotti 102* ☎ *0742/360978* 🖃 *DC, MC, V* ☉ *Closed Wed. No dinner.*

★ $ 🏨 **Hotel Palazzo Brunamonti.** This former early-Renaissance palace is built over Roman and medieval foundations, which you can still see in part. The hotel is very close to Piazza Silvestri, and is steps from good restau-rants and major sites. Room decor is simple—all the better for you to enjoy the architectural features. On your way to the lovely breakfast room you can admire the 18th- and 19th-century frescoes in the halls. The hotel entrance is under the arch at Via Piazza del Cirone and then left from Vicolo del Cirone (or just ring bell on Corso Matteotti). The owners and staff are exceptionally friendly and courteous. ⊠ *Corso Mat-teotti 79, 06031* ☎ *0742/361932* 🖃 *0742/361948* ⊕ *www.brunamonti. com* ⇨ *16* ⚬ *Dining room, some minibars, laundry service* 🖃 *AE, DC, MC, V* ☉ *Closed Jan. 7–mid-Feb.*

Montefalco

🔟 *6 km (4 mi) southeast of Bevagna, 34 km (21 mi) south of Assisi.*

Nicknamed the "balcony railing over Umbria" for its high, spectacular vantage point over the valley that runs from Perugia to Spoleto, Mon-tefalco began as an important Roman settlement situated on the ancient Roman consular road Via Flaminia. The town owes its current name—which means "Falcon's Mount"—to Emperor Frederick II (1194–1250). Obviously a greater fan of falconry than Roman architecture, he destroyed the ancient town, which was then called Coccorone, in 1249, and built what would later become Montefalco in its stead. Aside from a few frag-ments incorporated in a private house just off Borgo Garibaldi, no traces remain of the old Roman center. However, Montefalco has more than its fair share of interesting art and architecture and is well worth the drive up the hill.

Three of the four original gates still stand and provide a grand entrance to the town. The most majestic, the 14th-century Ghibelline **Porta Sant'**

Agostino leads to the church of Sant'Agostino, which houses quite a curious artifact: a mummy of a 16th-century Spanish pilgrim who never quite made the journey home. From the church, Corso Goffredo Mameli (the main street) heads straight toward the 13th- to 14th-century Gothic church of Sant'Agostino, which reopened in 2004 after extensive renovation. At the end of the Corso is the **Piazza del Comune,** surrounded by several Renaissance buildings, including the 14th-century Palazzo Comunale.

The municipal building, **Palazzo Comunale,** anchors one side of the main town square and dates back to the 13th century; a 15th-century portico was added later. At this writing, the palazzo is still undergoing restoration following the 1997 earthquake, but is expected to reopen by summer 2005. The palazzo's tower gives you the falcon's-eye view of southern Umbria. On a clear day you can see nearly 20 mi—as far as Perugia to the north and Lake Piediluco to the south. ⊠ *Piazza del Comune* ☎ *0742/378490* ⊗ *Closed for renovations at this writing; call for hours and admission price.*

At **La Strada del Sagrantino,** the tourist office in the Piazza, the staff will advise you on selecting a wine, direct you to nearby enoteche for tastings, and give you free maps to find your way around Sagrantino Road and some remarkable wine territory. They can also book you a room in a hotel, at a vineyard, in a hillside apartment, or at an *agriturismo,* a working farm. ⊠ *Piazza del Comune, 17* ☎ *0742/378490* ⊕ *www. stradadelsagrantino.it.*

Montefalco's artistic highlight is the 14th-century **Chiesa-Museo di San Francesco,** a church turned museum that enshrines the masterworks of some of the region's finest Renaissance artists. In tribute to the Franciscan order and the religious significance of the region, Pietro Vannucci, known as Perugino, painted *The Annuciation and Nativity* in 1503 in splendid colors and with a glimpse of the Umbrian landscape in the background. The highly original and vivid fresco cycle of the *Life of St. Francis,* painted in 1450–1452 by Benozzo Gozzoli, compares favorably with those by Giotto in Assisi. (Find the *Blessing of Montefalco,* one of the fresco scenes, for a look at the town during Gozzoli's time). The small **Pinacoteca** wing, upstairs, contains religious paintings and altarpieces by local artists. In the basement there is a small collection of sculpture and fragments from various periods. ⊠ *Via Ringhiera Umbra* ☎ *0742/ 379598* ⊠ *€4; price may increase during special exhibits* ⊗ *Nov.–Feb., Tues.–Sun. 10:30–1 and 2:30–5; Mar.–May and Sept.–Oct., daily 10:30–1 and 2–6; June–Aug., daily 10:30–1 and 3–7:30.*

If you like Gozzoli's work, there's more in the **Convento di San Fortunato,** though it's in less pristine condition than that in San Francesco. The convent is a 15-minute walk outside the town walls: look for *Madonna with Saints and Angels* in the lunette over the doorway of the cloister chapel (left side) and the fresco of San Fortunato on the altar. Tiberio d'Assisi's *Life of St. Francis* (1512) is also in the cloister chapel. ⊠ *Follow signs from Via Giuseppe Verdi away from the center* ☎ *No phone* ⊠ *Free* ⊗ *Daily 9–12:30 and 3–6.*

🕭 **Tessitura Pardi.** Visit this factory to see how the cotton and linen textiles of Tessuti di Montefalco are woven. Call ahead to book an appointment. Bastardo is an easy stop between Todi or Spoleto and Montefalco, and not far from the Antonelli winery in San Marco. ⊠ *SS 316 7 km southwest of Montefalco; follow signs for Bastardo or Todi* ☎ *0742/9975* 🎫 *Free* ⊙ *Weekdays 9–1 and 2:30–5.*

Where to Stay & Eat

Montefalco is a good stop for sustenance: here you need to go no farther than the main square to find a restaurant or bar with a hot meal, and most establishments—both simple and sophisticated—offer a splendid combination of history and small-town hospitality. If you decide to hang around and play Bacchus, some of the wine producers, including Antonelli, have *casale* or mini-apartments near the vineyards that are usually rented weekly, but in low season may be available for just a weekend. Contact the Strada del Sagrantino office for rental information (☎ 0742/378490 or www.stradadelsagrantino.it).

¢–$$ ✕ **L'Alchemista Wine Bar and Olive Oil Bar.** "The Alchemist" is an apt name, as the chef's transformations are magical at this friendly place. Try the *molle della Valnerina,* baked saffron cheese from Umbria, *pancetta* (bacon), and zucchini—served only here. In summer, cold dishes to try are *panzanella,* a local vegetable salad mixed with bread, or the barley salad mixed with vegetables. *Farro* (spelt) soup made with Sagrantino wine is a local specialty. The selection of local wines is excellent and desserts are delicious: all are made on the premises and not too sweet. L'Alchemista is open all day, from breakfast through dinner. ⊠ *Piazza del Comune, 14* ☎ *0742/378558* ⊕ *www.montefalcowines.com* ▭ *DC, MC, V* ⊙ *Closed Thurs. Jan.–Mar.*

$ ✕ **Ristorante Il Coccorone.** This is a good place for a hearty meal. Local meats are outstanding, especially Chianina beef. The novel *pappardelle con sugo di Sagrantino* (wide noodles with wine sauce) is very good. Rub elbows here with local businessmen and bon vivants. The wine list is the most comprehensive in the area and includes Sagrantino secco, Sagrantino passito, and Montefalco Rosso. ⊠ *Largo Tempestivi* ☎ *0742/ 379535 or 0742/379016* ⊕ *www.coccorone.com* ▭ *DC, MC, V.*

$$ 🏨 **Villa Pambuffetti.** Zelda and F. Scott never had it so good. If you Fodor'sChoice want to be pampered in the refined atmosphere of a private villa, this ★ is the spot. Just outside the town walls, it's a short walk from all the town's sights. Guests appear to be part of the ambience, and dress on par with the elegance of the villa and of the excellent cuisine in the dining room. In winter you are greeted by the warmth of a fireplace as you enter the front door, in summer a pool cools you down, and cozy reading rooms beckon year-round. Cooking courses are given on the premises (one-day class or three-night stay/two-lesson package), and horseback-riding or golf trips can be arranged, as can shopping excursions for local textiles, cashmere, and ceramics. ⊠ *Viale della Vittoria, 20* ☎ *0742/379245* ⊕ *www.villapambuffetti.com* 🛏 *20*

rooms, 3 suites ⚭ Restaurant, in-room safes, minibars, pool, bar, meeting rooms ▭ AE, D, MC, V.

Shopping

The local Sagrantino grape produces a dry ruby-red wine with plenty of body, called Sagrantino passito. Interest in this wine has revved area production (⇨ "The Sagrantino Story" CloseUp box). Another wine unique to this area is Montefalco Rosso, made from a blend of grapes that varies but mixes Sagrantino with Sangiovese, Cabernet, Merlot, or other grapes. If you would like to try a local white wine, Grechetto is far more interesting than most of the whites that are produced in Frascati near Rome

In development and set to open in Spring 2005 is the **Centro Nazional Vini Passiti** (⊕ www.centrovinipassiti.it), which is dedicated to the sweet dessert wines produced throughout Italy. At **La Strada del Sagrantino** (⊠ Piazza del Comune, 17 ☎ 0742/378490 ⊕ www.stradadelsagrantino.it) the staff can advise you on selecting a wine and give you free maps to find your way around Sagrantino Road and some remarkable wine territory.

If you don't have a car or the time, you can walk to an *enoteca*, a wine shop and bar where you may sample wines from local wineries. Wine can be purchased by the glass and by the bottle. Try L'Alchemista Wine Bar (⇨ Where to Stay & Eat) or **Federico II Enoteca** (⊠ Piazza del Comune 1 ☎ 0742/78902).

Trevi

⑪ *5 km (3 mi) southeast of Spello, 16 km (10 mi) southeast of Assisi.*

Trevi, halfway between Assisi and Spoleto, cascades down the slope of a hill, the warm beige hues of its stone buildings set amid the silvery green olive trees that surround the town. Up above, the cupola of the Duomo crowns all that, as if to contain the town from growing upward into the sky, too. Trevi—no relation to the famous fountain in Rome that takes its name from the three streets (*tre vie*) that once met in front of it—is home to 7,800 inhabitants and makes for a pleasant stop. It calls itself the Olive Oil Capital, evidenced in its slopes of over 200,000 olive trees and the rather well-hidden Olive Oil Museum. It's an especially well-preserved town, despite earthquakes and attacks in AD 881 by Saracens and by Ungari invaders in AD 924. Most of the area's Roman ruins are in the Clitunno Valley below Trevi at Rocca di Fabbri, where the Sagrantino Road begins, because the Romans settled here near the river in the 3rd century BC. The best artworks in town are found in the local churches: San Martino and Madonna delle Lacrime.

Raccolta d'Arte San Francesco, often called simply the Pinacoteca, was built over a convent founded by St. Francis on the site where a donkey lowered itself to its knees to listen to him preach in 1213. The museum contains a good little collection of paintings by local artists. See the duo of saints by Lo Spagna (circa 1450–1528): one shows St. Cecilia (c. 1520), patron saint of musicians, holding pipes; nearby are a flute, tambourine, recorder, and at her feet, sheet music. Don't miss the vivid hues of Pe-

THE SAGRANTINO STORY

SAGRANTINO GRAPES HAVE BEEN USED for the production of red wine for centuries. The wine began centuries ago as Sagrantino passito, a semisweet version in which the grapes are left to dry for a period after picking to intensify the sugar content. One theory traces the origin of Sagrantino back to ancient Rome in the works of Pliny the Elder, the author of Natural History who referred to the Itriola grape that some researchers think may be Sagrantino. Others believe that in medieval times clever Franciscan friars returned from Asia Minor with the grape. ("Sagrantino" perhaps derives from "sacramenti," the religious ceremony in which the wine was used.) The passito is still produced today and is preferred by some. But the big change in Sagrantino wine production came in the past decades when Sagrantino secco (dry) came into the market. Both passito and secco have a deep ruby red color that tends toward garnet highlights with a full body and rich flavor.

Experimentation among local growers increased dramatically in the 1970s and 1980s when wine-makers opted to further develop production of the Sagrantino grape for dry table wine, which has been very successful, gaining prestigious classifications by the Italian government. Production of Sagrantino has increased rapidly: from 2001 to 2003 Sagrantino secco production doubled. In 2004 most producers were busy planting more acres. For the dry wines, producers not to be missed are: Terre di Capitani; Antonelli; Perticaia; Caprai. Try those labels for the passito as well, in addition to Ruggeri and Scacciadiavoli.

The wines, like their wine-makers, have their own personalities. Terre di Capitani is complex and has vegetable and mineral tones that join tastes of wild berries,

cherries, and chocolate—this wine-maker hand-pampers his grapes and it shows. Antonelli is elegant, refined, and rich. The Ruggeri passito is one of the best, so don't be put off by its homespun label. Caprai is bold and rich in taste, often sets the pace for the rest of the pack, and has the largest market share, including a high percentage that is exported to the U.S. Perticaia has a full taste with a surprising "up" finish that suggested some divine presence other than Sagrantino.

Some wineries are small and not equipped to receive visitors. Arrange your winery visits at **La Strada del Sagrantino** (✉ Piazza del Comune, 17 ☎ 0742/ 378490 ⊕ www.stradadelsagrantino.it) in Montefalco's main square. There you will see a display of the wines; you can pick up a map of the wine route and set up appointments, book accommodations, and then visit local enoteche. At the enoteche, ask the owner or sommelier to guide you to some of the smaller producers, too, as you will have difficulty finding them elsewhere.

Sagrantino di Montefalco is celebrated twice yearly in the town of Montefalco when it's in its nascent stage during September's Festa Della Vendemmia (Grape or Harvest Festival). You can attend exhibits, tastings, lectures to celebrate the grape harvest. When the wine is in its full rosy glory during the springtime, area grape farmers turn out for a parade through the streets and a tasting of past years' labors in the Piazza del Comune during the Settimana Enologica (Wine Week). Details can be obtained from the **Centro Agro-Alimentare dell'Umbria** (☎ 0742/344214 ⊕ www. umbriadoc.com) or the Strada del Sagrantino (⇨ above). Salute!

rugino's *Adoration of the Shepherds* (c. 1521) in the midst of an Umbrian landscape. Off in one wing is the **Olive Oil Museum,** with an illustrated history of the various uses of the olive and its oil. ⊠ *Convento di San Francesco, Largo Don Bosco* ☎ *0742/381628* ⊕ *www.sistemamuseo.it* ☜ *€3* ⊙ *Apr.–May and Sept., Tues.–Sun. 10:30–1 and 2:30–6; June–July, Tues.–Sun. 10:30–1 and 3:30–7; Aug., daily 10:30–1 and 3–7:30; Oct.–Mar., Fri.–Sun. 10:30–1 and 2:30–5.*

Halfway down the hill from Trevi is the **Madonna delle Lacrime** (Church of Madonna of the Tears), built in 1487, with works by Lo Spagna and Perugino. Over the altar is a portrait of the Madonna that is said to have shed bloodstained tears on August 5, 1485, giving the church its name. ⊠ *1 km (½ mi) south of town along main road leading up steep hill from highway (ring bell at convent next door)* ☎ *Pro Trevi, 0742/781150* ⊙ *At this writing closed for restoration until at least mid-2005; contact the Trevi tourist office, Pro Loco, about the scheduled reopening.*

On the site of **Sant'Emiliano** (Duomo) in about AD 192 a bishop knocked down a temple to ancient Roman goddess Diana Trivia. After the earthquake of AD 365 destroyed the Umbro-Roman village below, Trevi began to rebuild on top of the hill around the site of this church (then Holy Trinity). The Romanesque church, named for the Christian Armenian Emiliano who was martyred on January 28, 302, was constructed in the 11th century and restored in the 1990s. Its dome is what you see as Trevi's "crown" when you are in the valley below. A statue of Emiliano, who became the town's patron saint, is carried through town every January 27 in a torch-lit procession, followed by a series of floats made by local artisans. ⊠ *Via Beato* ☎ *Pro Trevi, 0742/781150* ☜ *Free* ⊙ *Daily 9–noon and 4–6. Hours can vary widely; call ahead.*

off the beaten path

TEMPIETTO E FONTI DEL CLITUNNO – South of Trevi is the so-called Tempietto ("little temple") del Clitunno, an early Christian church built from bits and pieces of Roman temples in the area. The badly worn frescoes, some of the earliest in Umbria, date from the 8th century. Farther down the road are the Fonti del Clitunno (Springs of Clitunno), named after a Roman river god. The springs were famous in the ancient world partly because of the healing properties of water, which was once more abundant. Pliny the Younger mentions them and Caligula visited on several occasions for the famous oracles. The remains of the Roman-era Tempio del Clitunno (Temple of Clitunno) are nearby. The waters flow from fissures in the rocks and collect in a shallow pond before passing on to an artificial basin that was created over a lake. The springs were created when the Romans diverted several rivers upstream, although an earthquake in the 5th century AD greatly reduced the water supply; they were used until the 19th century to supply water to run the mills in the nearby town of Pissignano. ⊠ *About 2 km (1 mi) south of Trevi* ☜ *€2* ⊙ *Apr.–Oct., daily 8:45–7:45; Nov.–Mar., daily 8:45–5.*

Where to Stay & Eat

During **Appuntamenti d'Autunno** (Autumn Festival), held throughout October, temporary taverns are set up in courtyards and buildings, and local restaurants feature historic menus.

★ **$$** ✕ **Taverna del Pescatore.** The unpromising location of this "fisherman's tavern" right next to the busy Via Flaminia belies the idyllic tranquillity often found inside, once seated on the terrace, with the clear stream of the Clitunno River flowing just beyond your wineglass. Sit back, listen for the birds in the trees, and keep an eye out for the fresh fish in the river, on which the menu is based each day. Preparations are clean and simple and at times wonderfully eclectic: one springtime favorite is stringozzi with wild asparagus tips, trout filet, and tiny, fresh tomatoes. ⊠ *Statale Flaminia Km 139* ☎ *0742/780920* ⊟ *AE, DC, MC, V* ⊗ *Closed Wed. Sept.–July, and 2 wks in Jan.*

★ **¢–$** ⊡ **Antica Dimora alla Rocca.** In a palazzo that dates back to 1650, this hotel has rooms with wood-beam ceilings, some elaborately painted, and tile floors. The penthouse suite has a sitting room with frescoes, and the "noble floor" has rooms with frescoes. Some rooms have lovely rooftop views. The restaurant, La Prepositura, seems most dependable if you select one of the daily prix-fixe specials, such as the Champagne Dinner for €49 per person. ⊠ *Piazza della Rocca, 06039* ☎ *0742/38541 or 0742/78925* ✍ *31 rooms, 2 suites* ♿ *Cable TV, bar, lounge, laundry service, Internet, some no-smoking rooms* ⊟ *MC V.*

SPOLETO

For most of the year, Spoleto is one more in a pleasant succession of sleepy hill towns, resting regally atop its mount. But for three weeks every summer the town dusts off its cobblestones and shifts into high gear for a turn in the international spotlight for the Festival dei Due Mondi (Festival of Two Worlds), an extravaganza of theater, opera, music, painting, and sculpture. As the world's top artists vie for honors, throngs of art aficionados vie for hotel rooms. If you plan to spend the night in Spoleto during the festival, make sure you have confirmed hotel reservations, or you may find yourself scrambling at sunset.

Spoleto has plenty to lure you during the rest of the year as well: the final frescoes of Filippo Lippi; the beautiful piazzas and streets with Roman and medieval attractions; and superb natural surroundings with rolling hills and a dramatic gorge. Spoleto makes a good base for exploring all of southern Umbria as Assisi, Orvieto, and the towns in between are all within easy reach.

Umbri tribes were the first to settle here, probably taking advantage of the protection provided by the steep and narrow gorge that runs along the back side of Spoleto's hill. As usual, the Romans were not far behind, fortifying the city walls and building an aqueduct across the gorge, which serves as a foundation to Spoleto's breathtaking Ponte delle Torri. By all accounts an important city, Spoletum (as it was called in Latin) turned back Hannibal in the 2nd century BC. Ancient churches set in silvery olive groves below either side of town testify to Spoleto's importance in the early Christian period, when it ruled over a sizable independent duchy. During the Middle Ages the town at one time had more than 100 towers, but when the rebellious citizens refused to pay taxes, most of towers were destroyed by *Barba Rossa,* the "Red Beard" from the north, who first set fire inside the courtyards to weaken the structures and then knocked them down. But as you walk around town you can still see evidence in the walls of houses. Your clues are the odd proportions or larger stones that once supported the heavier weight of the tower. In the 14th century the town fell under Church control, and La Rocca was built at its summit to enforce papal rule.

Exploring Spoleto

The walled city is set on a slanting hillside, with the most interesting sections clustered toward the upper portion. Parking options inside the walls include Piazza Campello (just below the Rocca) on the southeast end, Via del Trivio to the north, and Piazza San Domenico on the west end. You can also park at Piazza della Vittoria farther north, just beyond the walls. Also, several well-marked larger lots are just outside Porta San Matteo and near the train station. If you arrive by train, you can walk 1 km (½ mi) from the station to Piazza Garibaldi and the entrance to the lower town. Regular bus connections are every 15 to 30 minutes, or use the "trenino," as locals call the bus service added in 2004, to go from the train station to Piazza della Libertà, near the upper part of the old town, where you'll find the visitor-information office. Like most other towns made up of narrow, winding streets, Spoleto is best explored on foot, but do bear in mind that much of the city is on a steep slope, necessitating lots of stairs or arduous inclines. The well-worn stones can be slippery even when dry; wear rubber-soled shoes for good traction. Several pedestrian walkways cut across Corso Mazzini, which zigzags up the hill. A €2.60 combination ticket purchased at the tourist-information office allows you entry to the Pinacoteca Comunale, Casa Romana, and Galleria d'Arte Moderna. It's an excellent deal, since a combination ticket purchased directly from any one of these sights is €6.

A Good Walk

Begin your day at Piazza della Libertà, with a visit to the adjacent **Teatro Romano** ⓬ ☛ and Museo Archeologico (enter on Via Apollinare). From the ancient ruins it's a short jump to the **Galleria d'Arte Moderna** ⓭, a five-room collection with paintings and small sculpture that has won awards in past festivals. Return to Piazza della Libertà, walk up Via Brignone to Piazza Fontana, and go left on Via Arco di Druso, through the **Arco di Druso** ⓮. Up ahead is Piazza del Mercato, built over the ancient Foro Romano and once a busy market. (Today its offerings have trickled down to the odd bits of produce.) Take the street that leads up out of the piazza and make a quick left onto Via Visiale, crossed by several arches. On the right is the entrance to the **Casa Romana** ⓯. Continue along Via Visiale and then turn right onto Via Saffi. Just ahead on the left is Palazzo Arcivescovile, with the church of **Sant'Eufemia** ⓰ in the courtyard and a small museum. Via Saffi continues uphill to Via dell'Arringo, which descends to **Piazza del Duomo** ⓱. The **Duomo** ⓲ stands against a backdrop of hill and sky with **La Rocca** ⑲ towering overhead. After lunch, proceed from the Duomo up to Piazza Campello and take Via del Ponte, which loops around the base of La Rocca, passing the magnificent **Ponte delle Torri** ⑳. Walk across the bridge, and either circle back around La Rocca or continue along the shady paths of the Bosco Sacro (Sacred Woods) of Monteluco, on the hill opposite the bridge, and down to the church of **San Pietro** ㉑. From there, return the way you came or cross the highway and take Via Monterone back up into town.

TIMING   Spoleto is small, and its noteworthy sights are clustered in the upper part of town; allow a full day for a thorough exploration, including time to stroll around town and across the Ponte delle Torri. Note that the Casa Romana is closed on Monday.

What to See

⑭ **Arco di Druso** (Arch of Drusus). Built in AD 23 by the Senate of Spoleto to honor the Roman general Drusus (circa 13 BC–AD 23), son of the emperor Tiberius, this arch once marked the entrance to the Foro Romano (Roman Forum). Excavations to the side reveal the original street level. ⊠ *Piazza del Mercato.*

⑮ **Casa Romana.** Spoleto became a Roman colony in the 3rd century BC, but the best excavated remains date from the 1st century AD. Excavated in the late 9th century, the Casa Romana was not your typical Roman residence—according to an inscription, it belonged to Vespasia Polla, the mother of Emperor Vespasian (one of the builders of the Coliseum and perhaps better known by the Romans for taxing them to install public toilets, later called "Vespasians"). The rooms, arranged around a large central atrium built over an *impluvium* (rain cistern), are decorated with black and white geometric mosaics that are still mostly intact. The peristyle was framed by an archway that faced the valley. ⊠ *Palazzo del Municipio, Via Visiale 9* ☎ *0743/224656* ⊠ *€2.50; €2.60 combination ticket from visitor-information center includes Pinacoteca Comunale and Galleria D'Arte Moderna* ⊙ *Oct. 15–Mar. 14, daily 10–6; Mar. 15–Oct. 14, daily 10–8.*

★ ⑱ **Duomo.** The cathedral's 12th-century Romanesque facade received a Renaissance face-lift with the addition of a loggia in a rosy pink stone. The eight rose windows and the gold mosaic of the Benedictory Christ, dating back to 1207 and signed by Solsterno, are especially dazzling in the late afternoon sun. A stunning contrast in styles, the Duomo is one of the finest cathedrals in the region. Look under the largest rose window and you see two figures amid the five columns, "holding up" the structure; in the corners of the square surrounding the window, the four Evangelists are sculpted. Inside, the original tile floor dates from an earlier church that was destroyed by Frederick I (circa 1123–90). Above the entrance wall is Bernini's bust of Pope Urban VIII (1568–1644), who had the rest of the church redecorated in 17th-century baroque; fortunately he didn't touch the 15th-century frescoes painted in the apse by Fra Filippo Lippi (circa 1406–69) between 1466-69. These immaculately restored masterpieces—the *Annunciation, Nativity,* and the *Death of Mary*—tell the story of the life of the Virgin. The *Coronation of the Vir-*

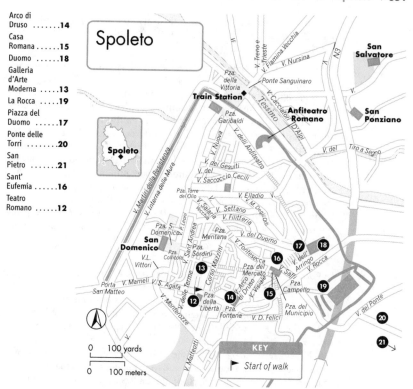

gin, adorning the half dome, is the literal and figurative high point. Portraits of Lippi and his assistants are on the right side of the central panel. The Florentine artist priest "whose colors expressed God's voice" (the words inscribed on his tomb) died shortly after completing the work. His tomb, which you can see in the right transept (note the artists brushes and tools), was commissioned by Lorenzo di Medici, "The Magnificent," and designed by Filippo's son, Filippino Lippi (circa 1457–1504). Another fresco cycle, including work by Pinturicchio, is the *Cappella Eroli* (Eroli Chapel) off the right aisle. Note the grotesques in the ornamentation, then very much in vogue with the rediscovery of ancient Roman paintings. The bounty of Umbria is displayed in vivid colors in the abundance of leaves, fruits, and vegetables that adorn the center seams of the cross vault and then in Poena, the old man clutching a grapevine with bunches of grapes, surrounded by shades of emerald and muted greens in a background of ultramarine blue. In the left nave, not far from the entrance, is the well-restored 12th-century crucifix by Alberto Sozio, the earliest known example of this kind of work, with a painting on parchment attached to a wood cross. To the right of the presbytery is the Cappella della Santissima Icona (Chapel of the Most Holy Icon), which contains a small Byzantine painting of a Madonna given to the town by Frederick Barbarossa as a peace offering in 1185, following his destruction of the cathedral and town three decades earlier. ⊠ *Piazza Duomo* ☎ *0743/44307* ⊙ *Mar.–Oct., daily 8–1 and 3–6:30; Nov.–Feb., daily 8–1 and 3–5:30.*

⑬ Galleria d'Arte Moderna. This five-room gallery contains the paintings and sculptures that from 1953 to 1968 won the Spoleto Prize, an honor given to significant works by renowned artists. Included are the original preparatory sketches for Alexander Calder's (1898–1976) *Teodelapio* (1962); the actual sculpture is near the train station. Don't miss one of Calder's portraits in wire, very different in style than his mobiles and heavier sculpture. Henry Moore is best known for his sculpture, but here you can also see some of his other media, including a collage. Other modern works are by contemporary Italian artists, such as Arnaldo Pomodoro, whose large golden globe sculpture, *Sphere Within a Sphere,* is on display in the Vatican courtyard in Rome. ⊠ *Palazzo Collicola,* ☎ *0743/46434* 🎫 *€4; €2.60 combination ticket from visitor-information center includes Pinacoteca Comunale and Casa Romana* ⊙ *Oct. 16–Mar. 15 daily 10:30–1 and 3:30–5:30; Mar. 16–Oct. 15, daily 10:30–1 and 3:30–7.*

★ ⑲ La Rocca. Built in the mid-14th century for Cardinal Egidio Albornoz, this massive fortress served as a seat for the local pontifical governors, a tangible sign of the restoration of the Church's power in the area when the pope was ruling from Avignon. Several popes spent time here, and one of them, Alexander VI, in 1499 sent his capable teenage daughter Lucrezia Borgia (1480–1519) to serve as governor for three months. The Gubbio-born architect Gattapone (14th century) used the ruins of a Roman acropolis as a foundation and took materials from many Roman-era sites, including the Teatro Romano. La Rocca's plan is long and rectangular, with six towers and two grand courtyards, an upper loggia and inside some grand reception rooms. In the largest tower, Torre Maesta, you can visit an apartment with frescoes inside. For most of the period from 1817 to 1982 La Rocca was used as a high-security prison, resulting in some badly damaged frescoes and prisoners' graffitti. But in 1999 the building was reborn as a museum that occasionally offers performances and temporary exhibitions. Future plans are to convert it to a Lombard museum with an additional perspective on the town's medieval history. A small shuttle bus gives you that last boost up the hill from the ticket booth to the entrance of the fortress. If you phone in advance, you may be able to reserve an English-speaking guide. ⊠ *Via del Ponte* ☎ *0743/223055* 🎫 *€4.65* ⊙ *Mid-Mar.–early June and mid-Sept.–Oct., weekdays 10–noon and 3–7, weekends 10–7; early June–mid-Sept., weekdays 10–7, weekends 10–9; Nov.–mid-Mar., weekdays 10–noon and 3–5, weekends 10–5.*

⑰ Piazza del Duomo. The piazza is stage-set perfect, a harmonious square
FodorśChoice enclosed on three sides by fine buildings, including the Duomo and the
★ small Teatro Caio Melisso, one of the first theaters built in Italy, with La Rocca behind and above it all. Try to arrive as the late afternoon sun catches the gold mosaics on the Duomo facade. In warm weather you can even dine outside on the square.

Pinacoteca Comunale. This museum contains a small collection of works from the 12th to the 18th centuries. Highlights include two 16th-century frescoes by a local artist known as Lo Spagna, which were detached from La Rocca, also *Magdalene,* by Il Guercino (1591–1666). The museum can be entered either from the main piazza or on the opposite side down the narrow Vicolo Terzo, which is off the Corso Mazzini. The location of the museum may change in 2005 or 2006; call before visiting. ✉ *Palazzo Spada, Piazza Sordini* ☎ *0743/43722, 0743/238920 Spoleto tourist office* 🎫 *€3; €2.60 combination ticket from visitor-information center includes Casa Romana and Galleria D'Arte Moderna* ⊙ *Closed Tues. and Oct. 15–Mar. 14.*

★ ⑳ **Ponte delle Torri** (Bridge of the Towers). Standing massive and graceful through the deep gorge that separates Spoleto from Monteluco, this 14th-century bridge is one of Umbria's most-photographed monuments, and justifiably so. The 750-ft-long bridge was built by Gattapone over the foundations of a Roman-era aqueduct and soars 262 feet above the forested gorge at its highest point—higher than the dome of St. Peter's in Rome. Sweeping postcard views over the valley and a pleasant sense of vertigo make a walk across the bridge a must, particularly on a starry night. ✉ *Via del Ponte.*

㉑ **San Pietro.** A walk to the church of San Pietro, at the foot of Monteluco, is a must and a pleasant excursion from town, either across the Ponte delle Torri and down the path to the right or out Porta Monterone and across the highway. The drama of life and death, of good and evil, are the real attractions here and are played out on the facade of this church that was rebuilt in the 13th century over earlier Christian, Roman, and Umbri holy sites. The carvings on the facade are among the best Romanesque carvings in the region, telling their story with simplicity and directness. Beneath the tympanum is a blank square, which presumably once held a mosaic, flanked by reliefs of Sts. Peter and Andrew, with a bull beneath each. Paired reliefs in the panels around the doors have peacocks mounted above allegories of work and of eternal life, and typical Christian scenes. The fates of two dying men, the just and the sinner, were sculpted on the church wall: the former being saved by St. Peter, with the devil held at bay; the latter has the scales of justice tipped toward the devil and is abandoned by the Archangel Michael to a pair of demons. A man's struggle with a lion suggests that this is one he might not easily walk away from. The interior of the church can be visited, but the showstopper is the exterior, usually illuminated at night. ✉ *Beginning of the Strada di Monteluco, 1 km (½ mi) south of town center* ☎ *0743/44882* 🎫 *Free* ⊙ *Hrs vary; call ahead.*

off the
beaten
path

SAN SALVATORE – The church and cemetery of San Salvatore seem very much forgotten, ensconced in solitude and cypress trees on a peaceful hillside with the motorway rumbling below. One of the oldest churches in the world, it was built in the 4th century, largely of Roman-era materials. The highlight is the facade, with three exquisite marble doorways and windows, one of the earliest and best preserved in Umbria; it dates from a restoration in the 9th century and has hardly been touched since. Inside is a 9th-century cross, studded in gems. ⊠ *Via della Basilica di San Salvatore, outside town, off Via Flaminia* ⊘ *Nov.–Feb., daily 7–5; Mar.–Apr. and Sept.–Oct., daily 7–6; May–Aug., daily 7–7.*

⑯ Sant'Eufemia. In the courtyard of the archbishop's palace with a partial view of the Duomo over the back wall, this austere ancient church dates from the 12th century. Built on the site of a Roman-era *insula* (city block), the plain Romanesque interior has a Cosmati mosaic altar and frescoes on the pillars. Access to the church is from the museum, and you will enter the gallery above the nave where female worshippers were required to sit. The gallery is a holdover from the Eastern Church and one of the few of its kind in this part of Italy. Admission to the church also includes a visit to the **Museo Diocesano d'Arte Sacra**, which has a bronze bust by Bernini of Barberini pope Urban VIII, who had been Bishop of Spoleto (1608-17) and donated this to the town in 1644. Have a look at some of the medieval painted wooden sculpture: a 14th-century St. Cristina in her red dress or the 15th-century St. Andrew draped in gold holding the church. The triptych of the Annunciation shows a peacock (once associated with the goddess Juno) on the roof above Mary. ⊠ *Via Aurelia Saffi, between Piazza del Duomo and Piazza del Mercato* ☎ *0743/23021* ⛛ *€3* ⊘ *Oct.–Mar., Wed.–Sat. and Mon. 10–1 and 3:30–6:30, Sun. 10–6; Apr.–Sept., Wed.–Fri. and Mon. 10–1 and 3:30–6:30, weekends 10–6.*

▶ ⑫ Teatro Romano. When the Romans colonized the city in 241 BC, they built this small 1st-century Roman theater that for centuries later was used as a quarry for building materials. The most intact portion is the hallway that passes under the *cavea* (stands). The rest was heavily restored in the early 1950s and serves as a venue for Spoleto's Festival dei Due Mondi. The theater was the site of a gruesome episode in Spoleto's history: during the medieval struggle between Guelph (papal) and Ghibelline (imperial) factions for control of central and northern Italy, Spoleto took the side of the Holy Roman Emperor. Afterward, 400 Guelph supporters were massacred in the theater, their bodies burned in an enormous pyre. In the end, the Guelphs were triumphant, and Spoleto was incorporated into the states of the Church in 1354. Through a door in the west portico of the adjoining building is the **Museo Archeologico**, with assorted artifacts found in excavations primarily around Spoleto and Norcia. The collection contains Bronze Age and Iron Age artifacts from Umbrian and pre-Roman eras. Another section contains black-glaze vases from the Hellenistic period excavated from the necropolis of St. Scolastica in Norcia. ⊠ *Via Sant'Agata, 18* ☎ *0743/223277* ⛛ *€4* ⊘ *Daily 8:30–7:30.*

Where to Stay & Eat

Restaurants in Spoleto are generally of much better quality than those in Assisi. Local truffles are served with abandon in season, and are shipped all over the country. Aside from the many midsize hotels and small, family-run inns, Spoleto has *agriturismo* (agritourist) accommodations that range from the rustic to the downright luxurious. The **Spoleto tourism**

office (📞 0743/238920) can advise you on different agriturismo options. Spoleto is known for outdoor sports and hiking; ask your hotel to assist you with booking bicycle and horseback excursions. If you're coming to stay during the Festival dei Due Mondi, book your room well in advance and be prepared for the high rates that accompany high demand.

$–$$$ ✕ **Apollinare.** Low wooden ceilings and candlelight in this former monastery of the 10th and 11th centuries make Apollinare Spoleto's romantic "in" spot. The kitchen serves sophisticated, innovative variations on local cooking: sauces of cherry tomatoes, mint, and a touch of red pepper, or of porcini mushrooms, to top the long, thin strangozzi. The *caramella* (light puff pastry cylinder filled with local cheese, served with a creamy Parmesan sauce) is popular. In warm weather you can dine under a canopy on the piazza across from the Archeological Museum. ✉ *Via Sant'Agata 14* 📞 *0743/223256* 🚫 *AE, D, MC, V* ☯ *Closed Tues. (except during the Festival dei Due Mondi).*

$$ ✕ **Il Tartufo.** As the name ("The Truffle") indicates, dishes prepared with truffles are the specialty here—don't miss the risotto al tartufo. But there are also choices not perfumed with this expensive delicacy on the menu. Incorporating the ruins of a Roman villa, the restaurant's decor is rustic on the ground floor with more modern furnishings upstairs. In summer, outdoor seating opens and traditional fare is spiced up to appeal to the cosmopolitan crowd attending (or performing in) the Festival dei Due Mondi. ✉ *Piazza Garibaldi 24* 📞 *0743/40236* ⌁ *Reservations essential* 🚫 *AE, DC, MC, V* ☯ *Closed Mon. and last 2 wks in July. No dinner Sun.*

$–$$ ✕ **Il Pentagramma.** This stable turned restaurant has terra-cotta floors, stone walls, and a wood-burning oven. Its fresh local dishes change seasonally. The farro soup has a new twist here: it is pureed and served inside a bread crust "bowl." Pastas might be *tortelli ai carciofi e noci* (artichoke-filled pasta with a hazelnut sauce) or, in summer, homemade fettucini served with sauce made from fresh vegetables and saffron. For your main course, you might try lamb in a truffle sauce, or—not to be missed if it's on the menu—roast pheasant. The stuffed zucchini flowers are lighter than usual, because they are baked (not fried) and filled with ricotta. The restaurant is quite central, off the Piazza della Libertà. ✉ *Via Martani 4* 📞 *0743/223141* 🚫 *DC, MC, V* ☯ *Closed Mon. No dinner Sun., and for about 2 wks after Christmas.*

★ **$–$$** ✕ **Ristorante Panciolle.** In the heart of Spoleto's medieval quarter, this restaurant has one of the most appealing settings you could wish for: a small piazza filled with lemon trees. Dishes change throughout the year, and may include pastas served with asparagus or mushrooms, as well as grilled meats. More expensive dishes prepared with fresh truffles are also available in season. ✉ *Vicolo degli Eroli 1* 📞 *0743/45598* ⊕ *www. ristoranteilpanciollespoleto.com* ⌁ *Reservations essential* 🚫 *AE, DC, MC, V* ☯ *Closed Wed. and last 2 wks in Nov.*

$ ✕ **Osteria del Trivio.** At this friendly trattoria with traditional Umbrian fare, everything is homemade and changes daily depending on what's seasonable. Dishes might include stuffed artichokes, pasta with *funghi sanguinosi* (a local mushroom) sauce, or chicken with artichokes. For dessert, try the homemade biscotti, made for dunking in sweet wine. There is a printed menu, but the owner can explain the dishes in a number of languages, and a complete meal from appetizer to dessert with house wine is likely to cost no more than €25. ⊠ *Via del Trivio 16* ☎ *0743/44349* ⊟ *AE, DC, MC, V* ⊗ *Closed Tues. Nov.–Mar.*

★ **$$** 🏨 **Hotel Gattapone.** Lucky Gattapone—this small, secluded hotel sits on the edge of the gorge separating the Rocca from Monteluco, overlooking the Ponte delle Torri. Wake up to wonderful views of the ancient bridge and the wooded slopes of Monteluco, and go for a morning walk around the Via del Ponte, which circles the base of the Rocca above. Interiors are done in modern style that's understated and tasteful, with beautiful wooden floors and comfortable leather furniture. ⊠ *Via del Ponte 6, 06049* ☎ *0743/223447* 🖨 *0743/223448* ⊕ *www.hotelgattapone. it* 🛏 *8 rooms, 8 suites* ⚐ *In-room safes, minibars, bar, meeting room, free parking* ⊟ *AE, DC, MC, V* ⑩ *CP.*

$$
Fodor's Choice
★
🏨 **Hotel San Luca.** The elegant San Luca is one of Spoleto's finest hotels, thanks to its commendable attention to detail, such as the hand-painted friezes that decorate the walls of the spacious guest rooms and the generous selection of up-to-date magazines for guests. Service is very gracious, and prices are surprisingly modest. Other attributes are its firm beds, and the fact that some of the rooms are wheelchair accessible. Enjoy an ample breakfast buffet, including homemade cakes, served on Deruta plates in a cheerful room facing the central courtyard. You can sip afternoon tea in oversize armchairs by the fireplace, and the hotel's rose garden provides a sweet-smelling backdrop for a walk. Its location at the bottom of town just inside the wall makes it ideal for cyclists (no steep hills to ascend); the hotel will give you route maps or help you book a guided bicycle tour. ⊠ *Via Interna delle Mura 21, 06049* ☎ *0743/223399* 🖨 *0743/223800* ⊕ *www.hotelsanluca.com* 🛏 *33 rooms, 2 suites* ⚐ *Bar, Internet, parking (fee)* ⊟ *AE, DC, MC, V* ⑩ *CP.*

$ 🏨 **Hotel dei Duchi.** This excellent, well-run hotel is a favorite among performers in the festival. It's in the center of town, near the Roman amphitheater. Some rooms have fine views of the city. ⊠ *Viale Matteotti 4, 06049* ☎ *0743/44541* 🖨 *0743/44543* ⊕ *www.hoteldeiduchi.com* 🛏 *47 rooms, 2 suites* ⚐ *Restaurant, bar, meeting room, free parking, some pets allowed* ⊟ *AE, DC, MC, V* ⑩ *CP.*

¢–$ 🏨 **Hotel Clitunno.** A renovated 18th-century building houses this pleasant hotel in the center of town. Cozy bedrooms and intimate public rooms, some with timbered ceilings, have the sense of a traditional Umbrian home—albeit one with a good restaurant. The hotel staff is glad to light the fireplace in Room 212 in advance of winter arrivals. Upper-floor rooms look over Spoleto's rooftops. The "older style" rooms, which have wood ceilings, iron beds, and nicer textiles, are more attractive. ⊠ *Piazza Sordini 6, 06049* ☎ *0743/223340* 🖨 *0743/222663* ⊕ *www.hotelclitunno.com* 🛏 *47 rooms* ⚐ *Restaurant, bar, library, meeting rooms; no a/c in some rooms* ⊟ *AE, DC, MC, V* ⑩ *CP.*

¢ 🏨 **Aurora.** This simple little hotel, right on Piazza della Libertà, is run by the owners of the Apollinare restaurant, which is downstairs. The rooms are basic and clean. ⊠ *Via Apollinare 3, 06049* ☎ *0743/220315* 🖨 *0743/221885* 🛏 *22 rooms, 1 suite* ⚐ *Bar; no a/c in some rooms* ⊟ *AE, DC, MC, V* ⑩ *CP.*

¢ ⊞ **Azienda Agrituristica Bartoli.** Just 13 km (8 mi) southeast of Spoleto, this agriturismo offers simple rooms with private baths in a converted farmhouse, with common kitchen and TV rooms. There is also an apartment that sleeps six. Rooms look out onto the green valleys below Monte di Patrico. Rent by the night or the week, with half or full board. There are ample hiking trails in the area, and horses are available with or without guides. Ask about truffle hunting in fall or winter. ⊠ *Località Patrico, 06049* ☎ *0743/220058* ⊕ *www.agriturismobartoli.it* ⥲ *11 rooms* ⑂ *Horseback riding; no a/c, no room TVs* ▭ *No credit cards* ⑃ *MAP.*

The Arts

In 1958, composer Gian Carlo Menotti chose Spoleto for the first **Festival dei Due Mondi** (Festival of Two Worlds; ⊠ Piazza Duomo 8 ☎ box office: 0743/220320, 800/565600 toll-free in Italy ⊕ www.spoletofestival. it), a gathering of artists, performers, and musicians intended to bring together the "new" and "old" worlds of America and Europe (there was once a corresponding festival in Charleston, South Carolina, but it is no longer connected to Spoleto's festival). The annual event, held in late June to early July, soon became one of the most important cultural happenings in Europe, attracting big names in all branches of the arts—particularly music, opera, and theater—and drawing thousands of visitors. With so much activity, the small town gives itself over entirely to the festival—events are staged in every possible venue, from church cloisters to the Roman Theater, and street performers abound. The closing concert (always free) takes place on the Piazza del Duomo.

At any other time of year, you will notice the changes brought by the festival—Spoleto is far more cosmopolitan than other towns in the region, its people more welcoming—and undoubtedly you will see traces of past festivals: old promotional posters hung in virtually all the shops and hotels, and modern sculptures left to the city in its art gallery and on permanent display outdoors. These include Alexander Calder's enormous bronze *Teodelapio* sculpture in front of the train station, Anna Mahler's *Sitting* in Piazza della Signoria, and *Geodesic Dome* by Buckminster Fuller (1895–1983) in the Parco della Passeggiata. Tickets for all performances should be ordered in advance. Full program information is available beginning in February.

Outdoor Activities & Sports

Biking

The pretty countryside around Spoleto is well suited for bicycling, with terrain that ranges from flat country roads to steep mountain paths. The **Spoleto tourist office** (⊠ Piazza della Libertà 7 ☎ 0743/238920) publishes an excellent pamphlet, *In Bicicletta nello Spoletino* (*Bicycling Around the Spoleto Area*), which details routes, distances, and levels of difficulty in Italian and English. You can get the pamphlet directly from the tourist office or from some hotels and bike shops. Many hotels are cyclist-friendly, with garage space for you to store your bike and knowledge of some of the local guides and major tour companies. Less-athletic cyclists may want to consider a hotel at the base of Spoleto near the wall so that you don't have to huff and puff up the hill on your re-entry. Bicycles can be rented at **Scocchetti Cicli** (⊠ Via Marconi 82 ☎ 0743/44728), open Monday through Saturday 9–1 and 3:30–8 (call ahead to reserve).

Hiking

Pick up a map of local roads and trails from the **Spoleto tourist office** (⊠ Piazza della Libertà 7 ☎ 0743/238920) and head out for a stroll in the country or a hike up the mountainside. Trails on **Monteluco**, a hill just across the Ponte delle Torri, wind steeply through the thick Bosco Sacro (Sacred Woods), passing caves and hermitages abandoned by spiritual seekers who have lived here since the time of St. Francis.

Horseback Riding

Horses can be rented with English-speaking guides at the **Centro Ippico La Somma** (⊠ Frazione Aiacugigli-Montebibico, about 15 km [9 mi] south of Spoleto ☎ 0743/54370), open daily 9:30–noon and 3:30–7.

Shopping

Spoleto's main shopping street begins as **Via Fontesecca** (near Piazza del Mercato) and continues down the hill, changing names several times. **Aracne** (⊠ Vicolo Primo di Corso Mazzini 2 ☎ 0743/46085) specializes in fine lace and embroidery. **Mobilia** (⊠ Via Filitteria 3 ☎ 0743/45720) is one of Spoleto's many antiques shops. Spoleto's tiny open-air **produce market,** open Monday through Saturday 8–1:30 has dwindled to practically nothing in Piazza del Mercato, but the nearby **Arco di Druso** has plenty of antiques. The second Sunday of every month sees the **Mercato delle Brisciole,** with antiques and crafts vendors taking over the streets of Spoleto's historic center. Down the road in Pissignano, the region's best **antiques fair** is held the first Sunday of each month.

> **en route** The road east from Spoleto (S395) goes 19 km (12 mi) to the Nera River, then turns north and becomes S209. As you climb higher, the olive groves that produce Spoleto's fine oil give way to chestnut trees and forests populated by wolves, porcupines, and owls. When you reach Cerreto di Spoleto, take the long way around to the S320, passing Triponzo, for the best views. Most minor roads are not in the best of shape, but they reward you with dramatic mountain scenery.

SPOLETO ENVIRONS & NORCIA

Spoleto is the obvious starting point for a visit to the eastern edges of Umbria, as few roads cut across the rugged mountainous terrain that quickly rises from the Valle Umbra. Roads narrow and the towns get smaller and farther apart as you break out off the well-traveled path between Assisi and Spoleto, but great rewards await. Spring brings milder weather with wildflowers at their finest, but truffle hunters should consider winter excursions. The main attractions are Norcia, a town known for black truffles and pork products, and for the road you take to get there, full of breathtaking views across unspoiled verdant mountain landscapes. To the east of Norcia, and extending into the Marches, is the Parco Nazionale dei Monti Sibillini, one of Italy's best nature reserves.

No less inviting is the Valnerina (Valley of the Nera River), which has its own protected nature area and stunning scenery. Lest any part of Italy be without an interesting church, the Abbazia di San Pietro della Valle sits like a gem amid the lush greenery of the valley.

Norcia

㉒ *48 km (31 mi) east of Spoleto, 99 km (62 mi) southeast of Perugia.*

A good day trip from Spoleto, Norcia is synonymous for most Italians with legendary sausages and prosciutto and the great tradition of butchers who have surgical precision with knives. (It's no coincidence that Norcia is also where one of Italy's first and more important schools for surgeons was founded.) In fact, from Rome to Rimini a *norcineria* is a place where sausages are made and sold, and a *norcino* is a pork butcher. (Under the circumstances, it is no wonder that the locals call themselves *nursiani.*) However, in recent years Norcia has produced fewer pigs, and Italians in the know say that most of the pork is imported from elsewhere. But pork products are still the biggest draw to Norcia, which also has fine truffles, a solid tradition of cheese making, plenty of delicious baked goods, and chocolate. The Sagra del Tartufo, the Black Truffle Festival, is usually held in late February.

Norcia is the birthplace of St. Benedict (San Benedetto), the founder of Christianity's first monastic order, and the town is surrounded by stupendous, lush mountainous terrain. In fact, the main reasons to visit Norcia are to enjoy the natural beauty, to go on a truffle hunt, or to take a cooking class. It's also a great place for kids to unwind, with nearby rafting and bicycling.

The local sights are clustered around Piazza San Benedetto. The 14th-century church of **San Benedetto** was built over the purported birthplace of the saint and his twin sister, St. Scolastica. Both are represented in statues set into the facade, which in turn must have been constructed over the remains of a Roman house, visible in the church crypt. Don't miss the fascinating set of nine medieval round stone vessels, once used to measure grain, that rest on a shelf under the portico on the Via Mazzini side. ⊠ *Piazza San Benedetto* ☎ *0743/817125* ✉ *Free* ☉ *Daily 8:30–12:30 and 3:30–6:30.*

Off to the side of San Benedetto, the **Duomo** bears the scars of repeated redecoration necessitated by frequent earthquakes over the centuries. The locals now adhere to strict building codes and height limitations. ⊠ *Piazza San Benedetto.*

The superb **Castellina,** the sturdy papal palace, holds the **Museo Civico,** which offers more than the usual drab collection of local work. The Della Robbia terra-cotta of the Madonna, a rare example in this region of the work of the masterful Florentine family, and a 13th-century *Deposition,* made up of several wooden statues, are worth the admission alone. Don't miss the Etruscan collection, acquired in 2002, that is displayed on the ground floor; artifacts from this former private collection are choice (some of Norcia's wound up in Spoleto); look for pottery with vivid geometric designs or the black-glazed pottery. ⊠ *Piazza San Benedetto* ☎ *0743/ 817030* ✉ *€3 museum, €4 with archeological site* ⊙ *Oct.–May, Tues.–Sun. 10–12:30 and 3:30–6; June–Sept., Tues.–Sun. 10–1 and 4–7.*

Parco Nazionale dei Monti Sibillini

㉓ *About 46 km (29 mi) east of Spoleto.*

Norcia lies within the boundaries of the Parco Nazionale dei Monti Sibillini, an unspoiled mountainous ridge that straddles the border between Umbria and the Marches region. Just southeast of Norcia is **San Pellegrino,** source of one of the country's most famous mineral waters. The main road that winds its way through the mountains, eventually crossing the border into Le Marche, passes through **Castelluccio,** a pretty town known nationwide for its lentils and their spectacular flowers in late spring. You're not here for the towns, though, but for the park, which, weather permitting, offers some of the country's best hiking and other outdoor activities, like skiing or spelunking. Ask about hiking to 2,173-meter (7,129-foot) Mt. Sibilla; it was on this mountain in ancient times that one of the famous prophetesses, or sibyls, for whom this park is named, lived in a cave. The maps issued by the Club Alpino Italiano (CAI), available at newsstands, are great for orienting yourself in the park.

The **Cooperativa Monte Patino** (☎ 0743/817487 for reservations), open weekdays 9:30–1:30 and 3:30–6, offers guided tours in English, including excursions to villages and isolated churches and hiking in the Parco dei Sibillini. A full-day food-shopping tour called **Sentiero Sapori** (Flavor Trail; €7.75) focuses on visits to artisanal workshops and cheese and sausage producers. If you prefer to travel without a guide, try the **Casa del Parco** (⊠ Via Solferino 22, Norcia ☎ 0743/817090 ⊠ Via Santa Caterina, Preci Alto ☎ 0743/937000). Both offices, open daily 9:30–12:30 and 3–6, have free maps and brochures about the Umbrian side of the national park.

Where to Stay

¢ ▦ **Rifugio Perugia.** You won't have a private room in this *rifugio di montagna* (mountain refuge)—in fact, you'll have to share with three people and you'll likely be sleeping in a bunk bed. But if you enjoy the atmosphere of a cozy mountain retreat and of getting together over a last bottle of wine, do join in (and get the seat near the guy with the guitar). Rates of €16 a person include sheets and bath towels. ⊠ *Località Canapine, about 22 km (14 mi) southeast of Norcia, 62039* ☎ *0743/823019, 368/646189, or 335/7010781* ✉ *rifugioperugia@libero. it* ⊅ *35 beds* ♨ *Restaurant; no a/c, no room phones, no room TVs* ⊟ *MC, V* ⊙ *Closed Nov. 1–Easter.*

Abbazia di San Pietro in Valle

24 *35 km (22 mi) southeast of Spoleto, 44 km (27 mi) southwest of Norcia.*

It's hard to believe that this remote building once served as one of the region's centers of Christianity, but the remnants of one of the fortresses that protected it, still visible in the distance, testify to its earlier importance. Column capitals in the apse and a 1st-century BC altar near the back door suggest that the 8th-century abbey was built over the ruins of a Roman temple. After it was sacked by the Saracens, Otto III began the restoration of the abbey in 996, which was completed by his successor, Henry II. The bell tower was built in the second half of the 11th century, the graceful cloister was added in the 12th century, and late in the 12th century frescoes were painted on the walls of the nave. Restored in 1995, the frescoes are considered important examples of Romanesque painting. The unknown artist who painted them preceded Giotto in trying to break away from the Byzantine style through realistic and vivid details. The main altar is a rare example of 8th-century Lombard bas-relief, which includes representations of the lord who commissioned the piece and the artist himself, called Ursus. To the right is a 3rd-century BC Roman sarcophagus containing the remains of Faroald II of Spoleto, the duke who built the abbey after having a vision of St. Peter. Note that the southern road going up to the abbey is easier to navigate than the northern road, which is unpaved. ⊠ *S209* ☎ *0744/780316* 🖃 *By donation* ☉ *Oct.–Apr., daily 10:15–12:30 and 2–5; May–Sept., daily 10:15–12:30 and 2–6. If it's closed, ring at the custodian's house, about 1 km (½ mi) south of the abbey.*

off the
beaten
path

Down at the bottom of the Valmarino (SS. 209) is the town of Ferentillo, and next to it, the Nera River. Cross a little one-lane ancient bridge over the river and take a short walk up the hill to **LE MUMMIE DI FERENTILLO** (The Mummies of Ferentillo) – , on the bottom level of the church of St. Stefano. The mummies are the bodies of about 30 people who died between 1500 and 1871. They were buried in this cemetery and mummified by a rare natural occurrence—not by elaborate preparation—wherein a microfungus attacked the corpses, preserving the skin and some other bits. The odd mix of dead companions includes a lawyer who was punched to death, his murderer on the other side of the room, and some Chinese pilgrims. This unlikely group is united in death in a single room, with lots of skulls in the background. ⊠ *Chiesa di Santo Stefano a Precetto* ☎ *0743/54395* 🖃 *€2.60* ☉ *Nov.–Feb., daily 10–12:30 and 2:30–5; Mar.–Oct., daily 9–12:30 and 2:30–6.*

Where to Eat

$–$$$ ✕ **Piermarini.** In the tiny town of Ferentillo, 4 km (1½ mi) south of the Abbazia di San Pietro in Valle, this is the local place for your Umbrian truffle experience, especially in winter (truffle season). Traditional, no-nonsense dishes include a truffle omelet, which allows the truffles to be enjoyed without other competing flavors. Second courses include grilled kid, lamb, and roasted pork. There is a garden for outside dining in good weather. ⊠ *Via Ancaiano 23, Ferentillo, 18½ km [11 mi] northeast of Terni, 31 km [19 mi] southeast of Spoleto* ☎ 0744/780714 ▤ AE, D, MC, V ⊘ *Closed Mon. and 1 wk in Jan.*

Shopping

Pick up some cheese—or truffles, in season—at the **Boutique del Pecoraro** (⊠ Via San Benedetto 7 ☎ 0743/816453). Local cheeses, salami, and truffle products are on plentiful, redolent display at **Norcineria Ercole Ulivucci** (⊠ Via Mazzini 4 ☎ 0743/816661), closed Monday in even years, Tuesday in odd years. For cakes and pastries, head to the shop at **No. 13 Corso Sertorio** (☎ 0744/816623), closed Sunday. As its name implies, **Norcineria Fratelli Ansuini** (⊠ Via Anicia 105 ☎ 0743/816643), closed Tuesday, stocks a full range of the local pork products. Well worth a visit is **Tartufi Moscatelli** (⊠ Corso Sertorio 42 ☎ 0743/817388), renowned for its truffles.

SOUTHERN UMBRIA

It's a short drive from Spoleto to Terni, but tempting diversions along the way include one of central Italy's finest abbeys and the refreshing Lake Piediluco. Hold your breath while river rafting at the foot of the tallest falls in Europe, and then recover while driving through olive groves to sleepy Amelia—Umbria's oldest town—before stepping into the medieval past of Todi. Finish off your visit to the province in Orvieto, with its unforgettable Duomo and wine that has pleased locals for 3,000 years.

Terni

25 *33 km (21 mi) southwest of Spoleto, 70 km (45 mi) southeast of Orvieto.*

Although a convenient jumping-off point for Lake Piediluco and the Marmore Falls, the attractions of Terni are less impressive, as the town was heavily bombed by the allies in World War II because of its weapons and metals industry—not the kind of place you would associate with St. Valentine, who was born here about 175. A church on the south side of town marks his burial place.

Terni is not bereft of art, and the local **Pinacoteca Comunale** has Benozzo Gozzoli's *The Marriage of St. Catherine*, as well as several noteworthy modern paintings. ⊠ *Via del Teatro Romano 13* ☎ *0744/59421* ▦ *€3.62* ⊘ *Tues.–Sun. 10–1 and 4–7.*

Just a few blocks from the Pinacoteca is the round church of **San Salvatore.** It was once thought to have been a Roman temple, on account of its dome and oculus, a circular hole in the dome meant to represent the all-seeing eye of heaven. ⊠ *Via del Teatro Romano* ☎ *No phone* ▦ *Free* ⊘ *Daily 9–noon and 4–6.*

The basilica **San Valentino** is south of town. St. Valentine (one of them) was born in Terni in about 175. He was made Bishop of Terni by San Feliciano (which explains the presence of both as sculptures over the main portal inside Foligno's cathedral). Under the persecutions of Emperor Aurelian, Valentine was sentenced to death and beheaded on February 14, 273, on the Via Flaminia in Rome—away from Terni to avoid a popular uprising. In 313 Constantine's edict ordered a basilica constructed on the site of his tomb, later destroyed by the Goths. The present basilica was constructed from 1605 to 1618. A legend, which this church notes is "Anglo-Saxon in origin," is that Valentine would give lovers who visited him a flower from his garden, as a symbol of the love that would consecrate their future marriage. Valentine is the patron saint of lovers, of married couples, and of Terni. ⊠ *Via Papa Zcaria 12* ☎ *0744/274508* ☜ *Free* ☼ *Daily 9–12 and 4–6.*

off the beaten path

CASCATA DELLE MARMORE – The road east of Terni (SS Valnerina) leads 10 km (6 mi) to the waterfalls at Marmore, which at 541 feet are the highest falls in Europe. A canal was dug by the Romans in the 3rd century BC to prevent flooding in the nearby agricultural plains. Nowadays the waters are often diverted to provide hydroelectric power for Terni, reducing the roaring falls to an unimpressive trickle, so check with the information office at the falls or with Terni's tourist office before heading here. On summer evenings, when the falls are in full spate, the cascading water is floodlit to striking effect. This is a good place for hiking, except in December and January, when most trails may be closed and only Piazzale Byron and the Belvedere Superiore (overlook) are open to visitors. *Information office:* ⊠ *SP79, 3 km/2 mi east of Terni* ☎ *0744/62982* ☜ *Free* ☼ *Light displays: May, weekends 8 PM–10 PM; June–Aug., daily 8 PM–10 PM; mid-Mar.–Apr. and Sept., weekends 8 PM–9 PM.*

LAGO DI PIEDILUCO – The road east from Terni (SS Valnerina) continues to Lake Piediluco, a nice spot to rest and get your feet wet. The lake is the prettiest in the region, surrounded by steep, forested hillsides. There are facilities for boat and canoe rental, as well as waterskiing and sailing.

Outdoor Activities & Sports
Rapids near the Cascata delle Marmore make for good water rafting for all skill levels; inquire at the **Centro Rafting Le Marmore** (⊠ Belvedere Inferiore ☎ 0330/753420 or 0337/729154), open daily from mid-March to October. Rafting is available to those between the ages of 15 and 55 and weighing less than 220 pounds. A descent, with a brief class beforehand, takes about two hours.

Narni

26 *13 km (8 mi) southwest of Terni, 46 km (29 mi) southeast of Orvieto.*

Once a bustling and important town at a major crossroads on the Via Flaminia, Narni is now a quiet backwater with only the wind and the occasional tourist invading its quiet hilltop streets. Modern development is kept out of sight in the new town of Narni Scalo, below. This means that you will find the old part safely preserved behind, and in the case of Narni's subterranean Roman ruins, beneath, the town's sturdy walls.

For a look at Narni underground, contact the **Associazione Culturale Sub-terranea** (☎ 0744/722292) to set up a tour in English (🖾 €3.60).

The **Duomo** originally had three aisles, but a fourth was added to the right of the church to incorporate a 6th-century shrine of San Giovenale, the patron saint of the town. As a result, the Via Flaminia passes through the church. A 9th-century mosaic over the shrine is partially visible. ⊠ *Piazza Cavour* ☎ *0744/722610* 🖾 *Free* ⊙ *Daily 8–12:30 and 3–7.*

Piazza Garibaldi, the town's main square, is built over the **Lacus,** a large late-medieval cistern with vaulting and remains of the Roman-era stone pavement. ⊠ *Below the Piazza Garibaldi.*

The town's big artistic attraction is an altarpiece by Domenico Ghirlandaio (1449–94), *The Coronation of the Virgin,* in the Sala del Consiglio of the **Palazzo Comunale.** Opposite the altarpiece is a loggia by Gattapone. ⊠ *Piazza dei Priori* ☎ *0744/715362* 🖾 *Free* ⊙ *Daily 9–1 and 3–5.*

For centuries Narni was protected from invasion by its lofty perch above the Nera River and by its imposing **Rocca** (fortress) built by Cardinal Albornoz in the 14th century. Little now remains of the interior decoration of the castle, but the architecture and the views make the walk uphill worthwhile. ⊠ *Via del Monte* ☎ *0744/715362* 🖾 *Free* ⊙ *Apr.–Sept., Fri–Sun. 10–7; Oct.–Mar., call ahead for hrs.*

The 12th-century church of **Santa Maria Impensole** is well worth a visit for its finely carved facade. Under the church, excavations have revealed an 8th-century church built over a Roman temple that was converted into a crypt for the church above. There are also two Roman cisterns, one of them in especially good condition. ⊠ *Via Mazzini* ☎ *0744/242226* ⊙ *Daily 9:30–noon and 4:30–6:30.*

The former **Monastero di San Domenico** is now the town library. Around the back, underneath the monastery, an entrance leads to a Romanesque church with frescoes from the 13th to 15th centuries. In the adjacent remains of a Roman building with a cistern is a cell used during the Inquisition. On its walls are graffiti left by prisoners. ⊠ *Via Mazzini* ☎ *0744/747203* 🖾 *Free* ⊙ *Weekdays 9–noon.*

Amelia

㉗ *50 km (31 mi) southeast of Orvieto.*

Amelia has the distinction of being the oldest town in the region, with archaeological evidence from as far back as 1100 BC. The little town's main attraction, the bulky **walls** that still surround it, shows that the Umbri knew a thing or two about fortifications—the walls are more than 20 feet thick at some points.

Admire the town walls from a path that leads from Porta Romana around the perimeter of the town, or walk up the main road to the brick **Duomo,** at the top of the town. The original church built on this site in 872 was another casualty of Frederick II and was rebuilt later. The facade is made of travertine and pink terra-cotta. The interior, modified in the 19th century, is decorated with two Turkish flags won in the Battle of Lepanto. Although it now serves as the Duomo's bell tower, the unusual **Torre Civica** (circa 1050) was built before the church. Its 12 sides were thought originally to represent the signs of the zodiac, but were later designated as the Twelve Apostles. If the proportion speaks to you, perhaps it's because the height of the tower equals the sum of the widths of the sides. There are fine views from the top of the hill that look over other hills, poplars, pines, vineyards, and olive groves. ⊠ *Piazza Duomo* ☎ *0744/981453* 🎟 *Free* ☉ *Daily 10–1 and 4–6:30.*

Don't miss **Museo Archeologico di Amelia,** opened in 2001, Umbria's second largest archeological museum after Perugia's. A rare full-length bronze statue of Germanicus, brother of Claudius and father of Caligula, is the prize here. You can get another look at him from the floor above. The displays are attractive and descriptions are informative (in Italian only; English translations are in the works). ⊠ *Piazza Augusto Vera* ☎ *0744/ 978120* 🎟 *€3.60* ☉ *Oct.–Mar., Fri.–Sun. 10:30–1 and 3:30–6; Apr.–Aug., Tues.–Sun. 10:30–7.*

en route The road northwest of Amelia (S205) passes first through **Lugnano in Teverina,** with its important Collegiata di Santa Maria Assunta. The facade is the region's best piece of Romanesque architecture. The interior is mostly undecorated, apart from a handsome Cosmati mosaic floor, which has complex geometric patterns. Just a couple of miles ahead is the town of **Alviano,** where an important nature reserve, good for bird-watching, has been established at the nearby lake. The road continues through Baschi, westward (13 km [8 mi]) toward Orvieto, and east (28 km [17 mi]) to Todi.

Giove

 12½ km (8 mi) southwest of Amelia, 9½ km (6 mi) south of Lugnano in Teverina, 24 km (15 mi) west of Terni.

The little town of Giove was named for the Roman god Jupiter (Jove) and for a famous temple in his honor that once stood here. Largo Macalle, next to the castle, has a beautiful view of the valley below, especially at sunset as you are looking west. Just outside the town is a convent with a Madonna by Perugino. The road continues to **Attigliano,** where the modern church of San Lorenzo the Martyr gives an idea of how all the churches in the region might look had they been built in the previous century.

Giove has an interesting 16th-century **Palazzo Ducale,** with 365 windows— one for each of the days of the year—and a peculiar spiral ramp large enough to allow horse-driven carts to enter the building through the front door and reach the upper floors. The castle is closed to the public. ⊠ *Piazza XXIV Maggio.*

need a break? If you arrive between September and May, head to **Caffe di Notte** (⊠ Largo Macalle ☎ No phone), an outdoor café that opens at 5:30 PM and serves into the wee hours; it has a lovely view of the valley below and serves simple sandwiches and drinks at very reasonable prices.

Todi

㉙ *34 km (22 mi) south of Perugia, 34 km (22 mi) east of Orvieto.*

As you stand on Piazza del Popolo, looking out onto the Tiber Valley below, it's easy to see how Todi is often described as Umbria's prettiest hill town. Legend has it that the town was founded by the Umbri, who followed an eagle who had stolen a tablecloth to this lofty perch. They liked it so much that they settled here for good. The eagle is now perched on the insignia of the medieval palaces in the main piazza. But historical evidence suggests that the Umbri didn't find an empty nest; Iron Age remains dating from 2700 BC make it the oldest settled area in the region. The usual Etruscan to Roman progression followed, and Todi rose to prominence in the 13th century, when it ruled over the *comune* (township) that included Amelia and Terni. Aside from the view and charm of the streets, there are also two small but worthwhile museums. Todi is best reached by car, as the town's two train stations are way down the hill and connected to the town by infrequent bus service.

Built above the Roman Forum, **Piazza del Popolo** is Todi's high point, a model of spatial harmony with stunning views onto the surrounding countryside. In the best medieval tradition, the square was conceived to house both the temporal and the spiritual centers of power.

On one end of the Piazza del Popolo is the 12th-century Romanesque–Gothic **Duomo,** which was built over the site of a Roman temple. The simple facade is enlivened by a finely carved rose window. Look up at that window as you step inside and you will notice its peculiarity: each "petal" of the rose has a cherub's face in the stained glass. Take a close look at the capitals of the double columns with pilasters: perched between the acanthus leaves are charming medieval sculptures of saints— Peter with his keys, George and the dragon, and so on. You can see the rich brown tones of the wooden choir near the altar, but unless you have binoculars or request special permission in advance, you cannot get close enough to see all the exquisite detail in this Renaissance masterpiece of woodworking (1521–30). The severe, solid mass of the Duomo is mirrored by the Palazzo dei Priori (1595–97) across the way. ✉ *Piazza del Popolo* ☎ *075/8943041* ✇ *Free* ⊗ *May–Sept., daily 8:30–12:30 and 2:30–6:30; Oct.–Apr., daily 8:30–4:30.*

A staircase on the Piazza del Popolo leads to the Palazzo del Popolo and the entrance to the **Pinacoteca di Todi.** The first room is devoted to the history of Todi; the collection includes religious garments, local coins, Roman relics, Etruscan pottery, and more-recent ceramics from Deruta. The highlight of the Pinacoteca is the *Coronation of the Virgin* by Lo Spagna. ✉ *Palazzo del Popolo, Piazza del Popolo* ☎ *075/8944148* ✇ *€3.50* ⊗ *Nov.–Mar., Tues.–Sun. 10:30–1 and 2–4:30; Apr. and Oct., Tues.-Sun. 10:30–1 and 2:30–6:30; May–Aug., Tues.–Sun. 10:30–1 and 4:30–6.*

Via di Santa Prassede heads down to the northern part of town; although called the *borgo nuovo* (new quarter), it includes two 14th-century churches and many well-preserved old buildings. Piazza del Popolo is thought to have been built over the remains of the town's Roman Forum, but the only ancient ruins visible are the so-called **Nicchioni** (large niches) that make up one side of Piazza del Mercato Vecchio, now used as a parking lot. ⊠ *Follow the signs from Corso Cavour.*

Near Piazza Jacopone is the **Chiesa di San Fortunato.** Had the church been completed, it might have looked like a small version of the Duomo in Orvieto. But the project was never realized. Legend has it that Lorenzo Maitani (circa 1275–1330) was given the job but was murdered by the jealous Orvietani to ensure that no other Duomo could rival their own. Aside from the carved doorway and captivating angels attributed to Jacopo della Quercia (circa 1371–1438), the church remains more impressive for its sheer mass than its makeup. The whitewashed interior is remarkably free of any Gothic atmosphere. Under the main altar is the crypt of the local saint Jacopone da Todi (circa 1230–1306). ⊠ *Piazza Umberti I* 🕾 *No phone* 🎟 €6 ۞ *Oct.–Mar., Mon. 10–1, Tues.–Sun. 10–1 and 2:30–5; Apr.–Sept., Mon. 10–1, Tues.–Sun. 9:30–1 and 3–7.*

The lane to the left of the Chiesa di San Fortunato exit leads to a public garden, where you'll find a few benches and all that's left of the Rocca, the papal fortress. Follow the signs for the winding path that descends to an unexpected Renaissance treasure, the church of **Santa Maria della Consolazione.** Thought to have been inspired by designs by Bramante, it was begun in 1508 but not finished for another hundred years. The perfect symmetry it has is heightened by an almost neoclassical purity of form and proportions. ⊠ *Piazza della Consolazione* 🕾 *075/8943120* 🎟 *Free* ۞ *Apr.–Sept., daily 9–1 and 3–6; Oct.–Mar., daily 10–noon.*

Where to Stay & Eat

$–$$ ✕ **La Mulinella.** If it weren't for all the other tables around, you'd think you were a guest at the home of Signora Irma, who has been making bread and pasta for 35 years. If you intend to go on to *secondi* (second courses), beware of the primi piatti, which include dishes such as *tacchino farcito d'uva* (turkey stuffed with grapes) or stewed wild boar. Portions are generous, so share a dish of her light-as-a-feather *gnocchetti* or tagliatelle in a goose sauce, and save room for the simple desserts. ⊠ *Località Pontenaia 29* 🕾 *075/8944779* 🖃 *MC, V* ۞ *Closed Wed.*

$–$$ ✕ **Ristorante Umbria.** Todi's most popular restaurant for more than four decades, the Umbria is reliable for sturdy country food, plus a wonderful view from the terrace. In winter try Etruscan or a legume soup, and homemade pastas with truffles, game, or *palombaccio alla ghiotta* (roasted squab). Steaks, accompanied by a rich dark brown Sagrantino wine sauce, are good as well. ⊠ *Via San Bonaventura 13* 🕾 *075/8942737 or 075/8942390* 🖃 *AE, DC, MC, V* ۞ *Closed Tues. and July.*

★ $ 🖸 **Fattoria di Vibio.** A cluster of old stone farmhouses set on a ridge north of Todi has been converted into this gracious and relaxed country compound, with painters' views of the vineyards and valleys below. Hike the country roads or relax poolside in summer; you can while the evening away at candlelit tables outside on the lawn or, on chilly nights, in front of the ample stone fireplace. For families or extended stays, the two independent cottages, with maid service and full use of hotel facilities, are a good deal. ⊠ *Località Buchella, Doglio, Montecastello di*

Vibio 06057, (12 km [7 mi] northwest of Todi) ☎ 075/8749607 ⊟ 075/8780014 ⊕ *www.fattoriadivibio.com* ⇆ *10 rooms, 3 suites, 2 cottages* ⚹ *Dining room, pool, mountain bikes, paddle tennis, bar, Internet; no a/c* ⊟ *AE, DC, MC, V* ☯ *Closed Dec.–Feb., bookings of 1 wk or more only July–Aug.* ⦿ *MAP.*

★ $ ▦ **Tenuta di Canonica.** The affable hosts here, Daniele and Maria Fano, have retained the architectural integrity of this brick farmhouse and medieval tower in the Tiber Valley. You're bound to marvel at the exposed stone walls, high-beam ceilings, brick floors, and terra-cotta tiles, all in soothing colors. Guest rooms are filled with family furniture and antique pieces. You can hike or ride on horseback through olive groves, orchards, and the forest on the grounds. ⊠ *Località La Canonica 75–76, 06059, 5 km (3 mi) northwest of center* ☎ 075/8947545 ⊟ 075/8947581 ⊕ *www.tenutadicanonica.com* ⇆ *10 rooms, 3 apartments* ⚹ *Dining room, pool, bar, library; no a/c, no room TVs* ⊟ *MC, V* ⦿ *CP.*

Shopping

Todi's local sweet, available in most pastry shops, is *panpolenta* (coffee cake made with corn flour and ground almonds). Local ceramics are available from several boutiques along Corso Cavour. The town also hosts one of Italy's most important annual antiques fairs (usually two weeks around Easter). For the dates and venue, contact the tourist office.

ORVIETO

The natural defenses of an enormous plateau rising 1,000 feet above the flat valley proved very attractive to settlers in central Italy as far back as the Bronze Age, making Orvieto among the oldest cities in the region. The Etruscans developed the town considerably, carving a network of 1,200 wells and storage caves out of the soft tufa (volcanic stone) of the mount on which the city was built. By 283 BC the Romans had attacked, sacked, and destroyed the city, by then known as Volsinii Veteres. Perhaps they were attracted by the golden Orvieto Classico made from grapes grown in the rich volcanic soil of the valley below—a wine the town is still famous for today.

Charlemagne (742–814) changed the name to Urbs Vetus, from which the modern name derives. The town rose steadily as an independent commune in the late Middle Ages. When the Guelphs won decisively over the Ghibellines in the 14th century, Orvieto passed under the control of the papacy and was subsequently used by the popes as a refuge from enemies or the summer heat of Rome.

In addition to wine and some of the best restaurants in the region, Orvieto has much to offer: the celebrated Duomo, with Italy's finest Gothic facade, is worth the trip alone. Inside are masterly frescoes by Luca Signorelli (circa 1450–1523)—stunningly restored—perhaps the most underrated in the entire country. A couple of good museums and some excavations round out the sights.

The festival highlight of the year is the Festa della Palombella on Pentecost Sunday (the seventh Sunday after Easter). In this unique take on a fireworks show, a tabernacle with images of the Madonna and the Apostles is set up on the steps in front of the central doorway of the Duomo. A white dove attached to a cable strung across the piazza slides down and ignites the fireworks.

Exploring Orvieto

Orvieto is well connected by train to Rome, Florence, and Perugia. It's also adjacent to the A1 superstrada that runs between Florence and Rome. Parking areas in the upper town tend to be crowded. There is ample parking in the lower town, near the railway station, and on the other side of town in Campo della Fiera (at the end of SS71).

In the 19th century, the steep grade led the Orvietani to build an ingenious funicular that runs from the train station up the side of the hill and through the fortress to Piazzale Cahen. It runs every 20 minutes, daily 7:15 AM–8:30 PM, and costs €.80. Although the workings have been modernized, there are a few pictures in each station of the old cog railcars, which were once run hydraulically. Keep your funicular ticket, as it will get you a discount on admission to the Museo Claudio Faina. Bus 1 makes the same trip from 8 AM to 11 PM. From Piazzale Cahen, bus A runs to Piazza del Duomo in the town center.

A *biglietto unico* (single ticket) is a great deal; for €12.50, you get admission to the four major sights in town—Cappella di San Brizio (at the Duomo), Museo Claudio Faina, Torre del Moro, and Orvieto Underground—plus a combination bus–funicular pass or five hours of free parking.

A Good Walk

Piazzale Cahen, where there's a large parking lot and the funicular station, is a good place to begin. A quick walk around **La Rocca** will give you an idea of just how far you have come from the valley floor. The fortress is now a public garden with great views from its battlements. Nearby are the **Pozzo di San Patrizio** 30 ☞ and the ruins of an Etruscan Temple. Cross Piazzale Cahen and walk up Corso Cavour, which cuts through to the center of town. Only about halfway up, as the streets narrow and plaster and stucco are replaced by stone, does Orvieto begin to resemble the other hill towns in the region. Off to the right, Via San Leonardo leads to Piazza del Popolo, where there's a good little market on Thursday and Saturday mornings, as well as Orvieto's most handsome civic building, the 13th-century Romanesque-Gothic **Palazzo del Popolo** 31 .

Return to the Corso and take Via del Duomo to the left, which leads past several gift shops selling local ceramics and curves toward Piazza del Duomo. The spires of the **Duomo** 32 just come into view, along with a glimpse of the marvelous multicolored facade that extends skyward, an effect that is heightened once you arrive at the piazza. Stop in at the nearby tourist office for tickets to the Duomo's Cappella di San Brizio to marvel at the fresco cycle by Luca Signorelli. Around the corner is the Museo Archeologico, with a disappointingly sparse collection that is poorly maintained—only a must for hard-core Etruscan fans, who by now will probably have seen much better relics elsewhere. In the part of the building that juts out at the far right is the **Museo Emilio Greco** ㉝, housing a worthwhile collection of bronze sculptures and sketches by the contemporary Sicilian sculptor, who made the doors of the Duomo. The **Museo Claudio Faina** ㉞, directly across from the entrance to the Duomo, has a beautifully arranged collection of Etruscan sculpture and jewelry; it's worth the admission price just for the views of the facade of the Duomo from the second-floor hallway. Back on the Corso is the 14th-century **Torre del Moro** ㉟, with a bell at the top with the 24 symbols of the arts practiced in Orvieto. With all the activity focused around Piazza del Duomo, you're likely to find the rest of Orvieto relatively quiet, except during the *passeggiata* (evening stroll), which is particularly thick along the Corso in the evenings. Before you leave Orvieto, don't miss the chance to have a look at its impressive tufa caves.

TIMING　The main sights in town can be seen in a full day; allow plenty of time for the Duomo and the Cappella di San Brizio, although a day and a half might do better to enjoy Orvieto at a more leisurely pace and to explore the local cuisine and perhaps pop into a winery. Thursday and Saturday are market days in Piazza del Popolo.

What to See

off the beaten path

CROCEFISSO DEL TUFO – This 6th-century BC Etruscan necropolis, about 2 km (1 mi) down Viale Crispi, doesn't have the frescoes that other Etruscan tombs are famous for, and the relics that were buried within have long since been taken away (mostly to the Museo Claudio Faino). But the walk here is pleasant, and it can be interesting to see the type of site from which nearly all our knowledge of Etruscans comes. Names of the deceased are carved into the stone architraves above tomb chambers. ⊠ *1½ km (1 mi) from Piazzale Cahen, down Viale F. Crispi (SS71)* ☎ *0763/343611* ⊠ *€2* ☉ *Daily 8:30–dusk.*

㉜ **Duomo.** Orvieto's Duomo is, quite simply, stunning. The church was built Fodor'sChoice　to commemorate the Miracle at Bolsena. In 1263, a young priest who ques-
★　tioned the miracle of transubstantiation (in which the communion bread and wine become the blood and flesh of Christ) was saying mass at nearby Lago di Bolsena. His doubts were put to rest, however, when a wafer he had just blessed suddenly started to drip blood, staining the linen covering the altar. The cloth and the host were taken to the pope, who proclaimed a miracle and a year later provided for a new religious holiday—the Feast of Corpus Domini. Thirty years later, construction began on a *duomo* to celebrate the miracle and house the stained altar cloth.

It is thought that Arnolfo di Cambio (circa 1245–1302), the famous builder of the Duomo in Florence, was given the initial commission for the Duomo, but the project was soon taken over by Lorenzo Maitani (circa 1275–1330), who consolidated the structure and designed the monumental facade. Maitani also made the bas-relief panels between the doorways, which graphically tell the story of the Creation (on the left) and the Last Judgment (on the right). The lower registers, now protected by Plexiglas,

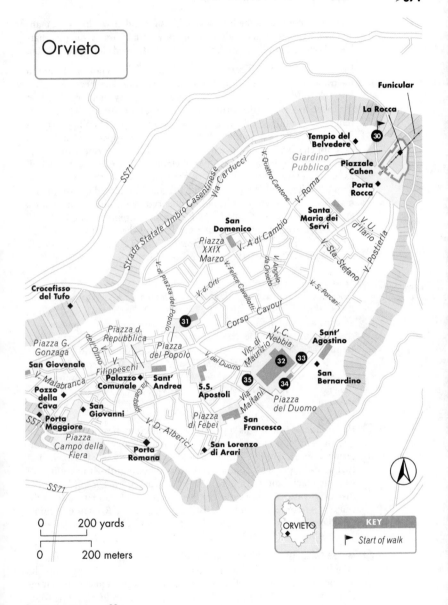

Orvieto

Funicular

La Rocca

Tempio del Belvedere ◆ 30

Giardino Pubblico **Piazzale Cahen** ◆

Porta Rocca ◆

Santa Maria dei Servi

V. Quattro Cantone

V. Carducci

V. Roma

V. U. d'Ilario

V. Posterla

San Domenico

Piazza XXIX Marzo

V. A. di Cambio

V. d. Orti

V. Angelo da Orvieto

V. Felice Cavallotti

V. Sta. Stefano

V. S. Porcari

Crocefisso del Tufo ◆

Strada Statale Umbro Casentinese

V. di Piazza del Popolo

Corso Cavour

31

Piazza d. Repubblica

Piazza G. Gonzaga

V. dell'Olmo

San Giovenale

V. Filippeschi

V. Malabranca

Pozzo della Cava ◆

San Giovanni ◆

Porta Maggiore ◆

SS71

Piazza del Popolo

V. del Duomo

Palazzo Comunale ◆

Sant' Andrea ◆

V. Garibaldi

S.S. Apostoli

35

V. Maitani

San Francesco

Piazza di Febei

V. D. Alberici

Porta Romana ◆

San Lorenzo di Arari ◆

Piazza Campo della Fiera

SS71

Vic. di Maurizio

V. C. Nebbia

32 33

Sant' Agostino

34

San Bernardino ◆

Piazza del Duomo

ORVIETO ◆

KEY	
▶	*Start of walk*

0 — 200 yards

0 — 200 meters

succeed in conveying the horror of hell as few other works of art manage to do, an effect made all the more powerful by the worn gray marble. Above, gold mosaics are framed by finely detailed Gothic decoration.

Inside, the cathedral is rather vast and empty; the major works are in the transepts. To the left is the **Cappella del Corporale,** where the square linen cloth (corporale) is kept in a golden reliquary that's modeled on the cathedral and inlaid with enamel scenes of the miracle. The cloth is removed for public viewing on Easter and on Corpus Domini (the ninth Sunday after Easter). In the right transept is the **Cappella di San Brizio,** or Cappella Nuova. In this chapel is one of Italy's greatest fresco cycles, notable for its influence on Michelangelo's *Last Judgment,* as well as for the extraordinary beauty of the figuration. In these works, the damned fall to hell, demons breathe fire and blood, and Christians are martyred. Some scenes are heavily influenced by the imagery in Dante's (1265–1321) *Divine Comedy.* ⊠ *Piazza del Duomo* ☎ *0763/342477* ⛪ *Church free, Cappella Nuova* €3 ⊙ *Nov.–Feb., daily 7:30–12:45 and 2:30–5:15; Mar. and Oct., daily 7:30–12:45 and 2:30–6:15; Apr.–Sept., daily 7:30–12:45 and 2:30–7:15.*

need a break?

Orvieto has plenty of spots to grab a quick bite—a boon in off-hours, when restaurants are closed and sightseers get peckish. **Gastronomia Carraro** (⊠ Corso Cavour 101 ☎ 0763/342870), closed Sunday, has an excellent selection of local cheeses and sausages. For a snack or coffee on tables outside, check out **Bar Sant'Andrea** (⊠ Piazza della Repubblica ☎ 0763/343285). Across the piazza is the odd-looking 12-side bell tower of the church of Sant'Andrea. Wonderful gelato in large scoops is to be had at ivy-shaded alfresco tables at **L'Archetto** (⊠ Piazza del Duomo 14 ☎ 0763/341034), closed mid-December through February.

★ ③④ **Museo Claudio Faina.** This superb private collection, beautifully arranged and presented, goes far beyond the usual museum offerings of a scattering of local remains. The collection is particularly rich in Greek- and Etruscan-era pottery, from large Attic amphorae (6th–4th century BC) to Attic black- and red-figure pieces to Etruscan *bucchero* (dark, reddish clay) vases. Other interesting pieces in the collection include a 6th-century sarcophagus and a substantial display of Roman-era coins. ⊠ *Palazzo Faina* ☎ *0763/341511* ⛪ *€4.50* ⊙ *Oct.–Mar., Tues.–Sun. 10–5; Apr.–Sept., daily 9:30–6.*

③③ **Museo Emilio Greco.** Another medieval building built by a pope on leave here from Rome, 13th-century Palazzo Soliano was for many years the location of the Museo dell'Opera del Duomo, a fine collection that includes works by Signorelli and other notable names like Simone Martini and Arnolfo di Cambio. But the art treasures have been locked away during an interminable restoration. Meanwhile, the ground floor has been made into the Museo Emilio Greco, a good-looking space filled with sculpture and sketches that the prolific Sicilian artist Emilio Greco (born 1913)—who also made the doors for the Duomo in the 1960s—donated to the city. ⊠ *Piazza del Duomo, Palazzo Soliano* ☎ *0763/*

344605 ⊠ €2.50 ⊘ Apr.–Sept., Mon.–Fri. 10:30–1 and 2–6:30, weekends 10:30–1 and 2:30–7; Oct.–Mar., daily 10:30–1 and 2–5:30.

off the
beaten
path

ORVIETO UNDERGROUND – More than just about any other town, Orvieto has grown from its own foundations—if one were to remove from present-day Orvieto all the building materials that were dug up from below, there would hardly be a building left standing. The Etruscans, the Romans, and those who followed dug into the tufa (the same soft volcanic rock from which catacombs were made), and over the centuries created more than 1,000 separate cisterns, caves, secret passages, storage areas, and production areas for wine and olive oil. Some of the tufa removed was used as building blocks for the city that exists today, and some was partly ground into *pozzolana*, which was made into mortar. The most thorough **Orvieto Underground tour** (⊠ Tourist office, Piazza del Duomo 24 ☎ 0763/341772) is run daily at 11 AM and 4 PM out of the Orvieto tourist office; admission is €5.20. The tour, which is in English, is about an hour long. If you are short on time but still want a look at what it was like down there, head for the **Pozzo della Cava** (⊠ Via della Cava 28 ☎ 0763/342373), an Etruscan well for spring water, open Wednesday through Monday 8–dusk; admission is €3.

❸ **Palazzo del Popolo.** Built in tufa and basaltic rock, this was once the town hall. Restoration work in the late 1980s revealed the remains of an Etruscan temple underneath, and it now holds the conference center and the state archives. ⊠ *Piazza del Popolo.*

▶ ❸ **Pozzo di San Patrizio** (St. Patrick's Well). When Pope Clement VII (1478–1534) took shelter in Orvieto during the Sack of Rome in 1527, he had to ensure a safe water supply should Orvieto come under siege. Many wells and cisterns were built, and the pope commissioned one of the great architects of the day, Antonio da Sangallo the Younger (1493–1546), to build the well adjacent to the Rocca. After nearly a decade of digging, water was found at a depth of 203 feet. Two one-way spiral stairways allowed donkey-driven carts to descend and return without running into one another. Windows open onto the shaft, providing natural light in the stairwells. There are 248 steps down to the bottom, but you'll probably get the idea after just a few. The well was once compared to St. Patrick's Well in Ireland. The name stuck, and the Italian "pozzo di san patrizio" has come to represent an inexhaustible source of wealth. ⊠ *Viale Sangallo, off Piazza Cahen* ☎ *0763/343768* ⊠ *€3.50* ⊘ *Oct.–Mar., daily 10–5:45; Apr.–Sept., daily 9:30–6:45.*

❸ **Torre del Moro.** It's hard to imagine a simpler, duller affair than this tower in the center of town. It took on a little more character in the 19th century, when the large, white-faced clock was added along with the fine 14th-century bell, marked with the symbols of the 24 arts and craft guilds then operating in the city. The views, however, are worth the climb. ⊠ *Corso Cavour at Via del Duomo* ☎ *0763/344567* ⊠ *€2.50* ⊘ *May–Aug., daily 10–8; Mar.–Apr. and Sept.–Oct., daily 10–7; Nov.–Feb., daily 10–1 and 2:30–5.*

Where to Stay & Eat

At this writing, the **Azienda Agricola Palazzone** (⊠ Località Rocca Ripesana, 5 km [3 mi] from Orvieto ☎ 0763/344166) winery, which makes some impressive wines, plans to make guest rooms available in its medieval manor house by summer 2005.

$–$$ ✕ **Le Grotte del Funaro.** If you can't do the official hour tour of Underground Orvieto, dine here instead inside tufa caves under central Orvieto, where the two windows have splendid views of the hilly countryside during the day. The traditional Umbrian food is average, but with good, simple grilled meats and vegetables and pizzas. Oddly, the food is outclassed by an extensive wine list with top local and Italian labels and quite a few rare vintages. ⊠ *Via Ripa Serancia 41* ☎ *0763/343276* ⊕ *www.ristoranti-orvieto.it* ✍ *Reservations essential* ▭ *AE, DC, MC, V* ☺ *Closed Mon. and 1 wk in July.*

Fodor'sChoice ✕ **Il Giglio D'Oro.** A great view of the Duomo is coupled with superb food. Eggplant is transformed into an elegant custard with black truffles in the *sformatino di melenzane con vellutata al tartuffo nero.* Pastas, like *ombrichelli al pesto umbro,* are traditional, but perhaps with a new twist like fresh coriander leaves instead of the usual basil. Lamb roasted in a crust of bread is delicately seasoned with a tomato cream sauce. The wine cellar includes some rare wines. ⊠ *Piazza Duomo, 8* ☎ *0763/341903* ▭ *AE, DC, MC, V* ☺ *Closed Wed.*

★ ✕ **Trattoria La Grotta.** The owner has been in this location for over 20 years, and locals are still fond of him. Franco has attracted a steady American clientele without losing his touch with homemade pasta, perhaps with a duck or wild boar sauce. Roast lamb, veal, or pork are all good. Desserts are homemade. Franco knows the local wines well and has a carefully selected list, including some from smaller but excellent wineries, so ask about them. ⊠ *Via Luca Signorelli, 5* ☎ *0763/341348* ▭ *AE, DC, MC,V* ☺ *Closed Tues.*

★ **$$$** ▦ **Hotel La Badia.** One of the best-known country hotels in Umbria occupies a 12th-century building that is a former monastery. Vaulted ceilings and exposed stone walls establish the rustic elegance in the guest rooms. The rolling park around the hotel provides wonderful views of the valley and the town of Orvieto in the distance. ⊠ *Località La Badia, 05018 Orvieto Scalo, 4 km (2½ mi) south of Orvieto* ☎ *0763/301959* ▦ *0763/305396* ⊕ *www.labadiahotel.it* ⇋ *21 rooms, 7 suites* ♨ *Restaurant, 2 tennis courts, pool, bar, meeting room* ▭ *AE, MC, V* ☺ *Closed Jan.–Feb.* ¶○¶ *CP.*

$ ▦ **Albergo Villa Ciconia.** Below Orvieto and well hidden in the business zone is a Renaissance villa once owned by a family with ties to Queen Cristina. In summer, cool off in the pool after a day of sightseeing; in winter, bask in the glow of the enormous stone fireplaces designed by Ippolito Scalza (1532–1618) in your own little hideaway. The restaurant food is only adequate and service could be more polished, so you'll do best if you stick to simple, traditional dishes that are reasonably priced and order a good bottle of wine. But where else will you find those fire-

places? ✉ *Via dei Tigli, 69, 05019* ☎ *0763/305582* 🖷 *0763/302077*
⊕ *www.hotelvillaciconia.com* 📠 *12 rooms* 🌢 *Restaurant (closed Mon.),*
minibars, no room TVs, pool, café, wine bar, piano, babysitting, dry clean-
ing, laundry service, free parking, some pets allowed ⊙ *Often closed*
Jan.–Feb.

¢–$ 🏨 **Grand Hotel Reale.** The best feature of this hotel is its location in the
center of Orvieto, across a square that hosts a lively market. Facing the
impressive Gothic–Romanesque Palazzo del Popolo, rooms are spacious and adequately furnished, with a traditional accent. ✉ *Piazza del*
Popolo 25, 05018 ☎ *0763/341247* 🖷 *0763/341247* 📠 *32 rooms*
🌢 *Bar* ☰ *MC, V* 🍽 *CP.*

Enoteche

Orvieto has been known for white wine since its beginnings. There is
evidence that the Etruscans grew grapes in the rich volcanic soil in the
valley below and then fermented their wine in the cool caverns dug out
of the tufa atop the hill. The Romans made special efforts to bring the
local wine, which they blended with water and spices, down to Rome.
Things had not changed by the early 16th century, when Signorelli was
paid in part with wine for his work on the Cappella di San Brizio.

Orvieto Classico is the best-known wine in the region, it is no longer
one of Italy's best. However, it is pleasantly drinkable and light. You
will also have the chance to taste different types of Orvieto, from the
well-known dry Orvieto Classico to the less-commercialized *abboccato*
(semisweet) and the intensely flavored, sweeter *muffato*.

Begin your tastings at these *enoteche* (wine bars), *cantine* (cellars or wine
shops), and *vinerie* (wineries). At **Cantina Foresi** (✉ Piazza del Duomo
2 ☎ 0763/341611), closed Tuesday November–February, hundreds of
bottles are stored in the cool earth of the cellar. The few outdoor tables
are a great place for a light snack while sipping. In addition to wine served
all day long, **L'Asino d'Oro** (✉ Vicolo del Popolo 1 ☎ 0763/344406),
closed October–March, serves lunch and dinner, with a different soup
and first course every day and plenty of cold snacks between meals. At
La Bottega del Buon Vino (✉ Via della Cava 26 ☎ 0763/342373), closed
Tuesday, a window in the floor looks down into the caves.

Many area wine producers create excellent variations of the standard
Orvieto Classico wine. Close to town and highly recommended is
Azienda Agricola Palazzone (✉ Località Rocca Ripesana, 5 km [3 mi]
from Orvieto ☎ 0763/344166), where you can sample Muffa Nobile—
a warm golden sweet wine with a rich taste caused by the fungus that
is cultivated—Grechetto, and Orvieto Classico Superior that has been
aged longer than most and has a richer taste than the mass-produced
Orvietos. This wine-maker has also won awards for his Armaleo, a rich
ruby red. **Castello della Sala** (✉ Località Sala, 20 km [12 mi] north of
Orvieto ☎ 0763/86051), owned by the Antinori group, produces white
wines of high quality. Housed in a 14th-century castle, this is an especially interesting place to try out some of Orvieto's new-style wines—
Cervaro della Sala, Grechetto, and Chardonnay—all aged in oak barrels.

Shopping

As do other towns in the region, Orvieto has its fair share of pottery re-
sellers, along with a few genuine shops selling Orvietan-style pottery,
bright-white vessels with hand-painted motifs. **La Torreta** (⊠ Corso
Cavour 283 ☎ 0763/340248) has a kiln right in the shop and will custom paint something for you on the spot. The copies of ancient ceramics that were made by **L'Arte del Vasaio** (⊠ Via Pedota 3 ☎ 0763/
342022) were good enough to fool the curators of a famous museum,
which displayed them as the real thing.

Established in 1907 to provide work for impoverished women, the tradition of lace-making, or *ars wetana,* has flourished in Orvieto. Using
designs inspired by the reliefs on the facade of the Duomo, the patterns
of Orvietan lace are unique and distinctive. Specializing in *merletto* (lace)
products, **Duranti** (⊠ Corso Cavour 107 ☎ no phone) maintains the high
standards set by one of the sustainers of the tradition during the last
century, Eleonora Duranti. The Moretti family has long been associated
with lace-making in Orvieto. Their products can be admired at **Ditta Moretti
Merletti** (⊠ Via Duomo 55 ☎ 0763/41714).

Orvieto is a center for woodworking, particularly fine inlays and ve-
neers. Corso Cavour is lined with a number of artisan woodworking
shops, the best known being the **Michelangeli family studio** (⊠ Via
Michelangeli 3, at Corso Cavour ☎ 0763/342377). The imaginatively
designed objects range in size from a giant *armadio* (wardrobe) to a simple wooden spoon. If all those Michelangeli flourishes don't quite suit
you, head over to **Patrice,** (⊠ Via Michelangeli 4 ☎ No phone) who has
a shop full of imaginative items that he has made, from crafts for children to trompe-l'oeil intarsia windows in wood.

ASSISI, SPOLETO & SOUTHERN
UMBRIA A TO Z

*To research prices, get advice from other travelers, and book travel ar-
rangements, visit* ⊕ *www.fodors.com*

AIR TRAVEL

There are no direct international flights into Perugia's Aeroporto
Sant'Egidio, the only major airport in the region, and connections to
domestic services are required if you wish to travel all the way by air to
Umbria. Flights to Perugia are operated by Alitalia from Milan's
Malpensa Airport, by Meridiana from Florence's Amerigo Vespucci
Airport at Peretola, and by Air Vallée from Rome's Leonardo da Vinci
at Fiumicino. Because only Alitalia offers a daily service, arrival through
Milan is much more convenient than through either Florence or Rome.
🖪 Carriers **Alitalia** ☎ 848/865641 ⊕ www.alitalia.it. **Meridiana** ☎ 119/111333 ⊕ www.
meridiana.it. **Air Vallée** ☎ 0165/303303 ⊕ www.airvallee.com.

AIRPORTS

The closest major airports are Rome's Fiumicino (officially Aeroporto
Leonardo da Vinci), Pisa's Galileo Galilei, and Florence's Peretola (of-

ficially Aeroporto A. Vespucci). Tiny Aeroporto Sant'Egidio, 12 km (7 mi) east of Perugia, has flights to and from Milan, Florence, and Rome.

🛪 Airport Information **Aeroporto A. Vespucci** (known as Peretola) ☎ 055/3061700. **Aeroporto Galileo Galilei** ☎ 050/500707 ⊕ www.pisa-airport.com. **Aeroporto Leonardo da Vinci** (known as Fiumicino) ☎ 06/6594420 ⊕ www.adr.it. **Aeroporto Sant'Egidio** ☎ 075/592141 ⊕ www.airport.umbria.it.

BUS TRAVEL

A number of private bus lines operate within the region and offer service to and from major cities in Tuscany and Lazio. Perugia's Sulga line runs between Rome's international airport and Perugia. The Sienese company SENA makes city connections between Tuscany, Umbria, and Lazio, and Florence, Siena, Perugia, Orvieto, and Rome. Spoletina operates buses both within the city of Spoleto and between a number of the main towns of the region, including Perugia, Assisi, Norcia, Terni, and Foligno.

🚌 Bus Lines **SENA** ⊠ Piazza Gramsci, Siena ☎ 0577/283203 ⊕ www.sena.it. **Spoletina** ⊠ SS Flaminia Km. 127.7, Spoleto ☎ 0743/212208. **Sulga** ⊠ Strada dei Cappucinelli 4/d, Perugia ☎ 075/5009641 ⊕ www.sulga.it.

CAR RENTALS

If you don't arrive in the area with a rental car from a major airport or town elsewhere in Italy, the best place to pick up a rental vehicle is probably Orvieto, accessible by train and by bus from both Florence and Rome.

🚗 Agencies **Avis** ⊠ Via XX Settembre 80/d, Terni ☎ 0744/287170 ⊕ www.avis.com. **Europcar Italia** ⊠ Lungonera Savoia 12/c, Terni ☎ 0744/282652. **Hertz** ⊕ www.hertz.com ⊠ Via 7 Martiri 32/f, Orvieto ☎ 0763/301303 ⊠ Via Cerquiglia 144, Spoleto ☎ 0743/46703.

CAR TRAVEL

The region is easily reached from the Rome–Florence autostrada (A1), which has exits at Orte, Orvieto, and Perugia. The main highways within the region run south from Perugia (E45) to Todi and Terni or southeast from Perugia to Assisi, Spello, Foligno, and Spoleto (via S75) and Terni (via S3). Orvieto lies above the Rome–Florence autostrada (A1) and is also connected to Todi by a country road (79 bis).

EMERGENCIES

In an emergency, dial **113** for paramedics, police, or the fire department.

Pharmacies take turns staying open late or on Sunday; for the latest information, consult the list posted outside each pharmacy, or ask at the local tourist office.

TOURS

Fully licensed English-speaking guides are available for groups or for individuals in many towns throughout Umbria. Full- and half-day tours may be booked with fixed rates through the regional Association of Tourist Guides.

🛈 **Associazione Guide Turistiche dell'Umbria** (Umbrian Association of Tourist Guides) ☎ 075/815228 ⊕ www.assoguide.it.

TRAIN TRAVEL

Although three train lines connect most of the towns, the stations are often a couple of miles from the towns themselves. Slow trains on the Rome–Ancona line make stops in Narni-Amelia, Terni, Spoleto, Trevi, and Foligno, while the Terontola–Foligno line connects Foligno, Spello, Assisi, and Perugia. Slow trains on the Rome–Florence line stop in Orvieto. Ferrovia dello Stato, the Italian state railway, has information about train schedules and fares, including a prebooking service.

🚂 Train Stations **Ferrovia dello Stato (FS)** ☎ 848/888088 toll-free within Italy ⊕ www.fs-on-line.it.

VISITOR INFORMATION

🚂 Tourist Information **Assisi** ✉ Piazza del Comune 12 ☎ 075/812534 ⊕ www.assisi. umbria2000.it. **Bevagna** ✉ Piazza Silvestri ☎ 0742/361667 ⊕ www.bevagna.it. **Foligno** ✉ Porta Romana 126 ☎ 0742/354459 ⊕ www.foligno.umbria2000.it. **Montefalco** ✉ Via Ringhiera Umbra ☎ 0742/379598 ⊕ www.foligno.umbria2000.it. **Narni** ✉ Piazza del Popolo 18 ☎ 0744/715362 ⊕ www.terni.umbria2000.it. **Norcia** ☎ 0743/828173. **Orvieto** ✉ Piazza del Duomo 24 ☎ 0763/341772 ⊕ www.orvieto.umbria2000.it. **Spello** ✉ Piazza Matteotti 3 ☎ 0742/301009 ⊕ www.foligno.umbria2000.it. **Spoleto** ✉ Piazza della Libertà 7 ☎ 0743/238920 ⊕ www.spoleto. umbria2000.it. **Strada del Sangrantino** ⊕ www.stradadelsagrantino.it. **Terni** ✉ Viale C. Battisti 7/a ☎ 0744/423047 ⊕ www.terni.umbria2000.it. **Todi** ✉ Piazza del Popolo 34/35 ☎ 075/8945416 ⊕ www. todi. umbria2000.it. **Trevi** ✉ Piazza Mazzini 5 ☎ 0742/781150 ⊕ www.foligno. umbria2000.it.

UNDERSTANDING FLORENCE, TUSCANY & UMBRIA

THE ARTLESS ART OF
ITALIAN COOKING

YOU ARE STAYING WITH friends in their villa in a windswept olive orchard above Florence. After a day in town—a morning at the Palazzo Pitti, afternoon in the Brancacci Chapel—you have returned to rest. In the garden, you find your hostess lifting heavy tomatoes into a basket, the acrid smell of their skins wafting up in the gentle September heat. You pick basil and tug figs from a tree that warms its back against the 14th-century kitchen wall. Inside, you watch your hostess rinse greens in the quarried stone sink. The tomatoes are still sunwarm when she scoops them, chopped, into a blender with the basil and a stream of olive oil; she pours the mixture into a faience bowl over steaming pasta. You eat at the kitchen table, pour wine from a crockery pitcher, and wipe your bowl with torn chunks of flour-flecked bread. Over the greens your hostess drizzles more olive oil and a bit of rock salt pinched from an open bowl. The figs melt in your mouth like chocolate. A scalding syrup of Arabic coffee streams from the *macchinetta*, and you're ready for a midnight survey of the olive groves.

Simple, earthy, at once wholesome and sensual, as sophisticated in its purity as the most complex cuisine, as inspired in its aesthetics as the art and architecture of its culture, Italian cooking strikes a chord that resonates today as it did in the Medici courts. Its enduring appeal can be traced to an ancient principle: respect for the essence of the thing itself—nothing more, nothing less. Like Michelangelo freeing the prisoners that dwelt within the stone—innate, organic—an Italian chef seems intuitively to seek out the crux of the thing he is about to cook and flatter it, subtly, with the purest of complements. To lay a translucent sheet of prosciutto—earthy, gamey, faintly redolent of brine—across the juicy pulchritude of a melon wedge is a stroke of insight into the nature of two ingredients as profound as the imaginings of Galileo.

Considering the pizzas, lasagnas, and red-drenched spaghetti that still pass for Italian food in many places abroad, it's no surprise that visitors to Italy are often struck by the austerity of the true Italian dishes put before them. The pasta is only lightly accented, not drowning in an industrial ladle-full of strong, soupy sauce. And while there may have been a parade of vegetable *antipasti,* the salad itself bears no resemblance to the smorgasbord of Anglo-American salad bars—it's a simple mix of greens, a drizzle of oil, a spritz, perhaps, of red-wine vinegar. If you've just come from Germanic countries, you'll notice a lack of Maggi, the bottled brown "flavor enhancer" that singes the tongue with monosodium glutamate, on the table. If you've come from Belgium, you'll miss the sauceboat of Hollandaise. And if you've come from France, you may shrug dismissively at the isolated ingredients you're served, saying as other Frenchmen before you, "But this is not really a true *cuisine. . . .*"

* * *

H, BUT IT IS. Shunning the complexities of heavy French sauces and avoiding the elaborate farce, Italian cuisine—having unloaded the aspirations of *alta cucina* onto its northern neighbors when Catherine de' Medici moved (chefs and all) to Paris—stands alone, proud, puristic, unaffected.

The Italians' pride comes in part from a confidence in their raw ingredients, an earthiness that informs the appreciation of every citizen-connoisseur, from the roughest peasant in workers' blue to the vintner in shoulder-tied cashmere: they are in touch with land and sea. In the country, your host can tell you the source of every ingredient on the table, from the neighbor's potted goose to the porcini gathered in the beech grove yesterday. In the city, the market replaces the country network, and aggressive shopping will trace the genealogy of every mushroom, every artichoke, every wooden scoop of olives. And in balconies overhanging the seashore, the squid floating in their rich, blue-black ink were bought from a fisherman on the beach at dawn.

Careening in your rental car down the western coast, clinging to the waterfront through sea-shanty villages that cantilever over the roaring surf, you feel a morning lag: your breakfast of *latte macchiato* and sugary *cornetto* has worn away. A real espresso would hit the spot; you hurtle down a web of switchbacks and pull into a seaside inn. You sip aromatic coffee and watch the waves. An hour passes in reverie—an aperitif, perhaps? Another hour over the Martini rosso, and you give in to the impulse, adjourning to the dining room. The odor of wood smoke drifts from the kitchen. A nutty risotto with a blush of tomato precedes a vast platter—austere, unembellished—of smoke-grilled fish, still sizzling, lightly brushed with oil, and glittering with rock salt. At the table beside yours, when the platter arrives, the woman rises and fillets the fish dexterously, serving her husband and sons.

* * *

THERE'S A WHOLESOMENESS in the way Italians eat that is charming and contagious. If American foodies pick and kvetch and French gastronomes worship, Italians plunge into their meal with frank joy, earnest appreciation, and ebullient conversation. Yet they do not overindulge: portions are light, the drinking gentle, late suppers spartan with concern for digestion uppermost. It's as if the voice of Mamma still whispers moderation in their ear. They may, on the other hand, take disproportionate pleasure in watching guests eat, in surrounding them with congenial company, in pouncing on the bill. (This wholesome spirit even carries into the very bars: unlike the dark, louche atmosphere of Anglo lounges and pubs, in Italy you'll drink your *amaro* in a fluorescent-lit coffee bar without a whiff of sin in the air.)

Yet for all their straightforwardness, Italians are utterly at ease with their heritage, steeped from birth in the art and architecture that surrounds them. Without a hint of the grandiose, they'll construct a still life of figs and Bosc pears worthy of Caravaggio; a butcher will drape iridescent pheasants and quail, heads dangling, with the panache of a couturier. Consider the artless beauty of ruby-raw beef on an emerald bed of arugula, named for the preferred colors of the Venetian painter Carpaccio; pure white porcelain on damask; a mosaic of olives and pimientos in blown glass; a flash of folkloric pottery on a polished plank of oak.

In fact, it must be said: a large part of the pleasure of Italian dining is dining in Italy. We have all eaten in Italian restaurants elsewhere. The food can be superb, the ingredients authentic, the pottery handmade and linens imported. Yet who can conjure the blood-red ocher crumbling to gold on a Roman wall, the indigo and pastel hues of fishing boats rocking in a marina, the snow flurry of sugar papers on a café floor? These impart the essence that—as much as the basil on your *bruschetta*—flavors your Italian dining experience.

Inside the great walls of Lucca, you are lunching—slowly, copiously, and at length—in the shade of a vaulted portico. Strips of roasted eggplant and pepper steeped in garlic and oil; tortelloni stuffed with squab in a pool of butter and sage; roasted veal laced with green peppercorns; blackberries in thick cream. The bottle of Brunello di Montalcino, alas, is drained. It has been a perfect morning, walking the ramparts, and you have found the perfect restaurant: a Raphaelesque perspective of arcades and archways, pillars, porches, and loges spreads before you. The shadows and lines are strong in the afternoon sun; you admire from your seat in the cross breeze. It's only slowly that you realize that this Merchant Ivory moment has a sound track, so organic to the scene you hadn't noticed—but now you feel goose bumps rising on your neck. It is Puccini: a young woman is singing, beautifully, from a groined arcade across the square, accompanied by a portable tape player.

". . . Ma quando vien lo sgelo . . . il primo sole è mio . . ."

("But when the thaw comes, the first warmth of the sun is mine.")

Your coffee goes cold, untouched until the song, the moment, is over—and, in all its multifaceted magnificence, your Italian meal comes to a close as well.

— Nancy Coons

PORTRAIT OF
TUSCANY & UMBRIA

JUST AS TUSCANY AND UMBRIA straddle the boot, so is their contribution to the Italian jigsaw massive and inescapable. Their influence pervades Italian culture and percolates far beyond, to the extent that their impact has been felt throughout European and even world history. Tuscany—and to a lesser extent Umbria—saw the birth of humanism, that classically leaning, secular-tending current that blossomed in the Renaissance and to which the West owes its cultural complexion. In the graphic arts, architecture, astronomy, sculpture, engineering, art history, poetry, political theory, biography—in every field of human endeavor—the achievements of the people of these regions have loomed large. The Italian language itself is Tuscan, owing largely to Dante's use of his local dialect to compose his *Divine Comedy*. When Italy became a modern state in 1865, Florence was the natural choice for the national capital until Rome's entry six years later.

Although it's hard to think of any other area that has seen such a dense concentration of human achievement as Tuscany and Umbria, it's equally difficult to find anywhere so riven by conflict and factions. The strange thing is how neatly the periods of maximum creativity and bellicosity coincided. Was the restless, innovative impulse a consequence of the social turmoil, or the principal cause of it? It is surely no accident that Tuscany and Umbria in general and Florence in particular contain the most quarrelsome elements ever thrown together, as a cursory flip through some of the names in the local annals can testify: for example, the Florentine Niccolò Machiavelli, who became a very synonym for the Devil (Old Nick); and Savonarola, whose energetic career pitched church and state into headlong confrontation, igniting the famous "bonfire of the vanities" in Florence's main square,

site of the Dominican friar's own incineration not long afterward. Perugia was populated, according to the historian Sigismondo, by "the most warlike people in Italy, who always preferred Mars to the Muse"; and the very street names of Florence and Siena recall the clash of medieval factions. Outside the towns there is hardly a hill, stream, or mountain pass whose name doesn't evoke some siege, battle, or act of treachery. The historic rivalry of Guelph and Ghibelline never reached such intense acrimony as in these seemingly tranquil hills, and nowhere was allegiance worn so lightly, with communes and families swapping sides whenever their rivals changed theirs.

The sense of opposition is alive in Tuscany and Umbria today. You can witness it on every two-toned marble church front. Feudal and commercial, Renaissance and Gothic—the antagonism is embedded in art history, revived in every discussion of the background of every great work. It is a fixed feature of the local scene: the Sienese are still suspicious of the Florentines, the Florentines disdainful of the Sienese, while Siena itself seems to live in a permanent state of warfare within its own city walls, as any spectator of the Palio and the months of preparation that precede it can testify. Outsiders contribute to the debate: for Mary McCarthy, Florence was manly, Siena feminine, and visitors take sides whenever they lay down their reasons for preferring Florence to Siena or vice versa.

Walking through the city streets of present-day Florence, you can't fail to be struck by the contrast between the austere and unwelcoming external appearance of the palaces and the sumptuous comforts within, or by the 21st-century elegance and modernity of the Florentines in the midst of thoroughly medieval churches and piazzas. Florence is a modern industrial city, and the Florentines themselves perennial modernists, their eyes fixed firmly in front. This helps to explain both their past inventiveness and the ambivalent attitude they hold toward that same past, composed of roughly equal parts ennui and fierce pride. To its inhabitants, that the city of Florence stands on a par with Athens and Rome is self-evident: to them tourism, which feeds on the past, is reactionary, decadent, and often intrusive, making a burden of the historical heritage. It is tolerated as a business, in a city that has a high regard for business—but it is only one of many. In Italy, Florentines are reckoned the most impenetrable, cautious, and circumspect of Italians, a reputation they have held since the days of the Medici. Nevertheless, Italians have coined a word—*fiorentinità*—to refer to the good taste and fine workmanship that are flaunted here, in a city renowned for its leather goods, handbags, shoes, jewelry, and a host of famous brand names. Pucci, Gucci, Ferragamo, and Cellerini are just four of the high-profile craft-turned-fashion designers that exude fiorentinità. Neither are the region's cuisine and fine wines to be taken lightly. Talk to any Florentines about these present-day aspects of their civilization, and they will perk up and debate enthusiastically; mention their past glories and they will stifle a yawn.

* * *

OTHER TUSCAN CITIES possess the same compelling mix of elements: what Tuscany's older centers share is an immaculate medieval setting, modern life taking place within the shell of the past; what divides them is a complex mental set. Needless to say, they all were rivals at one time or another, and each prevailed in distinct spheres. Pisa, for example, was one of Italy's four great maritime republics, its architectural style visible wherever its ships touched port. Once the most powerful force in the Tyrrhenian, it lost its hegemony on the sea to its trading rival, Genoa, and its dominance on land to Florence. Pisa

owed its prestige to a university that bequeathed a scholarly, scientific, and legal tradition to the town, and to its location on the River Arno, though this position much later was responsible for its being one of the most devastated cities in World War II. Skillful rebuilding has ensured a relatively harmonious appearance, however, and the city would still hold plenty of interest if the Torre Pendente (Leaning Tower) had never been built.

Livorno, on the other hand, the main Tuscan port of today, is the Pisa that never was. By Tuscan standards it is a recent affair, developed as a sea outlet for Florence after Pisa's port had silted up. Livorno reveals a highly un-Tuscan cosmopolitan character, a result of 16th-century growth that brought immigration. Livorno's most famous son, the sculptor Amedeo Modigliani, for example, was brought up speaking French, Italian, English, and Hebrew, though in other ways this hard-drinking Bohemian didn't typify the soberly respectable citizens for whom Livorno is best known. Also heavily bombed in the war, the port wasn't restored as tastefully as Pisa, though it can at least boast a vigorous culinary tradition, with its range of fresh seafood.

South from Livorno stretches a riviera of varying degrees of summer saturation, including numerous select spots where sun- and sea-bathing can be enjoyed in relative peace. The island of Elba—scene of Napoléon's nine-month incarceration—is today more likely to be somewhere to escape *to* rather than *from,* and together with the islands of Giglio and Capraia, it offers everything from absurd overdevelopment to true isolation.

Lucca, the principal enemy of Pisa during the Middle Ages, has been called "the most enchanting walled town in the world." The city's formidable girdle of walls has resisted the intrusions of modern life better than any other Tuscan center and contains within a wealth of palaces and churches wildly out of proportion to the size of what is, after all, a small provincial town. Much of Lucca's present-day success is based on, of all things, the manufacture of lingerie.

A much weightier substance—gold—forms, together with antique furniture, the basis of the wealth of the less imposing town of Arezzo. Such worldly items again form a counterpoint to the fact that this town has produced more than its fair share of pioneers in literature (Petrarch, Pietro Aretino), art (Vasari), and music (Guido d'Arezzo, also called Guido Monaco, inventor of notation and the musical scale).

Arezzo shares a university with Siena, another Tuscan town preserved in the aspic of its medieval past. It is said that there are three subjects you should avoid if you're in a hurry while in Siena: wild pigs (a prized quarry for hunters), the Palio (an object of fanatical zeal), and the battle of Montanerti (Siena's moment of military glory—a perennial obsession). To the rest of Italy, Siena is best known for its banks and its mystics—a characteristically incompatible duo—while its foreign visitors are more enchanted by the city's artworks, its easy pace of life, and the pleasing hue of its rose-colored buildings.

Prato and Pistoia, a short roll up the autostrada from Florence, have traditionally fallen within the sphere of that city's influence. Prato combines some choice examples of Renaissance art and architecture with a strong industrial identity, mainly based on its wool exports; Pistoia, on the other hand, was renowned for its ironwork, and its citizens for their murderous propensities.

* * *

ACROSS THE REGIONAL boundary in Umbria, the hilltop town of Perugia is dominated by the cold Gothic stone of its major monuments, its secretive alleys and steps, yet its animating spirit is among the most progressive and trend-setting in Italy. Within its medieval walls the town hosts one of Europe's prime jazz festivals, a modern tradition that has taken its lead from the international Festival dei Due Mondi (Festival of Two Worlds) at nearby Spoleto. As in Tuscany, modernity lives alongside medievalism in Umbria, a case not so much of collision as coexistence. In the same spirit, the imposing monuments of its towns were built by a new wealthy mercantile class in the teeth of almost uninterrupted warfare throughout the Middle Ages. Spoleto, Gubbio, and Orvieto owed their influence not so much to their continual brawling as to their interchange of goods and ideas. A university was founded in Perugia as early as 1308, and it was the small Umbrian town of Foligno that published the first edition of Dante's *Divine Comedy*. The belligerence of the age paralleled an intense spiritual activity, championed by such towering religious figures as St. Francis, St. Clare, St. Benedict, and the locally venerated St. Rita (as well as the more worldly St. Valentine)—a legacy nowhere so apparent as in the town of Assisi.

Although many of the urban centers of Tuscany and Umbria have cleanly defined boundaries beyond which the countryside abruptly begins, the towns harmonize with the surrounding landscape more closely than anywhere else in Italy. Even if devoid of museums or souvenir shops, the hinterland holds as much of the region's quintessential character as the cities of Tuscany and Umbria, and such unsung treasures as Todi and Bevagna are as revealing as anything seen in the galleries. This is your chance to immerse yourself in the region's less tangible pleasures, to rest your eyes on the gentle ocher stone of villages artfully situated above vine-strung, neatly terraced slopes. From the wine-producing hills of Chianti to the Carrara mountains where Michelangelo quarried to the soft contours of the Vale di Spoleto, the tidy cypress-speared landscape displays a weird inertia like some illustration from a fable. It has a geometric precision that underlines the strict rural economy practiced by the Tuscan and Umbrian peasants, for whom every tree has its purpose. The Tuscans in particular have long been considered the most skilled and intelligent of Italian farmers, having created for themselves a region that is largely self-sufficient, producing a little of everything, and excelling in certain areas, not least in wine production, for which the Tuscans have nurtured one of the most dynamic wine regions of Italy.

Like the great examples of urban architecture, the country in Tuscany and Umbria presents, for the most part, an ordered, rational, controlled appearance. It is the crust of civilization concealing the greatest paradox of all in this heartland of reason and classical elegance. For buried underneath lies a much older, earthier civilization of which most visitors to the region are oblivious. In every respect the ancient Etruscan civilization that flourished here was opposed to the values of the Renaissance, its vital, animistic spirit murky, dark, and mysterious to us, mainly known from subterranean tombs and wall paintings. Almost erased from the face of the earth by the Romans, the Etruscan culture—its centers scattered throughout Tuscany and Umbria (Perugia, Orvieto, Chiusi, Roselle, Vetulonia, Volterra, Cortona, Arezzo, and Fiesole were the main ones)—was central to the history of Tuscany and Umbria. Like the Hermes Trimegistus incongruously placed on the marble pavement of Siena's cathedral, the Etruscans are a mischievous element amid the harmony of Renaissance Tuscany and Umbria. Their precise influence is unclear, but it may well turn out to have been the contentious and destructive spirit ever-present in the golden age of these regions, harassing, hindering, entangling. Alternatively, it may have been the restless worm of invention, the defiant individuality that brought about the triumph of art in the face of adversity—which is, after all, the greatest achievement of Tuscany and Umbria.

— Robert Andrews

ARTISTICALLY SPEAKING: A GLOSSARY

You can increase your enjoyment of Italy's artistic treasures by knowing a few art and architecture terms.

Apse: A semicircular terminus found behind the altar in a church.

Atrium: The courtyard in front of the entrance to an ancient Roman villa or an early church.

Badia: Abbey.

Baldacchino: A canopy—often made of stone—above a church altar, supported by columns.

Baptistery: A separate structure or area in a church where rites of baptism are held.

Baroque: A 17th-century European art movement in which dramatic, elaborate ornamentation was used to stir viewers' emotions. The most famous Italian baroque artists were Carracci and Bernini.

Basilica: A rectangular Roman public building divided into aisles by rows of columns. Many early churches were built on the basilican plan, but the term is also applied to some churches without specific reference to architecture.

Belvedere: A lookout point; the word means "beautiful view."

Campanile: A bell tower of a church.

Capital: The crowning section of a column, usually decorated with Doric, Ionic, or Corinthian ornament.

Chiaroscuro: Literally "light/dark"; used to describe the distribution of light and shade in a painting, either with a marked contrast or a muted tonal gradation.

Cinquecento: Literally, "five hundred," used in Italian to refer to the 16th century.

Cortile: Courtyard.

Cupola: Dome.

Duomo: Cathedral.

Fresco: A wall-painting technique, used in Roman times and again in the early Renaissance, in which pigment was applied to wet plaster.

Gothic: Medieval architectural and ornamental style featuring pointed arches, high interior vaulting, and flying buttresses to emphasize height and, symbolically, an ascent to heaven.

Grotesques: Decorations of fanciful human and animal forms, embellished with flowers; first used in Nero's Golden House and rediscovered during the Renaissance.

Loggia: Roofed balcony or gallery.

Maestà: The Virgin and Child enthroned in majesty, often surrounded by angels, saints, or prophets.

Mannerism: Style of the mid-16th century in which artists—such as Pontormo and Rosso Fiorentino—sought to replace the warm, humanizing ideals of Leonardo and Raphael with superelegant, emotionally cold forms. Portraits in the mannerist style feature lively colors and often strangely contorted bodies.

Nave: The central aisle of a church.

Palazzo: A palace or, more generally, any large building.

Perspective: The illusion of three-dimensional space that was achieved in the early 15th century with the discovery that all parallel lines running in one direction appear to meet at a single point on the horizon known as the vanishing point.

Piano nobile: The main floor of a palace (the first floor above ground level).

Pietà: Literally "piety"; refers to an image of the Virgin Mary holding the crucified body of Christ on her lap.

Predella: A series of small paintings found below the main section of an altarpiece.

Putti: Cherubs, cupids, or other images of infant boys in painting.

Quattrocento: Literally "four hundred"; refers to the 15th century.

Renaissance: Major school of Italian art, literature, and philosophy (14th century–16th century) that fused innovations in realism with the rediscovery of the great heritage of classical antiquity. After Giotto introduced a new naturalism into painting in the early 14th century, Florentine artists of the early and mid-15th century such as Masaccio and Fra Filippo Lippi paved the way for the later 15th-century realism of Botticelli and Ghirlandaio. The movement particularly flourished in Florence and Venice, but most other Italian cities were participants as well. Some scholars believe that the movement cul-minated in Rome with the High Renaissance (circa 1490–1520) and the masterpieces of Leonardo, Raphael, and Michelangelo.

Rococo: Light, dainty 18th-century art and architectural style created in reaction to baroque. Tiepolo was the leading painter of the style.

Romanesque: Architectural style of the 11th and 12th centuries that reworked ancient Roman forms, particularly barrel and groin vaults. Stark, severe, and magisterial, Romanesque basilicas are among Italy's most awe-inspiring churches.

Triptych: A three-panel painting executed on wood.

Trompe l'oeil: An artistic technique employed to "fool the eye" into believing that the object or scene depicted is actually real.

BOOKS AND MOVIES

Books

The musings of some well-known travelers who visited Tuscany and Umbria when travel was as much ordeal as vacation make for entertaining reading. Many keen observations in Henry James's *Italian Hours* (offered in many editions, including *Traveling in Italy with Henry James: Essays*) and D. H. Lawrence's *Etruscan Places* still hold true, and their experiences put modern travel into an interesting perspective.

For background, *The Italians*, by Luigi Barzini, is a comprehensive, lively analysis of the Italian national character, still worthy reading although published in 1964. More recent reflections on Italian life include *Italian Days*, by Barbara Grizzuti Harrison, and *That Fine Italian Hand*, by Paul Hofmann, for many years *New York Times* bureau chief in Rome. For a general historical and art-history framework, begin with Harry Hearder's *Italy, a Short History*, which covers 2,000 years in fewer than 300 pages, and Michael Levey's clear and concise treatments of the Renaissance, *Early Renaissance* and *High Renaissance*. The history of the Renaissance—the great artists and political figures and turbulent power struggles throughout the region—make great reading when told by Christopher Hibbert, in *The House of Medici: Its Rise and Fall*. Two wonderfully written and beautifully illustrated volumes on that most vaunted of artistic periods are John T. Paoletti and Gary M. Radke's *Art in Renaissance Italy* and Evelyn Welch's eloquent *Art and Society in Italy 1350–1500*. *The Civilization of the Renaissance in Italy*, by 19th-century Swiss historian Jacob Burckhardt, is the classic study of the culture and politics of the time.

You can learn about the Renaissance from those who actually lived it in *The Autobiography of Benvenuto Cellini*, Giorgio Vasari's *Lives of the Artists*, and Machiavelli's *The Prince*. Some more recent studies of famous Renaissance and baroque figures offer fine opportunities to enter into lives lived centuries ago. Ross King's highly anecdotal *Brunelleschi's Dome* tells in detail about the making of Florence's fabled cupola. R. W. B. Lewis fleshes out the details of perhaps Italy's most famous poet in *Dante*; also worth a look in the Penguin Lives series is Sherwin Nuland's *Leonardo da Vinci*. A more scholarly, but eminently readable, biography is *Leon Battista Alberti: Master Builder of the Italian Renaissance*, by Princeton Renaissance historian Anthony Grafton. Although the title is somewhat of a misnomer (as it's more about father than daughter), Dava Sobel's *Galileo's Daughter* artfully brings to life the brilliant astronomer and his devotion to his family, particularly his firstborn, Suor Maria Celeste.

Novels and historical fiction often impart a greater sense of a place than straight history books: George Eliot reconstructs 15th-century Florentine life in *Romola*; Irving Stone's best-selling *The Agony and the Ecstasy* romanticizes the life of Michelangelo but paints an enduring picture of Renaissance Florence; Umberto Eco's *The Name of the Rose* is a gripping murder mystery that will leave you with tremendous insight into monastic life in Italy. Lovers of detective stories are likely to be highly entertained by the antics of Aurelio Zen, Michael Dibdin's bumbling detective. It's best to read them in order, as he builds on characters and situations; each novel is set in an Italian city. The series commences in Perugia with *Ratking*. Florence is the setting for two of Magdalen Nabb's entertaining thrillers: *Death in Autumn* and *Death of a Dutchman*.

Some English-speaking visitors have chosen to settle in Italy long-term, and the resulting expatriate memoirs make up their own literary subgenre. In *A Tuscan*

Childhood, Kinta Beevor lovingly recounts growing up in a castle near Carrara between the two world wars. Those with a yen to buy a dilapidated farmhouse and restore it can check out the experience of Frances Mayes in *Under the Tuscan Sun: At Home in Italy* (as well as in *Bella Tuscany* and *In Tuscany*). Matthew Spender's *Within Tuscany: Reflections on a Time and Place* and Lisa St. Aubin de Terán's *A Valley in Italy: The Many Seasons of a Villa in Umbria* are both rewarding reads. Tim Parks's *Italian Neighbors* tells with candor and good humor of the contemporary expatriate life in Verona.

If you truly want to understand the Italian psyche, learn about the national passion for *calcio* (soccer). Tim Parks made his own soccer odyssey with the Verona club and recorded his experiences in *A Season with Verona*.

For glimpses of the Tuscan landscape, pick up Harold Acton's *Great Houses of Tuscany: The Tuscan Villas* or Carey More's *Views from a Tuscan Vineyard*. The glories of historic Italian gardens are caught in the ravishing photographs of Judith Chatfield's *Gardens of the Italian Lakes* and Ethne Clark's *Gardens of Tuscany*.

Although every year there are more and more cookbooks on Italian food, Waverley Root's *Food of Italy,* published in 1977, is still a handy (if not infallible) reference. Faith Heller Wilinger's *Eating in Italy* helps to guide you to the good food and restaurants, and Burton Anderson's *Best Italian Wines* helps guide you through wine lists.

Movies

You'll recognize the idyllic scenery of central Italy in numerous English-language films, including *Under the Tuscan Sun* (2003), the Academy Award–winning *The English Patient* (1996), Kenneth Branagh's *Much Ado About Nothing* (1993), and Bernardo Bertolucci's *Stealing Beauty* (1996). Indispensable and not at all dated are Merchant/Ivory's *A Room with a View* (1986) and *Enchanted April* (1991), which depicts the awakening spirits of four English women who have rented a villa in Tuscany. The scenes of Florence are a good reason to see *Up at the Villa* (2000), a slow-moving story about a young English widow in Italy at the start of World War II. *Tea with Mussolini* (1999) is Franco Zeffirelli's love letter to a group of Anglophone women who helped raise a character very much like the director himself in pre–World War II Tuscany.

CHRONOLOGY

ca. 1000 BC Etruscans arrive in central Italy.

ca. 800 BC Rise of Etruscan city-states.

510 BC Foundation of the Roman republic; expulsion of Etruscans from Roman territory.

ca. 350 BC Rome extends rule to Tuscia (Tuscany), the land of the Etruscans.

ca. 220 BC Umbria, the land of the Umbri and later Etruscans, comes under Roman sway.

133 BC Rome rules entire Mediterranean Basin except Egypt.

49 BC Julius Caesar conquers Gaul.

46 BC Julian calendar is introduced; it remains in use until AD 1582.

44 BC Julius Caesar is assassinated.

27 BC Rome's imperial age begins; Octavian (now named Augustus) becomes the first emperor and is later deified. The Augustan Age is celebrated in the works of Virgil (70 BC–AD 19), Ovid (43 BC–AD 17), Livy (59 BC–AD 17), and Horace (65–8 BC).

14 AD Augustus dies.

65 Emperor Nero begins the persecution of Christians in the empire; Sts. Peter and Paul are executed.

117 The Roman Empire reaches its apogee.

165 A smallpox epidemic ravages the Empire.

ca. 150–200 Christianity gains a foothold within the Empire, with the theological writings of Clement, Tertullian, and Origen.

212 Roman citizenship is conferred on all nonslaves in the Empire.

238 The first wave of Germanic invasions penetrates Italy.

293 Diocletian reorganizes the Empire into West and East.

313 The Edict of Milan grants toleration of Christianity within the Empire.

410 Rome is sacked by Visigoths.

476 The last Roman Emperor, Romulus Augustus, is deposed. The Empire of Rome falls.

552 Eastern Emperor Justinian (527–565) recovers control of Italy.

570 Lombards gain control of much of Italy, including Rome.

590 Papal power expands under Gregory the Great.

ca. 600–750 Lucca is chief city of Tuscany.

774 Frankish ruler Charlemagne (742–814) invades Italy under papal authority and is crowned Holy Roman Emperor by Pope Leo III (800).

ca. 800–900	The breakup of Charlemagne's (Carolingian) realm leads to the rise of Italian city-states.
1077	Pope Gregory VII leads the Holy See into conflict with the Germanic Holy Roman Empire.
1152–90	Frederick I (Barbarossa) is crowned Holy Roman Emperor (1155); punitive expeditions by his forces (Ghibellines) are countered by the Guelphs, creators of the powerful Papal States in central Italy. Guelph-Ghibelline conflict becomes a feature of medieval life.
ca. 1200	Lucca appears strongest of Tuscan cities. Religious revival in Umbria centers on activities of St. Francis of Assisi and the foundation of the Franciscan order. Umbria takes the lead in art and architecture, attracting Pisano, Cimabue, Giotto, Simone Martini, and Lorenzetti.
1250	Florence takes the cultural and financial lead.
1262	Florentine bankers issue Europe's first bills of exchange.
1264	Charles I of Anjou invades Italy, intervening in the continuing Guelph-Ghibelline conflict.
1290–1375	Tuscan literary giants Dante Alighieri (1265–1321), Francesco Petrarch (1304–74), and Giovanni Boccaccio (1313–75) give written imprimatur to modern Italian language.
1309	The pope moves to Avignon in France, under the protection of French kings.
1376	The pope returns to Rome, but rival Avignonese popes stand in opposition, creating the Great Schism until 1417.
ca. 1380–1420	Umbrian cities ruled by *condottieri*.
1402	The last German intervention into Italy is repulsed by the Lombards.
1443	Brunelleschi's (1377–1446) cupola is completed on Florence's Duomo.
1469–92	Lorenzo "Il Magnifico" (1449–92), the Medici patron of the arts, rules in Florence.
1498	Girolamo Savonarola (1452–98), the austere Dominican friar, is executed for heresy after leading Florence into a drive for moral purification, typified by his burning of books and decorations in the "bonfire of vanities."
1504	Michelangelo's (1475–1564) *David* is unveiled in Florence's Piazza della Signoria.
1513	Machiavelli's (1469–1527) *The Prince* is published.
1521	The Pope excommunicates Martin Luther (1483–1546) of Germany, precipitating the Protestant Reformation.
1540	Pope Paul III consolidates rule of Umbria with other Papal States.
1545–63	The Council of Trent formulates the Catholic response to the Reformation.

ca. 1700 Opera develops as an art form in Italy.

1720–90 The Great Age of the Grand Tour: Northern Europeans visit Italy and start the vogue for classical studies. Among the famous visitors are Edward Gibbon (1758), Jacques-Louis David (1775), and Johann Wolfgang von Goethe (1786).

1796 Napoléon begins his Italian campaigns, annexing Rome and imprisoning Pope Pius VI four years later.

1801 Tuscany is made the Kingdom of Etruria within French domain.

1807–09 Tuscany is a French *département*; Umbria is annexed (1808) to French empire as département of Trasimeno.

1815 Austria controls much of Italy after Napoléon's downfall.

1848 Revolutionary troops under Risorgimento (Unification) leaders Giuseppe Mazzini (1805–72) and Giuseppe Garibaldi (1807–82) establish a republic in Rome.

1849 French troops crush rebellion and restore Pope Pius IX.

1860 Garibaldi and his "Thousand" defeat the Bourbon rulers in Sicily and Naples.

1861 Tuscany and Umbria join the Kingdom of Sardinia, which becomes the Kingdom of Italy.

1870 Rome is finally captured by Risorgimento troops and is declared capital of Italy by King Vittorio Emanuele II.

1900 King Umberto I is assassinated by an anarchist; he is succeeded by King Vittorio Emanuele III.

1915 Italy enters World War I on the side of the Allies.

1922 Fascist "black shirts" under Benito Mussolini (1883–1945) march on Rome; Mussolini becomes prime minister and later "Il Duce" (head of Italy).

1929 The Lateran Treaty: Mussolini recognizes Vatican City as a sovereign state, and the Church recognizes Rome as the capital of Italy.

1940–44 In World War II, Italy fights with the Axis powers until its capitulation (1943), when Mussolini flees Rome. Italian partisans and Allied troops from the landings at Anzio (January 1944) win victory at Cassino (March 1944) and force the eventual withdrawal of German troops from Italy.

1957 The Treaty of Rome is signed, and Italy becomes a founding member of the European Economic Community.

1966 November flood damages many of Florence's artistic treasures.

1968–79 The growth of left-wing activities leads to the formation of the Red Brigades and provokes right-wing reactions. Bombings and kidnapings culminate in the abduction and murder of Prime Minister Aldo Moro (1916–78).

1992 The Christian Democrat Party, in power throughout the postwar period, loses its hold on a relative majority in Parliament.

1993 Italians vote for sweeping reforms after the Tangentopoli (Bribe City) scandal exposes widespread political corruption, including politicians' collusion with organized crime. A bomb outside the Galleria degli Uffizi in Florence kills five but spares the museum's most precious artwork; authorities blame the Cosa Nostra, flexing its muscles in the face of a crackdown.

1994 A center-right coalition wins in spring elections, and media magnate Silvio Berlusconi becomes premier—only to be deposed within a year. Italian politics seem to be evolving into the equivalent of a two-party system.

1995 Newly appointed Lamberto Dini takes hold of the government's rudder and, as president of the Council of Ministers, institutes major reforms and replaces old-line politicians.

1996 A league of center-left parties wins national elections and puts together a government coalition in which the Democratic Party of the Left (PDS), the former Communist party, comes into power for the first time in Italy.

1997 Political stability and an austerity program put Italy on track toward the European Monetary Union and adoption of the single European currency. A series of earthquakes hits the mountainous interior of central Italy, severely damaging villages and some historic towns. In Assisi, portions of the vault of the Basilica di San Francesco crumble, destroying frescoes by Cimabue.

1998 Romano Prodi's center-left government, widely praised for its economic policies and lack of scandals, is brought down by a no-confidence vote in October, when the Reformed-Communist Party (PCI) withdraws its support for Prodi. The center-left regroups and forms a new government under Massimo D'Alema, leader of the former Communist Party, who in large part continues Prodi's policies.

1999 Rome continues preparations for the Giubileo (Holy Year) celebrations in 2000 with an array of public-works projects.

2000 The Jubilee of the third millennium is proclaimed by Pope John Paul II. Millions of pilgrims flock to religious sites throughout the country.

2001 Media mogul Silvio Berlusconi is elected prime minister for the second time.

2002 The lira is supplanted by the euro as the currency of the land.

VOCABULARY

English	Italian	Pronunciation

Basics

English	Italian	Pronunciation
Yes/no	Sí/No	see/no
Please	Per favore	pear fa-**vo**-ray
Yes, please	Sí grazie	see **grah**-tsee-ay
Thank you	Grazie	**grah**-tsee-ay
You're welcome	Prego	**pray**-go
Excuse me, sorry	Scusi	**skoo**-zee
Sorry!	Mi dispiace!	mee dis-spee-**ah**-chay
Good morning/ afternoon	Buongiorno	bwohn-**jor**-no
Good evening	Buona sera	**bwoh**-na **say**-ra
Good bye	Arrivederci	a-ree-vah-**dare**-chee
Mr. (Sir)	Signore	see-**nyo**-ray
Mrs. (Ma'am)	Signora	see-**nyo**-ra
Miss	Signorina	see-nyo-**ree**-na
Pleased to meet you	Piacere	pee-ah-**chair**-ray
How are you?	Come sta?	**ko**-may **stah**
Very well, thanks	Bene, grazie	**ben**-ay **grah**-tsee-ay
And you?	E lei?	ay **lay**-ee
Hello (phone)	Pronto?	**proan**-to

Numbers

English	Italian	Pronunciation
one	uno	**oo**-no
two	due	**doo**-ay
three	tre	tray
four	quattro	**kwah**-tro
five	cinque	**cheen**-kway
six	sei	say
seven	sette	**set**-ay
eight	otto	**oh**-to
nine	nove	**no**-vay
ten	dieci	dee-**eh**-chee
eleven	undici	**oon**-dee-chee
twelve	dodici	**doe**-dee-chee
thirteen	tredici	**tray**-dee-chee

fourteen	quattordici	kwa-**tore**-dee-chee
fifteen	quindici	**kwin**-dee-chee
sixteen	sedici	**say**-dee-chee
seventeen	diciassette	dee-cha-**set**-ay
eighteen	diciotto	dee-**cho**-to
nineteen	diciannove	dee-cha-**no**-vay
twenty	venti	**vain**-tee
twenty-one	ventuno	vain-**too**-no
twenty-two	ventidue	vain-tee-**doo**-ay
thirty	trenta	**train**-ta
forty	quaranta	kwa-**rahn**-ta
fifty	cinquanta	cheen-**kwahn**-ta
sixty	sessanta	seh-**sahn**-ta
seventy	settanta	seh-**tahn**-ta
eighty	ottanta	o-**tahn**-ta
ninety	novanta	no-**vahn**-ta
one hundred	cento	**chen**-to
one thousand	mille	**mee**-lay
ten thousand	diecimila	dee-eh-chee-**mee**-la

Useful Phrases

Do you speak English?	Parla inglese?	**par**-la een-**glay**-zay
I don't speak Italian	Non parlo italiano	non **par**-lo ee-tal-**yah**-no
I don't understand	Non capisco	non ka-**peess**-ko
Can you please repeat?	Può ripetere?	pwo ree-**pet**-ay-ray
Slowly!	Lentamente!	**len**-ta-men-tay
I don't know	Non lo so	non lo **so**
I'm American/British	Sono americano(a)	**so**-no a-may-ree-**kah**-no(a)
	Sono inglese	**so**-no een-**glay**-zay
What's your name?	Come si chiama?	**ko**-may see kee-**ah**-ma
My name is . . .	Mi chiamo . . .	mee kee-**ah**-mo
What time is it?	Che ore sono?	kay **o**-ray **so**-no
How?	Come?	**ko**-may
When?	Quando?	**kwan**-doe
Yesterday/today/tomorrow	Ieri/oggi/domani	**yer**-ee/**o**-jee/do-**mah**-nee

This morning/ afternoon	Stamattina/Oggi pomeriggio	sta-ma-**tee**-na/**o**-jee po-mer-**ee**-jo
Tonight	Stasera	sta-**ser**-a
What?	Che cosa?	kay **ko**-za
What is it?	Che cos'è?	kay ko-**zay**
Why?	Perché?	pear-**kay**
Who?	Chi?	kee
Where is . . .	Dov'è . . .	doe-**veh**
the bus stop?	la fermata dell'autobus?	la fer-**mah**-ta del ow-toe-**booss**
the train station?	la stazione?	la sta-tsee-**oh**-nay
the subway station?	la metropolitana?	la may-tro-po-lee-**tah**-na
the terminal?	il terminale?	eel ter-mee-**nah**-lay
the post office?	l'ufficio postale?	loo-**fee**-cho po-**stah**-lay
the bank?	la banca?	la **bahn**-ka
the . . . hotel?	l'hotel . . .?	lo-**tel**
the store?	il negozio?	eel nay-**go**-tsee-o
the cashier?	la cassa?	la **kah**-sa
the . . . museum?	il museo . . .?	eel moo-**zay**-o
the hospital?	l'ospedale?	lo-spay-**dah**-lay
the first aid station?	il pronto soccorso?	eel **pron**-to so-**kor**-so
the elevator?	l'ascensore?	la-shen-**so**-ray
a telephone?	un telefono?	oon tay-**lay**-fo-no
Where are the restrooms?	Dov'è il bagno?	do-**vay** eel **bahn**-yo
Here/there	Qui/là	kwee/la
Left/right	A sinistra/a destra	a see-**neess**-tra/ a **des**-tra
Straight ahead	Avanti dritto	a-**vahn**-tee **dree**-to
Is it near/far?	È vicino/lontano?	ay vee-**chee**-no/ lon-**tah**-no
I'd like . . .	Vorrei . . .	vo-**ray**
a room	una camera	**oo**-na **kah**-may-ra
the key	la chiave	la kee-**ah**-vay
a newspaper	un giornale	oon jor-**nah**-lay
a stamp	un francobollo	oon frahn-ko-**bo**-lo
I'd like to buy . . .	Vorrei comprare . . .	vo-**ray** kom-**prah**-ray
a cigar	un sigaro	oon see-**gah**-ro
cigarettes	delle sigarette	**day**-lay see-ga-**ret**-ay
some matches	dei fiammiferi	**day**-ee **fee**-ah-**mee**-fer-ee
some soap	una saponetta	**oo**-na sa-po-**net**-a
a city plan	una pianta della città	**oo**-na **pyahn**-ta **day**-la chee-**tah**

a road map of . . .	una carta stradale di . . .	**oo**-na **cart**-a stra-**dah**-lay dee
a country map	una carta geografica	**oo**-na **cart**-a jay-o-**grah**-fee-ka
a magazine	una rivista	**oo**-na ree-**veess**-ta
envelopes	delle buste	**day**-lay **booss**-tay
writing paper	della carta da lettere	**day**-la **cart**-a da **let**-air-ay
a postcard	una cartolina	**oo**-na car-toe-**lee**-na
a guidebook	una guida turistica	**oo**-na **gwee**-da too-**reess**-tee-ka
How much is it?	Quanto costa?	**kwahn**-toe **coast**-a
It's expensive/cheap	È caro/economico	ay **car**-o/ay-ko-**no**-mee-ko
A little/a lot	Poco/tanto	**po**-ko/**tahn**-to
More/less	Più/meno	pee-**oo**/**may**-no
Enough/too (much)	Abbastanza/troppo	a-bas-**tahn**-sa/**tro**-po
I am sick	Sto male	sto **mah**-lay
Call a doctor	Chiama un dottore	kee-**ah**-mah oon doe-**toe**-ray
Help!	Aiuto!	a-**yoo**-toe
Stop!	Alt!	ahlt
Fire!	Al fuoco!	ahl **fwo**-ko
Caution/Look out!	Attenzione!	a-ten-**syon**-ay

Dining Out

A bottle of . . .	Una bottiglia di . . .	**oo**-na bo-**tee**-lee-ah dee
A cup of . . .	Una tazza di . . .	**oo**-na **tah**-tsa dee
A glass of . . .	Un bicchiere di . . .	oon bee-key-**air**-ay dee
Bill/check	Il conto	eel **cone**-toe
Bread	Il pane	eel **pah**-nay
Breakfast	La prima colazione	la **pree**-ma ko-la-**tsee**-oh-nay
Cocktail/aperitif	L'aperitivo	la-pay-ree-**tee**-vo
Dinner	La cena	la **chen**-a
Fixed-price menu	Menù a prezzo fisso	may-**noo** a **pret**-so **fee**-so
Fork	La forchetta	la for-**ket**-a
I am diabetic	Ho il diabete	o eel dee-a-**bay**-tay
I am vegetarian	Sono vegetariano/a	**so**-no vay-jay-ta-ree-**ah**-no/a
I'd like . . .	Vorrei . . .	vo-**ray**

I'd like to order	Vorrei ordinare	vo-**ray** or-dee-**nah**-ray
Is service included?	Il servizio è incluso?	eel ser-**vee**-tzee-o ay een-**kloo**-zo
It's good/bad	È buono/cattivo	ay **bwo**-no/ka-**tee**-vo
It's hot/cold	È caldo/freddo	ay **kahl**-doe/**fred**-o
Knife	Il coltello	eel kol-**tel**-o
Lunch	Il pranzo	eel **prahnt**-so
Menu	Il menù	eel may-**noo**
Napkin	Il tovagliolo	eel toe-va-lee-**oh**-lo
Please give me . . .	Mi dia . . .	mee **dee**-a
Salt	Il sale	eel **sah**-lay
Spoon	Il cucchiaio	eel koo-kee-**ah**-yo
Sugar	Lo zucchero	lo **tsoo**-ker-o
Waiter/Waitress	Cameriere/ cameriera	ka-mare-**yer**-ay/ ka-mare-**yer**-a
Wine list	La lista dei vini	la **lee**-sta **day**-ee **vee**-nee

MENU GUIDE

English	Italian
Set menu	Menù a prezzo fisso
Dish of the day	Piatto del giorno
Specialty of the house	Specialità della casa
Local specialties	Specialità locali
Extra charge	Extra . . .
In season	Di stagione
Cover charge/Service charge	Coperto/Servizio

Breakfast

English	Italian
Butter	Burro
Croissant	Cornetto
Eggs	Uova
Honey	Miele
Jam/Marmalade	Marmellata
Roll	Panino
Toast	Pane tostato

Starters

English	Italian
Assorted cold cuts	Affettati misti
Assorted seafood	Antipasto di pesce
Assorted appetizers	Antipasto misto
Toasted rounds of bread, fried or toasted in oil	Crostini/Crostoni
Diced-potato and vegetable salad with mayonnaise	Insalata russa
Eggplant parmigiana	Melanzane alla parmigiana
Fried mozzarella sandwich	Mozzarella in carrozza
Ham and melon	Prosciutto e melone
Cooked sausages and cured meats	Salumi cotti
Filled pastry shells	Vol-au-vents

Soups

English	Italian
"Angel hair," thin noodle soup	Capelli d'angelo
Cream of . . .	Crema di . . .
Pasta-and-bean soup	Pasta e fagioli
Egg-drop and parmesan cheese soup	Stracciatella

Pasta, Rice, and Pizza

English	Italian
Filled pasta	Agnolotti/ravioli/tortellini
Potato dumplings	Gnocchi

Semolina dumplings	Gnocchi alla romana
Pasta	Pasta
with four cheeses	*al quattro formaggi*
with basil/cheese/pine nuts/ garlic sauce	*al pesto*
with tomato-based meat sauce	*al ragù*
with tomato sauce	*al sugo* or *al pomodoro*
with butter	*in bianco* or *al burro*
with egg, parmesan cheese, and pepper	*alla carbonara*
green (spinach-based) pasta	*verde*
Rice	Riso
Rice dish	Risotto
with mushrooms	*ai funghi*
with saffron	*alla milanese*
Noodles	Tagliatelle
Pizza	Pizza
Pizza with seafood, cheese, artichokes, and ham in four different sections	Pizza quattro stagioni
Pizza with tomato and mozzarella	Pizza margherita
Pizza with oil, garlic, and oregano	Pizza marinara

Fish and Seafood

Anchovies	Acciughe
Bass	Persico
Carp	Carpa
Clams	Vongole
Cod	Merluzzo
Crab	Granchio
Eel	Anguilla
Lobster	Aragosta
Mackerel	Sgombro
Mullet	Triglia
Mussels	Cozze
Octopus	Polpo
Oysters	Ostriche
Pike	Luccio
Prawns	Gamberoni
Salmon	Salmone
Shrimp	Scampi
Shrimps	Gamberetti
Sole	Sogliola
Squid	Calamari
Swordfish	Pescespada

Trout	Trota
Tuna	Tonno

Methods of Preparation

Baked	Al forno
Cold, with vinegar sauce	In carpione
Fish stew	Zuppa di pesce
Fried	Fritto
Grilled (usually charcoal)	Alla griglia
Seafood salad	In insalata
Smoked	Affumicato
Stuffed	Ripieno

Meat

Boar	Cinghiale
Brain	Cervella
Braised meat with wine	Brasato
Chop	Costoletta
Duck	Anatra
Lamb	Agnello
Baby lamb	Abbacchio
Liver	Fegato
Pheasant	Fagiano
Pork roast	Arista
Rabbit	Coniglio
Steak	Bistecca
Sliced raw steak with sauce	Carpaccio
Mixed boiled meat	Bollito misto

Methods of Preparation

Battered with eggs and crumbs and fried	. . . alla milanese
Grilled	. . . ai ferri
Grilled (usually charcoal)	. . . alla griglia
Raw, with lemon/egg sauce	. . . alla tartara
Roasted	. . . arrosto
Very rare	. . . al sangue
Well done	. . . ben cotta
With ham and cheese	. . . alla valdostana
With parmesan cheese and tomatoes	. . . alla parmigiana

Vegetables

Artichokes	Carciofi
Asparagus	Asparagi
Beans	Fagioli

Brussels sprouts	Cavolini di Bruxelles
Cabbage	Cavolo
Carrots	Carote
Cauliflower	Cavolfiore
Cucumber	Cetriolo
Eggplants	Melanzane
Green beans	Fagiolini
Leeks	Porri
Lentils	Lenticchie
Lettuce	Lattuga
Mushrooms	Funghi
Onions	Cipolle
Peas	Piselli
Peppers	Peperoni
Potatoes	Patate
Roasted potatoes	*Patate arroste*
Boiled potatoes	*Patate bollite*
Fried potatoes	*Patate fritte*
Small, roasted potatoes	*Patatine novelle*
Mashed potatoes	*Purè di patate*
Radishes	Rapanelli
Salad	Insalata
vegetable	*mista*
green	*verde*
Spinach	Spinaci
Tomatoes	Pomodori
Zucchini	Zucchini

Sauces, Herbs, and Spices

Basil	Basilico
Bay leaf	Lauro
Chervil	Cerfoglio
Dill	Aneto
Garlic	Aglio
Hot dip with anchovies (for vegetables)	Bagna cauda
Marjoram	Maggiorana
Mayonnaise	Maionese
Mustard	Mostarda *or* senape
Oil	Olio
Parsley-based sauce	Salsa verde
Pepper	Pepe
Rosemary	Rosmarino
Tartar sauce	Salsa tartara
Vinegar	Aceto
White sauce	Besciamella

Cheeses

Fresh:	Caprino fresco
	Mascarpone
	Mozzarella
	Ricotta
Mild:	Caciotta
	Caprino
	Fontina
	Grana
	Provola
	Provolone dolce
	Robiola
	Scamorza
Sharp:	Asiago
	Gorgonzola
	Groviera
	Pecorino
	Provolone piccante
	Taleggio
	Toma

Fruits and Nuts

Almonds	Mandorle
Apple	Mela
Apricot	Albicocca
Blackberries	More
Black currant	Ribes nero
Blueberries	Mirtilli
Cherries	Ciliege
Chestnuts	Castagne
Coconut	Noce di cocco
Dates	Datteri
Figs	Fichi
Green grapes	Uva bianca
Black grapes	Uva nera
Grapefruit	Pompelmo
Hazelnuts	Nocciole
Lemon	Limone
Melon	Melone
Nectarine	Nocepesca
Orange	Arancia
Pear	Pera
Peach	Pesca
Pineapple	Ananas
Plum	Prugna/Susina
Prune	Prugna secca

Raisins	Uva passa
Raspberries	Lamponi
Red currant	Ribes
Strawberries	Fragole
Tangerine	Mandarino
Walnuts	Noci
Watermelon	Anguria/Cocomero
Dried fruit	Frutta secca
Fresh fruit	Frutta fresca
Fruit salad	Macedonia di frutta

Desserts

Custard filled pastry, with candied fruit	Cannoli
Ricotta filled pastry shells with sugar glaze	Cannoli alla siciliana
Ice cream with candied fruit	Cassata
Ricotta filled cake with sugar glaze	Cassata siciliana
Chocolate	Cioccolato
Cup of ice cream	Coppa gelato
Caramel custard	Crème caramel
Pie	Crostata
Fruit pie	Crostata di frutta
Ice cream	Gelato
Flaked pastry	Millefoglie
Chestnuts and whipped-cream cake	Montebianco
Whipped cream	Panna montata
Pastries	Paste
Sherbet	Sorbetto
Chocolate-coated ice cream	Tartufo
Fruit tart	Torta di frutta
Apple tart	Torta di mele
Ice-cream cake	Torta gelata
Vanilla	Vaniglia
Egg-based cream with sugar and Marsala wine	Zabaione
Ice-cream filled cake	Zuccotto

Alcoholic Drinks

On the rocks	Con ghiaccio
Straight	Liscio
With soda	Con seltz
Beer	Birra
light/dark	*chiara/scura*

Bitter cordial	Amaro
Brandy	Cognac
Cordial	Liquore
Aniseed cordial	Sambuca
Martini	Cocktail Martini
Port	Porto
Vermouth	Vermut/Martini
Wine	Vino
blush	*rosé*
dry	*secco*
full-bodied	*corposo*
light	*leggero*
red	*rosso*
sparkling	*spumante*
sweet	*dolce*
very dry	*brut*
white	*bianco*
Light wine	Vinello
Bottle	Bottiglia
Carafe	Caraffa
Flask	Fiasco

Nonalcoholic Drinks

Mineral water	Acqua minerale
carbonated	*gassata*
still	*non gassata*
Tap water	Acqua naturale
Tonic water	Acqua tonica
Coffee with steamed milk	Cappuccino
Espresso	Caffè espresso
with milk	*macchiato*
decaffeinated	*decaffeinato*
lighter espresso	*lungo*
with cordial	*corretto*
Fruit juice	Succo di frutta
Lemonade	Limonata
Milk	Latte
Orangeade	Aranciata
Tea	Tè
with milk/lemon	*col latte/col limone*
iced	*freddo*

INDEX